Religious Fascism
The Repeal of Section 28

Garry Otton

Published by
Ganymedia

Also by Garry Otton

Sexual Fascism
Ganymede Books, 2001

Religious Fascism: The Repeal of Section 28
First published in 2014
By Ganymedia Ltd

Cover designed and illustrated by Garry Otton

Garry Otton, 2014
All rights reserved
ISBN: 978-0-9541131-2-4

This book is sold subject to the condition that it shall not, by way of trade or otherwise, be lent, re-sold, hired out or otherwise circulated in any form other than that in which it is published and without a similar condition including this condition being imposed on the subsequent purchaser.

Contents

Introduction: Page 9

Chapter One:
Closing the floodgates with Keep the Clause! Page 15

Chapter Two:
The assault on 'family values' Page 80

Chapter Three:
The Board of Social Responsibility Page 133

Chapter Four:
Praise be the Lords! Page 179

Chapter Five:
How to spot a homosexual Page 247

Chapter Six:
Church militants at war Page 303

Chapter Seven:
The Results Page 365

Chapter Eight:
Keeping marriage and schools for Christians Page 407

Chapter Nine:
Curtains for Section 28 Page 491

Epilogue:
The emergence of a new religious militancy Page 503

Acknowledgments

I would like to thank Robert Canning for his help reading and correcting the manuscript and other members of the Scottish Secular Society for assistance, support and advice.

"Section 28 has become really a badge of shame in the eyes of a very important part of our community and I think we're right to remove that".

First Minister, Donald Dewar.

For Mrs Abbott, for all her efforts in teaching me to walk tall, wash my clothes in Comfort, read the Daily Telegraph and stand up for the Queen.

Introduction

Taking the stand in her sky-blue twin-set, Prime Minister, Margaret Thatcher addressed a sea of waving Union Jacks at the Conservative Party Conference of 1987 to declare to rapturous applause: "Children, who should be taught to respect traditional moral values, are being taught they have the inalienable right to be gay".

The right-wing press couldn't have agreed more. Fuelling public anger and exposing a trend they labelled 'political correctness' in 'loony left' Labour councils, they attacked initiatives such as the one in Ealing which offered support to young gay people by posting notices advertising a gay switchboard. Conservative MP Harry Greenaway declared the move "wrong". The press went on to vilify 'proselytising' homosexuals; printing exaggerated stories of black lesbian self-defence groups and gay sex being taught in schools. Education Secretary Kenneth Baker sent a circular to all state schools forbidding teachers from "advocating homosexual behaviour".

The 'militancy' of Labour-controlled inner-city councils in London was a media catch-phrase as stories were delivered to shock: Haringey's 'courses on homosexuality' in nursery and primary schools; Hackney council's twinning arrangement with France, West Germany and Israel substituted for the Soviet Union, East Germany and Nicaragua, and their 'banning' of the 'discriminating' word 'family' from council literature; Ealing council's removal of books deemed racist or sexist from its local libraries and an Inner London Education Authority school in

Kennington's discouragement of competitive games and the introduction of protest letter-writing into the school curriculum.

The Conservatives responded with a campaign of billboards that begged: "Is this Labour's idea of a comprehensive education?" The posters showed, in red, the covers of three books written for teachers: *The Playbook for Kids About Sex; Young, Gay and Proud* and *Police – Out of School.*

Behind the rhetoric, much darker forces were gathering, destined to be exposed by an unworkable piece of legislation that would divide the nation.

Section 28 was an amendment to the Local Government Act, 1986 and enacted by the Local Government Act, 1988. It hatched from a Department of Education and Science circular, DES206/86 on 6 August 1986, stating: "There is no place in any school in any circumstances for teaching which advocates homosexual behaviour, which presents it as the 'norm', or which encourages homosexual experimentation by pupils". The essence of this message was born again into a re-draft of a Private Member's bill, introduced into the House of Lords by Lord Halsbury in 1986 called: 'An Act to Refrain Local Authorities from Promoting Homosexuality'. The bill was led for the Conservative Government by the Earl of Caithness, a 'family values' campaigner who quit politics after it emerged he had been involved in an extra-marital affair with a lady he met at a tea dance. (His wife later took a gun and shot herself).

Dame Jill Knight, Conservative MP for Birmingham, Edgbaston, chairperson of the Child and Family Protection Group, introduced the bill - demonising English local authorities, which in those days had more control over education - into the House of Commons. It fell through lack of Government support and the announcement of the impending 1987 general election. Knight insisted: "There is evidence in shocking abundance that children, as young as five, are being encouraged into homosexuality and lesbianism in our schools on the rates and against the wishes of parents". Margaret Thatcher thought the bill might be misrepresented and even "unnecessary".

Clause 14, as it was known, (before becoming Clause 27, then Clause 28, then Clause 29 before going back to being Clause 28 again), was tabled by Tory backbencher David Wilshire, MP for Spelthorne during the committee stage of the Local Government Bill on 8 December 1987. (It was a Clause at this stage because it was in a bill being put before Parliament to pass. Acts of Parliament have Sections, therefore it became Section 28. To make things more confusing, Section 28 was sometimes referred to as Section 2a after the section that was inserted into the Local Government Act). In debates over the bill in the House of Commons, there was much talk of buggery and the corruption of children. Commons drunk Sir Nicholas Fairbairn, MP for Perth and Kinross, who died of liver failure in 1995, branded homosexuality 'a pathological perversion'. Just three Conservative MPs were brave enough to vote against the clause: gay MP Michael Brown (later outed by the *News of the World*), Andrew Rowe and Robin Squire. In 2009, David Wilshire, who was separated and lived in Somerset with his partner, Ann Palmer, admitted to using parliamentary expenses to pay £105,000 over three years to Moorlands Research Services, a company he owned with Palmer running his office. He insisted it was approved by the authorities, but after a meeting with the Conservative Chief Whip, he announced he would not be standing as a candidate at the next election.

Clause 28 was championed by Jill Knight and accepted and defended by former Conservative Prime Minister, Michael Howard, then Minister for Local Government, who told the Commons that gay switchboards and youth groups were "precisely the sort of activities against which this clause is directed". It was debated on 8 December before being swiftly presented to the House of Commons on 15 December 1987, shortly before their Christmas recess. It was introduced into the 1988 Local Government Bill which was ostensibly about the compulsory tendering of school services and became widely known as Section 28 when, on 24 May 1988 - with controversial additions after Section 2a of the Local Government Act, 1986 - the Queen gave her Royal Assent to the first explicitly anti-gay measure introduced to Britain in the 20th century. Cancelling each other out, Scottish First Secretary Donald Dewar 'paired' with Nicholas Fairburn and stayed away from the vote. Edwina Currie, MP for West Derbyshire, later told *Gay Times* that "there was a feeling among some of us that we'd gone too far that night". Michael Howard also later expressed regret at its introduction.

By the end of the year, accompanying the law's passage, a firebomb went off at the offices of London's gay newspaper,

Capital Gay. Far from condemning the action, Conservative MP Dame Elaine Kellett-Bowman stood up in the House of Commons to voice her contempt for gay sex and declared that it was "right that there should be an intolerance of evil". What followed were a dramatic increase of attacks on gay men and another bombing of a gay bar in Rochester with teargas.

The first effect of Section 28 was to give the gay rights' movement a new public profile in the media. During one parliamentary debate, three lesbians disrupted proceedings by abseiling from the public gallery into the House of Lords. On another occasion newsreader Sue Lawley famously tried to deliver the ITV *Six O'Clock News* with the classic understatement that they had "rather been invaded" after lesbians had burst into their studio. Nicholas Witchell was forced to sit on top of a lesbian as Lawley struggled to deliver an item on the council tax over her muffled shouts.

As the subject of homosexuality rose in prominence at a time when the age of homosexual consent was still fixed at the age of 21, new groups like the Arts Lobby formed. These were a group of prominent actors who challenged the clause and joined thousands of protesters as they marched in London on 9 January 1988. There were 32 arrests. In February, 15,000 marched in Manchester and in April, 20,000 joined the march in London. Many saw the impending legislation as a piece of Tory bloody-mindedness, defining gays as second-class citizens and reminding young gays they were 'unacceptable'.

Section 28 stated that: "A local authority shall not (a) intentionally promote homosexuality or publish material with the intention of promoting homosexuality; (b) promote the teaching in any maintained school of the acceptability of homosexuality as a pretended family relationship". It would be invoked more than 30 times to prevent projects going ahead and went on to polarise conservative and liberal opinions on morality, right across the nation.

Although Section 28 was an unworkable piece of legislation in law, it presence ensured many erred on the side of caution. When Calderdale library service in Yorkshire attempted to ban the *Pink Paper*, they agreed to stock it after human rights group Liberty applied for a judicial review to clarify the law in 1995. East Sussex County Council banned a directory for schools as it listed a gay organisation. Telford Lesbian and Gay Youth Group were closed down but won their battle with Shropshire County Council after councillors reviewed the group's funding and decided they had not breached any law. A Head cancelled a touring play featuring a scene where a gay man 'came out' and Leeds College of Music and Essex County Council both banned gay and lesbian groups from meeting on their premises. The nearest anyone got to bringing a council to court was a nurse – backed by the Christian Institute – who claimed that Glasgow City Council's funding of an AIDS support charity was promoting homosexuality. She failed.

Section 28 existed only - as its backers admitted - as a measure of control and self-censorship.

Section 28 was most likely illegal under the European Convention for Human Rights (ECHR), contravening the act on two counts: One stating that everyone is entitled to respect for their private and family life, and the other stating that everyone has the right to an education. The statement on education had already been interpreted as meaning children were entitled to one which encompassed the whole spectrum of society. David Pannick, an eminent English QC writing an opinion for Justice, a human rights organisation, insisted that any interference with freedom of expression must be sharp enough to be understood. Section 28's muddled reference to 'promoting' homosexuality failed that test. With the ECHR emphasising important features like pluralism, tolerance and broad-mindedness in society, he believed Section 28 could have easily been knocked out in a court, never mind a Parliamentary debate!

Section 28 was never introduced into Northern Ireland, and on its imposition in Scotland Brian Finch from Glasgow exercised his wit in the letters' pages of the *Herald*: "This law was imposed on Scotland by the predominantly English Parliament in Westminster on the grounds that, because southern Tories were having a panic attack, we Scots must be compelled to eat the same medicine as our neighbours. In exposing an equally daft argument Sir Walter Scott once asked if, because the south of England was largely flat and suited to growing wheat, Scotland must be levelled and the cultivation of oats be proscribed".

As a former speechwriter to the Conservative Scottish Secretary, Michael Forsyth, newspaper columnist, Gerald Warner remembered Section 28's introduction somewhat differently. "Section 28 was not passed by Margaret Thatcher as an anti-homosexual measure. Her instincts were libertarian and she only sanctioned this legislation in response to the concern of large numbers of parents over a torrent of extravagantly obscene homosexual literature which had invaded some schools".

The attempt to repeal Section 28 began in Scotland in 1999 and unleashed the longest political debate in the history of the Scottish Parliament. It was a debate that exposed church leaders determined to sound relevant in a nation no longer holding them in their thrall. It divided Scotland on the subject of homosexuality. As the Scottish Executive began its countdown to repeal, a coalition of religionists, Conservatives, 'concerned parents', top businesspeople and newspaper editors like Martin Clarke of the *Daily Record* united under the 'Keep the Clause' banner to fight the government in a campaign led by a former editor of the *Scottish Sun* and Scotland's richest man, Brian Souter. As 'Keep the Clause' billboard posters were erected all across Scotland, lesbians, gays, bisexuals, the transgendered and those who simply looked different became targets for abuse. Newspapers were filled with 'Keep the Clause' advertisements and propaganda. Cardinal Winning compared gays to Nazis and publicly declared an international conspiracy as headlines referring to 'gay cliques', 'gay propaganda' and opponents' claims of 'anti-gay victories' - offensive to gays as 'anti-Jew victories' had been to Jews in Nazi Germany – filled the Scottish press. Most of the stories detailing the worse excesses of the campaign were withheld from the rest of the nation as different editions were printed south of the border. At the height of the campaign, newspapers recruited professional spokespeople to offer their opinion on how repeal would make children vulnerable to AIDS and sexual abuse. Letters' pages published views that advocated violence against gays and demonstrated the vilest homophobia. Anatomical drawings were published at the time purporting to show a homosexual's distinguishing features. As Souter prepared his private referendum, police began reporting an increase in attacks on gays, 'Keep the Clause' became a playground catchphrase and less fortunate victims of the prevailing homophobia took their life, were beaten and in some cases murdered. As hard it was denied, the brutal campaign was initiated, sustained, fuelled and driven by the darker forces of religion in a country struggling to come to terms with a new, more secular millennium.

Chapter One
Closing the Floodgates with Keep the Clause!

"She was 31 and I was 17,
I knew nothing 'bout love; she knew everything".
Bobby Goldsboro

Between 1996 and 2006 I was engaged in a ten year project, monitoring the Scottish media's treatment of sexuality which in part made up the contents of my first book, *Sexual Fascism*, published in 2001. My efforts appeared monthly under the title the *Scottish Media Monitor*, first in *Gay Scotland*, then *Cruise*, before finally settling down in *ScotsGay* magazine. Five years either side of the turn of the century was an extraordinary period to chronicle attitudes to sexuality in Scotland. My column captured everything in Scotland's sexual landscape from the insidious peddling of religious propaganda by media columnists to seemingly benign stories twisted by the forces of unnecessary conservatism, like the man arrested with a snake down his trousers in Ayrshire; the furore over a female doll found with a penis; a woman warned to remove a display of male dolls standing too close together in her window in Moniaive, Dumfriesshire; a spray developed to detect traces of sex; a public toilet in Aberdeen with an alarm to detect if two men might be occupying it at the same time. It was a time when Scots actor Robert Carlyle joined a band of unemployed men from Newcastle to stop short of doing *The Full Monty* and radio stations banned the pop group Bloodhound Gang from 'doing it like they do' on the *Discovery Channel*.

Just months after my column had begun, Thomas Hamilton tragically gunned down a classroom of children and their teacher at a school in Dunblane. But it was not the issue of how readily a madman might purchase a gun that kept the media busy. Whilst there was no evidence Hamilton sexually molested children in his care, or was himself gay, the tragedy was sexualised to the extent gay men were subsequently swept up in a tidal wave of moral panic. Scoutmasters and gym teachers, boys' club managers and priests were dragged across the pages of the Scottish press in frenzy. One 'sex beast' after another was 'caged.' A 24-year-old was jailed for three months after being found on school grounds in Paisley and a 77-year-old man was sentenced to four years for taking pictures of kids at the seaside in Ayrshire. Public toilets, saunas, parks and swimming-pool changing areas throughout Scotland became flash-points of moral warfare. A swimming-pool attendant warned parents "all their children are at risk" and was reported in a tabloid begging more staff to patrol open changing-rooms. "The only way to clamp down on this kind of thing", he said, "is by fitting screens to the top and bottom of cubicles and security guards watching at all times". A perceived threat to children from 'perverts' was trumpeted by tabloid campaigns such as the *Daily Record's* 'PervertWatch' campaign and the *News of the World's* 'Name and Shame' allowing the media to fuel moral outrage at even legitimate means of sexual expression. Most prominent amongst these campaigns was the attack on 'Channel Filth'; Channel 5's late night depiction of erotica, and the *Daily Record's* 'SmutWatch' campaign. An increasingly politicised church, fearful of moral decay and advances in sexual liberty and expression succoured these campaigns. A major victory for the Church and their media cronies was the banning of an exhibition of erotica in Glasgow. Any review of my book, *Sexual Fascism* was shunned by the *Herald*, *BBC Scotland* and the *Dundee Courier*, the latter publication refusing because the book "contained sex".

It was in this confused sexual age, before the new millennium, that the Labour Party in a newly-devolved nation saw fit to dispense of a legally-unworkable English Act they felt deserved no place in Scotland. The task fell into the lap of Communities Minister, Wendy Alexander.

It should have been *so* simple.

On 2 March 1999, the Bank of Scotland announced it was setting up a telebanking operation with controversial American TV evangelist Pat Robertson. There were protests outside the bank's headquarters and hundreds of customers closed their accounts. Larger institutions such as West Lothian Council, the

Closing the Floodgates with Keep the Clause!

Scottish Trades Union Council and even the new Scottish Parliament threatened to do the same. The bank's share price dropped almost four per cent. The Bank of Scotland turned to Jack Irvine of Media House, PR consultant and former guitarist with eighties pop band BA Robertson to manage the affair. (At the time, Irvine's company shared its name with a US Christian group Media House International whose mission was – in a touch of irony - to advance God in the world through the media). Media House boasted "unique relationships with major multinational companies, playing a crucial role in the decision making process of key management teams throughout the world". Irvine, who claimed to be a specialist in handling public relations crises, told the press: "The deal will definitely go ahead. The bank will continue to do business on the bank's terms, which are ethical terms and which are well known. Everyone it does business with will abide by these ethical terms".

Pat Robertson owned a mammoth media, educational and legal empire in the USA with an estimated value of a billion dollars. Robertson's message was carried daily in his *700 Club* programme on his very own *Family Channel*, (now owned by Disney), broadcast on almost 10,000 cable systems throughout the US reaching some 59 million homes, more than 10 times the population of Scotland. Robertson also ran Standard News, a secular news bureau working in tandem with Reuters. Regent University, founded by Robertson, had on its campus a school for journalists and lawyers. Funding for the University also came from Coors beer through the Coors Foundation. The American Center for Law and Justice (ACLJ) and the European Centre for Law and Justice (ECLJ) were legal advocacy groups founded by Robertson to aggressively promote the Christian Right agenda through the courts. Using leased and chartered jets, lawyers could come and go at a moments notice.

In 2010 the European Court of Human Rights in the Lautsi *versus* Italy case, ruled in support of Mrs Lautsi, that her children had a right to be educated in state schools without crucifixes on the walls. In support of the Vatican, the ECLJ filed a brief in support of Italy's appeal. A year later the ruling would be completely overturned by a higher chamber of the same court.

Pat Robertson was introduced to Bill Hendry, the Bank of Scotland's executive vice-president (and later the Managing Director of Corporate Banking for North America) at a New

RELIGIOUS FASCISM

York cocktail party hosted by Cardinal John O'Connor. Hendry was described by Simon Fluendy in the *Mail on Sunday* as "an ultra conservative Catholic" who "infuriated feminists by pronouncing that God is certainly a man". The pair hit it off right away. As chairman of Drive Financial Services - a firm based in Dallas, Texas, purchasing sub-prime contracts from more than 10,000 dealer partners throughout the USA and exceeding $2.4billion of retail instalment loans - Hendry announced in 2006 that Bank Santander had entered into a deal with Halifax Bank of Scotland plc and selected members of Drive's management to acquire 90% ownership stake in his company. The company lists Habitat for Humanity, offering interest-free loans to eliminate poverty housing, as a recipient of support. The organisation "seeks to demonstrate the love of God through practical action" claiming "it is our Christian faith that motivates our mission. We witness to the power and love of Jesus Christ each time we build a house, strengthen communities, and make people aware of families in need".

Before too many customers withdrew their money from the Bank of Scotland in protest at its hook-up with evangelist Pat Robertson - placing their accounts with competitors such as the Royal Bank of Scotland or Clydesdale Bank - the deal had to be aborted. Jack Irvine flew out with Bank of Scotland boss Peter Burt to meet Pat Robertson and explain personally. Robertson was advised by Scottish lawyer, Peter Watson, Irvine's partner in a lobbying company called Tactical Response (not to be confused with a US company of the same name offering one day courses on operating Kalashnikovs). Robertson reacted angrily, labelling Scotland a "dark place" overrun by homosexuals, and in an Internet broadcast gasped: "In Scotland, you can't believe how strong the homosexuals are, it's simply unbelievable!" While Bank of Scotland was reported offering to buy out Robertson's £30m stake in the venture; compensation was put at anything between $9m and $16m. After Jack Irvine stridently challenged the bank's critics, Tim Hopkins from Scotland's Equality Network said: "I think it is outrageous that the Bank's response to so many people's concerns is to attack them".

It would not be the last of Pat Robertson's pronouncements against homosexuals. In 2011 he told viewers of his *700 Club* programme that a mild earthquake on the east coast of the America was God's revenge on people "who act kind of gay",

Closing the Floodgates with Keep the Clause!

adding: "All across the Eastern seaboard there are men who get manicures, wear designer eyewear and know about thread counts. God finds this somewhat gay-like behaviour confusing and He responded by getting mildly peeved... God will strike back at people who act sort of gay with all kinds of mild responses. If you keep getting pedicures and facials, you can expect two to three inches of rain and some really hot humid days in your future... God looks at people who get their panties in a twist after a little shaking and He says to Himself, 'Wow, that's really kind of gay'."

Not everyone agreed with a boycott of the Bank of Scotland. Journalist Nick Gates in the *Scottish Daily Express* accused Bank of Scotland critics of being "hypocrites" and "most un-Christian". He dismissed the enterprise as "a relatively small-scale arrangement with a television evangelist..." and expressed sympathy for "the unfortunate wheeler-dealers who thought they were just doing their jobs".

One of many conservative, religious contributors enjoying an absurdly disproportionate profile in Scotland's media was Gerald Warner. In the *Scottish Daily Mail*, he blasted: "Political correctness is now the greatest threat to freedom in Scotland", describing institutions withdrawing their accounts with the Bank of Scotland as "the petulant gestures of politicians indulging an obsession". He described the suggestion that heads might roll at the Bank of Scotland: "grossly unfair". Surely, he begged, Robertson couldn't look "any more bizarre than the motley coalition of politically correct militants who have unravelled the deal...? We cannot sit idly by and watch minority pressure groups and their allies secure an absurdly disproportionate profile in the media..."

In his own column in the *West Highland Free Press*, Professor Donald MacLeod of the Free Church also accused gays of having too powerful a voice; declared a "sudden terror of human rights and civil liberties organisations" and refused to drop a few coins in a tin supporting Amnesty International. MacLeod cried: The way the "gay lobby has forced" the Bank of Scotland to "renege" on its deal "scares the living daylights out of me". Macleod wrote that Robertson's views were "remarkably similar to what orthodox Jews, Christians and Muslims have believed for centuries... They're shared by Scotland's eight hundred thousand Catholics, its one-and-a-half million Protestants, its two million

Partick Thistle supporters and the remaining non-descripts who spend Easter Sunday in the pub or on the golf-course... Gays are no longer content just to have their civil rights. They are giving their own sexual preference a quasi-religious status and demanding that any comment which causes them distress be treated as blasphemy. Their audacity has already yielded handsome dividends... Scotland is already a country in which homosexuals wield enormous power. They are shouting us down and denying us space... Scottish gays have tasted blood..."

Responding to Donald MacLeod, Marjory Smith of the Highland Lesbian Group wrote to the the *West Highland Free Press* to explain: "Lesbian and gay people... are born and brought up in the same society as everyone else and - think on this - some of us also absorb and fully assimilate the same monolithic oppression, which has so sadly permeated the mind of Donald MacLeod. A free spirit doesn't come in a bottle". Recounting an experience counselling a woman living in the Highlands, she added: "A lesbian Catholic woman's life has been totally blighted by her amalgamation of this repression. She knows she's lesbian, but can't accept it any more than Donald MacLeod. She has been in and out of mental hospital. Just when she seemed to be getting better the church got a new priest with similar understanding, caring, views to Donald MacLeod's, and she's back to square one".

The *Scottish Daily Mail's* columnist, Colette Douglas Home wrote: "Robertson has made millions out of God... He is against liberals, gays, feminists, Hindus, Moslems and President Clinton, but has links with bloody dictators like former President Mobutu of Zaire. The Jewish Anti-Defamation League says he brings to cultural disagreements 'a rhetoric of fear, suspicion, even hatred'... To see (the Bank of Scotland) throw its lot with the fast-talking, buck-raking, evangelical American is as shocking as seeing a maiden aunt take up with a snake oil salesman".

As a business, the Bank of Scotland soon recovered from this setback. After a failed bid to merge with NatWest Bank in 2001, the bank took over the Halifax Building Society in a £30 billion merger to form HBOS. Bank boss Peter Burt, who was also a non-executive director of Shell, was awarded a knighthood for his services to banking a few years later in the 2003 New Year's Honours list before retiring from his post as deputy chairman of HBOS. Sir Peter Burt later became executive

Closing the Floodgates with Keep the Clause!

chairman of US investment bank, Gleacher Shacklock and, despite a lack of experience in the TV industry, was offered the job of chairmanship of the newly-merged commercial broadcaster ITV in 2004.

The Halifax Building Society and Bank of Scotland's merger initially turned out to be a huge cash cow. In 2003 HBOS made £4billion in annual profits but was criticised in 2004 when the bank announced it was on course to beat that figure, making profits of £142 every second. The bank had already informed its 20 million customers that their bank account charges were set to rise when on some accounts the time it took to clear a cheque rose from two to six working days. The Office of Fair Trading protested. Such profits were made in a climate of a record number of people being made bankrupt and a national debt that showed the average Scot owing £13,380.

The Bank of Scotland found itself in the news once again after the *Sunday Times* claimed it had obtained papers showing that the Bank of Scotland's treasurer and managing director, Gavin Masterton CBE had arranged, between 1999 and 2000, a loan for an associate to buy shares in Dunfermline Athletic Football Club of which Masterton was also a director. It was claimed Masterton gave a guarantee that the shares would be bought off him before the loan had to be repaid; then, in 2001 – after Masterton had retired from the Bank of Scotland with a £250,000-a-year pension - the shares were later acquired by Stadia, a company Masterton owned. The Stadia group later collapsed with reported debts of £25m. A man in charge of corporate lending racking up losses of millions of pounds in his own private ventures in four years would have been a major embarrassment had it not been for the Scarborough Development Group – a company that also used Jack Irvine's Media House for its PR - setting up a new company, SDG Caledonia, to take over Masterton's stake and a share held by venture capitalist company, 3i for a nominal sum. The Bank of Scotland was then able to recycle the debt. The associate's loan application from the Bank of Scotland Corporate Banking offered £69,250 at 1½% above base rate, with no security, no arrangement fees and interest payments deferred until the end of the three-year loan period. After two years, a letter from solicitors for Wood Investments (of which Masterton was a director) declared they would arrange with the Bank of Scotland to have the loan account cleared using funds from Stadia which left them in control of Dunfermline Athletic Football Club. The *Sunday Times* claimed that a letter from Masterton discussed with his associate a realignment of shares in Stadia on the basis of a firm called Charlotte Eighteen holding 75%. Charlotte Eighteen appeared on paper to be a director-less offshore company in the British Virgin Islands. In 2014 the *Record* claimed nearly all of Masterton's £12.2million loan had been written off by his bank.

Gavin Masterton and Brian Souter both had a stake in a legal services and executive search firm called First Scottish Group Ltd. A row broke out after £400,000 was transferred from the company to Masterton's company Dunfermeline Athletic FC without Brian Souter's permission. It was reported in the *Mail on Sunday* that Souter had ordered Masterton and the then First Scottish managing director John Yorkston - who was also chairman of Dunfermline Athletic - to repay the cash before forcing them both to resign from the company's board. The paper received a statement from Masterton saying he continued "to enjoy a strong working relationship" with Brian Souter and added: "The £400,000 was a series of inter-group transactions which were repaid as agreed".

Bank of Scotland's attempt at doing business with Pat Robertson was not the first time the bank would work under the threat of a boycott. Councils across Scotland once again felt pressure to sever ties with HBOS in 2006 after the collapse of the Christmas hamper company, Farepak. Not just council staff, but an estimated 150,000 people faced an impoverished Christmas after losing savings estimated at £35m without any hope of compensation. HBOS, the principal banker of Farepak's parent company, European Home Retail (EHR), had refused to extend the company's overdraft facility, leading to the company's collapse. Shares were suspended in August, but the company continued to take payments for Christmas hampers from customers until mid-October. Labour MSP, Dr Elaine Murray said: "Like many colleagues, I have been contacted by constituents – mainly women in part-time or low paid employment – who invested with Farepak with the purpose of saving to provide their children and grandchildren with a decent Christmas. These hardworking, prudent people, who prefer to save rather than take out a loan or use a credit card do not know how to explain to their children that Santa won't be coming this

Closing the Floodgates with Keep the Clause!

year". HBOS offered to donate £2m toward a rescue fund for Farepak customers. Administrators for Farepak warned customers they may get as little as 4p for every £1 they paid into the scheme. After news of the collapse, Sir Clive Thompson, chairman of EHR, blamed HBOS before embarking on a luxury holiday in Argentina.

Not until 2012 did a High Court judge suggest HBOS should "seriously consider" contributing more money to the £2m it had put into a distress fund in 2006 for Farepak's customers. Mr Justice Peter Smith went on to accuse HBOS of taking a "hardball approach" to its customers. HBOS, becoming part of Lloyds Banking Group, eventually agreed to pay £8m in compensation, which would mean Farepak customers recovering half of what they had contributed.

Sir Peter Burt's merger with the Halifax turned out to be poisonous. Now HBOS was the biggest mortgage lender in the UK, and, as such, vulnerable in the face of any recession or severe downturn in the property market. That's exactly what happened on Thursday, 18 September 2008, when, after the company's shares plunged to dangerous levels, after high level government talks, Lloyds TSB announced it was taking over HBOS. The Bank of Scotland had been established in 1695, was the first bank to issue paper currency in Europe and opened its first overseas office in 1975 in Houston, Texas. During the credit crunch of 2009, Parliament's Treasury committee chairman, John McFall castigated bankers, blaming them for making "an astonishing mess of the financial system". The Chancellor at the time, Alistair Darling, had to defend the Bank of England's secret loans of £61.6bn to the Royal Bank of Scotland and HBOS, in an emergency statement to parliament. He said that any leak of the matter would have put the whole country's financial system in jeopardy.

On another occasion, the Bank of Scotland was forced to issue a publicly apology was after they were accused of lending money to the sex industry. They had financed a deal in which the *Daily Express* owner, Richard Desmond had sold 45 of his magazine titles, including *Asian Babes, Readers' Wives, Mother-In-Laws, 60 Plus* and *Big Ones* to Remnant Media for £20m in 2004. The bank had lent £5m to Remnant, run by Simon Robinson and Aroon Maharajh. The Bank of Ireland had to withdraw from the deal after the Catholic Church and Irish women's groups protested. It seemed that the deal had not come to the attention of those higher up the Bank of Scotland's ladder until it had already been agreed. Some speculated that Desmond had sold the titles to impress the Government and media regulator Oftel he was a suitable candidate to buy the right-wing broadsheet, the *Daily Telegraph*, which was up for auction. Eventually, the Barclay twins, owner of the *Scotsman* beat the *Daily Mail* and General Trust in purchasing the title.

By 2012, the Bank of Scotland was found guilty by the Financial Services Authority of very serious financial misconduct before taxpayers had been forced to bail it out to the tune of £20 billion. It escaped a fine in excess of £17million to protect the taxpayer who, by now, owned 41 per cent of what was HBOS. Former directors Peter Cummings, who was reported benefitting from a £660,000 pay-off and a £6million pension, and Andy Hornby, who went on to run gambling company, Gala Coral, both escaped criminal conviction despite pressure from Iceland, a country that underwent a financial collapse. Peter Cummings was fined £500,000 and banned for life from working in the City by the Financial Services Authority (FSA). By the following year, a Parliamentary Commission on Banking Standards saw former chairman Lord Stevenson and past chief executives of HBOS, Sir James Crosby and Andy Hornby blamed for "catastrophic" management failures that led to the bank's downfall and a £20.5 billion bailout funded by UK taxpayers. The commission slapped them on the wrist by concluding that the three men should never be allowed to work in the financial sector again.

On 29 October, 1999 Minister for Communities Wendy Alexander, Labour MSP for Paisley North told a gathering at Glasgow University that it was time for Section 28 to go on what was supposed to have been a low-key affair after the Bank of Scotland's embarrassing climb-down over Pat Robertson. First Minister, Donald Dewar's special adviser John Rafferty had encouraged Alexander to leak details to the press the previous day, which allowed the story to appear in the *Daily Record* and the *Scotsman* that morning. All political parties except the Conservatives agreed it was time to kick Section 28 off the statute books. Wendy Alexander had addressed an Interpride conference a week before on Friday, 22 October, but despite news reports to the contrary, never mentioned the possibility of repealing Section 28 to them or any other lesbian, gay, bisexual or transgender

Closing the Floodgates with Keep the Clause!

group. With a Local Government Ethics bill being prepared for debate both north and south of the border, and the fledgling Scottish Parliament seeking to make some modest and inexpensive reforms; it seemed like a good time to break the news. Like the controversial poll tax, previously introduced by a Conservative administration, Scotland would be a testing ground for repeal. There were also more pressing reasons to initiate repeal across the whole of the UK in the 1997 Treaty of Amsterdam. Article 13 entitled the European Commission 'to take appropriate action to combat discrimination based on gender, racial or ethnic origin, religion or belief, disability, age, or sexual orientation', and 'appropriate action' under Article 6, Title 1, included the heavy penalty of suspension of voting rights of an offending member state of the Council of Ministers, while that state continued its financial contribution to the European Union.

Born in 1963, Wendy Cowan Alexander started out as a medical student at Glasgow University before changing her course to history and economics and becoming a political researcher at Westminster for MP George Galloway. With an MBA in business administration and an £80,000 a year job as an international management consultant, she was just the sort New Labour was after. As a special adviser to Donald Dewar at the Scottish Office she played a substantial behind-the-scenes role in 1998, turning Scotland's new politics into a reality. But it was the repeal of Section 28 that almost brought down the fledgling Scottish Parliament and sent 'Wee Wendy' into the wilderness. She was later dubbed 'the minister for everything' after taking on the portfolio of Minister for Enterprise, Transport and Lifelong Learning under Jack McConnell. Although variously described as a "gerbil on amphetamines" and a "pint-sized policy powerhouse", this daughter of a Church of Scotland minister considered herself a Presbyterian, went to church on Sunday and longed to have a family. The end of a brief relationship with Chicago-based Presbyterian pastor, Calum MacLeod was blamed on her workload.

Donald Dewar's advisor, David Whitton leaked the news first to the *Scotsman* and Wendy Alexander spilled the beans to the audience at Glasgow University. By the time the news broke Whitton was in Ireland with First Minister Donald Dewar. But it was the headline in the *Daily Record* that led him to warn Dewar there was going to be a problem.

RELIGIOUS FASCISM

Before anyone had even seen the consultative document outlining repeal of Section 28, conservative politicians, religionists and press commentators pounced. The *Scottish Daily Mail's* editorial thought repeal was to be "deplored" and declared children were being turned into "pawns of political correctness – it is downright immoral". The tabloid underlined its support for the Scottish Executive legislating on issues of "substance", legislation tailored "to the needs and wishes of the Scottish people... Section 28 is not in that category". They insisted the Executive were doing "devolution a disservice" and quickly launched its campaign to fight repeal on the back of a well-worn 80's cliché: "'POLITICALLY-CORRECT CRUSADE' TO SCRAP CLAUSE 28". As well as the liberal education minister Sam Galbraith and health minister Susan Deacon, the tabloid turned on Communities Minister Wendy Alexander and declared her on a "personal crusade... to defy church leaders..." They stated she had signalled "her determination to allow the promotion of homosexuality in schools..." In so doing, she had defied "furious opposition from across society". One of these was a rather matronly deputy leader of the Scottish Conservatives and Kirk elder, Annabel Goldie, who warned: "The churches represent a very wide and important section of opinion and they should not be taken lightly". Hinting at an inferior status of homosexual relationships, she added: "I'm in no doubt whatsoever that a happy marriage is the best possible outcome for anyone". (Sadly, marriage was something that had eluded Miss Goldie who once famously addressed Wendy Alexander in Parliament before she married, "as one spinster to another").

The Scottish Parliament was in its infancy. It took up its powers on 1 July 1999. The Scottish Executive, the devolved government of Scotland, was a Labour/Liberal Democrat coalition responsible for proposing most legislation, (Executive Bills) whilst the Parliament could amend such legislation or throw it out. The Parliament's committees, which consider the general principle of Bills and detailed amendments to them, was independent of the Scottish Executive and was able to call on Ministers to account for policies. The Committees could introduce their own legislation (Committee Bills), as could individual MSPs, (Member's Bills). However, without the support of the Executive, these Bills faced an uphill struggle to find Parliamentary time.

Closing the Floodgates with Keep the Clause!

The *Daily Record*, Scotland's bestselling, Labour-supporting red-top tabloid was furious it had not been given more warning of the announcement to repeal Section 28 and fired a warning shot with the headline: "GAY SEX LESSONS FOR SCOTS SCHOOLS", calling it: "Another unnecessary blunder". They argued that "the reaction of most right-thinking Scots will be to ask if our ministers and MSPs have nothing better to do... Spending taxpayers' money on the promotion of homosexuality... gay 'propaganda'." Certainly the *Record* would appear to have nothing better to do, returning to the subject again and again over the coming months. The tabloid reckoned the Scottish Executive wanted to create "the most politically-correct country in Europe". Their own agony aunt, Joan Burnie wondered how the repeal of Section 28 would eliminate bullying of young gays and suggested MSPs had far more urgent business to deal with! "It's not as if homosexuality is something which dare not speak its name in schools", she huffed, adding: "Playground jibes about dykes went over my head at 13! God knows adolescence is confusing enough without 'Sir' or 'Miss' standing up in class and urging everyone to come out and be glad to be gay". Echoing Margaret Thatcher at her conference speech in the eighties, she said she was afraid teachers would promote being gay as a "better alternative than the boring old heterosexual lifestyle... Besides, as Michael Portillo and a thousand public school-boys can testify, sexual preferences can change". Finally, she spluttered: "We have enough straight teachers preying on their young pupils without the gays joining in".

Alan Cochrane, writing for Scottish editions of the right-wing broadsheet, the *Daily Telegraph* begged: "I try – I really do – to understand...," challenging Wendy Alexander to support her "ridiculous claims... Where is her evidence that Section 28 encourages intolerance...? Next take her claim that Section 28 prevents teachers from counselling the victims of 'homophobic' bullying and ask her: how so? Give us one example of a teacher who could not help the victim of such bullying because he or she feared being thrown in jail because of this piece of legislation". Without offering any particular reason why it should remain either, Cochrane went on to mock Wendy Alexander's performance as "laughable... Sanctimonious arrogance... Inflicting a new morality upon us". He asked: "Which good cause will suffer as a result of money being switched to fund homosexual organisations?" Cochrane was lazy, glossing over the real difficulties teachers – if they could be bothered - had in dealing with homophobia in and out of school. A survey by Dr Ian Rivers, a senior lecturer in social psychology asked 200 gay men and women about their experiences in school. The eminent doctor was concerned there had been no material collated since 1984 on bullying. He found that those subjected to psychological bullying, such as stares or ostracism, were more likely to leave school than those physically attacked. He found 28 per cent admitted being bullied by *teachers* due to perceived sexual orientation. Post traumatic stress disorders affected one in six bullied pupils with symptoms ranging from nightmares, panic attacks and flashbacks. The Department for Education and Skills was collating information at this time and would later estimate in its report, *Homophobia, Sexual Orientation for Schools: A Review and Implications for Action*, published in 2004, that 125,000 pupils in England were attracted to people of the same sex (this was based on a Scottish survey of 5,854 pupils, carried out to evaluate the needs of sex education in Scotland which found 3.2% pupils admitted they were attracted to members of the same sex). The study found homophobic remarks was the insult of choice in schools; homophobic attitudes were developed by some boys to gain credibility with their peers; that homosexual boys were at risk of physical violence; homosexual girls were commonly ignored by their friends; more than half of gay and lesbian adults had considered harming themselves as a result of bullying at school with two in five having done so or attempted to at least once; two-thirds of gay pupils were truanting to avoid abuse and sporty girls were at risk of being labelled lesbian. The report called on schools to adopt policies to tackle homophobia and challenge unhelpful stereotypes of gay people.

Scottish Conservative list MSP the late Phil Gallie had other ideas. He was more concerned with the 'damage' to children by the repeal of Section 28 and began sending letters to school boards and Parent Teacher Associations, telling the *Ayrshire Post*: "The only chance of defeating this move, which will damage our children, is by extending the debate". He would get his wish.

Glasgow's *Evening Times* began: "Gay people have every right to be recognised as equal..." before compromising their view with a resounding: "But..." It was "too great a risk to our youngsters", adding that homosexuality shouldn't be promoted

Closing the Floodgates with Keep the Clause!

anyway before opining about the need to discuss "stringent measures against sex offenders" which would help "pubescent teenagers' at the most vulnerable time of their lives".

Mrs Ann Allen, one of the most outspoken social conservatives in the Church of Scotland and convenor of its ridiculously-named 'Board of Social Responsibility' advised: "In the education of children, the promotion of homosexuality would be as wrong as the promotion of heterosexual promiscuity". Lyndsay MacIntosh, the Scottish Conservative's law and order spokeswoman insisted: "Children have more than enough to deal with at school without having to consider alternatives to proper, monogamous, heterosexual relationships". In *Scotland on Sunday* she stated firmly how she didn't want anything that "could encourage experimentation".

The *Scottish Daily Mail* used a picture of Communities Minister Wendy Alexander with a ferocious gait under the headline: "Minister faces a backlash on plan for gay lessons in schools", while Aberdeen's *Press and Journal* found the same news "widely welcomed". The *Mail* also let columnist Gerald Warner off his lead to yap across the page, cocking his leg up against anything gay. He was scathing of Wendy Alexander's speech to Glasgow University. "It belongs to the politically correct, gesture politics of a student union", he wrote, adding that her "absurd title as 'Minister of Communities' made her a caricature of political correctness" and then accusing Scotland's First Minister, Donald Dewar of "hysterical soundbites that we expect from Outrage! or Peter Tatchell". He frothed: "What's so wrong about protecting our children from moral corruption?" Working himself up into a frenzy, Warner described the mood accompanying the Scottish Executive's bid to abolish Section 28 with the Ethical Standards in Public Life bill as a "wave of hysteria". The imposition of an "unpopular and immoral measure upon the British people". He believed the Government was launching a "propaganda offensive" to obscure the fact that "Section 28 is an important protection for the most vulnerable members of society - our children - against moral corruption funded by the taxpayer and, in extreme cases, the predatory activity of paedophiles". This, he believed, was a clause that "prohibits propaganda in schools", and asked: "What is wrong with that? Why should it be the responsibility of a local authority to promote any kind of sexuality?" He ordered local authorities not to "control their constituents' sex lives". Blaming "the mushrooming number of early teenage pregnancies" on too much sex education, he gushed: "Children who can neither read nor write properly already spend far too much time having so called sex education beamed at them". (Unfortunately, not the sort of sex education that worked in the Netherlands which boasted a rate of teenage pregnancy six times lower than Scotland's). Warner waved a stick at "moral anarchy in our schools" throwing open their doors to "homosexual missionaries..." before adding: "School libraries may be flooded with books representing homosexual 'lifestyles' as normal, or 'cool'." (He ignored the dozens of religious missionaries that were already invading Scottish schools, some of them presenting six-day Creationism as normal, promoting abstinence-only and homophobia, often without parent's knowledge). He even accused the Executive of attempting to "nationalise children" and "asserting the right of the state to indoctrinate them with homosexual propaganda in school..." Gerald Warner stormed: "Using children as guinea pigs in politically-correct projects of social engineering, insisting that they be made accessible to homosexual proselytisers at an impressionable age – that gets to people where they live... It alarms and angers countless thousands of parents, while depriving them of the right to control... the health of their children". He recalled how Section 28 had been "reluctantly" introduced to prohibit an "abuse of public money in grants to homosexual groups". Warner believed that the former Prime Minister Margaret Thatcher was a woman "...never inclined to indulge in moral crusades..." reminding readers that her "instincts were libertarian; sexual morality, in her eyes, was a private matter". In this they were unlike the instincts of Mr Warner who frequently turned sex into a contested zone to fight his own political battles in his newspaper columns. Putting aside the need for sex education to communicate knowledge and skills, enabling young people to make informed decisions, Warner hijacked it for an opportunity to impose his prescriptive model of Catholic, conservative sexual and personal morality. Warner was also somewhat shy about Margaret Thatcher's religious leanings. She gave sermons and dropped Biblical references into her speeches, once telling BBC Radio 4's *Today* programme in 1987: "The fundamental reason of being put on this earth is to improve your character that you are fit for the next world". Her late

Closing the Floodgates with Keep the Clause!

husband Denis insisted her deep religious conviction was one of her fundamental driving forces.

There were bigger players ready to come to the fore in the battle to retain Section 28 in Scotland. Cardinal Thomas Winning, or 'Red Tom' as he was sometimes known because of his dress, was born in 1925 in Craigneuk near Motherwell, the only son of an unemployed miner and steel worker. Growing up in a more sectarian Scotland than today, he admitted to having had to hide his religion on more than one occasion to protect him from bullies. His homophobic rants led many to wonder if that wasn't all he was hiding. In his book *This Turbulent Priest: The Life of Cardinal Winning*', *Scotsman* journalist, Stephen McGinty wrote of his early life: "Winning slept with his father in one bed, while in another Margaret (his sister) slept with her mother. The sleeping conditions were common for an ordinary family at this time but a search for the reticence that Winning junior would attach to sex, even within the confines of marriage, should begin on the thin mattress of his sleeping arrangements. Winning never minded sleeping with his father, irritated only by his steady snoring, but the lack of room and, more crucially, privacy meant he rarely saw his parents kiss or even embrace. It was a subject Winning was always reluctant to discuss; in his family, sexual intercourse was strictly for the services of procreation."

US psychologist Professor Adams at the University of Georgia undertook serious research into the link between homophobia and homosexuality finding an astonishing 80 per cent of men who were homophobic had secret homosexual feelings. A plethysmograph, (a device attached to the penis to measure its circumference), expanded in four out of five men claiming they were heterosexual after they had been shown homoerotic images. Professor Adams began to describe homophobia as a form of latent homosexuality. This couldn't have been more evident than in the case of the crazed Soho gay pub bomber, David Copeland, who feared he might be gay. Brought up as a child near the Aldershot army base, he had been bullied for being small. Although dyslexic and a loner, he achieved nine GCSEs at the age of 16. Dr Philip Joseph, a consultant forensic psychologist who interviewed Copeland extensively said: "His problems stem from his sexual insecurity and his inability to cope with the examination at the growth clinic". (His small sexual organs embarrassed him). "...People who fear they are homosexual often join very heterosexual organisations. Right-wing organisations are very homophobic", Joseph added. Copeland was a member of the British National Party (BNP) and police found in his bedsit literature from the US-based, white-supremist Christian Identity Movement.

For any gay person wanting to follow the teachings of the Catholic Church, Winning was at great pains to explain the "joy and peace in living the virtue of chastity". In Stephen McGinty's book, his sister Margaret explained: "He knew what he wanted to be and knew girls didn't come into it".

The views of the Catholic Church on the subject of homosexuality are found in *The Catechism of the Catholic Church*. It draws a clear distinction between what are called 'homosexual tendencies' and 'homosexual acts'. Homosexuals are required to lead a chaste life, controlling themselves through prayer and self-mastery in order to find the only 'freedom' that really matters: freedom from sin.

In the recruitment of teachers, sports coaches, foster carers and the military, Winning believed discrimination against gays was "not unjust". His views on homosexuality were controversial, describing it once as "a disorder... that's got to be... dealt with". On the repeal of Section 28, he told the press: "I worry that any repeal will be presented by the so-called 'gay-rights' lobby as victory in their battle to have the disorder that is homosexuality placed on the same footing as marriage and family life. We have already seen this tactic used before. Before the election (of Tony Blair's Labour administration) we were told that all legislation would be given the 'family test' – namely, would a given policy benefit the family? If not, it would have no place on the new government's agenda. Yet... the families of Britain were left to come to terms with the idea that predatory male homosexuals would be able to indulge in dangerous, immoral acts with their 16-year-old sons, while our legislators washed their hands of the whole issue, proclaiming it to be a question of freedom and equality". (The predatory ways of heterosexual *men* indulging in dangerous, immoral acts with their 16-year old *daughters* were overlooked). As a Christian, Blair regularly read the Bible and sent aides and civil servants ahead of him to find churches to worship in on a Sunday. Behind the scenes, he witnessed the deep divide homosexuality created between influential militant and moderate religionists in government.

Closing the Floodgates with Keep the Clause!

To illustrate the pitfalls of the 'disorder' called homosexuality, Winning relied on discredited statistics used by far-right American Christian groups and advised that the repeal of Section 28 would reduce the life expectancy of children. Using the tactics of the political right, he expressed his certainty that people did not want "their council tax used to fund facilities for gay and lesbians which they do not enjoy for their own children". Winning declared the repeal would leave adolescents in a "fog of confusion" over their sexuality before suggesting, with a sudden and surprising passivity: "Now is the time for reflection, not for knee-jerk reactions", but a knee-jerk reaction was exactly what Scotland would receive from Winning. A frequent spokesman for Scottish Catholics, Monsignor Tom Connolly, quickly stepped in to take the edge off Winning's harsh words, assuring readers of the Edinburgh-based broadsheet, the *Scotsman:* "If people feel the Cardinal's words were discriminatory I am sorry, and I am sure he would be sorry too". But Cardinal Winning wasn't.

Scotsman journalist, Stephen McGinty, who prayed for him every Sunday until the day he died, wrote in his book: "Cardinal Winning was no saint. He could be arrogant, a bully and a sexist. He disliked homosexuals, distrusted many politicians, and considered Donald Dewar... a 'bigot' – a charge to which he himself lay open. In financial matters, he was at best woefully uninterested, and at worst incompetent, and his tenure as Archbishop of Glasgow coincided with the creation of a £10million debt that almost bankrupted the diocese."

In the final hours of the 20th century, human rights campaigner, Peter Tatchell sent an open letter to Cardinal Winning at the Archdiocese of Glasgow. The letter begged Winning to apologise for 2,000 years of Christian homophobia. Tatchell wrote: 'The Catholic Church will shortly mark the Millennium by celebrating 2,000 years of Christianity. But many lesbians and gay men will not be celebrating with you. We will be mourning two millennia of Christian homophobia, which has inflicted terrible pain on homosexual people. Your church has incited prejudice, discrimination and violence against queers for 20 centuries. Over the last 2,000 years, church homophobia has led to hundreds of millions of homosexuals worldwide being rejected and reviled by their families, driven to depression and suicide, discriminated against by anti-gay laws, and condemned to death for sodomy. The Catholic Church has never expressed any remorse for its persecution of queers. The millennium is an opportunity to atone for the genocide inflicted on us. We ask you to express your sorrow for the church's crimes against queer humanity, and to offer your apologies to the gay community. Leviticus 20:13 demands that homosexuals be put to death. For over 1,800 years, the Christian churches followed this Biblical injunction, sponsoring a Homo Holocaust involving the mass murder of queers. We were stoned to death in antiquity, burned alive during the medieval era, and, in this country, hung from gallows until the mid-nineteenth century. This slaughter of homosexuals took place with the official blessing of Popes, Cardinals and Bishops. While the church no longer advocates the death penalty for gay lovers, it still preaches a gospel of sexual apartheid, arguing that homosexuality should not be accorded the same moral or legal status as heterosexuality. This straight supremacist doctrine is used to justify the abuse of queers as second-class citizens. Most Christians, including yourself, continue to support discrimination against gay people with regard to the age of consent, marriage, employment, Section 28 and fostering and adoption. The time has come for Christian contrition. An apology for the suffering inflicted on lesbians and gays by the church is long overdue. We call on you to make this gesture of truth and reconciliation'. Tatchell's efforts were ignored by the Scottish media and snubbed by Winning.

But churches – plagued by scandal and dwindling congregations - had problems of their own. The Glasgow-based broadsheet, the *Herald* released the results of a poll that found 44 per cent of the public thought religion had only "a minor part" to play in their lives and only eight per cent of young people said it "was a major part of their lives". There were some who felt a major victory, such as the retention of Section 28, would underline Christian authority and gain credibility for the Church. With the repeal of Section 28 looming, religionists seized the opportunity. Press releases from religious organisations flooded newsrooms. The *Scotsman* reported two Scottish schools were buying an education pack "which encourages children as young as 14 to act out homosexual roles in the classroom". The video in question showed young people talking about 'coming out' and their experiences of gay relationships; venturing no further than showing a few images of young gay couples kissing. At one point, pupils are asked: "Michael is 15 and his boyfriend wants him to

Closing the Floodgates with Keep the Clause!

have sex. He really wants to, but he is nervous. Michael knows he should use a condom, but doesn't know where to go for help. What should he do?" The *Scotsman's* education correspondent, Tom Little began working himself up into a lather: "The pack, which includes a video and costs £35, encourages children to empathise with characters such as a married man who is caught 'cottaging,' a bisexual grandmother and a sado-masochist. In one game pupils are encouraged to play 'Spot the Heterosexual'." Little suggested that one character in the pack, named Karl, advised: "Try experimenting with other boys and girls and see who you feel most comfortable with".

The *Scottish Daily Mail's* report wrongly described Karl as gay (presumably after what the Honorary Member for Meriden, Mrs Spelman had told the House of Commons in her speech). *The Mail* claimed Karl said: "To attain sexual satisfaction, try experimenting with both boys and girls to see who you feel most comfortable with". In fact, the character said: "People try and see as many girls as possible, until they find the girl they are most attracted to". He then went on say that gay lads deserved the same opportunity.

Tom Little's report in the *Scotsman* was one-sided. He summoned responses from Monsignor Tom Connolly of the Catholic Church and also enlisted the help of Valerie Riches who helped found the Responsible Society, now the 'Family Values' group, Family and Youth Concern, (described in this report as an "independent think-tank)", who said: "This puts concepts and activities into the minds of youngsters they would not normally think about. That is a dangerous thing to do in a child as young as 14". Ian Bainbridge from the Christian Institute, a Newcastle-based religious lobby group described as a "charitable research foundation", declared the pack, "one of the worst examples of its kind..." and Brian Monteith, the Conservative's education spokesman decided it was "a breach" of Section 28.

The pack, produced by the Avon Health Authority funded agency, Health Promotion Service in Avon, was called *Beyond A Phase: A Practical Guide to Challenging Homophobia in Schools*, ungenerously described by the *Sunday Times Scotland* as "a video that encourages schoolchildren as young as 14 to experiment with gay sex". Despite the fuss, of the 76 education packs sold in England, only two were supposed to have been sold to secondary schools in Scotland: One in Fife and the other in Inverness. Even then, both schools denied ever having used them. A Highlands Council spokesman said the pack "was inappropriate and schools would be advised not to use it". This is a shame. In a study by Neil Duncan he found a close link between homophobia and violent attitudes towards women and anyone perceived as vulnerable. He found that boys who were 'nice' to girls were often perceived as 'gay'. Not a culture that bodes well for any young men entering into human relationships... of any kind.

In another report, Tom Little joined Frank Urquhart in the *Scotsman* to comfort "Mrs Hill" of the Scottish School Boards' Association "when it was revealed that two Scottish schools had already bought a teaching pack which asked teenagers to empathise with sado-masochists and 'cottaging' – soliciting for gay sex in a public toilet". With the Scottish School Boards' Association gearing itself up for a major role in the anti-repeal campaign, Mrs Ann Hill appeared to ignore the fact no Scottish school had expressed any intention of using the pack, adding: "What I don't want to see happening is teachers being forced into having to promote any type of sexual activity, whether homosexual or otherwise". The *Dumfries & Galloway Standard* reported how "Dumfries-based chief executive, Ann Hill had said present legislation went far enough in that it allowed discussion about sexuality in schools". Hill suggested she had no problem with children playing the part of a prostitute, but was "absolutely appalled" they might be forced to play "a black lesbian gay in a wheelchair" or "a bisexual granny". Attention was drawn to on-line petitions being drawn up by "a group of Christian primary school teachers" and "a group of student teachers". *TES Scotland (Times Educational Supplement)* noted: "The SSBA as moral guardian is not a pretty sight..." In his letter to The *TES Scotland*, Martin Flynn from Motherwell imagined children being "immersed in homosexuality discussions..." He explained: "Many teachers view the practice of homosexuality as a complete abomination. Many parents and pupils are aghast at the thought of discussing such a disorder... Parents and pupils are sick to the back teeth of liberal-minded people foisting their morality on to them. The alliance of Christian churches who wish to prevent discussions on homosexuality among the young as part of the curriculum speaks for the vast majority of the Scottish people. As a parent and teacher I stand beside Thomas Winning's view of things. Lord Jesus, give me the courage to continue".

Closing the Floodgates with Keep the Clause!

Gay kids often faced appalling levels of homophobia in schools. Not always from other children. On the subject of counselling gay schoolchildren in the *Herald*, Hugh McLoughlin of Bellshill, describing himself as a "humble schoolteacher" at a North Lanarkshire Catholic comprehensive school, asked why teachers should "be ready at the drop of a hat to abandon all their commitments to counsel children who are massively egocentric, compulsively self-indulgent, and totally insensitive to the needs of anyone except themselves?"

Readers of Scottish newspapers were already well-accustomed to the opinions of Christian campaigners, lobby groups and moral conservatives embellishing reports on sexual issues. For example, toward the end of 1999 there was a £600,000 Scottish sex education project undergoing research in Tayside and the Lothians. Alongside quotes from the project's principal investigator at the Medical Research Council's social and public health sciences unit, based at Glasgow University, the *Scotsman* threw in the comments of the Catholic Church's Monsignor Tom Connolly who blasted: "Telling young people about using condoms and safe sex is wrong, wrong, wrong..."!

From being illegal in Scotland up to 1981, homosexual intercourse had at last progressed into a topic that Scots could discuss openly. The debate over the repeal of Section 28 was played out in letters' pages across the nation. Alisdair C Sampson wrote in the *Herald:* "I have come to the inescapable conclusion that one of the most discriminated against groups in society are people like me – white, heterosexual males… I can say absolutely nothing critical about the views or actions of… those of a sexual orientation which is not of my choosing". That didn't stop George Cooper of Baillieston who warned teachers in Glasgow's *Evening Times:* "If any of my boys come home from school talking about loving other boys, I will remove the teacher's teeth without anaesthetic".

As the Section 28 story unfolded, religionists and social conservatives found loyal friends in the English editor of the red-top tabloid, the *Daily Record*, Martin Clarke and his political editor, Ron MacKenna. The tabloid focused on a "GAY RIGHTS CASH ROW", which the gay sexual health group, Phace West "caused" by "handing out free condoms to gay men at Strathclyde Park, a well-known area for gay pick-ups"; and on the supposedly "graphic pornographic images and lurid descriptions of gay sex" on the Phace West website. Colin Hart from the Christian Institute, a group already planning to establish itself in Scotland, faithfully registered their disgust, as did Mrs Anne Allen from the Kirk's Board of Social Responsibility. She declared money for health education, HIV and AIDS prevention was being "diverted into the promotion of sexual activity". Attention was drawn to "critics" – mentioning no names – who "fear the project will further cash in when the Government scraps Clause 28".

Martin Clarke had a formidable reputation as editor. In 2006, Jane Thynne wrote in the *Independent:* "All newspaper editors attract colourful tales from the journalists they employ, but few can boast of death threats. Few can have bashed a phone as forcefully against a wall as he is known to have done (when talking to "Donald fucking Dewar"). Few can shout so loudly that their nose begins to bleed... Clarke's editorial demeanour has attracted a range of tributes from former colleagues – 'vile', 'offensive', 'appalling', 'obsessive', 'childlike' and 'foul-mouthed' being the less flattering". At his morning conferences, journalist Alexandra Blair, who worked with him when he was editor of the *Scotsman* told the *Independent:* "He would start by saying, 'You're all a fucking disgrace and one of you is going to be fucking sacked this week,' and the terrible thing was, one of us usually was". On the other hand, there have been associates who have described him as a sensitive and charming chap who admires Paul Dacre, the editor of the *Daily Mail. Scotsman* journalists told the *Independent:* "He can be an energising, dynamic force, but he's not a stickler for accuracy and he's not at all rigorous about detail. He thinks readers will have amnesia but Scotsman readers don't". Another said: "...He spent too much, drank too much, smoked 60 Silk Cut a day, went clubbing so much he was badly hung over in the morning, and alienated staff in the most dramatic way". On Martin Clarke's approach to Section 28, a journalist told the *Independent:* "He got it right. He recognised that most working-class, left-voting Scots were tiny-minded and conservative about social issues". Clarke's brutish opinions were captured in his column in the *Scotsman,* when he wrote of Comic Relief comedians Lenny Henry and Dawn French: "If Lenny Henry really wants to make a contribution to the underprivileged he could put his wife on a diet and pay off the national debt of a small African nation with the money he saves on cream cakes and

Closing the Floodgates with Keep the Clause!

those Terry's Chocolate Oranges she advertises. Incidentally, do they pay her cash for that or just send round a lorry-load once a month?"

A senior reporter at the *Daily Record* later told me he sensed a lot of effeminate characteristics about Martin Clarke. He said at reporters meetings he didn't remember anyone supporting him during his campaign to retain Section 28 with most people left "wondering just what was going on". However, ageing columnists already on the tabloid needed little persuasion to get behind Martin Clarke's anti-gay campaign. The *Daily Record's* so-called 'Voice of Authority', a dickie-bowed religious columnist called Tom Brown wrung his hands. "Who are the first people you would want to help? Children? The shivering old folk? Poor families? The homeless? Homosexuals? How did they get priority…? How come an insidious minority with a perverse agenda commands the attention of a new minister…? We were not told about a hidden policy to expose our children to harmful propaganda". He bitterly opposed the genuine efforts being made to challenge homophobia in schools, adding there was no reason "to expose schoolchildren to corrupting smut like the teaching aid *Beyond a Phase*, which aims to 'challenge heterosexism and homophobia' in schools. It pursues the familiar homosexual tactic of rubbishing heterosexism and repeats the lie that those who oppose homosexuality are 'homophobic' – and their 'hatred' is a disguise for their own homosexuality. How is that supposed to make young people feel about their heterosexual parents?" Tom Brown thought the proposed repeal of Section 28 would turn "acceptance into flaunting" and stubbornly declared: "Being normal is natural". He stormed: "Homosexuals cannot accept the unhappy status their way of life forces on them. They want the impossible – everything that comes with a normal, natural family relationship". The *Daily Record* went on to print a reader's letter congratulating him on his views.

Christians went on the attack. In the *Lochaber News*, Andrew Holmes of the Highland Christian Schools Trust wrote to the paper to say he'd found local authorities "appointing homosexual school workers to target pupils who are unsure of their sexuality". And "homosexual youth workers… appointed to promote homosexuality and help young people to 'come out'. In some cases," he added, "the aim is to work with children as young as nine…" On the issue of homophobic bullying, Holmes was unyielding. "...This constitutes childish cruelty in the same way that children use other derogatory terms to insult one another. It does not constitute homophobic bullying. Liberal legislation is making our nation a place of darkness..."

Glasgow's *Evening Times* had Mrs A M H, "a happy, fulfilled mother and grandmother" recalling something she had read somewhere about an "eminent Swedish psychologist" who claimed "many boys" who "doubted their masculinity" grew up "normal" if they were "left alone, without undue pressures..." Mrs A M H nonetheless stepped up the pressure herself, begging "all religious and child-welfare organisations to make forceful vociferous protests against the Scottish Parliament's proposed legislation to abolish 'Section 28'." According to Mrs A M H, homosexuality led "our children... more often than not to a sad, unfulfilled life and increased dangers of AIDS".

Things were really flying over the cuckoo's nest by the time you reached Cairnbulg in Aberdeenshire! R S Stephen from the Orthodox Presbyterian Church penned a warning to the *Fraserburgh Herald*. "Labour MSPs have announced that the Scottish Parliament will legislate soon to enforce the teaching of homosexuality in Scotland's schools. This will repeal the Tory article 28 which forbids this teaching since the Bible calls sodomy an 'abomination'. Leviticus 20.13... Now that the Scots Parliament has voted to have prayers to Satan and demons 91 for, 7 against and 13 abstentions on the 9.9.99 and is now legislating Sodomy as a wonderful thing like Pergamos did, then Satan's Seat is also across from Arthur's Seat in Edinburgh up on the Mound in the Assembly Hall. 9.9.99 is 6666 upside down as Satanists always do things and 91 = 7 x 13 and that's the devil's number to perfection (7). I mentioned that in a letter to the (Fraserburgh) Herald a few weeks ago and on my way to deliver it I picked up a bill and was astonished to find it was for £91! The odds are infinite against these numbers especially as one of the voting computers in the Parliament had to be knocked oot to achieve them and the by-election took one MSP oot of the debate! One Tory MSP commented this is 'astonishing and rather chilling'. God now will deal with the Parliament and the nation as He did Sodom with nuclear fire... Have a nice day, albeit a chilling one".

The *Fraserburgh Herald's* editor, Alex Shand lent Mr Stephen's his support in his editorial, agreeing this was no laughing matter: "There are times when I am disgusted by the

Closing the Floodgates with Keep the Clause!

society in which we live..." He was "absolutely horrified" over attempts to repeal Section 28 and wasn't at all surprised "men and boys who are gay are much more likely to be assaulted than those who are 'normal'." Because, he explained, gays are encouraged to be proud of whom they are while there were "still an awful lot of people in the country who take the Biblical view and want nothing to do with any of it". Shand took the opportunity to mention he was "disgusted to see these two men cuddling each other on television..." Shand's editorial went on to express his opinion on one of several stories circulating about gay dads. "And I was even more outraged when I heard them trying to argue that the child will have an upbringing every bit as loving and secure as it would be in a normal family home. Absolute garbage! ...It will be picked on and bullied – and it will be these two men who will have been directly responsible for it".

The *Fraserburgh Herald* offered a welcome platform for some of the emerging homophobic panic. One 'Regular Reader', withholding their name and address wrote: "Sir, It makes one wonder at the attitude of the Prime Minister to the Clause 28, as a man with children himself. It is time that people put the word gay back to its proper use, it has been hijacked to give queers a sense of respectability in a way of life that is neither natural or healthy. The term homosexual Christian is comical, they would be as well to say a Christian thief or a Christian murderer. As a parent I strongly object to the removal of Clause 28. I do not want that taught in schools. I am not impressed with the performance of the Scots Parliament, to crown all that, the rates are to rise ten per cent. Where do they think people are to find it?"

In Glasgow's *Herald*, Michael Naughton from Aberdeen asked: "What is so wonderful about promoting a way of life that would lead to social disintegration, and ultimately extinction, if it came to be adopted by a large proportion of the population?"

John Kelly of Edinburgh told the *Herald:* "I am prepared to believe that there are some unfortunates who cannot help their immoral behaviour, but I also believe that there are very few of these and they need psychiatric help, not encouragement in their vice".

J Lach-Szyrma bestowed upon the citizens of Dundee his contribution through the *Courier:* "Many would appear to have a mental picture of John Inman mincing around in *Are You Being*

RELIGIOUS FASCISM

Served when the word 'gay' is used. In truth, the correct word to be used is 'sodomist'."

A boxer, paratrooper and former shipyard worker George McCaulay took a particular interest in the fight against repeal of Section 28. He believed the world was being taken over by gays and "ugly butch dykes". He was determined his two sons received a moral upbringing and were both shown in BBC Two Scotland's *Counterblast* programme, jumping in lochs and using pulleys attached to trees. Catherine Lockerbie interviewed him in the *Scotsman* and gained further insight into his opinion of women: "I think they're bitches, and we are bitch-busters", he said proudly. He challenged women to a debate on TV: "Come on girls, if you're hard enough, let's have you!" He scoffed: "Women's vanity is overwhelming. Very few women have the ability to be beyond the material in life... Man has a certain strength and consistency of emotion which makes him better suited for steering the ship of family".

McCaulay's views on the establishment of youth camps held a special appeal for right-wing columnist Gerald Warner who believed they would reassert "the values of integrity, heroism and all-round manhood". He enthused: "Servicemen, sportsmen and workers from the emergency services would act as instructors. At age 15, all boys would attend a three-week camp with no girls attending, to undergo exercises in hardship, discomfort and solitude... This experience would culminate in a form of graduation ceremony, acting as a rite of passage into manhood..." He imagined, "just when Johnny should be coming to terms with his sexuality and developing a crush on the boy sitting at the next desk, a bunch of macho militarists is threatening to drag him out into the open air and encourage him to climb trees and act generally like a character in the Just William books – which, of course", he mocked, "have been banned from the school library". Gerald Warner was unhappy with the changes that had taken place in the library since he had left school. "A generation ago, schoolboys learned heroic values from the adventure stories of such authors as G A Henty. Books like that should return to school libraries, displacing Trainspotting and Jennifer Lives with Bob and Carol and Ted and Alice".

Susanne Boesche's book, *Jenny Lives with Eric and Martin*, in fact, never saw the inside of a children's library. It was discovered in the eighties by the Tory press in a teacher's resource centre

Closing the Floodgates with Keep the Clause!

before it helped fuel the introduction of Section 28 following such headlines in 1986 as "VILE BOOK IN SCHOOL", *(Sun)*, "SCANDAL OF GAY PORN BOOKS READ IN SCHOOLS", *(Today)* and the expressed opinion that gays were "propagating" their "peculiar practices at the public expense", *(Sunday Mirror)*.

On the subject of youth camps, Gerald Warner delighted in the "...moral formation of young men". And "since the proposed training would be compulsory, it would be important to ensure the less physically robust pupils were encouraged to develop their fullest potential, rather than be humiliated". For the girls he promised: "...Self-respect, self-reliance, and homemaking skills (regardless of the screams of establishment feminists who eat out in expensive restaurants), financial management and many other useful preparations for careers and marriage". Leaving the women screwing the tops on jars of chutney, Warner turned to men: "We need to rekindle the aspirations celebrated by Rudyard Kipling in his poem If, a hymn to heroic masculinity: 'Yours is the Earth and everything that's in it, / And – which is more – you'll be a Man, my son!'" Warner was sure that the proposal would not find favour with the "politically correct". And a good few others, no doubt!

A Christopher Black of Edinburgh expressed some remarkably similar ideas to George McCaulay in his letter to the *Scottish Daily Mail*, following their columnist Colette Douglas Home's response to the apparent out-performing of boys by girls in traditionally male subjects at school. He wrote: "As with all things wrong with this country, a sizeable proportion of blame can be attributed to the Government's incessant crusade to embrace political correctness. The opprobrious onslaught of 'feminist' propaganda and the negative and weak images of the male gender, which boys of an impressionable age are constantly subjected to from the media, has a profoundly demoralising effect on them".

Before the crippling campaign against the repeal of Section 28 had properly emerged in December 1999, First Minister, Donald Dewar's chief of staff, John Rafferty was suddenly sacked from his post. The Labour spin-doctor admitted he was behind lies that a militant pro-life group had made death threats to Health Minister Susan Deacon for her comments on abortion. Rafferty was a devout Catholic and held the post of development officer for the Archdiocese of Glasgow. His support for gay rights and pro-abortion stance infuriated his boss, Cardinal Winning who had him brought in to rescue the Archdiocese after Winning's mismanagement saw it plunge into debts of around £10m. The *Daily Record* recommended "self-publicist Rafferty was kept on a tight rein and had to follow the masterplan set up by those advising Winning on his finances".

Then, on the morning of Friday, 14 January 2000, Scotland awoke to news that a former bus driver-turned-business-tycoon, Brian Souter, who had contacted his PR man Jack Irvine soon after reading Tom Brown's article, pledged to bankroll the Scottish School Boards' Association's campaign to prevent the repeal of Section 28. "Why can I not give £500,000 to help protect children?" Souter begged. The *Scottish Mail* announced: "The money he has pledged will come from his charitable trust The Souter Foundation, and will finance an intensive four-month campaign headed by the Scottish School Boards' Association".

As it was a devolved issue, the fledgling regional assembly, the Scottish Executive, planned to repeal Section 28 in its consultation document Ethical Standards in Public Life. The Ethical Standards in Public Life (Scotland) Bill was launched in November 1999, based on the principles set out by the Nolan committee. Riding on the back of a wave of optimism for a new, progressive Scotland in Europe and not reckoning on an orchestrated backlash from her opponents, Communities Minister Wendy Alexander said of Section 28: "We believe that legislation is unjust, reactionary and has no place in the Scotland of tomorrow". Brian Souter was having none of it.

Under editor, Bruce Waddell, (later to be an editor of the *Daily Record)*, Brian Souter enjoyed the editorial backing of the *Scottish Sun* which reported: "Mr Souter reckons the Scottish Executive is going soft over the move to scrap Clause 28, which prevents teachers from telling kids about gays and lesbians". Columnist Anvar Khan wrote in the *Herald*: "...Cash should not be used as a bully... I don't remember anyone voting for Mr Souter... The good book warned against the evil of a prosperous man's smash". Peter Tatchell of Outrage! asked in the *Sunday Mail*: "If Mr Souter has that kind of money to spare, why doesn't he spend it compassionately on flats for the homeless, computers for Scotland's cash-strapped schools, or equipping the NHS with urgently needed cancer scanners?" The *Scottish Daily Express* wondered: "How does all this eccentricity of dress, mixed with a

Closing the Floodgates with Keep the Clause!

ruthless cattle dealer's head for figures and profit margins, square with a private family life at his home in Ochtertyre where they say grace before meals, and regularly attend church?" Souter answered his critics in the *Sunday Times's, Ecosse* supplement: "If we were to apply the values of the Sermon on the Mount to our business we would be rooked within six months. Ethics are not irrelevant, but some are incompatible with what we have to do, because capitalism is based on greed". He dismissed it as "a dichotomy, not hypocrisy". With ex-editor of the *Scottish Sun* Jack Irvine on Souter's payroll to launch a campaign to fight repeal, the First Minister, Donald Dewar was forced to step in, quickly sidelining Communities Minister Wendy Alexander. Iain MacWhirter wrote in the *Herald:* "The Communities Minister had frankly found herself out of her depth, faced by the fundamentalist trinity of Brian Souter, Cardinal Winning and Jack Irvine, Scotland's foremost homophobic columnist". Scottish National Party (SNP) MSP Roseanna Cunningham cuttingly remarked in the *Scottish Sun:* "No doubt he (Donald Dewar) is worried that she may not be able to handle everything under all this new pressure".

Tycoon Brian Souter had courted Jack Irvine, the boss of PR firm Media House, after spotting his column in the *Scottish Mirror*. Irvine was renowned for his homophobia, for example, commenting on equalising the age of consent for gay men: "A pretty young boy of 16 can't vote for his local MP, but he can now be buggered by him... So equality is the key, is it? In that case, shouldn't 16-year-olds get the vote, be eligible to become, say, policemen? No? Why not? Because they're not mature enough. But they are deemed mature enough to be bum chums for sleazy old pervs". Irvine later trotted out an apology for his remarks in the *Sunday Herald:* "I have a long standing friend and client who is gay. I helped him when people wanted to 'out' him. I'm not homophobic. I have gay friends". Jack Irvine, who also expressed a mistrust of "muesli-eating" types, was recruited to run the 'Keep the Clause' campaign. In an academic study of lobbying in Scotland, his methods could be summarised by his own comments: "I go to clients and say we come at it from two levels. There's the political-intellectual level, and then we have the guys who go in with the boots on and kick politicians' brains out". Irvine's PR firm, Media House already had the *Scottish Mirror's* sister paper, the *Daily Record* on its books and had been hired by Stagecoach's bank, the Bank of Scotland, to rescue it from the mess it got itself into after forming links with televangelist Pat Robertson. Irvine's chief fixer was David Macauley. Macauley was in regular contact with Ann Hill from the Scottish School Boards' Association while he was head of Scotland Against Drugs (SAD). There was a lack of support for Macauley's stern just-say-no message in Scotland's war against drugs and he later resigned from his job.

Brian Souter – or 'Soapy' as he was sometimes referred to in the press after 'The Broons' cartoon character, Soapy Souter – was a little different from the traditional, conservative, Presbyterian Scottish businessmen that looked down from gilt frames across polished tables of dusty boardrooms. Born in 1954, he represented the sort of 'new money' that benefited from Margaret Thatcher's culture of accumulate and speculate even though he supported the Scottish National Party (SNP). It started with just one bus that he, his sister and her first husband used to ferry workers around building sites before a cash injection from a Canadian uncle and his father's redundancy money helped them on the way to the dizzying heights of a stock flotation in April 1993, raising more than £1 billion. His company, Stagecoach, eventually became a public transport firm in the FTSE 100 index chalking up £96m profit in 1999. Brian Souter was Scotland's richest man and a prominent member of the evangelical Church of the Nazarene based in Kansas, USA. The Nazarenes had their own publication house distributing their message across the globe. Interviews with ministers at the Church of the Nazarene confirmed that before taking communion, boys would have to be 'cured' of their homosexuality. In the UK, they boasted 5,000 adherents in 100 churches mainly in Perth (Souter's home town), Glasgow, and the northwest of England, where its headquarters was located. The church dictated that 10 per cent of believers' incomes should be given to the Church. Souter did not always give his donations directly to the Church but channelled his money through The Souter Foundation, offering support for projects engaged in the relief of human suffering in the UK or overseas, particularly those with a Christian emphasis. One such donation was a bus that stopped every Thursday afternoon at Musselburgh harbour to catch children going home from school, encouraging them onboard to attend a 'cell group'; "hanging out,

Closing the Floodgates with Keep the Clause!

using Playstation, watching films, chatting and most importantly, getting into the word of God and learning about Him".

Brian Souter's company, Stagecoach, also donated money to a city academy in Grimsby. He was prevented from doing so in Scotland, where where entrepreneurs and firms were not permitted to take control of schools. In 2008, Stagecoach donated £500,000 for a gym in the Oasis Academy in Wintringham, a school for 1,100 pupils run by the Christian group, Oasis Community Learning (OCL). Along with funding from the local authority and the education department, OCL paid £2million to help run the school with funding from the Souter Charitable Trust poured into the Oasis Trust which co-ordinated OCL's Christian work. By 2008, OCL was running nine academies across the UK.

Sunday sermons of the Church of the Nazarene were in the hellfire and brimstone tradition. The Church's application form for membership required those who joined to "endeavour in every way to glorify God by a humble walk, godly conversation, and holy service" and "abstaining from all evil, seek earnestly to perfect holiness of heart and life in the fear of the Lord".

For the most part, Brian Souter lived in a £1million mansion in Perth with his wife Betty and their children, or at their weekend retreat at Ochtertyre, Crieff. It was far removed from the life enjoyed by a large proportion of his customers in Northern England whom he once described as "the beer-drinking, chip-eating, council house-dwelling, Old Labour-voting masses". Brian Souter owned the bus company, Stagecoach, along with his sister Ann Gloag, once Scotland's richest woman. At the time, Souter was planning to buy a 35 per cent stake in Italy's largest bus company, Sogin and with Prestwick airport already in his grasp, dreamed of setting up a network of airports. Stagecoach bought the largest provider of coach, tour and sightseeing services, the second largest bus operator in North America, Texas-based Coach USA; run by executive chairman Larry King with operations headed by chief executive officer Frank Gallagher. Coach USA stretched across 35 states and Canada with a fleet of more than 6,500 motor coaches and 3,000 taxicabs. The company operated down the eastern coast to Florida, including Orlando and Miami, then through the south along Route 10 from Jacksonville to San Diego through Houston. It served most of the top convention destinations in the USA and had dozens of major contracts such as in Elko, Nevada, the mile-deep gold mine where it delivered 50,000 workers a day to the goldface. After Stagecoach acquired Coach USA on 26 July, 1999 it went on to add another 15 businesses and moved into the capital of the USA, Washington DC. One in three coaches, packed with commuters, going through New York's Lincoln Tunnel, belonged to Coach USA. Brian Souter's business empire stretched from Scandinavia to Africa, the United States and even Hong Kong where he owned a 60 per cent stake in the biggest commuter travel company, Road King. Ferries chugging across Auckland harbour and New Zealand Yellow Bus divisions bore Brian Souter's mark. By 2002, along with his sister Ann Gloag, Souter teamed up with the Bank of Scotland and property consultants Montagu Evans to form Highfield Properties (Holdings) in a £54million deal to acquire pension fund manager Hermes' portfolio of retail premises in UK towns. By 2007, the Bank of Scotland would acquire a 15 per cent stake of Paradigm Real Estate Managers, a £24million investment firm partially owned by Souter and Gloag. By investing directly in Paradigm, the Bank of Scotland would provide the company an additional £15million to play with. An expansion of Glasgow's Skypark, which the company partly owned, was first in its sights along with a development of luxury flats, a retail store in Giffnock and a business park near Edinburgh airport. At the time of the credit crunch of 2009, Stagecoach recorded bumper profits. While up to a thousand jobs were under threat at two of their English rail franchises, Souter gave away his £1.6million bonus package. The lion's share of £900,000 went to his Souter Charitable Trust to further his Christian causes and £623,000 went into Stagecoach's pension fund. Brian Souter and his sister, Ann Gloag were estimated to have a combined fortune of £700million between them.

In 2013, dressed in a powder blue jacket and white trousers, Brian Souter took to the stage to preach to an audience of evangelical Christians at Destiny Church in Glasgow; streamed live around the world on the Internet. He revealed how financier friend Colin McLean - whom he compared to John the Baptist for having the foresight to predict the 2008 economic crash - warned him not to invest in banks, thereby saving him millions. McLean was founder of investment group Scottish Value Trust. Souter explained to the audience: "In early 2008, I went to the

Closing the Floodgates with Keep the Clause!

Bank of Scotland and I met Peter Cummings who was running the bank at that time. "I said to him, 'Peter, what's going on with the banking business? There seems to be a lot of problems.'

"He said: 'Oh, there's nothing to worry about, we're going to make tonnes of money this year again. In fact, it's a great opportunity to buy some cheap stock'.

"Later in the year, I got into conversation with Colin McLean about it.

"He told me: 'The banks don't understand their own balance sheets and don't have any idea about the problems they are facing. There's going to be a liquidity crisis and the Scottish banks will probably not be here in 12 months time'.

"He didn't claim to have the gift of prophecy. But that was prophetic. After that, I thought, I'm not going to buy any more bank shares. Most of my friends filled their boots with the banks and lost an absolute fortune".

Back in 1999, Souter was Scotland's golden boy to the point he had even been appointed a 'champion of change' in Labour's drive to modernise local government. That was before he hired Jack Irvine to challenge the Scottish Executive over the repeal of Section 28. 'Keep the Clause' planned a £250,000 advertising blitz on television, radio and in newspapers to block repeal.

Brian Souter and his sister Ann Gloag were ruthless entrepreneurs. Souter expanded Stagecoach by blocking in the opposition's buses and offering lower, sometimes completely free fares. They frequently drove small operators off the road. It was often the leading topic in local papers as businesses went to the wall, crushed beneath the weight of a Stagecoach bus. Souter often forced drivers to take cuts or work longer hours for the same money. Facing a stream of referrals to the Monopolies and Mergers Commission, the MMC ruled that the company's behaviour was "deplorable, predatory and against the public interest". Souter's biographer, Christian Wolmar explained: "Souter might belong to a strict Christian sect but he is neither conservative nor homophobic". Wolmar did acknowledge, however, that Souter was a mass of contradictions. "He ensures his company has the best pension scheme in the industry - one that pays out to gay partners, incidentally" and was "the only chairman of a top 100 company to have sent in a corporation tax return in 1987 with 'Not for Trident', in line with his pacifist views, written on the cheque..." Once, as a loyal trade unionist working as a Glasgow bus conductor, Brian Souter went on strike. But that didn't stop him threatening to fly down scab bus drivers to break a threatened walkout in the East Midlands. Souter's brother David felt he pushed his drivers too hard and left the company. In Christian Wolmar's book *Stagecoach - A Rag To Riches Story At The Frontier Of Capitalism*, David Souter said: "Brian was very driven. He was only married in the late 1980s. He came late to that and had a very, very driven ethic on making the business work; more than I was comfortable with".

By the time millionaire Brian Souter had expressed his concern – an estimated £500,000 of it - the Catholic Education Commission unveiled a new document on sex education. For the first time they recommended that older children *could* actually discuss homosexuality. Glasgow's *Evening Times* reminded readers that the Church still considered homosexuality "depraved" and that it was "a trial" which could be helped by counselling. Without naming any, the tabloid insisted that "gay activists welcomed the Church's move". Helen Curry, secretary of the Glasgow Diocesan Union of Catholic Mothers told the *Evening Times* that the Catholic Church should be giving "guidelines on the modern times..." She presumed: "If it is coming from the Catholic education system, weighing heavily on morality, I cannot see how it could be objectionable".

With the recommendation that children in Catholic schools could discuss homosexuality, the *Scottish Daily Mail* rolled up its sleeves in defiance against the impending repeal of Section 28 by reporting the recruitment of children into the campaign in a string of events organised "by all the main Christian denomination churches and youth groups such as the Scouts and the Boys Brigade". If effeminate boys or tomboys hadn't curbed their behaviour now; they would soon have to.

Whilst any 'discussion' of homosexuality thrived in the school playground, it proved more difficult for the Catholic Church. Its presence within their ranks had been so heavily concealed; many had already died through risk-taking or ignorance. Nick Jackson of the London Ecumenical AIDS Trust working in the Diocese of Southwark claimed there had been a 'sanitising' of the death certificates of priests following revelations that many gay priests had died of AIDS.

In a letter to *Scotland on Sunday* Dave Berry from Edinburgh wrote: "The supporters of the clause make such a fuss about

Closing the Floodgates with Keep the Clause!

what schools might teach in sex lessons. If this is genuinely their concern then they are entirely missing the point of repeal. Section 28 does not say anything about which topics may be discussed in sex lessons, or which techniques may be used to discuss them. In fact it is so vague that it hardly specifies anything at all. It is primarily a statement of prejudice, and the law of a modern society should not include such prejudice. The supporters of the clause are also keen on 'family values'. But this phrase doesn't seem to mean loving the members of your family, regardless of their sexuality. Instead, it seems to mean forcing everyone to live the same way, even if this means living a lie".

According to the *Mail*, Souter "decided to make his stand after being shown shocking images of children being sexually abused on the Internet site run by a collection of gay groups who have said they would like to have a role in the education system". He told the *Mail*: "I have seen that material and, as a human being, I have been disgusted..." His comments were said to have alarmed the more liberal boss of Virgin Trains, Richard Branson, whose company was now 49 per cent owned by Stagecoach.

Souter insisted, "this is not homophobic" (Scottish editions of the *Daily Telegraph)* and pleaded: "We've got homosexual friends, I've had people with HIV in my house" *(Daily Record)* and "I respect their rights..." *(Scottish Sun).* Not everybody was impressed. His mildly camp demeanour, irregular dress sense and penchant for red Kickers shoes became a target for journalists. TV footage of a loner, skipping lightly across a car park at a Bank of Scotland awards ceremony before taking cover in his car earned him derision from gays suspicious of his motives. On the launch of his fleet of open-topped tour buses through New York, PR columnist for the *Scotsman*, Piers D'éere, wrote: "He dresses appallingly, giggles like a girlie, and mouths off cheerily about everything from gay marriage to low emission engines".

Red shoes or not; Brian Souter was no friend of Dorothy!

Under the heading: "Protect our kids", Brian Souter was given more publicity in the *Scottish Sun* to explain why he launched his "gay crusade". Reporter Kenny McAlpine wrote: "Souter, 45, has been offered backing by political groups in America, British trade unions and a number of 'disillusioned' Labour MPs and MSPs".

Nothing could stop US faith-based organisations fomenting fear and discrimination against gay groups operating overseas.

RELIGIOUS FASCISM

Following the exposure of links between US religious groups and the criminalisation of gay people in Uganda, who were threatened with life imprisonment and death sentences, a resolution was passed in 2010 in the California Senate stating: "There is a growing movement, supported and funded by some United States-based religious groups to further criminalize homosexuality globally. The Senate calls upon the United States Department of State to censure American citizens and organisations who contravene American foreign policy by demonstrated exportation of fear and misinformation to other countries". Nonetheless, soon after, the United Nations removed sexual orientation from a plea in a resolution that protected vulnerable groups from executions such as journalists, lawyers, different ethnic groups, faiths and linguistic minorities.

Souter claimed the reaction to his campaign "had been phenomenal. We have been contacted from parties in America backing the stance... We have also been offered money but we will check the sincerity and the background of the backers before we make a decision". The report added: "Mr Souter... has handed over his £1million to The Scottish School Boards' Association who are battling against the Government to keep the ban in force. SSBA treasurer Alan Smith said: 'We're acting to protect children and we should be allowed to use our democratic right for a debate on the issue from Scotland's new listening Government". The story was juxtaposed with one of retired Lieutenant General Sir Michael Gow, 76, who blasted moves to lift the ban on gays serving in the military and suggested that they be given their own regiment. "If we have to have homosexuals why not put them together. The Germans had Stomach Battalions where a soldier with a tummy complaint was put into a battalion with others who had a similar ailment. Something similar might be worked out for gays".

Scotland's *Sunday Herald* warned: "The London press have started asking the question: 'Are Scots the most repressed nation in Europe?' This is a view that we must challenge or else be prepared to live with for decades". Journalist and broadcaster Iain Macwhirter summed it up: "Here was an opportunity to strike back at the homosexualists, the 'slobbering queers' as they've been described by Jack Irvine of the PR firm Media House. Souter provided the cash, Cardinal Winning the legitimacy, and

Closing the Floodgates with Keep the Clause!

the *Daily Record* the publicity. The 'Keep the Clause' campaign was born".

After the Prime Minister Tony Blair gave his full backing to the repeal of Section 28, the *Scottish Sun* declared it would "lead to homosexuality being promoted in schools" and revealed Souter's intention to spend his last penny on the campaign. Souter told the Murdoch-owned tabloid: "If I have to use all my money and go and live in a council house I will".

Brian Souter enjoyed the support of two of Scotland's most popular Glasgow-based, red-top tabloids, the *Scottish Sun*, (edited by Bruce Waddell), based at Kinning Park and the *Daily Record*, (edited by Martin Clarke), at Anderston Quay, along Glasgow's Broomielaw. "As a married couple with four children, my wife and I welcomed New Labour's commitment to the family..." Souter told the press.

However, the Rt Rev Michael Hare Duke, Bishop of St Andrews, Dunkeld and Dunblane in the Episcopal Church in Scotland was not going to play ball when he advised the *Scotsman*: "If we begin with the Bible, the slogan 'family values' rings hollow as a prescription for social conduct... Jesus explicitly told (his disciples) 'Anyone who comes to me without hating father, mother, wife, children, brothers, sisters, yes and his own life too, cannot be my disciple' (Luke 14, 26)".

The *Daily Record* editor, Martin Clarke generously gave Souter space to exercise his opinion in an essay entitled: "The majority have rights too, Mr Dewar". Souter filled it with his concerns for a beleaguered "majority".

In his essay, Brian Souter gave away something of himself. A kid who had been mocked at school for his "face full of plooks". Now he was a man challenged by a society he claimed "chipped away at the foundations of our traditional values". These were values that Souter trusted; personal values that had been a lifetime's investment for a small boy struggling to emulate his strong father. This was a successful man, a family man and most importantly, a heterosexual man. But Souter rarely expressed his need for such values in the first person singular, demonstrated by remarks from his essay: "*We* have watched with dismay... *The people* of Scotland have a right... Important values as far as *the people* are concerned... *We have* no shortage of *volunteers* who are... desperate to show *their* support... determined, like *us*, to make this Government listen to the voice

RELIGIOUS FASCISM

of *the man in the street*... The *Scottish people* are not in the mood... This pressure is coming from *parents and grandparents* with a lifetime of experience... Passionately felt opinion from *ordinary men and women*... The message from *the Scottish people* is very clear... My principal reasons for getting involved are the concerns expressed *by friends and family, all of whom are ordinary people* in similar positions *to ourselves...* " (Italics mine).

At the same time as Brian Souter's essay was published, news reports revealed a dramatic rise in male suicides in Scotland, a proportion of which, of course, were a result of confusion over sexual orientation. Souter insisted: "The 'Gay is OK' message should not be directed at teenagers who are coming to terms with their gender and may be confused for a period of time". But according to a report at the time by Edinburgh University's Centre for Theology and Public Issues, *The Sorrows of Young Men: Exploring the Increasing Risk of Suicide*, the proportion of deaths of young Scotsmen attributed to suicide had risen from one in nine in 1984 to one in four in 1998, just fourteen years later. Suicides had become more than the combined total of deaths from road accidents and drugs.

Whatever Brian Souter's concerns, however, as a family man it didn't appear to be 'gay lessons' his son Scott needed protecting from. In 2007 15-year-old Scott drove his father's sports car the wrong way down a one-way street without insurance. Then, in 2009, at 18, he was fined for being drunk in public in Stirling, and on another occasion, after a lot to drink at a party, he rounded up several of his friends and chased a stranger by car. After forcing him to stop, he punched 20-year-old, Philip Johnston about the head and face for making fun of his family and his father. Souter's counsel tried to persuade the Sheriff to let him off after telling the court how his father ordered him into anger management and alcohol counselling sessions. After leaving his victim battered and bruised, he was ordered to pay £200 and a further £400 compensation to his victim.

Soon after Brian Souter's essay, Catholic Church spokesman Monsignor Tom Connolly told Glasgow's *Evening Times*, Mr Souter "reflects a fear that is clearly shared by parents across Scotland". Sensing a new strident tone coming from the Church the *Sunday Herald* predicted this would be "one of the biggest divisions between Church and State in recent history".

Closing the Floodgates with Keep the Clause!

Scotland was a devout country. Religious tourism was estimated to be worth anything between £80million and £100million with visitors travelling to such sites as St Giles' Cathedral in Edinburgh, the Orphir Round Kirk in Orkney, Rosslyn Chapel outside Edinburgh, the Pictish memorials in Shetland and the island of Iona. Home Secretary Jack Straw had already expressed his fear that religious fundamentalism might exert an undue influence on the Scottish parliament in a Cabinet committee which began hammering out devolution policies in 1997. It gave birth to a curious anomaly whereby health and home affairs were devolved to the Scottish parliament yet the issue of abortion remained a reserved power of Westminster.

As Souter rallied his troops, his ally, the Christian Institute, installed itself in Edinburgh. Their PO address turned out to be 15, Northbank Street in Edinburgh: the headquarters of the Free Presbyterian Church (the notorious 'Wee Frees').

Those supporting the retention of Section 28 would miss no opportunity to promote the message that Section 28 had to stay. Even BBC Radio Scotland's early morning news programme, interrupted daily by religious proselytizing in its *Thought for the Day*, became a target for some religionists to shoehorn in their message. On the issue of Section 28, Bishop of Motherwell, Joseph Devine begged for "tolerance" before insisting: "Let the people have their say". To help them, he went about gathering a petition in support of the retention of Section 28 from local churchgoers. As president of the Catholic Education Commission, Devine continued to provoke controversy by insisting, in 2005, backed by the church's blueprint for schools – *A Charter for Catholic Schools* - that homosexual teachers should have their promotion opportunities limited and be barred from working in Catholic schools. He made the headlines in Scotland, once again, in 2008 after claiming at a lecture that the gay community were aligning themselves with victims of the Holocaust to make it appear they were under persecution. He warned his audience there was a "huge and well-orchestrated conspiracy" taking place and "we ignore the gay community at our peril". Asked how parents should handle homosexuality, he advised that he "would not tolerate that behaviour" and finished by telling his audience he was looking for a fight.

Gays didn't need to try and align themselves with victims of the Holocaust: They *were* victims. Although the statutory criminalisation of homosexuals in Germany by Section 175 of the penal code had existed since 1871 and only repealed in 1994, it was under the Third Reich that the law was enforced with the formation of the Reich Office for the Combating of Homosexuality and Abortion which led to the persecution, castration murder and subjection to medical experiments of homosexuals. Although Section 175 was almost repealed in the preceding Weimar regime, *Sexualwissenschaft*, the science of sex was branded a 'Jewish science' and its Jewish exponents were forced into exile. During the Berlin Olympics of 1936 the Gestapo began systematically raiding gay bars and closing down the dozens of gay publications. According to Günter Grau in his book *Hidden Holocaust?* the number of homosexuals sentenced by Nazi judges between 1933 and 1945 was roughly fifty thousand, and internal documents of the Nazi leadership showed that some five thousand were deported to concentration camps. After liberation, homosexuals were judged to have been properly imprisoned once it was understood Section 175 of the penal code was not introduced by the Nazis. Their time in concentration camps was treated as a criminal record and revealed to employers. To add insult to injury, whilst former SS guards were allowed to declare their time in the camps in calculating their pensions; gay inmates had *their* time deducted.

Bishop Devine's views were challenged on BBC Scotland News (which wrongly suggested a majority had supported the retention of Section 28). The camp bishop was shown shrugging his shoulders, pointing to the sky and begging: "Don't shoot the messenger... Don't blame me... It's Him!"

Sarah-Kate Templeton, the *Sunday Herald's* religious affairs correspondent wondered at religionists' "unprecedented campaign" against "promoting homosexuality" in schools. Mrs Ann Allen from the Church of Scotland's powerful Board of Social Responsibility claimed to have 80 per cent of their members onboard vindicating her concerns over the promotion of "the homosexual practice". Rev Bill Wallace, former convenor of the Board told the *Scotsman:* "Genital sexual acts should be within the marriage bond and nowhere else". The *Sunday Times Scotland* pointed out that Souter would be "joined by representatives from the Muslim and Jewish communities". (The Scottish Council of Jewish Communities, in fact, supported repeal along with many Muslims and ex-Muslims). Templeton's

Closing the Floodgates with Keep the Clause!

article had Labour councillor, Bashir Maan explaining "most Muslims will send their children to Catholic schools if Section 28 is repealed... People like me have been trying to say stay together but this leaves me defenceless". The *Daily Mail* gave over a two-page spread to the Muslim Council of Britain's Secretary General, Iqbal Sacranie. But was this really the picture? Muslims were already attending Catholic schools in large numbers, not necessarily because Catholic education advocated the retention of Section 28, but because – for one thing - they wanted to send their daughters to same-sex schools. Such an alliance was a marriage of convenience. As president of the Catholic Education Commission, Bishop Joseph Devine was to tell the press, long after the Section 28 debate had died down: "Around 80 per cent of the pupils attending St Albert's Roman Catholic Primary School in Pollockshields, Glasgow are Muslim. It's a Catholic school in name only. It is a complete absurdity. What I would like is for the education authority to create a school for Muslim children". (That might have unsettled some 13 per cent of Sikh children who also attended St Albert's school). The *Herald* columnist Ms Anvar Khan was shocked by Muslims she saw standing incongruously with what seemed a discriminatory campaign and wrote: "The gang's getting bigger". Sufficiently satisfied with the way the campaign had been gathering momentum, Cardinal Winning was moved to declare: "It is heartening to see Christians from so many denominations coming together on this".

In Birmingham, more than 60 people took part in a candlelit vigil on the steps of the Town Hall in protest at the imposition of Section 28 in the UK. The local newspaper promptly claimed Section 28 had been breached since the council had loaned them a sound system. A similar vigil in Lincoln was photographed by a small group of British National Party members.

The gay community in Scotland, on the other hand, took the campaign very quietly with no high profile demonstrations to justify the 'militant' label lavishly applied by certain sections of the press. Tim Hopkins of Scotland's Equality Network began to play a lead role in campaigning against the well-funded efforts of Brian Souter's 'Keep the Clause' campaign, but the quiet, unassuming Englishman was largely unknown to tabloid readers. Much of the press focused instead on the already vilified London-based human rights campaigner and gay activist, Peter

RELIGIOUS FASCISM

Tatchell. The *Scottish Daily Mail* wrote: "The leader of militant gay campaigners Outrage, said: (Brian Souter) 'is behaving like the business leaders in the Deep South of America who funded the Fifties campaign to maintain racial segregation. I hope commuters, trade unionists, churches, politicians and companies that support gay human rights will boycott Stagecoach'." The *Mail* added: "The Scottish School Boards' Association which is set to front the campaign was bombarded by abusive and threatening phone calls from pro-homosexual groups yesterday. But the backlash among homosexuals against Mr Souter's £500,000 donation was overwhelmed by opposition from the silent majority of people who oppose the government's decision...

"The backlash from the gay lobby took a sinister turn as it emerged that Ann Hill, the chief executive of SSBA, had received abusive and threatening phone calls from militant gay rights campaigners".

By Christmas of 1999, the faithful were helping lift Cliff Richard's *Millennium Prayer* to number one in the British pop charts by buying up stocks and giving them away to churches. George Michael, who had released his single *Outside* based on his experiences of arrest by an undercover cop in Hollywood, called the exercise a vile exploitation. The *Daily Record* turned on the "sleaze-hit star" in fury. The paper labelled his video "outrageous" because "one scene shows two actors playing Los Angeles policeman kissing" and another depicted "gay and lesbian sex". They accused George Michael of "poking fun at the scandal" suggesting, "some people believe (the video) glamorises open air sex". In support of Cliff Richard, the tabloid insisted: "...When it comes to music, like everything else, the majority is always right... If Cliff is a 'vile exploiter,' what are you George?" The *Daily Record* listed all the hits where they thought George Michael "plumbed the depths" in his videos, dragging in the Catholic spokesman Tom Connelly to praise Sir Cliff as "an icon of goodness; a wonderful guy". Yvonne White, co-ordinator of the Cliff Richard Fan Club in Glasgow said: "George Michael has been involved in so many scandals that the *Lord's Prayer* probably makes him squirm with guilt". 'Old Mother Burnie' passed judgement on "vile" George Michael's "other record... the personal one which affronts common decency", chastising him for "imposing his own lewd lifestyle on young fans" and

Closing the Floodgates with Keep the Clause!

castigating him for "committing an illegal, homosexual act in a park's public loo". She reprimanded him for "exploiting something far more offensive than religion" before the *Record* asked readers to phone them and register a vote: "Do you agree with George Michael or Cliff Richard?"

Cliff Richards' subsequent victory should have come as no surprise to anyone.

As a registered charity, the Christian Institute received donations to help it promote its particular brand of "Christian values" receiving a staggering £496,581 as "gifts" in 2000. Its deputy director, Simon Calvert pounced on two "offensive books" in a Strathclyde University teaching programme. Calvert claimed: "These books are guaranteed to stoke up an interest in children in sexual matters they would otherwise not have had" and insisted, "children aged 10 were being given inappropriate sex education". In a report in the *Falkirk Herald*, Falkirk Council was "slammed" for "promoting sex in schools" and very soon morally conservative Labour councillors were attacking the work of parliamentary members of their own Party as they set about repealing Section 28. In the council chambers at Falkirk a debate raged over whether or not they should debate Section 28 at all before Falkirk's Provost, Dennis Goldie, got his way. He even dipped into his own pocket to pay for the hire of the Town Hall in Falkirk for a summit meeting, smugly informing the *Falkirk Herald* "he spoke for the vast majority of people in Falkirk". Before opening proceedings had begun, Provost Goldie was already speaking out against repeal and read what he described as "facts" from the *Daily Record*. The minister of Grahamston United Church leapt to his feet to remind Goldie: "As chairman of the meeting you should remain impartial". A parent lashed out: "I've got two kids and I feel it's my duty to teach them good moral and Christian values. You can call me a bigot if you like but I've no time whatsoever for these homosexuals". Alastair Horne, minister at the St. Andrew's West Church in Falkirk, said he strongly commended the council for voting against repeal, saying: "The Bible was clearly against homosexuality". One young gay lad in the audience bravely spoke up to say: "opponents of the plans should be 'ashamed' of themselves". All the same, a show of hands, taken at the end of the meeting, showed the vast majority of the 100-strong crowd - which included a handful of schoolchildren in a crowd mostly recruited from local churches -

were clearly in support of Dennis Goldie and the council. Whilst emphasising how much he abhorred discrimination and wasn't homophobic, at the Policy Committee Goldie voted against repeal in what turned out to be a very close call: four against; three in favour. The religious had tasted blood.

By now, the debate was already spilling out of council chambers into pubs, canteens, living-rooms and even colleges across the country. Although the National Union of Students in Scotland's Women's Officer wanted to "encourage both local authorities and students to promote understanding and tolerance", the *Falkirk Herald* helpfully pointed out she was not backed by Yvonne Harley, Falkirk College's student president.

While the Labour ministers at The Mound (where the parliament met in Edinburgh) tried to portray a united front in supporting repeal, the local press in Falkirk discovered notification of a 'Keep the Clause' meeting produced on local Labour Party headed notepaper.

If the letters chosen for publication by the editor of the *Falkirk Herald* were anything to go by, George Guthrie and Dennis Goldie did indeed enjoy massive support. Bert Smith of Hallglen wrote: "Our council at this time is to be congratulated on the democratic stance they have taken on this controversial subject by providing a platform for public debate".

Peter Moodie of Arnothill, Falkirk wrote: "It is pleasing to see that, at long last, the many shades of opinion on this topic are at last being aired... I was; however, somewhat surprised and disappointed to read the contribution from Duncan McClements... Duncan's principle reason for repeal of Section 28 is that it is 'discriminatory'. On that point I can agree with him whole-heartedly as surely it is right to discriminate against that which is evil just as we would discriminate against murder or rape. The gay lobby has been so successful over recent times in brainwashing society into believing that rejection or opposition to homosexuality somehow equates to discrimination of gays, that normally sensible people like Duncan can trot out such rubbish under the guise of Christianity. Abhorrence of unnatural practices does not equate to homophobia!"

H J Lynch from Larbert wrote: "...Balanced information about homosexuality can be given easily within existing Religious Education... A point correctly made by Provost Goldie. The Provost is also correct in stating that the public would not be in

Closing the Floodgates with Keep the Clause!

favour of ratepayer's money being used to fund gay/lesbian groups... Holy Scripture roundly condemns homosexuality/lesbian practices (Romans 1:24-27 and Corinthians 1:7). How can MSPs (Wendy) Alexander and (Susan) Deacon hope to reduce HIV/sexually transmitted diseases when they are openly supporting gay rights and teenage sexual promiscuity". Although not made clear in the *Falkirk Herald*, Hugh J Lynch was a vociferous supporter of 'Keep the Clause', chairman of the Larbert Labour Party and a member of the Christian Family Action Movement. He had recently retired from the position of rector of St Mungo's Roman Catholic High School in Falkirk and had served as an assistant director of education.

Extracts of a letter to the Scottish Executive and local MSPs from ministers and elders of different churches were also carried by the *Falkirk Herald*. "Our many years of experience as servants to our communities has involved ministry to people with a variety of sexual orientation. In the Name of the Lord whom we serve, we have always sought to treat each person with the love and compassion that we feel Jesus would have demonstrated. We make this point so that you will understand where we are coming from - we are not homophobic..." (But...)! "We believe the promotion of homosexuality and homosexual propaganda in schools will only facilitate the exploitation of the most vulnerable in our society... Some of us have written as individuals and are aware of the case you are putting forward in the guise of being: 'committed to the principles of equal opportunities and to tackling exclusion in all walks of life in Scotland. These principals apply to sexual orientation as much as to differences of sex and race'. We have consulted the Scottish Executive's publication Standards in Public Life; Consultation of the Ethical Standards in Public Life (Scotland) Bill along with information published by other agencies such as in the Christian Institute's booklet entitled 'Bank-rolling Gay Proselytism' - all of which you are probably familiar with. Taking the whole scenario into context we feel your arguments are unconvincing and influenced in measure by minority pressure groups". The letter was signed by representatives of local branches of the Free Church of Scotland, the Church of Scotland, the Evangelical Church, the Dawson Mission, the Pentecostal Church, the Baptist Church and a retired rector of Graeme High School.

RELIGIOUS FASCISM

Irked by the bank-rolling of religious proselytism, Mr A Irvine of Falkirk was a lone voice in support for repeal on the *Falkirk Herald's* letters' page: "As someone who attended the public meeting in Falkirk Town Hall on Monday, 31 January 2000, hoping for an intelligent, informed debate... I have to say that I am absolutely astonished at the events which occurred. Never before have I heard such a torrent of ill-informed prejudice, hatred and downright bigotry in the name of Christianity. I lost count of the number of speakers who began 'I am a Christian and I have no desire to force my beliefs on anyone who is not' and who then proceeded to do exactly that and at some length... In the week that new statistics revealed that more HIV infection is being spread by heterosexual activity than by homosexual activity, we were subjected to the same old 'gay plague' arguments... These intolerant and bigoted people... have mobilised themselves vocally in support of this misguided cause..."

Dennis Goldie - censured for comparing a political rival to serial killer Harold Shipman and in 2002 reportedly calling another member of the council a Nazi – later faced some rather outspoken claims against him made by fellow councillor Billy Buchanan. Anne Smith QC (before becoming the Hon Lady Smith), a representative of numerous Christian causes was appointed to represent Falkirk Council in the court where it was agreed Buchanan should be silenced. Never far from controversy, Goldie was also reported taking advantage of Tory 'right-to-buy' legislation when he purchased five former council houses and set himself up as a landlord.

Goldie would later be nominated as Labour candidate to replace the Independent MSP Dennis Canavan who stood down in the 2007 elections. Come the Scottish election in 2007, Falkirk West chose to elect an SNP candidate to represent them. Labour lost to the SNP in the Scottish elections by just one seat. Ironically, the SNP had been helped to win with £625,000 of Brian Souter's money, the largest donation in its history.

Falkirk might have just managed to pull off its portrayal of Christian sobriety throughout the 'Keep the Clause' campaign but for a deeply religious Catholic man from the town, Robert Mochrie, who, under pressure of a struggling business and a difficult marriage, bludgeoned his wife and four children to death

Closing the Floodgates with Keep the Clause!

before taking an overdose and hanging himself. It was discovered he had been regularly visiting a female prostitute in Cardiff.

Whilst moral conservatives were joining militant religionists to rock Falkirk, similar tremors were felt in nearby North Lanarkshire. As a pointer, Larkhall in Lanarkshire was a town where street parties were banned if Glasgow's Rangers won the Scottish football cup. The protestant town of 10,000 had a fence painted red, white and blue. It was reported that each time the local authority tried to repaint it, the fence was reverted to its original unionist colours. When cable TV boxes were painted green, (the colour of rival Catholic football team, Celtic), there was such an outcry; the company had to repaint them grey. A key figure in Lanarkshire was SNP councillor Richard Lyle. He had already nailed his sexually conservative colours to the mast when he told the *Scottish News of the World* he didn't want the local Strathclyde Park, which had a small section cruised by gays "becoming another Clapham Common". Richard Lyle was religious and a major critic of important sexual health work that involved handing out condoms there. One prominent doctor, committed to improving sexual health in Scotland, left the country in exasperation shortly after to work abroad. This solid Labour heartland led by the so-called 'Lanarkshire mafia' of old-Labour men also planned a vote in response to the Scottish Executive's moves to repeal Section 28. Richard Lyle had appealed to the Policy and Resources Committee to allow a 'conscience vote', rather than a political one. Convener Councillor Jim McCabe agreed. This did not produce the result Richard Lyle wanted. North Lanarkshire Council actually voted to respond to the Scottish Executive with their support for repeal of Section 28 by ten votes to five. So, because over 25 per cent of the vote was against repeal, he evoked the council's 25 per cent rule that meant it had to be debated again to a full council on 17 February 2000. Director of administration John O'Hagan tried to argue against the use of the 25 per cent rule. He said it only applied to matters discussed by committees and since this subject was not normally delegated to the Policy and Resources Committee, but sent there on a special basis, he argued the 25 per cent rule could not apply. Richard Lyle was however delighted when three Labour members voted to debate an amendment by Councillor Harry McGuigan. After talking to West Church Men's Association, Lyle had his opinion further vindicated. He implored in the *Wishaw News:* "...This is definitely not a homophobic move... I believe, as a parent and in all conscience, that this clause should not be repealed".

After a stormy debate at the full council meeting at North Lanarkshire Council an overwhelming 42 to 19 councillors voted to keep the clause, safeguarding parents from the "promotion" of homosexuality in schools. After the meeting, Lyle was satisfied that "other councils may now take a similar stand" and smugly told the *Scottish Daily Mail:* "Wendy Alexander has made a fool of herself".

It was seen as something of a presentational error that the Scottish Executive hadn't made more of the fact that 13 of Scotland's local authorities supported repeal against only three wanting to keep it on the statute books.

Gerald Warner frothed in his *Scotland on Sunday* column: "That vote represents Old Labour values, from the days of coal in the bath and short shrift for nancy boys in the miners' welfare. In contrast, New Labour in Edinburgh epitomised by Wendy Alexander, Susan Deacon and incongruously, Sam Galbraith ('Trust me, I'm a dad!'), has lost all sense of reality. These people do not realise that most parents look forward to spending the Sundays of their twilight years visiting their grandchildren in a conventional family home, not at the bedside of their son in an Aids hospice".

In Rutherglen's the *Reformer*, the Christian Institute's Colin Hart was quoted saying "some councils... were spending inordinate amounts of money promoting homosexuality in schools". He warned of "serious problems" in Scotland once Section 28 was repealed and that "the situation would get out of control".

In East Kilbride, hundreds of churchgoers were being urged to sign a petition against repeal by Catholic Bishop Joseph Devine. Printed in the *East Kilbride News*, the petition read: "We the undersigned wish to express horror and dismay at the proposal by the Scottish Parliament to repeal Section 28 of the Local Government Act of 1998 thus allowing homosexuality to be promoted in primary schools". Local MSP Andy Kerr attacked the media for peddling such inaccurate information. Ian Bell's column in the *Scotsman*, announced: "...The time has come to call a halt to the wanton promotion of Christianity in our schools... If rights, duties and offensive teachings are at issue, when might

Closing the Floodgates with Keep the Clause!

we expect the Scottish executive to disentangle religion from education? The only propaganda supported by law in our schools is propaganda on behalf of religious faith in all its baffling, pernicious variety".

By March 2000, *Scotland on Sunday*, a broadsheet supporting 'Keep the Clause', had headlined: "Souter pays family to sue on Section 28". Yet, judging by the remarks of a 'Keep the Clause' spokesman, they appeared to still be looking for one: "We will seek to bring a test case and we will need a parent or a family to do that. If any family wants to take part in the opposition to the Executive over Section 28 then we would ask them to approach us". *Scotland on Sunday* was defiant and confident that "parents will take fight against policy on sex education to the European court".

Lawyers for 'moral' campaigners soon turned on sex education material aimed specifically at gay men, many who had grown up *defined* by their sexuality. *Gay Sex Now* was a booklet that used a language already understood by gay men of all ages; emphasising safer sex practices. With HIV infections for gay men in Scotland dropping below those of heterosexuals, sex education programmes aimed at gay men were already vindicated. Turning the pages of *Gay Sex Now*, *Scotland on Sunday* reporter Stephen Fraser appeared surprised to find a black and white photograph showing "two men engaged in a sex act". (It was a small photo of the back of a naked man holding another man's legs apart). Fraser sniffed: "The text alongside discusses, with a degree of gusto and in explicit language, the nature of the experience and goes on to discuss the level of risk of catching HIV involved in the practice of anal sex". But apart from using the measured tones of a report in the *Lancet*, how *was* sex supposed to be discussed if not with some gusto? There could be no meeting of minds between moral conservatives and sex educationalists, despite sharing the stated aim of 'protecting children'. Whilst many moral conservatives insisted on protecting 'children' from homosexuality altogether, many gay 'children' had already sought and found it for themselves! It was to *those* young people and gay men that sex educationalists like Glasgow-based Phace West needed to present - without moralising – an important message: safer sex.

Young gay men are known to seek out information from a number of sources: anything from sex magazines to the Internet; what they can find out from friends, sexual partners or read about on the back of toilet walls. Add to that an element of surreptitious experimentation, brief encounters with bisexuals and married men, and a young gay man can soon find that he is, willing or otherwise, enjoying sex with multiple partners. The booklet *Gay Sex Now* succeeded in getting a wide range of safer sex messages to a wide range of gay men. It made no assumptions about how much sexual experience the reader might already have had. However useful the booklet might have been as a teaching resource for helping gay kids, it was never destined for schools. There was much to commend in the booklet's tackling of a number of taboo subjects with which gay men were confronted with in sex magazines, on the Internet, or in the free, gay lifestyle magazines picked up in pubs and clubs: explaining different reasons for using condoms; negotiating through situations where condoms might *not* be used; how to put one on; using condoms in open relationships; what to do when relationships break up; contact ads; the pressure of finding sex in clubs; oral sex; sex with women; sex on holidays; and, before the booklet was dismissed by the reader as just another health education lecture, anything else that might be doing the rounds in any number of chat rooms or school playgrounds: cruising; S&M; drugs; watersports; rimming; scat. *Gay Sex Now* clearly stated in the introduction: "You might disagree with some of the things you find written here. This booklet isn't about telling gay men what to do". In that, this small, square booklet was profoundly honest, but *Gay Sex Now* became famous - not for providing useful information for those who enjoyed gay sex - but as a tool used by the Christian Institute to stall the repeal of Section 28. The moment *Gay Sex Now*'s jism had ejaculated across the face of the Christian Institute's disgusted director, Colin Hart; the charity set its sights on suing Phace West who published it.

The Christian Institute had a sound homophobic agenda. As EC members prepared to ratify Directive 565 later in the year, outlawing discrimination against gay people in the workplace, the Christian Institute proved itself to be one step ahead; mailing out information responding to the consultation process undertaken by the Department for Education and Employment on the directive, begging support in their efforts to prevent legislation guaranteeing gays equality in employment.

On 14 March 2000, the *Daily Record* headlined: "LABOUR REBEL WARNS OF GAY PREDATOR RISK". They reported: "A Labour MP has warned youngsters will be targeted by

Closing the Floodgates with Keep the Clause!

predatory gay teachers if Section 28 is scrapped". Falkirk East MP Michael Connarty told Carlos Alba at the *Record*: "vulnerable pupils could be 'groomed' by unscrupulous gays" and claimed: "I have seen a situation where a teacher - to everyone's knowledge - groomed young boys who seemed to be leaning in a particular direction... I am conscious there are militant gays who believe it is their role to recruit other people to adopt their way of life..." He didn't want to see anything that encouraged "any kind of sexual activity among young people". Tony Blair's official press spokesman, Alistair Campbell accused the *Daily Record* of telling lies. The *Record* responded with a spiteful double-page spread simply headlined: "STAY OUT OF IT, ALISTAIR". The story sat alongside another story by Carlos Alba, this time warning of "controversial... radical proposals to overhaul Scots Law" that would give gays "new rights". It was, in fact, fairly mundane proposals to equalise the law governing inheritance and housing. The *Scottish Daily Mail* emboldened the words of a spokesman for Cardinal Winning who told them: "What we are seeing is the militant homosexual agenda being pushed from all angles". In future, the Prime Minister's spin-doctor was careful to describe himself only as a parliamentary 'source' while a furious Tony Blair turned on the Scottish press, calling them "unreconstructed wankers"!

Two days later, Carlos Alba reported for the *Daily Record* how education committee member, Lib-Dem MSP Ian Jenkins remembered his days of being a teacher when pupils often drew a blank when he referred to their 'mum' or 'dad'. This led the teacher to use the term 'folks at home'. The *Record* editorial accused him of taking "political correctness to ludicrous lengths by saying teachers should not even talk about 'mums' and 'dads'." (Of course, nobody said they couldn't). A spokesman for Cardinal Winning said Jenkins' comments were "extraordinary". Margaret Nicol, vice-president of the Educational Institute for Scotland (EIS) who also gave evidence to the Scottish Executive, sided with Ian Jenkins. She doubted whether children would understand 'family values' and felt the best course of action was not to promote any relationship as ideal. The *Scottish Daily Mail's* editorial interpreted this as telling teenage boys: "Feel free to experiment with homosexuality; there is nothing better on offer". Alan Smith, the treasurer of the Scottish School Boards' Association (SSBA) was predictably appalled: "If teaching is not about values and traditions, what is the point of education? I am appalled".

Trying to find out how much support there was for the retention or repeal of Section 28 was, of course, extremely difficult. Douglas McNicol cuttingly wrote in his letter to the *Herald*: "...There is little point in trying to discuss a matter of sexuality and its social implications with someone whose education thus far hasn't stretched him or her much beyond the level of a bright chimpanzee". One "senior MSP" was quoted in *Scotland on Sunday*, saying: "It's running at 20-1 against. And these letters are not from nutters". With research showing much of what people learnt about sex was from the media, none of this was surprising; nor that so much of Scotland had been seduced by a salacious and voyeuristic interest in real-time shagging and tabloid prurience, the inspiration of drunken, emotionless encounters piqued by a sense of dirtiness and shame; shrouded – just like Scotland's media - in a crust of moral conservatism.

It was reported that a petition headed 'Protect Our Children', organised by Vera Cowie, a 75-year-old Dundonian grandmother and devout Baptist was getting enormous support from the public in shopping centres. A forest of statistics professing to display the measure of Scotland's tolerance began to set the nation ablaze.

Rather than simply asking people whether they supported Section 28 or not, an Aberdeen School Board troubled itself to send parents some historical background to Section 28, together with a summary of the Executive's position and seven questions covering teaching of tolerance, dealing with homophobic bullying, discussion of homosexuality in class, the review of guidelines and whether safeguards were necessary. They were surprised, following a 10-day period for parents to respond and all the negative publicity from 'Keep the Clause', to receive just 14 returns! Only five wanted to keep Section 28. However, with backing from Brian Souter, the Scottish School Boards' Association claimed that out of 1,000 parents, 97 per cent were against repeal. A Scottish Television poll for *Scotland Today* claimed 4,672 callers revealed only 18 per cent wanted Section 28 repealed. (Viewers had been asked to call in between 1pm and 5pm on a Friday afternoon). On the other hand, a National Opinion Poll (NOP) survey commissioned by Channel Four,

Closing the Floodgates with Keep the Clause!

south of the border, revealed a 61 per cent majority in favour of repeal.

The Scottish Executive had been preparing - not a measure of how many people were for or against repeal - but a *consultation* document. There was little harmony anticipating the results. In the *Big Issue in Scotland*, Dorothy-Grace Elder wrote: "Massive piles of protests over Section 28's repeal are thumping onto every MSP's desk. Almost all are against schools being permitted to 'promote' homosexuality". The Government later claimed they had received 2,350 responses with as many as 1,762 in favour of scrapping Section 28! The figure was later upped to 85 per cent in support of repeal. The *Scottish Daily Mail* was dismissive, calling it: "A figure that was immediately derided by critics as 'ludicrous'." Ignoring the plethora of petitions and organised responses from Churches, its editorial cried: "…There is a strong suspicion that pro-abolition pressure groups must have contributed disproportionately to that exercise". The *Daily Record* declared that "gay activists" had been "bombarding MSPs with e-mails. They are bidding to persuade MSPs that the public is opposed to the controversial law - despite opinion polls which show less than a third of the Scottish public want it changed". In fact, in response to the threat of further organised campaigns by Churches, the Equality Network had urged and succeeded in persuading an otherwise apathetic gay community to send letters and e-mails to the Executive, which included some quite moving personal experiences, of bullying and homophobia in schools. The Equality Network had appealed over the Internet for support for what they saw was fast becoming "simply a numbers game". The *Daily Record* scoffed: "Hundreds of letters didn't even bother trying to disguise that they had been e-mailed in response to the Equality Network plea".

After the responses for the consultation exercise had been broken down, the *Scottish Daily Mail* reported bitterly: "The gay lobby hijacked the official consultation process on Section 28 and over-whelmed the wishes of most of the population…" Scottish Tory education spokesman Brian Monteith said the consultation exercise had been disgracefully hijacked by gay activists and Cardinal Winning used his reserved space in the press to call it "disgraceful". The Executive received responses from interested parties in a number of countries, all of which did not have any equivalent to Section 28. The *Record's* editorial stomped: "Whose opinion matters more to Scottish government ministers – the Scottish people or an international gay network? ...There must be some politicians in Scotland who still believe in representing the people." They wheeled one in. Tory MSP Phil Gallie told the *Daily Record:* "I think they are pretty desperate. They are a very committed minority group set on pushing their own ideas. Any pressure group is capable of outshouting the silent majority". David Macauley, of Jack Irvine's 'Keep the Clause' campaign added: "This just reinforces our belief that they are trying to destroy the democratic process. The continued distortion of this issue by the gay lobby knows no bounds".

The *Scottish Daily Mail* described it as a "revelation" that the "Edinburgh-based Equality Network... e-mailed thousands... demanding action from members across the UK". They claimed: "The Equality Network refused to comment". But The Equality Network's Tim Hopkins corrected this: "We never refuse to comment - we were never asked! Everyone in Scotland had an equal chance to respond to the consultation exercise. We know that some churches encouraged people to write in opposing repeal. It's not surprising that, of those who understood the issues and are actually affected by Section 28, the majority were in favour of repeal. That's what we would have told the *Mail*, had they bothered to ask".

When it came to mobilising support, the Churches took some beating. A couple of years later, for example, in June 2002 the Catholic Church responded to what was supposed to have been a consultation exercise on education carried out by the Scottish Executive. The Catholic Church's full-time parliamentary lobbyist, John Deighan attempted to blitz the Executive with e-mails in defence of sectarian schools, suggesting priests, congregations and lay members might highlight the need for recognition of parents as the first and foremost educators of their children and the right for families to have their children educated in accordance with the beliefs of the family. And again, in 2006, the Catholic Church distributed 100,000 flyers offering a free text-messaging service operated by volunteers from the Scottish Catholic Church's headquarters in Glasgow. It was expected to mobilise followers by alerting them to radio and television talk shows on moral issues a few minutes before they were broadcast, urging them to call in. With Scotland's alleged 700,000 Catholics, 230,000 estimated as attending church regularly, organisers were

Closing the Floodgates with Keep the Clause!

hoping for at least 20,000 subscribers with costs borne by the Church's communications budget. An "insider" explained to *Scotland on Sunday:* "People in the Church want to make their views known, and they are tired of the airwaves being dominated by a minority of people and their anti-religious views".

The Executive tried to respond to the furore by sending out a draft circular to head teachers across Scotland setting out the context in which sex education should be taught in schools along with advice on the curriculum. It was promptly attacked by 'Keep the Clause' for including the words 'stable family' and not mentioning marriage or heterosexuality.

With a remarkable brass neck, the *Daily Record's* editorial begged its readers to write to First Minister, Donald Dewar. "Write to him, fax him, e-mail him and tell him exactly what you think about his plans. To make it easier, we've printed a ready-made letter you can cut out, sign and send". The tabloid's letter begged its readers to express their "deep unease" at the "promotion of homosexual activity in schools", (despite no such promotion ever having been under discussion). Some became quite carried away with the idea of 'promotion' with Gerald Warner calling Wendy Alexander the woman who "promoted the idea of Section 28". The *Record* cynically warned: "You can bet the repeal lobby are already organising a letter-writing campaign to get their view across". It also insisted: "Our poll... makes nonsense of the Government's so called consultation process which yesterday claimed to have received 75 per cent of its submissions in FAVOUR of repealing the ban". The *Daily Record* commissioned Scottish Opinion to call 940 people and screamed the result from its front page: "2:1 AGAINST GAY LESSONS... Forget all the posturing from the politically correct classes. Forget all the po-faced lectures from ministers who think they know better than you do. Forget all the insidious propaganda that tries to portray Brian Souter - and anyone else who opposes its repeal - as a gay basher. Scotland does NOT want to allow the teaching of gay sex in our schools". Jack Irvine from Media House smelled victory and warned the *Scotsman:* "...We will accept no wishy-washy compromise. We regard this as a fight to the death..."

But it wasn't 'Keep the Clause' that would suffer the casualties.

RELIGIOUS FASCISM

Derek Ogg QC, marginalised to a column in *ScotsGay* magazine wrote: "A careful read of Scottish (yes, that's what I said, Scottish) history will show a despicable and shameful record of vilification, marginalisation and ultimate persecution of minorities in our land of fair-minded folk. One of the earliest ever opinion polls conducted under a modern system took place in Scotland in the 50s. The result was 64 per cent in favour of the proposition 'that blacks be sent home to their own country'. Given that a huge part of that number voting was made up of ordinary working class Scots men and women it must have made any black person then here quake in their shoes. Opinion polls on hanging, homosexuality, and abortion have all in Scotland historically shown us up as a nation to be a bunch of mean-minded, vengeful and unforgiving bigots. Our documented persecution (and murder) of Catholics, or anti-Semitism and our persecution of gypsy travellers over three hundred years is curiously absent from school history syllabuses, which instead favour a macho recollection of the battles of the most inept and corrupt royal dynasty, the Stuarts, in European history".

There was a flood of opinion polls, the results of each one endorsing a particular paper's editorial stance in the debate over the repeal of Section 28. Supporting 'Keep the Clause', *Scotland on Sunday* predictably waded into the fracas with the results of *their* poll. "Today's ICM poll in this newspaper, echoing other tests of public opinion over the last few days, reinforces the fact that a clear majority of people in Scotland do not want to see Section 28 repealed".

The *Scottish News of the World* stretched itself beyond the very narrow confines of its own representations of sexuality to declare: "Now we've polled the people who count - the kids themselves..." Without disclosing how many or even how they phrased the question, the paper boldly announced "three quarters of Scotland's schoolkids believe that there is no place for gay lessons in the classroom". Evidently drawn up by hand-wringing old hacks who believed gay sex was about to be 'promoted' in schools, the *Scottish News of the World* reported: "Kirsty Laird, 17, from Glasgow thinks Catholic schools and gay issues don't mix. She said: 'Religion at Notre Dame makes it hard for sexuality to be discussed - mainly because the teachers are embarrassed. If it comes up it's quickly swept under the carpet but I'm not sure that promoting a gay lifestyle is the answer". Only 10 youths of 16

Closing the Floodgates with Keep the Clause!

and 17 appeared to have been polled. "Jamie McCaig and pal Tom May, both 17, are happy to keep Section 28", the tabloid boasted. Jamie, from Newton Mearns, Renfrewshire, said: "The politicians went to school a long time ago, and are out of touch with what it is like now". Tom said: "Sex is far more openly discussed, so there is no need to take it into school". Robbie McCellan, 16, a fifth year student at Kelvinside Academy, said: "I don't think that it would make any difference if Section 28 was abolished. It seems to me that the system works fine as it is". Another Kelvinside Academy pupil, Ollie Shields, 16, from Cambuslang, added: "I agree with Robbie. Sexuality is not really something that I think should be dealt with in the classroom. It is a private matter, and our teachers would be too embarrassed to talk about it. The only time it has really been discussed is in the light of this recent controversy."

The *Scottish Daily Mail* printed the results of what they claimed was the "biggest and most comprehensive poll conducted on Section 28" finding "less than a third of Scots" wanted Section 28 repealed. "Only among voters aged 18-24 are there more who favour abolishing Section 28". Scottish Opinion Limited's results, also loudly trumpeted by the *Daily Record*, had the *Mail* celebrating in bold on their front page: "SCOTLAND SAYS NO TO GAY SEX LAW ABOLITION". Scottish Opinions claimed to have asked 1,104 members of the public the loaded and profoundly dishonest question: "Do you think the Scottish Executive is right to repeal Section 28 of the Local Government Act which prohibits the promotion of homosexuality in schools?" With the debate for repeal of Section 28 in England and Wales also looming in the House of Lords, the *Mail* issued a stark warning to Prime Minister Tony Blair and his Cabinet colleagues in London: "They risk a similar wave of public revulsion in England over their determination to delete the law from the statute books". Under the heading, "voters support ban", there was again praise from a host of predictable sources. A spokesman for the 'Keep the Clause' campaign cheered: "This is tremendous news. It confirms in the most comprehensive way that the majority of people in Scotland do not want the repeal…" Alan Smith, executive treasurer of the SSBA was convinced that "the hearts and minds of the majority of people are clearly in favour of keeping Section 28". And a spokesman for Cardinal Winning believed that "once again scientific sampling proves that the silent majority of Scots have genuine fears about the policy". Writing in the *Scottish Daily Mail*, Gerald Warner declared his opinions on the matter proved "beyond dispute", begging: "Why are Scottish politicians contending frenziedly to secure the votes of the three per cent of the population that is homosexual, while ignoring the potential votes of the large majority?" However, when in 2002 opinion polls showed the Tony Blair government in a good light he switched to being a little more circumspect: "Sophisticated psephological exercises, opinion polling and trawling of focus groups are still less reliable political guides than human instinct". The *Scottish Daily Mail's* editorial decided, "the only honourable and democratic course for the Executive is to bow to the wishes of the people". But what people? Their own poll showed massive gaps in the way different generations had responded. A majority of under-35s – Scotland's future - predictably displayed more progressive attitudes to homosexuality and thought Section 28 should go.

Carlos Alba, in the *Daily Record* produced a nail-spitting report on the Scottish Executive's consultation exercise, dismissing it as a "STITCH-UP"; a "shameless fix" and "clearly rigged by the gay lobby". "Forty gay groups and dozens of quangos - including the British Potato Council - were also asked for their views. But the public were frozen out". The tabloid reported: "All 129 MSPs were consulted individually on the controversial plans, and Equal Opportunities and Local Government committees were also invited to respond. That meant that Labour MSPs Johann Lamont and Michael McMahon, who are on both committees, were asked for their opinion three times". Not that this would have made much difference: A week later, Catholic MSP for Hamilton North and Bellshill and a former steelworker, Michael McMahon, was serenaded in the *Daily Record* for being the first to publicly break ranks on Section 28. Communities' minister Wendy Alexander MSP pointed out in the *Sunday Herald:* "80% of teachers who responded to our consultation about this are in favour of repeal. There have been more than 2,300 responses so far. We are being accused of not listening to public opinion but, in all, 85% of those who responded backed the repeal of Section 28 as humane, tolerant and right for the new Scotland".

The Scottish Executive's consultation process was altogether different from a poll, inviting individuals and

Closing the Floodgates with Keep the Clause!

organisations to put their case to MSPs over a period of six weeks. Missing the point entirely, the dickey-bowed former religious correspondent, Tom Brown, in the *Daily Record*, declared the results "overwhelmingly against scrapping Section 28... So what was the point of the 'consultation process'?" The Scottish Executive was not like Westminster, where the whole theatre of democracy took place in the House of Commons. In Scotland consultation can take place over many weeks involving different organisations. Not exactly tabloid material. Or was it? The *Daily Record* slid their balls across the abacus. "More than 40 gay groups were consulted including the Glasgow-based Bi-g-les group which came under fire last month for posting gay porn on the Net". And "it later emerged that gay campaigners had mounted a campaign to distort the results". The Executive's consultation process came under intense scrutiny by the tabloids. There were some grounds for concern too, not least the haste in which the Executive confirmed its intention to repeal Section 28, just two working days after the close of the consultation process. On Friday, 21 January the *Scottish Sun* joined in, bellowing across its front page: "SO WHAT HAVE GAY LESSONS TO DO WITH THE PRICE OF SPUDS?" They wrote: "More than 6,000 copies of the Ethical Standards in Public Life Bill were sent out to groups last November... There were 2,300 responses". The tabloid had been selecting some of the many groups who had been sent consultation papers: "The British Potato Council... The Deer Commission, ferry company Caledonian MacBrayne, the Association of Chartered Certified Accountants, the Welsh Office, the Royal Botanic Gardens, Arthritis Care Scotland and Alzheimer Scotland Action on Dementia". Objections from individual members of the public were excluded from final figures. Donald Dewar tried to explain to the Executive the difficulties of consultation over such a sensitive issue and the weighting given to various types of opinion, for example teachers, members of the public, the Church and gay groups.

Two days after the Scottish Executive announced the results of its consultation process, the *Kirsty Walk Show* on BBC One Scotland commissioned a poll carried out by MORI that found 56 per cent in favour of repeal compared to only 29 per cent against. They also found only 15 per cent agreeing with Cardinal Winning's claim that homosexuality was a perversion. 69 per cent did not. More surprisingly, it found fewer than half of the

RELIGIOUS FASCISM

Catholic head teachers - 47 per cent - backed Winning's views on homosexuality. The *Herald's* political cartoon had a Catholic pontiff holding a small megaphone marked 25 per cent, bellowing: "Let the moral majority be heard!" Behind him, he was about to be swallowed up by an enormous megaphone marked 75%.

The *Sunday Herald* discovered it was as much about how a question was worded as anything else. Reporting on the MORI poll, they wrote: "While a huge majority of 83% are in favour of sex education including information on homosexuality, 60% remain opposed to the 'promotion' of homosexuality as defined by the controversial Section 28, which the government proposes to repeal. The contrasting results show how the debate on Section 28 is distorted by the language of the act which means local authorities cannot 'promote the teaching of homosexuality'." The poll made clear that 60 per cent disagreed with Winning's interpretation of homosexuality as a perversion with only 32 per cent of Catholics supporting it. It was, of course, still alarming that a poll could show even one third of Scots agreeing with him, but as the *Sunday Herald* made clear in its editorial, "an alarmingly high 43% of Scots do not think that children should be taught the facts of life, including homosexuality".

The *Daily Record* was determined to discredit *any* poll that disagreed with them. The tabloid scoffed: "A BBC poll... showed Scotland's head teachers backed the repeal of Section 28. But only half of the country's 300 secondary school heads took part in the survey carried out for The Kirsty Wark Show". (This was a bit rich since the *Record* claimed *its* poll asked only 940 out of a Scottish population of around eight million)! Grace Wallace demonstrated where a large proportion of the results were coming from; dismissing the results and penning a response to letters' pages of the *Scottish Daily Express*. "The majority of head teachers in Scotland do not want the law repealed - surely somebody should listen to them...? The Bible clearly teaches that it is unnatural to practise homosexual acts".

The *Daily Record* was impervious. "FACT: Every single poll of the subject finds that Scottish parents oppose repeal of Section 28 by a majority of two to one". The influential businessman Brian Souter expressed a touch of remorse for the First Minister but remained quite emphatic: "I feel sorry for Donald Dewar's

Closing the Floodgates with Keep the Clause!

postie, - his back must be breaking but the message from the Scottish people is very clear... Either they please the very influential three per cent of citizens who find Section 28 offensive or risk the wrath of the other 97 per cent..."

The 'Keep the Clause' campaign set up a chat forum on its website. Unfortunately for them, the gay community magazine the *Pink Paper* clicked on it to notice that the "vast majority of responses in the past two days have been pro-repeal, and openly gay-friendly. Of a total of 73 messages posted from 31 January to 2 February 2000, 57 were in support of repeal - with just 16 homophobic or anti-repeal".

The whole poll business soon began to turn in on itself. Dr James M Wilson of Glasgow University's Management Studies Department wrote to the *Herald:* "I seem to be missing a subtle distinction that Saturday's Herald finds between one poll's '80% endorsement' and another's 'four out of five'. One warrants a front-page 'Huge support for Cubie' headline (an independent committee that was looking into student finance) while the other sinks to the last column of an inner-page continuation of a headlined 'Souter faces backlash' article. Seems to me that an 80% result ought to constitute the same level (huge or otherwise) of support regardless of the issue. I have for several years past taught a session on 'How to Lie with Statistics' to our MBA and management students. I do so appreciate such a good, bad example for teaching presentation. Thank you".

Memories of the Soho gay pub bombing by 23-year-old BNP supporter David Copeland the year before, in April 1999, were still fresh. Fuelled by right-wing extremism and insecurities about his own sexuality, he planted a nail-bomb in the busy Admiral Duncan pub in London's Soho. In the carnage that ensued, three people were killed and over 80 injured with 13 sustaining serious injuries including two with traumatic amputation of limbs. So too were memories of the violent murder of 35-year-old Michael Doran less than five years before, during the summer of 1995 in Glasgow's Queen's Park. A gang of three lads and a 14-year-old girl were on a 'queerbashing' rampage, putting a hammer through one man's head, beating another so badly he was unable to walk and, finally, murdering Michael Doran. Michael received 83 blows to his body. They stabbed him several times in the groin, stamped on his face until they had broken every bone in his head and left him in the bushes, choking to death in his own blood. With their clothes still bloodstained, the gang joined friends at a nearby party, bragging about what they had just done.

Whilst the media wrestled with the findings of opinion polls, others took their opinions onto the street. Reports circulated of name-calling, victimisation and queerbashing. For anyone who, by dint of fate, was effeminate or openly gay, everything was about to change. For them, at least, Scotland was to become a very dark and dangerous place. As each day passed there were more newspaper stories; more barracking from columnists; more readers' letters; more voices of outrage; each one more shrill than the last. No-one could escape the tension in the gay bars, or the gossip. In Glasgow gay bar Delmonicas, someone said they had been verbally abused on a bus by a group of lads shouting 'Keep the Clause'; some drunk had spat at someone outside The Waterloo; someone else added they had been jumped upon leaving another gay bar. Before catching the last train or moving on to another club, the landlord called: "Go carefully, lads," as he collected their empty glasses.

Chapter Two
The Assault on Family Values

"Understand – won't you try to understand my point of view
Understand – c'mon and try a little, try a little, try a little please do".
The Communards

Whilst the Scottish media threw themselves wholeheartedly into the brawl, none participated quite so vociferously against repeal and its supposed "sustained assault on family values" as the *Daily Record* under the editorship of Martin Clarke. The tabloid was part of the Trinity Mirror newspaper group and exposed a chilling totalitarian, heterosexual environment; aggressive as it was intolerant. Journalists from the paper privately expressed their horror at the hateful 'Keep the Clause' campaign to the National Union of Journalists, but remained silent throughout Clarke's intimidating reign as editor. In an unusual spectacle, newspapers turned on each other. A *Sunday Herald* editorial blasted: "It is regrettable that the over-simplifications and misinformation are encouraged and inflamed by first and foremost The Daily Record and some other tabloid newspapers, which criticise the parliament for ineffectiveness yet seem content to pursue the uninformed, oafish politics of the barstool". Seizing every opportunity to promote support for 'Keep the Clause', the *Daily Record's* editorial shrieked: "Free speech for everyone… So we weren't wrong when we predicted yesterday what the reaction would be… You have to admire the man's (Brian Souter's) bravery. Dissent isn't something that tends to go down very well these days. Scotland's most tedious newspaper – and there's some competition for that title – accused him of trying to influence 'free and open debate'. …You have to wonder what planet these people are on… The gay pressure groups operate thanks to council hand-outs and private donations… Only the feeble and discredited Tories are prepared to oppose the repeal of the gay lessons ban in Parliament". (Aided by a privileged and influential Church, powerful businesspeople and most of the Scottish press!) Of the likely backlash against Souter, the *Daily Record* warned "Brian" to beware. The *Sunday Herald* was scathing. "They long ago forfeited the right to be treated as a serious newspaper".

Former Religious Affairs Correspondent, Tom Brown - or 'Brigadier' Brown, as he became known in *ScotsGay* magazine; a sobriquet earned from his recollections of life in the Boys Brigade - wrote a regular column for the *Daily Record*. His opinions on what he described as "the sad, seedy perversions" of homosexuals was already in the public domain. "...We Boys' Brigaders goose-stepped to our drill hall, we always regarded the rival youth army as 'cissies...' none of that nonsense for your decidedly butch Boys' Brigade members. Our uniform was... spit-and-polish boots, a belt and sparkling buckle... In Kirkcaldy we were so manly we refused to wear the pansy little pillbox hat. Nothing nancy-boy there. And DEFINITELY no hanky-panky in the well-drilled ranks - or out of them". He wasted no time lambasting the "politically-correct politicians and the gay lobby" before settling down to give Brian Souter a make-over: "At home, he is just another parent – with four young children, three at state schools – with every father's worries about his children's future", he gushed. Souter was just doing something "for all parents". Brown soon revealed how he *really* saw this campaign developing: "People v Politicians". And, echoing former Conservative leader Margaret Thatcher's campaign to empower groups likely to remain faithful to the cause of Conservatism, he praised "parent power..." warning, "with the money from his charitable trust, the Souter Foundation, there will be an intensive four-month campaign of demos, multi-media advertising and lobbying". This was supposed to counter "the well-funded, articulate gay movement with its access to the highest echelons of government". It was an extraordinary assertion to make given the efforts of the late Baroness Janet Young, patron of the well-funded Christian Institute, who had successfully scuppered MPs proposals to repeal Section 28 in England and Wales in the *elected* House of Commons, by blocking reform in the *un-elected* House of Lords. As for support in the "highest echelons of government", where was it and what had they achieved? Most equality legislation concerning gays had, until this time, been foisted upon the UK by Europe. The Equality Network,

The Assault on Family Values

supporting gay equality in Scotland on a budget of £3,000-a-year, was hardly "well-funded" compared to 'Keep the Clause', which, along with Souter's money, was reported to have received offers of financial support from political and religious groups in America. When it came to influence, the Christian right had a well-established strategy of developing lobbying skills, placing young Christians as researchers with MSPs, hoping they would become politicians or civil servants that would go on to shape policy from a Christian standpoint. The Christian Institute and Christian Action Research and Education (CARE) operated in this way within the House of Commons and House of Lords. With around 20,000 members, the Evangelical Alliance already had its own lobbyist in place in the Scottish Executive. His name was Jeremy Balfour and was reported in *Scotland on Sunday* saying: "I suspect the only advantage we have (over other people) is that Christians are slightly better informed than the bulk of society and have a better understanding of how politics works". By 2013, CARE, the Christian Institute and the Evangelical Alliance were collecting £2m in annual income. According to a Theos think-tank report by Andy Walton in the same year, entitled: "Is there a 'Religious Right' emerging in Britain", Christian Concern also boasted an annual turnover of £2m, although this was quite paltry compared to the £38,000,000 generated by the Alliance Defence Fund in the USA. Andrea Minichello Williams of Christian Concern and Christian Legal Centre was reported saying that, along with cheques of £20,000 to £50,000 landing on her desk from supporters, the Alliance Defence Fund gave her groups "£1,000 here and a £1,000 there". Walton's report acknowledged that Christian groups had a "symbiotic relationship" with some elements of the press, inflating their voices and exaggerating their influence.

Whilst religionists were already well placed in the Scottish media there was not one out lesbian, gay or bisexual prepared to counter the 'Keep the Clause' propaganda. Nonetheless, the *Daily Record* insisted; "all Mr Souter is doing is evening up the odds a little for the silent majority". In another editorial, the *Record* thought "Brian… big enough to look after himself, but in case he needs a hand…" they would be there to offer support "against allowing homosexual propaganda in schools". And support him they did! After spitefully turning on "trendy cheerleaders in unpopular papers…" for criticising Souter's involvement in "sensitive matters", the *Record* publicly reassured him with their advice to "ignore them". Heady with what they perceived to be such clear support from the "majority" of "ordinary people", their divisive, homophobic campaign gathered pace. "... PROMOTING homosexuality in schools is now official government policy... Outside Government, the well-funded gay pressure groups will continue their noisy campaign to have the section repealed. We warned from the outset that there would be a backlash on this issue from the majority of ordinary people who do not hate homosexuals, but who do NOT want their children taught about them at school". On what should be done about the "sensitive issue" of repealing Section 28, *The Record* trumpeted their demands to the Scottish Executive: "They should quietly drop it before it does any more damage".

While Scotland lagged behind much of Europe on gay equality, it was still going too far for columnist Tom Brown who enjoyed parading his bigotry across the pages of the *Daily Record*. "Taking gay liberties to the extreme... Enough is enough", his headline shrieked. "This may seem perverse..." he began his back-handed compliment, "but I have no problem with giving equal legal rights to homosexual partners... Or, for that matter, if they are the financially-dependent home-maker - the role that women used to have". Brown was commenting on news stories of the rights (or rather lack of them) awarded to gay couples. Julian Dykes, a victim of the Soho nail bomb attack on a gay bar was compensated after losing his wife Andrea while Gary Partridge was denied compensation under the Criminal Injuries Compensation Scheme despite suffering appalling injuries and losing *his* gay partner. In another case, after his partner, whom he had cared for over a long period, had died, Martin Fitzpatrick fought hard and won his case in the House of Lords against eviction from the house he had shared with him for 20 years. Such variants in the progress towards equality did not perturb the mean-spirited 'Brigadier'. "What worries me is that this will be taken as capitulation to the homosexual cause. ...The signal to demand more".

Gays were increasingly seen in the media grouped together under one common heading. And everything 'they' argued was portrayed as a 'demand'. It was small wonder that so much of the public began to fear that 'gays' were somehow at the root of the 'problem' in much the same way that Jews were made a scapegoat

The Assault on Family Values

for much of Germany's problems before the Second World War. Anti-Semitism was once quite commonplace in the media and the *Daily Record* was no exception. In a gratuitously anti-Semitic report in 1899 on German picture-postcards a correspondent wrote: "An excellent one was a drawing in which faces were designed out of Jewish names – for instance, 'Moses' written in a round and flowery hand would be transformed into a wonderful Israelite type... It was not actually cruel, the spirit was of fun and derision than of anger; but it was most unkind, for the fun carried a bitter dart, doubtless, to poor Jewry's heart".

'Brigadier' Brown picked up on a misleading report that had appeared in the *Daily Telegraph,* which sensationally and falsely implied that the gay rights organisation Outrage! had issued a new policy statement, shortly before a vote on the age of consent in the House of Lords, suggesting the next stage of their campaign was the legalisation of public sex and sex in public toilets. "Gay groups seek to legalise gay sex in public lavatories", the *Telegraph* had cried, after rehashing a law reform submission Outrage! had submitted to the Home Office Sex Offences Review Team a year earlier. Brown outlined what "they" (gays) were going to do next: "Now that sex between males is acceptable in private - and, it seems, on the telly - they want to legalise it in public lavatories, saunas and 'cruising' areas". He sniffed: "If they have their way, it won't be safe to spend a penny. ...Streets where promiscuous homosexuals pick up partners will become no-go areas. Now they have been allowed to parade down Princes Street and take over the Millennium Dome, anything goes in public". (The route of the Gay Pride march, agreed by the police, skirted Edinburgh's main shopping street, Princes Street and the 'take over' of the former Millennium Dome by gays had been highlighted by a brouhaha in the press when a school cancelled a trip to see the Dome after gays had organised an event there, which included the Gay Men's Chorus). Brown would not give ground on his inflammatory language. Under a photo of Peter Tatchell appeared the caption: "Out of order: Peter Tatchell's outrageous demands give homosexuals a bad name. No doubt the politically-correct pink-brigade - with its advance guard in the Scottish Cabinet and Parliament - will say this is homophobic scare-mongering. Not so... The 'gays,' and their friends in power, are their own worst enemies, because they simply do not know when to stop pushing".

RELIGIOUS FASCISM

The language Tom Brown used against gays was not out of place in the Scottish media. It vilified the minority, portraying them as a threat to society and to the welfare of the young, asserting they were part of an international conspiracy, associating them with disease and corruption and played on the public's fears and prejudices. At the time, Britain had no incitement to hatred laws to protect lesbians, gays, bisexuals or the transgendered from the press. Brown continued: "Is it any wonder that there is a backlash from the majority, who say the line on decency and protection of family values has to be drawn somewhere...? We already know to steer clear of places like the 'Pink Triangle' in the Broughton Street area of Edinburgh and certain pubs in Glasgow and elsewhere. Isn't that enough...? What the gay lobby and their friends in government have failed to realise is that the tolerant majority have now woken up to the fact that the increasing demands of homosexuals and their permissive pals can never be satisfied. They have decided to draw the line - here and now".

In one of the 'Brigadier's' frequent blasts at homosexuals, he cried: "Hell is a night out in the company of Dale Winton, Graham Norton and Julian Clary - a worse Hell would be a night IN with them". The *Daily Record* provided a computer-simulated picture of Brown wearing his familiar dickey-bow, sandwiched between entertainers Dale Winton and Graham Norton. The *Record's* sister paper, the *Sunday Mail* praised Steven Flannery and Michael Johnston, a gay couple who opened Glasgow's Bar 10 and ran the Brunswick Hotel in its Merchant City. "Neither are political animals. They don't go on gay rights marches, display banners, or wear 'right-on' gay badges". They were decent. Normal. Invisible.

Joan Burnie, or 'Old Mother Burnie' – as the *Daily Record's* convent-educated agony aunt became known in *ScotsGay* magazine – never sought to question the *Record's* efforts to undermine repeal of Section 28 in her columns. A parent apparently wrote to her and explained how her young son had tried to kill himself after being bullied at school. The parent claimed teachers had dealt with the subject "sensitively". Joan seized the moment: "You're right"; she gleamed. "Schools have a responsibility to protect ALL their pupils from bullying. Clause 28 shouldn't and doesn't come in to it..." But the incident had taken place before Section 28 had become such a burning issue,

The Assault on Family Values

threatening to persuade teachers to err on the side of caution and avoid getting involved in cases of homophobic bullying.

Burnie's demonstrated a somewhat restrained view on sexual matters. "Where once cameras stopped dead at decency and the bedroom doors, now they glide right in and linger lustily through every grunt, groan and simulated orgasm", she sniffed. Burnie built her reputation despising erotica, chastising TV soaps where gay sex was "glamourised" and - unusually for a self-proclaimed 'agony aunt' – labelled a transsexual "he, she or it" and another, a "freak". It was during this time Burnie answered a letter on her problem page from "a normal 17-year-old" with a girlfriend who spilled out his love for another boy at his college. After dismissing it as a "pash", 'Old Mother Burnie' suggested, "some things are better left unsaid. So go on being friends, but don't try to force it into something else".

Another letter in the midst of the Section 28 furore chastised Joan Burnie for having any sympathy at all. "I feel you should be sacked as an agony aunt because of your attitude to gay people – you tell them they can't help being gay, but they can. They are NOT born that way. Men are born with male parts and women with female ones. The only reason anyone is gay is because it is fashionable and trendy. If you just told the truth and said it was wrong and perverted, you might do some good for a change". The correspondent didn't offer any explanation on why it had become "fashionable and trendy".

The *Daily Record's* code of morality had remained unchallenged for decades. Stories of a sexual nature outside heterosexual marriage were usually branded controversial, sleazy or sick. The tabloid's campaign against the repeal of Section 28 was relentless; its opinion bullish; its tone ever more shrill as it remained convinced it could do anything it liked with impunity.

The *Record* announced that: "A controversial new scheme has been launched to help protect pupils from gay-bashing". Sensible enough! Particularly after a University of London report had shown 82 per cent of English and Welsh schools were aware of anti-gay bullying (although only six per cent made reference to it in any anti-bullying policies). The *Record* pulled the "controversial" scheme apart. "... Education groups have slammed the policy as 'political correctness' gone mad", they cried. The so-called "education groups" the *Record* had referred to included the Campaign for Real Education whose spokesman

RELIGIOUS FASCISM

Nick Seaton told the *Herald* the very idea "resembles a witch hunt in a lot of respects". Only he wasn't referring to the *victims* of bullying! The truth behind the story was that teachers had simply been asked to "monitor" attacks and "register" verbal abuse. 'Critics' who wanted Section 28 to stay insisted in the *Record:* "We deplore bullying wherever it is directed and would never encourage prejudice or unjust discrimination against people of homosexual orientation". A 26-year-old Scot put them right in his letter to the *Herald* from his new home in London. He claimed he had been "verbally abused, spat upon, beaten up and had stones thrown" at him on his way home from school on "a virtual daily basis". He asked how many other children might have left Scotland for the same reasons. Judging by what little research was available from organisations left to pick up the pieces: thousands! The *Fraserburgh Herald's* prolific letter writer, R S Stephen offered a firm solution: "Christians have the answer to bullying in the restoration of the school belt... Proverbs 22.15".

Brian Souter's charity, The Souter Foundation came under the spotlight after questions were raised over the rights of charities to offer financial support to political campaigns. The *Record* turned on Glasgow's Gay & Lesbian Centre, also registered as a charity, disclosing how "gay groups registered as charities are fighting tooth and nail for the removal of the controversial clause". The Centre had been openly campaigning for the repeal of Section 28, a law that had, after all, prevented its members from receiving appropriate sex education in schools. Support for the campaign appeared in the Centre's newsletter *Centrepoint*. Since the Centre received donations, Brian Souter wasted no time insisting to the *Record* that he should be at liberty to do the same and donate money to the "heterosexual community" in support of *their* campaign.

The *Record's* editorial team did everything in their power to help Brian Souter make his point. Gay news stories sometimes received interesting juxtapositions. "£1m CAMPAIGN TO HALT U-TURN ON GAY LESSONS" was one of them, sitting next to: "Pink planes to take off". At a time when Brian Souter's £1m contribution was on everyone's minds, Martin Langham had "convinced" financial backers "to provide tens of millions of pounds for his new venture...", a gay airline company.

Another newspaper supporting the retention of Section 28 was the *Scottish Daily Mail*, edited in Scotland by Ramsay Smith.

The Assault on Family Values

The tabloid already had a staggering record of, not just homophobia, but misrepresenting diverse expressions of lawful sexuality in vile rhetoric. An editorial described Brian Souter's "huge campaign to protect children" as "a public-spirited gesture which will be welcomed by parents throughout Scotland," adding, "the attempt to open up schools to homosexual propaganda is the personal crusade of Wendy Alexander, Minister of Communities...", adding that her boss, "Donald Dewar, who absurdly described Section 28 as a 'badge of shame,' may live to regret the day he provoked this unnecessary confrontation".

The owners of the *Daily Mail*, the Rothermeres, had a past which sat rather uneasily with the 'family values' agenda espoused by its then London editor, Paul Dacre and Scottish editor, Ramsay Smith. Apart from the reputation of the first Viscount Rothermere's links with wartime Nazis, his son Esmond married three times and the third Viscount, Vere, lost his virginity in a brothel, kept a mistress, drove his wife, Bubbles, to champagne and pill addiction and lived as a tax exile in France. Jonathan, the latest Viscount fathered an illegitimate child in New Zealand. The *Daily Mail* so desperately wanted to prevent the Labour Government from repealing Section 28 and equalising the age of consent for gays that it employed a team of journalists to work full-time on the issues. The *Daily Mail's* double-page feature on the Scottish Executive's efforts to abolish the legislation screamed "SECTION 28: THE GREAT LIE". The article was aided by propaganda from the Christian Institute and clouded in bigotry. The *Mail* used its editorial to celebrate the article by journalist Steve Doughty, underlining how Section 28 would "prevent lessons being used to promote homo - sexuality" *(sic)*. It begged readers: "Imagine what would happen if (Section 28) is abolished and the floodgates are opened". Their editorial advised: "Read the gay 'educational material' on these pages that is presently being pumped into British schools and ask yourself: Why is this Government so obsessed with promoting homosexuality still further? Why is a Government that does nothing for marriage and the family so obsessed by gay rights?" Doughty's article focused on 'educational material' so-called 'family values' campaigners had gathered together for the benefit of the press. The Grampian Health Board's guidelines on sex education received special attention. Shocking enough to "teach homosexual liaisons as equal relationships with marriage...

Teachers of children aged 11 and 12 are asked to make the point: 'There are many types of sexual relationships, eg cohabiting, marriage, same-sex, heterosexual, celibate...' Teachers are told that it is necessary to provide 'positive images' of homosexuals". This guide was revealed as part of "the mass of gay propaganda that could be fed to schoolchildren if Section 28 is abolished..." Readers were informed this was "presently being pumped into British schools". The following week, its editorial insisted the material was "the kind of propaganda already being disseminated, even before the law is changed". Far from being 'gay propaganda', the material was, in fact, designed to reach young people who already identified themselves as gay and who might otherwise have been denied help, counselling, support and information to protect them from sexually transmitted infections, including HIV at a time when rates of HIV infection were particularly high amongst young people. The *Mail* warned that the Grampian Health Board had told teachers that "the idea that Aids can be prevented by sexual fidelity or marriage is strongly rejected". The editorial fumed: "Teachers are told not to mention marriage as a solution to HIV". The article was designed to strike fear and trepidation into the minds of parents and emphasised that the health education material "includes books produced with hundreds of thousands of pounds of public money designed to indoctrinate children with the claims of the gay equality lobby and to override the law that forbids the teaching that pretended homosexual families are as good as any other..." It was claimed the material "included advice to teenagers on homosexual practices they might try and guidance on 'cruising', or seeking casual gay sex in public places". It was also claimed it contained "material describing sexual-practices such as sado-masochism in crude and obscene terms". The use of the word 'indoctrinate' was used when 'educate' would have been more accurate. Constant references were made to a 'waste of taxpayer's money'. A Birmingham health guide for young people was also criticised for featuring "material that promotes homosexuality... widely published at great public expense and aimed at schoolchildren". In actual fact, the booklet contained nothing more than a discussion on homophobia and a list of gay and lesbian helplines. (Steve Doughty failed to mention that the subject of homosexuality formed just three pages of the 152-page booklet). Using language that tried to express gay sexuality as a perversion that deserved only to be hidden from sight or cloaked in shame, he warned he had even found "a 'feedback' page" that included "glowing recommendations for the services of gay advice groups". The guide was dismissed as "the promotion of homosexuality to children as young as five". The *Mail* posed a serious threat to the education of young gay and bisexual people who were already familiar and practising gay sexuality in different circumstances. Their efforts targeted not just the Grampian region and Birmingham, but health services in London, Avon and Glasgow.

Glasgow's Phace West, which provided valuable help to gay youngsters, was slammed for informing youngsters "that seeking gay sex in public places is called 'cruising'." (Most already knew). The *Mail* sniffed: "the language used throughout is crude and obscene". But was the tabloid right to question the careful attempts to get important information across to the right people in the right language? Hidden in the copy and much later in the feature was an admission that the material was "not written specifically for teaching children" but "young men". Providing outreach work to young gays at this sensitive time proved particularly difficult when every effort was under the media's microscope. The *Mail's* editorial sniped: "One homosexual group that enjoys council support and aims to offer advice to boys aged 16 and over, promises that newcomers to its meetings will be allowed a two-week period of grace before others are allowed to try to have sex with them…"

When, in 2001, Michael Portillo stood for leadership of the Tory Party, *Mail* journalist Steve Doughty produced an article on why the MP, who had confessed to having had gay sex in the past, was wrong about wanting to repeal Section 28 in England and Wales. Sebastian Sandys, a journalist for gay magazine, *QX* wrote: "I have spoken to Steve Doughty on a number of occasions about Section 28. I know that he knows that Section 28 is irrelevant to schools in England and Wales. I know that he knows that sex education is the responsibility of school governors and not local authorities. And I know that he knows he is running made-up scare stories to make a political point. All journalists have to live with their own ethics but I cannot for the life of me see how Steve Doughty at the Daily Mail can see himself as anything other than a duplicitous scumbag writing homophobic crap at his masters bidding".

RELIGIOUS FASCISM

Despite solid support from so many religionists, the *Scottish Daily Mail* became impatient with those from the Church of Scotland who appeared reluctant to jump on the 'Keep the Clause' bandwagon. An editorial congratulated Cardinal Thomas Winning who "minced no words in denouncing Labour's plans to abolish Section 28... The Cardinal will have felt wholly secure with his uncompromising stance as it will have found widespread support within his church. Can the Moderator of the Church of Scotland, the Right Rev John Cairns, feel similarly sure-footed today? We think not... Many may find Cardinal Winning's language harsh, in a country which seeks to treat all minorities with equal respect. These days – rightly – gays expect to live their lives untroubled by the prejudice and hounding which they had to endure in less tolerant times. That said, doesn't the Cardinal have a point...?" Brushing aside their assurance that those "less tolerant times" had passed, the *Mail* added: "Winning had reason to urge the silent majority to rise up".

The gay community newspaper, the *Pink Paper* declared how they were "stunned by the sheer audacity and strength of the conservative forces fighting to keep this bizarre law..." They claimed they had received a call from a teacher from a State school "upset and offended" that the *Daily Mail* had used his comments to portray him as supporting Section 28. (It was not unusual to read apologies in the *Mail* for comments they had made in error).

The *Pink Paper* had the opportunity to reveal the sheer hypocrisy of Associated Newspapers when they reported how senior executives from the group were locked in talks with organisers of the annual London gay festival, Mardi Gras, for four months. They had been negotiating the production of its official magazine. The report revealed: "News of the Daily Mail's plans to profit from the biggest promotion of homosexuality in Britain will horrify its conservative 'blue rinse' readers who are being urged daily to put their names to a printed statement to be sent to MPs about Section 28". As the *Pink Paper's* editorial explained: "If you want 'gay proselytising and promotion' - Saturday 1 July is your day... So whilst the Daily Mail condemns the lives of teenage gay people in its campaign against Section 28, Lord Rothermere, the 33-year-old inheritor of the Daily Mail empire, must have given his agreement to make money from our community".

The Assault on Family Values

The *Scottish Daily Mail* wheeled in Dr Kate Pickering, benignly labelled "a mother of three children aged between nine and 12". She was, in fact, a Conservative Party political activist from a surgery in Drumchapel. Pickering opened with the predictable opening gambit of many a homophobe: "I... have some good friends who happen to be gay... The last thing I want to appear is homophobic because I am certainly not. But... I do not want homosexuality to be promoted in schools... I have found myself having to explain to the children what 'gay' is. In doing so I have had to tell them the truth". (Not such a bad thing for a doctor, surely)? After much hand-wringing, Dr Pickering huffed: "Now people like Wendy Alexander wish teenagers to be exposed to homosexuality... Talk of 'urges' and 'expressions of love' is adult intellectual liberalism... She is not a parent..." and "with all respect to the gay and lesbian lobby, they are not parents either..." With all respect to Dr Pickering, of course, many were!

The idea that parents should be the sole providers of information on sexuality had now resurfaced. It was once promoted by fascists and outlined in this essay in a 1942 edition of *Der HJ-Richter*, an 'educational' newspaper of Hitler Youth Justice: "The Reich Youth Leadership should refrain from mass instruction of young people themselves in (homosexuality) as in the area of sex in general. Individual members of a yearly age-group are so different in their development and mental grasp that any mass instruction would lead to undesirable consequences. Such instruction must be given by the parents on an individual basis. No other educational institution can relieve parents of this naturally given task. Only they are fully suited to perform this task in their children's education. ...A merciless struggle should be waged against homosexuality in general. Homosexuality does not weaken a nation only through the loss of births; it also involves a degeneration or inversion of normal feelings, a feminization of man and a masculinization of woman. It thus puts at risk a nation's healthy behaviour and therefore its very future. Young people, as bearers of this future, have a right to demand a ruthless struggle against all symptoms of degeneracy".

In a letter to the *Scottish Daily Mail*, D Hopper of Blyth, Northumberland snapped: "As a practising Christian and grandmother, I applaud the House of Lords stand on Section 28. Moral and sexual teaching should be given by parents, not teachers. Along with Blair and his cronies, the bishops see nothing immoral in homosexuality. They should read Luke 16, verses 19 to 25, and beware".

Led by stories of "teachers having affairs with their teenage pupils", Dr Pickering wrote: "We have to accept that some of those teachers are going to get into emotional difficulties, even fall in love. It is asking far too much of them to take this on". Peter Dickson, secretary of the Educational Institute of Scotland (EIS) and principal guidance teacher in an East Dunbartonshire secondary school for 25 years begged to differ. He told the *Sunday Times Scotland* "Sex education in Scotland is usually taught under the banner of 'personal and social development'. ...What we teach is pretty bland. Many teachers shy away from discussing homosexuality altogether".

Already commanding a regular spot in *Scotland on Sunday*, Gerald Warner was frequently chosen by the *Scottish Daily Mail* to write for them. Eighties' metaphors, like 'politically correct' and 'loony left' turned like well-fingered prayer-wheels in his copy. "They are at it again", he stormed over a commissioned study of religious bigotry inspired by research showing men with Irish surnames 26 per cent more likely to die of heart attack, serving more prison sentences and suffering more mental illness. "Fresh from provoking public outrage over Section 28, the politically correct brigade in the Scottish Executive are launching yet another initiative as part of their attempts to nanny us into bland conformity – their target this time is religious discrimination in Scotland... So far as Christianity is concerned, they had better move fast while there are still some representatives left from the various denominations who have not been driven to atheism or Buddhism by the likes of Bishop Richard Holloway". (The then Bishop of Edinburgh was an outspoken critic of homophobia). Warner accused the "equality freaks" of pinpointing "an issue that was important 70 years ago but is of negligible concern now". Also renowned for a bigoted stance towards homosexuality, he was joined by former Tory MP, Phil Gallie who sniffed: "I don't need a consultation exercise to tell me that bigotry in the West of Scotland has been on the decline". The prospect of a repeal of Section 28 sent Gerald Warner into overdrive. Turning on the "elected dictatorship on The Mound" and the "stubborn arrogance of the Executive in persisting with this policy against public opinion" he asked: "What more legitimate aspiration could Scottish parents have than to protect

The Assault on Family Values

their children from homosexual propaganda?" Warner rarely let the facts get in the way of his arguments.

In a debate that seemed to depend so much on the publication of 'facts', it was surprising how often, when referring to gay people, the *Mail* was wrong. When Conservative MP John Redwood told a Party conference in 1992 that Hackney Council had wasted £31,000 on a lesbian bereavement course, the figure turned out to be, in fact, £31! His special advisor, MP James Gray, was forced to apologise, using his appearance on BBC 2 in June 2000 to add: "Most people want the age of consent for homosexuals to be 21". Not according to a Gallup poll commissioned by the *Daily Telegraph:* 65 per cent said they wanted the age set at 18 and 26 per cent at 16.

The *Scottish Daily Mail* flooded its pages with 'facts' and commentary supporting the retention of Section 28. They claimed Section 28 was brought in following fears "some Labour councils, particularly in London, were spending large sums promoting homosexuality in schools. The most famous example was the children's book, Jenny Lives with Eric and Martin". Just one copy of this book, published in Denmark in 1981, was held in a teaching resources library in London. Contrary to the media's vivid imagination, no-one instructed that teachers should use it with children. Author Susanne Bösche told the *Pink Paper:* "I was really shocked at the way it was used in England and the way it was called homosexual propaganda. You must have very little confidence in your teachers in England if you think they will use propaganda or promote anything". Her daughter Louise, who featured in the book as Jenny, was now aged 23 and lived with her boyfriend. Eric and Martin (real names Lars and Henrik) were still together and lived in Spain. The *Daily Mail* spun an entirely different tale of "the book that became the symbol of gay propagandists". They also insisted that one of the original publishers was "threatening" to "rush out an updated version" as soon as Section 28 was lifted and would make sure that "every school which wants a copy will get a copy". The *Mail* "tracked down" 'Jenny', 'Eric' and 'Martin' and apparently found "all three are united in their opposition to the idea of homosexuality being promoted to young children in schools". Author Susanne Bösche was reported being "furious at the way gay campaigners used her book".

RELIGIOUS FASCISM

Jenny Lives with Eric and Martin also shocked the *Daily Record*, of course. "Jenny is sitting on a bed, clutching a doll, beside the couple, who are asleep, naked, in each other's arms", they gasped. Quite apart from anything else, Denmark does not share Scotland's prudery over children seeing grown-ups naked. *Record* reporter Steve Smith declared that the book "was the reason the Thatcher government introduced Section 28 in 1988". The tabloid also reported a "pledge" by "gay activist" Neal Cavalier-Smith - who was, more accurately, a director of gay publishing house Prowler Press - saying: "I'll make sure every school in Scotland has a copy of *Jenny Lives with Eric and Martin*". A spokesman for Prowler Press assured me they were only *considering* reprinting an updated version of the book. The *Daily Telegraph*, on the other hand, insisted the book *'Colours of the Rainbow'*, published in 1986 and used by Camden and Islington Health Authority was the primary reason for the introduction of Section 28. That would have been difficult: the book was not published until 1996!

While the press wallowed in piety and displayed a certain enthusiasm for Bibles taking the place of rational discussion on sexuality in schools, they turned a blind eye to passages that, had they appeared anywhere else, would have been roundly condemned as unsuitable for the classroom, especially Ezekial 23:20 which explained with some frankness: "There she lusted after her lovers, whose genitals were like those of donkeys and whose emission was like that of horses. So you longed for the lewdness of your youth, when in Egypt your bosom was caressed and your young breasts fondled".

The idea that homosexual material was being stockpiled for schools was another 'fact' too far for the *Daily Record* which stomped: "FACT: Homosexual lobbyists and publishers are already waiting in the wings to churn out gay propaganda for our schools". Such an insult was not only inflammatory, but also untrue. Simply replacing references to gays with references to Jews amplified how insulting and inflammatory these remarks might have been for some gay people; turning the copy into propaganda more befitting the Third Reich: 'FACT: Jewish lobbyists and publishers are already waiting in the wings to churn out Jewish propaganda for our schools'. A letter from Ian McLaren Thomson in Glasgow to the *Herald* dismissed such comparisons outright: "…There is a vast difference between

The Assault on Family Values

berating an individual for what he or she does by choice, and hounding someone to death for being born black or belonging to Judaism".

Another regular columnist in *Scotland on Sunday* promoting 'Keep the Clause' was Mrs Katie Grant. Conservative, Catholic and a former pupil of St Mary's convent, Ascot, her opinions were regularly bought by, amongst others, the *Scottish Daily Mail*, the *Sunday Times Scotland* and BBC Radio Scotland. Portraying herself as a simple parent, she begged Donald Dewar to join her "outside the school gates. It is here, where buggy-pushing mothers, and quite a few fathers, wait to collect their offspring..." Here, she reassured him, he would hear "reasoned debate". Before launching into her rant, she rattled out a string of apologies on behalf of the parents. "These men and women are not ranting homophobes. They are not political activists. They are not out to cause trouble or make life difficult for anybody. They are just parents whose main concern is to safeguard their (mainly heterosexual) children's mental, physical and sexual health". Unfortunately, what Mrs Grant's argument lacked in substance was compensated for in emotive gestures. She was convinced repeal would "allow those who want to play sexual politics with children's sexual education to go ahead". What she had successfully ignored was the Church's and the conservative media's own efforts to use children's sexual education to pitch *their* political battle. She was also investing her trust in a religious leader whose sexual experiences were at best limited. Mrs Grant's fears bubbled to the surface. What if gay people started "pushing their own agenda..." in schools? How would they be stopped? "Most parents will tell their children that sometimes men fall in love with men and women with women. Parents do not want teachers to deny these feelings exist. But whilst children are at school, most parents emphatically do not want their children to be taught about homosexual techniques or life styles". This widespread ignorance of homosexuality prompted the Executive to announce its intention to post a leaflet on homosexuality to every household in Scotland aimed at the people who most needed it: adults like Mrs Grant. She leant heavily on fear and distortion whilst regurgitating familiar Conservative propaganda into the minds of the credulous and gullible. "Let us not forget why Section 28 was introduced in the first place," she wrote. "It was introduced because councils in London who wanted to promote a homosexual agenda used schools for their own very particular political purposes. Under the guise of 'education' they introduced materials that went beyond a point which parents found acceptable. The Section was not brought in to discriminate against homosexuals and when homosexual groups accuse worried parents of being homophobic it simply demonstrates their utter contempt for the truth. For the truth is that parents are a tolerant lot who are being used as political pawns. It is not children's welfare that concerns the increasingly vociferous and militant gay lobby. It is a desire to exert their political muscle".

Members of the so-called 'gay lobby' were considerably less militant than Mrs Grant who, whilst picturing herself benignly standing outside the school gates, was, in fact, proselytising in the columns of a popular newspaper. As a pro-hunt supporter, she was not beyond joining marches and demonstrations either, and, after the ban on foxhunting in Scotland, expressed her willingness to break the law and go to jail. All that the repeal of Section 28 was designed to do was ensure that the learning took place *inside* the school, properly and impartially delivered by qualified practitioners. Under a picture of a group of women outside the school gates, the caption for her story read: "Gates of learning…"

In an article Katie Grant once wrote on the First Minister Donald Dewar's plan to allow people to decide how the government spent its spare cash in a consultation exercise, Mrs Grant created a "virtual group" of people to raise their concerns with the First Minister. "And how we laugh when one of the children in the group quite innocently asks if his consultation falls into the same category as the consultation over the repeal of Section 28. The child points out that the words 'con' and 'consultation' begin in the same way".

Criticism of Katie Grant was provided by Elizabeth Welsh from Ayr who managed to fire at her from the letters' pages in *Scotland on Sunday* over her piece on marriage and her suggestion that "most gay couples do not desire 'exclusive faithfulness'! Where does she get that from? The common thread that runs through her comments and those of Betty Souter is homophobia, linked, worryingly, with the promotion of 'family values'."

Katie Grant was once again lurking outside the school gates contemplating the future of St Mary's Episcopal Primary School in Dunblane. In a double-page spread in the *Scottish Daily Mail*,

The Assault on Family Values

her opinion was exercised on: "A tale of two schools... Parents and teachers have made a success of running St Mary's by themselves. So, why should they be forced to surrender this freedom when one other Scottish school (where the Education Minister sends his children) will still be allowed to carry on running its own affairs?" Small children were dragged in to support her emotive argument. "As usual, it is the children who get right to the heart of the issue. And when what is under threat is the school they loved, their questions are clear and direct. Why, the pupils of St Mary's want to know, does Sam Galbraith (the Education minister) want to stop their parents and teachers from continuing to run their flourishing school? 'Shouldn't the Scottish parliament be proud of us?' asked 11-year-old Robert when I visited the school this week. 'Why do they want to change things when they are just fine as they are?' whispered a worried looking Rachel, 10'." Sam Galbraith's children attended Jordanhill School, which, by ancient charter, remained outside local authority jurisdiction. The Conservative Government introduced opting-out legislation on the back of its 'parent power' programme. St Mary's Episcopal Primary School, with 66 pupils, however was resisting pressure from the Labour administration to go back under local authority control. "...If he is going to destroy, as one child put it 'the essence of our school', it would be only courteous to attempt to explain, to that person, the reason why... Over coffee in the staff room, this is what sticks in their gullets: In a secret ballot, 97 per cent of those who voted wanted to retain the status quo. These people are not political proselytisers; just people who are passionately concerned for the well-being of their school... Labour's election mantra of local solutions for local issues rings pretty hollow in the ears of these primary schoolchildren and their parents. They point out that one of the reasons cited for abandoning opting out - that too few parents put themselves up for election and that the school board could be hijacked by a few vociferous and bossy people - has not happened, nor is likely to happen at St Mary's". Mrs Grant's idea of education could have more usefully illustrated boxes of chocolates. She found St Mary's "located at the top of a small lane, the pretty, stone-built school with its gable roof and white door exudes an aura of efficient, homely cosiness".

Katie Grant's interest in St Mary's school was more than just the passing interest of a 'concerned parent' of course. St

Mary's, famed for its no-nonsense approach to teaching with an emphasis on the 'three Rs' was a school that had won its independence under reforms introduced by a Conservative Government. Brian Monteith MSP wrote about the debate that had taken place in the Scottish Executive in his political diary for Wednesday, 22 March 2000 in the *Herald*. It was what he described as the "first stage in principle of the Education Bill which is supposed to be about raising education standards but reveals Labour's vindictive side. It will snuff out the independence of St Mary's Primary School in Dunblane whilst maintaining the independence of Jordanhill School in Glasgow. I make this the main subject of my speech while also raising Section 28, greater choice in State schools and stronger powers for the General Teaching Council". Parents of the school were already preparing to take a test case to the European Court of Human Rights where parents hoped to argue they had a right to respect for their private and family life, including the right to choose the kind of education they wanted for their children. This was the same ploy campaigners hoped might prevent the repeal of Section 28.

Even on the subject of gamekeepers in her column in *Scotland on Sunday* she managed to attack gays: "When political correctness (should it not, correctly, be political rectitude?) is confined to asinine rules about calling someone a 'sissy' in the playground (the Scottish Executive has decreed this to be a hanging offence); it can be viewed simply as a joke. But when it begins to contaminate the legislative process it ceases to be a joke and becomes a threat".

Gerald Warner could also be counted on to echo Mrs Grant's opinion, as he did in *Scotland on Sunday*. "St Mary's Episcopal Primary School at Dunblane is to be sacrificed to the principle that there is no room for clever-clogs in an inclusive education system".

The *Daily Mail* offered unqualified support for any efforts to prevent the repeal of Section 28. At the Stagecoach AGM in September 2000, shareholders gathered in Perth to find a copy of *On Stage*, the company's magazine on their seats. It carried one advertisement, promoting the *Daily Mail* and its sister newspaper the *Mail on Sunday*.

Letters published in the *Scottish Daily Mail*, of course, largely reinforced the opinion of the newspaper. Visiting his local

The Assault on Family Values

surgery, P McMullin of Jedburgh was "horrified to see a large poster in the toilets and leaflets in the waiting area which advertised 'free condoms and lube' which could be posted to gay men. The message was in full view of any child who happened to be there. Doubtless we should be pleased the NHS is so well-funded", he sniped.

David J Wilson of Woolwich in London imagined recruiting impressionable youngsters in after-school clubs was to become part of a secret gay agenda: "As happened in the U.S and Canada, after-school clubs for gay recruiting are the secret agenda after the removal of Clause 28".

A. Parker of St Andrews in Fife - no stranger to the letters' pages of tabloids - squealed: "I have just visited the website of Stonewall and was horrified to discover the extent of the orchestration for the repeal of Section 28/2a. If Donald Dewar is not happy with Brian Souter, I don't see him being just as angry with Stonewall. The propaganda from Stonewall admitted that they have a growing number of like-minded MPs... is it any wonder Brian Souter and the silent majority are on a hiding to nothing, when our Government is full of homosexuals and lesbians".

A. C. of Fochabers demanded: "We don't want compromise. We want the clause to stay before we are a society where the lunatics are running the asylum, with Dewar as the biggest maniac in charge".

Associated Newspapers successfully distributed a free newspaper throughout Scotland. On the whole, *Metro Scotland* avoided mimicking the vociferous moralising of its sister paper, the *Daily Mail*. However, there were some baffling coincidences on the letters' pages of English and Scottish editions of the *Metro*. On Monday, 3 July 2000, for example, nine out of 10 letter-writers in the London edition shared the same names or initials as those in the Scottish edition - despite having altogether different addresses. M Lester of London E4 wrote to the London edition about police rapid response units - but another M Lester, this time from Livingston, West Lothian, wrote about the NHS in Scotland.

The *Daily Mail* didn't have it all its own way. It was alleged their highly popular astrologer Jonathan Cainer had resigned and joined the *Daily Express* over the *Mail's* attitude to homosexuality and single mothers.

RELIGIOUS FASCISM

Scotland's popular broadsheet, *Scotland on Sunday*, labelled the response to Brian Souter's ferocious 'Keep the Clause' campaign "an insidious one", fanning the flames with a sympathetic editorial: "Indeed Scotland has always cherished and admired independence of thought and action by its citizens. To suggest, as some commentators have, that we are a nation of anti-homosexual bigots is fatuous". The paper nonetheless attacked gays for "vacuous and totemic flag-waving" and sneered at "Alexander's personal crusade..." adding: "Let us be unequivocal here. If Scottish children were being given access to explicitly *hetero*sexual imagery or ideas in the state education curriculum, similar concerns, voiced by the majority of voters in this country, would arise". But *this* was fatuous. Children were *not* being offered pornography of *any* kind. That would have contravened teaching practice guidelines already in place and resulted in disciplinary action. The editorial opined: "Let us remind ourselves why the government in 1987 introduced Section 28. This was a response to the disturbingly graphic portrayals of homosexual activity which were appearing in teaching materials distributed throughout schools in some of London's left-wing boroughs". In another editorial on Section 28, *Scotland on Sunday* advised: "Donald Dewar and Wendy Alexander, the minister for communities, may come to regret their lamentable decision to make Section 28 a tub-thumping exercise in political correctness". Brian Dempsey of Outright Scotland challenged the paper on their inaccurate reporting after the broadsheet described Section 28 as "the clause that forbids the promotion of homosexuality" in schools. Dempsey explained it was a law that forbade the promotion of the acceptability of homosexuality as a pretended family relationship. He also challenged their exaggerated description of "disturbingly graphic portrayals of homosexual activity... in teaching materials distributed throughout schools" and urged readers of the broadsheet to "have a look" at the book, *Jenny Lives with Eric and Martin* for themselves.

Along with his frequent articles in the *Scottish Daily Mail*, the totemic flag-waving political reactionary; right-wing, Catholic columnist Gerald Warner had a weekly column in *Scotland on Sunday*. Barely a week went by without him using it to allude to the subject of homosexuality. It offered him the chance to repeat the story on how communities minister Wendy Alexander had responded to her schoolfriend's experience of being bullied at

The Assault on Family Values

school. The story haunted her as the media consistently referred to repeal as her 'personal campaign'. According to Warner, announcing the Executive's intention to repeal Section 28, Alexander told her audience: "Tomorrow... the first phone call I will make will be to that schoolfriend to tell him... 20 years on, kids at that same school in Renfrewshire will have a better chance of growing up at ease with themselves and the world around them". Warner scoffed. "Cue violins... pass round the Kleenex... Hollywood would love it. '(Say, is Tom Hanks available to play this Scottish guy that gets a hard time from the machos in the football team? How about Julia Roberts as this Alexander broad...?)'"

Gerald Warner frequently returned to the subject of homosexuality in his columns with a fiery passion. In one column Warner declared: "Homofascism is now, aggressively and shamelessly, the ideology of the Scottish Executive and parliament..." Quite where this so-called 'homofascism' had been manifesting itself was unclear. In a column headed: "In the name of democracy it's time to do the decent thing", Warner hit out at the media supporting repeal. "Under the self-appointed leadership of loud-mouthed progressives occupying the commanding heights in the media, Scotland has drifted for the past few decades in a miasma of moral indifferentism..." His column rocked with an unshielded hate and loathing of homosexuality; unfettered by the absence of legal constraint. "The turning point..." he warned, "was when they came for the children. The attempt to repeal Section 28 is an aggression by homosexuals and fellow travellers against our children. It is as simple and wicked as that. Pressure groups want to proselytise in schools, to recruit adolescent boys at an age of confused identity, vulnerable to the false comfort offered by homosexual missionaries... The material directed at children is pornographic to the vilest degree..." Turning on Wendy Alexander's slight lisp, he added: "The useful idiot fronting this offensive is Wendy Alexander, the thirty-something Minithter for Communitieth with the mindset of a 1980s student activist".

Gerald Warner's attacks on Wendy Alexander were frequently personal and sexist. Another of his articles was headed: "Where are the visionaries to lead us out of the Wendy House?" He rounded on the "wee pretendy parliament..." and asked: "Why are we ruled by a gang of cooncillors *(sic)* and fat women from social work departments?" He suggested Wendy Alexander "interprets her portfolio as trampling upon the wishes of the community. As she stood at the lectern, shrilling, pouting and finger-wagging (two fingers would have sufficed to convey her message to the despised Scottish public), she personified the arrogance and hubris that characterises the Scottish Executive... Alexander is living testimony to the unwisdom of abolishing the ducking-stool".

When confronted by Grampian Health Board's recommendation that resources advocating monogamy and marriage as a *solitary* solution to HIV should be avoided, Gerald Warner flew into a rage. "These are the dark forces which will blight the next generation if a stand is not made against them. Every opinion survey registers massive opposition to this programme for the systematic corruption of the nation's children". He issued a sharp warning. "...This is not a democratic government... A head of steam is building up, of public resentment against the mendacious charlatanry both of the devolution settlement and of the strutting homosexual lobby. This mood will not now be reversed; the longer it is frustrated, the heavier the penalties that will be exacted from those twin enemies of Scottish decency".

Religionists opposed to the repeal of Section 28 jumped on Pope John Paul II's visit to the Holy Land to demonstrate how strong the links were between followers of Christianity and those of Islam and Judaism. Leaders of most religious factions shared the growing revolt against the adoption of gay rights. *Il Papa's* expressions of regret for some of the Catholic Church's wrongdoings throughout history - excluding its treatment of gays, of course – signalled a new religious coalition bolstered by features in certain sections of the media from Asian commentators reflecting a new surge of ethnic militancy within their own communities who were voicing moral concern over the erosion of the traditional family. There were threats that more Asian children would be sent to Catholic schools and local MPs and MSPs supporting repeal might lose their seats at forthcoming elections. Michael Portillo, when he made a bid for the Tory leadership, suggested that, if elected, he would look at the issue of Section 28 again. Capitalising on the new bond of friendship between Conservatives and immigrant communities, Lord Tebbit, a former Tory party chairman told the *Daily Mail:* "If we are to become more inclusive to racial minorities, as we should, we must recognise that this is one of the few things that bind us together across all other lines. The black evangelical churches and the Islamic organisations all agree on the need for this law".

Gerald Warner mocked the Pope's expression of regret for the Catholic's role in history that "led to the deaths of Jews by Christians at any time and in any place..." He wrote: "Being Catholic means always having to say sorry: about the Crusades, about the Inquisition, about Galileo; sorry for having been so insensitive as to contradict Luther and Calvin; for not rewriting history to slander Pius XII; above all, for continuing to promote - however mutely and incoherently - traditional moral values. Sorry about all that". (Sorry, he wasn't). "The Pope's visit to the Holy Land has had the predictable outcome of demonstrating that appeasement fuels the appetite of the moral blackmailer..."

Warner scoffed at claims that the Catholic Church was silent in the face of the holocaust and insisted: "The innocence of the late Pope has been established beyond doubt: so far from being complicit in the murder of Jews, by his personal intervention he saved 860,000 potential victims". Warner was particularly ruffled by the Pope's apology for "sins that have injured the dignity of women". He claimed the Church had "refused to support the degradation of women into mere units of economic productivity". He added the Church had "upheld their right to the security and dignity of lifelong marriage... implored them not to poison their bodies with chemicals in pursuit of the imagined benefits of artificial infertility or of promiscuity and erosion of self-respect; above all, not to turn their wombs into abattoirs by resorting to abortion".

There were deep concerns over the absence of any apology for the treatment of sexual minorities by the Catholic Church over the millennia. In 1988, an Italian gay man, Alfredo Ormando had set himself alight in St Peter's Square in protest at the Church's attitude to gays and later died from his injuries. Leader of the Italian gay rights group Arcigay, Franco Grillini hit out at John Paul II: "The Vatican is asking forgiveness for everyone except gay people, who have suffered the most at the hands of the Church".

Attempts to repeal Section 28 united religionists of all persuasions. Brian Souter's wife, Betty, a former social worker, also shared her husband's deeply held religious convictions that bound them to the Church of the Nazarene. She was pictured looking rather dour in *Scotland on Sunday*; sitting bolt upright, dressed in black and looking away from the camera. Her 17-month-old son, Calum, one of four children, (the others were Amy, 10, Scott, 8, Fraser, 6) was pictured playing on the tartan carpet in her traditional Perth home.

Not all of their children's traditional upbringing would necessarily save them from the attentions of the police. In 2007, a 15-year-old Scott Souter would be banned for driving his dad's sports car the wrong way down a one-way street without insurance. Then, in 2009 he received an on-the-spot fine for drinking in a Stirling street. Weeks later, brandishing a copy of the *Scottish Sun*, he was pictured emerging from a court following charges of assault. The *Sun* described how "boozed-up Scott Souter, 18, piled into a car with pals and chased down Philip Johnston's motor before launching a vicious attack on his victim". 20-year-old, Johnston, who'd left a party in Glenfarg, Perthshire after an argument, was battered repeatedly about the head before he was forced to abandon his car and flee. Scott Souter told police: "A group of boys made fun of my dad" and "they shouted wanker at me". Brian Souter hired lawyer Paul McBride QC to help his son avoid further punishment. The court was told Scott was already attending an Edinburgh clinical psychologist for sessions in anger management and help dealing with alcohol. McBride explained that Scott had already had the embarrassment of a conviction; nonetheless, he was forced to pay his victim £400 in compensation for his injuries.

Brian Souter had complained to the Press Complaints Commission through his lawyers Levy & McRae following the *Scottish Sun's* story "Stagecoach son nicks dad's car" which was printed a week after Scott had turned 16, saying it had been intrusive and an embarrassment for Scott and that the story had only appeared because his father was a prominent figure. The complaint was not upheld.

Betty Souter's newspaper interview began by applauding the Labour party for its commitment to "family values". But, for this Scotswoman - who had met husband Brian at a religious holiday camp - Labour had now gone too far. "As a parent" she was "particularly concerned" with "quick divorces, legitimising illegitimacy...," (the Scottish Executive had just written the word 'bastard' out of the statute books), "abolition of the married

The Assault on Family Values

couples' allowance and the repeal of Section 28". She added: "There is a phase which young people go through in which they may feel attracted to members of the same sex and which most grow out of. I am deeply concerned that young people passing through this phase may be exposed to influences which can be harmful to them and encourage them into lifestyle choices which they may regret in later life". It was not the first time the Souters had mentioned the challenge of a 'homosexual phase'. Betty's solution was the church: discipline, obstruction, censorship and, of course, the celebration of 'family values'. "That young people can be influenced by their environment and nurtured into homosexual activity is a very real possibility which must be avoided". She was convinced that Scotland's parents carried her opinions unanimously. "I chose to send my children to a State school because I wanted them to live in an inclusive society and receive an open, cosmopolitan education. I do not see why I should be forced to consider private or Catholic education because of this politically correct government". Her attack on human rights campaigner, Peter Tatchell was vitriolic. "The hysterical reaction from Peter Tatchell on this issue has only served to confirm my worst fears concerning a hidden agenda. I cannot understand why a 35-year-old English bachelor" - he was 48 at the time – "who shares his life with three other men" - but not in the traditional married context Betty couldn't see her way round – "has such an interest in Scottish schoolchildren". He had no 'interest' in Scottish schoolchildren at all, other than to ensure they had somewhere to turn if they thought they might be gay. "I believe that traditional marriage is the best environment in which children can be born and raised. I am entitled to this belief and I am entitled to teach my children these beliefs and values, and I don't want same-sex relationships presented to my children as having the same moral value". This was precisely why - with attitudes such as these doing the rounds - gay kids needed access to support in schools.

James Baker expressed his outrage over the interview in the letters' page of the next edition of *Scotland on Sunday:* "There is a mass collusion amongst heterosexuals to deny that these atrocities are happening in good god-fearing heterosexual families. And there is no Section 28 equivalent to prevent teachers teaching about all that, they just collude in the silence.

RELIGIOUS FASCISM

Perhaps it helps Mrs Souter's purpose to draw our attentions away from such unpleasantness".

In the same paper, L Richardson of St Andrews wrote: "I saw a phrase which read 'In disagreement, fight fair - no name calling'. Christians are not to bear false witness against their neighbours - and that includes innuendo".

Based in London with editorial offices in Glasgow's Kinning Park, the *Scottish Sun* was yet another tabloid hammering home a morally conservative message between busty, young page three girls and advertisements for premium-rate phone lines. The *Scottish Sun's* editorial opened: "Section 28 is one of the most precious safeguards in Scottish society. It blocks right-on thinkers from foisting the mechanics of homosexuality on children in the classroom".

A former *Record* night editor in the early 80s, Jack Irvine became the first Scottish editor of the *Sun* in 1987. Bruce Waddell, who formerly worked for the *Falkirk Herald*, was hired by Irvine as a sub-editor of the *Scottish Sun* before becoming its editor. What Bruce Waddell and Colin McClatchie, who ran Rupert Murdoch's News International's Scottish operation, failed to understand was that young people were already familiar with some of the "mechanics". It was only a proper understanding of them that was missing. Murdoch admitted he not only chose editors of the *Sun* and its then sister paper *News of the World*, but exercised a hands-on approach to editorial policy. Rupert Murdoch not only owned Zondervan, the world's biggest publisher of Bibles, but he went on to donate an undisclosed six-figure sum for the Pope Benedict to visit the UK in 2010. His son James enjoyed a private audience with the Pope and for further donations Murdoch received a Papal knighthood. As for his tabloids, instead of opting to floor the competition with a refreshingly liberal, lively, informed and forward-thinking opinion on sexual education, the *Scottish Sun* pocketed Souter's gold and delivered a sermon in its editorial: "God put his own son in a household with a mum and dad... We are the ones who are today grateful to Brian Souter, the raiding of his charitable fund, and the righteous stirring of sensible Scots everywhere. To use a Biblical term, the thought of removing Section 28 is an abomination. To use another, the idea deserves the same fate as Sodom and Gomorrah". The *Sun's* editorial exhorted: "What better use of charitable money than to turn the tide of muddle-

The Assault on Family Values

headed thinking that assaults young minds?" Without considering the thousands of lesbian, gay, bisexual and transgendered men and women, closeted or otherwise who already had children, the *Sun* cried: "Those of us who go with the 90 per cent majority in our sexuality are the ones who have children to worry about... Cabinets, the legal profession, showbiz and, let it be said, newspapers all have open doors to gay people..." The editorial scoffed: "They have followed the call of their genes and by and large have forfeited the joy of children... Are we homophobic to reflect this? Not at all".

The *Scottish Sun's* resident homophobe was former SNP MP Jim Sillars. Sillars was a former deputy leader of the SNP and married to Margo MacDonald MSP who had her own column in both the *Sunday Post* and Edinburgh's *Evening News*. Sillars was obsessed with the idea that older homosexual men wanted to keep a stock of young men to bugger. Turning on the "fanatical homosexual lobby" he furnished *Scottish Sun* readers with a somewhat unique insight into the real reason why gay men wanted Section 28 repealed: "...Test tube births on a scale of millions, with the sperm of homosexuals conveyed artificially to women's ovaries, in order to give homosexuals full rights to have children. That test tube world is the only logical conclusion of the Tatchellite campaign of full and equal rights". Perth SNP MSP Roseanna Cunningham - despite later making a name for herself tabling a motion against gay adoption in the Scottish Parliament in 2006 - tried to set the record straight in the *Scottish Sun* over the "unbelievable palaver" about Section 28 and tackled the issue of 'promotion' head on. "People are either gay or they aren't – they don't become so just because someone else says it is OK to be so. Of course, in our society, the real problem is saying that it is OK to be gay". Sillars was unmoved and later in the debate lambasted the Labour administration because they "bow the knee to fanatical minorities while holding the majority in contempt".

Another Rupert Murdoch title, the *Scottish News of the World*, which ceased publication in 2011 following a widespread phone-hacking scandal, treated sexuality with as much prurience as its daily paper, the *Scottish Sun*. SNP leader Alex Salmond wrote a regular column in the Sunday paper and put his weight behind his Party's commitment to equality for all. "The problem with Section 28 is that it states a homosexual lifestyle is unacceptable. That creates an atmosphere in which bullying and discrimination can flourish. That's bad for our children and for society, and is why it should be repealed". In another newspaper poll, the *Scottish News of the World* asked 500 people in the street during the debate on the repeal of Section 28 and found 58 per cent thought children should be made aware of homosexuality during school lessons. Yet 51 per cent thought Section 28 should be kept and 50 per cent had no problem with homosexuality as long as it wasn't flaunted. 38-year-old Andrew Vint demonstrated to the tabloid exactly why teachers needed to be free to discuss homosexuality in schools when he argued: "I don't think children should be made aware of homosexuality at school. I've already e-mailed First Minister Donald Dewar to let him know how strongly I feel. Clause 28 should not be repealed. Parents should have the final say in their children's education. Homosexual sex should never have been made legal. It makes me sick to even think about it – it's disgusting and morally wrong. I don't want anything to do with it, I would never condone it and I don't want my children taught about it".

In another Rupert Murdoch paper, the *Sunday Times Scotland*, edited by *Scottish Daily Mail* columnist Colette Douglas Home's husband, Mark Douglas Home, recognised in its editorial that "the alliance of Brian Souter and Cardinal Winning is the first example this side of the Atlantic of money and evangelism combining so powerfully to challenge government policy", adding: "In one respect Mr Dewar and his minister, Wendy Alexander, have brought this crisis on themselves... He must do more to appease the legitimate fears of parents by producing draft new guidelines forbidding any crudely explicit, pornographic or inappropriate sexual teaching materials in schools".

Scottish editions of the *Daily Telegraph*, a right-wing broadsheet, boasted journalist Alan Cochrane as their homophobic mouthpiece. In an editorial headed, "Tony's militant tendency", it shook the armchairs of the reactionary right with the extraordinary assertion that: "New Labour is more left-wing, more anti-British and more unrepresentative of the nation than any previous administration" and declared "Section 28 is the most prominent example". The Bishop of Liverpool James Jones had a point to make and one suitable enough to be printed in the *Telegraph*: "Kant said we should test the ethics of an action by applying to it the maxim: act as if this were to be the law universal. If homosexual practice were to become such, the

The Assault on Family Values

species would not be in a position to recreate itself. Further more, physiologically, the genitalia are manifestly designed for the opposite and not the same gender".

Clifford Langley wrote to the editor of the *Telegraph* to explain things from the missionary position: "To a non-homosexual man in the normal world, homosexuality does not offer itself as an addictive vice - as churchmen sometimes appear to think - but as an unenviable inability to be attracted to women, hence eliminating one of the chief pleasures of being alive".

From the same stable as the *Daily Record*, although with a much smaller circulation in Scotland than in England, the daily tabloid, the *Scottish Mirror's* position under editor Murray Foote was considerably less reactionary. "We at the Mirror are a liberal bunch. Not for us the bigoted rantings of our lesser rivals", they boasted. Although, not so liberal when two Leeds players, Ian Harte and Gary Kelly – albeit in national editions - celebrated a goal with a kiss. "...A full smacker on THE LIPS? We don't think so", they sniffed.

Most of the press failed to realise how painful their stories and headlines were to such a vulnerable minority at this time, not least the *Scottish Mirror* which headlined "ANTI-GAY VICTORY", over claims of a government "U-turn". Once again, trading 'gay' with 'Jew' or 'black' lent a greater clarity to the offending material. After the *Mirror's* headline: "Clause 28 has to be scrapped...," its editorial hid a contradictory message: "It is one thing to avoid offending the gay lobby - but quite another to ignore the wishes of the people of Scotland". The *Mirror's* editorial begged: "...While we disagree with the 'Keep the Clause' campaign's objective, we still believe Brian Souter is owed a debt of gratitude from ordinary Scots for bringing this debate into the open". Its editorial vainly pleaded with the "middle ground" to "lend their voices to the call to scrap the law". Their editorial insisted: "The Labour Executive assured us that Clause 28 would be scapped – and scrapped it should be".

After Brian Souter announced he was bankrolling a referendum, the *Scottish Mirror's* editorial insisted: "Prime Minister Tony Blair...knows that the Thatcherite law is blatant discrimination and has absolutely no place in Britain in the new millennium... However, last May we elected 129 politicians to make new laws for a new Scotland - and to do the job differently from Westminster". The *Scottish Mirror's* morally conservative, boot-boy, columnist of choice was the PR man hand-picked by Brian Souter to run the 'Keep the Clause' campaign, Jack Irvine. Irvine was born in Lennoxtown in 1949 and went to Eastbank Academy in Glasgow. He trained in journalism at the *Glasgow Herald* before working at the *Stirling Journal* and the *Irvine Herald* and playing guitar in BA Robertson's band producing such hits as *Bang Bang, Knocked It Off* and *To Be Or Not To Be*. Irvine used his column in the *Scottish Mirror* to express his virulent homophobia. He started up Scottish editions of the *Sun* in 1987 and with the help of his deputy Steve Sampson, earned a reputation as the Rottweiler of Glasgow journalism. One former employee remarked that Mr Irvine was "a man who would not be lost for words or thoughts even if you took the top of his head off and scooped his brains out". Two years later, Irvine was promoted to managing director of News International's Scottish operations at their base in Kinning Park in Glasgow which produced Scottish editions of the *Sun, News of the World*, and *Sunday Times*. Aidan Smith in the *Scotsman* wrote that the ex-editor "played fast and loose with the old journalist's axiom: 'Never let the facts get in the way of a good story'." He left News International to become managing director and editor-in-chief of Rangers Football Club's largest shareholder, David Murray's the *Sunday Scot*. It was a massive flop and folded after just 14 weeks in 1991. In his new job promoting the Mirror Group's titles, including the *Daily Record*, Jack Irvine rose to notoriety once again as the man behind a virulent campaign against their main competitor, the *Scottish Sun*. As well as serving private, Media House served a wide range of public clients besides Brian Souter's Stagecoach, Coach USA and Ann Gloag's Mercy Ships. They have included the Princess Royal Trust for Carers, Scottish Countryside Alliance, John Menzies plc, Lexmark International (Scotland) Ltd., Levy & McRae solicitors, Mackays stores, The Malcolm Group, Data Discoveries Ltd., Scottish Radio Holdings plc, Hilton International, Tamaris plc, THUS plc, WestSound Radio, John Letters (Scotland) Ltd., Independent Women and Infocell amongst others. Media House were also involved in various projects with Aitken Holdings Ltd., Glasgow Bar Association, Reid Furniture Company Ltd., the Christian Blind Mission (CBM) and the Carnyx Group, publisher of the Scottish media marketing magazine, the *Drum*.

The Assault on Family Values

Two pages in the *Scottish Mirror* gave Jack Irvine the opportunity to explain his "personal view" in patronising tones on the repeal of Section 28 in the form of an open letter to Communities Minister Wendy Alexander. "I believe you are one of the best things to have happened to Scottish politics," he began. "You are clever, honest and energetic and would seem to have a brilliant future. In addition, from the two brief times I have met you, I found you to be a thoroughly agreeable woman, not something I could say about many politicians. However, your one fault, and it may recede with experience, is that you don't want to listen to ordinary people. I'm a wee bit worried that your young, malleable mind is being influenced by the elite company you keep in Glasgow's West End". Irvine relapsed into chauvinism. "Maybe successful businessmen make you nervous", he wrote. "Firstly, let me say I am writing this to you neither as a newspaper columnist nor the boss of a PR firm. I am writing to you as the father of two children – a boy aged 13 and girl of 11. Before I was a father... I was the stereotypical, hard-drinking, hard-living newspaperman of popular legend... One night I was working on a story about a young runaway boy whom an evil gang of paedophiles had murdered and, as I read the horrifying evidence from the court, the tears welled up in my eyes. I had to walk away from the desk to compose myself. Every parent who is reading this knows what I am talking about... It was therefore not surprising that I received a call from one of my longest standing clients just before I headed-off on an assignment to New York at Christmas. It was Brian Souter and he told me that he and some friends had been reading some of my recent Mirror columns. He had paid particular attention to the aggressive stance I had taken against the Government's proposed lowering of the homosexual age of consent..." (Irvine wrote that the prospect of an equal age of consent was an opportunity "for a slobbering old queer to have his evil way with you... And remember, the next time an old fruit gets caught with his hands in a 14-year-old's pants, he will probably get off when he lisps: 'but I thought the boy looked 16)'." Irvine continued: "He (Souter) asked if I would co-ordinate a Keep the Clause campaign... It took me all of one second to agree... We're just two Scots laddies who were brought up in council houses... As the war of words rages between the camps, Brian and I are getting tired hearing the protestations of the many gay activist groups. No matter how tiny a gay lobby group – two members will suffice – normally, objective journalists will devote acres of newsprint to their views".

Wendy Alexander hit back, wasting no time in reminding him in the *Scottish Mirror:* "This law is also being repealed in England and Wales. I don't believe Scots want their country to be seen as a last bastion of bigotry... You suggest this policy has suddenly been sprung on Scotland. You know this is not true. Repealing Clause 28 has been Government policy since Labour's General Election victory in 1997... Listen to the experts. Childline takes around 7,500 calls every year from children who are being bullied. Another 500 children ring who are troubled by their sexuality".

Ian Bell commented with an element of exasperation in his column in the *Scotsman:* "...Matters have passed the point of lunacy when we are supposed to take moral guidance from a former executive of the Sun newspaper". Jack Irvine set up his PR company, Media House in 1991. Crisis management had a key role in the company's profile which included the Scots nurse Lucille McLauchlan who was accused of murder in Saudi Arabia, Brian Dempsey's overthrowing of the Celtic football club board, the unpopular Newcastle Football club directors and of course, the Bank of Scotland's aborted tie-in with US tele-evangelist Pat Robertson. The 'Keep the Clause' campaign was run from Media House's headquarters at 16 Robertson Street in the heart of the red light district of Glasgow. Along with his offices in Glasgow, he had premises in Edinburgh, London and New York. His other company was Tactical Response, which advised companies dealing with hostile attacks on their share price. He lived then in Whitecraigs with his wife, Maureen and two children, Chris, 13 and Rebecca, 11 and was responsible for another £250,000 campaign in support of fox-hunting for the Scottish Countryside Alliance. Of the latter campaign, the *Herald* obtained a leaked document suggesting the campaign was largely bankrolled from England to the tune of £130,000 and £205,000 for their public relations campaign. Scottish expenditure was more than double its income since the income from Scottish supporters was listed as only £110,389. Although the Countryside Alliance did not deny the allegations, when confronted by the *Herald*, Allan Murray, director of the Scottish Countryside Alliance was reported to have told reporters: "It's none of your damn business". Set up in 1998 to cover a wide range of countryside

The Assault on Family Values

issues, the Scottish Countryside Alliance spent a disproportionate amount on the 'red coats' support of blood sports at the expense of more pressing concerns of a rural economy in crisis. It was with some irony that one of the central themes of their campaign turned out to be the idea that fox-hunters were a vulnerable minority that needed protection from the majority.

After a disagreement with its editor, Jack Irvine's regular column in the *Scottish Mirror* no longer appeared, leaving Irvine more time to concentrate on the 'Keep the Clause' campaign.

Another tabloid, the *Scottish Daily Express*, edited by Kerry Gill and in direct competition with the *Scottish Daily Mail*, appeared only lukewarm in its response to repeal. "Name-calling and intemperate language... has damaged the country, setting group against group and individual against individual..." The *Express* editorial at the start of the Section 28 furore focused on the issuing of guidelines. "Some will criticise ministers for isolating teaching about homosexuality, a far cry from the 'inclusiveness' the Executive tells us it desires in the new Scotland. But desperate times require desperate measures and ministers may at least succeed in drawing the poison from the affair. Section 28 should, by all means, go, but most sensible and neutral people want to know what is going to replace it. While 99.99 per cent of teachers can be trusted to be responsible, there may always be an exception who will have to be tackled".

The popular Scottish Sunday tabloid the *Sunday Mail*, like the *Record*, another Trinity House title at the time, took a quick *volte-face* over issues of sexuality a few weeks before Souter announced he was bankrolling the Scottish School Boards' Association's efforts to prevent repeal of Section 28 when Peter Cox from the *Scottish Mirror* took over as editor. Under former editor Jim Cassidy the *Sunday Mail* had been excruciatingly Victorian about sexuality. Cassidy was the brother of Tom Cassidy who worked with Jack Irvine on the 'Keep the Clause' campaign and was close to senior members of the Catholic hierarchy, including Cardinal Winning. The *Sunday Mail's* editorial now spelt out its support for the repeal of Section 28: "Dewar learns how to lead from the front... His vision for Scotland's future, outlined in today's paper, is for fairness and justice for all – and that includes gays". The paper's columnist Melanie Reid pinpointed the latching on to the issue of 'promotion' of homosexuality. "Moral traditionalists like that description. They portray Clause 28 as a last bastion holding back a wall of filth from the ears of our innocents. As if its lifting would mean our kids would get 10 hours tuition a week in how to look like Julian Clary". Their editorial begged: "What on earth is happening to our normal tolerant Scottish society? You would think the Anti-Christ had just been appointed new teacher for Primary Two... We are talking about the scrapping of... Section 28... It was introduced by the Tories, let us remember, to soothe Middle England's fears about everything you can't buy in Sainsbury's... Axing it will not allow beasts incarnate to wander through our schools corrupting our children and turning us into a nation of cottaging gays... The right-wing English-based Daily Mail tells us gleefully that of the 2,300 groups asked for their views on Section 28, a full 40 were gay. Indeed. And the other 2,260 were heterosexual!"

Owned by the Barclay brothers, the *Scotsman* was an Edinburgh-based broadsheet in support of repeal. "This newspaper does not accept that Scots are prejudiced", its editorial insisted confidently. It was another about-turn for a paper once edited by the ferocious editor of the *Daily Record*, Martin Clarke in 1997, albeit for little more than a year. Alan Ruddock took the helm and was in the editor's seat until February 2000. Under its editor-in-chief, the Paisley-born former editor of the *Sunday Times*, Andrew Neil, editors changed frequently and pro-repeal Tim Luckhurst – a former advisor to Donald Dewar - would end up out on his ear after only a few months, finishing up, toning down his act, writing a column for the *Scottish Daily Mail*. Rob Ballantyne, Stagecoach's head of PR also served time as assistant business editor of the *Scotsman*. Ritchie MacLaren proudly related in his Diary in the *Scotsman* how he was "travelling by bus – not Stagecoach, since some of my best friends are gay..." Over the paper's support for repeal, Rev Dr Alistair P Donald from New Deer, Aberdeen wrote to the *Scotsman*, asking: "Have you taken leave of your senses?"

Robert Neil kept up some light-hearted observations watching the Scottish Executive at work for his column in the *Scotsman*. "Somehow, listening to MSPs talking about – you know – 'it,' is like hearing your favourite aunt at the Christmas table suddenly change the conversation from Brussels sprouts to orgasms... Wee Phil (Gallie), the Tory justice spokesman, ambled forth from the backwoods, claiming he didn't have an axe to

The Assault on Family Values

grind. But nobody believed him. In an ill-advised allusion, he said his postbags had been bulging.... Andrew Wilson (SNP) got fed up with his ramblings, and said: 'Are you, Phil Gallie, in favour of the equalisation of consent or not?' He was not. But the message from the overwhelming majority was: 'Not tonight, Philistine...' Another Conservative, John Young, who thinks the Karma Sutra comes with a chapati, said that in all his years on Glasgow council, sex had only been mentioned once. And, even then, it was just somebody asking what it was like. John is a genuinely nice man, and hardly anybody's idea of a bigot. He said of Mr (Jim, Scottish Lib Dem leader) Wallace: 'I just wonder if he isn't advocating sexual licence'. No, John, you won't need a licence. That's the television".

The *Scotsman* balanced its liberal view with a feature by Tim Williams: "...This crisis offers an opportunity for the new parliament to be seen as responsive and relevant to the Scots as they are, and not as they were imagined to be by the self-deluded intellectuals who saw self-government as the high road to a more liberal Scotland". An editorial in the *Scottish Daily Express* agreed. "The Scottish Executive has largely brought the brouhaha on itself by assuming too much and knowing too little about what kind of country Scotland is". Tim Hopkins of the Equality Network had his response to Williams's feature printed in the *Scotsman*. "Unlike the UK, Ireland's law now treats gay and straight people entirely equally. There is no Section 28, there is an equal age of consent, and gay people are protected by law from discrimination. Ireland's repeal in the last ten years of all laws which discriminated against gay people shows it is entirely possible for a country to accommodate both those with strong religious views, and gay and other minorities. Just as the Act of Settlement stigmatises Catholics and must be repealed, Cardinal Thomas Winning should acknowledge that a law which condemns the 'acceptability of homosexuality' stigmatises gay people and must be repealed". But Cardinal Winning responded to requests for sound-bites from the media; not gays.

The *Scotsman's* Conal Urquhart attempted to field the opinion of the very people the repeal of Section 28 would affect: schoolchildren. But the City of Edinburgh Council education department advised head teachers not to let senior pupils talk to the paper. However, Balerno High School showed no such timidity and revealed a high degree of intelligence amongst the ten pupils the broadsheet questioned on the issue. None of them believed a rounded education would have any bearing on their sexuality. Hannah Stevenson, 17 insisted: "You shouldn't make laws to deal with emotions". There was little sympathy for Cardinal Winning's "stupid and ignorant" belief that homosexuality was a perversion. Ewan Connolly, 17 revealed: "It's not seriously discussed, it's joked about because people are embarrassed about it. Today is the first time that we have talked about it". This was echoed in the *Herald* with a letter from Daniel Donaldson in Glasgow: "When I was taught in school, I was shown a video of babies in buckets to highlight the 'evils' of abortion, under sanction from the Catholic Church. Upon reflection this was an event that should never have been allowed to happen. I find the Cardinal's hypocrisy on the issue of education unbearable. If a Catholic school can show a traumatic and powerful video about abortion, featuring pictures of babies in buckets, then what is the big problem about teaching about homosexuality?" This was wickedly summed-up by Muriel Gray in the *Sunday Herald*. Due to the constraints of his faith, she criticised Cardinal Winning for his lack of experience. "He has never had sexual relations, never had to live alongside and compromise with a partner, never had children and felt the responsibility, joy and pain that accompanies that gift. Not even has he had the mundane experience of ordinary working life and the associated problems the rest of us struggle with every day. He has, therefore, through no fault of his own, the intellectual maturity of an average 16 or 17-year-old".

The *Herald*, Scotland's most popular broadsheet had always adopted a fairly conservative approach to sexuality, but now backed the Government. "Changing the law would be as likely to lead to 'gay sex lessons' as to naked abseiling with red squirrels". Compare that with a *Herald* leader in 1997 which advised that the Church's "...apparently controversial interventions in politics are actually of the greatest value to us all". Such an opinion would still be carried by a plethora of morally conservative and religionist commentators, all of whom now wrote regularly for the paper: Stewart Lamont, John Macleod, Patrick Reilly and Michael Fry to name a few. In the middle of the debate over the repeal of Section 28 the *Herald* printed a commissioned piece by Graeme Woolaston, a gay arts consultant who occasionally reviewed books in the paper. Not known for particularly liberal

The Assault on Family Values

views on sexuality, either, Woolaston was a safe and respectable homosexual that was occasionally permitted to grace the broadsheet with his commissioned opinion. Amongst his submissions he even attacked human rights activist, Peter Tatchell in a letter, adding: "In the area of personal relationships, the gay community has much to learn from straights". Woolaston detested the views or attitudes sometimes attributed to 'the gay community' which he insisted were held by "only by a vocal minority" and added: "There's no doubt that many gay activists have done immense damage to their chosen cause by antics which suggest that, out of sight of heterosexuals, gay life is a freak show... Let a gay march consist of 5,000 sober, cheerful men and women, and one bearded nun, and you can bet your life that the next day the bearded nun will be in all the newspapers..." And the illustration used to accompany Woolaston's sober commentary in the oldest newspaper in the English-speaking world? You got it in one... A bearded nun!

There sometimes seemed an element of restraint in the *Herald's* handling of the affair under its Editor Harry Reid who had written books on the Church of Scotland. On the other hand, Deputy Editor, Kevin McKenna once told the *Guardian:* "I am a Catholic, proud of my faith and happy to acknowledge Benedict XVI as supreme pontiff, Vicar of Christ, Bishop of Rome and a thoroughly decent old chap". Reflecting on Section 28's roots, its editorial advised: "True, the silly, right-on actions of a 'loony left' council or two played into Tory hands but (Section 28) was going to have its day sooner or later". Bill's political cartoon showed two gay men at a bus stop with the caption; "I don't care where it's going. I'm still not taking a No. 28".

Tom Shields and Ken Smith noted in their Diary in the *Herald* that young Nathan, from the hit drama *Queer as Folk*, was spotted climbing on board a Stagecoach bus "Presumably Brian did not object to taking a fee for his bus being used in the series..." The Channel Four programme *Queer as Folk* went out at 10pm every Tuesday night throughout the debate. The bright orange billboard posters of 'promiscuous' Stuart, boyfriend Vince and 'under-age' Nathan advertised the programme in Scotland. The new series, *Queer As Folk Two* featured Nathan bullied at school, unsupported by his teacher. The planting of erotica in the car of a devout Catholic to help Vince secure promotion over his religious rival in one scene angered some Catholics. G Hunter from Clydebank demanded in a letter to the *Record:* "Anyone believing Section 28 should be repealed... should watch Queer as Folk, now receiving its second screening on Channel Four... (it shows) gay pornography... (and) a scene depicting child abuse".

During the Section 28 debacle, many of the leading protagonists were profiled - Brian Souter, his wife Betty, Jack Irvine, the Scottish Schools' Board Association's Ann Hill and, of course, Cardinal Winning. In a Channel Four programme profiling Winning shortly before the repeal of Section 28, they made much of the fact that the voice of Catholics was not being heard. This was an extraordinary assertion compared to the silence imposed on Scotland's so-called 'proselytising, militant gay activists'. Where were they? The Scottish media, of course, had marginalised gay people so much that there was no recognisable face to feed off. The profile of Peter Tatchell, by Michael Tierney in the *Herald's* Saturday magazine might have been an exception had not the charismatic member of the gay rights group, Outrage! been based in London. With all the talk of well-funded militant gay organisations, Tierney revealed Tatchell lived "on about £5,000 per year". For a campaigner who had been vilified for so long by the media, it turned out to be a disappointing profile. Tierney labelled the lifelong pacifist a "militant gay rights activist..." from the outset. Fortunately, a more measured side to Tatchell's quest for repeal was also revealed: "His proposed guidelines for incorporation into the Section 28 repeal bill (which he has sent to First Minister Donald Dewar) to specify that: schools should not promote or encourage any form of sexuality; all sexual orientations must be discussed in an honest, factual manner; pupils should be offered practical advice on how to refuse and report unwanted sexual advances, practise safe sex to stop the spread of HIV, and how to sustain happy, fulfilling relationships..." Perhaps, such a calm and measured response from Tatchell was not what Tierney had expected. With a hint of disappointment, he wrote: "For all his erudition he possesses a kind of self-centred, I-know-best account of, well, just about everything. He's gripping and illuminating but he's also a bit sour, a bit dour. Stumbling around in a perpetual dungeon of righteousness, it can't be much fun being Peter Tatchell". Over his opportunity to interview Peter Tatchell, Tierney mused: "Finally, I'm in with the out crowd..."

The Assault on Family Values

The letters' pages of the *Herald* was always a lively platform of debate over Section 28 and special 'Letters about Section 28' pages appeared more than once to handle the huge postbags. This was one of the few papers that made a serious attempt at affording a wide-ranging and balanced view of opinions right across Scotland and beyond. Andrew M Fraser, Convener of the Committee on Public Questions, Religion and Morals of the Free Church of Scotland wrote from The Mound in Edinburgh on 22 March 2000. His Church had recently been split down the middle in another church schism and threatened to disappear altogether. He referred to the repeal of Section 28 as "not one of human rights but of morality". Without proof he declared that Section 28 was "an effective deterrent" brought in by a Conservative Government to curb local authorities that "were spending large sums of money promoting homosexuality in schools and in other areas…" Where? How? He didn't say, but went on to reveal there were "statistics to show that on many occasions local authorities have drawn back from this because of a fear of prosecution under Section 28". His real agenda was only too apparent. "Where do we want Scotland to go? Once we were known as the land of the Book (Bible). Our values, our laws, were based on God's blueprint for human society. It made for an upright, honest, diligent, compassionate society. Much of this is being eroded as both God and His blueprint have been largely dismissed".

Aidan McLaughlin from Glasgow had his letter to the *Herald* printed on another day when lack of space meant letters on Section 28 had to be rolled over onto another page in the broadsheet: "Before Section 28, how many people campaigned to have a law along those lines introduced in the first place? Before Section 28, how many times did we hear Brian Souter, the Cardinal, Jack Irvine, Michael Fry (a Conservative journalist who wrote frequently for the *Herald*), et al, on this issue? Before Section 28, how many complaints did the Scottish education authorities receive from parents about their children being indoctrinated with homosexual literature, forced to act in homosexual plays, etc…? The answer bears a passing resemblance to the first letter of 'opportunist' only it's bigger and fatter".

From the same stable as the *Herald*, the *Sunday Herald* was just a year old when the story of the Scottish Executive's intention to repeal Section 28 broke. It was difficult to find the

RELIGIOUS FASCISM

Guardian in Scottish newsagents, so - bar the *Daily Sport* – the *Sunday Herald* was as liberal as Scotland got! Under editor Andrew Jaspan, the broadsheet pitched itself solidly behind repeal. Its editorial warned: "We stand on the edge of darkness... We all need to choose where we want to be. This is no time for equivocation". They gave space to Bishop Richard Holloway whose liberal opinions courted regular chastisement in the Scottish press. He wrote with great candour: "It is nurture rather than nature that breeds homophobia: but what is unassailably true is that religion has been the main breeding ground for hatred of homosexual people; and it is the modern emancipation of gay people that presents one of the biggest problems for religious institutions in our day... The darkest stain on the historic record of Christianity is the persecution and murder of the homosexual community down the ages. And there is a direct connection between Christian crimes against gay people and the few biblical texts there are on the subject". Holloway was scathing of the Church's interference in affairs of the State in Scotland. "There was one reason why I suggested, before the election of the Scottish Parliament, that it should be a strictly secular body that left religion to the faith communities and governed impartially without favour to any of them. None of the other church leaders agreed with me, of course, but my most trenchant critic was Cardinal Winning. I now think I know why... Cardinal Winning may have a perfect right to deny homosexual rights within the Roman Catholic Church, which people can choose to leave if they want to; he has no right to interfere with the laws and civil rights of Scotland, from which gay and lesbian people cannot abstract themselves".

The *Sunday Herald* columnist Muriel Gray was also scathing of the 'Keep the Clause' campaign for "kick-starting one of the most disgusting and blood-chilling displays of intolerance this country has seen in decades... It's beginning to get frightening. The indignant rage the Daily Record often puts to delightful effect when it rails immovably against a genuine injustice has in this instance evolved into something quite revolting. The pages of hatred, deliberate rabble-rousing and fire-stoking of society's most uninformed are getting scarier by the day, making one wonder at what point the paper will be giving away pull-out, sticky-backed pink triangles and inviting concerned parents to slap them on the perverts' backs". Muriel sniped at *Scotland on*

The Assault on Family Values

Sunday for taking on a "medieval stance", but saved her best for the mother of the clause that became known as Section 28. "Had Jill Knight been prevented from slipping in her wicked little addition to the Local Government Act in the first place, what do we think would have happened in the last decade? Would teachers now be coming to school in black bondage gear and Stetsons, with The Village People blaring from the stereo of their Nissan Micras? Would an entire generation of heterosexual boys and girls have decided that Mrs Smith's interesting lessons on anal sex were so utterly convincing they went against their instincts to be gay...? If anyone ought to be getting annoyed with the man, whose Christian decency manifests itself in a habit of ruthlessly crushing the life out of small rival businesses, then it should be the teaching profession".

The *Sunday Herald* delighted in a political cartoon showing a priest addressing a bemused class of kids in a sex education lesson: "...So remember children never, never talk to strange blokes in frocks who reject women and push their morals and lifestyles on others, okay...?"

In January 2000, journalist Iain Macwhirter, a broadcaster and columnist for the *Sunday Herald* wrote: "It's been a week of moral panic in the small pond of Scottish media... A senior editor - not of this paper - turned to me solemnly and asked: 'Could we all have got it wrong? Is this what Scotland is really like...?' Ministers and MSPs... are frankly afraid of the power of Trinity House and the West of Scotland media. The Scottish Executive has no team of rapid-reaction media rebutters capable of countering the nonsense issued daily from Anderston Quay," (home of publishers Trinity House and the *Daily Record*)... "Some MSPs are worried that homophobic prejudice might indeed be more prevalent in Scotland than anyone had previously believed. The metropolitan media has heard and drawn the hasty conclusion that Scotland is over-run by sexual bigots - that, like the Republic of Ireland in the 1930s, Scotland is being revealed as an intolerant and inward-looking theocratic state dominated by religious moralists. There is a kind of infantilism about the booze and football culture of urban Scotland, and an inability to cope with complicated issues. But there are many faces to Scotland, and that is only one... Only a tiny handful of MSPs have been attracted by the Keep the Clause campaign and none has spoken out in its favour. MSPs will be given a vote on conscience -

Dewar has promised not to whip his troops into line - but the result is a foregone conclusion. Section 28 will go. This has all been a chimaera, a delusion of democracy that has put the wind up the liberal establishment. It has all been a bad dream, and it's time Scotland, and its media, woke up". A number of MSPs like Dennis Canavan (who also supported Section 28's repeal) agreed that this was an issue of conscience. He wrote in the *Herald:* "But why should free votes be confined to issues of 'conscience'? There should be more free votes in the House of Commons and in the Scottish Parliament. Instead of members being told how to vote, they would have to listen to the arguments and make up their own minds".

Publishers of the *Beano* comic and Dundee's the *Courier*, DC Thomson also produced a conservative Sunday tabloid, the *Sunday Post*. In his round up of events in the Scottish Parliament, Campbell Gunn asked: "How did Wendy get it so wrong?" He wrote: "MSPs postbags have shown what Mr and Mrs Average think of the plan. Tory leader David McLetchie says the letters he had been receiving are running roughly 20-1 against repeal... So why has the Executive gone to all this trouble to repeal Section 28? Why indeed?" Columnist Margo MacDonald MSP delivered some balance, writing in the *Sunday Post:* "Suppose everyone is laughing at the repeats of Are You Being Served on TV? And the youngest lad in the family minces across the room, wrist flapping a la John Inman? Would the adults present throw up their hands in horror, worry that a young man is being led down the primrose path, and turn off the telly in protest at how homosexuality is being promoted through such a nice harmless character as John Inman's Mr Humphries?" Margo MacDonald agreed Section 28 should be "dumped" because it was imprecise and asked: "What does 'promotion of homosexuality' mean?"

On the Readers' Page of the *Sunday Post*, M Robertson from Aberdeen had something to say about the teaching pack tackling homophobia that no Scottish local authority had been brave enough to use. "It's shocking to learn how children are being robbed of their innocence by being taught explicit details and encouraged to role-play gays and lesbians. I don't want my daughter coming home from school and giving me a lesson on lesbianism".

Dundee's the *Courier* could not stomach the repeal of Section 28. Its editorial advised: "(Education minister) Mr

The Assault on Family Values

Galbraith is unequivocal on one point: repeal 'definitely will not lead to homosexuality being promoted'. How he can be so certain is a mystery. The law already forbids what the minister says will not happen, so a puzzled parent might wonder why the Executive is putting itself through the mincer". Clumsy innuendo was as far as this paper appeared to want to take the subject of sex. It will surprise few that the *Courier* banned a review of my first book *Sexual Fascism*, about the treatment of sex in the Scottish media, because "it contained sex".

An insider at the *Big Issue in Scotland*, a magazine distributed on the streets of Scotland told me that the editorial staff had been "shocked" at the media coverage put out by certain sections of the media over the repeal of Section 28. One of the positive things that came out of the campaign was the eventual lifting of this magazine's ban on gay chatline ads, imposed as a result of pressure from moral conservatives, anti-porn campaigners and religionists.

BBC Scotland News Online hosted an informative question and answer section for all ages. Iona Bain in Edinburgh wrote: "I am only 11 and I am concerned about this issue. Why should we be disregarded as unfit to take part in Scotland's future? If anything we should be the front people in this discussion".

A R M in Edinburgh demanded to know of the Internet news site: "Are homosexual people disabled and/or dysfunctional? If so why shouldn't young people be made aware of the difficulties they and their parental families have to face? Social education on helping and understanding people who have physical and mental disabilities already exists. Where lies the difference...? I am a father with a 15-year-old son and there has never been a time where our young folk have been bombarded through your medium with blatant sexual innuendo and perversion. It is time the decent family-minded folk in this land stood up and SAY an emphatic NO..." A R M received a sharp reply. "Research published in 1993 found that Scottish school pupils did not think they received adequate education on sexual matters. It's worth noting that it also found they learned about what they did know from two main sources, neither of them the classroom. These were their friends and the media. Neither source is noted for its 100% accuracy – and neither is subject to Section 28."

RELIGIOUS FASCISM

The gay press had an important part to play too. At the time of the Section 28 debate, there was only one Scotland-wide magazine for lesbians, gays, bisexuals and the transgendered in Scotland: *ScotsGay*. The magazine's editor, John Hein's editorial at the start of 2000 warned: "It looks as if the backlash is on its way. The forces of darkness and ignorance represented by organised superstition in Scotland have condemned the Scottish Executive's modest proposal to repeal Section 28". An editorial in the *Pink Paper*, a free UK-wide broadsheet for the gay community, reflected with a sigh how much England was now also being affected by the campaign as the poison spread south of the border: "Wading through mile upon mile of objectionable invective issuing from the right-wing press in the past week, one could be forgiven for doubting if any progress has been made for gay people in the last decade". *Boyz* magazine for a younger gay readership reckoned: "Going by some reports over the last few days, you'd think the government were proposing compulsory buggery for all. 'Bizarre gay games your children will be forced to play' screamed The Sun; 'School video tells children to try gay sex', added The Sunday Times". In response to similar campaigns printed in the *Daily Mail* and the *Daily Record*, UK readers of *Boyz* were asked to fill in, cut out and send a coupon emphasising support by Childline and the NSPCC to "DUMP SECTION 28!" to their local MP. Mike from Bournemouth called the Backchat column in *Boyz* to say: "...Are these people all mad? Do they still seriously believe that talking to teenage kids about homosexuality may turn them gay? It's like the fucking dark ages". And 'Trouser Monster' of Stoke offered: "In our local newspaper, it says a report states that more heterosexuals than gays are now getting HIV, which means the safe-sex message has worked. I doubt though that we'll see headlines saying 'Heterosexual Plague Sweeps The Country,' like they did when it was a 'gay plague...'."

In *Punch*, a magazine owned by Harrod's boss Mohamed Al Fayed, whose son was killed alongside Princess Diana in Paris, he opined how he wanted paedophiles to be "castrated and publicly hanged in Trafalgar Square". His opinion of the Government over their plans to scrap Section 28 was equally severe. "Not only are they encouraging monsters to prey on kids, they also want to teach schoolchildren that it is OK to be a pervert. This is ample proof that this government has been infiltrated by liberal-minded idiots who support any minority group against the interests of the

The Assault on Family Values

public at large. What is the future for the culture of a country when the minister for culture (Chris Smith MP) is photographed at one of Prince Charles's parties posing proudly next to his boyfriend?"

Section 28 dominated phone-ins like former *Sun* editor Kelvin Mackenzie's radio station, *Scot FM*.

Whilst the *Scotsman* and the *Herald* carried letters from both sides of the argument, tabloids like the *Scottish Sun*, the *Scottish Daily Mail* and the *Daily Record* ensured an overwhelming majority of letters were shown supporting the 'Keep the Clause' campaign. When the subject of a transsexual cop had come up for debate in the *Daily Record* under a different editor, readers appeared not nearly as conservative with most of the letters printed supporting the PC in her efforts to just be allowed to get on with her job.

All Scottish newspaper's letters' pages were filled with outrage over the repeal of Section 28. George A Lamont of Carnoustie wrote in the *Herald*: "Thank God for Mr Brian Souter, father, Christian, and supporter of the silent, normal majority in its dispute with the Scottish Executive. God Bless him...! Most normal people find the high-profile behaviour of the 'Homo' activists offensive, especially that displayed during their demonstration in Edinburgh last year. Pedestrians, many of whom were mothers with young children, were compelled to witness hirsute men dressed in mini-skirts and tutus, their beards velcroed together as they passionately embraced in public. One can only imagine their repulsive practices, spawned in the 'bath houses' of San Francisco and London public toilets". His letter also appeared in *Scotland on Sunday*.

Alan Fraser Reekie, a Scotsman living in Brussels, tried to inject a sense of proportion in the *Herald*. Shocked at allegations of schools being flooded with "immoral and insidious propaganda", he hit back in his letter: "As a resident for many years of Belgium – a country with a predominantly Catholic population, but with constitutional separation of Church and State – let me reassure you and them that any such suggestion is completely absurd, as it has certainly not occurred here although there is nothing remotely resembling Section 28 to prevent it. But that is probably because the topic of homosexuality provokes little controversy here. For example, the current issue of the leading local radio and TV listings magazine in French, Télémoustique, has half a page on the 'Lesbian and Gay Film

Festival' which is now being held in Brussels' main publicly-funded Arts Centre".

Unsatisfied with the quality of the debate, the Rev Dr Alistair P Donald of New Deer, Aberdeenshire wrote: "...The acids of political correctness have in this case corroded the standards of objectiveness and fairness..."

John Oates, from Scotland's Catholic Education Commission wrote to assure everyone that "Circular 9/1988, which accompanied the Local Government Act 1988, said: 'Section 28 does not affect the activities of teachers. It will not prevent the objective discussion of homosexuality in the classroom or the counselling of pupils concerned about their sexuality'." Which begged the question: Why then weren't Catholic schools discussing it? He finished by insisting repeal meant only "the promotion of homosexuality in schools".

For some, the Catholic Church was infallible. Donald Morrison pointed that out to the *Scotsman:* "Catholicism is a system that works with captivating logic... which is its divine origin and preservation from error".

An exasperated Anne Marie Pyemont from Denholm wrote to the *Southern Reporter* from the Borders: "How can we protect our children from being drawn into the world of the homosexual lifestyle that is not normal? We can not. All we can do is to speak about our concerns so that we can protect our children from losing their own sexuality".

In their concern for schoolchildren, Frank Burrell and George Cuthill, Presidents of the Galashiels and Hawick branches of the Church of Jesus Christ of Latter-day Saints wrote to the same paper to advise "material already prepared to be sent to schools shows that repeal of this law will open the floodgates of totally undesirable material to be taught at a time when they are most vulnerable and open to suggestions that, if followed, can lead to a life of misery and bitter regret".

The *Scottish Sun* also encouraged readers to write in on the subject. They printed nineteen letters under the heading: "Don't let gay lessons defile our kids before they even start to live", with only one letter supporting repeal.

"I'm not homophobic but..." began Alan Sloane of Kennoway, Fife, "I believe there should be more emphasis on promoting the family, not sexual minorities". (Since homosexuality had never *been* promoted in schools and Mr Sloane

The Assault on Family Values

was presumably a confirmed *heterosexual*, one wonders why he felt the need for *further* promotion of heterosexuality).

"I've brought my two daughters up to accept every type and race of person they'll meet, but I don't want them taught about homosexuality in school", wrote Annette Irvine of Glasgow.

"It's disgusting to want to promote gay sex in schools. ...If everyone was gay then the human race would die out in about 90 years", added Thomas Hay of Edinburgh.

"Parents should be able to explain homosexuality to their own children when they think their children are at the right age to hear it", wrote Ronald Munns of Perth. (But hear what? Hopefully not everything Mr Munns had learned about sex from the *Sun*).

"I would have taken my daughter out of school if she'd have been taught that sort of thing", spluttered James Taylor of Penicuik, Midlothian.

"Children should be left alone to enjoy their innocence", declared Mary Archibald of Edinburgh who probably wasn't aware at that time of the Catholic Church's record on child abuse.

"Children have enough to worry about already with drink and drugs and violence", spat Jean Inch of Paisley.

"I don't have any kids myself but if I did and anyone tried to teach them about homosexuality I'd probably end up assaulting the teacher" threatened John McBride of Shettleston, Glasgow.

In the *Scottish Daily Mail*, Valerie Riches, director of the pro-marriage group Family and Youth Concern insisted: "We believe the repeal of Section 28 would be a victory for militant homosexuals and a retrograde step for children".

Archie Parker of St Andrews wrote: "I have three grandchildren under 13, and I certainly don't want them to even hear the word 'homosexual' from a teacher. Ms (Wendy) Alexander should remember it was the majority of straight people who elected her – and it is those people she should be representing".

Bestselling Scottish crime author, Christopher Brookmyre, author of *Boiling A Frog* which satirised Cardinal Winning as the scheming Cardinal Patrick Doollan, wrote to the *Scotsman* about "the assertion that this law's repeal is part of a 'sinister agenda' by homosexuals... Students of 20th century history may recognise the tactic of justifying persecution on the grounds that the persecuted are part of an ulterior conspiracy. It worked well in Thirties Germany, but another example can be found closer to home. The same 'sinister agenda' accusation was once levelled by the Church of Scotland against another oppressed minority: Catholic immigrants".

In the *Big Issue in Scotland*, Rev Paul King from Edinburgh, in favour of repeal, noted that, once again, "Christians are dragging their feet as they did with slavery and apartheid".

Iain Johnstone from Macmerry, East Lothian turned sex counsellor to advise in the *Herald:* "The purpose of sex is procreation, not recreation. This is not to say some fun may not be experienced in the process. Any other approach to sex is a perversion and its practitioners are perverts. This has nothing to do with religion, morals, or some obscure function that is open to many interpretations. An octopus may have fun with a set of bagpipes but it is not sex". The mind boggled.

John Kelly of Edinburgh turned his hand to science in the same paper to write: "The myth that homosexuality is part of one's nature (instead of a taste that is acquired) is clearly false, but hard to dispel, although people who claim this have had to invent the word 'bisexual' to explain why married men with children sometimes practise sodomy. Some even claim that there is a homosexual gene, ignoring the obvious fact that a gene which discourages breeding is bound to die out".

Rev David C Searle promoted ex-gay ministries in the *Scotsman:* "A friend, who is a minister of a large church in the United States, told me that a counselling service run by his church gets on average 40 appeals for help a week from men who have been enticed into homosexual practice in their adolescence by predatory older males, and who long to escape into a heterosexual lifestyle. Another friend, a consultant psychiatrist, tells me his research over many years (corroborated by fellow psychiatrists) indicates that a high proportion of practising homosexuals have been seduced into homosexuality in their formative years. It was on account of such solid and undeniable evidence that Section 28 was put on to the statute book".

As part of a 'silent majority' who were apparently not being heard, Douglas A Yates of Barrhead had his letter printed in the *Barrhead News:* "This is not being homophobic... Not surprisingly, anyone speaking out about the Scottish Executive's proposed abolition of Section 28 is 'branded' by the gay

The Assault on Family Values

movement as 'homophobic'. There is talk of the 'silent majority' being against the repeal of Section 28, but few will be found to actually put the proverbial head above the parapet to say so in fear of vilification by the politically-correct lobby. Are we becoming over tolerant as a society - a society where anything goes...? Let teachers educate children in the three R's, in languages and, by all means promote healthy lifestyles through sport and diet... I am against the repeal of Section 28 on the basis that the gay lobby is a very vociferous one - punching well above its weight... I urge you to write to your local MSP stating your view, that he may make a decision on the basis of the wishes of their constituents, rather than on any dictate from party whips". Mr Yates 'forgot' to mention in his letter that he was a Bishop of the Church of Latter Day Saints.

Once again, 'family values' campaigner H J Lynch from Larbert appeared in the *Falkirk Herald* to offer his advice to the Scottish Executive: "If they spent as much time and space defending the family, as they spend on promoting homosexual/lesbian activity, our society would be much healthier and far less crime-ridden".

After almost daily editorials and reports in support of 'Keep the Clause', on Saturday, 22 January 2000 the *Daily Record* declared in their editorial: "For once, we haven't got anything to say". Instead, they jumped on the bandwagon and offered two pages for its readers to express *their* homophobia. "Our great army of readers, say it for us", they declared. (And sometimes more than once in different papers)! Of course, out of the "avalanche of letters" sent to the *Record* - which editor Martin Clarke suggested was in the region of three or four hundred a day – surprisingly, only two demonstrated unequivocal support for the repeal of Section 28. The rest offered a painful litany of ignorance and misinformation on homosexuality fed by a paper that had spent many years establishing it. If ever there was an argument *for* the discussion of homosexuality in schools, it could be found in their letters.

"Truth is truth... Homosexuality is perverse". Alex and Gillian Gear, East Kilbride.

"...Tyranny of the minority". Steve Barlow, Isle of Mull.

"...Promoting filth". Joan Gray, Glasgow.

"I'm an Orangeman yet find myself agreeing with Cardinal Winning on this issue". Steven McLean, Glasgow.

RELIGIOUS FASCISM

"As a grandmother, I do not wish our children to be taught anything in favour of homosexuality. It's true what Cardinal Winning says. It is wrong and therefore sinful". M Morrison, Glasgow.

"As a socialist, I believe in civil rights for all people, regardless of colour, creed, nationality or sex. I believe homosexuals should be allowed to have equal rights. However..., (homosexuals) are against the teachings of God and nature". J McAleer, Glasgow.

"At one time gays kept their problems to themselves..." J Hoolahan of Blantyre.

"I'm sick of the in-your-face gay activists. They made their point - it's time they all just got on with their advantaged lives". John Murdoch, Helensburgh.

"I am not homophobic, but... the Government is trying to bypass the feelings of parents". Anne Bryson, Bellshill.

"Sex education should be left to the parents..." Brian McLean of Edinburgh (who astonishingly labelled himself "a practising homosexual").

"Homosexuality... should not be addressed by schoolteachers, but by the medical profession and clergy. It would be better if teachers were encouraged to get back to their traditional role of teaching reading, writing and arithmetic". M Lobban, Balloch.

"A child will learn soon enough about the existence of homosexuality, so do not let us be accused of warping their minds. Never let us be accused of misleading a child to the warped issue of mankind. Let us keep them holy and upright as long as possible". John Arkle, Crawford.

"We have Donald Dewar and Wendy Alexander trying to teach homosexuality to our children and, if that is not disgusting enough, we have Sam Galbraith robbing the education system of £2.5million and giving it to so-called opera singers who scream Italian songs no one understands. Roll on the next election". W Stewart, Greenock.

"Perhaps the silent Protestants and Catholics could stage a unified and dignified silent protest march up the Royal Mile to the Mound. They could be accompanied by concerned parents and other religious groups. Words on paper seem to be having little effect on this Government". Jennifer Brown, Dundee.

The Assault on Family Values

(Interestingly, more militant religionists would soon carry out such a protest).

"Courage, the homosexual self-support group, (actually, an evangelical anti-gay group), consider gay sexual practices to be dangerously addictive. School pupils would be badly misled if this serious difference of opinion among homosexuals was not presented in schools". G Pontier, Rutherglen.

In contrast, over in the *Scotsman*, James M Whitten, Brae from the Shetland Isles wrote: "I experienced something much more alarming recently while taking a party of Shetland pupils on a school trip to France. We stopped at a service station... Inside the complex, children were playing computerised games, one of which was to fire a gun at supposed enemies and 'eliminate' them. The children couldn't get enough of this. Then it struck me: we were four miles from Dunblane. How can we, as a society, find this form of 'entertainment' acceptable in the wake of a child massacre...? I can't help feeling that the biggest threat to our society comes from our toleration of violence, rather than emotional reactions to people's sexuality..."

William Drive of Milton of Campsie wrote to the same paper to add: "As a society, we should, of course, be charitable to those who have found it necessary to follow abnormal lifestyles..."

Martin Evans from Cley-next-to-the-Sea, Norfolk wrote in the *Sunday Times Scotland:* "Section 28? Of course it should be changed. We need to keep the population down".

Tom McCallum from Dumfries wrote in the *Southern Reporter:* "I suppose it is understandable that Peter Tatchell and Co. should want this dropped to fit in with their perverted style of life. ...We are on the slippery slope to much more child abuse, incest and even sodomy, all of which are criminal offences - and rightly so. I believe in calling a spade a spade and while one can have sympathy with the minority who are drawn to this abnormality - this perversion - that is no reason to abandon the safeguard that Section 28 provides". In a further letter printed in this Selkirk-based paper, McCallum revealed his Christian leanings and flawed logic: "I was taught that the first instinct of man (kind) - and all other life forms - was self-preservation, the second being the preservation of the species. The latter is normally achieved by copulation between a male and a female of each species, and God, in His infinite wisdom, associated this act with pleasure to ensure its success. He also decreed that any deviation from this norm was a perversion. Peter Tatchell and his ilk... are more to be pitied than laughed at - or mugged - for their unnatural inclinations. So more power to the Keep the Clause lobby".

Meanwhile, W M Hamilton from Largs warned in the *Largs & Millport Weekly News:* "A list is being prepared of all MSPs who voted for the repeal of Section 28".

On the evening of 14 January 2000, Cardinal Thomas Winning played host to some traditional entertainment at Glasgow's Hilton Hotel. Martin Clarke, the editor of the *Daily Record* was also there in a rather effervescent mood. Matthew Norman sniffed trouble in the *Guardian:* "Mr Clarke, who agrees with the cardinal about the splendour of Section 28, had a very jolly time, it seems, and shortly after dinner was in such high and raucous spirits that some police were invited to join him at the bar. This they did, and eventually he departed in their company. Not long after, Mr Clarke took an unscheduled holiday from work, telling colleagues that he was 'going to Cuba'. If so, and I suppose it's possible, his staff pray that the hot Havana sun may help him shake off the symptoms of a heavy cold he has borne with such stoicism for so long".

Chapter Three
The Board of Social Responsibility

"Billy feels contempt, indignant words from hypocrites.
To them it's God's revenge".
The Communards

The Scottish School Boards' Association, (SSBA), was established in 1991 during the last Tory administration with a political purpose. Their structures and procedures were specified in legislation. Whilst they received some government funding for training materials, they were expected to be supportive of Conservative policies, such as the self-governing status of schools at a time when the now defunct Parents' Coalition and the Scottish Parent Teacher Council were on the attack. Tory leader Margaret Thatcher's promotion of so-called 'parent power' succeeded in developing a growing mistrust of professional teachers and the local education authority's framework for sexual and moral education. What resulted, with a little help from some sections of the press, was a growth in the power and influence of school governors and parents.

At the time of the campaign against the repeal of Section 28, the SSBA represented 75% of schools in Scotland, but was an association whose executive was made up of representatives from only two thirds of the 32 local authority areas in Scotland. It had uncontested school board nominations and unfilled places on its executive board. It also provided an open door for anyone seeking to exercise their religious agenda.

Against a growing tide of mounting debts within the association, the Scottish Executive announced it would bail out the SSBA, an otherwise independent and non-statutory body, to the tune of £17,740. Weeks later, the SSBA announced Brian Souter's 'Keep the Clause' campaign would be fronting their campaign against repeal of Section 28 in Scotland.

It wasn't only in Scotland that school boards were seen to champion homophobia. Around the same time, the school board in Orange County California school district also feared the 'indoctrination' of gay lifestyles at El Modena High School. Students there had formed a Gay/Straight Student Alliance. The school board took away the decision of the high school administration to decide the club's fate and held public meetings - which became little more than a sounding board for the 'moral right' - before banning it. The Gay/Straight Student Alliance took the school board to court and, not without irony, cited an equal access law passed in the mid-eighties, originally designed to allow religious groups to meet in public schools. They won. 62 students and eight faculty members attended their first on-campus meeting on 10 February 2000. Student leader Anthony Colin said: "That so many faculty came was neat. Nobody talked about sex, but we talked about how people can come out as gay or bi in the face of all this hate". The next day, Orange County Unified School District trustees who had been forced to allow the meeting under the federal judge's ruling, added new requirements. High school students had to get written parental permission before joining any student group (an impossible requirement for gay students who were not out); there would be a prohibition on any discussion of sex in any school-sponsored club and there was now required a 2.0 grade average from any student who participated. Spokesperson Judy Frutig said: "The board will continue to try to protect the youth from ideas that are potentially harmful to them".

The announcement from the Scottish School Boards' Association's executive that they were to challenge the government's repeal of Section 28 with the help of Brian Souter's money signalled deep divisions within the SSBA. The motherly chief executive, Ann Hill took her place next to ex-*Sun* editor Jack Irvine at the press conference. When they were shown smiling together under a huge banner proclaiming 'KEEP THE CLAUSE' in blood red, columnist Anvar Khan waspishly wrote in the *Herald*: "...The moral future of the country may be in the hands of Max Clifford and Hattie Jacques". Mrs Hill suggested that Section 28 protected children from gay pornography. (Pornography is not mentioned in Section 28, and in any case, if 'protecting children from pornography' gay or straight was the aim of the SSBA, then Wendy Alexander's promise of 'guidelines'

The Board of Social Responsibility

would have been a more effective vehicle than Section 28, which only targeted homosexuality). The *Sunday Mail* reported: "The Scottish School Board Association chief executive Ann Hill has claimed that authorities are stockpiling homosexual material in readiness for use once the legislation is repealed". Ann Hill appeared more conciliatory in the *Scotsman* when she told them how a review of the guidelines might be enough to placate most of those opposed to repeal. She was quoted saying: "We are not against the repeal of Section 28 in principle... We are against the way it is proposed at the moment. It needs some tweaking". That was not how it appeared in the *Scottish Daily Mail*. They reported her saying: "We are totally opposed to the scrapping of Clause 28. We will announce further details of our campaign next week in Edinburgh". The full committee had not discussed the issue at this stage and were in fact split. It was six members for and six against repeal with SSBA president David Hutchison carrying the deciding vote.

James Forbes of Edinburgh added his voice in the *Herald* to calls for the resignation of David Hutchison (President of the Scottish School Boards' Association) from both the McCrone Committee and the General Teaching Council (GTC). "In six years as a teacher, I have not once been invited to vote, never mind stand for any school board election. The SSBA hold no mandate from Scotland's teachers. The teaching unions, whose delegates are elected from those of us who do the job... are clear in our stand for equality of opportunity. Mr Hutchison was one of the Secretary of State's nominees on the GTC yet he is president of a body which would deny Scotland's lesbian and gay pupils the same self-esteem enjoyed by heterosexual pupils... I resent paying my GTC registration fee for a person who does not trust the professional judgement of Scotland's teachers, yet holds power to decide their suitability to teach. David Hutchison should do the decent thing, resign, and stop dabbling in education".

In Rutherglen's the *Reformer*, the chairman of Stonelaw High School Board, Michael Fuller, blasted the SSBA for being trapped by the 'Keep the Clause' campaign while the acting head teacher of the school, John McDonald, when asked if sexual orientation was discussed in the classroom, admitted: "It would come up in the course of conversation but it's not part of our course content".

RELIGIOUS FASCISM

Teacher Tom Pow, a columnist in the *New Statesman* magazine, remembered his schooldays in a piece for the *Scotsman*. He recalled one boy in particular whose life had been hell. "Passing from class to class, whether in the playground or in a stairwell, other boys, some years younger, would give him casual punches, slaps or kicks. No-one stood up for him or offered him any kind of protection. That would be to side with the wimps. And all of us were terrified of the public face of our incipient sexuality. The most innocent act could lead to a scream of horror and chant of 'Poofter! Poofter! Poofter!' Like Abigail and her gang of witch accusers in Arthur Miller's The Crucible, it was better to join in than to leave yourself open to suspicion". And as a teacher in 1988 Pow remembered: "None of us had to push a tide of pornographic material back into our cupboards that year; nor is any such material straining for release now. If there is a classroom that has ever been a hotbed for sexual licence, neither I, nor anyone I know, has been in it. And yet, as a supporter for the retention of Section 28, cried on the radio this week: 'Enough is enough!'"

The *Sunday Herald* was one of a few papers that listened to gay kids who had been bullied for being gay at school. Ben Brown told Torcuil Crichton: "We had stones and bottles thrown at us and name-calling every day. When one of the girls went to her guidance teacher, he told her it was her own fault for hanging around with other gay people".

Andrew Johnson, co-director of the Equality and Discrimination Centre at the Faculty of Education at Strathclyde University wrote in the *Herald*: "Homophobia is a silent, taken-for-granted, deeply embedded discrimination witnessed in many forms. In principle and theory it is like racism, religious bigotry, and the rest: scratch the surface and generations of misinformation, ignorance, and educational silence gleam through. For the last 10 years I have taught very large classes of trainee teachers on issues of inequality, discrimination, and oppression. With my colleagues we have dealt with an analysis of how heterosexism and homophobia are reproduced and sustained. The combined numbers of students would run into several thousands, some being graduates, others undergraduates straight from school. Typically we have asked what the students learned at school about homosexuality. The overwhelming majority of students have indicated that they learned nothing or

The Board of Social Responsibility

next to nothing about such matters. It is no longer surprising to us when student teachers also tell us that they have been told that incidents related to homosexuality should not be dealt with lest it be seen as 'promoting homosexuality'. Three such instances, one including homophobic bullying, have been brought to our attention in the last three months. What we need to counter this silence is a Lawrence-type campaign (which challenged racism) against homophobia, even a formal inquiry! What we have is a campaign, nurturing moral panic from the media and hoarding sound-bites. Its growth and sustenance rely on well-cultivated educational ignorance, silence, and sometimes threats..."

The *Scottish Daily Mail* smugly reported "the Scottish School's Boards' Association has a unit to monitor bullying and it revealed there had not been one complaint about it in three years".

One of the other key figures behind the SSBA's vociferous opposition to repeal of Section 28 was its treasurer Alan Smith. Smith was a financial consultant with deep religious convictions who lived and worked in Paisley before becoming employed with Sun Life Financial of Canada. In Glasgow's *Evening Times*, morally conservative Smith attacked a board game, based on the popular TV show *Friends*. The report read: "The saucy nature of some questions has prompted Scottish School Boards' Association spokesman Alan Smith to urge the makers to clean up their act..." He claimed: "Dubious questions include 'where is the G-spot?', 'has anyone been injured during sex?' and 'does your mum know what a flavoured condom is?' Less repeatable subjects cover fancying your girlfriend's mother and various kinds of sexual behaviour". Alan Smith was reported suggesting the game was harmful. He said: "It's shocking children have access to this sort of unsuitable material". Under the headline "PARENTS IN FURY OVER RUDE QUIZ", five "fans" had their say. Maureen Kane, 24 of Royston called the game "shocking". Christine Curzon, 30 of Milton wanted to protect her godson. "I don't think he should know some of the things mentioned in the game". Janice Gallagher, 41 of Netherlee said: "Parents don't want their children to have access to cheeky questions". Young mum Adele Witkowski, 21 of Knightswood said: "Parents don't always read small print - it's up to the makers to warn about adult content in big letters on the front of the box," and there was just enough space for James Findlay, 53 of Newton Mearns to gasp "I'm shocked".

The SSBA executive faced a growing challenge from members who felt the Executive had properly consulted neither school boards nor parents. On Monday, 17 January 2000 a letter appeared from Joanne Beaumont, one of the 33 Executive Board members of the SSBA in the *Herald*. She insisted that the SSBA "supports the repeal of Clause 28…" with the rider that the Board had to have time to consult parents and consider the timing of Wendy Alexander's proposal of 'guidelines' once Section 28 was repealed. Communities Minister Wendy Alexander wrote to reassure the SSBA, a month before Souter had announced his involvement, if they wished, she would review and strengthen the guidelines in the wake of abolition. Ms Beaumont went on to quote the relevant minutes of the meeting and pulled no punches. "I certainly have not allied myself to any Church campaign, or any campaign to stop the repeal of Clause 28. I categorically refuse to lend support to any campaign in the absence of a thorough consultation with parents, and teachers, who also participate in boards".

Treasurer Alan Smith's angry response appeared the next day in the *Herald*. He was "extremely disappointed" with Ms Beaumont and told Glasgow's *Evening Times:* "She does not speak for the board".

A letter to the *Scotsman* from Scotstoun Primary School Board also went on the attack: "How dare Ann Hill… appear in the media purporting to represent school boards… when there has been absolutely no consultation on the matter with any school board whatsoever".

In a letter to the the *Herald*, Kim Connelly from Glasgow and 17 other signatories including a group of carers and parents felt the SSBA had "failed in any meaningful way to inform and consult parents like ourselves over this sensitive issue. Nor has it displayed any understanding or balance in the media broadcasts. The SSBA has created a moral panic and opened the door to prejudice and intolerance. Who exactly does Ann Hill, the Chief Executive of the SSBA actually represent?"

Pauline M Kelly in Glasgow wrote: "Unlike the Scottish School Boards' Association, the Scottish Parliament invited contributions to be made during the consultations period… The Scottish School Boards' Executive has put itself at the forefront

The Board of Social Responsibility

of a well-funded high-profile campaign to oppose repeal without initiating any formal consultation with school boards in Scotland".

Some boards, including the Bell Baxter High School in Cupar wrote to the SSBA in disgust. Others withheld their SSBA subscriptions or plotted to depose the association's leadership at their elections in March. Fife council was equally upset when it discovered the SSBA had accused it of buying graphic sex education material from Avon health authority in Somerset, a story that found its way into the newspapers. Fife council leader Christine May said they had requested a copy of the information pack, but returned it because of reservations about its content.

The chairman of Harris Academy School, Fiona Jurk wrote to Ann Hill accusing her of acting unconstitutionally and claimed there was no evidence the majority of parents supported the retention of Section 28.

In support of the SSBA, Dr Sam McKinstry wrote to the *Herald* to say: "On November 18 the Scottish Executive sent out some 6,500 consultation documents to community councils, local authorities and councils, certain churches, unions, health and education authorities, all private schools, and gay interest groups. The Executive's staff cannot furnish me with a complete circulation list, so no-one can say exactly who has or has not been consulted... or how comprehensive the process was. The consultation documents were still being distributed... in December... I can tell you that the chance of organisations such as these, which tend only to meet monthly, managing to discuss these documents and return them by January 14 was always going to be somewhat slim..."

As the press turned its attention to the SSBA fronting the 'Keep the Clause' campaign, pages from the SSBA website were mysteriously removed. Journalists trying to contact Ann Hill at the head office of the SSBA in Dumfries did so in vain. Callers were simply told by someone answering the phone: "No-one is giving anything out at the moment". Ann Hill had fled to Stornoway on the Shetland Isles "on business". Messages left on her answer machine went unanswered.

On Sunday, 16 January 2000, Derek Ogg QC made Brian Souter aware of the potential illegality of using charity funds to bankroll a political campaign. It was brought to light by the *Sunday Times Scotland* and repeated (this time drawing attention to

Ogg's sexuality) in the *Daily Record*: "Derek Ogg, who is gay, has written to the Lord Advocate..." Tom Brown, their dickey-bowed religious columnist wrote in the tabloid: "Brian Souter is 'very relaxed,' despite the vilification he has received from the gay lobby" and claimed Brian Souter had told him: "I'm not bothered about being labelled 'politically incorrect' – I'm in good company".

Within days, the Kirk Moderator Rt. Rev John Cairns threw his weight behind the abolishment of Section 28. "CHURCH LEADERS IN SPLIT ON GAY LESSONS", the *Scottish Sun's* front page squealed on Wednesday, 19 January. "Rev Cairns' support came as the Scots Executive revealed that three out of four people who responded to a consultation process on Clause 28, backed their plans to scrap it". The *Scottish Daily Mail* bellowed: "KIRK FURY AS LEADER BACKS GAY SEX LAW ABOLITION... The Right Reverend John Cairns was immediately accused by Kirk officials, ministers and politicians of losing touch with the views of most ordinary members of the church". This appeared to be as good a time as any for the tabloid to add bitterly: "The Moderator's comments come at a time when the Church of Scotland is suffering a dramatic decline in congregations. The latest figures showed membership had nosedived from 10 million ten years ago to just over 6,000,000 today". The Catholic Church wasn't exactly bursting at the seams with new members, either; something this campaign was not about to change.

The *Daily Record* accused the Kirk's Moderator, John Cairns of not showing "Christian solidarity – not to mention leadership – on such a clear moral issue". They even had the temerity to conclude: "There were suggestions from Kirk members that the Moderator was prepared to ignore the strength of public opinion because he did not want to upset his own gay friends". The *Record* declared an "embarrassing split" in the Church. One of the tabloid's favourite Church 'spokespersons', Mrs Ann Allen, the convener of the Kirk's ridiculously named Board of Social Responsibility was, of course, firmly behind the *Record* in keeping the clause and expressed her opposition to the views of the Moderator of the General Assembly.

If the very title, the Board of Social Responsibility sounded quaintly Victorian, its agenda could be described as patently medieval. In 2003, with a panel of ministers and psychiatrists, the

The Board of Social Responsibility

Kirk launched a study amid concerns it was not doing enough for people possessed of demons. The Catholic Church already had a number of priests in Scotland who performed exorcisms. The Board of Social Responsibility was one of the country's largest volunteer social work agencies employing around 1,600 people. Amidst controversy over its closure of homes for the elderly, they formed the Deliverance Group, which planned to look at how other churches performed exorcism, consider ways of funding ministers working in this field and tackle public scepticism.

The Kirk's Moderator, John Cairns did not speak for the Church of Scotland, since he was only a first amongst equals. Any judgement on the Kirk's position would have had to be determined by consulting its ministers and elders, a fact the *Record* hadn't missed before it went about putting words into their mouths: "The danger is... many Scots will believe that the Kirk is in favour of repealing Section 28. They may also believe that the Roman Catholic Church has more spiritual certainty, upholds standards of decency better and represents family values more and therefore has taken the moral high ground". The *Record* was driven to ask, "who REALLY speaks for the people in the pews of Scotland's kirks?" Quick off the mark, a Catholic spokesman told the *Record:* "We will not criticise the views of another Christian leader" but "we have been inundated with phone calls of support".

Scottish Socialist Party MSP Tommy Sheridan, the *Daily Record's* token "radical voice" pointed out in his column: "Priests are celibate – also a different sexual orientation to the majority". The tabloid wasn't listening. Smelling the scent of victory, on Wednesday, 19 January, its front page roared: "2:1 AGAINST GAY LESSONS". The *Record* celebrated with a chest-thumping editorial: "The people have spoken... The Record poll vindicated Cardinal Thomas Winning – who wants Section 28 retained and describes homosexuality as a 'perversion'." The praises flooded in from some predictable sources. "The Record would seem to have its finger on the pulse", gloated Jack Irvine, running Brian Souter's 'Keep the Clause' campaign. "The Record poll mirrors my own belief", said Tory spokesman Phil Gallie.

Mrs Anne Allen didn't get an easy time from Isobel Fraser on BBC Radio Scotland's *Good Morning Scotland* who tackled her on the church's so-called 'split' and her opinion on 'promoting' homosexuality. The religious stance of the *Scottish Sun* would provide Mrs Allen with a better window of opportunity to express her discomfort over the Moderator's support for repeal: "We are a broad church and he is entitled to his personal views". But she added: "...There will be many people in the church who will be deeply dismayed that he has made his views public when we want to encourage as much informed discussion as possible on this issue". Not everyone on the Kirk's Board of Social Responsibilty agreed with Anne Allen. One of its members was a certain retired minister by the name of Douglas Alexander, Wendy Alexander's father!

Brian Souter's spokesman, Jack Irvine dismissed Rt. Rev John Cairns, as "out of touch" and stressed: "Brian's view is that he does not approve of homosexuality. But that does not mean he does not love men and women who are homosexual". The homosexuals were feeling his 'love'.

The Moderator was more in touch than he had been given credit for and expressed his awareness of how the injustice of Section 28 had been instrumental in putting gay human rights firmly on the political agenda. It was somewhat ironic that the establishment of such gay groups as Outrage! and Stonewall owed much to the measure.

In the morning's edition of the *Scottish Mirror* on Wednesday, 19 January a selection of familiar faces were asked their views on getting rid of the clause. Jim Kerr of the band, Simple Minds "made it plain that he could never back the lobby supporting Section 28". Kerr and Simple Minds had contributed to *Red, Hot and Blue*, a project set up to raise funds to fight AIDS. Kerr told the *Scottish Mirror* "he would like to see more forward thinking in Scottish education. I think teachers have a part to play in this as well as politicians, in creating a society where everyone has equal rights". Jim Kerr was a wealthy entrepreneur. He had amassed a fortune estimated to be around £40m with interests in loft complexes, bits of restaurant chains, Internet start-ups, shareholdings in football clubs and a film company. Celebrity chef Nick Nairns, who had been battling to get a mention in the prestigious Michelin restaurant guides said of Section 28: "It is outdated and I find it offensive. The government is dead right – this is not about promoting homosexuality but informing children of reality". Others were more compromising. Millionaire Brian Dempsey, a devout Catholic wanted a "better debate". 54-year-old hairdresser to the stars, Taylor Ferguson, whose real

The Board of Social Responsibility

name was Henry, appearing on a Scottish news bulletin in a chic jacket with a leather stripe embroidered across it, added: "School education should not be about sex". Car dealer Arnold Clark, who, at 72 was a Church of Scotland elder and owner of Scotland's largest privately-owned company which was only £19m short of the £1billion turnover mark in 2001 and making £25m a year in profits, supported Section 28 but admitted: "Brian Souter shouldn't bankroll the campaign". A former RAF mechanic, Clark was knighted in 2004 for his services to industry and the community. He owned the largest independent car dealership in the UK and bought a luxury 1964 Bentley S3 Convertible once owned by Sir Elton John and a 1948 coupé Sedanca Bentley formerly owned by both Alfred Heinekin and Prince Rainier of Monaco. Sir Arnold Clark was placed tenth on the the *Sunday Times Scotland's* Rich List in 2006 with a personal fortune estimated at £385m.

The *Scottish Mirror* asked controversial comedian Bernard Manning for his opinion. Already known for his racist and homophobic patter, the tabloid reported: "…He let rip with a homophobic tirade branding homosexuals perverts. Most of it was unfit to print but he did say: 'We don't want our schools turning out a load of pansies'."

At the 'Keep the Clause' press conference that afternoon, David Macauley proudly trotted out their list of celebrity supporters: Catholic SNP MSP Fergus Ewing; the Optical Express chief executive, David Moulsdale; the former SNP MP and *Scottish Sun* columnist, Jim Sillars; the Scottish Muslim leader, Bashir Maan; the convener of the Scots Asians for Independence, Bashir Ahmed; celebrity chef Nick Nairn; Jim Kerr from the band Simple Minds; motor trader Arnold Clark; hairdresser Taylor Ferguson and Catholic Kwik-Fit boss Sir Tom Farmer. All it took was for the Scottish political editor of the *Mirror* to point out that "Nick Nairn supports the government" to have David Macauley sit down very abruptly. Within hours, Jim Kerr, Nick Nairn, Arnold Clark and Sir Tom Farmer were all publicly distancing themselves from the 'Keep the Clause' campaign. Jack Irvine's efforts to enlist the support of what writer Muriel Gray waspishly described as "D-list celebrities" descended into farce.

On behalf of 'Keep the Clause', David Macauley poured out his apologies to the *Scotsman:* "We are honourable people fighting an honourable cause. We are desperately sorry if we've embarrassed anybody. Our hearts and minds are in the right place..."

Jim Kerr was "shocked and amazed" claiming the campaign organisers had not even contacted him. He told the *Sunday Herald:* "The saving grace from all this is that most people were totally incredulous when they heard I was backing the campaign. The music business is the least homophobic and most idealistic industry you could find. God's sake, I've done charity work for AIDS and given money to the gay community... It was a bit Kafkaesque to hear you are backing something you've never opened your mouth about. I got on the phone to Cassidy and asked him what the f*** was going on". (Tom Cassidy was an executive at Media House who had held senior editorial executive positions in both Mirror Group and Express newspapers). "To their credit they were quick to admit they were wrong, but I was still angry and sickened". A spokesman for Sir Tom Farmer said: "It is not accurate to say Sir Tom is backing this campaign". It was later confirmed the campaign had enlisted the support of the Scottish Nationalist MSP Fergus Ewing; spectacle boss, David Moulsdale; former MP, Jim Sillars; SNP Glasgow councillor and businessman, (later to become MSP before his death in 2009), Bashir Ahmed and Bashir Maan, an immigrant from Pakistan, who, with his partner sold cut-price alcohol – forbidden to Muslims – from a shop in Glasgow before selling his shares to run a successful cash-and-carry business and become an unofficial spokesman for the 'Muslim community'.

The *Herald's* editorial responded with biting sarcasm: "It is reassuring to learn that Media House, the public relations concern, has applied the same rigour and attention to detail in checking the extent of celebrity support for the "Keep the Clause" campaign as it did in researching the implications for sex education in schools of repealing Section 28. The campaign has been badly mishandled and might well have reached its nadir..." Of the SSBA's Mrs Ann Hill, they were equally scathing: "Despite the comments of the chief executive of the Scottish School Boards' Association, there was proper consultation on repeal. Mrs Ann Hill's criticisms do not stand up to scrutiny... She implies that the Scottish Executive pulled the wool over parents' eyes. Yet the SSBA had already decided on behalf of school boards what they should think about Section 28. Anecdotal evidence suggests that many boards think differently.

The Board of Social Responsibility

The truth is that the SSBA, like many bodies before it, has been hijacked by people with an axe to grind. The latest accounts show that it received twice as much in grants from membership subscriptions and paid out close to the average pay for a teacher in directors' remunerations..."

The *Scottish Express's* political correspondent Angus Macleod reported how "SNP sources later indicated strongly that Mr Ewing had been carpeted by party leader Alex Salmond for not informing them of his action, and for going against party policy of supporting an end to the ban". It appeared all there was left of Souter's 'high-profile' celebrity supporters was a slightly camp 'hairdresser to the stars'.

Muriel Gray groaned in her *Sunday Herald* column: "Spare a thought for the thousands of honest, decent, moral and respectable gay people in Scotland, who for the last fortnight have had to endure the worst kind of personal attacks, a constant hurtful onslaught of bile from the press, the church and hairdressers".

Reporter Neil Mackay wrote advisedly in the *Sunday Herald:* "Well, the words 'fiasco,' 'disaster' and 'shambles' don't really leave even the most proficient of spin doctors much room for manoeuvre, so it's probably better to shut up". Jack Irvine told the *Sunday Herald:* "I don't want to talk to your newspaper as I thought its coverage of the issue was less than objective last week". (They had "highlighted some of Irvine's greatest work in his *Scottish Daily Mirror* column - including describing gay men as 'slobbering old queers,' 'bum chums' and sleazy old pervs)'." Aidan Smith in the *Scotsman* quoted one of Irvine's former colleagues on the defunct newspaper, the *Sunday Scot:* "Anyone in a tough-boy haircut who cuts his way through traffic in his Mercedes soft-top like Jaws and who loves the fact he lives in Whitecraigs, *the* suburb of Glasgow, is not going to spend too much time worrying about things. He likes upsetting people - that's his style".

In fact, Irvine claimed he was "acutely embarrassed" over the affair and had his first sleepless night in nine years. Media House claimed they had been the victims of a 'malicious fax'.

Although 'Keep the Clause' claimed they were already talking to a number of businessmen and public figures who wanted to commit themselves to their campaign, by Sunday night, 23 January, the SSBA were already threatening to quit the 'Keep the Clause' campaign. Treasurer Alan Smith tried to deny the rumours and insisted that no decision on accepting the offer of guidelines offered by the Executive would be taken until the Board met that Friday, reiterating his hard-line view that "guidelines are not statutory protection for children - that is only provided by Section 28".

On Monday, 17 January 2000, visiting the Orbiston Neighbourhood Centre in Bellshill; a camera crew filmed Cardinal Winning publicly calling homosexuality a perversion. He said: "I hesitate to use the word perversion, but let's face up to the truth about this situation. Are we now being asked to say what was wrong before is now right and they can go ahead and do it...?" Winning was not without his apologists. Hugh McLoughlin, who witnessed his remarks, told the *Herald*: "The media were supposed to be present to help publicise the work and ethos of the Orbiston Centre but, sadly, they had their own agenda. And it had nothing to do with Christian social action". McLoughlin rattled out Winning's defence. "During the previous week Mr Brian Souter had indicated his willingness to finance a campaign to retain Section 2a. On the previous day, the Sunday, Donald Dewar had been interviewed on TV and had defended Wendy Alexander in the face of mounting criticism of her inept handling of the proposed repeal of the law protecting children from homosexualist proselytising in schools. At the press conference in the Orbiston Neighbourhood Centre that Monday morning the media, and most especially a TV reporter, relentlessly harried Cardinal Winning for a comment, any comment, about the proposed repeal of Section 2a. His Eminence neither sought the opportunity to comment on the matter, nor had he come to Bellshill prepared in advance to do so. He was there, and he repeatedly tried to make this clear, to observe and to comment solely on the work of the centre. Exasperated, he finally made a few comments about Section 2a as much just to get rid of the media as anything. They clearly were not interested in the good endeavours of Mr Johnstone and his board to provide social services to the local community in a Christian but non-denominational *(sic)* setting so it was better that they should just go. His Eminence neither then nor at any other time called anyone a pervert. He stated that no matter how reluctant he was to do so - and if you take the trouble to look again at the interview on tape it is abundantly clear that he *was* reluctant - he had no choice but to clearly state that the homosexual act itself, that is buggery though he did not use the word, was a perversion. That statement is clearly in conformity both with the Roman Catholic Catechism and the civil law". According to Cardinal Winning's biographer, Stephen McGinty, Winning had already discussed in the car on the way there that if reporters asked him about Section 28 he would answer. His press officer, Ronnie Convery, who had worked at STV, tried to keep the cameras off him but failed. Winning was soon fielding calls from Charles Moore, the editor of the *Daily Telegraph* and a Catholic convert to write an opinion piece.

Four days later, on Friday, 21 January, without Hugh McLoughlin to give him his muddled support, Cardinal Winning - as guest of honour of the Cana Catholic family movement in Malta – once again let slip his opinions, comparing homosexuals to criminals and branding them 'perverted'. Cardinal Winning told the Maltese: "Today, society is facing a new threat, aided and supported by governments and politicians: the threat to equate homosexual partnerships with marriage. In my country at this very moment there is a national debate about this issue... I am glad to say that a broad coalition is now emerging to combat the threat which lies before us... Do not be complacent. All over Europe an active and militant homosexual lobby is pushing for greater power and the threat to the Christian family is very real... In place of the bombs of fifty years ago you find yourselves bombarded with images and ideas which are utterly alien". Martin Pendergast, chairman of the Roman Catholic Caucus of the Lesbian and Gay Christian Movement said: "The Cardinal's intemperate language, with words such as 'perversion,' places him out of line with even the Vatican's Congregation for the Doctrine of the Faith which said it deplores violence in speech or in action towards gays". Tim Hopkins, of the Equality Network in Edinburgh hit out: "Cardinal Winning's claims of an international conspiracy were reminiscent of the kinds of claims being made against the Jews 100 years ago". Even *Scotland on Sunday* issued a warning after their headline blasted: "Gay lobby compared to Nazis in new broadside by Winning... Cardinal Thomas Winning has compared the threat of the homosexual lobby in Europe to that of the Nazis in the Second World War, sparking widespread anger among politicians and gay rights campaigners. (He) drew parallels between a 'militant homosexual lobby pushing for greater power' and Italian and German bombers". Their editorial diluted its support for Keep the Clause to warn: "To compare the power of the gay lobby - as distasteful and misguided as he believes it is - with Nazism threatening civilisation in Europe in the 1930s is to invite the scepticism of many he might otherwise have counted as supporters. We would caution the Cardinal to bear this in mind as he continues to defend, as no doubt he will, his church's position". The *Scotsman* remarked how "his views appeared to resonate with those expressed by Pat Robertson, the right-wing American evangelist..." Winning hadn't actually mentioned Nazis by name, something for which *Scotland on Sunday* apologised the following week. Winning gave a languid apology too, suggesting his remarks were based on the idea of loving the sinner and hating the sin.

Iain MacWhirter observed in the *Herald:* "Intoxicated by what they believed to be an awakening of a Scottish 'silent majority,' the mask of moderation slipped. The leader of the Roman Catholic Church, Cardinal Winning, resorted to the queer-bashing rhetoric used by Mr Jack Irvine in his *Mirror* column".

What was not so widely known was how vociferously Winning had supported the fascists, led by Franco in Spain, when he was a boy. He saw the Spanish civil war quite simply as godless Communists assaulting and murdering the priests and clerics of the Roman Catholic Church. When Cambridge academic John Cornwell wrote his biography, of Winning's favourite Pope, Pius XII, *Hitler's Pope,* exposing him as an anti-Semite, Winning's defence of him appeared as an article in the *Daily Telegraph.*

The *Scottish Daily Mail* fell over itself in its rush to lend Winning some assistance, allowing him to say: "These stories are clearly intended to discredit me and my church over our stance on Section 28". *(Scotland on Sunday* was, in fact a virulent supporter of his campaign to retain Section 28). Winning claimed he was only referring to the invasion of satellite broadcasts.

Cardinal Winning had been planning to attend Mass at St John's Co-Cathedral in Valletta; followed by a lavish dinner at a luxury hotel, which had taken a year's planning by the Maltese people. It was suddenly cancelled. Joseph Mercieca, the Archbishop of Malta explained Winning had a Sunday appointment in Glasgow and his Sunday morning flight from

The Board of Social Responsibility

Malta to London had been cancelled. The Catholic Church in Malta said it was the connection from London to Glasgow that had been cancelled. Tracey Lawson wrote in the *Scotsman:* "A reasonable enough explanation until inquiries at Malta, Gatwick and Heathrow airports failed to give any evidence that the early flight... had ever existed, let alone been cancelled".

When Cardinal Winning arrived back in Glasgow he had a letter waiting for him. Opening the *Scotsman* he was confronted by an open letter addressed to him from a University graduate, working as a medical doctor in cancer research. He had required hospital treatment after having been assaulted leaving an Edinburgh gay bar the day after Souter pledged his million. "I was hit from behind with a baseball bat and I lost consciousness for several minutes. Whilst unconscious I was viciously assaulted by several people and suffered fractures to the bones of my face and lost several teeth. I have also been left unable to remember much about the events surrounding the attack... To make the remarks such as you do and believe that most of society possess the subtlety to understand their meaning reflects a naiveté about humanity which is no less than I have come to expect from you. You remark in newspaper interviews that most of society does not believe that Section 28 should be repealed. Your opinions were passionately expressed, but lacking in both intellect and articulacy. The duty of government in a democratic society is to aspire towards the creation of a society characterised by justice and peace. Supporting the customs and conventions of the masses does not necessarily assist in the creation of such a society. Millions of people in the UK read the Sun, but were its expressed editorial opinions to be adopted within government policy we would be living in a society considerably less tolerant and more violent. The teenagers who attacked me probably consider themselves to be good Christian boys, and your recent remarks will have done nothing to dispel them of their delusions. Were they to have had questions of gay, straight and celibate sexuality discussed in an intellectually informed environment at school, perhaps attacks such as mine would occur less frequently. So much for a Church claiming to give guidance to the young. Having been brought up in a Catholic family and having attended Catholic state schools in Greenock, I have always considered both yourself and your Church to be simply offensive. I now consider you both to be nothing short of evil. Yours sincerely, Dr S T".

Cardinal Winning was smug: "We condemn a lot of people because of their lifestyle – burglars for example. The fact that the prison population is bigger than any other part of Europe shows we condemn a lot of people for their lifestyle". A spokesman for Winning boasted that the Section 28 debate had given him the biggest postbag in 26 years.

Such intemperate language would be followed in years to come with the likes of the former Presbyterian SNP leader Gordon Wilson comparing his Party's support for gay marriage to 'state fascism'; former Church of England Archbishop, Lord Carey comparing anti-gay campaigners to Jews in Nazi Germany and Catholic Cardinal Keith O'Brien describing the implications of a human embryology law as "grotesque" and akin to "Nazi-style experiments". The Cardinal told BBC Scotland he wanted people to pay attention to the issue, adding: "Yes, I want publicity and I use strong language so that I'll get publicity". But none stirred more publicity than when gay rights group, Stonewall awarded O'Brien, 'Bigot of the Year' in 2012 for his contributions to the debate on equal marriage. He would go on to trump that the following year when it was revealed he had been less than frank about his own sexual proclivities with young seminarians.

A nineteenth century baronial mansion at Drygrange in Melrose filled with young men enjoying drunken parties, crushes on young 'pups', japes in the 'jakes' (communal bathrooms) and lights out in the dorms after a 'rager' (wild party) was Cardinal Keith O'Brien's undoing. Firstly, the Cardinal, irritable at not knowing exactly what priests had blabbed, scorned them, accusing them of vagueness before delivering his own mealy-mouthed apology vaguer than an apparition of Mary Magdalene. It was brief in his Ted Haggard moment, admitting his hypocrisy. "I've fallen below the standards expected of me as a priest, archbishop and cardinal", he confessed, adding: "In recent days certain allegations which have been made against me have become public. Initially, their anonymous and non-specific nature led me to contest them. To those I have offended, I apologise and ask forgiveness. To the Catholic Church and people of Scotland, I also apologise." The Catholic Church quickly whisked him away into hiding.

The Board of Social Responsibility

Although Cardinal Winning's comments comparing homosexuals to criminals provoked a good deal of anger, even amongst members of his own church, he never suffered the indignity of having his church described as 'split' as the Church of Scotland was in the *Record*, when its moderator declared his support for the abolition of Section 28. Instead, the *Daily Record's* editorial remarked how Winning had "found himself on the end of another tirade of abuse from people grasping at any straw with which to discredit him. Winning may have been ill-advised to compare the courage of the Maltese during the World War II to the courage needed to retain family values in the 21st century. But at no time did he compare the vocal gay lobby to the Nazis... They were so keen to latch on to any perceived lapse that Winning found himself misrepresented in most of the so-called quality Sunday newspapers. Meanwhile, most of Scotland's chattering classes were handed space in the same broadsheets to vent their outrage at The Daily Record for allowing readers to tell the Scottish Executive just what they thought of its plans to repeal Section 28. Despite trying to seize the high moral ground, their writers were left with egg on their faces". Cardinal Winning had at his disposal the best press manipulators. Dominic Ryan wrote in the *Herald*, in preparation of Winning's profile on BBC's *Frontline Scotland*: "He has a knack of being able to play the press, reeling in and playing the slack until headlines are moulded to his cause". The Cardinal refused to take part in the programme, but his spokesman Ronnie Convery faced a barrage of questions about Opus Dei, a right-wing faction that pledged to "contribute to the evangelisation of every sphere of society" and operated within the Roman Catholic Church. Opus Dei was formed in 1928 by Nazi-sympathiser, Jose Maria Escriva Albas who was canonised by Pope Benedict XVI in 2002. Its 80,000 members included priests and influential figures in both the media and government. Cardinal Winning had been reported stating his admiration for Opus Dei and Ronnie Convery admitted on the programme that he had once been a member himself. Convery denied that Cardinal Winning was at odds with the majority of Catholics and said: "It puts us in conflict with what you might call the forces of political correctness; it puts us in conflict with what you might call the siren voices of liberalism". Monsignor Tom Connelly explained to *Scotland on Sunday:* "Opus Dei is a fully approved part of the Catholic Church. It has the full support of the Vatican and enjoys excellent relations with the cardinal, who values the dedication and loyalty of its members. To describe it as a 'sect' or suggest it is somehow sinister is wilful distortion. It is also an insult to Cardinal Winning to suggest that he is under the influence of any 'group'." Many of Pope John Paul II's recent announcements were sourced to this faction; he made their top man a bishop and invited them to meetings. Father Fitzsimmons, of St John Bosco's Church in Erskine, Renfrewshire, who the *Scottish Daily Mail* dismissed as "a leading critic of the Cardinal's decisive moral leadership", claimed on the programme that the Opus Dei faction had secured access to the Cardinal and went on to criticise the Church leadership for allowing Opus Dei to build a closeted power-base in Scotland. Ronnie Convery hit back, shrugging off suggestions Opus Dei was right-wing and emphasising that it purely applied itself to the Pope's instructions. 60-year-old Father Fitzsimmons lost his patience and told the *Sunday Herald* he "didn't give a bugger" about his courting the wrath of the church hierarchy.

Of Winning, columnist Iain McWhirter wrote in the *Herald* that Catholics were "outraged, not just at his pejorative language, but his sheer opportunism. By what right did he hitch his church to a campaign organised by fundamentalist Christians, monomaniacal journalists and opinionated businessmen with more money than sense? I suppose that is a difficult question to pose in an organisation which has historically been based on the moral infallibility of its leaders... Of course, the whole affair could have been better handled by the Scottish Executive. The decision to move on Section 28 should have been delivered to the Scottish Parliament and not leaked to the press in a futile attempt to win the backing of the Daily Record".

As the letters poured in, in a special supplement printed in the *Herald*, Rev David A Keddie wrote: "The clod-hopping, black-and-white, judgmental, medieval, Aquinas-inspired dogmatic of the Cardinal is as insensitive as it is irrelevant".

Ian Bell, in his column in the *Scotsman*, contested the lies and stupidity behind Cardinal Winning's rhetoric. "First, as a matter of fact, you can neither be converted to nor cured of homosexuality. The medical and scientific evidence, far less the testimony of gays themselves, simply does not exist. Therefore any attempted promotion of a homosexual lifestyle - more tasteful, better dressed, better jokes, capable of painting the

The Board of Social Responsibility

Sistine Chapel - would be meaningless as well as entirely pointless. Or rather, entirely beside the point. Secondly, if this promotion-of-lifestyle gimmick is so effective, how do we explain the failure of the heterosexual lobby to prevent all those regrettable occurrences of the gay thing? How did they escape the promotional campaign? If it is truly possible to promote sexual orientation, why, given a world drenched in heterosexual imagery, are there gays at all?"

"Spot the campaigner", urged the *Herald* under a picture of a cheerful Cardinal Winning playing dominoes with three elderly ladies at the neighbourhood centre in Bellshill. Despite the photo-call, Winning was more interested in the campaign to support Section 28 and said: "What pains me about this whole situation is that the silent majority are so silent that the silence is deafening... I wish to God they would speak up for their society". He told the *Daily Record:* "Homosexuality is promoted every day. It's promoted by people who are on the streets, it's promoted by people who are attracted to others". The *Scottish Daily Mail* advised: "He warned that primary and secondary school children faced being exposed to 'explicit and perverted material' which could encourage them to become homosexual..." Courting public sympathy by steering the debate into the emotional arena of child sexuality, he added: "I am concerned that children might be converted by some of the literature. There's no doubt about it". Under a huge portrait of himself in the *Record,* Winning comfortingly smiled, "I'm no bigot", before showering Souter with his praise. "I am happy with his Christian commitment. I applaud the man". The free paper, the *Metro* reported Winning suggesting, "Mr Souter had been the victim of a witch hunt by Mr Dewar and gay rights activists". Repulsed after seeing erotic gay images found on the computer of Father Jim Nicol, a priest in the offices of the Scottish Marriage Tribunal, including some of Nicol getting a blowjob in his flat, Winning ignored medical research on homosexuality; thought it a 'lifestyle choice' and privately referred to them as 'sissies'.

When Prime Minister Tony Blair declared his support for the repeal of Section 28 in the House of Commons, Cardinal Winning was sitting in the public gallery after having being dropped off from the airport in a ministerial Rover with Ronnie Convery. The *Daily Record* was vitriolic. The headline: "Blair backs gay lessons", was provocatively dropped onto the front page.

RELIGIOUS FASCISM

"Tony Blair's decision to wade into the Section 28 row north of the Border is unfortunate and ill-advised", the *Record's* editorial raged. "Winning had to use a private entrance to Dover House to avoid gay rights campaigner Peter Tatchell, who had turned up to confront the churchman". The *Herald* columnist Anvar Khan sniped: "Some MPs have been taking the back door for years". Peter Tatchell had attempted to get Cardinal Winning to name the people he claimed wanted to 'promote' homosexuality in schools. In a letter to the *Scotsman* Tatchell pleaded: "Using religion to oppose equality echoes the actions of Afrikaner church leaders in South Africa under apartheid, who distorted Christianity to justify racial discrimination. Section 28 singles out homosexuality for special legal penalties that do not apply to heterosexuality. It is a form of sexual apartheid, which treats gay people as inferior, second-class citizens, and causes great suffering. Is that what Cardinal Winning wants? If not, why is he backing a bigoted campaign that is stirring up prejudice and intolerance?"

Glasgow Kelvin MP George Galloway, a friend of Cardinal Winning and one time columnist for the Catholic newspaper *Flourish*, joined the row by lambasting Cardinal Winning for calling homosexuality "a perversion". He told BBC Scotland's *Holyrood* programme that the description was "pernicious... I was disgusted by the use of the word, which could have dripped from the lips of any raving bigot... Cardinal Winning is not fit for the great office he holds... He ought to have known the atmosphere that it would help to create". The *Scottish Mirror's* headline blasted: "BOOT OUT THE BIGOT". A spokesman for Cardinal Winning told the *Scottish Daily Express* it was "quite inappropriate" to call the Cardinal bigoted. "He has made it clear that homosexuals should be treated like everyone else", which was of course untrue. A spokesman for the 'Keep the Clause' campaign, referring to Galloway, told the *Scottish Mirror*: "I don't think a prince of the church need worry about Labour's clown prince".

Cardinal Winning told the *Herald* that he had been "shocked and saddened" by the press coverage. Then, with the same debate looming south of the border in the House of Lords, Dr George Carey, the Archbishop of Canterbury joined the fray, backing the Cardinal with his remarks that Section 28 was also "a matter of concern" to him. The *Scottish Mail* quoted Dr Carey's "dramatic

The Board of Social Responsibility

intervention" over Section 28. "I condemn totally prejudice against anyone on the basis of sexual orientation. But I also resist placing homosexual relationships on an equal footing with marriage as the proper context for sexual intimacy". (Dr Carey, of course, merely 'intervened' in the debate as opposed to 'militant gays' who responded with 'hysterical reactions' and 'outrageous demands').

"Suddenly religion matters again in Scotland", columnist Tom Brown exclaimed hopefully in the *Record*. "For God's sake, people are actually speaking up for their beliefs. Those who claim to follow Him – whether they display the brainless, bigoted 'religion' of the football terraces, or the churchgoing, dressed-up Sundays-only sanctimoniousness of the 'unco guid' – have been getting God a bad name in Scotland of late... The Christian churches (because the Moslem and other ancient faiths are obvious exceptions...) are irrelevant to many, because they have had nothing relevant to say... So hallelujah for Cardinal Thomas Winning and Brian Souter... What puts them in the same pulpit is a shared belief in promoting what is right and wholesome and opposing what is unwholesome and perverse... I haven't lived a sheltered life – entirely the opposite, in fact – and I know the wide range of acrobatics and abnormal activities heterosexual couples can get up to... You don't have to be a prude to know some things are wrong".

Amongst the selection of letters the *Daily Record* printed, M B of Elgin wrote: "Thank you very much Daily Record for your wonderful achievement in campaigning to keep Section 28. Had you not printed all the readers' letters, the immoral people and the unsavoury Labour Government would have their wicked way already". The correspondent was joined by plenty of others as the *Record* emptied its mailbag and printed another selection of letters, allowing only one to show any compassion for the people most hurt by their vile campaign: -

"We shouldn't be too shocked at the Government. Surely it's been noted that there are several gay members of Tony Blair's 'Pink' Cabinet". Thomas Moran, Edinburgh.

"I cannot accept (Brian Souter) saying: 'I respect homosexuals as individuals and I respect their rights'. How can he, as a Christian, have respect for something God condemns?" Alex Lennox, Lochwinnoch.

RELIGIOUS FASCISM

"Brian Souter has done a wonderful thing for Scotland". Mary Potter, Bellshill.

"Why all this fuss over Section 28 when the biggest influence on our children – TV – is littered with homosexuals? We are, by our silence, making it all seem quite natural". T Stowe, Kilmarnock.

"To focus on homophobic bullying and make a special case of it is just as likely to exacerbate the problem as it is to diminish it". Bill McHaffie, Johnstone.

"How can brainwashing our kids with gay sex propaganda not create a whole new set of social problems?" J Brown, Glasgow.

"...The words used by the homosexual movement to describe themselves, their contrived scenarios and aims for legal privilege..." are "fallacious". Margaret MacDonald, Glasgow.

"...It is no surprise that the Government allows them into the armed forces. I can imagine the Last Post being sounded to the tune of Kiss Me Goodnight Sergeant Major". D Cooper, Glasgow.

"I would like to thank the Record for speaking up for the parents of Scotland... I am not homophobic but I want all children to be protected from the promotion of homosexuality". Mary Campbell, Uddingston. (Mary Campbell of Uddingston appeared again in the *Sunday Mail*: "As a parent, I will do everything I can to help keep out the filthy material that has already been printed, just waiting to be given to our schools in the guise of health education").

A Kennedy of Glasgow wrote: "What next in the name of equality – teaching children how the mind of a criminal, rapist or serial killer works, so they can try that out too?"

G Smart of Glasgow wrote: "I was appalled to read of the money and support handed out to gay groups by councils across Scotland. This is a shocking waste of public money. Let these communities fund their own lifestyles and stop trying to convert the rest of us".

Concerned of Ayrshire wrote on the "upraised voices screaming 'discrimination'... What a wonderful weapon this word has been for the furtherance of the homosexual cause and how skilfully they have used it".

D B of Paisley wrote: "Keep Section 28. I am 71 and no-one has ever asked me if I am illegitimate or gay".

The Board of Social Responsibility

The *Daily Record* had a one-word headline set aside for its cover on Friday, 21 January, accusing Labour MSPs of being "ROBOTS". Along with a coupon for readers to fill in and send to First Minister Donald Dewar expressing "deep unease", the editorial suggested "the row over Section 28 is fast turning into a calamity for Donald Dewar's Scottish Executive. Just how panicked it is can be seen by the response when we dared to ask some rank-and-file Labour MSPs what their view was on the move to repeal the section and allow gay sex lessons into Scottish schools. Within minutes the New Labour thought police swung into action. Pagers went off in the pockets of all 54 MSPs ordering them to duck the question". MSPs had been sensibly advised to ignore the *Record*.

Gerald Warner in the *Scottish Mail* found Labour MSPs were "expressing horror at the prospect of homosexuality being promoted in schools" despite no indication that homosexuality was ever going to be 'promoted' and the majority of MSPs clearly supporting repeal. The *Record* wrote: "Despite his (First Minister, Donald Dewar's) gagging order, more than 20 MSPs broke the ban and openly gave the Record their views on Section 28. However only two of them, Irene Oldfather and Gordon Jackson, refused to back the Government's line". And even then, "both claimed they had not yet made their minds up..." The editorial stormed: "...It was hardly surprising that the only MSPs willing to risk actually speaking to the dreaded newspapers were the ones who agreed with Donald anyway". Well almost. Under the picture of Wendy Alexander, MSP for Paisley North were the words: "DID NOT ANSWER".

Scotland on Sunday recorded "the unusual sight of Labour and SNP MSPs banging their desks for the two leaders as they both sat down" in their seats in the Scottish parliament. Iain Macwhirter wrote on the spectacle of Labour and Scottish Nationals moment of unity in the *Sunday Herald*: "When the Scottish parliament met... Dewar and Alex Salmond pressed home their advantage. In an uncharacteristic display of consensus, they joined forces to reassure parents that abolishing Section 28 did not imply that the Executive favoured the positive promotion of homosexuality in schools. It was an electric moment, and one of the most significant episodes in the short history of the Scottish parliament. But it was scarcely reported in the next day's press. The Record had by this stage begun a witch-hunt of MSPs seeking to 'out' those who didn't support the Executive line. It found none - but that only confirmed its suspicion that the entire parliament was founded on a conspiracy to promote 'gay lessons'."

The *Record* was adamant; not only its readers, but also Scotland did not want this "nonsense". Their agony aunt, Joan Burnie tried to contact Wendy Alexander but was left "distraught, devastated and dismayed" after her "humble request for an interview" was knocked back. "That it should be a woman makes it doubly hurtful", Burnie whined. "Wendy, Wendy, can't we kiss and make up?" she begged before remarking acidly: "...Don't you think the Ann Widdecombe hair-style and wardrobe is inappropriate for someone as young and sweet-natured as you?" Poor Wendy Alexander could do nothing right in 'Old Mother Burnie's' eyes. On another occasion, the so-called 'agony aunt' lashed out: "I'm surprised Father's day is still allowed. I should have thought Wendy Alexander and her Parliamentary pals would have banned it by now. After all, we can't have kids without fathers being made to feel that children with a daddy are better, can we?"

The *Record's* report by Gethin Chamberlain: "Gays target kids and teachers", plumbed new depths in hysteria. It reported a "publicly funded group, Healthy Gay Scotland, publishes a guide telling young men how to come out as gay... The group, funded by the Scottish Council for Voluntary Organisations, offers advice to young men on having sex in public places". It was, in fact, advice to young men who were *having* sex in public places. The *Record* declared: "Edinburgh-based Gay Men's Health, which receives £138,000 of public cash from Lothian Health, also publishes a guide offering advice on where to have sex in public and where to buy porn and sex toys". Worse... "Grampian Health Board publishes advice to teachers" and "advises that teachers should provide positive images of gays". None of the groups – apart from David Macauley from 'Keep the Clause' - were given the opportunity to challenge the report. Macauley was - of course - "appalled". The report declared: "Campaigners... are targeting teachers and pupils with homosexual propaganda. One gay group at the forefront of the campaign to scrap Section 28 has published a leaflet urging school children to try gay sex. A group calling itself Avert offers a range of information for training teachers and school governors. The site suggests open

The Board of Social Responsibility

discussions about homosexuality in class and offers links to other gay sites with instructions on gay sex practices. The Daily Record also discovered dozens of other websites with openly pornographic images masquerading as education material". Of those websites condoning violence and the murder of gays at this time, one of the most notorious was a 'Christian' one called *God Hates Fags*. Jim Mearns in Glasgow, unable to get his point across in the pages of the *Record*, wrote instead to the *Herald* about the website devoted to Matthew Shepherd, the young gay man mutilated and murdered in the USA and whose funeral had been picketed by Christians led by Fred Phelps a little over a year before in October 1998. Mearns advised the site "shows a photo of Matthew surrounded by flames, with a day counter and a statement that this shows the number of days he has spent in hell because of his unacceptable, unnatural lifestyle".

The *Record* found a new headline for its front page: "DEWAR DODGES HEAD-TO-HEAD TV GAY DEBATE", The First Minister, Donald Dewar had apparently "ducked" a challenge to enter into a live TV debate. Brian Souter had faxed Dewar with the following request: "I agree with Tony Blair's call for mature debate concerning Section 28, as I believe this sensitive and important family issue is worthy of proper discussion. I would therefore like you to consider debating the intellectual case for and against repeal with me in a public televised forum which would, I feel, be in keeping with our democratic traditions". A spokesman for Donald Dewar put it simply to the *Record*: "The First Minister doesn't believe this sensitive issue should be reduced to either a personality or gladiatorial contest".

On the moral panic that was now engulfing Scotland, in the *Scotsman*, Tom Pow quoted a piece from Stanley Cohen's book *Folk Devils and Moral Panics* and warned: "Societies appear to be subject, every now and then, to periods of moral panic. A condition, episode, person or group of persons emerges to become defined as a threat to societal values and interests; its nature is presented in a stylised and stereotypical fashion by the mass media; its moral barricades are manned by editors, bishops and other right-thinking people; socially accredited experts pronounce their diagnoses and solutions". That time had now come. The *Herald* called in Professor John Haldane, FRSA, FRSE and director of the Centre for Philosophy and Public Affairs at St

Andrews University to explain homosexuality to readers (...the paper omitted mentioning his Catholic connections. He became the author of *Faithful Reason: Essays Catholic and Philosophical* and wrote such articles as *Thomas Winning: Streetfighter for God* for the *Tablet*). In a piece linking homosexuality with anorexia, he made this analogy: "...The primary definitive use of sexual organs is intersexual, between male and female, and for the sake of reproduction. Does it also follow that this is the only legitimate use? I do not think so. Consider the analogy with eating. The organs of this are the mouth and digestive tract. Accordingly their primary definitive use is to consume food for the benefit of the body in general. Is this the only reason to eat? Evidently not. There is also the pleasure of savouring the taste and texture of one's meal as there is the pleasure of sharing the table with others. None the less, someone who divorced the practice of putting food in their mouth from the process of digesting it would be - and ought to be - judged perverse. Eating and spitting out, or vomiting up, adopted as general practices are pathological conditions. ...The primary function of sexual activity remains that of reproduction. Homosexual activity, like the intentional consumption of indigestible material or the continuing and deliberate regurgitation of food, is a misuse of natural human capacities. How serious a misuse is not a matter I feel competent to judge".

The *Sunday Mail*, the *Record's* more gay-friendly sister, edited by Peter Cox, supported the Government line and carried an exclusive declaring: "Catholic priest Gordon Brown is so sickened by his Church's stance on gays he has chosen to 'out' himself... He claims there is a significant underground gay movement within the Catholic Church in Scotland, with gay priests too scared to reveal themselves for fear of being expelled from their jobs and the Church". (That would include Scotland's next cardinal, Keith O'Brien). Father Brown said: "To say that homosexuality is a threat to family life is just nonsense. Who would consider a lifestyle which is considered to be second best"? The *Scottish Daily Mail* saw it somewhat differently and decided to run with the story from a different angle, declaring "the Catholic Church in Scotland was left reeling after a secret network of gay priests was exposed by one of its members". The Catholic Church in Scotland insisted Father Brown's sexuality would not be an issue as long as he continued to remain celibate. Father

The Board of Social Responsibility

Danny McLaughlin said: "Provided Father Brown does not indulge in gay sex then there is nothing to say that he is not living a good life... Considering it from a personal perspective seems to make him look at it in a slightly different way. Our position is quite clear. We are opposed to the promotion of homosexual activity as being equal to sex within a stable loving marriage. It is sad he can't accept that".

Letters poured in to the *Catholic Observer* to challenge Edinburgh's *Evening News* columnist, Father Steve Gilhooley's liberal stance on homosexuality. Before his book *The Pyjama Parade* was published, detailing the abuse he suffered at the hands of Father Francis Bligh who was jailed in 2001 for two and a half years and placed on the Sex Offenders' Register after admitting 10 counts of indecent assault on boys aged between 11 and 15, he was asked by the *Evening News* if he had published the book for money. "Do you want to come and see my hate mail?" he argued. "Or punch my name into the Internet and see all the slaggings I get? Or the bomb left under my car? And the flaming rags soaked in petrol left on my doorstep? Or pay for my broken windows? Anyone in Edinburgh knows that my auntie runs an orphanage in Bolivia. That's where my money for my *Evening News* column goes, and that's where money for the book will go too".

Years later, after the publication of *The Pyjama Parade* and after launching a scathing attack on the appointment of Cardinal Joseph Ratzinger who he claimed was trying to silence him in the *Irish Times*, Steve Gilhooley went missing on a 'soul-searching' trip to Ireland after announcing he would not be returning to the priesthood. He claimed in his article that "Rome's response was to deliver a threat to my archbishop that if he didn't silence me, they'd discipline him. I was treated as the perpetrator rather than the victim".

As the heat was cranked up in the progressively vile campaign to 'Keep the Clause' across Scotland, more victims surfaced.

Incidents of abuse and beatings became a common topic amongst those using Scotland's gay bars and clubs. Tim Hopkins of the Equality Network issued a statement in the wake of a Scottish Executive report that revealed gay men in Scotland's capital, Edinburgh were four times more likely to face violence than heterosexuals. He said: "Gay people in Scotland feel more alienated and vulnerable than a month ago. The whole issue has highlighted divisions in our society". 300 gay men had been interviewed and a further 50 completed questionnaires. Of those, more than half claimed to have encountered some form of harassment from strangers as a direct result of their sexuality, many were attacked near gay venues and 26 per cent said they had been the victims of physical assaults.

Using the editorial of *ScotsGay*, which was distributed free to gay and gay-friendly venues, editor John Hein warned: "Although the gay ghetto can give us a feeling of security, of being safe amongst our own kind, the very fact that we congregate in a relatively small area can allow us to be identified more readily by those who intend us harm. It's no coincidence that the number of queer bashings has markedly increased throughout Scotland..."

Notices were posted up in Edinburgh's gay establishments by the LGBT Community Safety Forum, a group set up at the suggestion of the local police. Headed: "Important Notice", they referred to an area known for cruising and read: "Lothian and Borders Police have advised of two serious assaults in the Royal Terrace/Calton Hill area in the early hours over the last couple of weekends. Both assaults have been carried out by groups of youths in their teens. It is believed that these attacks are related to the publicity over Clause 28. Please take extra care if you are in the area". Added to the warning at one venue in Edinburgh's gay quarter was the following advice: "There have also been reports of muggings at the nearby cash machines by a bottle wielding thug". It referred to a series of muggings at the cash machine near Planet Out. In one of the incidences it was claimed that a victim had been attempting to remove cash when a man approached asking: "Are you gay?" After responding: "Yeah, what of it?" a bottle was produced and smashed over the victim's head. The crime was not reported to the police.

Joan McAlpine wrote about a friend in her column in the *Sunday Times Scotland:* "He had been attacked in Edinburgh in the early hours of Saturday morning by a gang of teenagers. They first hit him over the back of his head with a blunt instrument and, while he lay unconscious on the pavement, kicked him violently and repeatedly in the face. The assault was so vicious he needed reconstructive surgery: several teeth were knocked out and bones were smashed. Seconds before the attack, he had left a gay nightclub... When he was well enough to pick up a newspaper, he read that Winning, the Scottish leader of the

The Board of Social Responsibility

church in which he was raised, had described gays as perverts... The morons who attacked my friend probably feel legitimised... A catholic priest who takes advantage of children in his care might reasonably be described as a pervert. Funny, I don't remember the cardinal using the word, or a variant of it, the last time such a case hit the headlines. When he did refer to the problem, he called child abuse a 'dreadful disease'. Call me pedantic, but there is quite a semantic difference between 'dreadful disease' and 'perverted...'."

Until 2009, Scotland was the only part of the UK not to have any legislation dealing with homophobic hate crime, (although it did for religion). Collating evidence of links between violence and intimidation against the gay community and the ongoing 'Keep the Clause' campaign was a project bravely taken up by Stuart Brown who produced a report to The East of Scotland Repeal Section 28 Group. He was challenged not only by the resistance of police to catalogue such crimes as homophobic – police preferring to log them only as assaults - but also by the reluctance of victims to speak out. Such difficulties were highlighted in the report when a man at the gay cruising area of Edinburgh's Royal Terrace in the early hours of the morning was attacked by a gang. He told police he had been waiting for his girlfriend and didn't want to press charges. Bob Sutherland of the LGBT Community Safety Forum told Stuart Brown: "There's something about being beaten up just because you're gay that can really mess you up psychologically. At the Switchboard we get a lot of calls like this. It's not like being mugged. You can get your head round that: They just want your money. But gay bashings - like racial attacks, I suppose - can profoundly affect your self esteem and confidence and remind a person that they live in a 'them and us' society. That's not a nice feeling".

In one of the reports collected by Stuart Brown, a man left Edinburgh's CC Blooms, a gay bar, in the early hours of a Monday morning in March 2000 and "as he got to the wee house on London Road, a large man abducted him, took him into the bushes near the house and raped him. The victim lost his wallet and a trainer".

Andrew O'Donnell, chair of the LGBT Safety Forum and an outreach worker conducting health promotion amongst male sex workers and men cruising for sex in the Lothian area, was contacted by police when attacks occurred. He insisted in the

East of Scotland Repeal Section 28 Group: "For over a year there's been nothing. There's been a bit of inter-rent boy violence but no gay bashings at all, not even rumours of attacks that haven't been reported to the police. Then all of a sudden in the last three months you've got all of these cases. It's just anecdotal evidence. Of course it is. That's all it can ever be probably, but it is happening and people are getting hurt".

In a collection of personal testimonials, *Caused by the Clause*, a document compiled by Ali Jarvis for Stonewall and released in November 2000, a gay man wrote: "Myself and my friends began to experience a great deal of homophobic verbal abuse from neighbours during and after the campaign, culminating in my house being broken into and vandalised and my car being first graffitied, then destroyed by these same people who'd been harassing us". Following the failure of the Scottish Executive to extend the definition of hate crime to include homophobia in 2006, Stonewall produced new research on the level of violence experienced by Scottish gays in and around the home. The document revealed disturbing evidence that, despite pleas to be moved out of an area or requests for action against perpetrators, abuse and intimidation was dismissed or downplayed by housing associations or landlords. Those interviewed reported being "harassed by late-night phone calls", "becoming a prisoner in your own home, having to sneak in and out" and "living in fear". Eddie, a 47-year-old Glasgwegian, had his windows broken and the words 'poof', 'queer' and 'baby murderer' scrawled across his front door over a period of some years and throughout the period when 'Keep the Clause' was active. The housing association ignored his pleas until he was forced to move himself out of the area.

Not all incidents of violence or harassment against gays made it into the public domain. The papers rarely took issue with the fact that in playgrounds throughout Britain; the word 'gay' had become a standard put-down. This had now been overtaken in Scotland by a new catchphrase: "Keep the Clause". Tim Hopkins of the Equality Network told the press: "We have heard that the words "Keep the Clause" are being used as a form of abuse against our people, who are having it shouted after them in playgrounds and on the street. What is happening in this country right now is truly frightening".

The Board of Social Responsibility

Indeed, the phrase 'Keep the Clause' had caught the imagination of schoolchildren across Scotland and its use had become widespread amongst them.

With such focus on the protection of children, vulnerable adults caught up in this campaign were easily ignored; one such group being gay teachers. Research from London University's institute of education estimated 17,000 gay, lesbian and bisexual staff in schools across the UK. Subject to inappropriate language, taunts of "Keep the Clause" from pupils and sometimes physical violence, many were unwilling to confront the issue for fear of antagonising parents. A report published by the Department for Education and Skills in 2004 found gay teachers overlooked for promotion and bullied by both pupils and colleagues.

In Stonewall's collection of testimonials, *Caused by the Clause*, a gay teacher who, through stress, had been forced to take time off work, explained how harmful the campaign had been for him and his partner at the time: "We are both 40 and live in Edinburgh. As the year and the arguments progressed I found myself getting more and more frustrated and angry, but with only a limited amount of energy to write to newspapers to try to refute the misinformation promulgated by Brian Souter and Cardinal Winning. I did write to the Cardinal – I was brought up a Catholic – but didn't receive any response. I also wrote to a couple of newspapers after reading particularly horrible and inaccurate pieces. I felt that I had to write to try to face up to the 'Keep the Clause' people and to show that we were people who lived ordinary lives in ordinary jobs and that we were not the monsters that Souter and others would have had people think. As a secondary school teacher who is not 'out' but who doesn't lie if asked, I found that my life was made hell by some pupils – mostly name calling – and that the school, while normally supportive, was inconsistent in its punishment of the people I managed to identify. I was told – by a deputy head teacher - that I was too sensitive; that I should 'laugh the remarks off'. I found that if the perpetrator was a troublemaker in other ways then he/she would be excluded, but if he/she was a 'good' pupil or if the parents objected and came up with the 'my boy/girl wouldn't do that' story, then the school backed off and gave the pupil the 'don't do it again' type punishment, (i.e. Next to nothing)".

The police expressed their disquiet by admitting violence against gays was on the increase. Fifty-year-old Alexander Noble from Bishopbriggs, near Glasgow, died in hospital four weeks after visiting a public convenience in St Vincent Street, Glasgow, a place well-known to some men who sought gay sex. He was spotted drinking in a nearby bar with a short, scruffy youth who called himself Stephen. Alexander had spent the day at Ayr races on 15 April, the day after the *Record* had been banging its drum over grants being awarded to gay groups. The couple then walked to the Crow Tavern near Noble's home in Coltpark Avenue, Bishopbriggs and left shortly before midnight. Alexander Noble lived alone. He was found next day slumped across the floor of his home with serious head wounds. A gold Accurist watch, a chain with a boxing glove-shaped pendant and an ID bracelet were missing. Police sought 'Stephen' and three or four occupants of a red or maroon Ford Fiesta that had parked outside Alex's house that night. The *Record* didn't report the murder, but instead devoted two pages to the gangland killing of 51-year-old Frank McPhie. Police later arrested 18-year-old Gary Fraser who was convicted of the culpable homicide of Alex Noble and sentenced to seven years imprisonment at the High Court in Glasgow.

At the same time, questions were also being asked about the nature of the brutal murder of 33-year-old unemployed Fraserburgh man, Brian Buchan. The body of Mr Buchan, a former pupil of Fraserburgh Academy, described by locals as 'a bit of a loner', was found at his flat in the town's Barrasgate Road. His face and back were repeatedly stamped upon and he had suffered horrendous injuries. Police were called to the flat by his friend Roy Smith who said he had found him lying dead that morning. Smith was arrested and charged with his death. Police say Smith had told them he'd been drinking the night before and couldn't remember if he was responsible for the killing or not, adding that he often did stupid things when he was drunk. He was convicted by a jury and sentenced to life imprisonment. Smith, of Lonmay attempted to challenge the conviction, his defence claiming the conviction was perverse as the court heard twenty-five witnesses claiming to have seen the victim after the time the Crown maintained he'd been murdered. Although Lord Justice General Lord Cullen agreed this was strong evidence, he threw out the legal challenge on the basis there was blood found on Smith's boots.

The Board of Social Responsibility

Against mounting evidence of a rise in homophobia and violence towards gays throughout Scotland, Brian Souter was adamant that the virulent 'Keep the Clause' campaign had nothing to do with it. In a column he wrote in the *Scotsman* he explained: "There is no empirical evidence to support such a claim and there are obvious reasons why Outright Scotland would try to make such a claim…" before adding, "most parents feel the gay lobby have no locus in the Section 28 debate…" Many gay parents were angered by his assertion. It was suggested perhaps only murderers were suitable for the post of Justice Minister since they were the only ones with any real experience. Souter was also interviewed on Scot FM, saying evidence of violence to homosexuals was only "anecdotal". He added that "homosexual acts from a scriptural point of view aren't right…" and that discrimination was commonplace in law since marriage discriminated against polygamists.

Cracks began appearing in the wall of the Scottish Executive's resolve to repeal Section 28. Donald Dewar promised that after the repeal of Section 28: "There will also be a review of the guidelines governing the type of materials used in schools which, if anything will be more rigorous". The prospect of more rigorous guidelines restricting and inhibiting the discussion of sexuality in Scottish schools was not likely to benefit children for whom the discussion of sex was already taking place more freely; more spontaneously outside school, in the playground and on the Internet. In any case, guidelines were issued to local authorities, not schools. Local authorities then have to decide what advice to pass on to teachers. Unlike in England and Wales, guidelines were not legally enforceable in Scotland. A briefing note issued by the Executive advised: "Schools are encouraged to take into account national and local authority advice, the views of the local community (including local church interests), the views of parents and, where appropriate, the views of pupils". But what if a school adopted a more liberal stance than ministers liked? Were they likely to find themselves courting the unwelcome attention of a media only too willing to act as the nation's moral guardian? And what of schools that took a more punitive approach? They would likely adhere to every letter of the repealed law with virtual impunity. Although it was left to HM Inspectors of Schools to monitor sex education, five years could go by without the school ever having seen an inspector. Baroness Janet Mary Young, fighting for retention of Section 28 in England and Wales in the House of Lords said on BBC's *Newsnight:* "A teacher should say what they believe to be true". Clint Walters, a young gay man, retorted in the *Pink Paper:* "If she is correct then comprehensive sex education boils down to luck! Section 28 was already in place when I was nine years old and I tested HIV positive when I was 17. What kind of luck did I have?" The late Baroness Young – or 'Old Tin Knickers' to some - was the first woman to lead the House of Lords and, as a stalwart Anglican, saw the Christian family as the bedrock for a well-regulated society. Born in 1926, the Baroness was a don's daughter, educated at the Dragon School in Oxford and recognised by her trademark grey suit and blouse buttoned to the top like a man's shirt with no tie. She was also an enthusiastic cricketer and rugby player at school. In 1950 she married Geoffrey Young and had three daughters. Later, she became deputy chairman of the Conservative Party and became Education Minister under Margaret Thatcher.

Whilst Baroness Young might have preferred homosexuality to remain 'the love that dare not speak its name' in the classroom, its growing recognition had been problematic for many. Writing about sex education, in a letter to the *Scotsman*, Dr Katie Buston, MRC Social and Public Health Sciences Unit found "a major constraint" in the discussion of homosexuality in schools. She wrote: "Some teachers even say they are reluctant to challenge homophobic comments made by pupils because of fears that they will fall foul of this clause. Also, in some sex education lessons, we observed teachers themselves joining in with the laughter surrounding such comments, engaging in homophobic teasing, pathologising homosexuality or reinforcing stereotypes or myths about gay and lesbians' sexuality... The voice of the young people identifying as lesbian or gay is rarely heard due to discrimination. We must recognise their existence..."

Torcuil Crichton wrote in the *Sunday Herald:* "If your own memory of sex education in school is of one of embarrassment and fidgeting - or a whole class giggling its way through a video - then you have a fairly accurate picture of what passes for sex education in Scottish schools today... Like most of the Scottish public, teachers had heard little or nothing about Section 28 until Brian Souter entered the fray..."

Jack Barnett, a teacher at Fraserburgh Academy added his views on sex education in the *Herald:* "Sex education is dealt with in secondary schools, increasingly in personal and social development programmes. These programmes contain units on alcohol, drugs education, both very contentious issues which parents believe we handle sensitively and appropriately. (I have not heard any calls for statutory guidelines for these areas)... It is not only guidance teachers young people will talk to. They will talk to teachers they trust. It is in building up this trust and not betraying it that marks out your professionalism, whether you are teaching history, English, or sex education. We are there to teach and support young people, there to create a safe learning environment. This is not an easy task. Any steps which make this task more difficult are not welcome. There have been periods since the announcement of the repeal that I have been very angry".

Peter Dickson, a senior guidance teacher with 25 years experience teaching sex education said: "A teacher facing a class of 30 pupils without proper materials is in difficulty... Schools play safe. The tendency is to take a bland line and not to raise issues that will cause problems for the teacher. The idea that these lessons ever went into detail on homosexuality is rubbish... What we are doing is not adequate for the needs of young people... Study after study has shown that young people want to talk about their emotions and feelings, but the teaching of sex education is not pupil-centred. It is based on a need to say that we are doing something so that when the school is inspected it can say the subject is covered".

The rights of children to receive sex education are upheld in the United Nations Convention on the Rights of the Child. Article 13 states: "The child shall have the right to freedom of expression; this right shall include freedom to seek, receive and impart information and ideas of all kinds..." Despite its ratification of the UN Convention, the UK systematically ignored the provisions. In January 1995, the Rights of the Child committee at the UN expressed their concern that parents were able to withdraw children from sex education classes and declared that insufficient attention was being paid to the rights of the child to exercise their rights and express their opinion.

Colin Dingwall's letter in the *Scotsman* was indignant: "There are about 700,000 Catholics in Scotland, or about 15 per cent of the population. It is reckoned that gay people make up about 10 per cent of the population, including a fair number of Catholics.

So... it is okay to provide a Catholic education for 15 per cent of the population to provide them with religious guidance, but not okay too for gay people to receive the sex education and guidance they need. This smacks of double standards".

With the promise of guidelines, the *Daily Record* pounced: "...MSPs could be asked to vote to repeal Section 28 - before they even see revised guidelines for schools". David Whitton, the spokesman for Donald Dewar, the First Minister, insisted that new sex education guidelines for teachers would be in place before Section 28 had been repealed. He reminded the press that the executive had always said it would revise the guidelines, but this would not take place until there had been full consultation with the teaching profession, parents and other interested parties. The Ethical Standards Bill, repealing Section 28, was expected to enter parliament and be put to a vote following its consideration at the committee stage. On Monday, 24 January, the *Daily Record* danced on their desks with "PARENT POWER: NEW GUIDELINES FOR TEACHERS", appearing in over four-centimetre high bold lettering across the page, declaring a: "LABOUR U-TURN ON GAY SEX LESSONS". This was, of course, misleading; since there was never any intention pupils would receive 'gay sex lessons'. Teachers who breached the proposed guidelines by allowing lurid or pornographic material into the classrooms would've been threatened with dismissal. The *Record*, in its effort to manage, constrain, manipulate, channel, re-route and deny sexual expression with a daily diet of sexual misinformation, homophobia and church propaganda claimed what it described as "their first victory". It was hailed as "a significant shift in Labour's position, in the face of widespread opposition to plans for repeal..." Changes to guidelines, previously promised *after* Section 28 was repealed, were now going ahead *before* repeal in the summer of 2000. The fact England and Wales had *legally enforceable* guidelines embedded in a National Curriculum was set to become the 'Keep the Clause' campaign's next challenge. They wanted Scottish guidelines to be enforced by law. In *Scotland on Sunday*, Gerald Warner suggested the Scottish Executive *wanted* guidelines unenforceable "...lest they might obstruct the proselytising activities of homosexualist activists in schools".

'Keep the Clause' reminded the Executive through the *Daily Record* that Brian Souter "wants something enshrined in

The Board of Social Responsibility

legislation, and he's willing to keep this up for six months or six years. He will spend every penny of his fortune fighting this if he has to". Then, the *Record* signalled the imminent arrival of a new and sinister twist in 'Keep the Clause's' campaign: A £1m advertising campaign, involving a national petition, TV adverts and billboards across the length and breadth of Scotland.

The Prime Minister's press spokesman, Alastair Campbell revealed that the Prime Minister Tony Blair was privately expressing concern over the media coverage of Section 28 in Scotland, which had, by now, made its way onto the front pages of newspapers across the whole of the UK. Campbell had said: "To read some of the papers in Scotland, you would think being gay was being put on the National Curriculum". Tony Blair pleaded for a "calm and rational debate". The *Daily Record*, a tabloid that had once been so loyal to Labour, scoffed: "…What's it got to do with him, anyway…" and issued a "warning" in its editorial: "Unfortunately for parents south of the Border, no English Brian Souter has had the guts to come forward yet and galvanise debate about the parallel legislation to repeal the section there. Donald Dewar and Wendy Alexander have already discovered that pinning your credibility to this politically correct crusade does not impress ordinary voters, however well it may go down with their chums in the chattering classes. Could it be that the Prime Minister has just made the same mistake?"

The front page of the *Herald* warned: A "tide of vitriol swamps Section 28". Indeed it had. The *Scottish Daily Mail* opened the floodgates, begging readers to "fill in the adjoining coupon…" and send it to them by letter, fax or e-mail. It simply read: "I oppose the abolition of Section 2A (Section 28) of the Local Government (Scotland) Act 1986".

Any suggestion by BBC's *Reporting Scotland* that the Scottish School Boards' Association were about to drop their objection to the repeal of Section 28 or that they had softened their stance in the face of proposed guidelines was blasted off the front page of "Scotland's champion" when the *Record* roared: "SCHOOL BOARDS WILL NOT BACK DOWN… Shoddy Beeb got it wrong… The BBC should hang its head in shame today… In a display of some of the most shoddy reporting ever to disgrace our TV screens, the BBC were prepared to devote a substantial chunk of their programme to a story based on the word of an anonymous malcontent who didn't even have the guts to speak

171

publicly". (This was rich coming from the *Daily Record;* making a living off the words of any number of anonymous malcontents)! But there was something of a warning shot fired across the bows of the SSBA when the *Record* added: "...hardly surprising, considering how betrayed the vast majority of Scottish parents would feel if the SSBA DID back down now". The SSBA were apparently adamant they "would go to the wire" rather than give in. Treasurer Alan Smith, a committed Christian, was spoiling for a fight, 'assuring' parents: "It's still all systems go. We won't let you down on this... I am concerned at elements in the media who are bent on misinformation..." Ann Hill chipped in: "My fear is that someone is trying to derail this campaign. We will not let parents down on this issue and it is thanks to people like the Record we are being able to take this forward". The *Record* insisted: "Only one of the 32-strong executive committee is believed to be against the campaign". The statement released from the SSBA after a tense six-hour confrontational meeting in New Lanark at 10.30pm on Friday, 28 January left the Saturday papers in a quandary with the SSBA promising to co-operate with the Executive and consult their members. Were they or weren't they still backing 'Keep the Clause'? Hours later, they confirmed - to the same BBC reporter whose work the *Record* described as "shoddy" – that the SSBA weren't, after all, backing 'Keep the Clause'. The *Record* hit back after the weekend with their most vicious attack yet on David Hutchison, the SSBA's president. He was described as having "egg all over his face after publicly claiming he would accept no money from Keep the Clause". They revealed the SSBA had, in fact, drawn up a £200,000 shopping list for Brian Souter to sponser five pet projects including an international conference. The letter signed by Hutchison said that the "SSBA share the concerns of many of the clients you represent and agree that a campaign needs to be fought..."

The *Daily Record's* faithful reporter Carlos Alba wrote how the Executive "was trying to foster discontent within the Scottish School Boards Association". His report claimed Joanne Beaumont "was the only member of the SSBA who had spoken out against the campaign publicly" and had been sent "two e-mails and a fax, pushing the Government's line, including a letter from Minister Wendy Alexander". They claimed the Executive had "wanted her to have something in writing" to take to the

The Board of Social Responsibility

SSBA's meeting on Friday. The *Record* turned to the SSBA's more compliant treasurer, Alan Smith, who told them: "Donald Dewar and Sam Galbraith have stepped in and have said they will have revised guidelines in place before a vote is taken. That is a big concession already and no one is in the mood to throw in the towel". The *Record* quoted another anonymous malcontent, described as "an SSBA insider", who told them: "Joanne is the only member who had expressed disquiet. The Executive obviously see her as the weak link..." Alan Smith later warned the press that guidelines were not going to be enough and demanded *statutory* protection.

In the face of such partisan views from the SSBA, questions were asked why ministers paid so much attention to them when there was an already longer-established widely-based parent group. The Scottish Parent-Teacher group claimed to have mailed 1,100 associations with its explanation of their support for the repeal of Section 28 and received only two negative responses.

In his column in the *Scotsman*, Ian Bell attacked the "moralising busy-bodies attracted to school-boards..." and asked: "Who gave the SSBA and its supporters, not least those who write to the editor of this newspaper, licence to speak casually, habitually, on behalf of Scottish parents? As a member of that constituency, hitherto oblivious to the association's achievements, I would be gratified to know who claims the right to debase my son's education, pervert simple truths, and attempt to turn him into a callous ignoramus who will never disturb their self-satisfaction. Not on my time".

Judy Hendry from Edinburgh told the *Scotsman*: "Ann Hill, the chief executive of the SSBA, reportedly states that it has been 'consulting regularly' since the proposed repeal was introduced. That's interesting: I have never been consulted on this matter, and neither has any parent I know... Until now, I had thought that school boards and, presumably, their organisation were in existence to represent parents' views. Obviously, I was mistaken; school boards and the SSBA appear to believe they are a law unto themselves".

The *Record's* sister paper the *Scottish Daily Mirror*, despite a much smaller circulation, headlined the findings of lawyer John Scott of the Scottish Human Rights Centre: "CLAUSE 28 IS ILLEGAL". Scott explained how the Court of Human Rights would first look at how the rest of Europe dealt with the issue -

all considerably more liberal than Britain - before adjudication. He felt a precedent had been set in 1976 when a group of Danish parents tried to stop sex education in school. The European Court ruled kids had a right to know what happens in society. A 'Keep the Clause' spokesman retorted: "It's an interesting theory but not one many distinguished lawyers would agree with".

Britain's duty to satisfy the European Convention of Human Rights was one of the considerations facing the Scottish Executive as they sought to find the right wording for the Ethical Standards in Public Life (Scotland) Bill which would repeal Section 28. Already, a resolution in the Council of Europe had proposed sexual orientation should be included in the European Convention of Human Rights. The amendment had been proposed by Dutch Senator Erik Jurgens and received the backing of speakers, not only from the UK, but Luxembourg, Belgium, Spain, Italy, Hungary, Poland and Turkey. Backing the move were the right-of-centre European People's Party, the Socialist Group and the Liberal Group. The conservative European Democratic Group opposed the move. In Scotland, more distinguished bodies began to add their voices to the repeal of Section 28, amongst them Ronnie Smith, general secretary of the Educational Institute of Scotland (EIS), a union with 40,000 members, and president Norman Murray of the Convention of Scottish Local Authorities.

John Foster, the General Secretary of the National Union of Journalists, after being briefed by Ann Coltart, their Equality Officer, appeared briefly on Clyde One, a Glasgow-based music radio station and attacked the widespread homophobia of newspaper editors.

The *Daily Record* sought every opportunity to discredit members of the ruling Labour and Liberal-Democrat coalition in the Scottish Executive. Another opportunity came on 26 January 2000, when they caught "DEWAR AIDE IN RED LIGHT SHAME". 38-year-old Philip Chalmers, a key figure in moves to scrap Section 28 had been convicted of drunk driving. "The Record can also reveal that when police officers caught father-of-three Chalmers drunk in charge, he had a woman in the back seat of his car". A senior police source informed the *Record* that there had been another woman in the back too. Chalmers denied it. The overly-moral tabloid must have been delighted when: "Chalmers admitted to bosses yesterday that the woman was

The Board of Social Responsibility

NOT his long-term partner and the mother of his three children". He had been caught with: "A lady who was not his wife - although she may have been somebody else's". The editorial added, not without a touch of sarcasm: "...We entirely accept Chalmers' claim that his companion was not... er... 'on the game'. No doubt they were merely discussing how best to sell the forthcoming repeal of Section 28 to the Scottish population". The *Scottish Sun* was less circumspect on its front page: "DEWAR AIDE AND HOOKER". The *Scottish Mirror* went one step further with the "FACE OF DEWAR AIDE HOOKER". A map marked the spot where Chalmers was first arrested on 7 January, labelled: "red light area". The *Daily Record's* office location was shown outside this area, even though his latest arrest was in Hydepark Street, a street they claimed was "used by prostitutes and their clients". Hydepark Street was, in fact the home of the *Daily Record's* new building at Pacific Quay, which, with more than a hint of poetic justice, for some time, overlooked a massage parlour. Upon his second arrest the *Record* declared: "...He wasn't so lucky and ended up losing his licence after Strathclyde Police caught him in another part of Glasgow's riverside red-light area". The *Record* suggested: "...Maybe he just got lost dodging the attentions of the many ladies of the night who tout for business in the streets surrounding Labour's Glasgow HQ". They sniffed: "It is, of course... very doubtful whether the locations of the incidents would have rung any bells with the unworldly First Minister". Chalmers resigned, blaming personal problems and "terrible press attention". The *Record* added in its editorial: "If the Press hadn't got involved, Donald's 'firm friend' would still be at work this morning, orchestrating - among other things - the Government's attempt to persuade Scotland it needs gay sex lessons in schools". The *Record* printed a picture of a woman getting into a car in Glasgow's red light area. Not Chalmers car and not the woman he was caught with. The tabloid was quick to add that this was the second minister with connections to the repeal of Section 28 to go, after John Rafferty who had been sacked for lying about death threats to Health Minister Susan Deacon. "John Rafferty, Dewar's chief of staff, and a major backer of the plan to reintroduce gay sex lessons to Scots schools, was fired for misleading the Press". (So far, no-one from the *Daily Record* had been fired for continuously misleading the public over so-called 'gay sex lessons'). Carlos Alba trumpeted: "Now the wheels have come off the campaign (to repeal Section 28) as the main driver has resigned in embarrassing circumstances". Dickey-bowed columnist, Tom Brown huffed at such "overbearing arrogance to believe the Scottish media and electorate can be manipulated by a pair of hirelings". He asked: "What was Chalmers... thinking of, openly frequenting such a well-known sleazy area?"

By a remarkable coincidence, a letter was published in the *Daily Record* from a woman who was told her husband's car had been seen parked in a red-light area. The *Record's* agony aunt, Joan Burnie advised: "It's possible there could be an explanation for him being in this district so frequently". (Visiting the offices of the *Daily Record* being one of them).

The tabloid's editorial wished Chalmers "a sordid goodbye" and wondered "where did Donald find his special advisers... a psychiatric clinic?" The *Record* was not best pleased with the police for not sharing the high moral ground with them. "For reasons best known to themselves, the police accepted he was not intending to drive the car and charged him with the lesser offence of being 'drunk in charge'." Sparing a journalist his blushes, the *Sunday Herald* noted: "Hacks who misbehave with ladies of the night in Glasgow have been warned to be careful after one horny writer went too far after a boozy night out in the Rogano. (An art-deco restaurant in Glasgow). He wound up in the back of a prison car after a particular touchy feely moment". 'Old Mother Burnie' shrieked in the *Record*: "What is it about men and prostitution? Heterosexual or homosexual, it's almost as much of a male 'hobby' as watching football. They're all at it".

Each day, the *Daily Record* dutifully applauded the efforts of 'Keep the Clause', filling their popular pages with their propaganda, until finally announcing: "Next week it will step up a gear with a national TV ad and poster campaign. Parents and focus groups are already being asked about their views on Section 28. Their responses will be added to the ad campaign and the comments printed on dozens of billboards across the country". A spokesman for 'Keep the Clause', (usually David Macauley or Jack Irvine) said: "We appeal to everyone in Scotland who is concerned about the future of our children - sign the petition and make the politicians listen". The *Record* ran a full-page advertisement with 55mm high letters in blood red, begging: "Protect our children. KEEP THE CLAUSE!" Using his own

The Board of Social Responsibility

column in the *Scottish Mirror*, Jack Irvine, running the 'Keep the Clause' campaign from Media House, shrugged off criticism from fellow journalists. "Ian Bell of The Scotsman says that all my problems stem from being so short... Better short and sexy than ugly and bald, Ian. The ailing paper's diarist, one Ritchie McLaren, also regaled readers with tales of how we used to work together choosing Page Three girls for another newspaper. (Scottish editions of *The Sun*). I'm sorry Ritchie, I can't remember you but after a while, all the t**ts looked the same... I look forward to the next Press Fund Lunch when these heroes of the free press can tell me to my face what they think of me".

Chapter Four
Praise be the Lords!

"Maybe one day they will understand.
There's more to love than boy meets girl".
Jimmy Somerville

Scotland was torched by the launch of 'Keep the Clause's massive newspaper advertising campaign on 26 January 2000. The top tabloid, the *Daily Record's* editorial celebrated by reminding its readers: "WHATEVER else you forget to do today, don't forget to sign your copy of the Keep the Clause petition on Page 12". Scotland's second best-selling tabloid, the *Scottish Sun* went one step further headlining: "SIGN UP IF YOU CARE FOR KIDS". The editorial made a point of explaining that: "The Sun is NOT homophobic" before delivering the caveat. "But we, like the vast majority of this nation, have strong reservations about allowing the militant gay lobby greater influence over the lives of vulnerable teenagers… In our book, children come before everybody else, including this country's powerful gay lobby". It was, of course, nonsense; but a very dangerous nonsense. There was and never had been a 'powerful gay lobby'. If there was, they had up until that point failed to deliver equality for gay people on almost every level with the majority of rulings on the fair and equal treatment of gay citizens in Britain delivered by European, not UK courts. Underlining the reason why everyone had a duty to turn to "page 18" and sign "Souter's gay petition" in the *Scottish Sun*, a news report from Kenny McAlpine focused on protecting "infants". The petition was presented as something of a saviour from the impending corruption of the nation's children. McAlpine reported: "The move came as a Labour MP warned that infants could face a pro-gay blitz if the ban is lifted. Stuart Bell (a Church estates commissioner and Middlesborough MP) claimed it was just the start of a gay revolution leading to a lower age of consent and homosexual marriage. He claimed that health authorities have stockpiled explicit videos and literature in readiness for a Commons vote..." The full-page advertisement in bright red for 'Keep the Clause' begged: "Protect our children" before providing ten spaces for signatures to be sent to 'Keep the Clause's freepost address in Perth. Despite the broadsheet's pro-government stance, the same advertisement appeared in the *Herald* a week later.

In some respects, Bell was right. The unequal age of consent left the UK in breach of a Convention of the European Court of Human Rights: 16-years-of-age for heterosexuals and 18 for homosexuals. That would not be put right until 2001. The restless passage of the ominously-named Sexual Offences (Amendments) Act 2000 only added to existing tensions over sexual expression. The House of Lords kept rejecting the provision until the House of Commons was forced to evoke the Parliament Act to push it through. The Scottish Executive had been established prior to the reintroduction of the Bill and since this was a devolved issue the consent of the Scottish Parliament under the Sewell Convention was required. Had it not been granted, it would not have been possible to use the Parliament Act and the human right would have been left to flounder at the feet of unelected toffs and clerics in the House of Lords. The first stage of equal marriage for same-sex couples – civil partnerships – would not be possible until 2004.

The *Scottish Daily Mail* also encouraged readers to send, e-mail or fax their opposition to repeal. A double-page spread featuring four different stories, planting an element of fear and suspicion into readers' minds about gays, appeared under the heading: "A matter for your consciences". Two days later the *Mail* claimed 3,000 coupons had arrived at their Glasgow office. In a story headed "Gay activists move in on Scotland", Ian Smith "discovered" gay groups "secretly planning how to promote gay issues on to school curriculums". (The Equality Network had suggested incorporating the needs of young gays into teacher training). 'Keep the Clause' told the *Mail:* "Many parents, particularly in ethnic communities, aren't fully aware of what is going on and we will do everything we can to inform them". They wasted absolutely no time at all. The very next day, a meeting was organised for a group representing all religions in Scotland.

Praise be the Lords

Once seen as the natural home of those opposed to immigration, conservative, right-wing groups showed a growing interest in uniting racial groups on moral issues, while liberals grew increasingly wary of the influx of conservative religionists threatening the development of liberal reforms. In the Netherlands, by 2004 there was growing unrest after the murder of Dutch film maker Theo Van Gogh, who challenged Islamic culture in film. There followed a spate of attacks on Muslim schools and institutions whilst, conversely, in the American presidential elections of that year, Republican George W Bush, heavily funded by conservative and religious groups, was swept to victory on the back of his opposition to gay marriage.

Amidst the hue and cry and to appease the growing revolt, the Liberal Democrat-led East Dunbartonshire council promised to take on board the views of parents before agreeing to support repeal of Section 28.

The *Scottish Daily Express* chose to report First Minister Donald Dewar's snub of Brian Souter's offer for him to attend the launch of his part-owned new airline service ScotAirways, formerly Suckling Airways, from his airport at Prestwick. Their editorial admitted having "every sympathy with those who fear repeal" and laid the blame at the feet of Donald Dewar and Wendy Alexander "who were determined to axe a law which had become virtually obsolete" adding, "we suspect Scots are not nearly as 'modern' in their thinking on the subject as Ms Alexander believes". If the selective process of choosing letters for publication was anything to go by, this was indeed the case. In a letter to the *Daily Mail*, Lloyd Mortiss wrote: "I and many other parents, feel strongly about this – to the point of keeping our children away from school until we know that they are there for one reason only, to be taught the three Rs".

David Tann wrote: "As a parent, I object to them being exposed to this sort of thing at a tender age. What next? Homosexuality being made compulsory?"

Chris Hall wrote: "I'm also a father (of two boys) and have no intention of letting them be exposed to teaching that shows homosexuality as anything other than abnormal behaviour".

Mrs Deanna McQue wrote: "Please, everyone, wake up and have your say. We need a good world for our children and grandchildren to grow up in".

RELIGIOUS FASCISM

Mr O Scarr wrote: "My wife and I endeavour to raise our boys in a Christian manner, in a loving, stable environment, and would prefer to decide where and when they are made aware of the unsavoury aspects of modern life... Please don't let them be exposed to the promotion of a sexual deviation".

A researcher turned to a newspaper columnist from the *Scottish Mirror* to discuss the ramifications of Section 28 on the radio. Brian Reade recounted life in his Catholic secondary school and the school disco where only girls from other Catholic schools were allowed. Where teachers would roam the floor with rulers ensuring a two-foot gap existed between dancers and where there was only one slow record played. That was when the lights had been turned up and they were circled by the Christian Brothers.

The *Record* printed an exclusive that declared Tony Blair had promised to give MPs voting on the repeal of Section 28 south of the border in England and Wales a 'free vote'. Many MPs had expected a human rights issue as sensitive as this would be 'whipped', forcing MPs to tow the party line. However, getting the Bill through the House of Commons would not be a problem. Getting it through the House of Lords, an unelected, Conservative-dominated second chamber, spiked with religious clerics, would. Baroness Young, leading the fight against repeal in the House of Lords in England had already promised to stage an exhibition of pornography in the House of Lords, an exhibition of material she and the Christian Institute believed were being stockpiled for use in schools. Lord Ahmed, a 42-year-old businessman already declared he would vote with the Tories after finding the Government's position on Section 28 conflicted with his interpretation of the Koran. Middle England's favourite, the *Daily Mail* threw open a page for Iqbal Sacranie, secretary general of the Moslem Council of Britain to warn: "Don't force law-abiding parents into revolt, Mr Blair". He was able to express his concern that "a small and unrepresentative pressure group appears to have seized control of the Government and is attempting to change the law in order to thrust on our children – and on the children of the rest of society – lifestyles and values which most people reject". Clydeside MP Jimmy Hood warned the *Herald:* "I personally find it very difficult to be whipped through the Government lobby without copper bottom guarantees that the promotion of homosexuality in our classrooms will be prohibited".

Praise be the Lords

Following the Scottish Education Minister Sam Galbraith's promise of consultation with parents and church groups on sex education guidelines, the Catholic Church got to work on a document they distributed to all Catholic churches, schools and organisations outlining the reasons why they opposed the repeal of Section 28. It was read from the pulpit of every Roman Catholic Church in Scotland on Sunday, 30 January 2000 and published in every community newsletter. Congregations were urged to sign a petition to 'Keep the Clause', to take it away and get 13 others to sign it too. The bishops outlined the Church's fears that taking away a law "that prohibits the promotion of homosexuality" and replacing it with guidelines, "risks leaving our children extremely vulnerable to the message that a homosexual lifestyle is an equally valid moral choice to marriage". The bishops' message asked people to "pray for our legislators..." Tim Hopkins of the Equality Network responded quickly: "A heterosexual marriage is clearly a better lifestyle than a homosexual relationship, for people who are heterosexual. But a homosexual relationship is just as clearly a better lifestyle than a heterosexual marriage for the minority who are gay. The Catholic bishops seem to want compulsory heterosexuality taught in our schools. Attempts to force gay people into heterosexual relationships simply cause misery for all concerned".

A *Scottish Daily Mail* editorial cursed Wendy Alexander for indulging in "undemocratic irrelevancies such as Citizens' Juries and repeal of Section 28". The paper must have been delighted with the opportunity to leave their stamp on the story of former Glasgow college lecturer Mary Collins who had been sacked for allegedly making an advance on two female members of staff before a court cleared her. The headline read: "Lecturer in lesbian probe in line for £50,000". Not only had this amount yet to be fixed, she was described as "celebrating again" after an earlier court victory. What was less clear was she was still out of work, "subdued", and had "expressed a desire to simply get on with her life".

The Anti-Bullying Network, based at Edinburgh University published its findings on 28 January. The manager of the Scottish Executive-sponsored network, Andrew Mellor indicated a "significant problem" in Scottish schools. Not specifically dealing with homophobic bullying, the report still found children as young as seven victims of it. In one primary school, a head teacher explained that words like 'poof' and 'gayboy' were commonplace amongst seven-year-olds. A 16-year-old described his experiences: "The others are always calling me names – like 'gay' and 'pooftah' and 'bummer'. They do this just because I don't enjoy football and the other stupid things, which they like. I can't stand it. I can't sleep at night. I've been staying off school and I just keep thinking about what they say. Maybe it's true, but I don't think it is. I like girls. I think I'm heterosexual". A mother described the experiences of her nine-year-old son: "He is a sensitive wee boy who doesn't enjoy sport. On a cold, wet, windy day he was standing shivering on the rugby field when the PE teacher came over to him and said: 'If you're just going to stand there shivering, why don't you do what you do best – go and play with the girls'." Jim Liddle, a teacher from Edinburgh wrote to the *Scotsman:* "I have sat at a hospital bedside tearfully comforting the parents of a young man who attempted to commit suicide because he believed he was 'intrinsically evil' and less worthy of life than some of his peers, who bullied him mercilessly".

A survey commissioned by the Scottish Executive and carried out between September and December 1998 revealed that out of 246 gay men in Edinburgh, half had experienced some form of harrasment and 26 per cent had been victims of violent attacks within 12 months. Only one in three victims of those attacks reported it to the police. This was in line with the results from similar surveys by Edinburgh City Council and Lothian and Borders Police that found gay men and lesbians were 14 times more likely to suffer physical assault than the rest of the population.

Scotland on Sunday printed a picture of the paint-sprayed graffiti covering the entrance to Queen Elizabeth II forest near Aberfoyle: Some of it read: "KILL THE GAY QUEERS".

The news of the day was the victory of Jörg Haider's right-wing Freedom Party, now the second most powerful Party in Austria and an attack in São Paulo's gay district in Brazil when a gang of 30 skinheads, including two teenage girls, went on the rampage. Armed with chains and knuckle-dusters they followed Edson Neris da Silva, 35, and his boyfriend, Dario Pereira, 30, as they left a bar. An eyewitness said the men had tried to run away, but when the gang caught up with them, they started to beat one of them with a chain. For 20 minutes, all the witness could hear was the sound of punches. Afterwards, they calmly walked away.

Praise be the Lords

Mr Da Silva who had just passed his vetinary exams, died at the scene.

Dan Arnott from Kirkcaldy was unsympathetic to reports of increased violence toward gays. In his letter to the *Scotsman*, he wrote: "May I suggest the alleged increase may be partly due to the disproportionate amount of TV programmes fronted by 'in your face' homosexuals? Their attempts at humour consist mainly of sexual innuendos and foul language and cause a great deal of offence to many of us in the heterosexual community". Mr Arnott might've been surprised to learn of the despair many gay people felt when such images of gay people were delivered purely for heterosexual entertainment. For every gay man with a camp demeanour; sharp wit and a heightened taste for fashion there was someone who was none of those things. Behind such rhetoric was a desire that homosexuality should have no voice at all. Jack Webster, a regular columnist in the *Herald* demonstrated just such thinking when he wrote: "What baffles and disappoints is the on-going display of exhibitionism in their campaign for freedom and recognition; they wished to be an accepted part of society, alongside the rest of us, without prejudice or fear of persecution. But no sooner do they gain that place in the mainstream of society they proceed to ghettoise themselves into a new-found separation. It is apparently not enough to be accepted and recognised for their similarities as human beings. They now wish to emphasise the difference of their inclinations".

The Christian Institute had been busy. On 28 January, the *Daily Record* filled a double-page spread with various teaching aids aimed at teachers working in sex education specifically dealing with the subject of homosexuality. "Trainee teachers in Scotland are being actively encouraged to promote homosexuality", shrieked a report by Jamie Macaskill. The Christian Institute had targeted a teaching college at Jordanhill, part of Strathclyde University. The *Record* dutifully displayed a collage of publications and web pages the Christian Institute had found, including books like *Taught Not Caught*, *Knowing Me, Knowing You*, *Lesbian and Gay Issues in the English Classroom*, and an Edinburgh gay guide. From the Internet they printed pages from the *Gay Sex Now* website, a 'coming out' guide for young gay men and the front page of Scotland's only gay magazine, *ScotsGay*. The caption that accompanied them on one side was: "This is what they push at our children now... how much worse will it be if Clause 28 is scrapped?" Turning the page was a 'Keep the Clause' petition form ready to sign. Nonetheless, for a tabloid so appalled by the discussion of gay, the *Record* remained as interested as ever in the comings and goings of gay folk. On this same day they carried such stories as the first openly gay serviceman in the UK's armed forces: "Gay sailor comes out of the cabin", popstar Mel C defending herself against rumours she was gay and a report of Mary Collins's employment tribunal: "Grope case lesbian wins sacking fight".

The *Daily Record* now reported Wendy Alexander had been "dumped", when in fact, with the focus of the debate shifting toward the provision of non-statutory guidelines, education minister Sam Galbraith had stepped in, beginning with a high-profile Sunday television interview urging parents to "trust me, I'm a dad". The *Record* was quick to point out that Jordanhill School in Glasgow, where Galbraith's children attended, was not under local authority control, (although the head said he would abide by council guidelines). Forgetting their support for protesters swaddling children in 'Keep the Clause' propaganda for pram-pushing protests, the editorial barked: "Politicians should always be careful about using their own children to prop up their propaganda". An 'inner cabinet' headed by Tom McCabe was set up to oversee the Section 28 crisis in Scotland with Wendy Alexander, Sam Galbraith and Lib-Dem Ross Finnie. The *Record* mocked: "We're all doomed! Donald Dewar has called up his private Dad's Army to battle for the repeal of Section 28".

After a classroom ceiling collapsed at Kings Park Primary School in Glasgow, the *Record* wrote: "The children of King's Park could teach Scottish Education Minister Sam Galbraith a lesson: Get your priorities right and find more money for our crumbling classrooms".

By 29 January, the Scottish School Boards' Association had publicly rejected Education Minister Sam Galbraith's offer of guidelines and demanded statutory protection for schools against 'gay propaganda' following their stormy three-hour meeting in New Lanark that had BBC *Reporting Scotland* upsetting the *Record* by prematurely suggesting the SSBA were about to accept an "olive branch". The SSBA agreed to continue taking Brian Souter's money and consult their members later, over the following two months. They later agreed to take up an offer by the Executive to participate with teachers and church leaders in a working group to reassess all aspects of sex education.

Both the *Record* and *Mail* announced the results of a MORI poll that showed 54 per cent in favour of keeping the clause. (The results, however, also showed most people *tolerated* homosexuality and that supporters of Section 28 were largely from an older age bracket).

37 prominent members of Scottish public life came forward to add their weight to repeal. Along with Paolo Vestri, director of the Scottish Local Government Information Unit; Mike Kirby, convener of Unison Scotland; Maggie Chetty, director of the Scottish Community Development Centre and Catriona Renfrew, director of commissioning for Greater Glasgow Health Board was Bill Spiers, the general secretary of the Scottish Trades Union Congress who called the clause a "symbol of discrimination". He also asked protesters to "calm down" and have a rational discussion. Baroness Young's contribution to that was reported in the *Herald* when she insisted her opposition to homosexuality was because "it was wrong".

Tory leader William Hague paid a brief visit to Edinburgh and capitalised on popular resentment to so-called 'homosexual promotion' in a radio interview: "The Parliament was not set up so Labour can make lawful use of public money to promote homosexuality in classes", he said. Hague had imposed a three-line whip in defence of Section 28 in the House of Commons in 1999 and sacked Shaun Woodward from the front bench when he refused to support it. While Hague was in Edinburgh, 'Keep the Clause' circled the Scottish parliament with a mobile advertising van bedecked in the words: "Dear Wendy, will your new guidelines give homosexual relationships the same moral value as traditional marriages?"

'Keep the Clause' contacted one of Scotland's most influential lawyers, Peter Watson of Glasgow firm Levy and McRae. The firm had acted as Pat Robertson's spokesman and legal advisor during his impasse with the Bank of Scotland and used the services of Jack Irvine's Media House. Watson's partner in his lobbying firm, Tactical Response, was Jack Irvine. Watson wrote to Wendy Alexander threatening legal action over the repeal of Section 28, since the issue of equal opportunities, they believed, was a matter for Westminster and outwith the powers of the Scottish Executive. "We'll see them in court", Jack Irvine was reported saying. The legal challenge, on the basis of counsel from former Scottish Solicitor General Paul Cullen QC was taken lightly. Section 28 was part of the Local Government Act 1998 and local government, along with education, was quite clearly a matter for the devolved Scottish parliament. Brian Souter was defiant and told *Scotland on Sunday:* "Money is not a material consideration. I'll go back and live in a council house if I have to. That's how strongly I feel about this", and, in direct reference to street riots over the poll tax, added: "If we have to, we are prepared to repeat some historical images on the streets of Scotland". Asked if he would be prepared to lead demonstrations, he said: "Yes... I am prepared to do that". The *Scottish Sun's* headline was shrill. Many who were openly gay in Scotland now genuinely feared for their safety: "STREET FIGHTER SOUTER TO LEAD GAY LESSONS DEMO". The *Sun's* editorial roared: "We hope MPs heed The Sun and the vast majority when they vote on Section 28 later this month. And ignore minority militant gays and the forces of political correctness". Gerald Warner joined the charge, blaming Wendy Alexander for provoking "hostility of the Scottish public on a scale unexampled since the poll tax" and mocked the "hapless Dither" (his nickname for the First Minister, Donald Dewar) before turning on Wendy Alexander with the words: "Verily, O daft wee lassie, with thy student politics thou has stirred up an hornet's nest against me and daily my feet slip on the skins of many bananas. Do thou, therefore, abandon the cause of them that are limp-wristed...?"

After Jack Irvine's Media House lost a lucrative account with accountants Ernst and Young, senior figures began having doubts about Jack Irvine's ability to maintain control of the 'Keep the Clause' campaign. Insiders claimed the *Daily Record* had disagreed sharply with Irvine over his claims that he pulled the strings in the newspaper's coverage of the repeal of Section 28.

In an exercise in damage limitation, in 2010, the *Herald* printed a long editorial following the departure of gay Glasgow City Council leader Steven Purcell following allegations of taking cocaine, cover-ups, paranoia, incoherent ramblings and a stay at a clinic treating people with drink and drug problems. It followed mounting fears that a network of powerful figures was running Glasgow from behind the scenes, including leading figures in the media. The *Herald* denied suggestions that editors were being less than candid about Purcell's departure through either being too close or buckling under pressure from Peter Watson and Jack Irvine's Media House. The *Herald's* publishers, Herald & Times Group used Peter Watson's firm Levy & McRae to ensure legality of editorial content. Watson and Irvine also acted for Steven Purcell. Peter Watson was one of four shareholders of Media House although claimed he held the shares as a representative of a trust for Jack Irvine's children. Following efforts to conceal Purcell's "chemical dependency", the *Sunday Herald's* article "criticising the tactics of Mr Watson and Mr Irvine" had to be checked by "a QC acting as an independent adviser, although still under the overall umbrella of the Levy & McRae contract with the Herald & Times Group". The *Sunday Herald* was forced to declare: "After the story's publication, the *Sunday Herald* was contacted separately by both Peter Watson and Jack Irvine... We printed a correction of one factual inaccuracy: we had said Mr Watson and Mr Irvine had left Scotland to go "on holiday" around the same time as Mr Purcell had left the country. In fact Mr Watson and Mr Irvine had both left on business trips to the Cayman Islands. We also printed a letter from Mr Watson complaining about our coverage. We agreed to print the letter to fulfil our duty to offer a right of reply".

Levy & McRae's website claim that "being networked at the highest levels and having access to major decision-makers is key to our success". One of their clients has been the Lord Advocate of Scotland, Elish Angionlini, an appointed member of the Scottish Government. On 5 February 2000, the *Daily Record* gave readers a rare break from Section 28, but on 7 February they were editorialising once again on "the latest salvoes from the PC brigade". In this case, it was over a piece in the Glasgow Gay and Lesbian Centre newsletter which claimed laws such as Section 28 were responsible for producing serial killers like Dennis Nilson and Jeffrey Dahmer. The *Record* reminded readers how the Centre "last year received almost £20,000 of your tax money" and dismissed their claim as "a new level of hysteria".

True hysteria manifested itself when protesters smashed the glass door of the Glasgow Gay and Lesbian Centre in Dixon Street. Although the floor was littered with shattered glass, no-one was hurt.

Inspired by what was happening in Scotland, organised opposition to the repeal of Section 28 across the border in England and Wales was growing. After the Archbishop of

Canterbury, George Carey had described such plans as "a matter for concern", Chief Rabbi Dr Jonathan Sacks and representatives from the Hindu and Muslim communities all agreed. Their opinions would not go unnoticed. More than 30 influential Labour figures were members of the Christian Socialist Movement, including the Home Secretary Jack Straw. Stuart Bell MP, who spoke on behalf of the Church Commissioners in the Commons wrote to Ann Taylor, the chief whip and advised her of a number of Labour backbenchers who were preparing to revolt against the party line in the House of Commons. Bell, a devout Christian told the *Daily Mail:* "How can Mr Blair allow another attack on the family". (Stuart Bell was author of the book *Paris 69,* about a man who had a promiscuous relationship with seven women). Since both Ann Taylor and David Blunkett MP - later to become Home Secretary in Blair's cabinet until he was forced to resign after fast-tracking his nanny's visa application - had voted against an equal age of consent at 16, it was no surprise to hear rumours of a 'free vote', allowing MPs to 'vote with their conscience'. There was fury amongst some MPs over this, more than perhaps many had anticipated and the idea was later dropped. David Blunkett wouldn't stop there. He was soon engaged in talks with church leaders to press for the supremacy of marriage to be installed in a set of guidelines that would be legally enforceable in England and Wales and later, proposing a law to make incitement to religious hatred a crime in Britain.

The Learning and Skills Bill received its third reading in the House of Lords at Westminster on Monday, 7 February 2000. It contained 118 clauses and eight schedules. Baroness Young led the debate for amendments to include the promotion of marriage over and above any other arrangements, including single mothers, with more than a little help from the Christian Institute. A slightly glazed former Conservative leader, Margaret Thatcher sat by Baroness Young throughout the proceedings. Young announced to the Conservative majority gathered in the House: "How dangerous to teach children, primary school children at the age of seven, about homosexuality which, apart from anything else, carries serious medical risks". Her views were backed by many of the Lords, including Lord Stoddart of Swindon who questioned whether the school was the right place for sex education under any circumstances. He rounded on gays "and their friends in high places" before quoting a passage in a document before him that

Praise be the Lords

read: "In what way have we been taught to be heterosexual"? This wasn't the sort of question the noble Lord felt anyone should be asking and gasped: "I thought heterosexuality was normal!" Dame Jill Knight, who was responsible for placing Section 28 on the statute books, claimed that the book *Jenny Lives with Eric and Martin* featured a six-year-old girl sitting up in bed with her naked father and his lover. Lord Harris explained that this was a collage and there were, in fact, three separate shots of the three on the front cover. Turning to Lady Young, he challenged her assertion that a video, *How to be a Lesbian in 35 Minutes*, had been shown in a handicapped school full of very young children and accused her of missing the irony of the title, which was to demonstrate that one *couldn't* teach someone to be a lesbian with a video, or even by giving one or two lessons in a classroom. He also explained that the lesbian youth meeting just *happened* to have been held in a special needs school. No handicapped or disabled children were actually present at the time. Lord Harris also challenged Lady Young's assertions that gay pornography was being stockpiled for use in schools once Section 28 had been repealed. The Education and Employment Minister, Baroness Blackstone challenged Baroness Blatch over the distortion of the facts surrounding the Avon Health Authority's teaching pack, challenging homophobia in schools which had Baroness Blatch leaping to her feet. "I hope you are not calling me a liar", she stormed.

Anthony Grey, a leading figure in the campaign to partly decriminalise homosexuality in the sixties wrote a letter to the editor of the *Pink Paper*. "I wrote to Baroness Young requesting her to furnish me with detailed evidence to back up her assertions that in 1988 'local authorities... were spending large sums of money promoting homosexuality', and were requiring schools to do so, with 'appalling material (being) given out to children'. I asked Lady Young to tell me which local authorities she was referring to; how much money they spent on 'promoting homosexuality'; what the 'appalling material' was; and what evidence she had that such material had actually been given out to children. Although I have sent her a reminder, Lady Young has not replied to my letter".

David Stevenson of Cambuslang had a similar letter printed in the *Herald*: "I responded to a letter from one of Mr Souter's acolytes and invited that person or Mr Souter to publish a list of the number of times prior to 1986 (ie, the introduction of Section 28/2a) when homosexuality had been promoted in Scottish schools. I have seen no response from either of these people or even Mr Souter's well-paid PR company on this question".

The *Daily Record* echoed Baroness Young's findings with "DAWN'S GAY LESSONS..." Actress Dawn French apparently revealed she was "giving her adopted eight-year-old daughter lessons on homosexuality". In an interview in gay magazine, *Attitude*, Dawn French confessed: "... If my friend Nigel has his boyfriend Mark come to stay, she's fascinated by them. She loves Nigel anyway, and she'll go and jump on the bed in the morning..." The *Record* grimaced: "French... allows little Billie to see her gay friends in bed together". The tabloid also turned on acting partner Jennifer Saunders, interviewed in the same magazine. Saunders had "spoken out in favour of homosexual education in schools. She claims the prevention of the promotion of gay issues in schools is 'fascist'." Speaking about Section 28, what Ms Saunders actually said was: "Most people didn't even know this law existed. It's dreadful. You can't legislate in that way. You have to stop nannying people. It's a kind of fascism".

With many Tories from the shires specially driven into the House of Lords for the vote, it was not surprising that a majority of 210 voted to throw out any attempt at scrapping the clause in England and Wales; only 165 voted for its repeal. Amongst those supporting the retention of Section 28 was the novelist Baroness P D James, three board members of British Airways, Viscount Slim, director of the holiday company Trailfinders and former defence minister Nicholas Soames. Baroness Young warned that without her amendment, marriage was put on a par with a relationship between two transvestites or even two paedophiles. As Baroness Young walked back along the aisle, Ministers reached out to congratulate her and pat her on the back. The *Scottish Mail* gloated: "A senior Minister last night paid grudging tribute to the way Baroness Young, the Tory leader of the Lords campaign to keep Section 28, has handled the battle. He said: 'She has marshalled the case brilliantly. The combination of Lady Young and The Daily Mail proved unbeatable'." As Members slowly filed out - Margaret Thatcher, Baroness Young, assorted men of the cloth and the former Conservative Scottish Secretary Michael Forsyth amongst them - the speaker announced the introduction of the Air Quality England Regulation 2000 debate amidst loud guffaws and shouts of "clear the House". The *Daily Mail* and *Scottish Daily Mail* both ran the same headline on their front page the following morning, spouting triumphantly: "PRAISE BE TO THE LORDS". The *Sun* commended: "A great victory for common sense has been won by the House of Lords. There wasn't a parent in the land who wanted to see the safety net of Clause 28 taken away. No one outside the pink lobby wants children to be taught that homosexuality is a natural foundation for family life". They had all missed an important point. Efforts to keep Section 28 on the statute books in England and Wales was, to a large extent, pointless, since Section 28 applied *not* to schools, but *local authorities*, whose control many had opted out of under measures introduced by - of all people – former Tory leader Margaret Thatcher.

Once the House of Lords had finished with it, the elected House of Commons at Westminster had the opportunity of debating the subject of repealing Section 28 once again before returning it back to the unelected chamber of the House of Lords for their approval. Measures to repeal Section 28 in England and Wales were now considered by many to be extremely unlikely. Even after beefing up the Labour minority in the House of Lords by creating 19 new peers; that still wouldn't have dented the majority of 45 peers in favour of keeping Section 28. Had repeal initiated in the House of Commons (and this is where many doubted so-called New Labour's commitment to equality), the measure could have been forced through the House of Lords like the equalisation of the age of consent had been.

The debate in the House of Lords finally provoked the first signs of gay activism. Members of the Lesbian Avengers hijacked a London bus, owned by Stagecoach, in Piccadilly Circus and sprayed it pink. They were all arrested and charged with criminal damage. Seven Lesbian Avengers later appeared in court. Two were found guilty of an offence under the Road Traffic Act; 'getting onto a motor vehicle whilst it is on a road' whilst two others had their charges dropped. Three others had to await sentence while reports were prepared for community service orders and probation. The Avengers claimed stipendiary magistrate, Mr Pratt, who presided over the case at Bow Street Magistrates' Court, had been unsympathetic. He insisted the five pay substantial compensation to Stagecoach, plus costs amounting to just over £2,000.

RELIGIOUS FASCISM

In a lecture for Amnesty International, the Most Rev Richard Holloway, Primus of the Scottish Episcopal Church and Bishop of Edinburgh said: "In some societies, gay people are executed for being who they are; in our society we practise a subtler form of persecution; we merely imply that they are so depraved, so perverted, as to be incapable of responsible, loving relationships, so that we dare not trust our children to them nor educate them about them; then we express false horror when they are bullied in our schools and mugged in our streets. All this because... we do not 'connect' the sophisticated intolerance of the House of Lords, say, with the active cruelty to gay people in our streets".

In Scotland, 'Keep the Clause' were forced to send out letters to everyone on their mailing list to inform them its freepost address had to be closed down, blaming an "organised gay rights campaign" which had sent "certain unsavoury and offensive items together with junk mail".

While his Stagecoach drivers began striking for better pay, Brian Souter issued a writ against the *Guardian* newspaper for £200,000 damages after it printed a cartoon by Steve Bell, in which Souter was depicted sharing the back seat of a Stagecoach bus with Cardinal Winning. With 'Just Married' marked on the back and a string of ballot boxes trailing behind, Souter claimed he had been depicted as a religious bigot. Souter later reduced the claim to £20,000 before dropping the libel action against the *Guardian* and Steve Bell altogether in 2002. A number of cartoonists, writers and historians had been preparing to make their way up to Scotland to defend Bell. Unfortunately for Souter, lawyers were hard pressed to find any precedent of a public figure suing a cartoonist. Souter claimed he had received 'assurances' from the *Guardian* that they had not intended to suggest he supported or represented extreme views. (Those 'assurances' had been sent to his solicitors at the very start of his legal action). Souter was forced to pay both sides' costs.

The debate in the Scottish Executive on Thursday, 10 February 2000 headed off cries for what the *Record* labelled the "Blunkett solution". Wendy Alexander and Education Minister Sam Galbraith had flown down to London to meet David Blunkett who had discussed the possibility of introducing statutory guidelines in Scotland. The debate was on a motion proposed by the Tories to put the repeal of Section 28 on ice.

Praise be the Lords

The *Record* editorial stated: "Our new Scottish Parliament has the chance today to put families first. Scotland will be watching". The tabloid was thrilled to see a break in the "cosy conspiracy with Labour and the Liberal Democrats" when the SNP – which enjoyed financial support from Brian Souter - started to "come to their senses". They called for protection against 'gay sex lessons' for parents to be enshrined in law. The SNP attempt to include legally enforceable guidelines was defeated in the Executive by 78 votes to 32. The *Record* sniffed: "The Labour/Lib-Dem motion calls for Scotland to be a 'tolerant, just and inclusive' society. That is an insult because Scotland has always been that". An Executive amendment pledging to consult widely on safeguards and produce revised guidelines on sex education was carried 88 votes to 18 with three abstentions. The Tory motion to put repeal on ice was defeated by 88 votes to 18, with three abstentions (SNP MSPs Winnie and Fergus Ewing and Andrew Welsh). Section 28 was now one step closer to repeal in Scotland.

The Scottish Executive agreed to set up an 'independent' working group including two religionists and a member of the Scottish School Boards' Association headed by Mike McCabe, director of education at South Ayrshire council. It was charged with reviewing advice and materials to be used on sex education in Scottish schools and to introduce a package of safeguards that would be introduced before Section 28 was repealed. Amongst those on the panel was a representative from the SSBA, Mr Jack Waddell, Vice Chairman of Williamwood High School, East Renfrewshire; the Rev John Laidlaw, Convener of the Church of Scotland Education Committee and Mr John Oates, of the Catholic Education Committee. As the Executive prepared to debate, and while a 'Keep the Clause' advertising van circled the parliament, nine women led by Brian Souter's wife, Betty, marched up the Mound for a photo opportunity with t-shirts spelling out the words: "DONALD WHY WON'T YOUR PARTY SUPPORT FAMILY VALUES?" Jack Irvine, who organised the protest while Brian Souter was on business in Hong Kong, warned the press Wendy Alexander was getting on the wrong side of "Scotland's mothers". Police interviewed Betty Souter, along with several other women, after they staged a protest in the parliament's viewing gallery. During the debate, Wendy Alexander, who was interrupted by Section 28 supporters, vigorously reaffirmed her commitment to repeal: "Section 2a, when all is said and done, remains a piece of legalised intolerance. The passage of time will neither heal it nor help it. It needs to go".

The next day, the *Scottish Daily Mail's* front page squealed: "BETRAYED... MSPs triggered a furious backlash last night by voting to support plans to end the ban on gay propaganda in schools. It was a wilful defiance of public opinion..." The editorial accused the parliament of having "broken its covenant with the people" before fielding comments from a string of religionists: The Catholic Church's Cardinal Winning, the Kirk's Ann Allen, the SSBA's Alan Smith and even Family and Youth Concern's Valerie Riches, who sneered: "Democracy doesn't appear to be beholden to the militant, homosexual lobby". Along with a new Scotland-wide 'Keep the Clause' advertising campaign, Brian Souter promised to consider financing a broad-based family values campaign if Section 28 was repealed.

M J Foinette and E C Campbell of Falkirk frothed to the *Scottish Mail* their civil rights had been "violated". Their concerns were "reinforced by the ejection from the public gallery during the debate on Section 28 of silent and peaceful demonstrators, and their later questioning by police, while supporters of the repeal of Section 28 were allowed to remain in the gallery and were not questioned by police".

Pauline McNeil MSP for Glasgow Kelvin appeared alongside David Macauley of 'Keep the Clause' on BBC's *Newsnight Scotland*. Pauline McNeil insisted the cabinet were not split over their wish to ditch the clause. Pictured on a large screen behind them in London, Peter Tatchell was able to add his support for the introduction of "non-judgemental" guidelines. In *Scotland on Sunday*, 'Keep the Clause' was reported saying Souter was "disappointed that Peter Tatchell and Outrage! have responded in such a bitter and vindictive manner. However, Tatchell's actions have uncovered a sinister agenda to promote homosexuality in our schools. We do believe militant gays would use the dropping of Section 28 to push extreme material of a distasteful nature".

When Sam Galbraith, Wendy Alexander and Frank McAveety, the deputy minister for local government met church leaders, there was no softening of their opposition to repeal. Turning on the institution of marriage, the Board of Social Responsibility's Ann Allen appeared blind to the fact that

Praise be the Lords

affording special rights to marriage in law was socially *ex*clusive, not *in*clusive before telling the press: "We want an understanding and implementation of social inclusion which recognises, respects and tolerates all views but is not imbalanced by the agenda of a minority, and so far the executive has been deaf to that plea". The *Record* interpreted the meeting as: "Wendy turns a deaf ear as Clause talks deepen". Alexander tried to explain that since Scotland didn't have a national curriculum, as in England and Wales; it has never had statutory guidelines. Despite already promising not to interfere with the way Catholic schools already taught religious and sex education, the Catholic Church insisted it would continue fighting against repeal of Section 28. Dr Ian Morris wrote in the *Herald:* "No guidelines are statutory. If they were they would be tram lines and would simply be laws. Statutory guidelines are oxymoronic just like militant pacifists and intelligent idiots". The Liberal-Democrats in the coalition remained firm, insisting First Minister Donald Dewar must push ahead with repeal and not compromise. Lib-Dem Ministers refused to speak to the press, while Keith Raffan; a senior backbencher insisted they would not back down. He was joined by Nora Radcliffe, the party's equal opportunities spokesperson, who told the *Scottish Mail:* "As a society we should trust teachers, not impose restrictions that force them to marginalize their vulnerable pupils".

Behind the scenes, there was a growing impatience with Donald Dewar at the Labour Party headquarters in Millbank, London. Whilst Downing Street had warned him to "get a grip", spin-doctors were now suggesting he might find himself being briefed against and advice withdrawn to a point where he might be forced to resign. A similar tactic had been used on the Northern Ireland Secretary, Mo Mowlam. Her appearance on gay Irish entertainer Graham Norton's Channel Four TV show was something that would never have been sanctioned by Labour's Millbank headquarters and was intended to embarrass her. She came back into political life after having a brain tumour removed, but senior Government aides said she "lacked the intellectual rigour" for the job.

The *Record* insisted: "The Section 28 battle will go on as long as Alexander and her colleagues in the Scottish Executive persist in their pig-headed determination to flout the majority will in Scotland". Described as 'bossy', a 'spinster', 'five-foot-nothing' and showered by a host of other uncharitable and misogynistic remarks, Wendy Alexander had been wounded by the continual bombardment of personal and sexist attacks against her. Alan Cochrane in Scottish editions of the *Daily Telegraph* called her the "accident-prone and politically myopic Miss Alexander". The *Record* suggested she was "riding high in the Department of Frump" and gave her a makeover, superimposing her head onto the body of a woman curled up on a couch wearing a white trouser-suit with lilac-strapped shoes. The *Scottish Daily Mail* chimed smugly: "Her attempt to win Press favour by telephoning a journalist to appeal for support for the repeal backfired".

Channel Four awarded Wendy Alexander a trophy and the title Parliamentarian of the Year in Scotland, but it was smashed to pieces as she got out of a car at Heathrow Airport. The following year, they awarded it to Baroness Young!

Katie Grant started her column in the *Scottish Daily Mail* praising Wendy Alexander for being "exactly the sort of dynamite" Holyrood needed and "a woman not easily deflected" after she generously hailed a taxi and offered Mrs Grant a lift home. A few more sentences and Mrs Grant shook her head. "Now I am worried". She chastised Alexander for treating the electorate "as if they were simply impediments" to her ambitions. She recommended she ought to "listen for a change" instead of applying "her now trademark finger-wagging and the 'I am in charge and I know best' school of oratory". After Wendy Alexander had been handed the responsibility of repealing Section 28, Mrs Grant baulked: "Then in rides Miss Alexander, bustling outrage at a perceived slight to the homosexual community and declares a crusade... Miss Alexander's message to parents seems to be this: that she is cleverer than they are, that she sees the world more clearly than they do, that their experience of life is not as broad, as enlightening, as visionary as hers. Pretty staggering stuff from somebody who is 36 and has no family responsibilities". Mrs Grant had decided "Miss Alexander had brought the "political process into disrepute", by pandering to a "vociferous minority".

With the prospect of a by-election in Ayr, Downing Street put pressure on the Labour Executive to come up with a solution that would get Section 28 out of the papers – and quickly. Labour chiefs ordered a leak blackout on a Cabinet sub-committee meeting. The *Record* printed a picture of Wendy Alexander - "the

Praise be the Lords

Minister famed for preaching to the public" - poking out her tongue and left journalist Ron Moore to bitch: "As recently as February 2, she was still happy to explain at length the Executive's plans to dump Section 28. Even on a Ministerial visit to Dublin, she still found time to bang on again about the issue. But yesterday, the normally loquacious minister was finally forced to bite her tongue".

The *Scottish Mirror's* Scottish political editor, Lorraine Davidson, was sent out on the streets of Ayr to listen to parents. She told BBC Radio Scotland the following morning, in a round-up of the early editions of the Scottish papers, how "relieved" she was now that parents could be reassured by news of impending amendments to the Ethical Standards in Public Life Bill.

An impressive list of 34 researchers from Scottish universities, including doctors, psychologists, sociologists and educational experts, including Dr Stephen Reicher, editor of the *British Journal of Social Psychology* penned a joint letter to the Herald on 16 February warning: "The very notion that one needs to 'protect' young people from homosexuality implies that it is a danger to youth. Equally, the idea that a 'homosexual lobby' seeks to prey on impressionable youth conveys the idea that homosexuals are a sinister menace. Such ideas are the root of intolerance, the wellspring of hostility, and they are a tragic descent into homophobic violence". On behalf of 'Keep the Clause'; David Macauley insisted parents would not be lectured to by "a bunch of academics". Peter M Spinney wrote to the *Herald* warning the academics "they should mind their own business". A further stack of letters challenged the "gaggle of socio-psychologists" for their support in repealing Section 28. Stuart Ainsworth, co-director of the Equality and Discrimination Centre at the Department of Educational Studies at the University of Strathclyde warned: "…History also teaches us that those of a dogmatic and totalitarian mentality have also targeted intellectuals for daring to speak out".

Not until 21 February 2000 had anyone closely resembling a 'spokesperson for the Scottish gay community', let alone a 'gay leader', been afforded space in Scotland's media to put the case for the repeal of Section 28. Tim Hopkins who led the Equality Network wrote a column in Jack Irvine's stomping ground, *The Scottish Mirror* and pointed out: "If Clause 28 picked out any other minority and banned schools from teaching that they were acceptable, it wouldn't last five minutes".

One anonymous submission for Stonewall's *Caused by the Clause* begged: "I was disappointed that there were so few major public or political figures opposing the 'Keep the Clause' position. Where were the key icons of Scottish social and public life – or did they just not want to get dragged into it?"

A £120,000 TV advertisement for 'Keep the Clause', due to run for three weeks from Valentine's Day was stopped by broadcasting watchdogs, the Broadcast Advertising Clearance Centre, after finding it too political. With shrieks of "PARENT POWER", the *Record* warned they would now take "the Keep the Clause battle to the streets of Scotland". In a sense, that is precisely what happened.

Full-sized black billboard posters with blood-red letters spelling out the words: KEEP THE CLAUSE quickly appeared all over Scotland in what was claimed to be the biggest advertising campaign in Scottish history. A friend of the Souters, mother of two, Ruth Clarkson from Perthshire was just one of six people used in the new billboards. She was pictured with the quote: "This Government doesn't care what we parents think". She told the *Record* her friends "didn't see me as the type of person who would get involved in something like this. I've got loads of friends who are gay and lesbian. I'm not homophobic..." Another "mother of two", Marie Fraser from Inverness was quoted on a similar huge billboard: "My son could be asked to take part in homosexual role playing in school. That horrifies me". A "grandmother of three", Sheena Grant of Inverness, looking down from her poster said: "Clause 28 protects my grandchildren, I don't believe guidelines will". Another "mother of two", Flora Junor from Milngavie, was quoted saying: "I believe in discussing homosexuality in schools, but scrapping Clause 28 is a step too far". As attacks on gays increased, homophobia became more vocal. In Scottish school playgrounds and amongst children, the catchphrase, "Keep the Clause" ceded other forms of abuse. It was heard everywhere. Columnist and mother, Muriel Gray wrote in the *Sunday Herald*: "For the first time in my life I feel frightened and insecure in my own country. I no longer have the confidence that the lunatic fringe will stay there. I walk my children to school past nauseating posters that regardless of being scorned by the decent majority, may nevertheless have some impact that will affect our future". Gay switchboards like the one in Glasgow claimed threats of suicide had almost doubled. The *Record* juxtaposed the story of 'Keep the Clause's new poster campaign with the headline: "Fury at plan to give gays status of married couples". The Executive were planning to introduce measures that would allow a gay tenant to inherit a tenancy when their partner died and legal control over affairs should their partner suffer head injury or mental illness. A spokesman for the Catholic Church shockingly announced: "We are against laws that give an impression that a homosexual relationship is equal to that of a heterosexual married couple because that promotes the acceptability of a homosexual lifestyle".

Ben Matthews wrote to the *Scotsman* to say: "Once a week, I take an evening bus through Morningside, in Edinburgh; lately, a group of young teenagers, who are also on this route, have identified me as being gay. This results in me being surrounded by the group of them, verbally harassed, and my space being invaded in an aggressive and threatening manner... If this is their behaviour to a stranger on a bus, it is easy to imagine what life must be like for any gay student who is at school with these bullies".

John Roberts, co-ordinator at The Steve Retson Project, which was based at the time at Glasgow's Royal Infirmary, providing counselling, support, health education, safer sex information and treatment for sexually transmitted infections for gay men hit out at the posters in Stuart Brown's Report to the East of Scotland Repeal Section 28 Group. "We've seen a number of people who have come through the Project who have been forced to face their sexuality because of this 'Keep the Clause' – all those billboards, the publicity surrounding Section 28... If you're happy with your sexuality, as most of us are, it's not a problem, but if you're just coming to terms with your sexuality, this is a complete nightmare. Horrendous! You've got 16 or 17-year-olds seeing the posters on the way home from school and then they're seeing it on the news. It's just very difficult for them. And they have to confront this every single day". Roberts described a typical case: "We had one young guy come along. He had been to his GP because he was suffering from depression and it turned out that it was all about this. It was just getting too much for him. He was in Lanarkshire, and

Lanarkshire is a difficult place to be growing up gay to begin with. His doctor managed to get him to see a psychologist, for want of a better word. The psychologist asked him 'have you had sex with women yet?' He said 'no'. She said 'well that's a bit like saying you don't like chocolate cake without tasting it!' Incredible! It just didn't help him at all. The end result was the guy went on medication. He's okay now. He's done a lot of counselling with us". Roberts added: "It's on the TV every single night and if you're 16, 17 or 18-years-old and going to school – that's how old this lad was - and you're seeing billboards that basically send out a signal that says 'gay men are perverts', however tactfully they try to put it, because that's basically the underlying message: 'Being gay is bad'. It's damaging. There have been loads of cases like this. As a Project, we generally meet folk from 28 to 35-years-old, but these last three months we've seen a lot of young people coming in to speak to our counsellors. It's gone up by about 25%. It's the teenagers that are coming in. Lots of schoolkids, that's the interesting thing".

In a collection of testimonials compiled by Ali Jarvis for Stonewall, *Caused by the Clause*, a young man from the north-east of Scotland wrote: "I found the whole experience of starting each day and seeing what was essentially my life judged in certain tabloid papers to be demoralising and saddening. I didn't know who these 'Keep the Clause' campaigners were with their hatred and angry letter-writing campaigns and found myself looking with fear at everyone with whom I came into contact. Was it the lady in the shop where I bought my paper? Was it the young guy next to me on the bus? They felt like a faceless threat all around me".

In another testimonial, a young Glasgow female wrote: "Passing the billboards with Souter's campaign against repealing the clause had a severe impact on me, making me feel that somehow I had less of a right to dignity and respect than any heterosexual".

A lesbian parent wrote: "Our daughter was going away for a weekend with her youth group. The children were all meeting up at the local train station for their outward journey. There were about ten 10 – 12-year-olds and various parental figures waiting to put them on the train with their leader. On the advertising hoarding on the platform opposite was a huge 'Keep the Clause' poster, hard to ignore but we all struggled to do so. I felt awful; felt I had to justify my parental rights and even suitability. I felt awful for my partner, our daughter, the other parents and the other children in the group. Nobody said anything pertaining to the poster…"

A gay man wrote to Stonewall to say: "Living in a small village in the north-east of Scotland and never reading a newspaper, I initially felt relatively untouched by this campaign. Only seeing events in the central belt on TV I felt I was in a part of the country that was taking the moral high ground and not lowering itself into the mire. No one around me was talking about this issue. Unfortunately I was wrong and was to be left aghast when circling a major roundabout in Aberdeen. There, in glorious bigoted technicolour, was a 'Keep the Clause' billboard poster of a mother proclaiming her fears for her son at school if the clause was not kept. I suddenly found myself wondering how many people could be influenced by this propaganda and what effect it may have on the attitude of parents to gays. I felt angry that this poster might make someone hate me, and make me afraid to be open about my sexuality in the future. Some days later, while circling the same roundabout, my spirits were lifted. Somone had thrown a pot of pink paint over the poster and painted the word 'bigots' in the bottom corner".

In another contribution for *Caused by the Clause*, a gay person remembered: "Each morning I was awoken by the alarm clock and instantly sick with apprehension as almost every day there seemed to be another hate-filled comment from the 'Keep the Clause' media machine to kick off my morning. Every helpful comment from the Scottish Executive or from our own campaigning groups seemed almost life-saving and helped calm the feeling of depression and nausea I felt daily".

Ali Jarvis who had collected the personal testimonials for Stonewall's *Caused by the Clause* was concerned that the public were making decisions and taking sides based on misinformation. "As it was, the poster campaign was perceived to hinge on 'triggers' that were deliberately emotive and whilst probably stopping short of outright lies, certainly implied some things that were far from true in order to provoke maximum public 'outrage'".

The socially conservative media had already lied, misrepresented, distorted and repressed many aspects of lawful sexuality. By igniting the vile rhetoric of the religious-right and socially conservative on homosexuality, the press had fanned the flames of moral righteousness. The fires of hate were now out of control. What was absent was the sort of provisions in law against incitement to hatred already established in other European countries. Had Scotland been the Netherlands, the newspapers would have most likely at this point been covering the arrest of a few tabloid editors, religious leaders and a handful of other individuals.

Section 28 had nothing to do with the protection of children. If that were indeed the case, campaigners might have demanded the adoption of the Dutch system of sexual education which saved children from sexual ignorance and delivered a teenage pregnancy rate around six times lower than Scotland's. The Dutch also had a lower incidence of sexual diseases, and - as studies proved - youngsters actually started to have sex later. This was confirmed in a report by the United Nations agency, UNICEF which reported that the Netherlands - which also boasted one of the world's lowest abortion rates - there was a sharp reduction in unwanted teenage pregnancies caused by "the combination of a relatively inclusive society with more open attitudes towards sex and sex education, including contraception". In the US and UK, which produced some of the world's *highest* teenage pregnancy rates, "contraceptive advice and services may be formally available, but in a 'closed' atmosphere of embarrassment and secrecy". Quite apart from that, schools teaching homosexuality as 'wrong' or 'sinful' didn't show an exemplary record. In one Minnesota middle school that carried out a 'no homo' policy, there were nine suicides by gay students in just two years. A 2008 study by the Suicide Prevention Resource Centre suggested at least 30% of American gay youth attempted suicide compared to just over 7% of heterosexual youth.

Muriel Gray wrote in the *Sunday Herald:* "I'm going back more than ten years here. It was a party in London and an amused, urban home counties chap was challenging a discussion between a gathering of five Scots, including myself, concerning our lust for devolved power. 'You know what will happen, don't you?' he laughed merrily. 'You lot will just end up fighting like children, the tabloids will run the country and the churches will turn you into a new Northern Ireland'. Five voices rose to a shout of outrage and indignation. Didn't this imbecile understand anything about the realities of our country? Didn't he realise how much more civilised, tolerant and self-evidently libertarian we were? Ha! Obviously not. For your information, choked one of us haughtily, poking a finger at his chest, the churches have no more power than they do in England, and as for the tabloids, in comparison to the disgusting, evil English Sun, the Daily Record is a model of populist decency. I remember nodding proudly at that one, before moving huffily back to the free bar and some tiny pastry things with bacon. The fact that the chap being shouted at was Peter Mandelson is only of mild historical interest".

The *Daily Record* resorted to begging in its editorial of 19 February 2000 to back the "three heavyweight" Scottish ministers pressing for statutory guidelines. The tabloid "understood" they were the Enterprise Minister Henry McLeish, Finance Minister Jack McConnell and Parliamentary Minister Tom McCabe who regularly attended Catholic mass. When MSP Malcolm Chisholm stood up to criticise the cabinet ministers for leading the apparent u-turn over Section 28, he was greeted with 'whooping cheers' from other MSPs. Wendy Alexander had sat quietly while the split had emerged at a cabinet meeting at Bute House on Tuesday, 15 February. The *Record* held out a withered olive branch: "It would reinforce the First Minister's reputation as a caring and humane leader in tune with the soul of Scotland. It would allow the ambitious Wendy a chance to repair some of the damage this affair has done to her promising career... But let us be clear: Scottish parents will not accept a fudge. At the very least the legal guidelines MUST make it clear that schools cannot present homosexuality as a viable alternative to traditional, heterosexual family life. That is NOT negotiable". The Executive found itself under intense pressure. The results of the SSBA's survey - not of just its own 1,700 members, but all 2,400 boards in Scotland - was thought to favour keeping the clause and North Lanarkshire Council, a Labour heartland, had also voted in favour of keeping the clause, at least until there were better safeguards. Along with letters already sent to Scotland's head teachers, Education Minister Sam Galbraith was now considering another letter of reassurance to every parent in Scotland. The *Scottish Express* began to sound like the *Record* addressing the "finger-wagging school of government", suggesting: "It's never too late to listen, First Minister... The Executive believed they could dump the law banning the promotion of homosexuality in schools with impunity. We told them this could not be achieved... Donald Dewar should take more notice of the three realists in his ministerial team, rather than listen to the shrill political correctness issuing from a few zealots". Alan Cochrane, in Scottish editions of the *Daily Telegraph* advised: "The simplest course for the Executive would be to get rid of the offending piece of legislation and bring in guidelines to more or less do the same thing, that is ban the promotion of homosexuality".

The *Record* went to the trouble of organising another survey by Scottish Opinions Limited who interviewed 576 adults from Ayr by phone and found almost half – 42 per cent – of potential voters in the forthcoming by-election said Section 28 was going to affect where they put their cross. With the public presumably following their opinions, the tabloid warned: "It is not too late". And it wasn't too late for the SNP's Alex Salmond who seized the opportunity ahead of the Ayr by-election and Labour Ministers leaking news of a split in their ranks, to suggest for the first time that he wanted statutory guidelines to replace Section 28. (Considering he led the nationalist party and Scotland was in the unique position of having no national curriculum or statutory guidelines, many thought the SNP leader should have been *defending* that position, not selling it down the river. This wasn't the first time the SNP would appease its religious supporters and let Scotland down on issues that went to the very heart of nationalism. Whilst the SNP made loud noises about its right to make legislation for Scotland, equalising the age of consent was also too much of a hot potato. In "very much a one-off", Alex Salmond begged Westminster to do it for them, even though it was a devolved issue and the Scottish Executive was entitled to do it!)

During 'Scottish Questions' in the House of Commons on 23 February, English Tory MP Desmond Swain claimed that the Section 28 row north of the border only supported the claim by US televangelist Pat Robertson, that Scotland was a "dark land" over-run by homosexuals. Columnist Ron Ferguson in the *Herald* warned: "Pat Robertson is alive and well and wearing a kilt in what he calls our 'dark land'." But a crack had appeared in the wall. Sensing a shift after the parliament's "arrogant decision" to repeal Section 28, the *Record* triumphantly announced a "CAVE-IN" on its front page. Donald Dewar was apparently throwing his weight behind "plans to give parents legal powers to stop gay sex lessons in Scots schools". Compromising Scotland's position of having non-statutory guidelines, a new legally binding clause was going to be added to the Ethical Standards in Public Life Bill. The *Scottish Mail* correctly forecast: "The war is far from over". There was a crisis in the cabinet over the wording. After three days the sub-committee still couldn't come up with a form of wording to suite both sides of the divide. Amidst threats of resignations and a potential split in the Labour/Liberal Democrat coalition, it was clear that collective responsibility could not be relied upon. The issue of gay sexuality was effectively threatening to tear apart devolution in Scotland. The *Scottish Mail* accused the Lib-Dems of "sabotage". The *Record* tore into MSP Susan Deacon for "leading a Lib-Dem revolt over Section 28". Their editorial spat: "We will not be fobbed off with a fudge or some feel-good phrases talking about happy families and stable relationships. We fail to see why Susan Deacon should be allowed such influence since her brief is health, not education or local government. We do not know what kind of politically-correct world she lives in, but it is well-known that she has not bothered with marriage as her own family arrangement... She only made it as a Labour candidate on appeal and, on her performance so far, she would be no great loss... (The Liberal Democrats) like Susan Deacon, are out of touch. They should be ignored – just as they tried to ignore the Scottish people". Journalist Ron MacKenna's report was just as nasty. "It is Deacon's opposition that is causing the biggest problem. She has attacked her colleagues for even considering giving in to public opinion. The rookie minister... has struggled badly and has blundered regularly. She was suspected of leaking details from last week's crunch cabinet meeting... Her relationship with BBC political producer John Boothman has also caused eyebrows to be raised..."

Ministers who had backed repeal of Section 28 through thick and thin were understandably upset to find the goalposts being moved the moment their back was turned. It wasn't just the form of words that was holding up publication of the Bill containing repeal of Section 28. The presiding officer, Lord Steel had yet to sign a certificate of legislative competence. His office claimed that he had done it four days before. The *Scotsman* sighed: "It is as well that Scotland's minorities do not depend entirely on the Scottish executive for their defence".

RELIGIOUS FASCISM

The *Scottish Express's* editorial cried indignantly: "...(Donald Dewar) refuses to say exactly what he means by a 'stable family life'. Is he talking only about the traditional, married family, or not...? We predicted such a shambles at the very beginning. It gives us no satisfaction to say we were right".

On Thursday, 24 February, the same day Jack Irvine announced he was giving up his weekly column in the *Scottish Mirror* to concentrate on 'Keep the Clause', there were extraordinary scenes at Holyrood as Tom McCabe moved round the Chamber speaking to his own Labour backbenchers and Lib-Dem MSPs, clinching a deal that would accept Donald Dewar's replacement clause in the Bill on "the value of stable family life". The First Minister's timetable was shifted around before issuing an emergency statement on the matter. After he had made it, condemnation from the Catholic Church was swift. Cardinal Winning gasped: "Stable family life is not defined and therefore could be interpreted to include homosexual or lesbian domestic arrangements". Gerald Warner in *Scotland on Sunday* went one step further, announcing the "formal ending of democracy in Scotland". Journalists like Alf Young in the *Herald*, waiting for the media onslaught, warned: "It is time the gauleiters of Anderston Quay" (where the *Record's* offices were based in Glasgow), "who printed their presumptuous ultimatum over the page from 'Amanda grins and bares it' and opposite 'Love Cheat Husband Has A Dram Cheek Too', were told they are not the custodians of Scotland's morals, nor the democratically-accountable arbiters of what should – or should not – be enshrined in law. It's time the Daily Record was summarily disabused of the notion that it either runs the Labour Party or dictates Scottish public opinion". They weren't listening. The *Record's* front page bawled: "DEWAR BOTTLES OUT ON GAY SEX DEAL". The *Scottish Sun* cried: "INSULT" and the *Scottish Mail* shrieked: "NO DEAL". The *Record* attacked Donald Dewar and asked: "Is he really the man for the job?" The capacious, ranting editorial accused him of allowing "the politically-correct amateurs he's foolishly appointed to his cabinet..." including the "fanatical" Susan Deacon and "the pro-gay commissars in his Executive crucial days to rally their forces and prevent any meaningful climbdown". Brian Souter told the *Record*: "We have to ask ourselves, who have the Government been listening to – gay pressure groups or Scottish

Praise be the Lords

families?" Jack Irvine dismissed the Bill as "clearly written to placate the militant gay rights lobby".

As Donald Dewar toured the Ayr constituency in preparation for the by-election, a "source" told the *Record:* "Donald's canvassing consisted of him being chased up closes by old ladies furious at what he was trying to do with Clause 28. He got the picture".

As the by-election in Ayrshire approached, the *Ayrshire Post's* front page reported the plight of Nicola Ferguson, a local resident who had graffiti sprayed over her home which spelled out the words 'lesbians' and 'whorehouse'.

In the *Record* there were pictures of a man sticking up a thumb, saluting a woman collecting signatures for 'Keep the Clause' and another of a woman, smiling as she signed the petition on the streets of the west coast town of Ayr. The *Scottish Sun* pictured crying two-year-old baby Logan Hunter, in his pram holding up a 'Keep the Clause' leaflet, and advised that teaching schoolkids that "two gay parents are as good as a married mum and dad is an insult to every mum and dad in Scotland". The *Daily Mail* included a report by Daniel Jeffreys on a new biography by Tom King of music chief David Geffen, called *The Operator.* Entitled "The Rise of the Velvet Mafia" Jeffreys' feature put a spin on Hollywood's "ugly secrets". The article portrayed one of the films produced in Geffen's studios, *American Beauty*, "as a caustic and dark attack on heterosexual family life". Jeffreys declared: "Last year's Oscars had Gods And Monsters with Ian McKellen and Brendan Fraser, which pushed the notion that gay soldiers are the truest heroes in battle". He remarked that Geffen's parties at Fire Island, a gay resort in the state of New York, were a "place the Velvet Mafia meet to indulge in extraordinary bacchanals". He recalled a time when "they had little power in the movie business and not even a fraction of the political clout they have today" and added how the book "allegedly reveals that Geffen and his fellow gays were determined to get their revenge on the heterosexual establishment..." While Jeffreys' echoed the sort of anti-Semitic remarks that once claimed Jews controlled the movies, they didn't deter Pope Benedict XVI from signing up to Geffen's label to do a recording in 2009.

By Saturday, 26 February, police were called in to investigate a gay men's health website after a complaint "from a member of the public". English Tory MP Nick Johnston demonstrated his outrage on the pages of Scottish editions of the *Daily Telegraph:* "If this was a genuine site to educate people about the risks of HIV I would welcome it, but it is not. This site does raise questions with the planned repeal of Section 28, about the availability of this sort of material in the classroom". Johnston had contacted Scottish Lord Advocate; Colin Boyd QC who advised him it was a matter for the police.

Glasgow's Strathclyde Lesbian and Gay Switchboard received approximately 6,000 calls in 1999 and noted that during that year the number of calls had risen by 24%. Their co-ordinator said in the Report to the East of Scotland Repeal Section 28 Group: "This increase of 24% is not normal. It's not just people getting 'the winter blues', or part of any normal seasonal increase. Many callers are specifically mentioning the (Keep the Clause) poster campaign". Without releasing it directly to the press, Glasgow's Strathclyde Lesbian and Gay Switchboard sent a statement to MSPs on the call logs and evaluation of caller statistics they had assessed for the three months to February 2000. They added: "Many callers are expressing fear and intimidation regarding the level of the media reporting in connection with the repeal of Section 28 (Section 2a) and in particular with the advertising campaign being run by the Keep the Clause organisation. In many cases callers are expressing feelings of increased isolation and exclusion from mainstream society. Callers are thinking carefully before coming out to family, friends and work colleagues given the reactions to the current debate. Some callers are regretting having 'come out'. Some callers express thoughts of suicide".

The Grampian Lesbian, Gay and Bisexual Switchboard which covered the Highlands noted a similar increase since the campaign had started but wouldn't at first be drawn on the cause.

An outreach worker for Reachout Highland, engaged in offering safer sex advice and distributing condoms in areas where men were meeting men, recounted a potentially dangerous incident in the Report to the East of Scotland Repeal Section 28 Group. "We were being verbally abused by a crowd of people, men and women. We felt that it was going to escalate. To avoid a very, very nasty situation we had to leave very quickly. It was a homophobic incident – connected to the work we were doing and us being gay men". His boss Jacqui Brown added: "We've been doing outreach work for the last two years and this is the first time that such abuse has escalated to the level that staff had felt unsafe, so unsafe that they couldn't do their work. I can't help feeling it's all to do with the Keep the Clause campaign".

The following day there was an incident in Inverness when two gay teenagers were attacked. A man in his 40s had grabbed one of them by the crotch; then punched him in the throat. The Reachout Highland outreach worker said in the Report to the East of Scotland Repeal Section 28 Group: "The lads were really shaken up when they came into our office. It's a very serious incident and really bizarre that myself and another worker should have an incident and then, all of a sudden, there's another one the next day".

By Sunday, 27 February 2000, Cardinal Winning was writing for the *Scottish Mail on Sunday* praising the "silent majority... standing up for traditional values" against the "collective deafness" of MSPs. Winning preached: "The Church, realising how essential to children is the stable union for life between a man and a woman, has made it one of the events in human living which can expect special and continuous help from Jesus Christ... All of a sudden people are finding the courage to stand up for traditional values. The silent majority are finding their voice, and that gives me grounds of hope that Christian values are still strong among our fellow Scots..."

At this time, on 7 March, across the Atlantic, the state of California was preparing to vote in support of Proposition 22, an initiative to ensure no-one would recognise a gay civil union, led by a coalition of religionists and part-funded by the Catholic Church to the tune of $350,000. The $10m campaign was backed by TV advertising and headed by Senator 'Pete' Knight. They succeeded in getting their proposition into state law. On the same day, Cardinal Winning's lecture in London was interrupted by a peaceful protest organised by Outrage! The Cardinal's theme for the 12th annual Cobb Memorial Lecture was social justice, respect and solidarity and was held in St Mary's Catholic Church Hall in Croydon, South London. Charles Cobb was a First World War conscientious objector. Twenty minutes into Winning's lecture, extolling the importance of respecting other people, Peter Tatchell stood up and asked: "Why don't you respect gay people? Why do you oppose human rights?" The Cardinal ignored him, trying to continue while six members of Outrage! walked onto the platform holding placards. One member was arrested but later released without charge. Peter Tatchell said later: "Inviting the Cardinal to give this lecture is an insult to the memory of Charles Cobb. Whereas Cobb took a stand against injustice, Cardinal Winning endorses the injustice of anti-gay discrimination". The *Record* reported how Outrage! had "invaded the platform" and a spokesman for Cardinal Winning emphasised how the demo had interrupted the Cardinal's talk on opposing the death penalty and Third World debt.

In the early hours of Sunday morning, 5 March, police charged four individuals - three male youths of 18, 17 and 16 and a 15-year-old girl - for an attack on a 33-year-old gay student at Edinburgh's Royal Terrace. The student had been alarmed by the seven-strong gang's homophobic comments and attempted to leave the area before he was punched and kicked to the ground. He managed to pick himself up and get into the middle of the Royal Terrace. Three cars passed without stopping. He managed to call a girlfriend who, in turn, alerted the police in time for them to track down the gang who had congregated up on Calton Terrace Brae. Bob Sutherland of the LGBT Community Safety Forum said: "I've no idea exactly what they (the accused) said to the police, but what the police said to me, quite clearly, was they believed the attack was motivated by the publicity over Clause 28".

That day, the Sunday papers had the results of the Scottish School Boards' Association's consultation with their boards. Details had already landed on the desks of pro-Section 28 papers a week before. Alan Smith had told *Scotland on Sunday* then: "This shows the leadership of the SSBA were right to oppose the Scottish Executive's proposed repeal of Section 28". And in the *Scottish Mail* he said: "This is the voice of parents. This sends out the message to Ministers – why are you touching this issue? Why are you tinkering with this law at all?" A week later and *Scotland on Sunday* reported: "Almost 90% of the 777 school boards which responded... voted either to 'Keep the Clause' altogether, or to keep it until they had consulted on Scottish Executive guidelines to replace it". The *Record* headlined: "PARENT POLL SHOWS HUGE SUPPORT TO KEEP CLAUSE". But did it? The SSBA posed three choices: (1) Section 28 should be repealed; (2) Section 28 should remain in place until the Scottish Executive have fully and formally consulted upon and agreed revised guidelines; (3) Section 28 should not be repealed. There was also advice that school boards should consult as widely as possible with the parents they were supposed to represent. In most cases, there was insufficient time. The *Sunday Herald* discovered that out of the 2,400 ballot forms sent out, only a third of the school boards had responded. Only 46 per cent of these supported unqualified retention of Section 28. A further 40 per cent supported repeal if replacement guidelines were consulted upon and agreed, and 11.5 per cent supported unqualified repeal. Donald Dewar expressed no objection to sensible safeguards. Tim Hopkins of the Equality Network was able to explain in the *Herald:* "The SSBA did everything they could to produce a result opposing repeal of Section 28. Instead, 51.5% of the school boards that responded support the Executive's position. The Equality Network wrote to the SSBA on January 23 to request a meeting to discuss the issues surrounding appeal. The SSBA have not even done us the courtesy of a reply. That is how open-minded they are on Section 28. The information on Section 28 that the SSBA sent to school boards was far from balanced, and was chosen to encourage responses opposing repeal. It failed".

From inside the Scottish School Boards' Association there emerged a power struggle. The *Scottish Mail's* Ian Smith labelled the SSBA ringleaders "a small but powerful pro-repeal faction" within the Board's executive. Getting rather tired of Alan Smith's and Ann Hill's clumsy efforts at PR, the executive made a decision that if anyone was going to speak to the press in future; it would (and should) be the chairman, David Hutchison. Alan Smith was asked to resign. The *Record* was livid! Turning on Hutchison, Jack Irvine shrieked at the *Record:* "*He* must resign!" Reporter Pete Richardson cuttingly wrote: "The new mouthpiece for the SSBA has rejected claims he has gagged vociferous opponents and is pushing for a weaker policy". When the *Record* suggested the vote was an overwhelming one in favour of keeping the clause, Mr Hutchison retorted: 'Overwhelming is going a bit far I think'."

The front page of the *Scottish Mail* on 7 March revealed "MOSLEMS' GAY LAW BOYCOTT" after "religious leaders threaten schools exodus over Section 28 repeal" in a report by Hamish Macdonell. Mazhar Malik, convener of the education committee of the UK Islamic Mission told the Scottish parliament's equal opportunities committee, as it took evidence, that Donald Dewar "was destroying Scottish society", and Moslems "would insist on the creation of their own schools". The *Mail's* editorial highlighted the loss of votes. "This is not a fit of pique, but a boycott that is likely to persist permanently". The Catholic Church joined them with a strongly worded written submission declaring that the mention of 'the value of stable family life' in the Bill replacing Section 28 was actually worse than repeal of Section 28 itself! Ann Allen leapt in with Gordon Macdonald of Christian Action Research and Education (CARE) and Mr Jeremy Balfour of the Evangelical Alliance to protest that Moslems were not "some weird right-wing fundamentalist group".

Amongst the religionists opposing repeal of Section 28 in Scotland was a breakaway branch of the Free Church of Scotland, called the Free Church of Scotland (Continuing). 63-year-old minister, Maurice Roberts from Inverness had been working with hard-line US preacher Joel Beeke and changed their rules to welcome followers of Theonomy into their church. The cult believed adulterers, gays and unruly children should be publicly stoned to death. The way the newspapers had it, only the Episcopal Church, the Quakers and two ministers from the Church of Scotland's Education Committee appeared to publicly back the Scottish Executive's plan for repeal.

Church of Scotland homophobia was once again highlighted a year later in the summer of 2001 in a survey of fifty ministers, worshippers and dozens of church youth workers carried out by the Kirk's National Youth Advisor, Steve Mallon. An astonishing 75 per cent of ministers stated their disapproval of gays. Mallon admitted: "The Church is incapable of welcoming people who are divorced or separated, as well as those who are gay". Again, in 2002, it was whispered that Margaret Ferguson lost out on the opportunity of breaking into the ranks of one Scotland's top boys' clubs and becoming the Church of Scotland's first female Moderator after she conducted a private ceremony and blessed a lesbian couple's long-term relationship.

To the fury of 'Keep the Clause' campaigners, most trade unions pledged support for the *repeal* of Section 28. The *Daily Mail* however, was eager to counter this setback with: "Workers back gay law". The *Record* added, "Dewar is hit by new poll blow... UNION MEMBERS TELL LABOUR: KEEP CLAUSE 28". Pollsters Progressive Partnership, commissioned by Brian

Praise be the Lords

Souter's 'Keep the Clause', sampled 518 trade union members between 18 February and 1 March. 60 per cent disagreed with the repeal of Section 28. In addition, 'Keep the Clause' commissioned a poll in Prime Minister Tony Blair's constituency of Sedgefield. 718 people over the age of 18 were asked if they supported or opposed the repeal of Section 28. They were asked at the same time: "To what extent do you support or oppose local authorities being permitted to promote the teaching in schools of homosexuality as acceptable?" The System Three poll found 71 per cent in favour of keeping Section 28 and nine per cent in favour of 'gay lessons'. Cardinal Winning, Baroness Young and Colin Hart of the Christian Institute were all on call to register their satisfaction with this result.

The *Daily Record* never tired of finding new ways of maligning the First Minister, Donald Dewar. Pictured through a telephoto lens and straining to hear through his headphones during a parliamentary debate, he was pictured next to an ageing cartoon character called Geri the Cleaner from Disney's *Toy Story 2*. Readers were expected to appreciate the similarities.

Avoiding the impending by-election in Ayr, Prime Minister Tony Blair arrived in Scotland and addressed the Scottish Labour conference in Edinburgh on 10 March. Cabinet Minister Mo Mowlam headed for the seaside town of Ayr in his place, only to be met by a battalion of Brian Souter's huge billboards. One featured Labour's Wendy Alexander with her fingers in her ears and the words: "THE LISTENING GOVERNMENT ISN'T LISTENING... 66% of parents voted in favour of keeping the clause". After Mowlam attacked Souter for spreading misleading propaganda, the *Scottish Mail* promptly turned on her: "Mowlam fans flames of gay law campaign". The *Record* smugly declared: "...It's ludicrous to suggest that a few Keep the Clause posters and leaflets in Ayr will materially affect the outcome of the election. If Labour lose it will be because of their arrogant refusal to listen to the silent majority". It was more than a few. The town was *saturated* with massive billboards and leaflets promoting the 'Keep the Clause' campaign.

Contributing to Stonewall's *Caused by the Clause*, a collection of personal testimonials, a woman wrote a touching testimonial: "I had been away. I was so pleased to touch down at Prestwick Airport and head on home to Ayrshire. On the train people chatted and interacted with each other, so different from

215

London. It was a huge relief to be back. But then on the train, each face, one by one, became hidden by newspapers and instead of faces I was confronted by an array of Scottish tabloid newspaper headlines demanding that Labour must 'listen to parents', 'protect our children' and presenting gays as a threat to young people. I was literally boxed into my seat by these newspapers. It sounds daft but I ended up staring out of the widow, weeping. It was such a shock to be confronted with this all at once, it felt utterly alienating. I am so proud of Scotland, but it no longer feels like home in quite the same way. I feel betrayed that our politicians would not take a strong and decisive stand against the bigots. Sometimes it is hard to see a future for myself here anymore".

Delivering his first speech to the Scottish Parliament, Tony Blair set aside prepared text to spontaneously attack the "corrosive cynicism" of sections of the Scottish media and the 'Keep the Clause' campaign, labelling it "scaremongering nonsense... Drugs are the real threat to our children; not the phoney threat plastered all over those Clause 28 posters. I've never seen anything more astonishing." Brian Souter responded by suggesting 180 English schools had already bought the Avon teaching pack, encouraging homosexual role-playing and teenagers to experiment with their sexuality. Tony Blair referred to Souter's poster campaign as "some of the most astonishing propaganda I have ever seen in my life" and defended his First Minister saying Donald Dewar was "the most decent man I know in politics. Too decent, perhaps, for some commentators, who don't come up to his kneecaps in stature of integrity". The *Scottish Mirror* editorial was filled with praise for Blair's performance. "Donald stutters, Tony states. Donald dithers, Tony acts. Donald ducks, Tony stands his ground to be counted". The *Scottish Express* front-page led with: "SOUTER'S GAY LAW 'LIES' TO PARENTS". Brian Souter was reported saying: "I am quite angry that Tony Blair should come to Scotland and lecture Scottish parents in this way. We don't want lectures in Islington New Labour morality", before adding: "A lot of local authorities are driven by political correctness".

Responding to Tony Blair's attack on the press, Tom Brown wrote smugly in the *Record*: "Blair went out of his way to have a moan about journalists who displayed their passion to see the

Praise be the Lords

Parliament established and are 'now appearing to show an equal passion for knocking it down'. I plead guilty – and proud of it".

Tony Blair delivered a morale-boosting speech at the Scottish New Labour Party conference in Edinburgh, a series of uncompromising interviews and a Party broadcast which was supposed to show him shoulder-to-shoulder with his First Minister Donald Dewar and Scottish Secretary John Reid. At the conference he by-passed the press lunch table on his way to the podium before turning on them to say: "They cover something for four weeks and then accuse the politicians of being obsessed with it". Deeply offended by the 'Keep the Clause' billboards and their trailer-advertisments circling the parliament and MPs and MSPs wherever they went, he mounted the podium and confessed: "I've never seen anything more extraordinary. No wonder parents are concerned. They're told we're going to make kids have homosexual role-playing and gay sex education. And it's all Donald who is doing it, and refusing to listen. What utter nonsense. No child is going to be given gay sex lessons in school. Not under this Government. Not now. Not ever. That poster campaign has no proper place in serious political debate. We have not had Section 28 in English schools for six years". This was a point not carried by newspapers campaigning for its retention, but remained a fact. Most schools in England and Wales were no longer under local authority control and therefore outside the constraints of Section 28. Brian Souter again told Scottish Television: "I am quite angry that Tony Blair should come to Scotland and lecture Scottish parents this way". The *Herald* congratulated Blair on his keynote conference speech. "BRAVO, Mr Blair... To go on the offensive and nail the banal lie that repeal would lead to 'gay sex lessons' in Scottish schools". The *Scottish Daily Mail* accused Blair of being "cut off from the real world" and talking "poppycock". In an extraordinary editorial, the paper implored: "The Mail passionately believes that gays should be treated with tolerance and dignity. But we believe the majority have rights too..." They went on to report how a 'Keep the Clause' advertisement - depicting Donald Dewar, Wendy Alexander, Susan Deacon, Sam Galbraith and Jim Wallace in a spoof police line-up under the heading "WANTED: For failing our children" - had been "banned" in a magazine. The advertisement, appearing in *Holyrood*, had not been banned at all, as was revealed in the small print: the magazine had applied for a stall at the Labour Party conference and had to be refused after filing a late application.

Contributing to Stonewall's testimonials, a bemused gay female asked: "How on earth did the 'Keep the Clause' campaign get permission to display those posters? Such blatant attempts to promote fear and hatred should surely be illegal".

The Advertising Standards Authority (ASA) insisted there were no grounds for investigation under the British Codes of Advertising and Sales Promotion of the 'Keep the Clause' billboards plastered across the length and breadth of Scotland. From their offices in London, the ASA claimed the billboards were "unlikely to cause serious or widespread offence". Although confined to Scotland, 'Keep the Clause's campaign resulted in a total of 88 complaints to the ASA with the campaign reaching the eighth position in their top ten most offensive campaigns of 2000. (That compared with 23 complaints in 2008 against a TV advert for a hair-styling product using the words "thy will be done". The ASA ruled that it was offensive to Christians and that the advertisement should not be shown again). Compliance with the codes was judged on the content, medium, audience, product and prevailing standards of decency. Layla Wood, for the ASA claimed "complaints made under the codes' taste and decency provisions present the Authority with a special difficulty, if only because what appears decent to one reader may offend another deeply. Moreover, it is not the Authority's intention to act as censor". Three questions were posed, reaching the conclusion that allowed 'Keep the Clause' to display their posters throughout Scotland. "Will the advertisement offend the majority of people who see it; will it so deeply offend a minority that it is reasonable for their interests to prevail against the undoubted liberty of the advertiser to free expression; should the unoffended majority be prevented from hearing what the advertiser wishes to say?" The ASA claimed they "considered" the clauses in their codes that say: "Advertising should contain nothing that is likely to cause serious or widespread offence". They also stated: *"Particular care* (my italics) should be taken to avoid causing offence on the grounds of race, religion, sex, sexual orientation or disability". One of their Codes stated that advertisements might be distasteful without necessarily conflicting with this and urged advertisers to "consider public sensitivities before using potentially offensive material... The fact that a particular product

Praise be the Lords

is offensive to some people is not sufficient grounds for objecting to an advertisement for it". In poorer towns, the posters were particularly abundant, yet the ASA noted: "Advertisers should not exploit the credulity, lack of knowledge or inexperience of consumers". And on truthfulness: "No advertisement should mislead by inaccuracy, ambiguity, exaggeration, omission or otherwise". Keeping in mind the safety of gay kids in schools, their advice stated: "Advertisements should not show or encourage unsafe practices except in the context of promoting safety. Particular care should be taken with advertisements addressed to or depicting children and young people... Advertisements and promotions addressed to or featuring children should contain nothing that is likely to result in their physical, mental or moral harm".

Souter's posters had indeed caused widespread offense. In Scottish towns and cities many were defaced. An indignant Michael Naughton wrote to the *Herald*: "Here in Aberdeen there has been widespread defacing of pro-retention billboards with spray-painted obscenities..." A website was even set up entirely devoted to showing defaced 'Keep the Clause' billboards the length and breadth of Scotland.

In Stonewall's collection of personal testimonials, *Caused by the Clause*, a 41-year-old man from Glasgow wrote: "It made me realise how Nazi Germany came about... I kept thinking, 'this can't be happening; this is just so crazy'. One rainy night I stopped my car beside a billboard and ripped down a Keep the Clause poster. It made me feel great".

An angry Alison Borthwick from Falkirk used the *Herald* to hit back at complaints made by 'Keep the Clause' over the defacement of their posters: "Unlike the orchestrated, massively financed efforts of those wanting Scotland to employ discrimination, the tearing down and defacing of these adverts has been a spontaneous and unco-ordinated reaction. In Glasgow, a mother-and-toddler group removed those near their premises. A group of straight men with a ladder painted 'Lies' on one to the resounding applause of passers-by. Two brothers were applauded by bystanders for throwing paint-filled balloons at another in Ibrox car-park. All in broad daylight. In every town in Scotland, from Edinburgh to Inverness, Stirling to Ayr, etc, the stories are the same. None of the offending posters remain in Falkirk despite the anti-Government stance of the 'Labour' council. The anger of this majority of the public has gone mostly unreported..." And indeed it had.

Neil D Fletcher from Aberdeen wrote in the same paper expressing his concern for young gays: "I can only despair at what must be going through the minds of such young people today, when they look up at one of Mr Souter's billboards, or are told by Cardinal Winning they are perverts".

This would not be the first time the ASA would rule in favour of religionists. In 2006, an advertisement produced by the Gay Police Association (GPA) depicting a copy of the Bible beside a pool of blood was printed in the *Independent* newspaper accompanied by the slogan: "In the name of the father". The copy read that "in the last 12 months, the Gay Police Association has recorded a 74% increase in homophobic incidents, where the sole or primary motivating factor was the religious belief of the perpetrator". The ad provoked outrage amongst some Christian groups who claimed it singled them out as responsible for the increase in hate crimes. Along with Operation Christian Voice's Reverend George Hargreaves, the Lawyers' Christian Fellowship also registered a complaint, providing e-mail addresses and telephone numbers of police officers dealing with the case in an attempt to orchestrate a reaction from fellow Christians. Amongst the 553 formal complaints were bodies such as the Evangelical Alliance, Christian Watch, the Trinitarian Bible Society, The Fellowship of Independent Evangelical Churches, the Bible Theology Ministries and Conservative MP Ann Widdecombe who had converted to Roman Catholicism in 1993. Members of the GPA received death threats, e-mails which began: "Be on notice that your days left on this earth are limited". Quoting part of the postcode of chairman Paul Cahill's address, the message finished: "Homosexuals everywhere will tremble at this powerful message and repent of their perverted lives". Cahill claimed the theats only endorsed the GPA's message. The ASA ruled that the GPA had breached codes covering truthfulness, accuracy and offence in failing to back up its figures of an increase in faith crimes and implying that Christians were driven by religious motives to hate and abuse homosexuals.

In 2010, the ASA banned an advert for Antonio Federici Gelato Italiano desserts depicting two male priests about to kiss with the tag-line: "We believe in salivation". This followed widely reported stories of Vatican priests being filmed entering gay bars in Rome. After just six complaints the ASA ruled the ad distasteful for mocking the beliefs of those of religious faith, particularly Catholics.

The ASA's cautious conservatism would once again find itself in opposition to a campaign put out by a gay agency, however, there was a breakthrough when, after a lengthy battle, the gay men's health charity, Gay Men Fighting AIDs (GMFA) won a ruling to lift a ban on health promotion adverts containing words the ASA found offensive or obscene. The *Pink Paper* had received an anonymous complaint over an ad from a campaign run by GMFA called Relation Tips which featured the slogan: "We'd rather fuck than watch TV". The ASA ruled against it, yet the *Pink Paper* defied the ban in the interests of gay men's health and continued to run the ad. Eventually, with the aid of research, the ASA were persuaded that the frank language was useful and relevant in communicating an important message to gay men in getting a safer sex message across and overturned their former ruling.

It seemed astonishing that in one of Scotland's most marginal constituencies with a Labour majority of just 25 over the Tories, there would have to be a by-election at this time. Claiming he was bored with sitting on the government backbenches, tired of travelling to and fro from Edinburgh and wanting to devote more time to his family, just over six months into his job as MP, Ian Welsh announced he was resigning. In his council constituency of Prestwick St Nicholas, Welsh had been closely involved in the regeneration of Prestwick airport, once owned by Brian Souter. (Welsh went on to take up the post of chief executive and director of Kilmarnock Football Club). It was to be the Labour Government's first by-election since they had came to power. As preparations got underway, 'Keep the Clause' attempted to hire every billboard site in the town. Opening the *Ayshire Post* there would be three 'Keep the Clause' advertisements hammering home their message. A full page in the familiar red on black housestyle advised: "On Thursday 16th March your vote can help protect our children". One advertisement begged readers to "use your vote wisely", another simply read: "Vote for common sense". A meeting was held at the Quality Hotel in Burns Statue Square in Ayr inviting residents of the town to "hear the facts" and "listen to the truth". Unofficial posters were also posted up around the town in support of 'Keep the Clause' warning: "A vote for Labour is a vote for sodomy". While Brian Souter was on his spending spree in Ayr, 665 employees of his Stagecoach bus company held a one-day strike to protest over a disputed pay deal imposed on them and marched through the town.

Keeping the Clause wasn't the only Christian conflict played out in Ayrshire at this time. During the run-up to the election the *Ayrshire Post* reported a scuffle between 39-year-old Kenneth McCarvel and 53-year-old Carol McCann, a 'born-again' member of the evangelical New Life Church in Prestwick. Kenneth McCarvel claimed Carol McCann had continually put pressure on him to leave his church and join hers while giving him the run-around when he tried to get back his black, tasselled bikers' jacket he wanted for a forthcoming trip to Amsterdam. Mrs McCann said Mr McCarvel had made a sexually explicit comment to her on the phone and turned up in a taxi where he had to be restrained in a scuffle with two other men. She told the court McCarvel had shouted at one of the men: "You are dead meat! You are a dead man walking!" During the evidence, Mrs McCann said Mr McCarvel had told her God had talked to him when he visited Malta. Sheriff Neil Gow was unimpressed and fined him £125 for breach of the peace.

Angus Macleod penned a portrait of Ayr for the *Scottish Express:* "It is a long time since it was the smart holiday destination of Glasgow's wealthy merchant class, the days when well-bred ladies twirled parasols and men fretted over the cut of their dove-grey suits. Ayr still has the unmistakable whiff of a faded holiday resort, with its own theatre, crazy golf and candy floss stalls, wall-to-wall B&Bs and nursing homes... And everywhere there are images of Burns. The Naysmith portrait stares from packets of oatcakes, haggis, beer glasses, egg timers, tea towels and the most popular pub in town for tourists is the Tam O'Shanter. If there is such a place as Middle Scotland, then this is it".

Gerald Warner had other ideas in the *Scottish Mail:* "Ayr is a long way removed from the world of New Labour. It is a different planet from the Edinburgh bars and clubs frequented by the beneficiaries of repeal of Section 28. Ayr is no backwater; it is as modern in outlook as anywhere else in the country, but it still respects traditional values".

Praise be the Lords

Defending a majority of only 25 ahead of the Conservatives, the Labour candidate, Rita Miller, was presumed by many to be heading for a defeat, and not entirely because of Section 28. The closure of Carrick Street Halls, a community centre used by hundreds of elderly folk had been announced 13 days before polling day. The closure saved South Ayrshire Council £200,000 in running costs and paved the way for developers to build a shopping extension. Rita Miller was convener of the council's social services committee. Also confirmed a week before polling day was £5 millon of budget cuts in South Ayshire along with an above average rise in council tax. The textiles company Miller's husband used to run - of which she was secretary - had folded the previous year with 47 redundancies and debts to the local enterprise company. Rita Miller hoped to pose for cameras in front of the site where the first Scottish Parliament sat at St John's Tower. When she arrived, the gates of the park were padlocked and she had to be driven off at speed. It was bad luck, but there was more to come. The *Record* insisted: "Party chiefs were still refusing to admit the Section 28 fiasco was behind what is likely to be a disaster on polling day".

The *Scottish Mirror's* Lorraine Davidson reported: "You can usually tell a by-election town by the sea of red, yellow and blue posters on every available lamppost as the political parties slug it out. But the seaside town is instead bedecked in 'Keep the Clause' posters... Those Labour campaigners who bothered to take to the streets grumbled that instead of the usual chants of 'SNP' on the streets they had to run a gauntlet of homophobic abuse. They reported their leafleting was constantly interrupted by cries of: 'Get lost ya p**f.'"

The other candidates in the election were the founder of the Ayrshire Farmers' Market, John Scott who stood for the Conservatives, Jim Mather a former chartered accountant for the SNP, student Stuart Ritchie for the Liberal Democrats, shop steward James Stewart for the Scottish Socialist Party and Gavin Corbett for the Green Party. Others who stood were Kevin Dillan (Anti Cloning), Alastair McConnachie (UK Independence Party), Robert Graham (Pro Life) and Clif Botcherby, a radio vet who stood for the retention of Section 28. 64-year-old Harry McEachan, a night shift petrol-pump attendant from Largs failed to raise the £500 deposit to stand on a pro-Section 28 platform and was later arrested at Ayr Sunday market for breach of the peace as he gathered signatures for his petition. The kilted protester raged: "Suddenly, it seems criminal to be ordinary".

In his column in *Scotland on Sunday*, Gerald Warner pretended for a moment he was Tony Blair. "Hi, fellow Scots and web surfers...! I say to the corrosive Scottish media - the unreconstructed self-abusers - the Forces of Conservatism - The Daily Records of this world - don't think that you are going to knock us off course. Don't imagine that the greatest progressive project in the history of the world... is going to be derailed by a bunch of Rab C Nesbitts with typewriters. ...This is a listening government. Like - take Section 28, where we're listening to almost 3% of Scots - this is our flagship policy on social inclusion. I didn't grow up with a silver spoon in my mouth - in some subsidised council house, like the Brian Souters of this world. My kids - including the new arrival that Cherie and I are so very privately expecting - they won't inherit a fleet of air-conditioned buses. Or a castle in the Highlands. All this stuff about Section 28. Look - I mean - I'm a pretty straight kind of guy - it's complete and utter nonsense. Section 28 has nothing to do with sex, heterosexual or homosexual. It doesn't apply to schools or local authorities or to anything else. It hasn't for the past hundred years. Whether it is on or off the statute book doesn't make a blind bit of difference to anybody. That's why we are prepared to defy public opinion, lose by-elections - whatever it takes - to prove to parents how unimportant it is... This is a young devolved region. The future, not the past. A future for the many, not the few. For kids. For Scottish kids. Kids no longer under the tyranny of hereditary peers. Kids free of Section 28. Kids who can go behind the bicycle shed at 16 - even if they're not allowed to smoke before 18..."

Gerald Warner also used his column to make a swipe at Tony Blair's brief visit to Scotland: "To his embattled garrison in the Stalingrad that Section 28 has made of Ayr for Labour, Blair's dash through Scotland must have been dispiritingly reminiscent of the Führer's last visit to the Eastern Front". And turning on a minor altercation as Labour MSPs were taking their seats in Parliament: "Wendy Alexander, Minister for Communities and the Schools Curriculum That Dares Not Speak Its Name, found that Alasdair Morrison, Minister for the Highlands and Islands, was occupying the seat most exposed to the television cameras. La Alexander ('It's my party and I'll sit where I want to')

Praise be the Lords

brusquely ordered Morrison to vacate it. He, possibly due to unfamiliarity with the Sassenach tongue, refused; thereupon She Who Must Be Obeyed called in Messrs McCabe and McAveety to evict the Teuchter intruder - splendid ministerial PR, in full view of the corrosive cynics in the press gallery".

Rita Miller lost. The Labour party were defeated in Ayr. Gerald Warner could hardly contain himself over news of the Conservative victory in *Scotland on Sunday*. He aimed and fired at the "infantile Minister of Communities" Wendy Alexander. "Thank you, Wendy! The Tory revival that eluded Messrs Rifkind, Lang and Forsyth (former Tory Scottish Secretaries) has finally been triggered by your heroic indifference to electoral opinion. Wrap up carefully, my dear, when you go out into the cold (which is where you may often now find yourself) – you are very precious to Scottish Tories and, more especially, to Scottish Nationalists. It is to be feared that the damage done to The Party We Love by the sixth-form milk monitor who is its Communities Minister is potentially mortal... Thanks to the Ayrhead Wendy, the likelihood is that Alex Salmond and his woad-streaked marauders will leave many of their corpses on the stricken field, while even the Tories slope off with some rich pickings in their jaws... The Leader had persuaded his Scottish satrap, Donald Kerensky Dither (batteries not included), that in-your-face aggression was the key to making repeal of Section 28, the Holyrood Dome..." (a reference to the Scottish parliament building, the construction of which was already well over budget) "and the many other eccentricities of his administration acceptable to the public... No more Mr Nice Guy. Donald Schwarzendither is kicking ass. Instead of a nightmare marginal seat, Eastwood is now a role model ('Go ahead – er, ah – punk! Make my – um –day!'). You can almost hear the jingle of his spurs". Warner turned on Nora Radcliffe, the MSP for Gordon who had expressed her support for equality for gays in partnerships. "There is a vote-winner for you. Possibly with the co-operation of sympathetic local authorities, provision could be made for the romantically-minded to hold their wedding at the public convenience where the happy couple first met". He cruelly wrote of "homosexual 'rights'" as a daily preoccupation for the Scottish Executive "while influenza stricken patients lay on trolleys in hospital corridors".

RELIGIOUS FASCISM

The *Scottish Daily Mail* revelled in the results of the Ayr by-election. "SHAMED... Labour slaughtered in Ayr by-election after Section 28 fiasco and limp into third place behind Tories and the SNP". They danced over Labour's "humiliating defeat", a "devastating blow" that had them "beaten into third place". It was described as "the lowest ebb yet for Donald Dewar's troubled administration, Labour was trounced in a seat it won just nine months ago". They believed it would lead to "a full-scale inquest". Tory candidate John Scott's victory was won by a margin of 3,344 votes. They polled 12,580 votes, the SNP received 9,236, Labour 7,054, Scottish Socialist Party 1,345, Liberal Democrats 800, Greens 460, William Botcherby (Clif Botcherby, the radio vet and Independent supporter of 'Keep the Clause') 185, UK Independence Party 113, Pro-Life Alliance 111 and Kevin Dillon, the Independent candidate against cloning, just 15 votes. For all their crowing, the Tories gained only one per cent from the previous May election. There was a 57 per cent turnout with the SNP benefitting the most, increasing its share of the vote by nine per cent. Labour's vote dropped 16 per cent. Most parties agreed that Section 28 had ranked only fourth in their lists of voters' priorities: in fact, 60 per cent voted for parties in favour of repeal. Following remarks from David McLetchie suggesting Labour was obsessed with political correctness, the *Daily Telegraph* headlined his quote: "Section 28 'obsession made Labour lose in Ayr'." The broadsheet castigated the Scottish Executive's "mania for 'equality agendas'" in its editorial, adding with a hint of encouragment for its Conservative readership: "Solid results can be built on Ayr". The *Record* predictably added: "It was a massive – if not the only – issue on the campaign". Journalist, Bob Shields quoted Ayr resident, Willie Gibson: "Listen son, the only Section 28 I want is my seat in the stand at Hampden for Ayr's cup tie with Rangers". The *Scottish Mail's* editorial suggested; "political correctness was the root of Labour's downfall". In the same paper, right-wing columnist Leo Mckinstry reflected on the communist witchunts in America under former President Joe McCarthy. "While we might sneer at Senator Joe's quest to seek out alleged Left-wing traitors in every branch of the U.S. government, we are doing exactly the same today with those who supposedly refuse to adhere to the new dogma of political correctness".

Praise be the Lords

The *Scottish Daily Mail* reported Deputy First Minister Jim Wallace stating his belief that traditional marriage was the best environment to bring up children. In fact, what he actually said was that *marriages* were the most recognisable and widely accepted way of signalling to society a couple's commitment to each other and their life as parents. He also stated that families now took diverse forms. He announced a 34 per cent increase in funding for family support groups. The main grant of £447,000 went to Family Mediation Scotland, which helped couples with marital difficulties. 'Keep the Clause' declared it was a sop to public opinion that wouldn't work until the Executive gave a strong family values message. They countered suggestions that Section 28 hadn't played a major part in the outcome of the Ayr by-election by having their own exit poll conducted by Progressive Partnership, which showed 15 per cent of the voters - more than 4,700 and enough to have secured the seat for Labour - changed their voting intentions because of Section 28. They claimed 30 per cent of voters had been influenced by the Section 28 issue which, in the negative, would have been hardly surprising given every available advertising hoarding had been booked by 'Keep the Clause'. The poll was dismissed as flawed, particularly when it couldn't be shown in which way the voting intent had been changed.

The tabloids hunted down any story that could fuel the debate. The *Scottish Sun* captioned: "LET'S PUT A SQUEEZE ON GAY TOYS" after "cash-strapped council bosses splashed out hundreds of pounds on executive toys for gays". With the council logo on one side, the toys had 'Glasgow's Housing Facts for Lesbian and Gay Men' on the other. In fact, the 400 rubber toys in the shape of a house, handed out at Glasgow's stand at a housing conference, carried similar messages for the disabled and other tenants too. In another story, a former SAS man "flounced" into court facing assault charges "wearing lipstick and a frock" under the headline: "WHO DARES MINCE", after the nine years the transsexual spent with the elite Who Dares Wins regiment. The *Scottish Mail* reported: "John White, now known as Joanna, attended court in a blue chiffon skirt with a fluorescent green T-shirt, a bright pink hat, matching pink lipstick and carrying a Mini Mouse umbrella. He was given a two-year conditional discharge". In the *Record*, following TV entertainer, Graham Norton's attempt to mimic model Naomi Campbell on the catwalk, it was reported: "Norton looked more like a duckling waddling off to find his mummy". It was recommended he didn't give up his day job.

The *Sunday Herald* produced a timely report on the research of Professor Michael Lynch of Edinburgh University. "...The saltire, the true blue symbol of Scottish nationhood, was originally, er, pink". The first medieval representations of St Andrew's motif on Scotland's flag were undeniably pink in a picture of the funeral of King James III in 1488 and in the Book of Hours belonging to the sister of James II who ruled from 1437 to 1460.

In the midst of this religious-inspired moral crusade, the *Record's* agony aunt, Joan Burnie harked back to her wedding day. "Don't tell the teachers – especially the Union, the Educational Institute of Scotland", she snapped, "but I was once m*****d. Yes, now it can be told, although I don't wish to corrupt any vulnerable or impressionable young person by writing that filthy 'M' word in full. Even I am not that depraved... I know, I am thoroughly ashamed of myself and realise that such irresponsible behaviour must have irreparably damaged the lives of my son and daughter... Better yet, I should have gone the whole hog and turned homosexual just to provide them with something of which Ms Nicol's pals, (Margaret Nicol, Convenor of EIS Equality Committee), could wholeheartedly approve. Or maybe shoved them into care, less they might, in the EIS's words, 'alienate friends from different backgrounds'. Of course, this is the most ridiculous claptrap which we have yet heard from the teachers' representatives... Marriage, as far as I am aware, is still considered an honourable state".

Ms Burnie was a divorcee.

A letter also appeared in the *Record* on Joan Burnie's 'Just Joan' page, saying: "I have a real fear of homosexuals. I worry they will grab me and rape me. This is stopping me from going out at night, as I live in an area where there are a great number of so-called gays. They have taken over the local pubs and you cannot move for them. I have seen them looking at me in the street as well. Someone once told me that I was just the type they go for, being into sports and looking very manly. It is terrible that, in this day and age, someone shouldn't feel safe in their own neighbourhood because of these militant gay groups". Without doubting the authenticity of the letter, Burnie went on to reassure him: "I'm sure you are a very good-looking guy, but just as you could never fancy a gay man, I doubt any of them would want a straight one". On the subject of rape, she added: "When a man is raped, he is likely to be gay and his attacker straight and not the other way round".

The *Daily Record* felt drawn to challenge charges of prudery by promoting a guide called *Marriage Matters*. Written by 52-year-old Linet Smith, the tabloid reported: "A vicar's wife has penned a sex guide so parishioners can sizzle between the sheets… (Mrs Smith) says wives should wear flimsy lingerie to greet their husbands when they come home from work. And she recommends a lock on the bedroom door so couples with kids can conoodle in peace".

Pro-Section 28 newspapers continued to produce appalling examples of homophobia either in their reports, through insensitive juxtaposition of stories or abandoning any attempt at balance in their letters' pages. Mrs Anne Walker felt moved to write to the *Scottish Mail* to register a complaint: "Although most children in my daughter's class come from 'normal homes' with mums and dads who work hard, pay their bills and taxes, who receive no benefits and try to bring their children up to learn respect and manners, the head teacher says it's the minority who must not be upset".

Following the Ayrshire by-election, the European parliament voted in favour of a resolution that homosexual relationships should have equal status across the European Union. The Vatican issued a warning to Catholic politicians that they must not support any legislation that gave gay relationships equal status in law with marriage. In a communiqué of the Pontifical Council for the Family, of which Cardinal Winning was a member, it said: "Legislators and especially Catholic parliamentarians must not favour with their vote this type of legislation since it runs contrary to the common good". MSP Nora Radcliffe retorted: "You would think that the Catholic Church, which was persecuted for centuries, would not want other people to be persecuted". Cardinal Winning told the *Mail*: "This alarms all families in Scotland. The marriage-based family is the foundation stone on which this nation has been built. People are not prepared to stand idly by and watch these foundations being undermined". The paper dismissed critics of his message by suggesting they'd missed the point.

RELIGIOUS FASCISM

It was spring and the Chancellor of the Exchequer promised to deliver a "Budget for a fairer, stronger Britain. The *Record* grabbed the opportunity to carp: "His Budget theme of 'for the many, not the few' is one that some of Labour's Scottish representatives would do well to remember. Fighting for the few against the will of the many went a long way to getting them into a mess in the first place".

Jack Lovie of Irvine wrote in the *Herald:* "May I interrupt the avalanche of intellectual debate in your letters pages on the repeal of Section 28 to inquire if anyone has heard the first cuckoo?"

The *Record* called Tory leader Brian Monteith over a story about a new gay supporters' club for Hibernean Football Club. Monteith claimed he 'smelt a rat' and clicked on the club's website to read the exchanges between fans. His suspicions were confirmed. "It's riddled with homophobic jokes and I suspect a Hearts supporter with a sad sense of humour". On the *Record's* sports' pages a few days later, under the bold headline: "GAY PRIDE" was Colin Duncan's report: "Fans have last laugh as Hibs come from behind". He wrote: "Hibs latest and most unusual supporters club, The Gay Gordons, must have relished the mince along Leith Walk after this pulsating Edinburgh derby... Thoughout the 90 minutes the Hearts fans mercilessly taunted their rivals about their new-found backers. However, it was the Gay Gordons, who came out of the closet last week to pronounce their undying love for the Hibees, who had the last laugh. Apparently young Kenny Miller, who sported a new haircut for the occasion, is their icon but surely they could not have failed to have been attracted to the Gallic flair of Franck Sauzee. Indeed they would be well advised to start a pressure group aimed at persuading the Frenchman not to up sticks and quit at the end of the season... The smile on Yogi's face at the end of the match and the clenched-fist salute of boss Alex McLeish told you how much this victory meant to Hibs..." Craig Halkett's full-page photograph with the caption "Yogi bare" showed Hibernean footballer Yogi Hughes flashing his bum at the crowd.

Traditionally, sectarianism, racism and violence were more prolific in Scottish football than homosexuality, which remained hidden. Indeed, after this match between Hibernian and Hearts, an incident was reported to police after Heart's fullback, Gary

Praise be the Lords

Naysmith, was hit just below the eye with a missile midway through the second half.

In an attempt to set the record straight in the toxic atmosphere of repealing Section 28, the children's charity ChildLine organised a conference in Edinburgh for one hundred teenagers from all over Scotland to give them a say in the Section 28 debate. Thousands more children were able to add their voice in the debate during a live Internet link-up with secondary schools. They summed up the state of sex education in Scottish schools as a 'shambles'. Director of ChildLine Scotland, Anne Houston said that the overwhelming message from young people was that Section 28 should be repealed. Sadly, for one young person, it was already too late...

Dr Roger Lambert from Aberdeen wrote to the *Herald* with some disturbing news: "My brother is headteacher of a Catholic comprehensive school in a rural area and though of liberal views himself, he has found Section 28 a barrier to sensible informed debate in school about homosexuality. This was highlighted last Sunday when a very bright, sensitive 16-year-old boy from his school committed suicide. The reason was because he was gay and it would appear that he felt unable to approach anyone to talk about his sexuality... It is totally irresponsible for some sections of the media to attempt to influence public opinion with ill-informed campaigns on a subject as sensitive as this. Perhaps they should attend the inquest into the boy's tragic and needless death!"

Ethan, a highly sensitive, intelligent, young 16-year-old, attended a Catholic co-educational Grammar school where any support for young gays was non-existent and where he would learn to know of himself as a sinner, unnatural, immoral and an inferior human being. His diaries contained evidence of his lack of interest in girls, his dislike of sports and incidents of bullying. He had hung himself. If Ethan had struggled to vanquish evidence of his emerging sexuality in life, death only concurred with the enforced repression. The court session enquiring into the circumstances of his untimely death was held in private, closed to the public and press. No mention was made of Ethan's sexual orientation and a death by misadventure was recorded.

At a Scottish Executive enquiry on Monday, 20 March, it looked as though 'Keep the Clause' might've been ready to throw in the towel. Brian Souter and Jack Irvine stayed away, leaving a minister's wife, Mrs Anne Stewart and 'concerned father' Patrick Rolink, a school board member from Airdrie, to face the Scottish Executive enquiry to say: "We have accepted that Section 2a will be repealed". Not yet ready to move out of his £1m Perthshire mansion into a council house, as promised, Brian Souter was already planning behind the scenes to snare the Government with a major referendum on the issue. The next day, the *Scottish Daily Mail* announced an "unprecedented warning" as: "Churches unite against Dewar over Section 28". Even though the Church of Scotland had no official line on the matter, Mrs Ann Allen signed the letter on its behalf. The others signing the letter to First Minister Donald Dewar were Gordon Murray of CARE, Bashir Maan of the Muslim Council of Great Britain, David Anderson of the Evangelical Alliance, Rev John Fulton of the United Free Church of Scotland, Rev Kenneth MacLeod of the Free Church, Rev Angus Morrison of the Associated Presbyterian Church, Canon Mike Parker of the Scottish Episcopal Evangelical Fellowship, Parminder Singh Purba of the Central Gurdwara Singh Saba, Imam TH Shah of the UK Islamic Mission, Mr M T Shaheen, MBE of Glasgow's Islamic Centre, Rev William Slack of the Baptist Union, Armrik Singh Uppal of the Glasgow Gurdwara Council and Mr S L Gajree, President of the Hindu Temple in Glasgow. The *Scottish Sun* reported: "They also want to know whether the Scottish Executive – which wants to repeal Section 28 and allow gay lessons in schools – will move toward civil recognition for same-sex unions". The *Record's* Carlos Alba reported their demands of the First Minister: "...They urged him to halt moves to give gay relationships the same legal status as heterosexuals". The letter stated: "We sincerely believe that nothing less than the soul of Scotland is at stake... We genuinely fear that the current debate over Section 28 reveals a very real hostility on the part of some powerful lobby groups to the marriage-based family". Yusuf Islam, formerly Cat Stevens the pop singer, added his voice by claiming the Government's bid to scrap the clause was a further decline in morality. A 26,000-name petition organised by pensioner Vera Cowey and her husband Jim from Broughty Ferry, near Dundee was handed in to the Scottish Executive expressing "horror" at the planned repeal. They were joined by a 20-strong delegation handing in a petition signed by 320 Church of Scotland ministers.

Praise be the Lords

The Scottish Tory leader, Brian Monteith, sought to have a clause inserted into the Scottish Bill which would give the school boards a role in drawing up and monitoring sex education classes in schools and a legal right for parents to withdraw their children from classes they thought were inappropriate. Lawyers working for 'Keep the Clause' had argued that because parents in Scotland had no legal right to withdraw their children from sex education lessons, the Executive was in breach of the European Convention of Human Rights. The *Scottish Mail* astutely called it on 22 March a "plan for parent power on school sex lessons". SSBA treasurer, Alan Smith called it an "excellent idea". Ministers refused to budge and said they had no plans to change the wording of guidelines set to replace Section 28.

The plan for parent power that Alan Smith thought an "excellent idea" might have appeared less than excellent in the light of research showing that Scots parents were the shyest in Britain when it came to talking to children about sex. A study by Norwich Union Healthcare at this time found more than a third of parents with children aged between ten and 15 admitted they had not discussed issues surrounding puberty with them. The study also found 27 per cent of parents admitting sex was the most difficult subject to discuss with their child compared to 11 per cent in the south-east of England. Three quarters of parents assumed their children found out about puberty at school.

The Liberal Democrats were described by the *Scottish Mail* as "split over gay law 'obsession'" when Gordon Macdonald, a member of the party's Scottish executive "attacked his own party" two days before the Lib-Dem annual conference. He was reported being concerned that motions in support of repeal were swamping the conference. The report by their Scottish Political Reporter, Ian Smith cuttingly added: "The militant gay rights organisation Stonewall is also hosting a reception at the conference to thank the party for supporting gay rights". Smith claimed Macdonald was part of a "growing band" of Lib-Dem defectors. Macdonald was, in fact, a member of the evangelical Christian group; CARE (Christian Action Research Education).

At the beginning of March 2000 a deal had been struck in England and Wales between Church leaders and the then education minister David Blunkett. The Church of England and the Catholic Church had agreed to accept the repeal of Section 28 if a clause was inserted in the Learning and Skills Bill promoting 'marriage' and 'traditional family relationships' during sex education lessons. The *Record* had already heralded this as a victory with their headline on 3 March: "ENGLISH WIN TOUGHER GAY SAFEGUARDS". But the government were about to be double-crossed by religious militants. On Friday, 24 March, Baroness Young and her supporters blocked its passage through the unelected House of Lords. The *Daily Mail* dutifully reported Labour's failure to win approval for the bill by just 15 votes: "SEX LESSONS LAW IN CHAOS... Lords revolt boosts campaign against the repeal of Section 28... Tony Blair's bid to scrap the ban on gay propaganda in schools failed last night after peers rejected an attempt to buy them off". Souter was reported to have been "delighted". Baroness Young said: "I know I speak for the overwhelming majority of the population which does not want the promotion of homosexuality in schools". It was a disaster for pro-repeal groups. Not only would Section 28 remain on the statute books in England and Wales, but new guidelines on promoting marriage in sex education had now been added! With temporary amnesia blocking memory of their own obsession with the subject, the *Daily Mail* commented: "Ministers have failed to convince their core supporters that their obsession with gay issues is in line with the mood of the nation... With every defeat and setback, new doubts are raised over its judgement... New Labour hasn't anything better to do with its time".

The *Daily Record* groaned: "Blair is said to be so angry over his tenth defeat by the new-look Lords in just four months that he will risk another 'Tony's cronies row' to strike back". The *Record* had been studying the Prime Minister's "devilishly simple plan to get round the Lords' rebellion over Section 28 repeal in England..." Blair had asked his Cabinet members to look around party members and sympathisers for life peers to serve in the House of Lords. 19 were already recruited but Blair still needed a further 31 new peers for another opportunity, at least six months away, to defeat the inbuilt majority against repeal. Even after the Lords reform which abolished all but 92 hereditary peers, the Tories still had 232 peers in the Upper House to Labour's 182. Only a maximum of 50 could be introduced at a time. Under the heading: "Souter attacks Blair bid to pack the Lords", he claimed Labour were "obsessed with political correctness... They must be completely beholden to minority pressure groups to consider such a desperate course of action". A spokesman for the Catholics weighed in to declare the Lords were effectively being "silenced". And Tory leader David McLetchie added: "The Lords have defied him and hell hath no fury like Tony Blair scorned. Now he intends to bring them to heel by packing the house with Labour placements". The *Record's* editorial sounded off in a fury: "Unfortunately that still leaves Mr Blair with the small matter of a general public who are adamantly OPPOSED to repeal on both sides of the border. And no amount of foot-stomping, steamrollering or gerrymandering seems capable of helping him out there. But - as has become so very obvious since this row started - when did what YOU think ever matter anyway?" Tom Brown put his name to a piece claiming the Lords had been "bastardised".

Religionists and moral conservatives soon found another rich seam of support for their cause. The *Daily Mail* cleared a page for Labour peer Lord Paul. "We British Asians look with sorrow at the spread of divorce..." he sighed, "...and what might be taught about homosexuality... Jack Straw's wise words about the strength and resilience of the traditional Asian family will be welcomed by the millions of British subjects whose origins are in India, Pakistan and Bangladesh... We desperately needed the backing of our wives and children in those early days. Quite simply, we would not have survived and prospered without the support provided by marriage - proper, traditional marriage... We would certainly not have found the strength and the stability needed to build up mighty businesses and to plan for our domestic futures in our new homeland... That is why... the Government must... pay less attention to those trendy liberals..."

Lord Paul had come to Britain in 1966 to be with his daughter who had been dying of Leukaemia. "My wife and I were so heartbroken that we were determined to stay on to be near her. That is why I founded my business here instead of going back home to join the family firm". His remonstrations were contradictory. He voted with the Government and claimed single parents and families who had chosen to live together without marrying could do well for their children. "Who ever thought otherwise?" he begged. But, in support of marriage, he added: "Our instinctive feeling for marriage is strengthened by academic research which shows that children desperately need stability and continuity - and that those values are most likely to be found in God-fearing families built around proper marriages". Lord Paul begged: "Why does marriage not bring with it fiscal rewards - as it does in France and Germany?" In fact, the French believed they delivered a better system of sex education by keeping religion out of schools and their *Pacte Civil de Solidarite* permitted gays to financially benefit from civil unions. Lord Paul did not enjoy unanimous support. Ms Anvar Khan, a columnist in the *Herald* scorned: "We are small-town. Asking Scotland to talk reasonably on the global issue of homosexuality is like asking the characters in *High Road*" (a Scottish television soap) "to re-enact Jarman's *Caravaggio*... While Scotland stockpiles sandbags and corned beef in the war against homosexuality, the rest of the world accepts that the disco gene cannot stop dancing". Her remarks were made without the benefit of hindsight. Within four years, on the back of 'moral' issues like 'gay marriage', religionists would be rallying to support evangelical Christian George W Bush's election for presidency of the US.

The newly formed Multi-Faith Coalition, formed to do battle with the Scottish Parliament over the repeal of Section 28, claimed to include members of the Islamic, Chinese, Hindu, Sikh and Muslim communities. The group threatened to oust Labour MSPs such as Mohammed Sarwar, George Galloway and Ian Davidson who all had a high proportion of ethnic communities in their Glasgow constituencies. Ayub Khan, chairman of the coalition told the *Sunday Post* that MSPs "are not listening to what we want. We do not want Section 28 in our schools *(sic)* and don't want to see it repealed and homosexual liaisons placed on the same moral footing as traditional family marriage. One of the apparent reasons for teaching homosexuality in schools is to stop bullying and homophobia but we don't accept that. I was bullied at school because of my colour, and I don't believe any amount of teaching will ever stop bullying".

The gentle overtures played to ethnic minorities by right-wing newspapers like the *Daily Mail* were never likely to have lasted long enough for an encore, demonstrated when "the floodgates (were) thrown open" and refugees given temporary homes in Glasgow. "Taxpayers pick up the bills", the paper stormed. The *Daily Record* reported "a new influx of asylum seekers...", and warned of a "second wave of refugees set to arrive in Glasgow..." The right-wing British National Party

Praise be the Lords

needed little encouragement to begin leafleting the empty, hard-to-let houses at Sighthill in Glasgow.

Amongst the collection of testimonials compiled for Stonewall's *Caused by the Clause*, a lesbian parent and teacher from West Lothian wrote: "The implication on the posters that I am the threat/danger from which children need to be protected was awful. I felt angry and fearful. I felt that being visible and defending myself was a big risk... I was particularly affected by the very concerted drive to enlist ethnic minority communities in the 'Keep the Clause' campaign. I felt I was being divided from allies in work against discrimination and commitment to Equal Ops. I began to feel unsure of my welcome and suspected – and even expected - opposition and intolerance from ethnic minority communities. I now feel cautious about being 'out'. I feel that lots of fear has been stirred up in Scotland, including my own".

While the furore over the repeal of Section 28 rolled on, a scandal broke out in Scotland that did nothing to help Section 28 on its way. Just four letters graced the front page of the *Scottish Sun:* "SICK". 70's Scottish pop group the Bay City Rollers' drummer, Derek Longmuir had received 300 hours community service for alleged paedophilia. Longmuir's lawyer, Robbie Burnett retorted: "He is not a paedophile and is not someone who is terribly interested in child porn". But the media left little room for doubt. "Storm as Bay City pervert walks free", cried the *Scottish Mail* and "fury as shamed Roller escapes prison" the *Record* added. The head of Scotland Yard's Obscene Publication Branch, (later named the Paedophile Unit), Mike Hames, was dragged out of retirement to register his disgust. "This sends out completely the wrong message to those who might think of copying Mr Longmuir. It is not easy to track down people who are downloading child pornography from the Internet, but when you have brought that task to a successful conclusion, to find the defendant getting a sentence like this is very demoralising".

Longmuir, who had always been upfront with police officers about downloading 'porn' off the Internet tried to argue he had not 'made' pornography, but, in an equivalence to pulling a magazine down off the top shelf and opening it, was in possession. The court disagreed. Officers seized 73 floppy discs. 14 pictures out of 1,700 on the computer's hard drive were judged to be child porn and 117 pictures of a sexual nature, which, the *Scottish Mail* pointed out, "experts said included 27 of children being abused. Of those 27 images, it was accepted that four were downloaded by Longmuir". The *Herald* put it more simply, reporting material seized as: "...Discs containing more than 100 indecent images - many showing young children involved in sex acts - as well as dozens of indecent films, photographs and videos when police raided his home in September 1998". Longmuir, who now worked as a nurse and lived in a flat in Edinburgh, claimed an American friend had bought much of it in Portugal before it was made illegal. Sheriff Isobel Poole accepted this and noted significant extraneous circumstances in the case.

Derek Longmuir, wider in girth and without his blonde locks, had changed as much as the definition of 'decency' had in the three decades since the Scottish boy-band Bay City Rollers sang 'Keep on Dancing'. Then, the bare-chested and stripped teens reflected a style of British gay porn that flaunted a sexual confidence in the pages of UK teen magazines like *Oh Boy!* or *My Guy* in the late seventies. Pre-dating the import of the eighties 'macho man', such images would not just become passé: they would become illegal. The *Record* added: "What Edinburgh Sheriff Court did not hear about was his close relationship with a 15-year-old Portuguese boy..." It was a lad Longmuir had befriended and introduced to his own family. The *Scottish Sun* added: "Nelson Queiros met the ex-drummer when he was just 14. Nelson, now 17, told stunned cops: 'I love Derek'" when they burst into the flat. (This differed markedly from a story printed in 2008 in the same paper when reporter David Goodwin wrote police had "found terrified Nelson cowering in a corner when they raided the flat").

Letters poured in to the *Scottish Sun*. Duane Irvine, Alford, Aberdeenshire wrote: "This man deserves to be treated the same as any other pervert sent to jail and left to rot". Rosemary Thomson, Wishaw, Lanarkshire wrote: "As a mother I am horrified at the lenient sentence handed out to ex-Bay City Roller Derek Longmuir". George McLean, Alloa wrote: "Would you like to be nursed by him? I doubt it. ...I say he should have been put away for a long time". Alick Richardson, Falkirk wrote: "The sentence is a joke. He should have been sent to prison for a long time". J Simpson, Alloa agreed: "The sentence was a joke". D Carson, Cowdenbeath wrote: "It should be an automatic two to three-year sentence, then we might start to beat this disgusting

Praise be the Lords

practice". Two weeks later Scottish Television News were focusing their cameras on the front of Longmuir's grey and dismal flat at Queens' Mansions in Edinburgh. The *Record* reminded everyone how he had been "caught with a vile collection of porn", admitted to possessing "a mass of child-sex videos, indecent photos and computer images" and how "some of the snaps showed children as young as six being sexually abused". The 49-year-old psychiatric nurse was sacked from his job at Edinburgh Royal Infirmary before – in the words of the *Scottish Sun* - "a sheriff sparked outrage when she gave him just 300 hours' community service".

Not until some months later, in the middle of May, did another side of the story come to light, not from Derek, but Jorge Loureiro, a 28-year-old Portuguese boy Longmuir had adopted. He told the *Sunday Herald* that an obsessive American fan Derek befriended had framed him, telling the police there were sexual images on a laptop he had left with Derek. It was also revealed that floppy discs had been sent anonymously to Derek's flat a few days before the police raid. The paper reported: "The police also received further details about the items in Longmuir's flat from a long-term police informant with links to the Bay City Rollers who has served a jail sentence for underage sex with young boys". It emerged that police broke the Data Protection Act when they gave Jorge's address to a *Scottish Sun* reporter and one of the officers even gave a television interview before the case had gone to court. Derek had met Jorge when he came up to him begging for money. He was rewarded with a meal. Now married with two children and living in Edinburgh, Jorge had nothing but praise for the man who helped him. Jorge told the *Sunday Herald*: "Detectives asked me at least five times in the course of two hour interviews whether Derek and I ever had a sexual relationship. I kept saying no, that it was never like that, but they just kept on coming back to that question. They got increasingly angry when I wouldn't say yes and showed no interest in how Derek had rescued me and brought me up. I told them that Derek could hardly work computers... It wasn't even his..." Jorge's wife Michele said: "I think losing his job is what Derek has found most hard to take. He was a good and devoted nurse". Derek's lawyer, Robbie Burnett told the *Sunday Herald*: "I have been a solicitor now for 26 years and I have never come across such misleading, inaccurate and sensational reporting. The coverage of the case was disgraceful and I am very concerned that Mr Longmuir's employment is being decided on what the newspapers have said rather than the facts".

That wasn't the end of the story for Derek Longmuir. In 2008, the *Scottish Sun*'s front page headline blasted: "I WAS ROLLER DEREK'S CHILD SEX SLAVE". The story told how "tormented dad", Nelson Queiros, suffered "a decade of abuse" at the mercy of "pervert star" Longmuir. Queiros, who was described as "shy" and "regularly beaten by his drunken father" claimed, after he took paid trips to Longmuir's Edinburgh flat, was "driven to try to kill himself when the abuse became too much" and was quoted saying: "I have been to hell", adding, "I was frozen with fear when he first touched me, but there was nothing I could do. I was a small boy and I was completely helpless". Under the headline: "MONSTER LURED ME INTO EVIL WEB AT 13", Queiros, who claimed to be on "a cocktail of up to 16 tablets and anti-depressants a day" decided to go to police after "a three-day stint in hospital... as he battled his demons". He was quoted saying: "Derek started taking my clothes off and he performed a sex act on me before forcing me to do it to him. It was over after 20 minutes. I felt disgusted. I was petrified but I was small and weak I couldn't fight back... He told me if I didn't let him it would be worse for me because he would keep on trying again and again. I felt trapped. I had no escape. He kept me like a prisoner and I was his sex slave". The *Sun* reported: "Nelson said he threatened to throw himself from Longmuir's top-floor flat balcony in Edinburgh – but the pervert managed to talk him out of it". Nelson was reported saying: "He told me he would not touch me again but he was lying, he started again just days later. I felt that killing myself was my only escape. I'd started having suicidal thoughts from the age of 14. Twice in Portugal I threw myself in front of buses. I just wanted someone to listen to me and help me. But my family seemed happy because they were getting money. Derek even asked my mum for her bank details and she was happy to give him them. I have three sisters and four brothers and sometimes there was no food in the house and my mother would need money and I gave her everything that Derek gave to me... I tried to get extra time at work and asked the manager for more hours so I could stay away from the flat. Despite the fact I was a man physically, I still felt like a helpless boy. I had no energy to do anything about what was happening to me". Queiros was pictured with his partner, Yvette, who told the paper how he had "cracked under the strain and broken down in tears and admitted the whole sordid story". She also mentioned how he took violent mood swings and battered himself off of furniture.

Whilst Derek Longmuir was being attacked in the press, *Scotland on Sunday* swept in with another story supporting the retention of Section 28 on its front-page. "Souter pays family to sue on Section 28". (A little premature, perhaps, since he had apparently yet to find one). Brian Souter wanted to find a family willing to take Donald Dewar's administration to the European Court. The Sunday broadsheet also went on to describe the Scottish Nationalist Party's position as "very close to that of the Keep The Clause campaign" after the SNP national council had met and voted to table an amendment in Parliament to make guidelines – in their words - 'semi-statutory' by placing a duty on education authorities to 'have regard' to the proposed guidelines. The *Herald* said the SNP "affirmed support for the leadership's position in favour of repeal of the existing section coupled with a clause in the Ethical Standards Bill placing a responsibility on local authorities to heed the new guidelines currently being drafted". Asked on BBC 2's *Holyrood* programme whether the guidelines should mention marriage and "traditional family values", SNP leader Alex Salmond said that they should, but that they should also be non-discriminatory. This was nonsense, of course, since, as gays couldn't marry, or even at this stage, enter into a civil partnership, how could such an inclusion not be discriminatory? In the *Sunday Herald*, Iain Macwhirter wrote: "This should have been hailed by Keep the Clause as a great political victory and one that could force the Scottish Executive to think again. But instead, by calling a referendum on outright repeal, Souter left Salmond hanging in the air. The SNP leader will now have to condemn Souter's attempt to buy into the democratic process if he doesn't want to be accused of cynical opportunism".

The alleged theft by the *Mail on Sunday* of an article by broadcaster Nigel Wrench on 'barebacking', (anal sex without condoms) from the *Pink Paper* sparked a furious response from the *Pink Paper's* editor-in-chief, Mike Ross. He called for the resignation of Paul Dacre, the editor of the *Daily Mail* from his post on the Press Complaints Commission. (The PCC, made up of newspaper editors, was licenced by the government to adjudicate on complaints made against newspapers). The *Mail* was clearly unhappy about the transmission of HIV in casual sex, yet had done more than most to obstruct the work of organisations promoting safer sex. The *Pink Paper's* David Bridle blasted: "Associated Newspapers needs gay men in Britain to remain criminals and figures of hate for their readers. After all, who else would they target in their campaign to preserve the 'forces of conservatism'? ...Maybe Lord Rothermere should check his sales figures. Last month, the Mail had the biggest drop in sales of any national daily newspaper. It lost 27,000 readers - right in the middle of its virulent anti-Section 28 campaign. Not a huge loss by newspaper standards but maybe a small sign that its readers are just beginning to tire of homosexuality being thrust across their breakfast table every morning". In its Disclosures column, the *Pink Paper* explained their version of events. "The Mail on Sunday - or the Forger's Gazette as it is known so fondly in Fleet Street - asked if they might reproduce (Nigel Wrench's piece on 'barebacking)'. The Pink Paper said no... The Mail's hypocrisy about obeying the law will, of course, come as no surprise to those who have followed its approach to family values. While sternly preaching monogamy to its readers during the 1970s and 1980s, ageing proprietor Lord Rothermere was engaged in a prolonged adulterous relationship with a Japanese hand-model. The dowager Viscountess is now known to some disrespectful Mail staff as 'Lady Hand-job".

A group calling itself the Bigot Busters stormed the offices of Associated Newspapers and brought the newsroom to a standstill for 15 minutes. The *Pink Paper* reported how: "they chained themselves to furniture, let off foghorns and held up banners emblazoned with 'Daily Mail promotes anti-gay hatred'." Others cheated security officers and made their way up the balcony overlooking the vast atrium at the heart of the organisation.

The *Scottish Daily Mail* could barely conceal their excitement with its next headline: "CLAUSE 28: BLAIR IS SET TO CONCEDE DEFEAT... Tony Blair is ready to concede defeat south of the Border in the bitter struggle to scrap Section 28, the law which bans homosexual propaganda in schools". Hamish Macdonell, *The Mail's* Scottish political editor decided, "the revelation will now put immense pressure on Donald Dewar to

Praise be the Lords

follow suit in Scotland". A Downing Street spokesman, however, put the record straight for the *Pink Paper:* "Such reports are complete speculation. We remain completely committed to repealing Section 28, and will be looking at our options again in the light of (the) vote in the House of Lords. Anonymous quotes from alleged cabinet ministers will make absolutely no difference to this commitment". Nonetheless, the *Scottish Mail* was popping corks. "In what will be seen as an epic victory for campaigners for traditional family values, the Prime Minister has signalled to colleagues that he will abandon the fight if the House of Lords defeats the Government for a second time on the issue". The vote was expected, later that year, in June 2000. Hamish Macdonell warned: "Campaigners from all over Britain will now focus their energies on Scotland, raising the profile of the contentious issue yet further". Under the heading: "Climbdown over gay law", there was a good deal of tub-thumping: "The Daily Mail has led the way in campaigning for the retention of Section 28 which was introduced by the Tory Government to prevent left-wing councils spending public money on the promotion of homosexuality". No evidence of Labour councils 'promoting' homosexuality had ever emerged. Certainly, homosexuality was never promoted in Northern Ireland where Section 28 did not even apply. The *Mail* insisted: "Opinion polls show opposition to repeal in Scotland is even more widespread than south of the Border". The *Daily Mail's* version of events, with key dates marked out in the development of the campaign, pointed to "JAN 21" when the *Mail* revealed only one third of people supporting repeal. Their reports were becoming increasingly shrill, mixing conjecture with fact, commentary with reporting. They considered that the issue had become "a touchstone for many young modernisers on the Labour benches" and quoted Souter's PR man, Jack Irvine. "...If Tony Blair sees sense and calls a halt to this politically correct madness, Dewar's position will be untenable. It does sound like a re-run of the Poll Tax - good enough for Scotland but not for England. Strange Donald Dewar should be the man bringing Thatcherite tactics to Scotland". (Strange too, that a small group of men were supporting so vociferously an English law imposed on Scotland by the Thatcher Government, still greatly despised in Scotland). The *Scottish Mail's* editorial declared "repeal of Section 28 had become Labour's Poll Tax..." and "a seriously destabilising force in Scottish society". References to the highly contentious Poll Tax began to surface repeatedly. 'Keep the Clause' had already warned of riots in the streets similar to those initiated by the Poll Tax if Section 28 was repealed. The *Mail* advised: "It is time for the First Minister to bow to the settled will of the Scottish people and abandon this ill-advised initiative".

Andy Myles, a former chief executive of the Scottish Liberal Democrats spoke out at his Party's annual conference. Referring to Cardinal Winning, he said: "I am sorry, but you have shown an unworthy intolerance which is deeply regrettable. If gay men and lesbians are going to be accused of being perverts, then the person stating that is a bigot, there is no way out of it". A spokesman for Cardinal Winning scoffed in the *Scottish Mail*: "On the whole question of Section 28, Cardinal Winning speaks for a far larger part of the population than the Liberal Democrats". The *Scottish Sun* gasped: "Scotland's top Catholic Cardinal Thomas Winning was yesterday branded a bigot for trying to stop gay lessons in schools". The *Scottish Mail* was bitter. "An amendment calling for the proposed guidelines to replace Section 28 to stress 'loving marriage' was rejected. Lib-Dem activists voted for another amendment which expressed regret over the Keep the Clause campaign, accusing Stagecoach tycoon Brian Souter of a cynical attempt to buy public opinion…" (The term "activists", of course, was never applied to religionists within the Party promoting an agenda of so-called 'family values'). The *Scottish Mail* ignored Cardinal Winning's reference to perversion and pulled out the sectarian card, turning on Andy Myles to accuse him of "intemperate language which threatens to add a sectarian dimension to an already heated issue". The *Record* added how "the conference also confirmed the Liberal Democrat support for the repeal of Section 28, despite warnings from within their own ranks". Comments from party executive member Gordon Macdonald were added to support the *Record's* line: "I don't accept that all these people are misplaced in their concerns, which is the line that comes out of the Executive all the time". Only a few delegates backed an amendment with a Christian theme calling for guidelines promoting "loving marriage as the ideal". Nora Radcliffe, Liberal Democrat MSP for Gordon told the delegation: "It is frightening to witness how quickly a tide of bigotry and fear could be released". And Lanarkshire delegate Hugh O'Donnell compared 'Keep the Clause's

Praise be the Lords

"scurrilous campaign" to Bible belt fundamentalists in the US or the Taliban in Afghanistan.

Meanwhile, under its editor Martin Clarke, the *Daily Record* continued ruthlessly promoting its 'family values' agenda. Amongst the tabloid's 'Keep the Clause' propaganda was a piece on Beatles' manager Brian Epstein, "a manic depressive homosexual who worried constantly... haunted by inner demons - despite his incredible success". There was also a double-page moral tale on the destructive forces of relationships formed on the Internet. "LOVE.CON... Ian loses wife, job and savings after falling for fake beauty on Internet". Ian McLean from Paisley had fallen for an American girl who had probably not expected ever to meet her cyber lover. "Ian had been fooled by... a woman who looked more like the psychopath played by Kathy Bates in chilling movie Misery". She was neither unattractive or anything like the part actress Kathy Bates played in *Misery*, but a picture of Bates in her character-role was dropped in to help the story along anyway. The *Record* warned: "Already thousands of marriages are being ruined by the Internet" and moralising in its editorial, added: "The Internet may bring us all closer together, but as Ian McLean knows to his cost, an old-fashioned dinner for two is safer than a cyber-courtship any day". In another editorial the *Record* once again tried to hammer home the same moral message. "WARNING - the Internet can seriously damage your marriage...! It all seems like cyber-silliness, except that these Internet romances have led to real-life heartbreak. Lives have been ruined, families have broken up, wives and husbands have been dumped and children left behind. So be sure what your partner's getting up to on the home computer. They could be dialling up www.divorce.com". Promoting the Tory's 'family values' message, the *Record* also carried a picture of former Conservative Prime Minister John Major giving away his daughter. (Rather unfortunate given a later revelation of an extra-marital affair with fellow married MP, Edwina Currie). It topped a piece on marriage's fall from fashion. "It has got to the stage where almost 40 per cent of babies are now born out of wedlock... But it's not all bad news for the traditional family - four out of every five children still live in a two-parent home and 90 per cent of those parents are married to each other". But how much worse could it get? Even the *Record* was forced to admit; "the number of couples who choose to get married has plunged over the last four decades". The controversial Dr Adrian Rogers' of Family Focus, (a new front after being shunned by the Conservative Party), was given an air of respectability by the *Record:* "Not only are people not marrying, they are not having children - we simply aren't reproducing enough. These people who aren't getting married are going to face terribly lonely futures. There is a large element of loneliness that's going to hit them in their 40s". The *Herald* spelled out the research from the Family Policy Studies Centre more honestly. "Divorce rates are soaring, with more than two in five marriages now ending in the courts, while people are marrying at a later age or opting to cohabit or live alone". The 'Keep the Clause' campaigners apparently "declined to comment" when asked by the *Herald*, but the paper was able to drag out Catholic Church spokesman, Monsignor Tom Connolly of the Catholic Church who told them: "It is a very sad reflection on our society that we do not encourage people from a very young age to have any serious commitment or loyalty to marriage". He turned on former Spice Girl pop star Victoria Beckham and her footballer husband David Beckham and blamed them.

The outrage over the repeal of Section 28 continued to fill newspapers with endless column inches, dividing Scotland and keeping the 'Keep the Clause' campaign firmly at the top of the agenda before the campaign took a very sinister new turn.

Chapter Five
How to Spot a Homosexual

"Hey there boy
This prejudice and ignorance we can overcome..."
The Communards

On Tuesday, 28 March 2000, the *Scottish Daily Mail's* headlines spelt out a new stage in the campaign to prevent the repeal of Section 28 in Scotland: "LET'S PUT IT TO THE VOTE... £1m private cash for Scottish referendum over Section 28... 23 co-sponsors helping pay for the ballot". (The *Daily Record* reported 22). According to the *Record*, the costs - £950,000 before VAT - were to be split between the backers with Souter underwriting the total. 'Keep the Clause' deputy, Jack Cassidy refused to answer the pro-repeal *Sunday Herald* when they asked what brought this particular business group together and exactly how many were clients of Jack Irvine's Media House. He dismissed their questions as "irrelevant". Many of those putting their names forward as sponsors of the 'referendum' were part of the Entrepreneurial Exchange network, and at least four; winners of a top entrepreneur award sponsored by the *Herald*.

Brian Souter, of course, headed the list. He and his wife Betty were both members of the evangelical Church of the Nazarene based in Kansas, USA. As boss of Stagecoach, he had a personal fortune of over £565m at the start of 2000, making him Scotland's richest man. His spokesman explained: "His interests are his family, which he puts above everything else, Stagecoach, which is his baby, and Clause 28, his private belief".

Also down as a sponsor was Brian Souter's 57-year-old sister Ann Gloag, Scotland's richest woman - at her height richer than the Queen - with a personal fortune that was estimated at the time to have been more than £100m and an annual dividend payout of £4m. Leaving Perth High School without a single O-grade, she owned the £2m Beaufort Castle in Invernesshire (for which it was once reported she paid an annual council tax fee of £1,878) and a yellow Bentley with the number plate: 1 ANN. Ann Gloag's son Jonathan had tried to work in his mother's business but things didn't work out and he left to become a chef. He owned a £450,000 mansion on a hill overlooking Perth bought by his mother and had what the *Scottish Daily Mail* typically described as "a loving, pretty wife and three small sons". He was married at 21, three years after his mother's second marriage. Unsurprisingly, there were no announcements or pictures in the local press. The marriage was to his 17-year-old step-sister, Sarah, with whom he had lived and grown-up as a child. Sarah was the daughter of his mother's second husband, David McCleary. Jonathan was described as a devout, sensitive boy and supported his mother in her divorce with her husband Robin Gloag. Jonathan even went on to set up a bus company of his own before joining forces with Brian Souter to drive rival bus company, Highwayman, owned by Robin Gloag off the road. Jonathan stood to inherit the Stagecoach empire, but, on the night of 18 September 1999, at 28, Gloag's son walked a few miles towards his mother's home before taking his own life. He was found hanging from a tree. His father Robin Gloag's name wasn't mentioned at Jonathan's funeral. Ann and Brian's elder brother, the Rev David Souter, conducted the service. By 2007 there was another tragic accident when Jonathan's father Robin was killed after his silver Renault Laguna left the road near Perth and crashed into a field. His overturned car was spotted near a farm by a passing motorist. He was killed. Further tragedy struck in 2009 when Ann Gloag's 24-year-old son, Peter, was involved in a car crash. He was 10 and living in Kenya before being adopted and brought to Scotland for his education. The accident put him in intensive care and left him paralysed.

Amongst Souter's 'referendum' sponsors was another of Jack Irvine's clients: Thomas Blane Hunter, who also went on to earn the title of Scotland's richest man, estimated at the time to be worth around £400m. Only four weeks previously, Tom Hunter had been favourably featured in a profile in the *Scottish Daily Mail* and a report in the *Record* after his £5m donation to Strathclyde University to set up the Hunter Centre for Entrepreneurship. In a similar profile in another 'Keep the Clause'-friendly paper, *Scotland on Sunday*, Hunter claimed: "When

How to Spot a Homosexual

you have as much as I have, making another million isn't going to make a difference". Tom Hunter sold his Sports Division business to JJB Sports for £290m. He drove a blue, tinted windowed Bentley marked 2 TBH. His stake in Internet retailer Toyzone was valued at around £80m and his 20 per cent stake in the Reality Group netted him a further £7m in May 2000 when the company was sold to Great Universal Stores.

Afer a thirty-year marriage which produced two children, a scurrilous report appearing in the *Scottish News of the World* undermined any moral posturing when it alleged he had been caught in Room 3 of a £35-a-night motel on the M6 with fellow executive Mary Rigby. "They indulge their lust then talk about price of steak pies", the paper exclaimed rather piously. The tabloid suggested Mary booked the room under the false name of 'Mrs Barnes'. "But as many travellers will know, the dividing walls between rooms and the motel are not that thick, so the guest in Room 2 last Tuesday could hear everything going on next door. 'The headboard was banging against the wall,' said the guest".

Alf Young, a respected business writer and a personal friend of many of the sponsors of the referendum wrote in the *Herald*: "Tom Hunter says it doesn't really matter whether he thinks Section 28 should be repealed or not. 'This issue is now one of democracy'. Come off it, Tom. You believe there is a genuine majority in Scotland for keeping Section 28. I suspect there is an even more decisive majority in favour of higher taxes on the very wealthy, like you... Were that cause to be given the same PR welly Brian Souter and Keep the Clause have given Section 28, Tom, polls would soon be telling us a decisive majority of Scottish voters want you and I to pay higher taxes. Would you, Brian and all the other sponsors be willing to bankroll a referendum on that issue in the name of democracy? I think I know the answer to that one".

Along with Brian Souter's, Hunter's personal fortunes grew by around £3m in August 2000 when Edinburgh-based Orbital Software, a company producing Internet search engine software packages, confirmed a £70m stock market flotation. Tom Hunter had also invested £1m in Corporate Jets, based at the once Stagecoach-owned Prestwick Airport. His Lear jets were hired for around £1,600 an hour. By the summer of 2001, with Hunter's growing appetite for commercial acquisitions, and after forming a private equity fund, West Coast Capital, he was involved in a joint venture with property tycoon Nick Leslau's Prestbury Investment Holdings for the acquisition of £166m of real estate which included Babcock Park Industrial estate in Glasgow, a 1.7m square foot estate next to Glasgow International Airport, shops and offices in Kensington in London and a business park by the M4 near Maidenhead. West Coast Capital was the principal investment vehicle for the £260m he made selling Sports Division. He was, however; soon back on the high street with his new clothing chain, d2. For his 40th birthday in 2001, his wife Marion booked pop stars Stevie Wonder and Kool and the Gang for a private concert and fancy-dress party outside Monaco. Guests Brian Souter, dressed as Zorro and his sister Ann Gloag as Queen Victoria joined Virgin chief Richard Branson, Scots racing legend Jackie Stewart, TV star Jonathan Ross and many of Tom Hunter's closest friends drinking bottles of £400 chilled Chrystal champagne from a bar carved from solid ice depicting famous Hollywood stars. In 2002 he was ready to pull off his biggest deal since selling Sports Division in 1998 by leading a £168m buy-out of Granchester Holdings, which owned a series of retail parks across Britain. West Coast Capital teamed up again with the Bank of Scotland for the deal leaving it with significant stakes in property portfolios worth around £800m. By 2002, Hunter was trying to buy House of Fraser for £197m, waving a guarantee of payment from the Bank of Scotland, now part of HBOS after its merger with the Halifax Building Society, to persuade the company he had the money as well as bidding for a £700m retail portfolio. The Chartwell retail portfolio comprised 15 retail parks and five development sites. Hunter later unveiled another £200m deal, as HBOS confirmed it was a prolific and solid investment partner for Tom Hunter. In 2003, Hunter scooped £8m after paying £10m for 4.56m shares in the Selfridges stores group before making an offer to buy them out. Unfortunately for Hunter, Canadian billionaire Galen Weston made a higher bid, but after selling his stock for £18m, Hunter was on top again. He went on to make major investments in higher education and would eventually join forces with the Executive to fund £1.8m of research looking at the way primary school teachers were educated. HBOS, through its joint venture team, headed by Peter Cummings, joined forces with Hunter's West Coast Capital to capture Wyevale Garden Centres in 2006 and made further deals in commercial property including an approach to housebuilders Crest Nicholson with a £659m bid, but this was rejected. Under the name 'Mother Bidco', West Coast Capital and HBOS also teamed up with billionaire property moguls, the Reuben brothers to buy Britain's largest retirement home developer, McCarthy & Stone for £1.1billion. Although the bank's first deal with Hunter was in 2001, the relationship went back much further to the 90s when Peter Cummings first started working closely with Hunter and his sports business. In 2006, HBOS's joint venture team had secured twenty property deals worth £2.4bn of debt and equity, selling most of the debt to other lenders whilst keeping the attractive equity stakes.

Another successful entrepreneur that came forward to sponsor Souter's poll was Sir Tom Farmer, a devout Catholic, a personal friend of Cardinal Winning and a papal knight of St Gregory the Great. He was a former chairman of Scotland Against Drugs when David Macauley had fronted it. (Macauley later resigned before fronting 'Keep the Clause' for Jack Irvine and Brian Souter). Sir Tom Farmer established motor repair firm Kwik-Fit in 1971 and sold it to Ford in 1999 for £1billion making £77m on the sale. He also ploughed £6m into Hibernian football club where Jack Irvine had worked briefly as PR. Although still owning many of the bases from which KwikFit operated, he amassed further property developments including Norfolk-based Morston Assets, which planned a £150m development in Linlithgow, and by 2002 Farmer was seeking further planning permission from Falkirk council for a £150m enterprise on a vast 125-acre space owned by Morston Assets outside Falkirk. Farmer also made a substantial financial contribution to the SNP, donating £100,000 in the run-up to the 2007 election. Farmer told reporters he had done it to ensure "a more level playing field".

A less entrepreneurial figure amongst Souter's sponsors was the convener of the Church of Scotland's so-called Board of Responsibility, Anne Allen. Her soft, almost blurred, Hollywood-like, tilted portrait, frequently used in the Scottish press, concealed her evangelical zeal. Mrs Allen's views on homosexuality were already well-known within the Kirk and when Edinburgh council carried out a survey of homophobia Mrs Allen reportedly begged to know why people who were disgusted at the activities of homosexuals weren't also surveyed.

RELIGIOUS FASCISM

Jim Sillars, former MP for Glasgow Govan and deputy leader of the SNP also sponsored Souter's poll. He was a regular columnist in the *Scottish Sun*. His homophobic credentials were on show when he used his column to accuse gays of needing an age of consent as low as possible to keep a "stock of homosexual young males… to ensure a continuous supply of sexual partners. …Sex objects, to be used".

Another entrepreneurial sponsor was Gerald Weisfeld, connected to Tom Hunter through the retail trade, he had helped his wife Vera build up the 'What Everyone Wants' discount chain before selling it for £50m. His wife, born Vera Carlin was brought up on a tough Coatbridge housing scheme and started work in C & A before learning enough about the retail business to develop the stores with her husband. They sold up in 1990, and eight years later Vera was awarded an OBE. With plans to set up a base for their Weisfeld Foundation Charity, the couple, who already had homes in Australia and Stratford-Upon-Avon, paid £1.7m for Torr Hall in Bridge of Weir, Renfrewshire, which boasted its own lake, a helicopter landing pad, tennis courts, stables, ballroom, eight bedrooms, staff flat, coach house cottage and 50 acres of land. The mansion was designed by James Souter of Aberdeen in 1903. The Weisfeld Foundation donated around £1m a year to such charities as the Moira Anderson Foundation, Women's Aid, a home in Romania for people with HIV and the Mercy ships. In a departure from protocol, Princess Anne once accepted a private invitation to dine with Tom Hunter and the Weisfelds and even stayed overnight in Hunter's house in the south of France.

Another wealthy sponsor was David Moulsdale, millionaire chairman of DCM Holdings and owner of Optical Express, the fifth largest chain of opticians in Britain; Health Clinic; Specialeyes and Co-Op Eyecare in the UK. He was a close friend of Tom Hunter. Jack Irvine's Media House also worked for Optical Express. In 2002, they beat off stiff competition from Boots and Specsavers to acquire Health Clinic for £10m from administrators. The deal was part funded through shareholder funds with the rest coming in the form of a debt package from the Bank of Scotland. In an effort to use the Netherlands as a testing ground for rapid expansion into Europe, Mousdale bought two eye laser clinics from Free Vision Euro Eyes, one in Amsterdam and the other in The Hague.

How to Spot a Homosexual

Other wealthy sponsors included Pat and Alex Grant. They had both set up Norfrost in Caithness on a shoestring budget in 1972. They owned one of the largest refrigeration businesses in the world and were understood to be one of the UK's few manufacturers of chest freezers. Manufacturing white goods under the Norfrost and Aura brands, their customers included retail chain Dixons, Mars confectioners and Coca Cola. Although the couple had no children together, Pat's son by a former marriage, Clay was an occasional member of the International Church of Christ sect and evoked criticism when he attempted to post homophobic posters up in Edinburgh. Although no stranger to gay sex himself, he claimed to have been "tormented by guilt" and had tried to take his own life. Pat Grant was a close friend of Souter's sister Ann Gloag through the Scottish Business Trust.

Another sponsor was Hugh Adam, a trustee of the 'Keep the Clause' campaign and a former director of Rangers Football Club. Adam also ran the Rangers Pool Division. After spouting the almost obligatory: 'I'm not homophobic, but…' precursor in the *Scottish Sun*, he revealed that: "My difficulty is that I cannot persuade myself that homosexuality is other than an abnormality. That does not mean, of course, that its practitioners are diminished in any way as human beings. I know that there are many people with the same views as myself but decline to speak out for fear of being branded politically incorrect. I urge them to come out".

John Cameron, a Fife landowner and farmer who was chairman of the National Farmers' Union of Scotland also came forward as a sponsor of Souter's poll. He was also railway advisor to Brian Souter's Stagecoach and director of South West Trains. South West Trains became embroiled in a court battle when they refused to grant the partner of a lesbian employee subsidised travel in the same way they offered subsidised travel for partners of heterosexuals and, in a separate case, was fined £4million by the Strategic Rail Authority for offering unreliable services.

Another wealthy sponsor was Donald Macdonald, a crofter's son from the Isle of Harris who had worked his way to the top at Stakis Hotels before establishing a chain of hotels of his own: Bathgate-based Macdonald Hotels. In June 2000, they announced a £100m joint venture with the Bank of Scotland and Royal Bank of Scotland to build 10 upmarket city centre hotels. Macdonald Hotels announced an eight per cent increase in underlying pre-tax profits to £13.8m in 1999 and won the Scottish Enterprise top Elite award after notching up an 18% rise in operating profits. They were voted 'Scotland's fastest-growing company' two years in a row while pre-tax profits rose 15% to £7m in 2000. The group boasted an annual turnover of £40.6m. With 26 owned and 53 managed hotels, Macdonald Hotels became engaged in a joint venture with Sheffield University for a 110-bedroom hotel as well as a number of other ambitious hotel projects. Asked if the company was vulnerable to takeover, Macdonald was reported saying the board owned more than 30 per cent with probably another 20 per cent or 30 per cent in "very friendly hands". Those friendly hands included Scottish company Standard Life, Scottish Equitable, Scottish Mutual and Edinburgh Fund Managers. By 2001, together with the Bank of Scotland in a fifty-fifty joint venture, they purchased 48 upmarket, country Heritage Hotels from Compass in a deal worth around £235m and gained full control of its Barratt Resorts timeshare for £8.5m. In 2007 Donald Macdonald gave the SNP £30,000. Once the SNP were in power, Macdonald's planning application for his resort in Aviemore was speeded up to prevent the collapse of the project and save 300 jobs.

George Russell, the chief executive of Scotland The Brand, a company promoting Scottish products overseas, became a sponsor after being approached by Brian Souter with whom he had long-standing personal and church connections. George Russell told the *Sunday Herald:* "I'm not in the same church, but we follow the same Saviour". Scotland The Brand was established in 1994 as a division of Scottish Enterprise. It was semi-privatised in 2003 with Scottish Enterprise ceasing subsidies but retaining a director with enhanced voting rights. In 2004, members of Scotland the Brand voted to wind up the organisation before Scottish Enterprise took over the management of the Scotland the Brand mark for members and licensees. The Scottish Executive was criticised by chairman Nick Kuenssberg for undermining their success.

Bill Hughes, once the Treasurer and Deputy Chairman of the Scottish Conservative Party, a key figure in the Scottish division of the CBI and an elder in the Church of Scotland also stepped forward as a sponsor. He was also an architect of Scottish Enterprise as well as a chairman of Grampian Holdings, a company Jack Irvine also did PR work for. The *Scottish Daily*

How to Spot a Homosexual

Mail, proclaiming itself "the favourite newspaper of Britain's leading businessmen" claimed: "It was his Christian duty to support moves to retain Section 28". Hughes explained: "As a Christian, I believe in the sanctity of marriage and that the traditional family unit is critically important. It is the ideal state of affairs in which to propagate a child. This stance is strongly taken by our minister, Alistair Horne, and the membership of the church are totally behind him".

David McLetchie, leader of the Scottish Conservatives and MSP for Lothian was also a sponsor. McLetchie would be outspoken on later efforts to make marriage more inclusive for same-sex couples when he proclaimed: "Organisations fighting to preserve the traditional definition of marriage believe homosexual groups should not have the right to redefine marriage for everyone and that people should not be intimidated into going along with it because of political correctness". The Scottish Conservative Party had their Holyrood campaign bankrolled by the reclusive Monaco-based tax exile Irvine Laidlaw. Although not on the list of Souter's sponsors, Laidlaw became Scotland's second richest man in 2006 with a personal fortune estimated at £730m. He donated £2m to an Academy in Newcastle and wanted to donate cash to Scottish schools using the City Academy model introduced by Tony Blair, but this was rejected by Scottish ministers. He was later caught spending £27,000 on an orgy with one male and four female sex workers in the £6,000-a-night presidential suite of Monte Carlo's Hermitage Hotel. After details emerged he checked himself in to a sex-addict programme and donated £1million to help fellow "sufferers".

Other sponsors of Souter's poll were Sir David McNee, formerly Chief Constable of Strathclyde Police and Commissioner of the Metropolitan Police from 1977 to 1983 when Conservative leader Margaret Thatcher was Prime Minister, and Fergus Ewing, a staunch Catholic SNP MSP for Inverness East, Nairn and Lochaber and deputy shadow minister for tourism, small businesses and the Highlands and Islands. Also amongst the sponsors was James Peter Hymers Mackay, Lord MacKay of Clashfern, a former elder of the hardline Free Presbyterian Church of Scotland, a retired former Lord Chancellor from 1987 – 1997 and member of Prime Minister Margaret Thatcher's Cabinet. On later legislation, The Equality Act (Sexual Orientation) Regulations (Northern Ireland) 2006, which sparked a process ending discrimination on the grounds of sexual orientation in the provision of goods, facilities and services, he wrote in the *Daily Telegraph*, saying: "If, as I believe, the regulations are intended to make it unlawful to refuse to facilitate homosexual acts, then it is obvious that those who practice a faith that considers homosexual activity to be sinful are being subjected to a law that seeks to over-ride their consciences". While the impending legislation was being prepared, MacKay insisted: "It follows that such a person (a religionist) will not wish to undertake any activity that involves participating in or facilitating the carrying out of practices by others which he considers sinful for himself".

Mackay had his own element of notoriety to contend with. Attending the funeral Masses of Catholic friends, one of whom was a member of the judiciary in his role as Lord Advocate, was deemed so outrageous it caused a split in the Free Presbyterian Church. Mackay was suspended and the Associated Presbyterian Church had to be formed in 1989 to support greater 'liberty of conscience' and accommodate such supposed misdemeanours as Lord Mackay's.

Lord Mackay of Clashfern's most controversial move came in 2010 when, at 83, as a former Lord Advocate, Lord Clerk Register and honorary president of the Scottish Bible Society, whose official patron is the Queen, called upon Scotland's legislatures to take biblical teachings into account when applying the law and fronted a campaign to have Bibles sent to every court in the land! Copies were delivered to Sheriff Courts; the High Court; the Court of Session; the Faculty of Advocates; the Crown Office and offices of the Procurator Fiscal service. Mackay invited sheriffs and judges to re-familiarise themselves with biblical principles and act accordingly when presiding over court cases. He warned that "since the prosecution of crime in Scotland is at the instance of the Crown, the words taken from the coronation oath (accepting the Bible as 'Royal Law'), it also served as a reminder that the vital elements of justice and mercy are to be uppermost in the mind of a Crown prosecutor as well as in the mind of the judge". The National Secular Society's president, Terry Sanderson responded: "What Lord Mackay is proposing could put the Sharia laws of the Middle East to shame. He and the Scottish Bible Society make absolutely no concessions to the progress of legal thought over the past two millennia.

How to Spot a Homosexual

Killing witches and homosexuals and stoning adulterers are all clearly stated legal requirements in the Christian holy book. Are they seriously suggesting that Scottish sheriffs and judges should follow the Bible to the letter? How would the Scottish seafood industry fare if the biblical ban on shellfish were to be enforced? And would Shetland's knitwear industry flourish if there was a ban on garments made from two kinds of material, as required in the Bible?"

Other sponsors included Andrew Welsh, lay preacher and a chairman of the powerful audit committee of the Scottish parliament and Neil Hood, Professor of Business Policy, director of Strathclyde University's International Business Unit, advisor to Scottish Enterprise and a non-executive director of Kwik-Fit (whose former chairman was Tom Farmer) and Grampian Holdings (whose former chairman was Bill Hughes). They were joined by Vali Hussein, vice-principal of the Islamic Academy of Scotland who promoted research in Islamic Jerusalem. Hussein told the *Scottish Daily Mail* how his deep religious convictions led him to take a stand. "I firmly believe the promotion of homosexual acts is completely immoral and is a terrible thing to teach innocent children in schools. I do not want such things in schools. We respect family values and want children to grow up in a normal environment and not be brainwashed into thinking something abnormal is normal".

The *Scottish Daily Mail* assured: "There is not a fanatic, a crank or a so-called 'homophobe' among them". The *Record* crowed: "This time, Souter doesn't stand alone. He had put together an impressive bunch of backers from every walk of Scottish society who share his rage at the Government's arrogant refusal to listen to public opinion over gay sex lessons in schools. Along with church leaders, they include academics..."

Brian Souter promised a private 'referendum' so that everybody could have "THEIR" say. The *Record* spewed out its praise in another editorial: "There's one thing you have to give Brian Souter - he's got guts". Tim Hopkins of the Equality Network advised: "Brian Souter has just spent half a million pounds promoting misinformation about section 28 across Scotland - the biggest billboard campaign ever. Now he wants to measure whether his adverts have had an effect. That's not democracy. We elect our MSPs to examine issues carefully, weigh the evidence, and take a decision. That is democracy, and we believe that MSPs will make the right decision. The last thing we need in Scotland is the Americanisation of politics, where what matters is not the facts, but how many millions are spent on advertising and promotion. Children's welfare groups like Childline and Children in Scotland, and groups working in education like teachers, Directors of Education and the Church of Scotland Education Committee, support repeal of Section 28, because they know Section 28 benefits no-one, and does a lot of harm to young gay people. It would be quite wrong for MSPs to ignore that evidence".

It would prove a difficult challenge to persuade the electorate that there is good reason for their not being entitled to vote on issues of human rights – like hanging - and that MSPs are their representatives, not delegates, in Parliament. This issue worried the liberal-minded long before the surge of universal voting rights. In the nineteenth century, Napoleon III ordered plebiscites and whipped up the prejudices of the conservative majority whenever it suited him. A constitution protected by courts, out of reach of the majority, acts as a compromise in many countries. Donald Dewar did his best to explain that referendums were only used for great constitutional issues, such as whether the UK should be a member of the European Union or whether Scotland should have a parliament. Meanwhile, *Daily Record* editorials continued to spin the tale that "ample evidence" showed "unsuitable teaching material" was being prepared for the nation's children while the Government refused to listen. They warned: "If Mr Souter's devastating poster campaign got under the Government's skin, his decision to bankroll a nationwide referendum will send them right into orbit". When envelopes "filled with disgusting material" was found in envelopes sent to 'Keep the Clause's freepost address, the *Record* focused on the "Royal Mail workers" and how they had to be issued with protective gloves and clothing. The tabloid reported: "Gay rights campaigners are said to be behind the move" while the *Scottish Sun* reported "condoms – sent by gay rights activists fighting to scrap Clause 28". (It was reported elsewhere that envelopes containing condoms, excrement and hypodermic needles had been posted in England). So-called 'gay activists' in Scotland recommended Souter's ballot paper simply be torn up. Eager to receive whole boxes of signed petitions, the *Record* advertised a freepost parcel delivery address but soon found themselves in possession of a broken fridge, a garden gate, a large soggy mattress, wrapped bricks, boxes of stones and even a scrapped Volvo 440.

Media House's Jack Irvine once again demonstrated his ineptness in handling the affairs of 'Keep the Clause' when he was questioned on Scottish TV News. The reporter asked if the Electoral Reform Society (ERS) had agreed whether 'Keep the Clause' could go ahead with a 'referendum'. Jack Irvine assured the reporter documents had been signed before he was told that the Electoral Reform Society had denied it. He tried to explain that he hadn't meant *that* document, but *other* documents with *other* people involved, insisting he had an "agreement with them we are going ahead". A "stunned" Brian Souter cried to his cronies at the *Record* that there had been an "enormous breach of trust". The *Record* printed a picture of a blurred letter dated 3 March 2000 from the Electoral Reform Services (ERS) that "outlined a timescale and methodology that could be adopted for such a referendum" and an estimate based on a similar referendum once commissioned by Strathclyde Regional Council. Sources close to the ERS admitted that there had been some internal wrangling over the issue, with staff wanting to ditch it. The *Scottish Mail* declared: "So far we have witnessed Brian Souter and Cardinal Thomas Winning subjected to vicious abuse by politicians and commentators whose so-called liberalism has been exposed as downright intolerance. Are the co-sponsors of this referendum now going to be subjected to similar treatment? Will those who demonised Mr Souter as a maverick tycoon with more money than sense turn their vitriolic attacks on Tom Hunter, Sir Tom Farmer, David Moulsdale, Sir David McNee, Pat Grant and the rest? We hope not". Both the *Record* and the *Scottish Mail* printed Brian Souter's statement to back their story. He said: "Parents are angry that a social equality argument over sexuality, valid for consenting adults, is being applied to children". Demonstrating an admiration for European methods, he also defended his argument for a referendum by recommending that this was the way policies were decided in Switzerland. The *Scottish Mail* returned to the Scottish School Board's Association survey and tagged it on to the end of their story. "A survey conducted by the Scottish School Boards' Association of its members - representing 80 per cent of Scottish schools - has shown 90 per cent of parents are against repeal". In fact, less than half of school boards' members responded, representing a third of all school boards and a quarter of Scotland's 3,000 schools. 40 per cent wanted the matter put on hold until more information was available. This figure was lumped with 46 per cent who had not consulted parents or seen any detailed information on the subject and were either against repeal or recorded a split vote. When these figures were added together, of course, it was made to appear that 90 per cent supported the retention of Section 28. The *Record* was otherwise engaged with the antics of pop star Ricky Martin, pictured swinging his backside round to face the camera along with commentary on his "gay side-step". They wrote: "Latin pop idol Ricky Martin fuelled rumours that he was gay when he refused to discuss his sexuality on an American chat show. Ricky was happy to discuss his boozing and drug-using past", they added.

The *Scottish Mirror* featured a picture of Prime Minister Tony Blair standing next to First Minister Donald Dewar with the caption: "Is that a smile or is the knife in your back making me wince"? Their Scottish political editor, Lorraine Davidson wrote: "Furious Tony Blair warned Donald Dewar he would be hung out to dry in the battle to scrap Clause 28 - if he didn't halt the damaging row in Scotland". Tony Blair had apparently told Dewar he was on his own after Dewar complained his hands were tied on the issue because of the Liberal Democrats. Blair wanted him to end the row over the issue because the massive public backlash was proving too damaging.

The *Herald* could barely conceal its impatience with Brian Souter in their editorial. Calling his poll "a referendum too far…" they suggested: "If we had too many referenda we would be entitled to ask what the point was in having Government". Faced with the privatisation of water by a previous Tory Government, Strathclyde region itself had organised a referendum with an inevitable result. But the *Herald* explained: "Mr Souter has no mandate other than money (and a tricksy PR outfit)". Robbie Dinwoodie, their Scottish political correspondent explained: "In keeping with the way the whole campaign has been run, news of the development was given only to newspapers which have given editorial support to the campaign to halt the repeal of Section 28… Media House were approached for comment on reaction to the referendum plan, but they declined to return the call". Local Government spokesman Donald Gorrie reminded the *Herald* how school pupils would be denied a voice under Souter's proposal and columnist Iain Macwhirter wrote: "Brian Souter's plebiscite, if it happens, will cause deep divisions within Scottish society. The lies about 'gay sex lessons' being taught in schools will be spread again by billboard, tabloid and pulpit. The voice of the Scottish parliament drowned by the homophobic megaphones". Iain Macwhirter visioned "a head-count after a campaign of lies" and expressed a deep regret over Scotland's fledgling democracy's "inability to cope with popularism…"

In response to the promise of a 'referendum', the *Scotsman* commissioned two pieces, one from George Kerevan, the independent MSP, and another from *Sunday Times's* conservative columnist Allan Massie. Kerevan castigated Souter's "deep-seated religious beliefs" that encouraged "his sad, anti-gay obsessions". Allan Massie, on the other hand, showed a lack of interest in the whole affair. "I would rather the Scottish executive had had the sense to let the sleeping dog of Section 28 lie, till, disused, the clause mouldered". Mouldering away unnoticed it might have been to the likes of Allan Massie, but a smouldering reminder it was to the many gays, lesbians, bisexuals and transgendered who grew up in its shadow. Forgetting for a moment 'Keep the Clause's' contribution in all of this, Massie blamed Wendy Alexander, "who couldn't see the trouble ahead" for having "stirred things up and made what was not a political issue of any consequence a topic of fierce debate".

Only when Brian Souter attempted to bankroll his 'referendum' did the *Scottish Daily Express* wake up from its malaise in its editorial. "This newspaper has backed the democratic right of Stagecoach boss Brian Souter to oppose the Executive's plans to abolish legislation prohibiting the promotion of homosexuality in our schools. We have also recognised that he is allowed to pump his own hard-earned money into that campaign. However, his latest wheeze, to hold what he calls a referendum of the people of Scotland on the matter, marks a bleak day for the democratic process in this country".

The Electoral Reform Society further backtracked after reports from Scotland of more attacks on gays. A spokesman for Lothian and Borders police said: "There's certainly been an increase in homophobic attacks. Keep the Clause has had an effect".

RELIGIOUS FASCISM

Brian Souter told the *Scottish Daily Mail:* "It is outrageous that gay cliques within the Labour Party are now putting intolerable pressure on the Electoral Reform Society..." A letter pictured in the *Scottish Mail* from the ERS's deputy chief executive Sian Roberts outlined how it intended to conduct the 'referendum', but the paper failed to draw readers' attention to the top of the letter which clearly spelled out: "RE: POSSIBLE REFERENDUM". People naturally began to question if the 'referendum' would go ahead.

The finger of blame continued to be laid at the feet of 'gays' or a 'gay clique,' echoing MP Jimmy Wray's reference to a 'gay mafia' in the *Scottish Sun* and in the *Scotsman* where he advised: "People didn't vote Labour into power to allow the country to be run by a gay mafia. The public don't want to know what homosexuals are doing. This is the trendy minority trying to dictate to the majority, and it won't work". The *Scottish Sun* also reported: "Stagecoach boss Brian Souter last night accused a gay clique within Labour of trying to wreck plans for a referendum on Section 28". Echoing the Nazi treatment of Jews in the thirties when there were references to powerful Jewish cliques influencing government and of Jewish trickery, the *Scottish Sun* referred to "gay dirty tricks". The *Record* reported: "Tycoon Brian Souter accused the Government and the gay lobby of sabotaging the plan for the referendum..." Headlining the eruption of "fury" gays had caused, the *Record's* 8.5cm lettering declared Souter's efforts well and truly "POLL AXED" along with a picture of Brian Souter looking "concerned". The *Record* reported Souter claiming that "the gay lobby had managed to influence the U-turn..." This was also a clear reference to gay MP and ERS member, Stephen Twigg who denied spiking the 'referendum'. The *Record* was not amused. Its editorial spat: "The Section 28 turmoil has gone from unsatisfactory to downright sinister. It is now clear that powerful factions are determined that the people of Scotland will not have their say". The *Record* turned on the ERS. "If they refuse the people the chance to give their opinion on Section 28, they will be accused of showing partiality to the gay lobby. It would be a shame if such an important body lost its authority by caving in to a minority, no matter how influential... If the voters are not allowed to have their say now, they will have it sooner or later..."

How to Spot a Homosexual

Later, after things appeared to be "back on track" with the Electoral Reform Society, the *Record's* attitude changed: "The respected organisation had already signalled to Souter and his backers that they would go ahead with the ballot. But they staged a last-minute rethink which left them open to accusations that they were responding to Government pressure". All the same, the tabloid's editorial expressed utter contempt for any suggestion that people might tear up their ballot paper. The *Record* warned: "The Government is determined to do all it can to sabotage the referendum of the Scottish people on Section 28. So afraid are they of the will of the people that suggestions for a 'bin the ballot' campaign are being made at the highest level. They hope that if enough people boycott the referendum, the results will be discredited... The Executive is also likely to run into major problems if it tries to pay for such a campaign out of public funds". With a shameless disregard for its own contribution, the *Record* opined: "The longer the Section 28 dispute drags on, the worse the damage to Scottish society and relations between Parliament and the people. A responsible Scottish Government would be seeking to heal the divisions. Instead, day by day, they are making them worse".

R D Don from Girvan wrote to the *Herald* to wag a finger at the First Minister: "If he had been exposed to some of the evils that I have seen among 'gay' (there's nothing gay about depravity) communities around the world, he would not be so keen to encompass them in what he holds as 'normal' relations. More strength to Brian Souter. Thank God someone is prepared to stand up for decency. I for one will be pleased to receive his referendum form".

P Wardlaw from Carnoustie despaired: "Of course we cannot expect sense from Brian Souter - he's clearly a few coaches short of a bus fleet - but has the rest of Scotland gone completely mad too? How can we expect the rest of Europe to take us seriously as a modern nation if we act like refugees from the Middle Ages? God help us if we ever get complete independence - we'll be having public executions before you can say 'Cardinal Winning'".

The *Scottish Daily Mail's* editorial soon got agitated: "The Electoral Reform Society has stated it would only participate in the exercise if it advanced the cause of democracy in Scotland. The fact that it was not prepared to commit itself to the project last night is cause for alarm in that failure to proceed as planned would be seen as bowing to outside influences... The whole future course of democracy in Scotland is now at stake. The people must have their say".

Writing in the *Scottish Daily Express*, Keith Aitken wanted a "gentle" word with Brian Souter. "You evidently think you are doing us all a big favour by giving us a referendum. Actually, you are treating us with monumental insolence. Why? Two reasons. First, your actions imply that we, lacking your wealth, are incapable of making our democracy work properly. But our democracy is not an ailing company to be sorted out by a hostile bid. It's something that was fought for over generations by people with smaller pockets but bigger ideas than you. The idea they fought for was that public policy should be determined according to public rules, not private privilege. It is for the public to decide whether the rules are right, not for you. You are one five millionth of the Scottish public, and not a fraction more. The way our democracy works is that we elect an administration by reference to its broad policies and outlook, we let it get on with the job, and we change it at the next general election if we don't like what it has done. The fact that you evidently lack the patience for that process doesn't mean that the system isn't working, merely that it isn't delivering what you want... Secondly, it is an impertinence for you to suppose that you can hire voters like casual staff. Scotland is not a rotten borough that can be sent obediently to the polls at your feudal command... The simple truth, I rather suspect, is that you are proposing to confect a referendum for no more complicated reason than the belief that you can win it. Please don't be offended by that assertion. It is exactly the same motivation which has driven every politician who has ever called for a referendum. The difference, of course, is that we can get rid of politicians. I'm not quite clear how we get rid of you".

The *Daily Record's* Joan Burnie produced a piece on Scots who had been prevented from expressing their views. "To them it looks like a sinister, politically correct stitch-up - with everyone but those most involved having the First Minister's ear". The majority of people she spoke to, of course, applauded Souter's efforts. "Either that,", she wrote, "or they echo the feelings of those such as William Campbell, 71, of Dundee, who suspects this obsession with Section 28 is all a red herring, to 'cover up some far more serious issues". She advised: "The Government's priorities were questioned again and again, not least by Labour voters who fail to see why this single issue, above all others, must be tackled, when anyone can see there is so much that requires attention in our brave new Scotland".

Columnist Katie Grant was full of praise for Souter's referendum backers in the *Scottish Daily Mail*. "Not one of those supporting a referendum, from Tom Hunter to Vali Hussein, could be accused with any credibility of being homophobic or anti-democratic. You could not even call them part of the awkward squad". She generously saw the referendum as "a neat way out for Mr Dewar". Under a picture of one of the 'Keep the Clause' propaganda posters showing Donald Dewar with his fingers in his ears, Mrs Grant attacked the First Minister. "Dewar now appears to feel that democracy is more his enemy than his friend. The idea of a referendum seems to cause him some affront. This only serves to underline the general feeling that slowly but surely Donald Dewar is becoming more distant from the nation he governs. He is up there on the Mound, flanked by his Executive, living in one world. The rest of us are out here living in another... Quite what Dewar sees is a mystery - even, perhaps, to Dewar. The result has been that this erstwhile thoroughly respected astute politician is now perceived to be drifting along like a stick in a river, tossed about helplessly and occasionally getting badly snagged". Mrs Grant was also full of praise for the "nimble feet" of the Scottish Nationalist Party for shifting their position "to support statutory guidelines". But they were guidelines that supported a 'stable family' and not the 'one man; one woman' one the *Daily Mail* and Mrs Grant wanted. Also, in Scotland, sex education was part of a consultative process between parents and teachers and not governed by statute as it was in England and Wales, where parents and governors determined sex education as laid out by the provisions of the 1994 Education Act.

A letter printed in the *Scottish Mail* from Douglas Sampson from Melrose offered encouragement to Souter's sponsors. "Congratulations to the Scottish Daily Mail and Brian Souter, our champions for the silent masses of Scotland. Congratulations also to all those 'concerned individuals' who are organising and financing this Electoral Reform Society referendum on Section 28. The list reads well. In the absence of a House of Lords in

Scotland, might it not be a good idea to retain the services of these responsible citizens as a watching brief on this irresponsible Scottish Government?"

On Thursday, 30 March, 2000, across the border, the press concentrated on the frank exchange in the House of Commons over Labour's failure to repeal Section 28 in England and Wales between Prime Minister Tony Blair and the shadow minister William Hague. Hague challenged Blair with the words: "Just so we know what we have to do to get you to back off from this politically-correct nonsense, will you tell us, if the Lords defeat it one more time will you abandon it?" There was every prospect of a humiliating defeat in the Tory-led House of Lords. Unless a compromise could be reached, the whole bill - including the prospect of elected city mayors - would be lost. There was speculation that Section 28 could be entirely dropped from the bill. In London, mayoral favourite Ken Livingstone promised he would terminate Greater London Authority contracts with homophobic firms. This was a clear – albeit improbable - threat to Stagecoach, whose buses filled London streets. Ken Livingstone said: "I think Brian Souter's campaign in Scotland is homophobic. I would not countenance London buses becoming associated with that sort of cause". Souter snapped back: "It is none of Ken Livingstone's business".

In the House of Commons, Tony Blair took the safest route over Section 28 and told the Conservative leader he was simply "committed to the repeal of it". He added: "We in particular remain absolutely set against the mischievous propaganda campaign run against this that has suggested that, in some way, by repealing Section 28, children in our schools are going to have their sex education lessons changed... This campaign is based on people who don't want to come out and say they are prejudiced against gay people and so they hide behind the issue of child protection". The *Herald* reported how "Mr Hague consistently side-stepped the challenge from the Prime Minister, concentrating instead on the apparent contradiction that, if Section 28 did not apply to schools, then why did the Government want to repeal it". Jack Irvine, confident his own reputation for irrational behaviour was now behind him, gave his response in the *Scotsman* to the Prime Minister's labelling of opponents to the repeal of Section 28 as bigots. "Frankly, I find it an astonishing view for Blair to take, but it might suggest the level of stress that he and Donald Dewar are under over this issue, in that they are now making irrational statements".

The *Daily Mail* printed a "tongue-in-cheek" list of questions to put "New Labour's 'patriotism' to the test". They asked the question: "You believe in the family, so how do you help to protect it? A) Follow the German and French lead and give married couples huge tax breaks. B) Scrap the Married Couples Allowance and encourage schools to promote homosexuality. C) Make divorce illegal and adultery a criminal offence". If your scorecard showed all C's, Edward Heathcoat Amory's quiz suggested: "You are clearly a force of conservatism and will be deported with your home being donated to a Romanian gipsy". For the B's, you were "a perfect Blairite Briton" and scoring all A's you were asked to learn to be more modern.

Columnist, Edward Heathcoat Amory's right-wing aversion to the European Convention of Human Rights (ECHR) made him ideal *Daily Mail* material. He wrote: "Labour's obsession with incorporating European human rights laws into our legal system threatens to undermine every aspect of British life", adding: "Our slapstick comedy politicians have got Britain into another fine mess. Carried away by their desire to suck up to the rest of Europe, they have rushed to embrace the Human Rights Act". He fumed over the "vandalism that has undermined the Scottish judiciary" and singled out the ECHR as an "experiment". Scotland, he blasted, was "a political laboratory in which half-baked policies could be tried out". This "idiocy" was supposed to "undermine a system that survived 300 years of Union", and the "new Scottish parliament" was to blame. Producing a shopping list of horrors the Executive had produced, he added: "The Executive is increasing the rights of gay couples to give them parity with heterosexuals, rather than fall foul of the equal opportunities provisions of the Convention".

When Anne Smith QC, hired by the Christian Institute, claimed repeal of Section 28 could breach the European Convention on Human Rights because of a perceived lack of safeguards, the Christian Institute rushed to have her opinion sent to every Scottish MSP.

The European Convention of Human Rights (ECHR) had nothing to do with the European Union but was a convention of the Council of Europe that Britain signed up to in the forties. Both Conservative and Labour abided by the rulings of the

European Court of Human Rights with it incorporated into Scottish law.

"GAY RIGHTS AND THE END OF MARRIAGE", was Edward Heathcoat Amory's next hysterical assertion. "The changed law is certain to lead to a flood of other challenges, with gays demanding exactly the same rights as married couples in every field, from public housing to inheritance, from taxation to pension rights". With an illustration of a bomb being detonated, the caption ran: "EURO LAW TIME BOMB". The *Scottish Mail's* editorial imagined "a new tyranny of human rights" and "scenes from British life, a year or two from now: In a packed courtroom, the head of a public school is ordered to pay damages for the 'offence' of banning gay sex between his pupils... Meanwhile at a nearby office, staff turn up in jeans and trainers, knowing that their bosses can no longer insist on suits. Welcome to the brave new world emerging under the European Convention of Human Rights. Such examples of politically-correct lunacy could become almost routine". Robert Boyd, an education lawyer gasped in the *Scotsman:* "Sodomy after the age of 16 is going to be lawful and gay children at boarding schools may insist that they have the right to have sex with one another". John Scott, director of the Scottish Human Rights Centre accused him of scaremongering and explained that the key word in the convention was the right to an education. Scott advised that the ruling simply made it clear that a school couldn't expel a teenager and deny them their right to an education for having sex if they were over the age of consent.

The discovery of two Frenchmen 'marrying' in Edinburgh brought on a flurry of moral panic amidst the Section 28 debate. This administrative act took place in the French consulate. The legislation, containing all the legal benefits but none of the vows of matrimony was known as *Pacte Civil de Solidarite* (PACS) and was introduced by the French government in 1999. The *Scottish Mail* stomped: "A Scotsman and his gay French partner have become the first homosexual couple to be 'married' in Scotland". The Catholic Church leapt into the story with their frocks flying and "immediately demanded assurances from the Scottish Executive that similar legislation would not be introduced in Scotland". The *Mail* hinted darkly that Jacques Chirac's introduction of the PACS was met with objections from national and local politicians. Yet not enough to stop it becoming law.

How to Spot a Homosexual

Reporter Gavin Madeley gasped: "Up to 100,000 French couples are expected to sign an agreement over the next year". While this was left to appear as though thousands of gay couples were queuing to sign up, in reality, this figure also included straight couples. Cardinal Winning "asked for reassurances from First Minister Donald Dewar that the concept of marriage would not be broadened to include gay couples". A spokesman for the Catholic Church added: "Any move towards recognising gay marriages is an attack on the marriage-based family..." The cautious statement that appeared in the *Scottish Mail* by the spokesperson for the French Consul-General in Scotland, Anita Limido, was explained by the Consul-General's role as political observer in a climate of hostility towards gay men in Scotland: "This was a purely administrative act. We cannot comment as this is a private matter between two men".

Lothian and Borders police in Edinburgh, recognising the difficulties gays were experiencing in Scotland at this time, opened a special surgery in the gay area of the capital. The *Scottish Sun* quipped: "Send for the boys in pink".

The *Daily Record* issued "a simple pointer" to help establish someone's sexual orientation. Echoing the pseudo-science of phrenology whereby millions of Germans under Nazi rule had their head shapes, nose sizes, hair and eye colours measured to determine racial purity, the tabloid declared that men who were the youngest in a large family of boys "are more likely to be gay". There was a picture of a hand with advice on how to spot a gay. "...Gay men with several older brothers had an unusually 'masculine' second and fourth finger length ratio. But gay men with no older brothers had finger lengths the same as heterosexuals... Lesbians had a greater difference in length between their second and fourth fingers than 'straight' women". The *Daily Mail* did better and printed a double-page spread with an anatomical diagram of the human phalanges explaining: "Homosexual men have slightly shorter second fingers than straight men". And "lesbians tend to have the homosexual male characteristic of a shorter second finger". After ransacking picture libraries, a selection of photographs was found of "well-known figures whose sexuality - present and past - is, almost without exception, known". This was presented "in the interests of scientific debate - and public curiosity..." Included was Prince Edward whose picture, taken on his wedding day, showed his "index finger is clearly longer", indicating that he was, as the *Daily Mail* always suspected, completely straight. Similar research demonstrating at the time that gay men had bigger penises than straight men was ignored. R Bain of Balloch wrote to the *Herald* complaining; "one of my hands is homosexual and the other heterosexual. Fortunately in my case for most of the time the right hand does not know what the left hand is doing..."

Such discussion was not new. When, on 13 March 1996, Thomas Hamilton gunned down 16 children in a Dunblane school, the *Daily Mail* summoned a graphologist to reveal: "He was almost certainly a sexual misfit" with "homosexual leanings" because "...the lower loops of his handwriting lean heavily to the left".

A letter titled "gay myth" in the *Scottish Mail* repudiated the claim gays represented 10 per cent of the population, and, quoting from the *Sexual Behaviour in Britain* survey, insisted it was only "between 1 pc and 2 pc".

Continuing to stoke the fires of moral outrage, the *Record* turned on "Soap chiefs rapped for Eastbender". The homophobic headline was used to describe, not another flagrant demonstration of homosexuality, but a story on the broadcasting watchdog's criticism of BBC soap *Eastenders*. "The Broadcasting Standards Commission upheld two viewers' complaints, saying the show had gone 'beyond acceptable boundaries'". The storyline covered ten of the characters going to Amsterdam to celebrate Ian and Barry's joint wedding to Melanie and Natalie. The *Record* listed the almost relentless "drunken and promiscuous behaviour, sexual innuendo and drug-taking, before the watershed... In December's programme, Mel... was challenged to kiss men from six countries. Natalie... had to acquire three love bites. Her husband-to-be, Barry, was caught kissing his mother-in-law, Andrea. The rest of the men, wearing clown wigs, visited the red-light district to try to buy a prostitute for idiotic Robbie... who was violently sick after smoking a joint". Although such boisterous behaviour for a combined hen and stag weekend was fairly predictable, it was still too much for the *Record* and the two viewers whose complaints had been upheld. The tabloid warned how in 1999 "a survey for the Commission showed the proportion of people who believed there was too much sex on TV had jumped from 32 per cent to 36 per cent".

There were echoes here of a previous campaign, when, appalled by "lashings of flesh and fornication" and "unashamed salaciousness" on TV, the *Record* launched: SmutWatch. "We're not prudes, but..." the editorial explained, "every move they make we – and you – will be watching them".

On the evening of Friday, 31 March 2000, *BBC News Scotland* made the announcement that the Electoral Reform Society had abandoned its plans to conduct a referendum for Brian Souter. In the newsroom, Jack Irvine swivelled his chair round to face the ERS spokesman, Ken Ritchie. Then, in an unconcealed rage, called the ERS "spineless" and "gutless". Ritchie, visibly shocked at Irvine's language, expressed deep misgivings about the true motives behind Souter's campaign. Ritchie had phoned society members asking them if they wanted to get involved, and they hadn't. The *Herald* admitted they had also written to the ERS pleading for them not to go ahead. Ritchie tried to explain the complexities of balloting and wording sensitive issues such as this. He said it was not the Electoral Reform Society that took the decision not to conduct the referendum for 'Keep the Clause' but their professional balloters who didn't want to compromise their integrity. The ERS felt no-one could form a final opinion over repealing Section 28 until they had seen the guidelines that replaced it. Columnist and SNP politician, Jim Sillars in the *Scottish Sun* hit out at Labour for pandering to "fanatical minorities" and the ERS for showing itself "to be engaged in humbug. Its excuse for not holding a ballot on Section 28... pathetic". The commentary appeared under a clip of a newspaper headline: "Souter blames gay dirty tricks". The *Record* accused the ERS of a major blunder. "The guidelines in Scotland are a totally separate issue and will not replace Section 28. In its place will go a clause promising to promote stable family life".

The next day, the *Scottish Daily Mail* vented their anger on its front page: "SILENCED". The editorial stormed: "The majority voice has been snuffed out. Silenced". They reported how "a spokesman for Cardinal Winning", whom they described as "the leader of Scotland's Catholic community" had called it a "massive disappointment". The *Mail* tore into the ERS committee. "Liberal society with Tory share cheat at the helm", they spat at the society's chairman, former Tory MP Keith Best who was sentenced to four months in prison for making multiple applications for British Telecom shares. "As a lobby group for voting reform, the majority of ERS members are from left wing and liberal political backgrounds, with many Liberal Democrats on its ruling council". (Not something that bothered them *before* the ERS made its announcement not to support Souter's referendum. This was something the *Herald* took up, quoting a pro-repealer who wrote: "Last week the Keep the Clause people were extolling the society's reputation and boasting about its credibility, and clearly the society has looked at what it was getting into and decided to have nothing to do with it. That says much more about the Keep the Clause campaign's referendum plan than it does about the Society"). Jack Irvine told *Scotland on Sunday:* "If we had realised the kind of people they were we would never have got involved with them. They have presented an image of propriety and fair dealing and it turns out their chairman is a spiv". The ERS's gay committee member wasn't spared. "Stephen Twigg's views on Section 28 were made clear last month when he joined a pro-repeal march organised by homosexual groups. The Labour MP and ERS council member has made no secret of his homosexuality since he ousted Michael Portillo from the Enfield Southgate seat at the last election". In fact, Stephen Twigg had *always* been entirely open about his sexuality. The *Scottish Mail* finally called on Anne Allen from the Church of Scotland's Board of Social Responsibility so that she could round their story off with her extreme disappointment.

The *Scottish Sun's* support for Souter's campaign, under editor Bruce Waddell, was unwavering. "Clear. Concise. Democratic. What are they scared of? Are the people of this country so stupid to call this toss the wrong way...? Anti-repeal supporters were looking for a simple answer. Like: Yes, delighted. What time suits you? What they got was another affront to the democratic process".

Anyone would have thought the public had been deprived of its right to vote at the next general election. The reason 'Keep the Clause' campaigners were so vociferous in their fight to have a referendum was because they saw it is as their only chance of victory. The only political party to support them was the Conservative Party, which had been wiped out in the last election in Scotland and stood no chance of gaining any majority. Nonetheless, "furious Mr Souter" said: "From our feedback it's clear that the people of Scotland want a referendum. We will just have to find a way to give them the referendum they want".

How to Spot a Homosexual

The *Daily Record*, under its editor, Martin Clarke, launched an attack on the ERS, its executive director, Owen Thomas and gay committee member, MP Stephen Twigg. "ERS chiefs sabotaged poll... The Record can reveal it was the 15-strong ruling council which vetoed the plan... The name of the Electoral Reform Society has become a byword around the world for integrity, fair play and democracy. But not any more. Today, the men and women of that august organisation should hang their heads in shame at their craven decision not to organise the postal petition over Section 28... The Society's commercial polling arm bottled out after it discovered what a hot potato the issue has become in Scotland... Mr Thomas also fails to grasp the most essential point of all which is that most parents are not impressed with the concept of non-statutory 'guidelines' anyway. They want a law and are quite happy with the one they've got, thank you... In the meantime, Mr Thomas's excuses are so flimsy that the inevitable suspicion arises that somehow his organisation has been nobbled. We know, for instance, that one openly gay Labour MP, Stephen Twigg, sits on the society's ruling council..." Stephen Twigg told the *Record*: "I do not have to speak to you and I do not take kindly to being slagged off in your editorials". A "spokesman" for 'Keep the Clause' told the *Record*: "I have seldom come across such a gutless, spineless organisation. We can smell the fear coming through from every line of their letter". The *Herald's* editorial mocked: "After celebrities who backed but did not back the Keep the Clause and the ERS contracts that were signed but were not signed, Mr Souter's PR company has enough egg on its face to make a meal of it".

Stewart Lamont, a minister and former BBC radio producer for religious broadcasting, cloaking his homophobia in light commentary, opened his regular column in the *Herald* with a joke: "A minister goes into public lavatory in the centre of Glasgow, one of the type which is entered by a flight of stairs down from street level. He recognised the lavatory attendant as one of his parishioners and greets him cheerily. 'How are things with you, Geordie?' 'Nae verrra great, minister,' replies the man, grimly. 'This job used to be a pleasure when it was real gentlemen that used to come in here. Noo it's a' different. If it's no the gays coming in here to meet, occupying the cubicles, then it's they drug addicts, using the place to inject themselves, and selling their stuff to each other. You know, minister, when I get someone in here for a right good s***e it's like a breath of fresh air". Stewart Lamont wrote how he "felt a bit like a lavatory attendant this week", forced to listen to "debates about decriminalising drugs and abolishing the ban on promoting homosexuality in schools..." Lamont believed: "A majority in our society still believe that neither homosexuality nor drugs deserves to be promoted, so why not take their opinions into account in public policy while leaving people freedom to deviate in private? That way we show tolerance towards others but still demand high standards of ourselves, an approach which seems to me rather close to the teaching of Jesus. Of course, some may say that it's a double-standard, and in a way it is, because it has the double virtue of toleration and pragmatism, common sense and compassion".

In national editions of the *Daily Mail*, homophobia took the form of a review that had already appeared some months before, giving Daniel Jeffreys from New York another airing, this time, in a double-page feature under the bold headline: "HETEROPHOBIA" which described the Oscar-winning film *American Beauty*. The film was attacked as a "sinister attack on heterosexuality" by gays. The feature promised to reveal; "how Hollywood is demonising heterosexual life as part of a disturbing new pro-gay agenda". It explored the preposterous idea that "some time in the past ten years, a new theory gained currency among gays, especially in the entertainment business. This held that heterosexuality was a curse to be denigrated and mocked wherever possible and that gays could never win the power they craved in society without undermining heterosexuals whenever possible".

In a sinister development, Outcast, a gay political website, was suddenly closed. It followed a legal landmark case only days before when a university lecturer was paid almost a quarter of a million pounds in damages and legal costs by the Internet Service Provider, Demon, owned by Scottish Telecom, in an out-of-court settlement over material carried on the site. Outcast was a respected and nationally distributed gay political magazine run by volunteers with a circulation of around 10,000. It boasted contributions from many people who were sympathetic to gay equality: Ken Livingstone MP, Peter Tatchell and writer Mark Simpson. The ISP NetBenefit wanted an assurance from a solicitor acting for Outcast that they would not print anything libellous. "Obviously, no solicitor can give a guarantee like that", said editor Chris Morris who had previously taken Britain to the European court over its unequal age of consent law. The ISP admitted closing the site "following a complaint".

On Sunday, 2 April 2000, a trusted friend of pro-Section 28 campaigners appeared in *Scotland on Sunday*, (still under the editorship of John McGurk), to reveal how Brian Souter had spent £50,000 commissioning a computer firm to build "an up-to-the minute computer database of every voter in Scotland". He had commissioned a computer firm to build a database of almost four million Scots registered to vote. "The database - compiled from electoral records held by local councils - was finished on Friday and took the firm just five days to complete".

On the BBC's *Frost on Sunday*, Donald Dewar stood by his commitment to abolish Section 28 and challenged the pressure on him to define 'stable relationships' claiming that family life could not be defined as 'heterosexual marriage' because 50 per cent of Scottish children were born out of wedlock. The *Scottish Daily Mail* sniffed: "In fact the correct figure is 40 per cent".

Scotland was filled with uncertainty, even in the more liberal *Sunday Herald*. Broadcaster and journalist Iain Macwhirter asked: "Keep the Clause has been a bad joke. So why has this flaky organisation been allowed to run civic Scotland ragged this winter?" Derek Ogg QC asked in the same paper: "This is a major issue for Scotland. What if they decide abortion is next? Or capital punishment? Scotland will become a playground for millionaires who realise they can buy a change in the law". Iain Macwhirter warned: "Recently a number of political journalists have been discovering that discrete inquiries are being made about their own private lives. 'What's he like? Is he married? Is he divorced? Is he gay?' Even newspaper editors are being threatened by sinister figures on the fringes of Scottish media life. In the small pond of Scottish public life, this kind of thing can rapidly become poisonous. Some gay journalists are seriously thinking about leaving the country altogether. The referendum would have been - might still be - one of the ugliest political campaigns in mainland Britain since the Smethwick by-election in the 1960s. Naked prejudice would have returned to mainstream politics. In Smethwick, they chanted: 'If you want a nigger for a neighbour vote Labour'. I dread to think what they would have found this time to rhyme with 'poof' and 'queer'. The lies about gay sex lessons being taught in schools would have been - may still be - spread anew by this unholy alliance of egotistical businessmen, tabloid newspapers and the Roman Catholic Church. Homosexual teenagers would be victimised, gay teachers targeted, political opponents vilified".

In another worrying development, the Christian Institute revealed it was ready to sue Phace West, the Glasgow-based group that produced a useful guide to safer sex, *Gay Sex Now*. The Christian Institute believed Glasgow Council was illegally promoting homosexuality by paying around £50,000 a year to Phace West, which they claimed offered advice on homosexual practices to youngsters as young as 12. Lawyers acting for the Christian Institute had been instructed to stop the council from making any further payments and intended demanding Phace West paid back money it had been granted over a period of five years. Simon Calvert, of the Christian Institute, told the *Scottish Mail on Sunday:* "We are keen to see Section 28 is properly enforced. It has served as a deterrent and it is perfectly proper to see the law is applied". The *Big Issue in Scotland* asked Colin Hart, the Christian Institute's director, for evidence that Phace West had been giving adult material to children. Hart was quoted saying: "I don't have evidence. Some youth workers go into schools but I've never said they give the materials to 12-year-olds". In response to claims of misrepresentation, he added: "They've put their stuff in the public domain. We're putting our view. People are misrepresented all the time".

First, Strathclyde Police was forced to investigate after 'a complaint from a member of the public'. Then, the *Scottish News of the World* rubbished the guide under its headline: "THIS CRUDE ADVICE IS ON A GAY WEBSITE... AND YOU PAID FOR IT". In fact, all local authorities had a duty to supply appropriate safer sex information to communities. Placing the information on a website was more time-consuming than financially draining. The tabloid got Tory MSP Nick Johnston to condemn the site as "disgraceful and shameful... leaving little to the imagination". The fact that the campaign entitled Healthy Gay Scotland had been providing accurate and effective sexual health advice was laudable and exactly what a Tory Government policy statement in 1995 had prescribed.

How to Spot a Homosexual

After concentrating their efforts on the website set up by Phace West, the *Scottish Daily Mail* had to report in anguish: "'Pornographic' gay website will not face prosecution". They reminded readers that "the group, which receives £180,000 of taxpayers' money annually, has made material available to children as young as 12 with its easily accessible website. The site, with explicit photographs of naked men having sex with each other, was set up by Big-les, the youth branch of Glasgow-based Phace West". The paper was alarmed that "the procurator fiscal in Glasgow, after talks with the Crown Office, has decided against any prosecution". The Christian Institute's Colin Hart declared they would now consider a private prosecution against Phace West - an organisation set up to provide sex education to a specific minority group - "to close it down" but expressed a concern over "political interference". Tory education spokesman Brian Monteith agreed with the Christian Institute over the "pornography which is passed off as health advice", and also imagined "heavy-handed political interference". In a thinly veiled reference to Section 28, the Catholic Church asked what sanctions were in place to stop the material reaching children.

The *Sunday Times Scotland* carried the news that Brian Souter was now looking to the US to find a company to run his referendum in Scotland. Propounding the myth of a sinister clique undermining the majority, he was reported telling them: "If someone felt as strongly about repeal then they could launch a campaign. There's an enormous (amount of) money coming from the gay lobby group, who are even sponsored, sometimes, by people in the City". Patricia Nicol joined him on the sofa in his tartan-carpeted Victorian drawing room in Perth for an interview in the broadsheet. "A devout Christian, Souter is not comfortable discussing sexual mores with a stranger", she observed. "He avoids eye contact at first and seems awkward..." Pat Nicol asked him why he thought a half-hour's role-playing exercise at 14 was going to change a child's sexuality. Brian replied: "We all know that when children are going through a phase in their early teens, when they are coming to terms with their own sexuality, they often have a same-sex crush. Now when they are going through that difficult stage I think it would be wrong to send a child a message that 'gay is a good choice', because a perfectly normal heterosexual child going through that phase could be encouraged into a series of sexual experimentations that could actually be very damaging to them. It could leave them emotionally scarred and at risk from sexual disease. As a parent I don't want that for my children - I want them to be nurtured with things that are wholesome and good and conform to our traditional values". The interviewer emphasised that "he says he did not experience such a crush himself, but has a close friend who did". Adding: "He seems so awkward that I wonder how he deals with his children asking about sex. 'I'm just a normal guy,' he answers softly. 'It embarrasses me. The one time Amy asked me something I said, 'Your mother will tell you when she gets back from the shops'."

Then the *Observer in Scotland* announced: "Souter's new ambition is to buy Herald". Columnist Arnold Kemp, a former editor of the *Herald*, found, "although his spokesman, Jack Irvine, of Media House, dismissed the suggestion as fantasy, it is known that Souter has told friends that he is keen to buy the paper, perhaps jointly with his friend and fellow millionaire Tom Hunter, founder of Sports Division". The *Herald* was bought by the Scottish Media Group, which owned Scottish and Grampian TV for £110m. Irvine told the *Observer in Scotland:* "That's fantasy. He must have been winding somebody up" and re-affirmed Souter was willing to spend up to £2m on keeping Section 28 before dismissing his pledge to go back to living in a council house in Perth as hyperbole.

Back in February 2000, after Mike Kinski, the Stagecoach chief executive had resigned, Stagecoach shares had plummeted. £265m was lost in just 24 hours. Neither was it just a blip. On Tuesday, 4 April, amidst calls to boycott Stagecoach, news broke in the City of London that - as the *Herald* put it - "Stagecoach shares had hit the buffers with a grinding crash..." The *Scottish Mail* reported: "Stockbrokers' screens turned into a sea of red" after Stagecoach shares went into freefall. The Perth-based bus, rail and airport group, owned by Brian Souter and his sister Ann Gloag, employing more than 40,000 people world-wide, had warned that profits at its Coach USA acquisition were going to be worse than expected. They blamed difficult labour marketing conditions and a hike in oil prices. Coach USA, the largest provider of sightseeing and charter bus operations in the US, which had 16,500 coaches and 3,000 taxis and cost Souter £1.2 billion in 1999, was a price too high according to some analysts. The *Scotsman's* Business View hinted: "The US had been tipped as the market where Stagecoach would find major growth. But yesterday's news aroused fears that if it can't get it right in the US, then perhaps its strategy is faulty". Souter had already suffered the sudden departure of Coach USA chairman Larry King at the end of February and before that, chief executive Mike Kinski with a £1m 'golden goodbye' and a £1.4m pension provision. In Larry King's case, the *Sunday Herald* reported: "The theory goes that King deliberately pumped up the group's turnover ahead of its sale through a series of fast and loose acquisitions, 'just so he could persuade some sucker to buy it'." The *Record* reported Mike Kinski "quit after a series of boardroom fallouts with Souter. The antagonism reached a head in a row over the publicity Stagecoach was attracting through Mr Souter's high profile involvement with the bitter Section 28 controversy". In the *Herald's* Business Comment, they said: "According to one insider, it was a profound disagreement over strategy that led to Kinski's departure. The former ScottishPower director was said to want measures to boost earnings short term. Souter, on the other was said to have insisted on giving priority to growing passenger volumes at the expense of short-term profit. Amongst other business interests, Prestwick Airport in Ayr, also owned by Stagecoach, had been badly hit by the withdrawal of Federal Express. There had already been discussions in 1999 to sell Prestwick for £71m. Now it was up for sale with a book price of £21m. Stagecoach's Scandinavian subsidiary, Swebus was sold at a loss in October 1999 after a three-year struggle to make it pay and Souter had already pulled out of markets in Kenya and Malawi. Added to that, Souter wanted to be China's biggest bus operator and had a minority share in a toll-road business there called Road King, which had also turned out to have been a disappointment. To clear the air, Stagecoach announced the sale of its Porterbrook train-leasing arm to Abbey National for £1.4 billion. This was a controversial move since this highly profitable company had been contributing between a third and a half of the group's profits, providing a safe and steady income. Despite the much-hyped new share issue to pay for Texas-based Coach USA in 1999, Stagecoach was now saying they planned a £250m share buy-back. The City got nervous and £850m was wiped off the Stagecoach share value in two hours of frenetic trading. The shares tumbled 42 per cent in two hours, falling at a rate of £116,000 every second. Shares plunged 51¼p to a four-year low of 70¼p by the time the Stock Market closed. Although more people wanted to travel by train, Stagecoach was finding it impossible to pack more paying-passengers onto its overcrowded commuter trains. Added to that, South West Trains had to face a £5m cut the following year in its annual rail subsidy. Brian Souter and his sister Ann Gloag had £170m wiped off their personal fortunes. They were no longer Scotland's richest couple. Their new worth of £238m made them fifth behind Tom Hunter with an accumulated wealth of £400m. It was not often that Brian Souter was not available for comment to the *Record* but "a spokesman for Stagecoach" told them "Mr Souter was 'on an aircraft and uncontactable' while travelling abroad on business". Souter's friends in the press did their best to soften the blow. Hamish Macdonell, the Scottish political editor for the *Scottish Daily Mail* warned there would be "no end of funding for polls", referring to Souter's quest for a private company to administer a referendum in Scotland over Section 28. The paper praised him as the "tycoon with a £1m heart" over his gift of a heart scanner to Glasgow University. The *Record* also made a contribution, describing his donation as "typical of the generosity to charity shown by him, and, on an even greater scale, by his sister". Ann Gloag made what was believed to have been the largest single donation to a Christian charity in Britain: a £4m floating hospital for the Third World.

On Wednesday, 5 April, 2000, Stagecoach took another tumble with £190m wiped off the company's value, pushing it below the psychologically important £1 billion barrier. The sort of fury the City was now displaying was normally reserved for companies on the brink of going bust. The day had started badly with a slide in the share-price target from 210p to 85p and security house Goldman Sachs downgrading its rating of Stagecoach from 'market outperformer' to 'market performer'. Similarly, Morgan Stanley downgraded its recommendations from 'strong buy' to just 'neutral'. Stagecoach's value had been halved from around £2 billion in just two days. Fears were growing that Stagecoach could be in danger of a hostile takeover bid. The *Record* found an Edinburgh stockbroker to beef up the news. "This is not the end of the road for Stagecoach - there are still many good bits to the business". Gert Zonneveld, transport analyst at securities house WestLB Panmure was not so optimistic. He reported in the *Herald's* Business section that

How to Spot a Homosexual

Stagecoach should not have included in its exit price the £270m of Porterbrook train purchase commitments being taken on by Abbey National. The price was, he argued, only £1.17 billion and therefore at the bottom, rather than the top end of City expectations ranging from £1 billion to £1.5 billion. Once again Souter was unavailable for comment and Keith Cochrane, his new chief executive, was on a flight to Hong Kong for a board meeting of the Citybus subsidiary. The City was not best pleased. Brian Souter and his sister Ann Gloag dropped further to sixth place in the league of Scotland's richest and the *Herald* speculated that Souter might even take Stagecoach off the stock market.

Amidst rumours Brian Souter was going to make the company private, Stagecoach spent £6.4m buying back its own shares to halt a collapse in price. Stagecoach edged up 1.75p to 65p after it bought 10.25 million in the open market at 62p. Souter had a lot of explaining to do to, not just to the City, but his institutional investors: Standard Life, Mercury Asset Management and Franklin Resources. As the following *Scotland on Sunday's* Doug Morrison advised: "The buses are still running. So too are the trains. But for Stagecoach, as far as its share price and its relationship with the City are concerned, the wheels have well and truly come off".

Just over a week later, on Thursday, 13 April, the *Herald* reported "Stagecoach on the ropes" after another 10 per cent slide in the value of its already battered share price. Brian Souter failed to attend a 7am breakfast briefing for City transport analysts. In just two days, the stock market value of Stagecoach had nearly halved to £1.05 billion.

Weeks later there was another resignation at Stagecoach, this time by the non-executive chief executive Jim Leng who complained Souter was treating the company as his personal fiefdom. The much-respected businessman's resignation was not disclosed during or after an extraordinary meeting at Stagecoach in Perth. Instead, it was announced after the stock market closed for Easter. Leng was critical of the group's corporate governance and was supposed to have made his views known to Souter after the executive chairman of Coach USA, Mike Kinski's departure. The City saw Leng as the most independent director on the Stagecoach board.

There was still no let up in Souter's campaign to halt the repeal of Section 28. Another of the *Herald's* morally conservative commentators, a former Conservative parliamentary candidate and historian Michael Fry warned: "We're off along the road laid down by Hitler and Stalin" before signalling his willingness to "stand up and be counted" in support of Section 28. Fry insisted if referendum supporters hadn't taken up "the people's cause" against repeal, "somebody else would have". He believed that "during a quarter of a century, Scots have grown practised in their own form of civil disobedience: a quiet, steady refusal to take, if they do not want it, what is handed down to them from on high..." Referring directly to Section 28, he declared: "This is the latest example... Ministers and their sycophants shout about homophobia, yet Scotland does not seem noticeably more or less homophobic than other countries. Scottish homosexuals are fully tolerated, and nobody is calling for constraints to be placed on them. No, the worried ones are the parents. I dare say most parents... acquire a bias in favour of that form of social organisation, which is often commended by politicians, too... They tend to think it would be a great affliction if one of their children grew up to be a homosexual... Since homosexuals do not procreate, they only increase through recruitment. And Section 28 is a safeguard against recruitment. That line of reasoning, central in the campaign to keep the clause, does not rely on the money or character of its backers". The *Herald* was very generous to Michael Fry, opening up their offices for him to broker a new publishing deal, and, a week after he wrote this feature, Brian Monteith, the Scottish Tory leader was sharing with readers how he had enjoyed "Scottish crustaceans" in a late lunch with him.

The *Record* turned its attention on Health Minister Susan Deacon's plans to spend £150,000 on four new Brook Advisory Centres in Glasgow, Aberdeen, Dundee and Stirling to add to two already operating in Edinburgh and Inverness. The *Scottish Daily Mail* simply headlined: "Fury over new sex clinics for the under-aged". In 1998 there were 9,218 teenage pregnancies in Scotland, the highest in Europe. Of those, 4,033 were terminated. Of the 12,500 abortions that were being performed each year in Scotland, 4,000 were amongst teenagers. "Deacon faces pro-life fury over sex clinics", ran the headline. "They drew up plans to picket her in protest at the centres which offer contraceptives and abortion advice to girls as young as 12 without the permission or knowledge of their parents". Comments were fielded from

How to Spot a Homosexual

Monsignor Tom Connelly who told the *Record:* "Evidence is clear over the years that, the more the availability of contraception, the higher the number of pregnancies". Rose Docherty, development officer for the Society for the Protection of Unborn Children felt: "The abortion figures are going up and it's clearly time to go back to the drawing board". The fortunate Ms Docherty added: "we are living in a sex-saturated society". The *Mail* allowed "Miss Deacon" to explain; "Brook Centres do not promote under-age sex. They do provide essential information about all aspects of sexual health in a way which encourages young people to make informed choices". Her voice was drowned by a motley-crew of moral conservatives, 'family values' campaigners and militant Christians. Rose Docherty portrayed Scotland's history as one of sexual anarchy: "For years now the approach has been to give out more condoms and more information on sex to young people, but where is the evidence it is reducing the problems when the statistics are going up?" Tom Connelly agreed while Valerie Riches, the director of Family and Youth Concern declared that Susan Deacon's plan: "...Is a charter for underage sex". Truth was: Scotland had never demonstrated a liberal sex education in its schools and was still reaping the consequences.

The attacks in the media on the Health Minister, Susan Deacon, began when she started her drive to improve the sexual health of Scotland's teenagers. The ferocity of the backlash had caught her off-guard. The health minister was branded a nutcase by a spokesman for the Catholic Church, depraved by anti-abortion campaigners and morally suspect by the *Record.* They even went so far as to suggest in an editorial that Ms Deacon shouldn't be passing judgements on sex education because she wasn't married to her partner John Boothman and they had a child out of wedlock. (The *Scottish Mail* would primly refer to her as "Miss Deacon"). News that National Health Service bosses were using dance classes as a team-building exercises was the only excuse the tabloid needed to picture Susan Deacon alongside the headline: "FAT CATS GET DANCE CLASS ON THE NHS" and in another *Record* report by Carlos Alba, she was accused of "being the source behind a bid to destabilise the Scottish Cabinet".

A conference organised by Children in Scotland called: Developing a Sexual Health Agenda for Scotland's Children and Young People took a bold step. Professor Peter Aggleton, director of the Thomas Coram Research Unit, at the Institute of Education, University of London said: "Sex has become linked to infection and disease and in the case of young people at least, to unintended pregnancy. We are encouraged therefore to view sexual health in largely negative terms. It seems important to recognise that sexual health is, or should be, an affirmative concept, a state of well-being imbued with positive qualities, not merely the absence of those that are undesired. Sexual health must be concerned with the attainment and expression of sexual pleasure not with the repression of sexual energies and desires, still less with their denial". Aggleton went on to relate how he'd trawled the various agencies working with young people on reproductive and sexual health matters and found only one - the London Brook Advisory Centre - that made any reference to sexual pleasure. The *Sunday Herald* reeled in the notorious 'Sexfinder General', Monsignor Tom Connelly who said: "The adult world is obsessed with sex. It is time the adult world gave young people a sense of discipline". He insisted young people wanted "discipline" and a "decent code of conduct" and declared it the responsibility of adults to ensure children were not allowed to "lose the innocence of youth".

The *Record's* front page bellowed the result of yet another poll. Only this poll tried to ascertain whether the Scottish public actually *wanted* a poll on Section 28! A sort of poll about a poll: "We want vote on clause... 64 per cent of Scots tell Dewar they back referendum... and 60 per cent said they would vote to keep the law which bans the promotion of homosexuality in schools". This was heralded as "the biggest poll ever conducted on the issue". But readers were beginning to tire of the onslaught and no other paper followed up the story. Brian Souter reappeared to welcome the *Record's* findings. Scottish Opinion Ltd who - according to the *Record* - "Interviewed 1,426 adults across Scotland by phone from March 31 to April 4" once again conducted the survey. Jack Irvine said: "The Record has demonstrated it has totally understood the will of the people" while the editor of *ScotsGay* magazine, John Hein was quoted saying: "I'm sure the vote reflects the opinion of people after the lengthy and expensive campaign waged by Mr Souter". The poll was similar to one already carried out by the *Big Issue in Scotland* which showed a polarisation of views along age lines. In their poll of 1,304, conducted by the same company, over half of 18 to 24-

year-olds backed repeal while older voters became increasingly conservative and favoured its retention. The *Big Issue* also commissioned Progressive Partnership to poll head teachers and MSPs, which revealed widespread support for its abolition. The *Record* called the results "a blow to campaigners who want Section 28 axed". The tabloid's editorial insisted the "people's voice will be heard..." and stormed: "What will it take to get the stubborn Scottish government to unplug their ears and listen to the voice of the people...? From the moment they announced the repeal of Section 28, it has been obvious that they are flouting the will of the majority by siding with the gay lobby. Today, they have more evidence that they are driving a dangerous division deep into Scottish society. They have another think coming because this issue will not go away quietly... The sound of protest is growing too loud to be ignored". Meanwhile, turning the music up in Deacon Brodie's bar on Edinburgh's Royal Mile, the *Record's* political editor got up with two other *Record* reporters at a karaoke to belt out the Village People's gay anthem, *YMCA*.

In an award ceremony organised by media and marketing magazine the *Drum*, the *Daily Record* was made Scottish newspaper of the year for best news coverage. The *Record* beat its chest in celebration: "Scotland's champion leads the way in fighting to ensure the nation's real voice is heard... Our support for the campaign against a repeal of Section 28 has been a reflection of the very real fears across the country", adding; "the Record continues to be a caring, family newspaper". The chairman of the judging panel was former *Herald* editor Arnold Kemp, who wrote for the *Observer in Scotland*. Other judges were the USA's *Boston Globe* editor Matthew Storin; Endell Laird, former editor of the *Daily Record;* Cameron Grant, former chairman of the Institute of Public Relations; Giles Brooksbank, of the Institute of Practitioners in Advertising; and David Appleton, head of group media relations at the Royal Bank of Scotland. At the media awards, the former editor of the *Record*, Endell Laird, said: "The Daily Record takes news stories and gives them a good punchy angle". In London, the *Scotland on Sunday* won an award for best Sunday newspaper in the 2000 Newspaper Awards. Its editor John McGurk sat on the judging panel.

The managing director of merchant bank Noble Grossart was Sir Angus Grossart and its co-founder was Sir Iain Noble. Sir

Angus Grossart was chairman of the *Scottish Daily Record*. He hinted at his position on the repeal of Section 28 when he was reported saying to the *Sunday Herald:* "I have a lot of respect for Brian and... he has the right to do this". Noble Grossart's portfolio included Brian Souter's Stagecoach as well as the Church of Scotland. Indeed, the non-executive director of Noble Grossart Ltd and Lloyds TSB Group plc, Ewan Brown, had been a non-executive director of Stagecoach since 1988.

Sir Angus Grossart was Scotland's leading investment banker and a dealmaker whose influence reached into many boardrooms. He controlled large amounts of arts funding as chairman of the Heritage Lottery Fund in Scotland, served on the boards of brewer Scottish & Newcastle and the Royal Bank of Scotland and even became a director of David Murray's Murray International Holdings, which listed Noble Grossart as its merchant banker. (Jack Irvine had been both managing director and editor-in-chief of Murray's failed newspaper, the *Sunday Scot)*. Sir Angus Grossart was also chairman of the £1.1 billion Scottish Investment Trust (SIT). (Standard Life Investments were big institutional shareholders in both SIT and Stagecoach). Sir Angus went on to face angry shareholders when it was revealed the SIT, of which he was chairman, paid his merchant bank, Noble Grossart, more than £300,000 in corporate advice fees in 2001. But that was nothing compared to the fury unleashed over the payment of £2.5m of bonuses to four of his fellow directors of the Royal Bank of Scotland! Grossart sat on the committee approving the bonuses. There was a huge protest vote of 235 million shares (some £4bn of the bank's stock market worth) against him. His seat on the SIT board, held for almost a quarter of a century - almost three times as long as the nine-year maximum term considered appropriate - angered shareholders. It wasn't the only time a company was advised by Noble Grossart while its chairman, Sir Angus Grossart, sat on the board of that company. Edinburgh Fund Managers, where Sir Angus formerly held a position as deputy chairman, paid £229,000 in fees to Noble Grossart. As advisor to plant hire group Hewden Stuart, Deutsche Bank was dropped in favour of Noble Grossart, which went on to help sell the company to Finning International of Canada. Grossart was a director of Hewden Stuart. By 2004 Grossart joined Rangers owner and metals entrepreneur David Murray, Brian Souter and his sister, Ann Gloag in rescuing the former bus-builder operation, TransBus, later Alexander Dennis, in Falkirk. Nobel Grossart took a 30% share, and by 2008, Companies House was showing them unveiling an 81% leap in pre-tax profits to £14.7m. The *Herald* reported Chairman Sir Angus receiving an annual salary of £514,000 in 2008. Such a beneficial holding in Noble Grossart earned him dividends of £1.14m. In their accounts, they attributed their success to having only a small number of executives "engaging with clients whom we know and whose business we understand..."

It was a Scottish consortium backed by Peter Cummings, the head of corporate banking at the Bank of Scotland that bought Falkirk-based body and chassis business, Transbus for £90m in 2004. The Bank of Scotland chipped in with around £70m of debt and equity finance. The deal was led by merchant bank Noble Grossart, put together whilst Grossart was on the Iraq-Syrian border looking at castles left by Christian Crusaders. Pleased with beating off a shortlist of bidders at the eleventh hour, Grossart told the *Sunday Herald* that he had worked with Murray and Souter "almost telepathically". He added: "The bottom line is that we had been aware of it (TransBus International) for some time. We had been tracking it, and when we moved, we moved very decisively". Grossart and David Murray, (Rangers football club chairman, Murray enjoyed a close working relationship with Peter Cummings to help his significant metals, mining and property interests earn a personal fortune estimated at £650m in 2006), and would own about half of Transbus - renamed Alexander Dennis to reflect its bus-making roots - while Brian Souter and Ann Gloag would be minority shareholders with over 40 per cent. Murray's firm, Wishaw-based Multi Metals had been supplying steel to Transbus while Souter's Stagecoach had also been customers of the firm. The result was a company with annual sales at the time of £200m and a strong forward order book bought for £40m with the addition of their commitment to invest £50m of working capital into it.

Eton-educated Sir Iain Noble, who, with Sir Angus Grossart, founded Noble Grossart, invited controversy in 2003 when he was invited to talk to the pro-blood-sport Scottish Countryside Alliance, another outfit whose PR was handled by Jack Irvine's Media House. Noble owned an estate and hotel on the Isle of Skye and was chairman of the Skye Bridge Community, while Sir Angus Grossart was a financial advisor to the builders of the controversial bridge, the Miller Group. Reported in the *Herald*, Noble told the assembled audience how proud he was not to have English blood in his veins, something he felt the Scottish National Heritage would appreciate in its efforts to maintain "the purity of species". Discussing sex workers, he was reported saying: "Damn it, prostitution is the easiest thing for a woman to do who wants to earn a bob. But it doesn't mean it's the best". He also hit out at "English people..., buying up all the houses" before adding: "Damn it, it would be quite wrong if this continued. Who can stop it and how can we do it? Does that mean I must be a racialist? I think I have to confess that I am. It doesn't mean I don't like foreigners. I love them, all colours. I have many friends and even one or two black ones. But I don't want them to settle and create ghettos in my patch of the country. And I believe that SNH should approve of this instinct, because genetics are the key to everything". Sir Iain Noble and Sir Angus Grossart were both members of the rather Masonic-style, all-male gentleman's club in Edinburgh, The Speculative Society. Membership included large swathes of the Scotland's legal establishment as well as senior businessman, civil servants and bankers, including Lord MacKay of Clashfern, the retired former Lord Chancellor of Margaret Thatcher's cabinet and another sponsor of Brian Souter's 'private referendum' on the repeal of Clause 28. Sir Iain Noble died in 2010 after a long illness.

Standard Life, Europe's largest mutual life insurer was a big investor in Souter's Stagecoach along with Donald Macdonald's Hotel chain and Grossart's Scottish Investment Trust. Standard Life had to face disgruntled policyholders in 2003 when, as bonuses, endowments and final payouts from their pensions tumbled; executive directors reaped almost £2m in performance-related bonuses along with pension entitlements worth another £5m. Chief Executive Stuart Bell received a long-term incentive plan award of £110,000 in 2002 upon his retirement, and his £373,000-a-year pension was increased to £420,000 during the year. Despite tumbling stock markets and a number of cuts in payouts for its 2.6 million policyholders, in 2004 Standard Life announced 1,000 of its employees would loose their jobs while 35 of its top paid sales staff were taken on an all-expenses paid trip to Barbados. John Hylands, the finance director's remuneration packaged doubled, and Claude Garcia, president of Standard

How to Spot a Homosexual

Life's Canadian operation got a 24 per cent increase in total remuneration to £341,000, including a basic salary of £221,000 and bonus of £108,000. Standard Life's ousted Chief Executive, Iain Lumsden received £1.13m in salary and performance-related bonuses. His internally appointed successor, Sandy Crombie, got an £83,000 rise in total remuneration to £603,000 in his former post as deputy chief executive. When Crombie was promoted, his basic salary was increased from £480,000 to £600,000 and he benefited from a £5.5m pension fund. After the new Standard Life boss took delivery of his £65,000 red Carrera 2 Porsche, decorator George Ormiston revealed how, in 1990 he was forced to take Crombie to a small claims court over a £461 bill after Crombie's wife, Margaret, didn't like the colour of wallpaper her husband had chosen, resulting in him disputing the bill.

By the time of its AGM in 2003, Standard Life board members were being accused of being complacent, arrogant and clubby, and by 2004, the *Herald's* editorial was positively scathing: "Standard Life is earning a reputation as a complacent, haughty, and insular business run by a discredited executive management, one that has doubly let the members down by using some of their money to secure a financial reward when none has been merited". Eventually, in 2005, Sandy Crombie took a "principled decision" and agreed to forgo bonus payments of £500,000 whilst the rest of the directors hung on to theirs. (He later received a £2.75m increase in the value of his pension fund, taking it to £6.7m and was later appointed to run Creative Scotland).

Standard Life continued to upset members when chairman Sir Brian Stewart decided to 'divert' unused votes at the board elections to support established candidates. Ronnie Sloan, a semi-retired actuary who had twice stood for election, had challenged Standard Life over the issue. He believed if you voted for fewer than six candidates and wanted to give a thumbs-down to the ones not receiving your vote, you shouldn't have to tick a box preventing the chairman from doing what he wanted with the wasted votes. He complained that it should be the other way round and the box should be ticked if you *wanted* the chairman to cast your unused votes.

In 2010, Standard life was fined almost £2.5m after the Financial Services Authority found the company, under Sir Sandy Crombie, had been misleading some 100,000 of investors of its Pension Sterling Fund; telling its customers their money was a low-risk investment in cash when, in reality, most of their money was being ploughed into toxic mortgages.

In 2010, a small group of entrepreneurs, including Sir Angus Grossart, Brian Souter and Sir David Murray ploughed £10m into the Airdrie Savings Bank claiming the seven branch bank was an example of how a traditional bank should work. Souter was quoted in the *Scotsman* as saying "the public had become tired of the big-salary, big-profits culture of the larger banks and were seeing no benefits". He was also quoted saying: "I think people are very tired and angry of what happened with our banks in Scotland and I think this creates an opportunity in the future to build a new bank which is based on mutual principles. It's not going to be speculating in all kinds of strange derivatives and it's not going to be a bank that's going to be focused overseas, it will be a bank that's focused in Scotland – and really it's a peoples' bank". With details of how customers could then sign up, the story was little short of an advertisement. The paper said the bank was "inundated with calls from well-wishers across Scotland wanting to follow their example and open accounts" and named Sir Tom Farmer, financier Ewan Brown, food firm boss Alastair Salvesen and Souter's sister, Ann Gloag, as amongst those investing.

Sir David Murray went on to court controversy of his own after netting almost £5m in a land deal. Murray's property business paid £375,000 for land in Dalmarnock, Glasgow in 2005 and four years later, while property prices were plunging in a recession, the land was valued at £7.3m and sold to Clyde Gateway, a government quango, for £5.1m of taxpayers' money for the Commonwealth Games. Then, in 2012, after Murray's Rangers Football Club was sold with massive debts to Craig Whyte, which saw HMRC ringfencing £2.8m of the company's assets and the club's former lawyers, Levy & McRae taking a huge £35,000 bill to the Court of Session, the company was finally forced to go into administration.

Murray stood to benefit from the introduction of Holyrood legislation in 2012 that opened the door for his prime site at the old Waverley Market, a £50million shopping centre in the heart of Edinburgh, being sold for a pittance to his company Premier Property Group (PPG). It was likely to lead to the future of some 9,000 long-leases, many of them prime properties held in 'common good' trusts, succumbing to a similar fate under the

How to Spot a Homosexual

Long Leases (Scotland) Bill. Princes Mall was held by Sir David on a long-term lease after having been bought from a previous owner for £37million in 2004. The long lease, whereby PPG paid Edinburgh City Council only 1p-a-year rent under a £14million deal with the original developers in the eighties, was more than 175 years old and could automatically pass from Edinburgh City Council to PPG for a few pence. Edinburgh City Council's argument centred on the idea that granting leases, many of which are for 999 years, was just the same as bestowing ownership of the property.

By Friday, 7 April 2000, with mounting debts running into tens of thousands of pounds, the Scottish School Boards' Association looked like they were in trouble. Even the *Record* struggled to view it from a positive angle. It began after Mrs Ann Hill handed her draft business plan for the next three years to the Board's executive. Despite the plan listing an accumulated loss of £72,000, Mrs Hill still intended to claim £9,500 on top of her baseline salary of £38,000 a year with £4,620 to be added to her assistant's salary. She earned £10,000 for 100 days work back in 1995. Now, her salary had jumped to £38,000 for working 200 days a year, giving herself and her assistant a £1,200 a month rise for providing services that no longer existed! These fees were for managing the Furbie Foundation whose main backers were the Bank of Scotland and Scottish Power and which aimed to refurbish old computers in schools. Five of them had been installed in the 32-pupil Mouswald Primary School near Dumfries, which, coincidentally, Mrs Hill's children attended. But with Tony Blair promising new computers for all schools, Furbie ceased trading, more or less, back in December 1999, yet it appeared Mrs Hill had been accepting payments of £3,000 a month since January 2000. The press grumbled that Mrs Hill was on holiday in Cyprus and "not available for comment". John Bonington, an SSBA executive board member from Fife wrote to the *Herald*. "Despite asking, the Executive Board has never received proper reports and accounts of the Furbie scheme's actual operation over the last year. The full written report of the conduct of, and implications arising from, the Furbie venture which we expected tabled at our meeting in December of 1999 was not forthcoming, and continues to be unavailable to us". Ann Hill told the *Scotsman*, after receiving £1,200 a month in salary and bonuses for administration of the fund, she regarded the payment as a one-off fee rolled into her salary of £38,000, rather than individual monthly payments. She was suspended from duties.

The chief executive of the SSBA, Ann Hill and president David Hutcheson, both directors of the Furbie Foundation, now faced bankruptcy. The Furbie Foundation's third director was David Urquhart, a serving officer with Lothian and Borders police. The accounts showed the Furbie Foundation owing the Scottish School Boards' Association £24,000. Despite outrage from executive member John Bonington; treasurer Alan Smith and association secretary Frank Farrell suddenly reinstated Ann Hill on the eve of elections to its new executive board. Her duties, however, were restricted to an SSBA-organised profit-making international conference, Parents in Education Around the World. The SSBA hoped between 200 and 300 participants from 20 countries would pay up to £520 a head to attend.

Ann Hill was later cleared of any financial impropriety by an independent enquiry but became embroiled in further trouble when a £40,000 donation Ann Hill had asked Brian Souter for in January 2000 was withdrawn. The cash-strapped SSBA badly needed Souter's money. According to Jack Irvine, the matter was "under review".

Alan Smith, the SSBA's trusted ally of 'Keep the Clause' told the *Scottish Daily Mail* that President David Hutchison's future was in doubt and that an emergency meeting had been called to discuss this. The *Mail* reported: "He will face calls for his resignation and may be forced out over what has been seen as his 'conciliatory' attitude to the Executive over Section 28. Mr Hutchison has always been uncomfortable with his association's opposition to the repeal of Section 28, but members believe his close ties to Labour may also have influenced his views". Hutcheson gave evidence to the Executive's committee on the Ethical Standards in Public Life (Scotland) Bill but faced a vote of no confidence after he was accused of playing down the SSBA's opposition to the repeal of Section 28. He later denied a split in the association saying he supported the introduction of safeguards.

Ann Hill now appeared on the front of the *Scotsman's* education supplement with Jack Irvine, standing in front of his enormous 'Keep the Clause' poster under the caption "I am not prejudiced". Journalist Helen Silvis spoke to an apparently remorseful Ann Hill. "A brief silence as the question sinks in, then the down to earth voice begins to answer. But in the middle of a thought the steady tones crack, the voice tails off and tears well up..." Ann Hill begged: "There's not been a day in the last six weeks that I haven't cried".

Eventually, Executive Scottish School Boards' Association member Derek Robertson quit his post. He had not been happy about what had been going on and told journalists that he wasn't sure he would have been able to stay silent and keep a collective responsibility. He revealed how some school boards and local authorities were awaiting the new executive's recommended changes to roles, standing orders, and operational procedures before deciding to stay members. Accounts showed a near £30,000 loss in the year to December 1999. This would be further exacerbated by the withdrawal of the Scottish Executive's grant for their quarterly newsletter.

Following new elections, Alan Smith became the SSBA's new chairman and Ann Hill became its executive chairwoman. The SSBA, promising to stay non-political and non-sectarian, gained charitable status and increased its membership.

The *Pink Paper* reported: "It's now exactly two months since the Sun launched a phoneline poll asking readers to vote on whether they wanted to retain Section 28. Usually, the paper publishes the results of such polls within days. Funnily enough, we are still waiting".

The Working Group on Sex Education in Scottish Schools, a group of parents, teachers and church representatives had been set up by the Executive to look at the guidelines replacing Section 28 with the intention of preparing summary guidelines for teachers and a package of information on sex education in schools for parents. The *Scottish Daily Mail* cried: "Gay law fury as Galbraith group backs the repeal". Brian Monteith for the Tories warned in the *Mail*: "The infamous gay book for schools 'Jenny Lives With Eric and Martin' could easily be used by schools if the working group failed to recommend changes to the law. Nothing short of the specific legal right of parents to remove their children from sex education classes and granting greater powers to school boards in deciding the content of sex education materials will suffice". The Catholic Church's representative on the group, John Oates "objected to the report and asked for his objections to be publicly noted. He said it was wrong for the

Executive to repeal Section 28 without putting anything in its place which placed proper emphasis on the importance of marriage". The report duly noted Mr Oates's concerns. The *Scottish Mail's* editorial bemoaned that the working party had noted without comment the objection from the Catholic Education Commission on the omission of a reference to marriage and "the Executive's refusal to give any support or promotion to marriage at a time when family life is under concerted attack from all quarters in our morally disintegrating society". The *Herald's* editorial called it "sweet reason darkened by sour prejudice".

The *Herald* ran a report on The Society for the Defence of Tradition, Family, Property, (TFP). Formed in 1989, TFP was funded by private individuals and had 1,000 part-time members in Scotland; 4,000 across the UK. Their director Philip Moran linked homosexuality with paedophilia. 20,000 leaflets went out requesting donations of up to £25; enclosed were postcards that people were urged to send to the First Minister Donald Dewar. The letter stated: "If we do not stand fast for traditional moral values, you, your children and the Scottish people will suffer the dire consequences, both morally and socially. Homosexual acts are an unnatural vice and a moral disorder - they are sins that cry out to heaven for vengeance". Moran was dismissive of any consequences of his actions: "Of course, some will be upset by the truth, but sometimes the truth hurts", he was reported saying. Catholic Church spokesman Tom Connelly, while not willing to say "anything in support of TFP... couldn't wholly condemn them either..." because he "simply didn't know enough about them". The *Herald* found Jack Irvine taking much the same line: "He also refused to support or condemn TFP". The *Herald* suggested in its editorial that TFP "would be in deep legal water if, say, the word black replaced homosexual in the odious leaflet it has been distributing in Scotland... Unlike other newspapers (that seem to be leaving Section 28 behind in their damaging wake, having found new targets to replace a discredited campaign) we believe in full, fair, and open debate". But how true was that? The paper expected every submission for their letters pages to include the sender's name and address for publication, which was always likely to be weighted heavily in favour of those religious campaigners who were less shy of their predilection. In the pervading climate, the *Herald* supported the government throughout the debate in its editorial stance, yet reflected the opinions of both sides of the argument in its Letters to the Editor pages. E J Hart from Helensburgh wrote: "As a 14-year-old schoolboy newspaper deliverer in 1940 when one of the advantages was to have wee free keeks at the Glasgow Herald, and its stablemate the Bulletin much taken by the ladies as a more compactly sized pictorial journal (never a tabloid, oh dear, no). I have followed its fortunes ever since, save for war service... In all these six decades I have never experienced such opprobrium as has appeared in the Letters to the Editor page these seemingly interminable weeks..." Whilst the numerous religious columnists, stirred by the Section 28 debate in religious enthusiast Editor Harry Reid's *Herald* were not ashamed to express their homophobia, without one outspoken liberal with an unembarrassed grasp of sexual politics, was it balanced?

The *Sunday Herald*, a lot more confident about sexual issues, with a younger editor, supported Catholic Church liberal Father Fitzsimmons who put himself on a collision course with Cardinal Winning when he said: "Most priests don't want to risk putting their heads above the parapet but I can't stand by and say nothing while we have Winning supporting the retention of Section 28. It is the most malicious piece of legislation ever placed on a statute book and it has no place in a civilised country. We should imagine the words 'promotion of homosexuality' being replaced with 'promotion of Catholicism' or 'promotion of Judaism'."

The *Sunday Herald* was happy to give a voice to anyone who dared challenge the Catholic Church's position on sex and sexuality. Mark Miller, one of the world's highest paid comic book writers had just finished a DC comic book, *The Authority*, featuring gay superhero Apollo kissing Midnighter on the cheek. The *Scottish Sun* declared "fury at world's first homosexual comic heroes". The Catholic Church tore into the comic as an insidious attempt to present homosexual role models to adolescents. "This kind of material will serve to increase the justified anxiety among parents over the whole issue of lifting Section 28", a spokesman said, although quite how Section 28 would have done this wasn't explained. Mrs Ann Allen from the Kirk's Board of Social Responsibility declared in the *Record:* "Children need to be protected from this sex-mad society and to introduce such issues into comic books is very unhealthy". There was, nonetheless, a ripple of surprise when it was revealed Mark Miller was a lay priest! He told the *Sunday Herald:* "I'm shocked by the behaviour of the Church. It has been horrible and homophobic – medieval, backward and Stalinist. They seem to delight in victimising homosexuals. I can't believe my own Church is acting like this. It was pathetic the way they turned on me". In a separate story the *Sunday Herald* featured We Are Church, a pressure group that challenged Cardinal Winning's conservative stance within the Catholic Church. Ronnie Convery, Director of Communications at the Archdiocese of Glasgow fumed: "We Are Church is a small pressure group which has had almost no influence in England and Wales and will have even less influence here. This group betrays a faulty understating of the nature of the Catholic Church. The Church is not democratic. It does not claim to be democratic. Morality is not settled by a show of hands in the Catholic Church".

The *Scottish Daily Mail* hit back in support of Cardinal Winning over what it described as the "bitter personal attacks over his defence of family values". The bold headline declared: "Church leader targeted by gay activists over family values", suggesting: "Cardinal Winning has been targeted by a succession of gay rights campaigners and liberal politicians who accused him of promoting a Right-wing extremist agenda". Winning was slapped on the back for having "angered a wide-range of politically correct groups". The *Scottish Mail*, after having described Father John Fitzsimmons as "a maverick priest", brushed him aside. Cardinal Winning huffed: "Critics won't silence me". Shortly after, Father Fitzsimmons was summoned to a disciplinary meeting with his bishop, which was understood to have been at the behest of the *papal nuncio*, Archbishop Pablo Puente, the Pope's ambassador to Britain. He was forced to issue a public apology to Cardinal Winning or face suspension.

In the *Scottish Mail on Sunday*, Fidelma Cook interviewed a gay law professor's lover and his "bid for 'marital' rights". Break-ups are a messy business in anyone's books, and here was the *Scottish Mail on Sunday* savouring every detail of the untimely split of Joe Thomson, Regius Professor of Law at Glasgow University and Alastair Murdoch. Soon after meeting Joe in a "trendy Glasgow wine bar" Alastair was mentioned on invitations to parties and he was rubbing shoulders with a string of celebrities. "Scotland's leading expert on divorce law is embroiled in an extraordinary battle with his former gay lover that could lead to

How to Spot a Homosexual

full legal rights for partners in same-sex 'marriages'", reported the Sunday tabloid. Alastair Murdoch confessed, "the Lord Chancellor told me and my gay lover we should have the same rights as married couples. Now my lover has married a woman and left me penniless... We sat in Derry Irvine's drawing room (the Lord Chancellor, Lord Irvine) a few years ago discussing that very point. Both Joe and Derry agreed that the law had to change and would. I vividly remember Derry saying something had to be done to change the law to give us rights". Fidelma Cook added that Lord Irvine, with his responsibility for divorce law, "appears to underline the Government's determination to greatly increase gay rights". Alistair Murdoch had unwittingly handed the *Mail* the perfect opportunity to expose gays hobnobbing with 'influential friends.' "It was Joe's idea to offer (Lord Irvine) a Doctorate of Law and he wanted to get it in before Labour got in power. I seconded it. Nine months later, as Lord Chancellor, he came up to Glasgow with Alison to receive it. We had a very merry time". The *Mail* elaborated: "A whirlwind round of parties and entertaining. There were formal dinners and receptions of the Faculty of Advocates in Edinburgh, opening nights at the ballet and the opera and holidays in the Caribbean. Their friends and acquaintances included Princess Margaret's daughter, Sarah Chatto, Lord Rodger of Earlsferry, the Lord Justice General of Scotland; designer Jasper Conran; playwright Peter McDougal; BBC Scotland Controller John McCormick; former president of the Scottish Tories, Professor Ross Harper; and artists John Cunningham and George Devlin. Lord Irvine and his wife Alison... became close friends".

A letter from Bob Harper from Anstruther in Fife appeared in the *Scottish Daily Mail* adding to the growing clamour against 'gay cliques' working behind the scenes to undermine Brian Souter. After sniping at the "Scottish arm of the so-called independent body of the Electoral Reform Society" he warned Souter that "he must ensure there is no external manipulation of the stock market by Government or the minority groups that are forcing the repeal of Section 28 on to the public in Scotland without first consulting them as to their own wishes on the subject".

Along with a debate on the Sexual Offences (Amendment) Bill in the House of Lords, which was set to equalise the age of consent at 16, on Tuesday, 11 April 2000, there was a reading of the Local Government Bill in the House of Commons, which contained proposals to repeal Section 28 in England and Wales. In 1999, the Lords threw out the Sexual Offences Bill, equalising the age of consent, at its second reading. If they did the same again, it would become law in just over a month by way of the Parliament Act because the House of Commons had passed it twice. Tory frontbencher, Baroness Blatch insisted in the Lords: "Children's rights have given way to gay rights".

As for the Local Government Act, the elected Government in the House of Commons could have put back proposals to repeal Section 28 after the unelected House of Lords took them out. But because the measure had originated in the Lords, the Parliament Act could not be evoked on this occasion, so Section 28's repeal in England and Wales looked increasingly unlikely.

The *Daily Record* assured readers that repeal of Section 28 for England and Wales would be defeated when it was returned to the House of Lords and observed: "If that happens, it is believed Tony Blair will drop the issue until after the next election, putting pressure on Holyrood to follow suit". MPs objecting to the repeal of Section 28 in the House of Commons were advised they could take the day off. But the *Record* scoffed: "the ploy to keep the rebels away looked likely to fail - with two MPs set to abstain and another indicating he was virtually certain to vote against the Government". Urging MPs to stay away was made to appear necessary by a Government "keen to diffuse a backbench rebellion". One MP told the *Record:* "The problem is that someone decided they were going to make the abolition of Section 28 a crusade" and "we have lost the support of a large section of the electorate and... the support of Scotland's leading Catholic cleric". Efforts to contact MPs and MSPs, sending copies of *Gay Sex Now* along with Christian Institute propaganda had paid off. The *Record* named one of the rebels as 61-year-old Glasgow Baillieston Labour MP James Aloysius Joseph Patrick Gabriel Wray, better known as Jimmy Wray who told them: "It is my Christian belief that we should bring families up to teach them right from wrong. I fear for my children and I certainly don't want anyone to teach them that filth that's being thrown around. I have been wondering just exactly what they are going to put in its place because we don't want some of the literature in schools that we've seen. One quite clearly stated, 'Gay Sex Now'. There was all the filth on some of it, scheming and all the things you can do. Also there were pictures of people committing homosexual acts. I don't think in this day and age that we should be showing that... That's an insult to parents and certainly does away with family values. If that is going to open the floodgates by taking Section 28 away then it certainly won't be getting any support from me. And a lot of other people in the Party feel the same way... I don't want to know what homosexuals are doing in their home. I think that you've got to keep these values. Toilets are for public convenience not for people standing up then advertising cottaging... I don't give a damn what response I get from the rest of the Party. My morality is something that nobody is going to take away". Wray had recently made front-page news after being awarded damages against Associated Newspapers for branding him a serial wife-beater. He was pictured toasting victory with his third wife Laura and condemned his former wife Catherine's "evil" actions for making the claim in the *Mail on Sunday*. She had said he had held a knife to her neck and alleged she had received medical treatment for abuse suffered at his hands during their troubled marriage, which ended in divorce in 1998. Wray countered that she was an insecure drunk. When Jimmy Wray sounded off in one of the tabloids behind the 'Keep the Clause' campaign of his worries for his son, "wee Frankie", the *Herald's* editorial was cutting. "Do not fret, Mr Wray. You will not be required to write a parental note requesting that your boy be excused compulsory lessons in homosexuality".

Nicknamed I.R. Wray by *Private Eye* for his views on Irish Republicanism, Jimmy Wray stood down as MP at the 2005 elections and died in 2013 after suffering from Bowel Cancer.

The *Scottish Mail* reported the Scottish Conservatives' bid to "give parents a say over sex lessons" in the Scottish Executive. Tory education spokesman Brian Monteith intended to ensure parents had the legal right to withdraw their children from any class they disapproved of since children could only be taken out of a class for religious reasons. The *Mail* reported: "The move gained the backing of senior members of the Scottish School Boards Association... Alan Smith, chairman of the school board of St Andrew's Secondary in Paisley, said: 'This would be an excellent idea which would go a long way to reassuring parents and allaying their fears over repeal". The story was accompanied by another piece of scaremongering with the headline: "School heads are asked to give out gay newsletter". In *Connect*, a gay

RELIGIOUS FASCISM

newsletter distributed in Berkshire in the south of England were items such as a report on a gay pub in Reading which the *Mail* declared "has a website featuring pictures of naked gays, and another urging readers to join the Mr Gay UK contest". The programme had been broadcast on national TV.

The *Scottish Sun* reported how a "store manager axed for being HIV-positive won £250,000 compensation..." in an out-of-court settlement, while the *Scottish Mail* advised: "The case of 34-year-old Mark Hedley is expected to be the first in a wave of Aids-related claims which could cost businesses millions". Aldi, the German supermarket chain told the young manager, to stay away from work because his HIV status would be bad for business. The *Scottish Sun* immediately followed the story with a report: "Health chiefs in Lanarkshire yesterday blamed gay men for the biggest increase in HIV infection ever in the county". Half the new cases estimated appeared to have been caused by sex between men. Ten new cases overall. Health boards had already been condemned by churches and politicians for handing out condoms in a part of Lanarkshire's Strathclyde Park which had become popular for men seeking gay sex. Despite research having shown how the social stigma of homosexuality helped fuel the spread of HIV, North Lanarkshire Council SNP leader, Richard Lyle told the *Herald:* "...That does not mean giving out free condoms at what should be a tourist venue and family facility is the answer. I still believe that this may have the effect of encouraging homosexual activity at the park and this is wrong".

After the growing assault on gay people in Scotland by religious fundamentalists, it emerged that gay rights lobby group, Stonewall was planning to base one of their team on a part time basis in Glasgow, the *Record* launched a blistering attack, screaming:. "FURY OVER £1m LOTTERY GRANT FOR GAY GROUP". (There had been almost 2,000 lottery grants awarded in the twelve months previous, and out of a total of £246m, only £2.8m had gone to lesbian, gay or bisexual projects). Stonewall - which only "claims to have a staff of nine" - was attacked by reporter Simon Houston. He reminded readers of Stonewall's last show in London: "The star performer was Elton John - who shocked observers by performing a raunchy stage routine with male dancers dressed as cub Scouts". A picture of Elton dancing with them illustrated his point and was shown alongside Stonewall's director: "Activist: Mason..." (Angela

How to Spot a Homosexual

Mason). The National Lotteries Charities Board spokesman Robert Blow apparently "admitted" that Stonewall's grant was "a bit of a whopper". Lottery chiefs were portrayed as defending the award and attention was drawn to "healthy annual donations" already donated by the "increasing" number of gay businesses. The *Record* listed: "Richard Branson's Virgin group, NatWest bank and the huge American financial institution, JP Morgan". 'Keep the Clause' wanted to know whether the board "would be just as happy to award £900,000 to a group which promotes traditional family values" and Dr Adrian Rogers of Family Focus warned anyone not wanting to promote homosexual behaviour to stop buying lottery tickets. The *Herald* used quotes from Dr Adrian Rogers and Valerie Ritches, director of Family and Youth Concern. Ritches thought it "scandalous" and said: "If the lottery board had their heads screwed on they would give it to helping the lot of families. The family unit in Britain is breaking down and is in desperate need of support". A letter went out from Stonewall to its supporters begging donations to "match the bigots £ for £... They're rich and they're wrong".

In Moniaive, a small town in Dumfrieshire, 54-year-old Marcelle Bremner had her shop busted in a dawn raid by local police for displaying two male dolls in her window. Marcelle Bremner used to backcomb Dusty Springfield's bouffant before she went to live in a flat above the vacant shop and filled the window with Barbie-dolls. Police hammered on Bremner's door in a raid in the early hours of a Saturday morning insisting she removed a potentially illegal display of two Ken dolls. This followed a complaint from a member of the public of a "lewd and libidinous" display of "a graphic nature". *Scotland on Sunday* found "two Ken dolls, sitting suspiciously close to each other, staring out quite blatantly at passers-by, and wearing only Bermuda shorts". The *Scottish Mail* found them "naked but for their Bermuda shorts... sat in a shop window shamelessly flaunting their bronzed and perfectly sculpted bodies before passers-by..." and giving "more than a hint of the close nature of their relationship... Moral outrage followed swiftly and police were despatched to restore public decency". A WPC ordered Bremner: "Get those Ken dolls dressed. I don't want to see those two men beside each other!" *Scotland on Sunday's* Shan Ross wrote: "The display, which is housed in the double-fronted windows of Bremner's former clothes shop is festooned in pink and surrounded by Barbie memorabilia and every possible pink boudoir item imaginable". A spokeswoman for Dumfries and Galloway Constabulary said in a prepared statement that they would not be charging Mrs Bremner but it was also suggested she might want to reconsider how she displayed them.

It was Easter and the 'Sexfinder General', Monsignor Tom Connelly delivered a scathing attack on Cadbury's 'Squegg', a chocolate square egg, insisting only round chocolate eggs could symbolise rolling the stone from Jesus's tomb. A square one "made a mockery of the whole tradition". The *Scottish Mail on Sunday* referred to the egg as "shades of a new dark age". The eggs were milk, not dark chocolate, and besides, the name Easter was a corruption of *Eostre*, the Anglo-Saxon goddess of Dawn and a symbol of fertility and rebirth long before Christians hijacked the tradition. The *Mail* bemoaned the fact only half of Brits knew what Easter was supposed to be about anyway. "Possibly not since the early Dark Ages - before Pope Gregory sent missionaries to bring the word of God to these shores at the end of the sixth century - has our society been so ignorant about basic Christianity. This must be disturbing..." Their editorial warned: "In schools, the teaching of Christianity is being sacrificed on the altar of multiculturalism. Where religious instruction was once based on the Bible and its meaning, it now imparts a pick-and-mix smattering of the word's religions, loosely defined". The editorial lambasted churches for tamely giving in to the "politically correct", while in truth, it was no longer able to control its 'flock': The public were already turning away from organised religion in their droves.

Chapter Six
Militant Religionists at War

*"Love the kind you clean up with a mop and bucket
Like the lost catacombs of Egypt only God knows where we stuck it
Hieroglyphics? Let me be Pacific I wanna be down in your South Seas
But I got this notion that the motion of your ocean means 'Small Craft Advisory'
So if I capsize on your thighs high tide, be five you sunk my battleship
Please turn me on I'm Mister Coffee with an automatic drip
So show me yours I'll show you mine 'Tool Time' you'll Lovett just like Lyle
And then we'll do it doggy style so we can both watch 'X-Files'*

*Do it now
You and me baby ain't nothin' but mammals
So let's do it like they do on the Discovery Channel
Getting' horny now"*
    The Bloodhound Gang

'Keep the Clause' meetings were organised up and down Scotland to strengthen the backlash against repeal. Socially conservative, industrial towns were targeted. In a meeting organised in a hotel in Clydebank, four Christian activists convened a meeting. Sitting at the top table, 'concerned parent' Patrick Rolink wore a black shirt, but if that was supposed to carry any message it was somewhat tempered by Bill Lydon who stood up in a sky-blue knitted pullover of mixed fibres to introduce the 'Keep the Clause' crew, Pat, Hugh, and Ross, to a round of polite applause.

"I'm going to give you all the facts that have been withheld from you", Bill began proudly.

A woman from the local school board nodded enthusiastically in his direction, adding in a loud whisper: "We're gonnae hear some hot air, th' night!"

RELIGIOUS FASCISM

'Keep the Clause' had attracted 30-or-so goodly church folk, along with Sister Mary running her eyes down a 'Keep the Clause' leaflet, and packed them into a room at the Radnor Hotel in Clydebank. With the refusal by the Electoral Reform Society to organise 'Keep the Clause's referendum, Chairman Bill announced they were here because the "gay lobby" were getting their own way too much. He thought there ought to have been a referendum, but thanks to those "powerful pink people" and the "strong gay membership on the Electorial Reform committee... We can't"! (There was much tutting). Referring to MP Stephen Twigg, Bill named the man he thought responsible: "It's "Mr Twiggy!" (Laughs). Sweeping aside all doubt, Pat Rolink stood up and promised a referendum. "Within three or four days! he stormed. There were mutters of approval. "Everyone is going to get their say"! (Cheers).

Des McNulty, the local MSP wasn't able to make it, so he sent a letter to be read out. Bill was disgusted. "It was a fudge", so he wasn't going to read it. If there were any withheld 'facts' to be dispensed on this night; this wasn't one of them. It sparked trouble in the second row. A fiery woman from the Scottish Socialist Party got up to leave. "I'm not interested in your opinion. Des McNulty wrote that letter for everyone to hear and I wanted to hear it!" She finally got her way too. Des McNulty supported repeal and promised strong guidelines. Someone suggested the Dutch system of sex education. A woman spun round in her chair and spat: "And the world's highest abortion rate too!" A man shouted angrily: "They legalise sodomy of children! We don't want fornicators in Scotland! The Scottish majority won't have it!"

The 'moral majority' got their way. There was a vote and only four people showed their hands in support of repeal. Bob stood up and waved his fist in the air in defiance at 'New Labour' and repeated: "THE PEOPLE WILL HAVE THEIR SAY"! There was a thunderous applause. Coffee and biscuits piled up on a table by the door stopped them spilling out onto the streets to riot. Before I left, someone called Bob asked if I would be voting in Souter's referendum. I told him gay peoples' human rights were not up for negotiation. Bob smiled, shook my hand politely and warned me I would burn in Hell.

Where once, as the darling of the Scottish Trade Union Congress (STUC), Brian Souter had stood up and addressed the hall, now he was being targeted by them as "a threat to democracy". The STUC document stated: "Misinformation has been disseminated by the Keep the Clause campaign and certain unscrupulous sections of the media. This has led to an unprecedented rise in the number of homophobic attacks and harassment being reported and experienced by our gay and lesbian communities". Jack Irvine quickly dismissed the statement as "the work of a small clique of politically correct officials".

On Monday, 17 April 2000, and in preparation for the vote that day by delegates of the STUC, Hamish Macdonell reported in the *Scottish Daily Mail* how a new poll had revealed 60 per cent of union members were opposed to the repeal of Section 28: "How union chiefs ignored poll over Section 28 repeal". Most members of the teachers' Educational Institute of Scotland (EIS) and public health workers union Unison were in favour of repeal. The biggest majority against repeal came from the Amalgamated Electrical and Engineering Union with 85 per cent.

Producing only reports in support of Section 28 for the *Scottish Daily Mail*, Hamish Macdonell then declared a "blow to the Scottish Executive" when the Equality Network's Tim Hopkins, addressing a fringe meeting at the STUC "admitted for the first time yesterday they have lost the battle for public opinion and the people of Scotland do not support the repeal of Section 28". Macdonell insisted that such an "admission" from "a leader of the gay lobby" was a "clear indication the Executive is fighting a losing battle". 'Keep the Clause' described it an "amazing revelation". Far from it, since so-called "gay leaders" were under no illusion that the results of a 'referendum' – such as the one financed by evangelical Christian Brian Souter - were not likely to show support for the repeal of Section 28.

Rowena Arshad, an equal opportunities officer, told delegates Section 28 was "grotesque" and unprecedented in law since the days of Nazi Germany while the *Record* editorialised on Donald Dewar's speech: "He sniffed at the 'rhetoric' about support for family life. What is wrong with supporting family life?" Jim Friel, president of the printers' union, the GPMU charged Brian Souter with being an "anti-trade-union bigot" and said church leaders should be ashamed of lining up with those "who would not look out of place alongside the rednecks of Tennessee". The STUC pledged to call for legislation prohibiting

RELIGIOUS FASCISM

incitement to hatred in a bid to prevent the future persecution of minority groups.

After the debate at the STUC, not a single hand was raised in support of retaining Section 28. Jack Irvine was less than satisfied with this and was reported challenging Bill Spiers, the general secretary of the STUC: "I didn't ask how the nodding dogs at your congress voted. I asked what percentage of your members are in favour of repeal". Irvine e-mailed Spiers to call him a "New Labour luvvie" and questioned his left-wing credentials. Bill Spiers publicly accused Jack Irvine of using "aggressive" and "childish" tactics. Gerald Warner called the STUC in *Scotland on Sunday* a bunch of "gratified knuckletrailers" full of "Neanderthal prejudices".Elsewhere, Bishop Holloway told the National Youth Assembly that over the past six months he had been ashamed to be a Scottish Christian and at a press conference in Edinburgh City Chambers, Tim Hopkins of the Equality Network issued statements from Save the Children Scotland, Childline Scotland and the Edinburgh Voluntary Organisations Council, all backing repeal.

When 60-year-old Clive Soley, chairman of the Parliamentary Labour Party remarked that pensioners were more likely to vote conservative and were often racist, it was coupled with remarks by Peter Mandelson, chair of the election planning committee, who suggested there was no mileage to be had from chasing pensioners' votes. Tom 'Brigadier' Brown challenged the "gaffe that could cost Labour dear" and sought to exploit the apparent abandonment of their vote. "It reeks of the smugness and calculating opportunism of the New Labour pipsqueaks... So the elderly are offended when the Governments at Westminster and in Edinburgh seem more concerned with homosexual rights. While there is so much undone for the old, they have every right to get bitter at the sense of priorities that puts gay and lesbian issues at the top of the agenda". Donald Dewar hit back, calling it a "prejudiced" second-hand account of a Labour strategy meeting. He reeled off a list of reforms including the winter fuel allowance for OAPs saying: "The idea that we are writing off old age pensioners is grotesque and totally untrue. We are not writing them off, we are writing them in and writing them in big". The *Record* sneered: "He was eight pages into his speech before he got any applause".

Militant Religionists at War

The *Record* was more than pleased to print a letter from Steven P Took from Paisley who wrote: "The price of the Scottish Parliament, the Repeal of Section 28, Govan shipyards, the admission of 30,000 refugees, and now they're calling OAPs racist. I don't know who I'll be voting for come the next election, but it definitely won't be Labour".

At the same time as fanning the flames of fury against homosexuals, the *Record* found "trusting" 18-year-old Kevin Stevenson to tell his story under the headline: "...MY RETREAT INTO HELL". Stevenson claimed abuse at the hands of Tsering Tashi, or Timothy Mannox in the Samye-Ling Tibetan monastery in Dumfriesshire when he was 16. "Within a year Kevin's life lay in tatters, his confidence shattered by the cruelty and hypocrisy of the very people he had placed his faith in". When confronted, Timothy Mannox explained: "I wouldn't deny it. There was physical contact. We were intimate because we were sleeping in the same area" but felt it was "a bit heavy" to call his advances a sexual assault. That was not how the *Record* saw it and continued to report Kevin Stevenson as having been "assaulted". Stevenson claimed that Tashi lay naked beside him, saying: "He asked if I knew what spoons meant then he pulled me over behind him, and pulled my arm around his waist. Then he asked me if I knew what forks meant and pulled me on top of him so he was lying on his back and I was lying on top of him facing him". (In Buddhism, monks frequently circumscribe the rules governing celibacy by penetrating between the legs). Prominently displayed at the foot of the story, the *Record* begged: "HAVE YOU A STORY... about a retreat which turned into a hell at the Samye Ling Buddhist centre or any monastery? If so, call us on 0141 242 3251". Though it did not involve the sexual orientation they were hoping for, a story was soon forthcoming. *Record* reporter Vivienne Aitken reported: "MONK JAILED FOR ABUSING GIRL, 14". There was no mention of what Tenzin Chonjoe, 30 had actually done. Only the words of Daniel Travers, prosecuting: "The girl lay down on a bed with her feet up against the wall and he put his head on her stomach. After the assault, the girl got up and went outside. She was very shocked". In his defence, Margaret Payne said: "He said he was just giving the girl a massage which was acceptable in his culture but he now realises the English are more restrained and less trusting". Chonjoe was sentenced to three months and placed on the sex offenders' register.

By Thursday, 20 April, the Scottish Parliament Local Government Committee had published its Stage One report on the Ethical Standards in Public Life Bill, which included the repeal of Section 28, and presented to the rest of Parliament the general principles of the Bill based on the evidence committees had taken during March. There was unanimous agreement to proceed in repealing Section 28 before the Scottish Parliament prepared to debate the general principles of the Bill and vote on whether it should proceed. The only dissenting voice was one Tory member on the Committee, Keith Harding MSP. He was backed, amongst others, by most of Scotland's main national newspapers: The *Record*, the *Scottish Daily Mail*, the *Scottish Sun* and *Scotland on Sunday*. Jack Irvine huffed in the *Record*. "If the Parliament and its committee poodles do not listen to the views of Scotland's parents then Keep the Clause will not only continue its campaign but dramatically accelerate its activities". In the *Herald*, Irvine said the Committee "positively salivated over the gay rights group Stonewall and the spurious links they drew between Section 28 and homophobic bullying..." The *Herald* warned the debate had "reached new levels of bitterness".

The *Record* claimed "Donald Dewar is now facing an internal revolt by his own MSPs over Section 28" after the *Record's* Carlos Alba was told that ten Labour MSPs wanted guidelines to state that marriage should be promoted as an ideal in sex education classes. Another nameless MSP, supposedly worried about a backlash from his constituents, cried: "When people stop talking to you altogether you know that you are doing something wrong". The tabloid advised hopefully: "If they are backed by the Tories and the SNP, they would squeeze through by a single vote, inflicting the first defeat on the Executive". The *Record* had "learned" that 'marriage' was included on the original draft that Dewar took to a meeting of the Labour group. "But he was persuaded to drop it following pressure from a number of backbenchers - including Kate McLean, Rhoda Grant and Johann Lamont - who believed it would discriminate against single mothers". The *Record's* editorial described the Executive as "under siege" and insisted: "Donald Dewar cannot go on kidding himself any longer. He is now being told from all sides that his attitude on Section 28 is wrong". The so-called "rebellion" of

Militant Religionists at War

course, "delighted" a "spokesman" for the Catholics who declared: "All Christian people will be very pleased".

In their edition of Saturday, 22 April, a 57-year-old Ann Gloag, Brian Souter's sister, looking particularly glamorous and pushing boxes containing "120,000 reasons" why children should not be "taught about homosexual lifestyle issues" was pictured in the *Record* "making her first public appearance since the funeral of her 28-year-old son Jonathan who committed suicide" in September 1999. She was joined by a "pram protest" of 100 Christian activists, described by the *Record* as "concerned mothers" with their "children at the front" marching up to the Scottish Executive on the Mound. Unfortunately, as it was Good Friday, the Scottish Executive was closed. Using the 'I'm not normally the sort of person who would do this kind of thing' line adopted by parents depicted on the 'Keep the Clause' billboards, Ann Gloag begged: "I don't usually do this kind of thing so I'm like many of the people here. They are mothers and grandmothers with their children and grandchildren. These aren't the demonstrating type but they feel so strongly that they are willing to march. We chose Good Friday because it is a day when families are together". Wearing 'Keep the Clause' slogans and carrying placards, Gloag pushed her daughter Pam's one-year-old son Ross Macmillan in a buggy while his older sister Ashleigh, five, walked alongside. Over what was now widely believed to be "sexually explicit material entering the classroom", Anne Stewart, a mother-of-three begged: "The vast majority of people - and everybody I know - is not homophobic... It's about protecting our children. I've had a glimpse of the material and it appals me. It's a form of child abuse, robbing children of their childhood. Some of the material is aimed at primary school children. It's a sad day when that sort of stuff is being forced upon them". Out of sight in the *Record's* photo was Ayub Khan's Multi-Faith Coalition that had otherwise failed to gain much support from the Asian community. "Feelings against this Bill is so strong that it has united Sikhs and Hindus", he crowed. The *Record's* editorial was aimed at the Executive: "Surely, they cannot ignore a Good Friday procession... The First Minister's own consultation process was a flop which was hi-jacked by the gay minority - but 120,000 signatures is REAL consultation..." The *Record* demanded Dewar "should lend an ear now - before a national referendum proves how wrong he is". The *Herald* noted how Jack

Irvine, present throughout and carefully orchestrating the march, blocked access to Ann Gloag by newspapers unsympathetic to 'Keep the Clause'.

Scapegoating gays in the name of protecting children served only to let sexual offenders and predators off the hook. Gay men have never been the only source of predatory sexual assaults on children. Such narratives service moral panic; they don't contribute to answers. 'Perverts' or paedophiles have been eagerly absorbed by the media, be it a pathological loner or networks of male 'outsiders' utilising digital images and networks to bring otherwise externalised threats into the otherwise safe refuge of childhood, the home or schools of 'innocents'. Such an unyielding belief of an external threat may bind the demonstrators, but it concealed the over-riding fact that children are most vulnerable to sexual exploitation in the family home at the hands of parents, carers, siblings, relatives or someone they already know. It also concealed the primary locus of most violence; most sexual pain and dysfunction: the family. And just as the family, as a unit, can be so good at collusion and denial in instances of abuse, so too was it formidably misguided when it was united behind ignorance or misinformation.

Conservative shadow leader, William Hague had already addressed the Spring Harvest festival, attended by 9,000 fundamental Christians. Now, a few months later, he was back, addressing black church leaders at the 'Faith in the Future' conference in Brighton. They gave him a standing ovation after he called on the Government to allow national Christian TV and radio stations. Hague told them the state: "should be supporting the Judaeo-Christian values of our society, not undermining them", adding: "I believe we should support families with an explicit recognition of the value of marriage in the tax and benefit system" and calling for society to actively support Christian churches and charities before criticising the Labour Government for attempting to repeal Section 28. William Hague confirmed his strategy to rally the religious to the Conservative cause and met Texas University Professor Malvin Olasky, an influential advisor in the George W Bush presidential campaign. Olasky was quoted in the *Dallas Morning News* claiming churches and charities and not government should provide social services with "a spiritual dimension to assistance". Olasky was a vociferous supporter of

Militant Religionists at War

the poisonous 'ex-gay' movement which committed itself to turning gay people 'straight'.

Labour leader Tony Blair addressed a 6,000 strong rally organised by the African and Caribbean Evangelical Alliance assuring them of his support for faith-based charities. On the same day, the *Record* reported 30,000 Jehovah's Witnesses had "swamped" Perth. Their eighth annual festival was held in St Johnstone's football stadium. The tabloid emphasised how their presence added £1m in tourist cash.

Scotland's links with US Christian evangelism didn't just begin with Scottish Christians lending financial support to slavery and end in Americans returning the favour by donating cash to religious campaigns against equality in Scotland. Scotsman Rev George M Docherty was responsible for the addition of the words "under God" to America's Pledge of Allegiance, recited by millions of children across America every day. Docherty was minister until 1975 at the New York Avenue Presbyterian Church in Washington DC which presidents often attended. It began as a sermon questioning why – since the founding fathers had believed the nation's destiny to be divinely ordained – His name had not been mentioned in the Pledge. With Eisenhower's agreement, the addition of the words "under God" was introduced in 1954.

By Monday, 24 April 2000, the *Record* gloated: "DEWAR 'TOO SCARED' TO DEBATE CLAUSE PLAN". Failing to engage the First Minister Donald Dewar in a public debate, Brian Souter settled for appearing on BBC's Question Time with pop star Boy George. The *Scottish Daily Mail* hit out: "The BBC TV programme Question Time was accused of 'dumbing down' last night over its decision to include pop star Boy George as a panellist". The *Mail* made a point of the fact that Boy George, a regular columnist in the *Daily Express* newspaper, once sang: "All war is stupid". But there was a lot more to Boy George than the media were ready to admit. In his book 'Straight', (Arrow Books, 2005), George O'Dowd wrote of religion: "I wouldn't call myself religious, although I don't think you can ever escape the religious convictions passed on by your parents. My mother and father were always described in the press as 'staunch Catholics'. Mum would often take us to church when we were very young, and all of us kids went to Sunday school, but it was a way of getting us from under her feet. Mum and Dad were hardly strict about us practising our faith. Maybe having six kids to feed took precedence over faith, or maybe it was because, like a lot of people, they lost respect for the Church, as more of its indiscretions were made public. After my mother's mother passed away I discovered the horrors of her teenage years in a strict Irish convent. If she wet the bed she would be made to wear the wet sheet for the entire day and they were regularly made to feel disgusted with their femininity. My ex-boyfriend Michael was raised by the Christian Brothers in Ireland and suffered physical and mental abuse. That high-handed morality often creates the very thing it seeks to eradicate. Those who are the most disgusted by sex are often the ones who are the most consumed by it". His comments pre-dated the Catholic Churches' day of reckoning when barely a day would pass without some new revelation of child-sex abuse amongst its priests.

The *Sunday Times* suggested that Prime Minister Tony Blair was now ready to allow gays to adopt. Downing Street, on the other hand, dismissed this as "absolute rubbish". The *Record* wrote: "Critics say the strategy would force councils to treat all potential parents, including gays, the same". Felicity Collier from the British Agencies for Adoption and Fostering confessed: "The simple fact is there aren't enough families coming forward at the moment".

After Ulster Secretary Peter Mandelson was spotted in his ministerial chauffeur-driven car with his partner Reinaldo Avila da Silva, the *Record* pointed out that Peter Mandelson was "20 years older than Da Silva". After they had been caught "shopping together" the *Record* pursed its lips to describe this as a reflection on "the New Labour tolerance of unconventional relationships" before passing the smelling salts to the *Mail on Sunday* that discovered: "They spent the night at Chequers with the Blairs and their children".

On Wednesday, 26 April, the *Scottish Mail* headlined: "DEWAR HEART SCARE SPARKS CRISIS". The First Minister Donald Dewar was forced to go into hospital for major heart surgery, leaving Liberal Democrat leader and coalition partner Jim Wallace to stand in as deputy for three months. The *Scottish Express* reported: "secret crisis talks". 'Keep the Clause' hovered over the First Minister's bed. The *Mail's* editorial warned: "Mr Dewar can no doubt detect from his hospital bed the rumble of speculation about his future". With such concern for the First

Militant Religionists at War

Minister's well-being there was nothing left to do but turn on Wendy Alexander, who had 'steam-rollered' the repeal of Section 28 in with such "pig-headed determination". Days later they focused on "Dewar 'jumping the heart surgery queue...'", adding how the "First Minister (was) getting free private care on the NHS". The *Record's* 'Brigadier' Brown sniffed: "Small wonder signs of strain began to show".

The *Record* favoured Henry McLeish as successor, whom they once described as one of the three wise men along with the other former local government officers, Tom McCabe and Jack McConnell, who were credited for their willingness to listen to 'Keep the Clause'. Jack McConnell, the finance minister, was otherwise favoured at five to one, Wendy Alexander ten to one and Susan Deacon twenty to one. Iain Macwhirter wrote in the *Sunday Herald*: "Those ministers whom (Donald Dewar) regarded as his key modernisers - Alexander and Deacon - have been picked off. The 'lippy women' have been silenced, and pose no further threat. The Big Macs are now in charge, and their mouthpieces in the press are boasting about how chief whip McCabe is the 'king-maker'. It is assumed that McLeish will take over as king, though his reign may be relatively short. McConnell - the 'great communicator' - is warming up on the sidelines..." Tom McCabe threatened legal action against the *Sunday Herald* over claims that they had suggested he had leaked information to the *Record*. Years later, former Labour MP Lord Foulkes told the *Sunday Herald*: "Loads of people at Westminster could never understand how Henry (McLeish) became a minister of state even. He used to brief against colleagues all the time. He used to stab people in the back". McLeish replied: "These comments are beneath contempt and don't deserve any response whatsoever".

The *Scottish Daily Mail's*, editor, Ramsay Smith carried the headline on the front page: "SOUTER REFERENDUM FINALLY GIVES SCOTS VOTE ON SECTION 28". Smith's lap-dog Scottish Political editor, Hamish Macdonell dutifully wrote up his editorial opinion.

Brian Souter's glorified opinion poll was already under scrutiny. In Glasgow, legal advice was sought on how Souter obtained names on the electoral register, which was, in any case, 18 months out of date. David Macauley from 'Keep the Clause' explained the ballot paper for BBC Scotland News. There were just two questions: "I vote to retain Clause 28 (Section 2a)" and

"I vote to repeal Clause 28 (Section 2a)". ICM and a Bristol company called Vote IT had been hired along with John Cowdall, a former deputy returning officer for Britain's European elections. Vote IT had only been in existence for a year. The *Scottish Sun* reported: "Mr Cowdall said he expected the turnout to be somewhere between the 30 to 35 per cent for local elections and 70 to 75 per cent for parliamentary polls". While ICM assured there would be no accompanying notes to persuade anyone which way they should vote, Souter planned to spend £150,000 on another poster advertising campaign begging voters to KEEP THE CLAUSE. Tim Hopkins of the Equality Network called the 'referendum': "Offensive, undemocratic and discredited. It's like Ian Paisley running an opinion poll on the Good Friday Agreement. As an opinion poll, the whole thing has so many holes you could drain cabbage in it".

While John Cowdall, given the controversy, wanted Vote IT's premises kept secret, its location in the offices of a mail order company on the third floor of a Victorian red-brick street near Piccadilly Station in Manchester was soon public knowledge. The *Scotsman* found, "in the foyer of the building, the founder, sternly Victorian, a man who would clearly have no truck with non-heterosexuals, stares from a portrait" and noted that the mail order catalogue was "aimed at women of a certain age and modish men time-locked in 1976".

Despite being frightened into invisibility, the *Mail on Sunday* warned: "Security firm staff will police the poll count, which could be a target for mass protests by gay rights campaigners".

Since former *Scottish Mirror* editor Peter Cox was now editing the *Sunday Mail*, he had an opportunity to show he shared none of the views of his former columnist, Jack Irvine. The editorial blasted: "The so-called referendum on Section 28 that Brian Souter is bankrolling is exposed today as a total sham. He is pumping £1million of his money into a bizarre and ever-more-desperate attempt to buy into the laws of this country. The organisation he is using is a tuppeny-ha'penny outfit whose biggest contract so far is a poll on dustbins for the South Ribble Borough Council in Lancashire. Lined up against him is a 'Repeal the Clause' organisation with just £198 in the bank and debts of £400. They are so broke they have to ask people who don't want their leaflets if they can have them back". In fact, while Souter was spending an estimated £2m, Tim Hopkins had hastily convened Scrap the Clause. It had no office, paid staff, transport or even their own phone line. Their bank statement read: £198.24!

In preparation for Souter's so-called 'referendum', Jack Irvine's Media House announced the results of another poll showing 43 per cent of teachers of primary and secondary schools supporting the Government's efforts to repeal with 35 per cent opposed and 19 per cent undecided. Talking up the result, this appeared in *Scotland on Sunday* as: "...Less than half of Scotland's teachers back the government's attempt to repeal Section 28". The *Mail on Sunday* roared: "Teachers vote down repeal of Section 28".

In a very different poll, Dr Geoff Scobie, senior psychologist at Glasgow University charged Scots men with being too worried about being labelled gay to express emotions to each other. An opinion poll by NOP of a thousand men showed 62 per cent of Scots guys would not kiss a man while 23 per cent said they would only if they were extremely drunk or in the midst of celebrating a sporting victory. Glasgow's *Evening Times* accompanied the report with a picture of footballer Ally McCoist laying on his back on the pitch with team mate Paul Gascoigne leaning over to kiss him.

The media were still circling Donald Dewar who was well enough to attend the important debate in the Scottish Executive on Section 28 before his operation. The idea of Labour's coalition partner, a Liberal Democrat leader in charge of the Executive in Donald's absence sent shivers down the *Scottish Daily Mail's* spine. "The last thing we want is a Liberal Democrat in charge"; a Labour insider told them. The *Record's* editorial spat: "That's right, the man whose dismal little rabble came in fourth, with 14 per cent of the Scottish election vote, will be the face and leader of Scotland... Labour - the largest party in Scotland's parliament - will effectively be rudderless until (Dewar) gets back... if he gets back". Weighing up possible contenders, the *Mail* cast a wary eye over MSP Wendy Alexander "who will before long emerge from under the black cloud of Section 28". Thanks to the *Record*, 'wee Wendy' was now the most well known face on the Executive. In an editorial, they remarked bitterly: "Clause 28 may not have done Wendy Alexander any favours with the public - but at least it now knows who she is". The tabloid was already rushing to boost the profile of their favourite contender: Henry McLeish. Faithful reporter Carlos Alba obliged. A picture appearing to go back some years was captioned: "FAMILY MAN", which included McLeish's first wife Margaret and daughter Clare. Alba wrote that he combined "political talent with genuine decency". Whoring her own 'family-values' agenda to *Scotland on Sunday*, Mrs Katie Grant spat: "I notice that the unattached Ms Alexander has taken to bagging the seat next to the First Minister. I say to Donald, don't even think of it unless you want your life to be dominated henceforth by the wagging finger. I could make a joke about Warfarin here but good taste prevents me".

The *Scottish Daily Mail's* reporter Hamish Macdonell penned a report over "Wendy's talkshops", accusing her of "setting up a spate of quangos for cronies". These "cronies" were apparently proliferating at an alarming rate. "12 task forces, a rate of one a month... including funding to black and ethnic minority groups..." Wendy explained that volunteers who were only paid travel expenses ran most of them, like groups dealing with initiatives for the homeless.

The *Fraserburgh Herald's* editorial demanded: "Those MSPs who are refusing to listen to the voice of the people should resign immediately, and the first to go should be the Political Correct Wendy Alexander who has spearheaded the move to repeal Clause 28. Instead of wasting her time on irrelevancies such as Clause 28, and setting up Quangos for pals in the Labour Party, Ms Alexander in her capacity as Communities Minister should be doing something to deal with the scourge of drugs which is sweeping the country".

Attacks on "Miss Wendy Alexander" continued unabated, notably after the publication of the Scottish Affairs Committee report on poverty, which advised the Executive on the handling of poverty. The *Scottish Daily Mail* thought they had found something in the report that had criticised her and snarled: "'Headline-grabber' Alexander savaged by the spin-busters" while the *Record* sniggered: "WENDY'S ON THE RACK". A letter from David Marshall, Chairman of the Scottish Affairs Committee sharply rebuked the *Mail*: "I must protest about your coverage... in particular the way you chose to vilify Communities Minister Wendy Alexander. The report does not at any stage single out Miss Alexander for criticism of any sort. On the contrary the only reference to her... states: 'We are particularly grateful to the Minister for Communities... Her appearance marked the first occasion on which a Minister from the Scottish Executive gave oral evidence to a select committee'. The comment on 'headline grabbing initiatives'... was a caution rather than a rebuke and refers specifically to 'both the UK Government and the Scottish Executive', but makes no reference to individual ministers... The committee's hard work and positive recommendations to tackle the most serious problem in Scotland have been ignored in favour of unjustified personal attacks".

On Thursday, 27 April 2000, the Executive met to debate the general principals of the Ethical Standards in Public Life (Scotland) Bill, primarily concerned with codes of conduct for local councils but famous for including the repeal of Section 28. It would be just the first stage looking at the general principles of the Bill and a vote on whether it should pass on to the second stage. The *Scottish Daily Mail* bawled: "...The clause fails to mention marriage as the pre-eminent family relationship". The *Record* sobbed: "At one stage fewer than 30 of the 129 MSPs were in the chamber during the debate... The appalling attendance shocked on-lookers..." (Interestingly, the press were completely absent when the Scottish Executive debated domestic violence). With the press in full attendance for Wendy Alexander, she stood up to say: "Consultation is not about listening to whoever shouts the loudest or whoever employs the most sophisticated PR machines, nor is it about pulling out the largest cheque book". On 'Keep the Clause', she said: "What has been paraded has been simplistic and misleading. A campaign expensive to mount but perhaps with a cheapness all of its own... The tone and tactics of the Keep the Clause campaign has itself revealed why repeal does matter. For we seek a Scotland that looks to the future and does not allow itself to be dragged back to an indifferent and intolerant past which had too little room for inclusion and human solidarity". Education minister Sam Galbraith added: "When you start basing your judgment on behalf of minorities on opinion polls, then you have a very poor democracy".

SNP MSP, Nicola Sturgeon's column in the *Scottish Daily Express* pointed out that "in the Scotland's Schools bill, going through Parliament now, there is a clause that says: 'The Scottish Ministers may issue guidance to education authorities... and education authorities shall, in discharging those functions, have regard to any such guidance'. If the Government can include a clause like that in the schools Bill there is no reason why there should not be a similar provision relating to guidance on sex education. That would give parents a guarantee that the spirit of guidance would be translated into classroom practise. It's a simple idea, but one that will settle this argument". Proposing such an amendment to the Ethical Standards in Public Life Bill, the SNP would only succeed in surrounding sexuality with a covert warning sign that sent a message to teachers: 'Handle with care'. It was more tolerant ideas and relaxed attitudes that were needed, but these were harder to encourage now that such a poisonous and virulent campaign orchestrated by militant religionists and moral conservatives had now surfaced.

'Brigadier' Brown stormed in the *Record:* "The Parliament of closed minds and cloth ears sat in its cocoon on the Mound and shut itself off from Scottish public opinion". He accused Wendy Alexander of being "back in her most infuriating finger-wagging lecture style". He was furious that the Bill should've passed so effortlessly by 103 votes to 16 with five abstentions and despaired of the "number of Labour Ministers and MSPs" who want Section 28 retained, groaning in exasperation: "...They sat silent". He had a word of warning for the SNP who "backed the 'Scrap the Clause' Movement" in "a particularly weasel-worded way". Reminding them: "Stagecoach tycoon Brian Souter has put his personal fortune behind the 'Keep the Clause' campaign - as well as donating cash to the Nationalists. Will he be satisfied with their spokeswoman Nicola Sturgeon's oh-so-carefully worded formula 'The SNP supports the repeal, recognising that for some people this is an issue of conscience'?"

On Monday, 1 May, Gordon Currie's report in the *Scottish Daily Mail* showed the tabloid to be in a more strident mood: "Gay law mob stage protest outside Souter's church". The *Mail* declared: "Gay activists and far left campaigners yesterday staged a protest outside the church where Stagecoach millionaire Brian Souter worships. The mob waved placards and chanted homosexual propaganda as churchgoers arrived..." The *Herald* correctly referred to "protesters" and "campaigners" and showed a wide discrepancy over numbers attending the peaceful protest. The *Mail* imagined a "50-strong mob" while the *Herald* more accurately recorded "around a dozen members of the Perth and Dundee branches of the Scottish Socialist Party..." The *Mail* wrote: "Banner-waving members of the Scottish Socialist Party

Militant Religionists at War

marched on the church with gay rights leaders... The 50-strong mob thrust leaflets into the hands of worshippers". No "gay rights leaders" were in attendance. Through a history of marginalisation, the Scottish press wouldn't have known one if he/she or "it" - as one agony aunt had referred to a transsexual - had landed on a desk in their newsroom. At an Edinburgh demonstration, under a picture of marchers under a banner waved by the Scottish Socialist Party, even the *Scottish Sun* was forced to admit: "Peaceful Scots praised by cops". Rev David Souter who was at the church in Perth was given space in the *Record* to back his brother and say: "We ask 'Scrap the Section' to restrict their future demonstrations to activities involving adults to avoid situations where children could be intimidated". In fairness, it wasn't the Scottish Socialists who had bedecked their children in slogans and dragged them along to the demonstration as 'Keep the Clause' had done only days before to Holyrood.

Reverend David Souter appeared in the weekly *Deeside Piper*, reputed to be a favourite newspaper for the Queen's mother when it was delivered to her Birkhall holiday home at Balmoral. Locals were upset when it reported on a religious play in the nearby village of Midmar. A picture of a scene from the Midmar Passion Play, featuring Jesus on the cross, was accompanied by the rather casual headline: "Hanging around at Midmar". Rev David Souter "blasted" to the *Scottish News of the World*: "This is deeply insulting, awful. Someone really boobed. I never use the words blasphemy and hatred myself but people I spoke to have done in this case. A great number of villagers were offended. It's very sad and hurtful". The *Deeside Piper* editor took it upon himself to apologise for the *faux pas*.

Soon after, the *Scottish Daily Mail* reported: "...Another mob of gay and lesbian activists stormed into a public meeting held to discuss Section 28 in Paisley". This story was initiated by a press release from Jack Irvine which also made out that gays had somehow 'broken up' the meeting. The other version was that an employee of Glasgow's sexual health group, Phace West had been walking to the station to go to Glasgow when he came across the gathering in the centre of town. A woman was standing on a concrete block speaking about the need for Section 28. He was reported saying he thought it was the Tory party canvassing and climbed up on the next block along to say she was wrong. The crowd started calling him a paedophile. One member of the crowd was so threatening a policeman had to intervene. Two Socialist Workers Party members joined them before writing 'SCRAP THE SECTION' on a piece of card, holding it up and calling out that he was right. The altercation was soon dispersed.

UK editions of the *Daily Mail* continued to print features that would have been read in Scottish editions, all vilifying gays. They included a story proclaiming an underground gay propaganda network that operated in Hollywood; a feature on Richard Burton's drug-and-alcohol-ridden love for Elizabeth Taylor's former husband Eddie Fisher and another on Wallis Simpson's lover Jimmy Donahue, dismissed as a "spoilt, mother-reliant, homosexual misfit..."

After the *Scottish Daily Mail* had announced the launch of the 'Keep the Clause' "referendum on gay law" on Tuesday, 2 May 2000, the £100,000 "massive poster blitz" soon followed. The *Mail*, of course, praised 'Keep the Clause's "attempt to highlight their side of the argument..." One poster said: "MAKE THE GOVERNMENT LISTEN", while the other said: "MAKE YOUR VOICE HEARD". Gay rights organisation Outright Scotland advised gays to use the pre-paid envelope to insist 'Keep the Clause' took their name off their mailing list and demand confirmation this had been done. The *Mail* responded by chastising Outright Scotland for calling on the public to "disrupt the referendum". The *Record* begged readers to vote on "the law banning gay sex lessons in schools", reminding readers how the Scottish Executive's "undemocratic plan has backfired and now everyone has a chance to state their view... Let them not be swayed by minority pressure groups, but by the genuine feeling of the majority".

Commenting on the Scottish Parliament's first year, First Minister, Donald Dewar borrowed from Mary Poppins when he quipped: "Super-Parliamentary-Year, The-Media-Are-Ferocious". Donald Dewar admitted to having made mistakes in his first year, which was seized upon by the *Record*: "DONALD: I'VE MADE MISTAKES", they cried, offering him "4 STEPS TO PUT ONE OF THEM RIGHT". One of them was to fill in Souter's ballot paper and send it off. They even helped readers by showing them, with the aid of a photograph, which box they had to tick. Care officer, Anne McKnight of Howwood told them: "If any of my children was to tell me they were gay, it would not change my feelings towards them. We have nothing against gays, but we believe this sort of thing should be discussed at home".

In *Scotland on Sunday*, Gerald Warner marked the Scottish Executive's first year by sharing his opinion on "every malign instinct to make society more squalid by marginalizing marriage, normal family life and heterosexuality... People who want to safeguard children from sodomite propaganda are demonised as 'bigots'; an attempt to give the overwhelming majority a voice by referendum - the devise to which the parliament owes its own existence - is denounced as 'subverting democracy'. The very statute which will empower homosexuals to proselytise children is, by an extravagant inversion of truth, entitled the Ethical Standards in Public Life Bill". (A few years later, Warner would confess in one of his columns that "many polls are distorted or exaggerated". Presumably with the exception of Mr Souter's). In his fury he turned on the parliament apparently ready to bestow awards on the "Limp-Wristed Activists' Open Season on Pubescent Schoolboys..." before castigating women MSPs; calling them, "roly-polys with attitude".

Ronnie Liveston from Falkirk wrote to the editor of *Scotland on Sunday* demanding; "the teaching of the sexual aberrations of the genetically flawed should be outwith the teaching mandate to the very young".

A letter in the *Scottish Mail* declared: "On Section 28 we know what the word of God says about homosexual behaviour, and God is not bigoted or homophobic".

A "Regular Reader" with "name and address supplied" advised the *Fraserburgh Herald*: "The term homosexual Christian is comical, they would be as well to say a Christian thief or a Christian murderer".

The Scottish Socialist Party leader Tommy Sheridan and the elected leader of 800,000 trade unionists, Bill Spiers both threw down the gauntlet at a rally of trade unionists in Edinburgh, challenging Brian Souter and Cardinal Winning to a debate. With Brian Souter's TV debate with Boy George looming, 'Keep the Clause' scoffed: "We are certainly not going to run down the debate by taking on Mr Speirs and Mr Sheridan". Bill Spiers, general secretary of the STUC had written to ICM Research raising questions about the wording of the poll and what security arrangements were in place. The poll company was not able to guarantee the mail-shot would be given to the person whose name was given on the form. Neither could they guarantee someone getting a replacement form if they never received the first. And with an out-of-date electoral register, many young people, like students in short-term accommodation, were left disenfranchised.

In the Section 28 supporting *Scottish Sun*, Jim Sillars turned on the "arrogance" of "trendy-lefty... 'Witch'... Wendy". Sillars blasted: "...Before the homosexuals' good fairy Wendy alighted upon our Parliament, Scotland was populated by people like us - the uncaring and intolerant, who don't give a damn for anyone. We who have the temerity to disagree with Miss Alexander on Section 28, we who don't want the promotion of homosexuality in schools, are painted as thick know-nothings, bigots who live in intellectual squalor, unfit to deal with modern times".

On Wednesday, 3 May 2000, the *Record* announced: "Use your voice to speak for Scotland. From today, the voice of Scotland can make itself heard. The first ballot papers in the national referendum on Section 28 will start dropping through your letter boxes..." But beneath the 'Keep the Clause' slogan the *Record* now regularly carried, it warned readers: "Between now and the voting deadline of May 22, attempts will be made to downgrade and discredit the referendum. Already, the politicians and the gay lobby are trying to dismiss it as a 'flawed opinion poll'... The gay lobby want to disrupt the ballot". Familiar faces voiced their support for the poll. Ann Allen from the Board of Social Responsibility implored: "People who choose not to vote are not using a democratic right they have been given". Monsignor Tom Connelly begged people to vote "with their Christian conscience" and the Scottish Tory leader Brian Monteith promised he'll table an amendment demanding tougher safeguards. As the ballot papers were despatched from northern England to target four million voters in Scotland, the *Herald* begged readers to "junk this mail: Section 28 poll is bogus" and attempted to get a comment from 'Keep the Clause', but Irvine refused to speak to them. The *Herald's* editorial warned: "A strange and disparate company of people lurks behind this dubious document, including a cardinal of the Roman Catholic Church, a multi-millionaire bus owner, and a homophobic former tabloid journalist". Tim Hopkins of the Equality Network insisted "it's highly offensive that people should be asked to justify their human rights by sending a form back to a millionaire whom nobody ever elected to do anything". The *Scottish Mirror*, the *Record's* sister paper, recommended: "...Scrumple up the voting form and chuck it in the bin..."

Before the summer of 2000, there was something of Germany, 1935, in the air in Scotland. The *Scottish Daily Mail's* Scottish Political Reporter Ian Smith's report read like something out of *Der Stürmer*: "Keep the Clause campaigners raised fears yesterday that the powerful gay lobby was attempting to undermine the vote by questioning its legitimacy. Highly active gay and lesbian groups have already had a major effect on the repeal process by running a concerted e-mail campaign distorting the Scottish Executive original consultation process on Section 28 in favour of scrapping the clause. A spokesman for the campaign said: 'In view of the fact that gay and lesbian groups were so active in undermining the government's consultation and turning it into a farce and fraud, they would do well to allow the Scottish people a fair and free opportunity to vote. Why are they so scared of a referendum involving every voter in Scotland with a fair and open question? You have to ask what they are afraid of, or what they have got to hide'".

Backed by Baroness Janet Young, Souter's self-proclaimed 'referendum' still operated against heavy criticism. Now, many more new billboard advertisements were springing up over Scotland begging the public to "KEEP THE CLAUSE!" It was a shameful exercise in innuendo and misrepresentation that disguised bigotry and predjudice as social concern. The 'referendum' brought cases of triplicate forms, ballot papers sent to the homes of those deceased, and missing security envelopes. 79-year-old Dan McNicol on the Isle of Arran and his wife Irene received two forms each but they were addressed to a local caravan park 300 yards up the road. The following weekend's *Sunday Mail* further discredited the 'referendum' when they reported how 58,000 in Scotland had died since the old electoral roll Souter used had been compiled. They claimed Wendy Alexander and Donald Dewar wouldn't be getting ballot papers, 157 papers were delivered to a Vauxhall car dealership in Sighthill, Edinburgh and dad Brian Keith had voting papers sent to his 11-year-old son Niall and 15-year-old daughter Claire. The *Scotsman* printed a letter from Dr Gillian Hardstone from Lockerbie who asked: "Are we seeing the exclusion from the ballot of all who do not live in households that can readily be identified as a nuclear family?" Dr Hardstone claimed she hadn't received her ballot paper while those around her with a "Mrs" in their household had. The *Sunday Herald* pointed out that less than half of Scotland's young people would receive the 'Keep the Clause' ballots because of the out-of-date electoral register. Michael Taylor of East Lothian pointed out to the *Scotsman* how "the way in which a vote is cast can be seen without opening the envelope; all that is needed is to hold it up to the light. So, someone could destroy a vote if they did not like it". The *Sunday Mail* reported on a woman who received a paper for her late husband John, who had died 14 years ago. Mike McLean from Glasgow wrote to the *Scotsman* to say: "There are ten flats in our block, and ten ballot papers were delivered. Seven were for people who no longer lived at that address. I have lived at this address for just over 17 years. I did not receive a ballot paper. A friend, with five people in the household eligible to vote, got 16!" Professor Stephen Prickett wrote in the *Times:* "I received five copies of Brian Souter's referendum paper and, on the good old principle of 'vote early, and vote often' I completed and returned them all". Duncan MacInnes on Skye asked the *Herald:* "I have just received 46 questionnaires from Mr Souter: five for genuine family members and 41 for named people who do not live, and never have lived, here... Is this a record?"

Students, who were largely in favour of repeal, prepared to release a dossier showing at least 25,000 Scottish students would be denied a vote on Section 28. Mandy Telford told the *Herald:* "This is the most incompletely organised ballot in Scottish history. Our survey exposes Souter's poll as lacking in any democratic legitimacy".

The *Record* snapped: "NOTHING is perfect. But Brian Souter's referendum on Clause 28 is as close as we are likely to come in this world". Meanwhile, on the 'Keep the Clause' website, correspondence supporting repeal of Section 28 - a clear majority – were swiftly wiped, while pro-retention correspondence was left untouched.

On Saturday, 6 May 2000, the newspapers were reporting how Ken Livingstone had become London's first mayor. Leo McKinstry saw it differently in the *Daily Mail,* wondering what "henchman" Livingstone would appoint to his Cabinet. For the Greater London Authority's workforce he believed there would be a "far greater priority placed on race and gender issues than on

Militant Religionists at War

actually delivering services" and warned that Brian Souter with his Stagecoach buses running through London would be an "early target".

In London, local government minister Hilary Armstrong hinted that the Government had already given up hope of getting the repeal of Section 28 in England and Wales past the House of Lords and that it would have to wait until after the next election in 2001. Brian Souter gloated in the *Scottish Mail on Sunday* that it had been "an action packed week". Baroness Young attended a conference at London's Regent's Park mosque wearing a blue headscarf out of respect for Islamic tradition. London's Spectrum Radio's Dr Majid Katme spoke warmly of Baroness Young and told the audience: "Thank God we have got Baroness Young. We need a 1,000 people like her". He said homosexuality was "the greatest threat to mankind" and "lesbianism was spreading like wildfire. We must vaccinate our Islamic community against this threat". Dr Abel Abbas speaking on the medical outcome of homosexuality, said gays had a twenty-five to thirty-year decrease in life expectancy and "unfortunately, bisexual men pass the HIV infection to their innocent wives and to their offspring". With the aid of pictures showing lesbians in fetish gear and wearing strap-on dildos, he attempted to demonstrate the likelihood of damage to the female genitalia by penetration. Gary Steeler, Shadow Secretary of State for International Development extended the good wishes of Tory leader William Hague, and Chief Rabbi Jonathan Sachs sent a message of support.

Section 28 had started a war amongst newspapers. The *Sunday Mail* was losing patience with its sister paper, the *Daily Record*. The gentlemen's agreement that once restrained one newspaper from criticising another had been broken. Difficulties between Jack Irvine and *Scottish Mirror* editor Peter Cox became evident after Jack Irvine stopped writing his column in the paper. Now Peter Cox was editor of the *Sunday Mail*, there was a dramatic change of tone: "What chaos. What a shambles. What a total waste of silly Souter's £1million", the editorial blasted. Along with columnist Melanie Reid's step-by-step origami illustrations on how to make a dead duck out of Souter's ballot paper, Tommy Sheridan MSP invited everyone down to George Square in Glasgow for a public burning of the mail-shot. He wrote: "Let's have a referendum on whether the murderous nuclear arsenal on the Clyde should be closed down - surely a more important issue for our church leaders than Section 28? Brian Souter made his fortune from the Tory privatisation and deregulation of bus and rail services. Let's have a referendum on whether this rip-off of public assets should now be reversed. What really angers me is that Souter is splashing out £1million on a private referendum while his own workers are being forced to take strike action for a decent wage. Passengers in south-west Scotland have suffered two months of inconvenience because bus drivers - some earning as little as £4 an hour - have staged seven one day strikes. The dispute could be settled for just over £100,000 - one-tenth of the amount that Souter is forking out on his referendum". Columnist Melanie Reid recommended dumping Souter's "exercise in intolerance" in the bin alongside "the dead teabags, rotting potato peelings and the dog's toenail clippings". MSPs publicly tore up their ballot papers; delegates of a conference organised by the Lesbian and Gay Christian Movement publicly ripped up theirs and Bishop Richard Holloway tore his up during a sermon after insisting they were being delivered to "graveyards all over Scotland". Addressing the conference, Bishop Holloway said: "I want to ask your forgiveness for the way you have been hounded and persecuted by organised forces in Church and State down the centuries, down to our own day".

A. McDonald from Glasgow demonstrated to the *Record* the mercy some gay kids might've expected from some parents: "I am most annoyed at Tommy Sheridan urging people to burn their voting papers on Section 28. Our children are ours to teach about the dangers of homosexuality, but by all means counsel the abnormal".

Peter Donaldson from Dundee wrote to the *Scottish Daily Mail* to say: "Pictures of Tommy Sheridan burning ballot papers were reminiscent of that historic photograph of Hitler's Brownshirts burning books in Thirties' Berlin. Book burners and ballot burners are kindred spirits, and Tommy Sheridan is a dangerous man..." What the media continually failed to mention when showing this familiar film footage was that it was the burning of books and documents outside the Magnus Hirschfield Institute in Berlin, which was, before World War II, the largest centre of homosexual study in the world. At that time Berlin had a thriving gay scene with between 50 and a hundred gay bars and dozens of gay publications: *L'Amitie, Die Soune, Eros, Inversions,*

Militant Religionists at War

Der Strom, *Fanfare* and *Friendship and Freedom* to name a few. They were often filled with personal gay advertisements. Life in Berlin was very liberal; epitomised by Christopher Isherwood's *Goodbye to Berlin* and the film *Caberet*. There was even cross-party support in 1929 for a ban on all anti-gay laws. But it was too late. In February 1933 the Nazis seized power with a new message of moral certainty and used the media to further their propaganda of lies, slander and distortion. The gay centre and library was burnt and a model of the head of its Jewish leader was paraded through the streets on a stick. Some Nazis who were counselled at the Institute had their own reasons why they did not want their records becoming public. Bars and clubs were closed down and thousands of gays rounded up by secret police and murdered. Many were thrown into concentration camps before the war had even started.

I. Couper of Alexandria wrote in *The Scottish Daily Mail*: "Burning polling forms at a Stagecoach depot serves only to remind us how dangerous these socialist zealots are to the democratic process".

The *Scottish Mail* attacked the "maverick socialist MSP Tommy Sheridan". Along with a portrait of a smiling and "deeply religious" Brian Souter they asked: "Which of these two men would you support?" To run alongside a list of Souter's achievements, the "sun-tanned" Sheridan was chastised for being jailed for anti-poll tax protests, clenching his fist in salute when he was sworn in as an MSP, defecting from the Labour Party "to Militant" and for being "'a man of the people' who surrounds himself with celebrity friends". A "spokesman" for 'Keep the Clause' accused him of acting like "a fascist" and the *Mail's* editorial called him "contemptible... To see a former Militant activist burning ballot papers reminds us of where Mr Sheridan is coming from".

The *Daily Record* threw a party with two pages, headlines, photos and yet another editorial on Section 28. Sir Tom Farmer, a Catholic multi-millionaire and one of the sponsors of Souter's private 'referendum' had comments spread over two pages: "DON'T LISTEN TO THE COWARDS". The tabloid reported: "A coalition of homosexual activists and their New Labour supporters were branded 'faceless cowards' by one of Scotland's richest men last night over their attempts to smear the referendum on Section 28". The *Scottish Mail* joined in the kicking. Again, in the *Record* there was a photograph to show readers where to mark their cross on the ballot paper and a letter from Hugh Lynch, chairman of the Larbert Labour Party telling Tony Blair how he had been forced to resign over his efforts to repeal Section 28. "As a father of three children, you should be in the vanguard of the movements to disown these evil activities and to protect all children and families". He signed himself off as a member of the Family Action Movement, a new group promoting 'family values'.

The very next day a shamefaced *Scottish Daily Mail* was telling a different story: "Sir Tom Farmer, chief executive of Kwik-Fit, was quoted incorrectly as saying gay rights activists and sympathisers in the Labour Party were 'faceless cowards' undermining the referendum on the repeal of Section 28". The *Mail* was forced to admit they had "misrepresented Sir Tom's views. He did not criticise any homosexual or political groups…" Before insisting Souter had Farmer's full support for his mailshot, the *Record* wrote: "Sir Tom has asked us to make it clear that he was quoted incorrectly and that he never used these words, nor did he criticise any homosexual or political groups". It would not be the first or last time the *Daily Mail* was forced to make apologies for inaccuracies. Days later the paper was forced to apologise to the Prime Minister's official spokesman, Alastair Campbell after columnist Peter McKay suggested he had made a serious of criticisms of Gordon Brown. The *Mail* grovelled: "We accept that no such comments were made by Mr Blair's spokesman, and that the remarks were wrongly attributed to him. We apologise for the error". Following that, Paula Yates accepted libel damages from Associated Newspapers over allegations in the *Mail on Sunday*, which suggested she had become pregnant by the late Michael Hutchence just to ensnare him into a permanent relationship.

Counting down the days before the results of Souter's mailshot like excited children opening boxes on an advent calendar, the *Record* marked "13 DAYS TO GO" before publishing details of a "GAY SHRINE FOR WENDY". It was a sweet, innocent fan website set up by a young man offering his support to the beleaguered MSP with a few poems and some words of encouragement: "Cheer up Wendy, we love you!" It was set up by 26-year-old Jonathan Paisley from Ibrox, Glasgow but dismissed by the *Record* as a "bizarre tribute… flanked by cherubs and framed by ornate scrolls". This "exclusive", penned by Gethin Chamberlain, provided an opportunity to repeat how "anti-Clause 28 campaigners have already mounted an orchestrated e-mail campaign to distort the results of the Scottish Executive's consultation process on the issue". Of Wendy Alexander, Jack Irvine sneered: "I'm glad she's finally achieved gay icon status".

The next day the *Record* woke up with a start to find gay activists had apparently hijacked BBC Radio's *Thought for the Day*. This was a programme that interrupted the news every morning on BBC Radio Four to offer views from an entirely religious perspective. "Keep the Clause campaigners accused... BBC Radio Scotland of allowing their *Thought for the Day* spot to be turned into a political propaganda broadcast". Kevin Franz, general secretary of Action for Churches Together in Scotland had suggested on the programme that it wasn't too late for those opposed to the repeal of Section 28 to "sit and talk with his gay fellow citizen". Jack Irvine, on behalf of 'Keep the Clause' made an official protest to Blair Jenkins, BBC Scotland's head of news and current affairs, and told his pals at the *Record:* "I had not previously realised Thought for the Day could be used for political activism. I trust this is not the beginning of a trend and that Mr Franz simply slipped through your producer's net - assuming he/she had one".

On any contentious issue where the church wanted to put forward its view: *Thought for the Day* was a reserved space for clerics to do it. The religious speakers often made political points on the BBC's flagship news programme that no-one could question, a privilege not open to any other contributor on the Today programme. All too frequently this worked against those who opposed church teaching, and that usually included gay rights.

Broadcaster and columnist Ruth Wishart wrote in the *Herald* on the experience of Judith, a lesbian mother and teacher who had spoken on the radio. "...Making her thoughts public was a daunting prospect because of the poisoned atmosphere in which this debate is now taking place. Like very many Scots she has been utterly shocked by the venom and hysteria, fearful of the likely impact on her own child, distressed at the evidence of a strong current of homophobia uncovered among the population at large. She has had the good fortune, she says, to live a life supported by love and friendship, including that of the father of her child". Ruth Wishart hit out at 'Keep the Clause's "cacophony of disinformation". Over criticism of BBC Radio Scotland's *Thought for the Day*, she wrote: "For Jack Irvine to accuse Kevin Franz of politicising the referendum process is really pretty rich". She was equally scathing of the *Record's* 'apology' to Sir Tom Farmer. "For if the campaign organisers feel able to put false quotes in the mouths of their own supporters, you might imagine with what cavalier disregard for accuracy they might treat those who have dared to express a different view... This has been a very unsavoury mountain fashioned from a barely discernible molehill. And 18 months hence it will not be worth a single line in a single newspaper. Thank God".

On Thursday, 11 May, the *Herald* reported how, "gay rights activists... coloured the debate... by painting a normally white Stagecoach bus pink and festooning it with banners at Glasgow's Buchanan Street bus station". The *Scottish Daily Mail* painted the story in altogether darker colours. "Three arrested as one of Brian Souter's buses is targeted by activists... Gay rights vandals held after coach is covered in paint... Militant gay rights activists were arrested yesterday after a bus owned by Stagecoach tycoon Brian Souter was vandalised". With gays finally goaded into abandoning their Bacchanalian practices for some political action, Brian Souter hit back with sarcasm in the *Scottish Mail on Sunday*: "...Campaigners moved on from destroying ballot papers to damaging buses in their renewed attempt to spread their message of tolerance and democracy". Tory education spokesman Brian Monteith also jumped on the pink bus to make political capital: "These stupid actions only serve to undermine any argument that these people may have had and will, I am sure, serve only to convince more people to put pen to paper and to vote against repeal of the clause in the referendum". 'Keep the Clause' went one better: "Once again members of the public have been put at risk by the outrageous actions of mindless people hell bent on trying to pervert the democratic rights of the Scottish electorate in the Section 28 referendum".

As dearly as 'Keep the Clause' might have liked one, there was nothing in the way of a violent reaction from so-called 'gay militants'. Not until Saturday, 15 July, in the wake of a powerful cross-party alliance of peers and church leaders planning to overturn the repeal of Section 28 in England and Wales in the

Militant Religionists at War

Local Government Bill when it returned to the House of Lords, did an estimated 1,300 turn up to a demonstration led by Stonewall in Manchester. In an otherwise peaceful protest, a crowd forced a Stagecoach bus off the road. Apart from the activities of Media House and their cronies, Scotland remained calm. All the same, Brian Souter changed his mind about addressing the National Association of Pension Funds' conference in Glasgow, fearing he might be a target for so-called 'gay militants'.

When Brian Souter appeared on BBC's *Question Time*, the cameras portrayed a small, timid, soft and somewhat effeminate man shielded by an evangelical zeal. He insisted: "A man can only marry one woman. It discriminates against people who might want to be polygamists. It's that way because it's a moral issue and the law is backing up a moral case. That's what Section 28 is about". He was no match for Boy George who made an impressive performance in an unapologetic purple felt Fedora and full make-up. He responded: "If Brian was a wealthy racist, would we all be sitting here saying, he has the right to express his views?" They both appeared alongside Liberal Democrat leader Charles Kennedy, Lord Falconer and Labour MP Angela Brown, the first MP to 'come out' as gay. Souter defended his actions in carrying out an opinion poll claiming that a "cheque-book democracy is the only type of democracy we have ever had in this country". He chastised the committee structure of the Scottish Executive, accused the Executive of being too "Presidential" and propounded the myth that "political correct" local authorities were putting unsuitable material into schools, citing the book *Jenny Lives With Eric and Martin*. He didn't want homosexuals to "force their way into my home and indoctrinate my children with their lifestyle and ideas". His views brought derision and laughter from the London audience. Boy George - or "Mr George", as the *Daily Mail* insisted on calling him in their review - accused Souter of wasting his money on a campaign driven by "personal reasons" and asked: "Should I be kept away from my nieces and nephews in case I affect their lives?" Brian Souter failed to please the audience by accusing Charles Kennedy of talking "tosh", but the most rapturous applause was reserved for a young man in the audience who drew attention to the bombing by a young man of a gay pub in London's Old Compton Street. He said: "Section 28 has to go so that we can actually tell the young people that being lesbian or gay is OK, and frankly Mr. Souter you can hide in whatever sheep's clothing you want. You are a bigot"!

David Belcher, reviewing the programme for the *Herald* noted how "Perth bus baron Brian defended his funding of the Keep The Clause referendum with a series of baseless and somewhat paranoid assertions - ranging from 'You can be in favour of Section 28 without being a bigot' all the way to 'People are jackbooting their way into our homes and forcing an Islington morality on our children'. What was worse was that Brian had kicked off with a major *faux pas:* according to him, chequebook democracy is OK so long as the man beating democracy to death with his chequebook doesn't accept a knighthood for doing it. Jings Bri, you should immediately use your chequebook to hire a set of clued-up media handlers who'll stop you shooting yourself in the bahookey with ill-considered guff like that!"

On Friday, 12 May 2000, there was a set-back on the road to repeal of Section 28. The news headlines took everybody by surprise. Sex education *guidance* would become statutory. Wendy Alexander was on the line from Boston USA for BBC Radio Scotland's *Good Morning Scotland* along with the Equality Network's Tim Hopkins, David Macauley from 'Keep the Clause' and education minister Sam Galbraith. Donald Dewar had apparently agreed to the move before his operation. The Government had capitulated with an idea first voiced by Judith Gillespie, a spokesperson for the Scottish Parent Teacher Council and later adopted by the SNP. Backbenchers were stunned. Members of the education committee were taken aside and told of the climbdown, others were not likely to find out until they opened their newspapers first thing that morning. The *Sunday Post's* Campbell Gunn wrote: "The first they heard about it was from the media, after we were briefed on it. To say they were furious is an understatement". One MSP "incandescent with rage" told the *Herald:* "It is absolutely unbelievable. In terms of political strategy the question… is what on earth is going on".

Labour's chief whip, Tom McCabe and finance minister Jack McConnell had been pressurising cabinet ministers to climb down and sought and got the agreement of the SNP. The Executive tabled the amendment to the Standards in Scotland's Schools Bill. Sam Galbraith emphasised that these were not 'guide*lines*', which would govern the contents of statutory legislation - always rebuffed as contrary to Scottish practice - but

Militant Religionists at War

'guid*ance*' which govern the *conduct* of sex education in Scotland. The 'guidance' was to state that parents had to be consulted if sex education - appropriate to pupils' ages - were given to their children and that they could even remove them from classes, (although such a right already existed). Also muted was a possible redress for parents who objected to the content of sex education being taught. Defending himself against charges of capitulating to the Souter camp, Aberdeen's broadsheet, the *Press and Journal* headlined: "Galbraith says: I'm not interested in Souter". The broadsheet added: "The new concession, added with no public forewarning just hours before the Question Time programme, comes in an amendment to another piece of planned legislation, the Standards in Scotland's Schools Bill". The *Herald* editorial called it "a climbdown that we regret" as likely to "confuse as to assuage parents, particularly in the light of the Executive's semantics over what constitutes 'guidance' and what constitutes 'guidelines'" adding that "predictably, it was not enough to appease the mendacious tabloid 'Keep the Clause' campaign or its backers, Mr Brian Souter and his hapless PR adviser". The *Herald* challenged his "badly-organised, self-serving opinion poll" for "running out of bilious steam". The *Scotsman* called the amendment "more symbol than substance". 'Keep the Clause' told the *Scottish Express* that the Government had "completely failed to grasp the reality of the situation". The tabloid's editorial blamed ministers for "being forced to react rather than take the lead on this controversial affair". The Labour-supporting *Scottish Mirror* announced "Clause 28 law to be scrapped in weeks" and dutifully hailed the amendment "a victory for common sense". Iain Martin wrote cynically in the *Scotsman:* "We have had more cabinet positions on Section 28 than there are manoeuvres in the Joy of Sex".

Scottish Tory leader Brian Monteith shared his diary in the *Herald* and news that after a full day's Education Committee meeting on Tuesday, 9 May 2000: "The Labour members are oblivious that one of my motions is a direct copy of Labour's line at Westminster and unwittingly take great delight in ridiculing it because it includes the word marriage". Labour had been forced into such a compromise in England chiefly because of the unelected House of Lords, not because the majority of Labour MPs wanted the so-called 'promotion of marriage'. After Brian Monteith had been briefed on the Executive's climbdown, he wanted the credit for it: "They've just been briefed that Sam Galbraith has tabled an amendment introducing statutory guidance to the Education Bill and it bears an uncanny resemblance to the first section of my own amendment which was trashed two days before. I am both pleased and annoyed, and spend the next couple of hours ridiculing the Government for its welcome U-turn". In another diary entry Brian Monteith once again vented his fury over the Executive's apparent oversight of his contribution and stomped: "Rather arrogantly the Committee members still refuse to recognise that part of one of my amendments the previous week had said practically the same as the Ministers' latest offering but they had voted it down. So much for the so-called new politics... The SNP group predictably tries to take some of the credit for the cave-in..."

Mike McCabe, director of education for South Ayrshire Council, was to chair the working group set up to look at sex education 'guidance' for schools. A former Physics teacher, McCabe was a 50-year-old divisional education officer with Strathclyde Regional Council and married with three children. Police officer Jack Waddell, once a vice-chairman of Williamwood High School in Clarkston, Glasgow, and representing the Scottish School Boards' Association, became the working group's vice-chairman. Joining the group was the Rev Jack Laidlaw, a 60-year-old convener of the Church of Scotland's education committee who was married with four stepchildren. He was also a former teacher and college lecturer and adviser in religious and moral education to Tayside Regional Council. John Oates represented the Catholic Education Commission. He was married, with four grown-up children and a former head teacher of St Modan's school in Stirling and Keith Grammar School. Kim Connolly was vice-chairman of Hillhead High School board in Glasgow and director of the Scottish Parent-Teacher Council. Rowena Arshad was director of the Centre for Education in Racial Equality at Edinburgh University. John O'Keane was headmaster at Cardinal Newmain High School, Bellshill in Lanarkshire. Anne Pearson was head teacher at Park Primary School, Aloa, and Gill Mackay was a senior teacher at Dunard primary school in Glasgow. It should have been clear from the start that they were never destined to make any breakthrough in tackling the urgent question of sex education.

Militant Religionists at War

Iain Macwhirter in the *Sunday Herald* put the Executive's play on semantics in plain language. "Governments often make mistakes. To rule is to compromise and ministers sometimes have to look stupid to do the right thing. But it's rare indeed for an administration to be left looking stupid, mistaken, compromised and wrong all at the same time. But that's pretty much what the Scottish Executive achieved with its latest genuflection to the forces of homophobic conservatism... The distinction between 'guidance' and 'guidelines' is such a fine one it could keep teams of lawyers in work for years. If a parent objects to a lesson on homosexuality, can he or she now prosecute their local authority concerned on the grounds the authority has not observed the guidance? Discuss".

Lending as much support to Souter's 'referendum' as they could, the *Daily Record* revealed "a staggering 500,000 Scots" had already returned their 'ballot papers'. They claimed the Government had been "rattled", had "tried to head off a mauling... taken fright at the surge of popular feeling in favour of the Clause 28 referendum"; was "slowly and grudgingly... being forced to see sense" and "trying to wriggle off the hook on which they impaled themselves". The tabloid also expressed its dissatisfaction with the 'guidance' or 'guidelines' debate. "The more Education Minister Sam Galbraith tried to clear it up, the muddier he makes it. Either his heart isn't in it - or he doesn't fully understand it either". The editorial claimed the Executive's offer of 'guidance' was: "...Nowhere near far enough to buy off the Keep the Clause campaign". With the edges now sufficiently blurred between where 'Keep the Clause' ended and the supposedly independent *Daily Record* began, the tabloid demanded: "...A declaration of support for heterosexual marriage as the norm and a clear and enforceable ban on the promotion of homosexuality in schools". Political editor Douglas Fraser warned in the *Sunday Herald:* "The next monstering, over marriage, has only just begun". How right he was.

In the *Scottish Mail on Sunday*, Brian Souter stomped: "We have been trying for four months to obtain an honest answer to the simple question - do homosexual liaisons have the same moral value as traditional marriage? Wendy Alexander, Jim Wallace, Tony Blair and Hilary Armstrong have all refused to answer this straightforward question. My own response to this silence is very clear - no answers, no repeal!"

RELIGIOUS FASCISM

The *Scottish Daily Mail* also struck out at Sam Galbraith in their headline: "Minister's sop aims to derail Section 28 poll" and declared, in their editorial, that the Scottish Executive's attempt to undermine Souter's 'referendum' was "transparent" before confidently asserting: "Parents want discrimination - in favour of marriage". In fact, what the *Daily Mail* really wanted was discrimination *in* marriage.

The *Scottish Sun* was already celebrating a "landslide" victory for 'Keep the Clause's mail shot and gloated how ministers had "caved in to parent power". They believed the "people's ballot" had "put the wind up our masters" and added, "had it not been for those like Brian Souter and the Scottish Sun who hammered on Holyrood's dogmatic door, there would have been no let-up". They begged Scotland: "ONE SMALL STEP... NOW KEEP VOTING".

Anne Smith QC offered her religiously influenced legal opinion to the Christian Institute, advising that if teachers introduced anything that parents found offensive or disrespectful, they could take the education authority to court. On 4 March, Hamish Macdonell imagined in the *Scottish Daily Mail:* "Europe may rule out repeal of Section 28". Colin Hart of the Christian Institute warned they would be monitoring schools very closely if Section 28 were repealed. He said: "If the Scottish Executive won't protect our children, then parents will have to do it themselves... It is shocking families may have to go through the trauma of legal proceedings simply to protect their children from homosexual promotion. This is why the Christian Institute is promising to give every help it can to any parent who feels their human rights have been violated". Peter Watson of law firm Levy and McRae who advised 'Keep the Clause' said they would be happy to assist any Scottish parent who wanted to challenge repeal or any new clause brought in to replace it.

When, in England and Wales, the General Teaching Council (GTC) - made up of teachers, union officials and government appointed representatives - entered an equal opportunities clause in a professional code of conduct for teachers, the ever-vigilant Christian Institute's Colin Hart claimed it would side-step Section 28. The clause stated: "Teachers recognise diversity and work to ensure the rights of individuals to develop. They fully respect differences of gender, marital status, religion, colour, race, ethnicity, sexual orientation and disability. Teacher

Militant Religionists at War

professionalism involves challenging prejudice and stereotypes to ensure equality of opportunity". Colin Hart begged: "How will Christian teachers be able to work in state schools?" which predictably won him the support of Baroness Young and Tory MP Julian Brazier. The GTC's chief executive, Carol Adams suggested the Christian Institute had got the wrong end of the stick: "We're talking about a statement of professional values of teachers, not a set of instructions telling people what to do". She also denied it would be used as a "checklist" to assess teachers with. "It provides a context for the Council's advisory and regulatory work. Teachers are not required to sign the code".

On Saturday, 13 May, newspapers revealed a shocking new development. 'Keep the Clause' had found a willing Christian to challenge the Government. 27-year-old Mrs Sheena Strain of Allison Road, Govanhill, Glasgow was launching the first Section 28 court action imposing an injunction on the funding of all gay groups in Glasgow. The Court of Session in Glasgow was told that she objected to her council tax money funding homosexual pornography. She alleged the council funded gay health group Phace West to the tune of £140,729 up to 1999; distributed a pornographic booklet called *Gay Sex Now;* had a website run by a youth group called Bi-G-Les with members "as young as 12" that promoted "homosexual nurture" and portrayed homosexual acts as "exciting". Brian Souter explained to the *Scottish Mail on Sunday* the booklet "was being distributed in youth clubs". Mrs Strain said: "At a time when council resources are stretched, the local authority must ensure that funding is used in an efficient and appropriate way in order to benefit the wider community". Mrs Strain sought an interim interdict banning Glasgow City Council from any further funding of gay groups. While this was not granted, the council agreed - without informing any of the gay groups affected - to suspend payments until a full hearing. Sitting judge, Lord Philip said Strain had an arguable case but wanted it to be dealt with at a later date.

Charles McMillan, chief executive of Phace West, one of the main organisations targeted in this action explained: "The money we receive from the council all goes to counselling and support services including for those with HIV and their families. I believe our funding was totally misrepresented in court. Bi-G-Les, the bisexual gay and lesbian group mentioned, has a website with health information and advice which is funded by the Healthy and Gay Scotland group, not with our money. We only provide a youth worker who goes to their meetings and gives advice on topics including HIV and Aids".

As a 'research group' and a registered charity, the Christian Institute would inevitably face questions asked by the Charity Commission over its role in the legal action against Glasgow City Council. Despite the *Record's* insistence that David Strain's wife raised the action against the group, Strain himself appeared to be the one with the closest links with the Christian Institute. A clean-cut 25-year-old trainee Church of Scotland minister, it was he, not his wife, who was pictured in the *Record* and telling the *Scottish Mail:* "Glasgow City Council should be protecting children, not promoting homosexuality". He became involved with the Christian Institute - whose stated aim was to 'promote' Christianity - while he was at college. (Religious organisations had been infiltrating colleges and Universities up and down the country for some time). The English-based Christian Institute was highly connected, with Baroness Young a patron of the organisation. They had been looking for a Glasgow resident to take up a challenge to the council and were financially backed the Strains. David Strain's name was not on the petition because, as a student, he didn't pay any council tax. An answer machine at their home directed callers to Colin Hart, director of the Christian Institute. Hart was quoted in the *Scotsman* saying: "Both Sheena and her husband are very upset…" Mrs Strain's representative, Anne Smith QC, the same Anne Smith hired by the Christian Institute to claim Section 28 could be overturned in a European court, told the court Mrs Strain "is very concerned at the prospect of her council spending money on what would be an illegal purpose". The Christian Institute had apparently carried out an "investigation" at Strathclyde University's teacher training campus, which concluded that its courses actively promoted homosexuality. Their 'investigation' evoked the response of a letter to the *Herald* from the co-directors of the Equality and Discrimination Centre at the Department of Educational Studies at the university. "No such course existed then or now", wrote co-directors Stuart Ainsworth and Andrew Johnson. At a press conference organised by the Christian Institute in a hotel for whom Jack Irvine's Media House had done PR work, the tabloids and 'Keep the Clause' supporters were welcomed with open arms while a reporter from the *Herald* was barred. The broadsheet hit back. Their editorial admitted supporting repeal of "a deeply flawed and regressive piece of legislation introduced for the worst of populist, politically opportunistic reasons…" and glibly added, "our letters page attests to the fact that we have given both sides their say in a debate among the liveliest encouraged by and aired in the *Herald*. We believe in full and open debate and we do not seek unfairly to influence it in this or any other matter".

Phace West had already had a quarter of their £43,000 grant. The rest was to be stopped until after the hearing. So too the HIV carers group which was in receipt of only a quarter, (£9,100) of their grant. The £18,000 that had been awarded to the Glasgay arts festival was stopped and the remainder of the MCT Theatre Company's £2,200 grant was also stopped, after they had received only £1,700. "But £12,352 had been paid to the West of Scotland Lesbian and Gay Forum before yesterday's court hearing", the *Daily Record* found. Their friends at the *Scottish Daily Mail* claimed however: "The West of Scotland Gay and Lesbian Forum last year got £11,992 and was due to receive £12,352 this year from Edinburgh City Council". (This would have affected the Lesbian Archives – a national collection - held at Glasgow's Women's Library and the lesbian, gay, bisexual and transgender centre in Dixon Street, Glasgow which had already had its glass door smashed). The 25-year-old Strathclyde Gay Switchboard was expecting a one-off payment of £1,098 from the council for 2000. Their grant was also stopped with immediate effect. Robert Fox from Gay Switchboard told the *Herald*: "I pay my council tax. Like other gay people, I am a part of society who works and makes a contribution and like them I have a right to say how my money is spent". Mrs Strain wrote to Glasgow City Council to plead that MCT and Glasgay! were never mentioned in her original petition.

While the House of Lords blocked Section 28's repeal, the Christian Institute was also looking to proceed with a test case in England. They warned *Positive Nation*, a magazine for people living with HIV, that their actions would not stop at Glasgow. A spokesman for the Christian Institute, Ian Bainbridge, told them they were looking at a HIV health website run by Camden and Islington Health Authority claiming it was "irresponsible". The religious fundamentalists were on a roll.

David A Robertson from Dundee wrote to the *Herald* to tell readers what gays were not entitled to. "…The special privilege of the council supporting (to the tune of 71%) festivals such as Glasgay! Which are little more than celebrations of gay pornography..."

Sybil Brinham from Dollar wrote to the *Herald* adding: "...Your readers may be unaware that many other groups supporting sick, disabled, and disadvantaged people have never had council, or Government, funding..."

Donald Morrison from Edinburgh, a Christian Institute supporter, wrote to the *Scotsman* over Phace West's "other" activities "at public expense". He began: "In 1996-97, it distributed, free of charge, more than 123,000 condoms to homosexual men". It also "gives advice to young people about 'cruising' in public places with the intention of finding homosexual partners... If it promoted monogamous relationships, with a view to reducing HIV/AIDs, one might be sympathetic. It does not..." On the other hand, Christians had done little to encourage gay people striking up any relationships, let alone monogamous ones.

Stuart Morrison from Glasgow wrote to the editor of the *Herald*: "The latest 'Keep the Clause' jape, to force some patsy into a legal challenge to the funding of gay groups by Glasgow City Council, does serve one worthwhile purpose. It gives the lie, once and for all, to the idea that their sick, bigoted campaign is anything to do with 'protecting our children'. It proves, rather, that they are hell-bent on a homophobic crusade. Who's next, I wonder?"

The Federation of Scottish Theatre (FST) condemned the legal attempt to use Section 28 to halt local authority funding to gay and lesbian theatre companies and compared the aims of the 'Keep the Clause' campaign to the repressive regime of Nazi Germany. The FST had the support of such Scots actors as Robbie Coltrane, Richard Wilson, Bill Paterson, Peter Capaldi, Elaine C Smith and Peter Mullan. Elaine C Smith, best known for her role as Mary Doll in the television comedy: *Rab C Nesbitt*, said: "We're all here because this is the start. What's next? They take out homosexuality and put in Jewish, put in Asian, put in far left politics - where does it stop? We have to make our voice heard very loudly, regardless of how difficult it is". Elaine Smith was most likely remembering the words of the immortal poem: *First They Came for the Communists:* -

Militant Religionists at War

First they came for the communists, and I did not speak out - because I was not a communist;
Then they came for the socialists, and I did not speak out - because I was not a socialist;
Then they came for the trade unionists, and I did not speak out - because I was not a trade unionist;
Then they came for the Jews, and I did not speak out - because I was not a Jew;
Then they came for me - and there was no-one left to speak out for me.

Ironically, the poem had been attributed to Martin Niemöller, a fundamental Christian fascist; author of *From U-Boat to Pulpit* who went on to recount some of his ideals after he was forced to spend time in a concentration camp after losing favour with powerful Nazis. It was, in fact, also the homosexuals who were the first the Nazis came for: a fact omitted in this poem written in 1946.

At the Court of Session in Edinburgh on 6 July 2000, the pro-Section-28 newspapers heralded the sudden collapse of the Strain's case a victory for the Christian Institute! According to the *Scottish Daily Mail*, "Mrs Strain's lawyers agreed to settle the matter out of court on the condition a letter ordering groups not to use grants to promote homosexuality was sent to council-funded groups". The face-saving exercise was immaterial since the groups concerned had always denied having infringed Section 28 in that way anyway. The *Scottish Mail* sounded victorious. "Legal deal blocks cash for gay propaganda" after "Scotland's largest local authority was yesterday forced to issue new guidelines to pro-gay groups..." The *Scottish Sun's* Dave Finlay was even more radiant. "NURSE WINS 'NO GAY PR' PLEDGE... A nurse has forced council bosses to promise not to promote homosexuality... Furious Sheena Strain... took action after PHACE - an organisation which helps AIDS and HIV victims - was handed more than £140,000". (The group was called Phace West). Ann Smith QC for the Christian Institute told the court that Mrs Sheena Strain and Glasgow City Council had agreed to pay their own legal costs. Mungo Bovey QC, advocate for the four lesbian, gay, bisexual and transgender groups involved, thought otherwise and asked the court to award those groups' legal costs against Mrs Strain. Ann Smith QC insisted that the groups had not needed legal representation, as they could have left it up to the Council to defend their case, but the judge gave that argument short shrift and awarded costs against Mrs Strain. As a result, Mrs Strain (with the help of the Christian Institute) was forced to pay her own legal costs, plus those of the lesbian, gay, bisexual and transgender groups, probably a total of well over £10,000 (or £7,000 if you read the *Scottish Daily Mail*). Mrs Strain didn't put in an appearance in court as she was on holiday, leaving a rather bitter *Scottish Mail* to sneer: "Despite the strict rules introduced by Glasgow Council, gay groups yesterday heralded the withdrawal of Mrs Strain's petition as a victory".

A gay man living with AIDS wrote movingly to Stonewall with his personal testimony to be included in *Caused by the Clause*. "Being involved with Body Positive Strathclyde, I was more than a little worried when we temporarily lost our funding as a result of the vindictive court action brought under Section 28 (at a time when repeal had already been voted). However, we all quickly mobilised and came together to fight off Sheena Strain and the Christian Institute. Unwittingly the actions of Sheena Strain and others have brought us together and made us stronger. As a gay man living with full-blown AIDS, the whole episode has only strengthened my resolve to fight for the dignity of all people to live their lives in peace and respect".

Tom 'Brigadier' Brown wrote in the *Daily Record* that statutory guidance "still falls short on the recognition of marriage and does not give hard enough guarantees prohibiting the promotion of homosexuality". The *Scottish Daily Mail* cried: "Make sure you vote", while, in its editorial, the *Record*, referring to the Scottish Executive in bold headlines across the page, begged: "KEEP VOTING... THEY'RE ON THE RUN". The *Record* claimed Cabinet ministers had "admitted their latest move to defuse the row had failed". Apparently, "ministers said privately that their U-turn... had not gone far enough to satisfy worried parents". A "senior Parliamentary source" told the *Record:* "These bills are technically in the hands of the Parliament. Any backbencher can table their own amendments, and it shouldn't be too hard to produce an amendment backing marriage that would win support across the Parliament". The *Record's* editorial begged: "Speak up, please". The only Labour MPs so far that had said anything to support the *Record's* stance on promoting heterosexual marriage had been Jimmy Hood, Jimmy Wray and Michael Connarty. The *Record* went down on its knees: "There are some 129 Members of the Scottish Parliament. Is there just one of them who is prepared to be the voice of the people...? The weight of public opinion may force one of our MSPs - who are already under pressure from their constituents and traditional Labour supporters - to table a back-bench motion, amending the Standards in Scotland's Schools Bill to endorse marriage and prohibit promotion of homosexuality. Which of our MSPs will have the courage of his or her convictions?" before adding in bold: **"Which one will speak for the people?"** The tabloid was full of praise for the 'Three Wise Men', now re-christened the Triple Mac alliance; Henry McLeish, Tom McCabe and Jack McConnell who 'Brigadier' Brown insisted, "have never been happy with the mess made by Executive colleagues of the handling of the Section 28 furore". Brown also claimed "all three have been quoted as potential successors to First Minister Donald Dewar". The *Record* claimed "a group of around 20" were prepared to insert heterosexual marriage into the teaching of sex education. Although none of them publicly denounced repeal, rumours circulated of leaks to the press. Liberal Democrat Iain Smith suggested it might have been his former boss Tom McCabe. When news of a compromise was mooted in Labour ranks, Smith claimed he e-mailed Jim Wallace, leader of his party, the Liberal Democrats to express his dissatisfaction. He said McCabe had not been happy but "was a little surprised to find the contents of private ministerial e-mails and a private discussion between ministers featuring on the front page of the Daily Record, where apparently I'd been 'rapped on the knuckles' for mounting an e-mail campaign". The headline stirred the fiction of a 'gay conspiracy' and promptly 'outed' the Minister: "Gay MSP rapped for Clause 28 campaign by e-mail... Deputy Parliament Minister Iain Smith targeted all 21 of his colleagues in a move similar to that launched by gay groups across the globe".

Attacking the issue of sex education 'guidance' for teachers, the *Scottish Daily Mail* resorted to some now familiar lies: "If past experience is any guide... comments will be noted, while the powers that be order thousands more copies of Jenny Lives With Eric and Martin... Children who were not withdrawn from classes would undoubtedly share their information with classmates on the playground network... The present legislation offers total protection to children and does no harm to homosexuals. Parents are satisfied with the status quo; they want Section 28 to stay. Beyond that, an average of opinion polls shows around 65 per cent of the Scottish electorate wants to retain Section 28. In a democracy, that should be the end of the argument". In the same paper, Gerald Warner sniffed: "There is currently a Standards in Education Bill going through the parliament, but don't hold your breath. This Bill will be neutered by the acolytes of political correctness. The instincts of MSPs are to support the teaching unions in defending the interests of incompetent teachers and resisting the restoration of effective teaching methods in our schools".

In the *Sunday Mail* on 14 May, the paper showed a Stagecoach bus coming out of a ballot paper marked: "REFERENDUM YOU CAN DRIVE A BUS THROUGH". They declared: "Mr Souter's camp boasted that 500,000 voters have responded. But many of those returns are empty envelopes, or papers returned after the names were not known at the addresses". A Labour source told the *Sunday Mail:* "The turn-out has been terrible. The response is about 12 per cent, which is pathetic, and the longer it goes on the less likely people are to return these things". The *Scottish Mail on Sunday,* meanwhile, spun it their way, the headline roaring: "Section 28 poll to break one million". Then, "organisers have been inundated with more than 500,000 already..." 'Keep the Clause' shifted the goalposts by four days in order to get more ballot papers in. (The official deadline had been May 22, but it was now May 26). A full-page advertisement appeared in the *Sunday Mail* from 'Keep the Clause' showing which box voters had to tick to "prevent the promotion of homosexuality in our schools". Columnist Melanie Reid wrote: "I've been swamped by apparently respectable, decent people foaming at the mouth with vitriolic homophobia... I've heard things and read things that made me feel like I was stuck in the Dark Ages, not living in a tolerant Scotland in the year 2000... This, sadly, is what Brian Souter and his Keep the Clause campaign has done - empowered closet bigots to... well... to come out. 'Do you know what dirty old men do to little children, you evil woman?' one sweet old lady slavered down the phone at me... Then there was the kindly grandfather of four, who described himself as 'normal' and said I should be subject to a ritual hanging... Not to mention the various barns who suggested that all Sunday Mail reporters were 'poofs' and 'lesbians', encouraging 'an unstoppable tide of filth and dirt'. And those let me tell you were the clean letters. ...I cannot forgive Souter... the legacy of his so-called exercise in democracy - a hateful outpouring of bile and prejudice which has set Scotland back 20 years. Keep the Clause will be remembered by journalists for dirty tricks, the smearing and threats to 'out' gay people... The only consolation I can take is that it is the old and the middle-aged who are so full of venom towards homosexuality. Young people, happily, are totally relaxed and cool about the whole thing". The *Sunday Mail* claimed a record postbag, most of which were against Souter's mail shot. Margaret Docherty, a mother-of-three from Glasgow wrote: "I have lived out part of my life with one Hitler, I do not need another. Banish Section 28 - we do not want to see any pink triangles in Scotland".

"Has Labour hung Wendy out to dry?" *Scotland on Sunday* asked, following claims that Tony Blair had told her not to allow the repeal of Section 28 to become top of the agenda. Labour sources denied the paper's claims. As far as *Scotland on Sunday* was concerned, it was all 'wee-Wendy's fault and the full weight of the 'Keep the Clause' roadshow had to be laid at her door. The editorial turned on liberal factions in the Executive: "The plight of Wendy Alexander over Section 28 should be a salutary lesson to some of her fellows on the Scottish Executive. The health minister, Susan Deacon, springs to mind... All eyes are on the ambitions of finance minister Jack McConnell and parliamentary business manager Tom McCabe as Wendy Alexander finds herself increasingly sidelined within the Scottish Executive". The Sunday broadsheet chastised Alexander for her "adolescent posturing..." and launched an attack against Tim Hopkins of the Equality Network and "other gay community leaders" for "whipping up a hysterical homosexual backlash over a sensitive issue". They were all dismissed as "hugely irresponsible". The editorial insisted: "Such an ill-considered approach diminishes the valid concerns of gay people", which was an extraordinary statement for a newspaper not known for highlighting *any* concerns of gay people.

The *Scotsman* wrote of Wendy Alexander: "She can talk the hind legs of a donkey, the feathers off a pheasant, the spots off a leopard. She talks nineteen to the dozen, words gushing out of her pretty mouth like coins spilling out of a fruit machine".

RELIGIOUS FASCISM

Lorraine Davidson in Scottish editions of the *Sunday Mirror* spoke up for Wendy Alexander: "She has been vilified in some sections of the press in a poisonous, ill-informed debate of which we should all feel ashamed... Ministers sat in their offices whining that Brian Souter could spend £1million on a poster campaign arguing against the repeal. Never mind that they spend a million of our money every year on an army of spin doctors who sat back and did nothing, allowing themselves to be completely outflanked by three PR men from Glasgow. Wendy has paid a high price for doing the right thing. When she reflects on this ugly episode she should order a post mortem to ensure it's never repeated. She should ask why Brian Souter's PR man Jack Irvine can single-handedly take control of the news agenda in Scotland and dominate it for months".

Pat Grant, owner of the refrigeration company, Norfrost and one of the backers of Brian Souter's referendum was attacked in the same paper under the headline: "ICE QUEEN'S GAY SON". It was the tragic story of her 35-year-old son Clay's quest to be a "normal son" after revealing he had made attempts on his life following his experimentation with gay sex. Pat Grant was quoted saying: "I don't want anything more to do with him. I couldn't care less what he says or does. I've heard it all before. I pay his mortgage and his bills - he costs me £20,000 a year. I am not interested in rebuilding our relationship". Clay begged: "All I want to do is hug her. I just want us to be like a normal mother and son". Clay Garner, (Pat Grant's son from a previous marriage), was registered disabled and expecting to be made homeless. As Clay fell back into the clutches of fundamental religion, Brian Souter, with a personal interest in Clay's struggle to fight off his gay inclinations - spoke to Clay on the phone.

In a letter to Brian Souter, Tom Shearer from Broughton begged to know whether his own children might be traumatised by his campaign if one of them turned out to be gay. "Everyone was entitled to their views", Souter replied in a handwritten letter.

The *Daily Record* rushed to Pat Grant's defence: "ICE QUEEN'S SON FROZEN OUT IN STORM OVER CLAUSE 28". The tabloid printed an extract from a letter from Ms Grant's lawyers to her son. "You have again brought your mother into the public arena in a manner you know she finds distasteful. You... knew perfectly well that involving your mother in your... own lifestyle causes her offence..." The *Record* explained:

Militant Religionists at War

"Freezer tycoon Pat Grant is kicking her son out of his home after he spoke publicly about his gay past". The *Record* reported how Clay "drifted into the gay scene after a chance encounter at the Laughing Duck pub. He said the fact he was 18, but was physically underdeveloped with the body of a 10-year-old, made him 'God's gift to the gay scene'" and, "had affairs with several well-known figures in Edinburgh's gay community".

Despite some efforts within the Catholic Church to hold Cardinal Winning back from any further fighting with politicians, as their countdown to the result of Souter's 'referendum' continued, on Monday, 15 May, the *Daily Record* celebrated Winning's "support" for Brian Souter after "Cardinal writes to tycoon as 'gesture from one Christian to another'." The *Scottish Daily Mail* heavily promoted efforts to rally Catholics to vote: "Winning weighs in on Section 28... As leader of 750,000 Catholics in Scotland, Cardinal Winning's words carry enormous authority in encouraging people to send back their ballot papers". This was recruiting just about anyone whose forehead had been sprinkled with 'holy' water. Ten years later, the appearance of the Pope in Glasgow's Bellahouston Park struggled to fill it with a fraction of this number, around 70,000 were said to have attended and that was even after enlisting the help of Churches from across the border and Ireland. In his letter to "Brian", Cardinal Winning wrote: "I wanted to drop you a short line to offer you my support in this difficult time. In recent weeks you have been subjected to some quite unacceptable press coverage, which must have been difficult for both yourself and your family... Many of us believed that the New Scotland would be built on the best of our traditions: the family, creativity, humour, openness, hard work and generosity. We could never have foreseen that the marriage-based family would be one of the first casualties. It is particularly galling that those of us who have stood up for the family are branded 'uncaring'. The Archdiocese of Glasgow alone provides a vast network of care for all categories of disadvantaged people in our communities... the elderly, those with learning difficulties, the dying, the young homeless, drug addicts and many others. I can think of no human suffering in Scotland that we have not tried to alleviate in some way... It is a pity that those who brand us as 'uncaring' are so selective in their judgements".

Of Cardinal Winning's letter to Souter, William Tyler from Thurso wrote to the *Scotsman* to say: "This was a tremendous boost to those who cringe at the very idea of homosexuality being fostered on young impressionable children, many of whom have never heard of the word".

In truth, the media could no longer ignore the extent of a particular human suffering the Church was much less vocal about and increasingly finding it difficult to conceal: child abuse. Allegations were surfacing from within its institutions right across the globe. In Scotland, a string of allegations against the Poor Sisters of Nazareth had already been filed in the High Court in Aberdeen against Sister Alphonso, alias Marie Docherty. Former children from the orphanage lined up to provide testimonies of daily beatings, sexual abuse from visiting priests, the force-feeding of a little girl with her own vomit, the wrapping of bed-wetters in their urine-soaked sheets, the forcing of a little girl into a cold bath in the middle of an epileptic fit which Sister Alphonso was supposed to have described as "the work of the devil", lads being dropped into scalding baths and the 'cleansing' of menstruating girls by immersing them in baths filled with Jeyes disinfectant. One woman claimed Sister Alphonso had dragged her by her hair and beat her face against a wall so hard it broke her front teeth leaving only the stumps. Helen Cuister told a court that when she began menstruating, Sister Alphonso told her that it was 'God's punishment' for girls who did not behave and that her punishment would go on until midnight, when she would die for being so dirty. Louise Clark told the same court how she had been beaten mercilessly simply for not attending church. Sister Alphonso told the court how as a child she had pulled down her knickers and asked her father to hit her, and how as a sister in the Aberdeen home, she had given the girls a good talking to after she caught them watching forbidden TV programme, 'Top of the Pops'. The church stood by Sister Alphonso. A Scottish Catholic Church source told the press: "The view within the church is that she deserves sympathy, not more punishment. The church will rally round her." And it did. The Catholic Church appointed a team of leading lawyers, including former Solicitor General Paul Cullen, QC, while the Rt Rev Mario Conti, the Catholic Bishop of Aberdeen and Orkney, later the Archbishop of Glasgow, was its chief apologist, explaining: "Some practices which today seem excessive and even cruel would not have been viewed in this light years ago. These convictions do not, moreover, invalidate the great good which was done by Sister Marie in caring competently and appropriately for many thousands of children over the last 100 years". Still dressed in her nun's habit, Marie Docherty was found guilty of just four counts of cruelty and unnatural practices. Former care assistant Helen Howie, 75 was angry that she was not called as a witness. "She has made all these children out to be liars", she said, "but everything they said was true. A couple of times when my husband came to collect me from his work he had to pull her off to stop her beating the children. I called him many a time to take her away from the children". Docherty's age, state of health, lack of previous convictions and the time that had passed since the crimes took place were all taken into consideration. After whispering a polite 'thank you' to Sheriff Colin Harris, Marie Theresa Docherty was free to walk away. The *Scottish Mail* tried to "put this case in perspective" assuring readers that what Sister Alphonso did "was not in the same category as the more sordid offences involving paedophile priests and social workers", adding "there was no sexual element involved".

At the Court of Session in Edinburgh, allegations by 11 former pupils who claimed to have been brutalised by an order of Catholic monks, had their solicitor Cameron Fyfe claiming he was handling the biggest abuse case Scotland had ever seen. Allegations from former pupils of St Ninian's List D School in Gartmore, Stirlingshire described electric shocks administered from a device described as a type of generator kept in a boot room where boys had to hold on to a pair of wires leading from the machine. Central Scotland Police were involved in compiling a report for the Procurator Fiscal that also included complaints of regular thrashings, being forced to eat vomit, sexual fondling and serious physical abuse.

The *Big Issue in Scotland* told a particularly harrowing tale by resident John McCorry of the behaviour of the nuns from the Smyllum Park Orphanage near Lanark. "They warped our sexualities. We were told that the toilet - and even using the word toilet - was evil. We couldn't refer to any part of our body between the neck and knees as anything other than 'our front'. But as a result kids would get beaten for talking about their fronts. We would get beaten for asking to go to the toilet. It was institutionalised insanity... Boys who wet the bed were beaten all the time... They were forced to drink Epsom salts over and over again. But that ended up making them doubly incontinent. Most of the boys who suffered this ended up soiling themselves a few hours later. The most disgraceful thing I ever saw was one boy who was forced to walk up and down all day in the dining hall with his wet sheet under his arm. The sister who made him do this was shouting at us, saying, 'Why aren't you laughing at him?' There was the sound of forced laughter everywhere. The boy was crying. It was sadistic, sick, mental torture". The Catholic Church's spokesman Monsignor Tom Connelly had his secretary explain to the *Big Issue in Scotland*: "It's nothing to do with us any longer".

The *Daily Record* guaranteed Cardinal Winning a platform: "I have no objection to anybody. I'm supposed to live with my neighbour and I try to do that as much as I can. But I will not stand for this kind of behaviour which is now being regarded as wholesome and healthy... Homosexuality is promoted every day. It's promoted by people who are on the streets, it's promoted by people who are attracted to others. We only need to look at some of the pamphlets available to see just exactly what is in place to put into schools. I am concerned that children might be converted by some of the literature... I deplore homosexual acts. I hesitate to use the word 'perversion' but let's face up to the truth".

As Souter's 'referendum' approached, more 'Keep the Clause' posters went up on billboard hoardings and bus shelters. Full-page advertisements were taken out in the Scottish press and the addition of mobile billboards ensured no-one in Scotland could escape the homophobia. Whilst most of the ones in cities were defaced with comments like "Souter is a closet", 'Keep the Clause' had greater success in conservative, old-Labour strongholds. In towns and areas like Port Glasgow, Greenock, Motherwell or Pollock, on the outskirts of Glasgow, KEEP THE CLAUSE billboards outnumbered any other. On Paisley's Q96 FM, Gary Marshall listed some famous stars born in Scotland. When he came to gay singer and former Communards star Jimmy Somerville he added: "But you wouldn't want to mention that if you came from Pollock".

On Tuesday, 16 May, advisors to Brian Souter's mailshot, ICM Research, were commissioned to do another poll. Their poll had the *Record* trumpeting excitedly: "Labour head for hammering in Clause 28 poll... In a survey over the weekend, 1,000 voters were asked how they would vote on Clause 28. Of those who replied, 74 per cent would retain the clause. The same percentage said Parliament should have held the referendum". And, in a clever ploy to use the 'wasted' votes to support their campaign, he added: "Even among those who said they did not intend to vote, almost half want to see the clause retained".

Although 'Keep the Clause' had their eye on the Great Hall at Edinburgh Castle to declare the results, it was more likely to be the *Record's* canteen where they would be first heard. Historic Scotland declared the Great Hall had already been booked. Elton John, who criticised Cardinal Winning and wanted to stage an open-air concert on 30 July, 2000 had apparently beaten them to it.

Now John MacLeod stepped into the debate for the first time. The *Herald* columnist had struggled with his own sexuality against a tide of religious pressure and objections. The son of Professor Donald MacLeod of the Free Church, he was better known for references in his weekly column to "forbidden desires", describing gays as "unnatural... dangerous..." and "evil". He linked homosexuality to "promiscuity, instability, neurosis, substance abuse, suicide, untold depths of degradation, misery, self-loathing" and even declared gays "simply not equipped to live": a claim apparently "borne out by study upon study". MacLeod now warned: "There are so many bullies in Scotland today on the streets, in offices, in churches, and in assorted fields of public life but perhaps the most dangerous are the cheap newspapers and the power-drunk blackguards who run them. These bullies hold themselves accountable to none. They believe they run the country. Or that they know best who ought to run the country. Or, perhaps, that the country should be run the way it used to be run. Or, as that wicked joke of my schooldays ran, they do not care who runs the country, as long as she has big tits". He had been inspired by the discovery of a poem in his 1979 copy of the *Jordanhill School Magazine*, a touching, anonymous poem from someone bullied because he was gay. "Cheap papers like the Record, in its Der Stürmer campaign to retain Section 28, don't care who gets hurt amid their unceasing farrago of lies. Nor do they give a whit for representative democracy. They'd rather rouse the mob. And if you stand up to them, be you an appointed Minister, an elected

MSP, and ordained churchman, a journalist declaring the truth in his heart, they will hammer you into the ground... Do you know what's the popular taunt in Scottish schoolyards as I write?" he asked. "Keep the Clause! Keep the Clause!" After giving the *Record's* sister paper *The Sunday Mail* a piece of his mind for attacking his island home, on Harris, he remarked with indifference: "I don't care if the Sunday Mail votes me... Poof of the Decade"!

After Macleod was sacked from the *Herald* for suggesting murdered schoolgirls Holly Wells and Jessica Chapman might've been alive if they'd been in church, he wrote a new weekly column for the *Scottish Daily Mail*. Slipping back into a more homophobic style, he would go on to describe Dewar an "unmitigated disaster", adding, "His 18 months in office were dominated by the follies of his entourage, the indiscipline of his Executive and the poisonous, wholly unnecessary row over Section 28... Though a keen judge of talent, Mr Dewar had little insight into character, and Wendy Alexander – his most notable protégé, with vast brains, minimal charm and scant common sense – proved the administration's Achilles heel". As contradictory as ever on the subject of homosexuality, he would later write of Cardinal Winning: "It was brave of him to take on the gay lobby, one of the nastiest out, over the Section 28 debate..."

On Wednesday, 17 May 2000, reporter Glenn Campbell interviewed Brian Souter on Scot FM. The station's e-mail address was given out, and listeners were asked to send in their questions, but, according to Campbell, owing to Brian Souter's other commitments, the programme had already been recorded. Scot FM news picked up on Souter's oft-quoted position that he was not against homosexuality being discussed in schools; he just wanted Section 28 to stay. That evening, 'Keep the Clause's David Macauley attended a Scot FM phone-in with Jock Brown opinionating on Scotland sinking under the weight of "political correctness" and an Executive "going against the will of the people". Towards the end of the programme, a Swedish man defending the repeal of Section 28 was asked by Jock Brown if he might be offended at some of the labels used against Swedes, like 'liberal'. He said he wouldn't, but to call him gay was pointless because he wasn't and not to label the 'Keep the Clause' campaigners homophobic would make it impossible to label the men who persecuted Jews, Nazis. He was thanked for his point and cut off rather promptly.

Reporter Hamish Macdonell in the *Scottish Daily Mail* celebrated with some enthusiasm "one million ballot papers returned for Section 28... It's a turnout of 25 per cent". All very well, but one million votes was all it took for a Freddie Mercury look-a-like to win the TV contest, *Stars in Your Eyes!* It was of course no news at all; just a desperate bid to keep 'Keep the Clause' on the agenda in the run up to the inevitable announcement that they had 'won'. The *Record*, of course had the same story, backed by the comments of a 'Keep the Clause' "spokesman" who returned the compliment, gasping in feigned surprise: "Once again the Record is first with the news. These figures seem remarkable". Since the Scottish parliamentary building had not yet been completed, the Executive had been temporarily housed in the headquarters of the Church of Scotland. The *Mail* reported that Section 28 would be discussed at the Kirk's General Assembly after the Executive had temporarily transferred the Parliament to Glasgow. "Ministers and elders are being asked to underline the sanctity of marriage and to reiterate the Kirk's traditional stance on homosexuality. A report compiled jointly by the Church's boards of education and social responsibility will call on the Assembly to 'reaffirm the foundational nature of marriage'. The stage was being set for a war between Church and State; religion and secularism. The rights of religious same-sex couples to marry would be the new battleground. For now, social conservatives within the Church would focus their attention on preventing the repeal of Section 28.

Thursday, 18 May, turned out to be one of the few occasions Section 28 did not feature in a *Record* editorial but there was nonetheless another chance to blacken Wendy Alexander's name. She "was at the centre of a new storm... after she was accused of misleading Parliament". The £12.5m she announced for housing partnerships in Glasgow had already been announced the preceding year. Only now had the money been properly allocated. The *Scottish Mail's* editorial called for her head: "Does Wendy Alexander, Minister for Communities, imagine that the citizens of Glasgow came up the Clyde in a banana boat?" In her column, Joan Burnie had her say: "How perceptive of the Alexander parents all those years ago to christen their darling daughter Wendy - the name invented by J. M. Barrie for one of his characters in Peter Pan. Yes, very fitting indeed for someone like our clever Minister for Muck-ups... who not only makes up facts and figures to suit herself, but lives in a political Never Never Land". When it was Gerald Warner's turn in *Scotland on Sunday*, he scoffed: "Ministerial responsibility - does she know the meaning of the word, or does she think it is a technical term for a red box and a government car? Throwing an imaginary £12.5m at the dirt-poor housing estates of Glasgow exhibits all the sensitivity of a joker who tosses a metal washer into a blind beggar's cap... In the terms which Alexander impudently applied to Brian Souter's campaign, it has a cheapness of its own... Alexander's contempt for the Scottish electorate is axiomatic..." Warner went on to lambast Wendy Alexander as the "infantile minister... uncontrollable... politically correct" and "the Walter Mitty minister" who had a "finger-wagging distaste for the public which clings to such outdated totems as marriage, heterosexuality or the democratic claims of majority opinion..." Warner demanded Alexander "should be sent up the wooden hill without supper before this spoiled brat throws another tantrum or breaks something fragile - such as Labour's grip on power in Scotland... Virtual reality is her preferred domicile..." before demanding Wendy Alexander be "put beyond use".

The following week it was minister, Susan Deacon's turn in the *Scottish Daily Mail* when she was "under attack" for "misleading the public by repeatedly re-announcing spending plans to give the impression new money was being released".

Ron Ferguson, a Church of Scotland minister of St Magnus cathedral in Orkney and another religious *Herald* columnist, whilst generally pro-repeal, sometimes floundered on the same ill-informed judgements, ignorance and prejudices that drove the homophobes. Ferguson highlighted a paradox when he asked: "The Keep the Clause campaign insists that it is not motivated by prejudice against gays. Why, then, has it chosen a noted foul-mouthed homophobe to be its public spokesman?" He then castigated the peaceful gay rights group, Outrage! for being an "obnoxious gay militant tendency... as unlovable as it gets". Ferguson didn't say what he had based his judgement on, although whatever it was, it was most likely something he'd read in a newspaper. He went on to draw from history an argument to support the gay struggle against 'Keep the Clause': "Now think about the following personages: Socrates, Alexander the Great, Michelangelo, Leonardo da Vinci, Tchaikovsky, Marcel Proust, Sir Benjamin Britten, Gertrude Stein, Virginia Wolf, and Rabbi Lionel Blue. If a teacher tells the truth about these randomly chosen gays and lesbians, is he or she open to a charge of 'promoting' homosexuality under the terms of Section 28? Yes. (After all, we can't expect a poofter like Michelangelo, painter of the Sistine Chapel frescoes, to be as good a role model as Jack Irvine, can we?) As a parent, I sympathise with parents' genuine concerns, but whatever the question is, Brian Souter and Jack Irvine are not the answer".

Mary Rolls from Langholm had something to say about Ron Ferguson's suggestion that there were more heterosexual paedophiles than homosexual: "It is disingenuous to base such a poor joke on a misinterpreted fact. For even if we accept the gay claim that 10% of the population is homosexual, offences against boys still form a disproportionate part of the total and indeed this only reflects the historical preference of homosexuals. Greeks and Romans had their catamites; our Prime Minister's wife honoured with her presence a national gay ball where the cabaret featured 'Boy Scouts'." David Paisley from Glasgow hit back: "...Comments about the Elton John stage show and his use of Boy Scouts is merely inflammatory nonsense, especially when you consider that Britney Spears, in her school uniform, is one of the 21st century society's first great (hetero) sexual idols".

Jack Irvine, "in the interests of accuracy..." took great exception to Ron Ferguson in the *Herald:* "Mr Ferguson describes me as a 'noted foul-mouthed homophobe', and misquotes the phrase from my column as 'slobbering queers who want to get their hands on young boys' arses'. The thrust of my column was that the lowering of the age of consent was being misrepresented by the Blair Government as a matter of equal rights. I wrote: 'You know the tired old argument - if you're old enough to get married, you're old enough for a slobbering old queer to have his evil way with you'. I then went on to highlight the dangers of overly-liberal legislation encouraging boys barely into their teens being swept up into a homosexual lifestyle. I wrote: 'And remember, the next time an old fruit gets caught with his hands in a 14-year-old's pants, he will probably get off when he lisps,' But I thought the boy looked 16". Now Mr Ferguson might have a gentler, more polite name for older men who attempt to seduce young, impressionable teenage males and put their health, and possibly lives, at risk. For the moment, I'll stick to 'slobbering queers' until I can think of something more damning. For me to be homophobic, I would have to hate homosexuals. I don't. What I do dislike intensely are adults, homosexual and heterosexual, who force themselves and their sexual politics on children. Mr Ferguson may continue to pontificate from his island hideaway but here in the real world, Brian Souter and myself would prefer to focus on people like Mr Peter Tatchell who in 1997 wrote to the Guardian championing a book which challenged the assumption that all sex involving children is abusive. Mr Tatchell referred to the 'positive nature of some child-adult sexual relationships' and concludes, 'it is time society acknowledged the truth that not all sex involving children is unwanted, abusive, and harmful'. So Mr Ferguson should take his pick - Souter's traditional family values or Tatchell's sexual anarchy". The letter was signed and sent from: Media House Strategic Communications, 16 Robertson Street, Glasgow.

I notified Peter Tatchell who quickly responded in the *Herald:* "Does the Keep the Clause campaign endorse Jack Irvine's smears and slurs in this letter today? Are his McCarthyite tactics the official policy of those who lead the campaign to save Section 28? I ask these questions because Jack Irvine has sunk to new depths with his outrageous, false implication that I endorse child sex abuse. He quotes selectively from my letter to the Guardian in 1997, in a way that suggests I approve of sexual relationships between adults and children. I do not. In fact, my Guardian letter stated categorically that it is 'impossible to condone paedophilia'. What does it say about his character and integrity that he is prepared to ignore the facts and distort the truth? I have spoken out many times against child sex abuse and campaigned for better protection for vulnerable young people. In January, I wrote to Donald Dewar, urging him to amend the Bill repealing Section 28. My proposed amendment would require sex education lessons to stress the importance of 'mutual consent, respect, and love' and advise pupils on 'how to refuse and report unwanted sexual advances'. This would give young people greater confidence to resist sexual manipulation and exploitation. While it is true that I support an age of consent of 14 for both heterosexual and homosexual relationships, my motivation has been wickedly misrepresented. I do not endorse 14-year-olds having sex with anyone, especially not with adults. However, whether we like it or not, 14 is now the average age of first sexual experience. If two people of that age have a consenting sexual relationship, I do not believe they should be prosecuted and jailed. They need counselling and advice to help them make wise, responsible decisions. Jack Irvine's misrepresentation of my stance on these issues is evidence of the dishonest, scaremongering nature of the Keep the Clause campaign. Unless Cardinal Winning, Brian Souter, and other leading pro-Section 28 campaigners publicly disassociate themselves from Mr Irvine's scurrilous witch-hunting tactics, many people will conclude that such tactics have their *de facto* endorsement".

In Roddy Martine's column in the *Scottish Daily Mail*, he suggested that "such has been the venom expressed against (Rev Ron Ferguson) that he jokes he has had to take Edinburgh lodgings at a heavily-guarded flat belonging to one of his elders from St Magnus Cathedral on Orkney..."

In a clever PR exercise, the Scottish programme, *Scotland's Towns: Stirling* was cancelled, and, in its place was a timely profile on Brian Souter in a *North Tonight* special on ITV. Brian Souter in his trademark brown jacket, open shirt, red Kickers shoes and plastic carrier bag was followed around with his PR man Jack Irvine in tow. The *Scottish Daily Mail* was sufficiently satisfied with the programme to preview it in a story quoting his reactions to claims he was a bigot. Souter hit back saying: "I feel quite angry actually when people say that, because I know in my heart that I don't feel like that about any other human being and I don't have any of these prejudices. So I find it quite insulting". His language on the programme was benign. The same questions that popped up in interviews were given the same carefully scripted answers. The *Scottish Mail* might have been intending to follow their report up with a piece by pro-Section 28 Catholic writer "Katie Grant - Page 12" but instead, upon opening the paper at page 12, the reader found a piece by celebrity cook, Clarissa Dickson Wright on: "Why I'm so proud to be a spinster!"

The *Daily Record* reported how "randy ducks" were driving citizens of Forres in Moray mad with their behaviour, and there was "FURY OVER NAKED TEACHERS ON NET". These were courtesy of pupils at Peebles High School who had dropped pictures of the heads of a headmaster and two teachers onto the bodies of porn stars and posted them onto a "rogue" website.

RELIGIOUS FASCISM

Referring to the boys and not the noisy, excited ducks, the *Record* insisted: "If the culprits are caught they could be charged with breach of the peace".

By Friday, 19 May 2000, the *Record* headline blasted: "LABOUR REBELS TURN UP HEAT IN CLAUSE BATTLE". Led by the Catholic MSP, Michael McMahon, they were demanding Labour upheld "the traditional values of marriage" in legislation to replace Section 28. Following the Vatican edict, the MSP for Hamilton North and Bellshill tabled an amendment to recognise the importance of marriage to society while recognising the importance of 'preventing intolerance, stereotyping and stigmatising' of those who chose an alternative lifestyle. Their report advised: "Earlier this month, the Record revealed 10 Labour MSPs were set to rebel against the Executive unless marriage was properly recognised in legislation. But it is now believed that number has doubled... The decision to go ahead with the amendment came after a last-minute discussion with Labour chief whip Tom McCabe..." The *Scottish Mail* added: "It is understood Mr McCabe made no attempt to block the amendment, which some Labour members interpreted as a sign of tacit Executive support". Cardinal Winning also voiced his support for the amendment. In a feature in the *Spectator* magazine he accused the Executive of declaring war on marriage and the family.

Michael McMahon, who spent time as a parliamentary aide to Jack McConnell, controversially employed his wife, Margaret, and daughter, Siobhan, in his constituency office and benefited from the services of an intern paid for by Christian Action Research and Education (CARE). The organisation paid a bursary of £5,000 towards a 10-month training programme. McMahon explained to *Scotland on Sunday:* "Circumstances forced this on me, I can't pay staff enough to retain them and I've lost three members of staff in the last four years".

As the 'referendum' drew closer, a full-page advertisement in the *Daily Record* bellowed: "THERE'S ONLY 4 DAYS TO GO. So, if you want to prevent the promotion of homosexuality in our schools, make sure you vote to retain Clause 28. This is your opportunity to make the government listen". 'Keep the Clause' helped them along with a ballot form crossed in the appropriate place.

Militant Religionists at War

The *Scottish Daily Mail* found space for Mrs Katie Grant in the guise of a confused parent, pen in hand, wondering where she was going to put her mark on Souter's mail shot. "The envelope tumbled through the letterbox... And there it was, my chance to take part in the independent referendum... Now I could do one or two things... So I picked up a pen. But still a nagging doubt remained... I put down my pen. A little more thought was needed... The vilification of this man tells us something. It tells us that the opinions of those of us who are in the mainstream, who still want to uphold the ideal of the increasingly marginalized traditional family unit, believing, despite all its failures and imperfections, that it is still the best model for society, are not only unheard but despised. Small, vocal pressure groups with fashionable agendas have hijacked the political landscape. The mainstream has become the silent and silenced majority. My pen now hovered over the ballot paper".

Would she vote to retain the clause? Was the Pope a Catholic...?

"...If the Scottish Executive had not been so deaf to the concerns of parents, if the Communities Minister Wendy Alexander had not wagged her finger so often, if everybody who raised their head above the politically correct parapet had not been branded a bigot and homophobe in such a mindless way, then this referendum would not have got off the ground or, indeed, have been necessary. They can brand Brian Souter anything they like for spending his money on a referendum but it should not be forgotten that fellow signatories to the referendum included businessmen Sir Tom Farmer, Tom Hunter, former Metropolitan Police Commissioner Sir David McNee and representatives from a variety of religious organisations. Should they be branded homophobes and bigots too...?" Seemingly blind to the billboards that now covered Scotland, she continued, "if only the Executive had, like Mr Souter, asked us instead of shouting at us, the repeal of Section 28 would surely never have degenerated into such a bitter war? There is, of course, danger lurking here that nobody can ignore".

On the Isle of Lewis, the managing director of Isles FM, Rev Stanley Bennie was sacked from his morning show for playing the Bloodhound Gang's top ten hit *The Bad Touch*. The song included the lyrics: "You and me baby ain't nothing but mammals. Let's do it like they do on the Discovery Channel..."

RELIGIOUS FASCISM

and the line the *Record* picked up on: "Put your hands down my pants and I'll bet you feel my nuts". Non-executive director Iain Maciver left a memo stating: "The song The Bad Touch by the Bloodhouse Gang is banned from airplay on Isles FM. This is as a result of a majority decision at a volunteers meeting on May 10, and also by a majority decision of the board of directors. Offenders may lose their slots permanently".

Later, that summer on Isles FM, disc jockey Gordon Afrin was fired after he was caught smuggling a box of 250 condoms out to give away as prizes. Carol Massey was also sacked with Afrin for reading out information about the sacking on the news, and deejay Jim Black resigned in support after playing out with *The Bad Touch*. In response to Gordon Afrin's actions, a station insider told the *Sunday Mail*: "This is Lewis for goodness sake... Goodness knows what he was thinking about..." By the end of July, the hapless radio station prepared to switch over to the World Radio Network at the end of its broadcast, but a power surge meant the station instead broadcast an erotic channel. With his nose seemingly hovering over a bottle of smelling salts, volunteer Peter McKibben gasped to *Scotland on Sunday:* "The staff were horrified".

After the pink, Pekinese hugging authoress Barbara Cartland died, the *Daily Record* wept: "Fans of pure and innocent love will have to turn back to her astonishing library of 723 books if they want to keep living happily ever after. She may have looked like a pantomime dame, but Barbara Cartland made a fortune out of providing readers with an escape from our sex-driven society". Barbara Cartland once said: "If you read newspapers today you see things that our mothers and grandmothers would have been shocked and ashamed to read. It is sex, sex, sex all the time, and it is not what we want".

The *Record* also commented on a major shake-up of sex laws in England and Wales, some of which had been in place since Napoleonic times. "A very likely source of controversy is the question of men kissing in public, which is an offence punishable by up to five years in jail in England and Wales - but which isn't illegal in Scotland... Straw is expected to scrap that law, but Freda Lambert, of the National Board of Catholic Women, said: 'Men kissing in public is a homosexual practice and we oppose it. It would make us feel uncomfortable'."

Militant Religionists at War

The *Mail on Sunday* used the birth of Tony Blair's son Leo as an excuse to peddle its hard line on 'Family Values'. "Blair as the family man we elected", its editorial cooed. "As our exclusive MORI poll revealed a year ago, 'married with children' is still, overwhelmingly, the lifestyle to which Britons aspire, and more than seven out of ten of those questioned expressed concern that the traditional family seems under threat..." They wanted to know "why the Cabinet as a whole has seemed so strangely determined to advance a social agenda whose outcome, if not avowed objective, would be to put homosexual relationships on a legal and moral par with marriage". Gerald Warner, come hell or high water, was determined to find a way of connecting Leo's birth to homosexuality. "Oh, frabjous day! We shall not experience such a spontaneous national outburst of joy again in our lifetimes, unless Peter Tatchell falls into a combine harvester... And, speaking of spontaneity, there he was - the proud father - Tony the Bloke, casually dressed and absent-mindedly holding a coffee mug which happened to have a photograph of his children on it. His voice quavered with emotion, as the man who has voted 28 times to extend abortion marvelled at the miracle of childbirth. Family, family, family is the new mantra of the government that is repealing Section 28; that will shortly use the Parliament Act to lower the age of homosexual consent to 16; that has abolished the married couples' tax allowance;' and which is planning a bonfire of many existing laws relating to morality. Sometimes one feels there simply is not enough vomit in all the world to pay adequate tribute to Blairite hypocrisy". He went on to accuse Tony Blair of "ruthlessly promoting sodomy".

The *Scottish Daily Mail* printed a flood of letters supporting 'Keep the Clause'. "Section 28 prevents the promotion of homosexual lifestyles being peddled to our children. It has nothing to do with the tiny minority of self-pitying and self-obsessed teenagers who, annoyingly, label themselves 'gay' in our schools", wrote "name and address supplied".

Secondary school teacher, Avril Henderson from Houston explained how homosexuality would be 'promoted' in schools: "I know that the promotion of homosexuality would be much more widespread and subtle than simply an occasional lesson. The promotion would stretch right across the curriculum. Instead of as now, for example, a modern languages textbook graphic showing a heterosexual couple walking into a French hotel, it would soon be a homosexual couple. Or, instead of a heterosexual family shown in a kitchen design graphic, it would be a homosexual family. This would be the law and you had better believe the aggressive homosexual lobby would increasingly push for these sorts of changes. The drip, drip effect would, in time, change what today seems perverse into something seen as normal. Scottish parents had better wake up quickly or in the near future their sons or daughters will be new recruits for the growing number of homosexual and lesbian organisations in the country".

J Lynn from Inverness wrote: "It is just not normal family life and so it is wrong to impress upon children that it is normal. I agree wholeheartedly with the point that depicting homosexuals in school textbooks could become commonplace".

Charles Carpenter from Sutherland thought the powers that be could have instigated a referendum, "but, instead, they chose to dance to the tune of the militant gays and their headline-hogging, mealy-mouthed liberal sympathisers... I propose that we reciprocate that contempt by slamming the door in their faces the next time they call at our homes to solicit our votes".

The failure of the media to have fairly platformed any 'gay agenda' meant no gay leaders were known or even recognisable outside gay community publications. As such, there was nothing standing in the way of outright persecution of all homosexuals with little more than a few diagrams and television stereotypes to spot them.

Charles Palmer from Falkirk helpfully suggested: "As the law stands, a single letter to the head teacher at the beginning of term is all that is requisite to assure your child's withdrawal from sex education classes. Even an institution so unduly confident in its opinions as the Executive would be forced to take notice if confronted with empty classrooms".

Trevor Royle, historian and associate editor of the *Sunday Herald*, commentating after a group of scholars and politicians met in Aberdeen to study links between Scotland and Ireland, wrote in the *Guardian:* "As one representative put it, given the current predicament within the country the comparison might be better made with Iran". Indeed. It was, after all, virtually the only other nation to have unelected clerics sitting on its legislature.

Militant Religionists at War

As the results of Souter's poll fast approached, under the headline: "MEANINGLESS"! The *Sunday Mail's* Lindsay McGarvie spoke to Ken Ritchie, chief executive of the Electoral Reform Society who said, "eyebrows had been raised" at the way Brian Souter's mailshot had been conducted.

Still counting down with only "3 DAYS TO GO", the *Record* - the paper Muriel Gray described in her *Sunday Herald* column as "The Daily How-Much-Worse-Can-This-Paper-Get-Before-The-Idiots-Start-Noticing Record" - reported "campaigners were yesterday braced for a last-minute flood of ballot papers in the referendum over Clause 28". New billboard posters had gone up simply demanding: "VOTE TO RETAIN CLAUSE 28". The *Record* hinted: "No details of the poll will be released until counting is complete - but an ICM opinion poll this week found the Government was heading for a humiliating defeat".

On Thursday, 22 May, the *Daily Record* announced in over four inch high letters: "70% BACKING THE CLAUSE... More than 1.2million voting slips have now been returned..." The *Scottish Mail* chipped in with "in the region of two million or 50 per cent" and three days later: "...A massive 70-30 margin". With apparent surprise, a 'Keep the Clause' spokesman gasped: "If the Record's figures are right, then the Executive are heading for a humiliating defeat". The *Record* added: "There is huge public interest in the event, which will be covered by TV and radio stations from abroad". The *Scottish Mail* warned the result would be "substantially damaging" to Labour as it prepared for a forthcoming election. (An election was just over a year away). A 'Keep the Clause' "spokesman" told them: "...We are expecting a huge turnout when we announce the result next week".

Chapter Seven
The Results

So with patches on my britches
Holes in both my shoes
In my coat of many colors
I hurried off to school
Just to find the others laughing
And making fun of me
In my coat of many colors
My momma made for me
Dolly Parton

On Tuesday, 23 May 2000, the Christian Institute were telling the press how they expected demonstrations and protests at a public meeting discussing Section 28 at the headquarters of the Free Church the following day. The Christian Institute was invited to address the General Assembly by the breakaway faction Free Church of Scotland (Continuing). John Macleod, in his column in the *Herald* warned them: "There is... no room in the Christ's mansion for proto-fascist garbage". The Charity Commission for England and Wales admitted it had received complaints about inappropriate political activity by the Christian Institute but stressed it was not conducting a formal inquiry into the pressure group. The *Herald* reported: "The institute later claimed to have a very good relationship with the commission and said the 'defamatory' allegation in the Scotsman had been referred to its solicitors, who were calling for its immediate withdrawal". The *Scotsman* had reported that the Charity Commission was questioning the political activities of the registered charity. However, the Christian Institute was cleared of breaching its charitable status over its activities campaigning against an equal age of consent. The Commission's report stated that there was "no absolute prohibition on charities undertaking political activities" so long as such activities further "charitable purposes". The Commission warned such activities had to be reasonable and associated publications balanced and unemotive. Despite the Christian Institute equating equal rights for gays with the rights of Nazis, the Commission also declared that it is "appropriate for a charity established to promote the Christian religion to have publicised views on homosexuality". The Commission acknowledged the Christian Institute provided a practical and administrative research assistant to Baroness Young and employed people actively involved in Parliamentary lobbying. The Commission were, however, critical of some publications by the Christian Institute, notably *Homosexuality and Young People* and *Bankrolling Gay Proselytism: The Case for Extending Section 28*. With reference to the former, the Commission accused the Christian Institute of producing an argument in favour of preventing homosexual law reform rather than articulating a wholly Christian view. With reference to the latter they recognised it could be seen as "overly political for a charity publication". All the Christian Institute was asked to do was remove its motto, 'Influencing public policy', and list of aims that deviated from its original objectives, which had been the basis of its registration with the Charities Commission: To 'challenge humanism, relativism and other ideologies'.

Before the start of the Church of Scotland's annual General Assembly, Gerald Warner in the *Scottish Daily Mail* clicked his heels to demand they got on with "serious evangelising... Compassion may be Christian virtue; self-pity is not... This is not to single out the Church of Scotland for hostile comment; the same applies to all the Christian denominations, apart from those which are scornfully described by their unsuccessful competitors as 'fundamentalist'." Warner asked: "How can an unbeliever share the priorities of Christians? ...The major Christian denominations... want to learn from the outside world, when their responsibility is to teach it. It is a failure of confidence. It is the same malaise that prompts the Vatican to apologies for imagined faults committed centuries ago". He questioned the Church's apparent fear of being "irrelevant... Irrelevant to what...?" he gasped. "To the rabidly anti-Christian media? ...So called inclusive language, vandalising much loved hymns, will not bring a single convert but it will drive some existing members out".

The Results

Andrew McNeish from Glasgow, entering into a part-time pastorship, wrote to the *Mail* to say: "Thank you, Gerald Warner, for your concise, crystal-clear commentary..." He wanted to make it plain that no "recruitment system" could have tempted him to join up. "This is neither a post nor a career - it is a calling, to which thousands before me have responded. That has enabled the Kingdom of God to grow and it will continue to do so - with or without the established church systems".

Tom 'Brigadier' Brown wrote in the *Daily Record:* "The Kirk... shouldn't be saying 'tell us what to believe'. It should be giving this nation of non-believers something to believe in - whether that belief is popular and trendy, or uncomfortable and unfashionable".

On Wednesday, 24 May, after the Scottish Executive had been gathered up and planted temporarily in Glasgow, the Victoriana was laid out again for the Church of Scotland's General Assembly in the Assembly Hall on the Mound and broadcast every night on BBC 2. With Anne Allen "leading the debate" - as the *Scottish Daily Mail* put it - the fundamental Christian informed the gathering: "As a church we must ensure that people in the homosexual community are valued, loved and pastored. Whatever the term homophobic is understood to mean, it should not be a term that could ever be truthfully used to describe Christian people... This repeal was to herald a new Scotland free from discrimination and bigotry. If only it were that simple... In their determination to embrace liberalism and inclusiveness, the Executive has become entrenched in illiberalism... The political drive for equality should not mean that our culture and ethics are moulded by the demands of the lifestyle of such a tiny minority of our population". Borrowing from Oscar Wilde, Mrs Allen reminded everyone that homosexuality was the "love that dare not speak its name... Now it appears to be the 'm' word: Marriage". Propounding the message of sexual apartheid, she reminded *Record* readers: "Marriage is important to Christian people and we are not going to see it sidelined to another alternative status". She was wrong. Statistics published by the Catholic Church showed the numbers of weddings held in 1998 was just over half of that of ten years before. If the current trend continued, marriage would be a rarity within 50 years. Already, in France, civil partnerships (PACS) were already the preferred option for the majority of couples formalising their relationship. Rev Bill Wallace went on to declare himself "brow-beaten by political correctness" and eagerly put forward his amendment in support of heterosexual marriage. Although it was defeated, the General Assembly agreed a motion by former moderator Very Rev John Cairns not to hear differing viewpoints from the floor but to show a united front in opposing Section 28 and to support the promotion of marriage. The Assembly agreed to urge new legislation insisting on external monitoring of local government funding awarded to groups whose remit concerned sexual behaviour and health. After the debate, Mrs Allen insisted to reporters that no decision had been taken on whether the Kirk supported repeal of Section 28 or not and that Cairns's motion merely referred to whether or not the Assembly should debate it. Rev Graham K Blount, Scottish Churches Parliamentary Officer, wrote proudly to the *Herald*: "Nobody went over the top to grab headlines about bigots or perverts..."

The subsequent Church report sought a compromise between the two opposing bodies within it, stating: "The intrinsic worth or moral superiority of any relationship does not depend on any ceremony religious or secular, but on the way people treat and regard each other in that relationship. It should be made clear that love, trust, forgiveness and faithfulness are the most significant criteria by which all relationships are to be assessed".

The *Scottish Daily Mail* headlined: "Kirk issues challenge on repeal of gay law". The editorial begrudgingly supported the Kirk in switching its focus onto the promotion of a special status for heterosexual marriage: "Limply, it accepts Section 28's repeal as inevitable... If the Executive cannot comply with the Kirk's modest request, it will have marginalized marriage, making other relationships the statutorily-approved norm". Quite how granting equal rights to gay civil unions or single mothers would undermine the status of heterosexual marriage wasn't explained. All the same, 'Keep the Clause' now began throwing its weight behind the promotion of exclusively heterosexual marriage.

The *Daily Record's* editorial lambasted the Church of Scotland for being "weak and compromising" and "so afraid of being seen to condemn that they opted for a feeble fudge". Waking up from its worst nightmare, the *Record* noted that the Kirk "were strangely reluctant to pass an opinion on whether same-sex parenting is good or bad for children - and even seemed

The Results

to accept that in the near future homosexual 'marriages' will be legalised... Is it any wonder that, faced with a national church that does not seem to know where it stands on the crucial moral issue of the day, people are turning to other churches - or none at all?" Reporting from the Kirk's General Assembly, the tabloid reported how "the Rev Alastair Horne, from Falkirk, said he had been shocked to see two men kissing in a 12-certificate film he had watched with his children". He was quoted: "There are those groups who are promoting their views in many ways, many of them in-your-face... There are some in the homosexual community who are very vociferous. There needs to be a questioning of some of their funding - and yes, perhaps discrimination. They are actively promoting a lifestyle that the Bible does not".

The veteran religious correspondent, 'Brigadier' Brown, the *Record's* "voice of authority", reminisced: "Those were the days, when morals mattered, religion was front page news and Scotland listened when the Kirk thundered from the pulpit". Holding fast against a youthful optimism that faced new challenges, he begged: "Six years ago, I was at the Assembly which ruled that gay sex and 'living in sin' were against God's law. But they did not have the courage of their convictions and left the door open for yesterday's about-face. They shilly-shallied and failed to kill off the reports on taking the sin out of extra-marital sex and making the 'physical expression of homosexual love' acceptable. It was only a matter of time before the Kirk's traditional tolerance became acceptance of homosexual love and gay marriages - and that is what finally happened yesterday".

Yes. That's tolerance for you! Perhaps the Kirk should never have got into the tolerance business unless it was prepared to go all the way. Tom Brown continued his rant to gasp: "One minister even asked for guidance on whether homosexual marriage could now be regarded as a valid family relationship. Is that a question a minister who binds heterosexual couples in Christian marriage should even have to ask...? At least with the Roman Catholic Church you get spiritual certainty".

The *Record* reported the ability of homosexuals to bridge the sectarian divide: "Pastor Jack Glass has become an unlikely ally of Cardinal Tom Winning in the furore over Clause 28. The firebrand leader of the Zion Baptist Church has often in the past denounced the doctrine of the Catholic Church. But yesterday, he led a small demonstration outside the General Assembly in support of keeping the Clause... Around 20 members of Pastor Jack's church handed out leaflets headed 'Home-work not homo work in schools'."

The *Herald* was not very happy with the "Kirk's craven performance" either. Its editor, Harry Reid, was already busy writing his book, *Outside Verdict*, examining the alarming drop in the Church of Scotland's congregations. The paper considered the debate on Section 28 "essential for the nation" and described it "shameful in the extreme... So this is what it has come to. The unity of the Church of Scotland is above an issue of great moral, spiritual, and social importance". The Church was not completely silent. Its Church and Nation Committee took the unusual step of accusing Cardinal Winning of encouraging a "culture of contempt" for people in public office. Close to retirement, Harry Reid was soon to hand over the job of editing the *Herald* to Mark Douglas Home in July 2000.

Christianity magazine reported how single women who attended church increasingly gave up hope of finding a Christian boyfriend because of a shortage of men in their congregations. For every single man in his thirties who attended church there were two single women in the same age group. *Daily Telegraph* writer Anne Atkins suggested "muscular Christianity" would bring them back.

The Kirk's ambitions to promote heterosexual marriage fell foul of Liberal Democrats in the Scottish coalition government. The *Scottish Daily Mail* sniffed: "Executive refuses to promote marriage in schools" while Hamish Macdonell, their Scottish Political editor warned: "Mr Wallace's decision to reject the Kirk's request means the Executive is now in direct opposition to all churches in Scotland". Michael McMahon MSP proposed to alter Section 26 of the Ethical Standards in Public Life Bill. As it stood, it proclaimed: "It is the duty of a council in the performance of those of its functions which relate to children to have regard to the value of stable family life". McMahon's amendment added two paragraphs demanding local authorities have regard to "the important place of marriage in society and in raising children" and that councils "recognise the importance of avoiding intolerance, stigmatisation and stereotyping of children from alternative family units". The Catholic Church even offered to drop its opposition to the repeal of Section 28 if only the

The Results

Scottish Parliament accepted McMahon's amendment giving weight to the institution of marriage. The Catholic Labour MSP for Hamilton North and Bellshill's campaigning zeal was demonstrated in his bill for postage stamps that reached a staggering £12,574 compared to just £234 for Tory John Young. While Cardinal Winning was in Canada, the Church's parliamentary officer wrote to MSPs to say: "We are eager to see the end of the controversy which has seen the Church and the Parliament at loggerheads... I believe that an opportunity to draw a line under the issue exists in the form of the amendment..."

Whilst having a drink with colleagues, sitting near the door of the Drum & Monkey pub in St Vincent Street in Glasgow, Wendy Alexander MSP had her bag snatched. When she looked round, the bag had gone. "Politics can wait - just tell us what was in your handbag Wendy?" asked the *Scotsman*. It included her house-keys, credit cards and her mobile phone with 200 or so names in the phone book. Arrangements were made to have it cut off, "so anyone who wants to talk to me about Section 2a can't"; Wendy told them. The *Record's* editorial sniped: "It's probably typical of our chatty communities minister Wendy Alexander that she was too busy talking to notice somebody nicking her handbag in a pub. We only hope whoever stole Wendy's mobile phone has the sense not to dial any of the pre-set numbers, especially her own. It's for their own good - they'll never get her off again".

A five-hundred-strong crowd headed by Stonewall's Angela Mason delivered 60,000 signatures calling for Section 28's repeal to the door of 10 Downing Street. Peter Tatchell, declared gays were "never going underground", echoing the words on banners at the Manchester demonstration twelve years ago when Section 28 was first put on the statute books. Actor Michael Cashman then said: "We demand the same rights as other ordinary civilised human beings. They can round us up, gas us, or shoot us, but as long as heterosexual men and women continue to procreate we will always exist, and we will never surrender". TV personality Sandi Toksvig thanked her family for coming along: "That's my genuine family not my pretend family". And Angela Mason told the crowd: "Section 28 is about prejudice and nothing else and it has to go. No one, not the Christian Institute, not Baroness Young, not Brian Souter, is going to drive us back into the closet".

RELIGIOUS FASCISM

On Sunday, 28 May, *Scotland on Sunday* reported: "Section 28 amendment to fail". Their political correspondent, Murdo MacLeod wrote: "Scottish Executive ministers have hardened their line against a last-minute compromise on Section 28 repeal, ruling out backing for an amendment which would include the word 'marriage'". Catholic Michael McMahon's amendment was due to be considered an hour after 'Keep the Clause' revealed the results of their 'referendum'. The more liberal *Sunday Herald*, on the other hand, wrote: "New Section 28 climbdown imminent". They explained: "The Scottish Executive is preparing the ground for a third major concession on the repeal of Section 28. The combined effect of backbenchers, committee power and the churches is forcing it to reconsider its refusal to endorse marriage in sex education guidelines". After Wendy Alexander met with Labour MSPs to seek their backing, political editor Douglas Fraser wrote: "...Ministers now realise if they continue to back the 'stable relationships' wording they will in effect be asking MSPs to vote against marriage'". The *Sunday Herald's* editorial, however, stated: "It is ridiculous to make a law which forces one set of arrangements upon teachers and would-be parents: why not legislate to tell children racism is wrong, or that exercise is good for you?" In a call for fewer laws, they wrote: "So when MSPs vote against giving marriage a special place in the sex education curriculum, as we hope they will, it will not be because they are anti-marriage but because they are learning appropriate limits for legislative action". They emphasised: "A high proportion grow up with one parent in a broken home - the future King William included. That is the reality for young people. It is the reality teachers face up to daily - so why force them to teach that marriage is superior to all other domestic arrangements?"

The *Sunday Mail* braced itself for the results of Brian Souter's 'referendum'. "R.I.P. Section 28... 70% of Scots refuse to back Brian Souter's barmy mock referendum... But Souter is set to claim victory in his private ballot, even though only 30 per cent of voters bothered to respond". The tabloid also revealed how 38 voters in the village of St Catherines, Argyll had received ballot papers five days after the cut-off date and Deputy First Minister Jim Wallace had not received one, despite living in the same Orkney house for 16 years. In their Mailbox section, A.R. from Glasgow swept aside gay parents to write: "Homosexual

The Results

activity does not result in procreation, therefore homosexuals should have no say in how other people's children are educated".

In the *Scotsman*, Rev David A Collins wrote: "Brian Souter would do well to remember that when Pontius Pilate conducted an opinion poll, the majority cried: 'Crucify him! Crucify him!'" Which, according to Christian belief, turned out to be a jolly good thing for everyone.

Brian Souter threatened to take his revenge on both of Scotland's largest political parties, Labour and SNP, warning them of his intention to target the constituencies of every MSP who voted against McMahon's amendment. A fortnight after saying he would bow out of politics after the parliamentary vote on Section 28, he was quoted in the *Scotsman* saying: "If this amendment doesn't go through, the war will go on. We will target the constituencies of MSPs who have not supported marriage and family values. This campaign will go on up to the next election". The *Record* reported Souter had warned them "he would 'haunt' the party with Scotland-wide billboards denouncing them as the party who 'hate marriage...' and the hugely expensive campaign will continue up to the General Election..." The *Scotsman* claimed he was also threatening to withdraw his financial support to the SNP, estimated to be at £600,000 in recent years because of his anger at their reluctance to support his stance on Section 28. "It is still not too late", screamed the *Record's* editorial in desperation. They expressed fury at the Executive's failure to seize the "olive branch" and prevent the repeal of Section 28. "Labour's Scottish politicians botched Clause 28 from the very start. It seems they are hell-bent on botching it right up to the very end. Even when they are offered an acceptable compromise that will satisfy almost everyone, they spurn it". The *Record* remarked: "Souter's threat to mount nationwide retaliation at the next election, reminding voters of Labour's performance, has serious implications..." The "dull" debating participants in the 11-strong Local Government committee were all pictured: Colin Campbell, Kenny Gibson, Trish Godman, Donald Gorrie, Keith Harding, Sylvia Jackson, Johann Lamont, Michael McMahon, Bristow Muldoon, Gil Patterson and Jamie Stone. The *Record* described Liberal Democrat, Jamie Stone as "well thought of", since he was wavering and, according to the *Herald*, might absent himself from the meeting. Only Tory Keith Harding was expected to back the amendment. Souter spat: "This war will go on. We will target constituencies of MSPs who have not supported marriage and family values and we know our friends in the ethnic communities plan to the do the same". A "senior Labour figure" told the *Record*: "This has not been properly thought through. Those who have dug their heels in and think that if we win on Tuesday the matter is over are kidding themselves. What will happen next could be far worse. We could find ourselves forced into the spectacle of voting against marriage on the floor of the Scottish Parliament. It is entirely possible that a motion could be put forward on that basis by the SNP and the Tories. How would that look to voters? ...Everybody wants out of this war - the Church, the politicians, the newspapers - and everybody knows the 'm' word is the way out". An "Executive minister" talking to the *Scottish Express's* Scottish political editor Angus Macleod saw things differently. "The SNP may see an opportunity here. Together with the Tories, they could force us into a position where we look as if we were urging our MSPs to vote against marriage. We could end up looking for an escape route with the churches, the opposition parties, some of our own backbenchers, most of the press and Souter - armed with his referendum result - baying at us. It would be extraordinarily difficult for us to row back at that point and include the world 'marriage'". The *Scottish Daily Mail's* editorial warned: "...The legislators are now turning the politically correct ratchet a further notch by relegating the institution of marriage to just another lifestyle choice. This is effectively a whole new permissive agenda - beyond the Section 28 issue".

A letter sent to the *Herald* condemning McMahon's amendment contained an impressive list of signatories: Jane Chisholm for Couple Counselling Scotland, Maureen Lynch of Family Mediation Scotland, Sue Robertson for One Parent Families Scotland, John Findlay of One Plus, Judith Gillespie of the Scottish Parent Teacher Council and Alison Davies of Save the Children Fund, to which Brian Souter belonged and had already made a number of donations.

Judith Gillespie of the STUC wrote to the *Herald* to challenge the politicisation of the school curriculum and the SNP's attempt to insert the primacy of marriage into sex education guidelines. "...It is not acceptable, and never should be acceptable, for politicians to start dictating what children will be taught. If the promotion of marriage appears or does not appear

The Results

in the revised sex-educations guidelines as the result of political intervention, then it will be using what is taught in schools to mark a political victory for one side or other in the current political debate over a piece of legislation. The school curriculum must not be used in this way. Rather what is in the school curriculum should and must be left to the independent committee which is reviewing the sex-education programme".

On Tuesday, 30 May 2000, the day the results of Souter's much-hyped 'referendum' were to be announced at Edinburgh's Balmoral Hotel, the *Record* declared: "MORE VOTE FOR SECTION 28 THAN LABOUR". The tabloid confided: "...Of the 1.3million ballots returned, around 70 per cent have voted to keep the clause... It means more people have voted to keep the clause, which bans the promotion of gay lifestyles in schools, than backed Labour in last year's Scottish election". The *Scottish Sun* had the same spin on Souter's "£1million gay lessons referendum", a point the *Herald* hadn't missed: "Throughout the process of the referendum those newspapers which have backed the exercise have been fed information about the size of the count and the early voting returns in a way which would have been inconceivable in a legitimate, publicly organised ballot. Some newspapers announced the turnout weeks ago and result days ago. They will announce these figures all over again today".

With the majority of postings condemning 'Keep the Clause'; at 5.30pm that evening, the discussion board on their website was closed down.

The *Scotsman's* Scottish Government editor, David Scott, called the 'referendum' "one of the biggest moral issues in living memory" but noted how it was also "the first press conference in Scottish political history at which bouncers on the door were deemed necessary".

Reporter Alison Hardie attacked 'Keep the Clause' in the *Scotsman*. "It has fed its favoured newspapers with a diet of biased stories while ruthlessly cutting others, this publication included, out of the loop if the editorial line offended. And, while Keep the Clause cannot be blamed for some of the tabloids' worst excesses, few could reasonably argue that they did not fuel them. Those excesses hit an all time low earlier this year when The Daily Record chose to 'out' the already openly homosexual junior executive minister, Iain Smith. The rapacious appetite for backing Keep the Clause was evident yesterday as one political correspondent at the Record notched up his 50th such story. Because this campaign has been less about politics and caring for children's best interests and more about awaking the public's sleeping bigotry towards homosexuals through an aggressive PR offensive".

The *Scottish Daily Mail's* reporter, Ian Smith targeted Wendy Alexander as "the minister who started the controversy…" She was described as acting "defiantly" against "the biggest expression of public opinion ever seen outside a general election" and a woman who was to "take personal charge of the Executive's unpopular anti-marriage stance". Smith reminded his readers that, "1.2 million people, 30 per cent of the electorate, returned the postal ballot, outstripping the average turnout at local and European elections". He failed to mention, of course, the difference between having to get out to a polling station to vote and popping it in a pre-paid envelope! A "source close to Mr Souter" in the *Mail* threatened: "The campaign will target the constituencies of MSPs who have not supported marriage and family values and if Wendy Alexander puts herself in the frontline she has to be prepared for that". The irony of such a statement was in Brian Souter's continued funding of the SNP's war chest. With the party led by Alex Salmond, who claimed religion was the driving force behind his thinking and who went on to chastise Tony Blair for remaining quiet about his religion, religious candidates were regularly fielded. They would join the likes of Catholic MSPs like Roseanne Cunningham and Fergus Ewing, the latter who would go on to hold private talks with Souter's charity, the Souter Charitable Trust (SCT) – whose declared aim was "the advancement of religion" - to discuss a return to the discredited, pro-abstinence drug policy similar to one promoted by 'Keep the Clause's' David Macauley. Souter's charity proposed the administration of neuro-electric therapy – sending an electric current to the brain - to addicts, a controversial treatment developed in the sixties by Scottish neurosurgeon, Dr Meg Patterson. Amongst others, Baptist John Mason won the Glasgow East by-electon in 2008 before thanking everyone for praying for him. In 2009, Glasgow North East's SNP candidate, David Kerr was revealed to be a member of the controversial Opus Dei sect. Most controversial of the religionists was Osama Saeed. In 2008, amongst many handouts to religious groups, Salmond awarded £215,000 of public funds to the Scottish

The Results

Islamic Foundation (SIF); a company the SNP helped set up; led by Osama Saeed, the SNP's parliamentary candidate for the Glasgow Central constituency who was campaigning to secure the support of its large Muslim population. SIF included other SNP activists and members of Saeed's family. Osama Saeed had been heavily criticised for urging Dundee's Muslim community not to cooperate with Tayside Police's Special Branch community contact unit and for supporting the restoration of an Islamic Caliphate, which would absorb existing states around the world into a Shari'a 'superstate'. Saeed was also a strong supporter of separate Muslim schools. Most of the SNP's funding was earmarked for an IslamFest in Glasgow. SIF later received a further £190,000 from the Race, Religion and Refugee Integration Fund (RRRI) which supported organisations assisting ethnic minority communities despite being the only one of 33 organisations that was neither a company nor charity at the time they applied for funding. Osama Saeed not only promoted the homophobic ex-gay Muslim group The StraightWay Foundation but posted on his blog a recommendation for an anti-gay blog: Eye on Gay Muslims. Against sound professional advice, the site claimed: "You cannot justify homosexual activity in the light of divine revelation, and no doubt it is all sinful. Understand Islam properly, realise that even the identity of being 'gay' is problematic and un-Islamic, and repent to Allah, who is Forgiving, Merciful". The SNP went on to offer Saeed the opportunity to contest the Glasgow Central seat in the General Election.

Wendy Alexander had indeed put herself in the frontline. She not only defended the repeal of Section 28 against the might of Brian Souter's 'referendum' campaign: she was also in charge of the controversial Glasgow housing stock transfer scheme and electoral reform for local government. Her colleague, Susan Deacon had taken on anti-abortion activists and the Catholic Church with her plans to improve young people's sexual health leaving many to ask what the majority of men were doing? The male MSPs seemed to be better organised, acted in concert, formed alliances and apparently avoided difficult and controversial issues. The female MSPs were rarely seen preparing the ground politically, talking to backbenchers, chatting to journalists, leaking stories and making useful friends.

RELIGIOUS FASCISM

The *Scottish Daily Mail's* editorial accused the Executive of playing "fast and loose" with democracy and promised revenge at the next general election. It also repeated the words of their reporter Ian Smith when he wrote that it was going against "the biggest expression of Scottish opinion ever recorded outwith a general election..."

The "fury over sex swap Liz's NHS boob job" was a transgender story that caught the attention of the *Record*. Alongside a full-length picture of "sex-change dad-of-two Liz Rowe" in a short skirt, the tabloid found a 41-year-old mum who declared how she "had to fight to win expensive treatment for her son Gavin, a cystic fibrosis sufferer" and "criticised Liz's op". Unsurprisingly, the same story interested the *Scottish Daily Mail* which advised: "In a country where patients can lie on hospital trolleys for 24 hours, people are denied cancer drugs because of where they live and others die awaiting heart surgery, the NHS has paid for this 6ft rugby player to have a sex-change operation, then a new 38d bust". Exactly the same 41-year-old mum who appeared in the *Record* now appeared in the *Mail* to reiterate her disgust. The issue of Liz's transsexuality had been dealt with some years ago. She had spent 11 years on waiting lists; sometimes on waiting lists for waiting lists. She was treated as a woman without breasts. From Jarrow, a conservative Labour politician was given a sound-bite on breakfast show *GMTV* to declare no transsexuals deserved help on the NHS. Reports of how greedy clerics were creaming £45million a year off the NHS for their services or how much the NHS were spending on plush, new homeopathic hospitals and unproven homeopathy treatments were still some years away.

Pictures of 'Keep the Clause' announcing the result of their 'referendum' were carried on the national television news. With Jack Irvine pictured at his side, Brian Souter stormed: "We plead with the Government to respect parents' rights. We will not allow the politically correct minority to undermine the importance of marriage". It was then he delivered his iconic moment: plonking himself down in his chair in a gesture that hovered between petulance and high camp, a red-faced Souter thumped the table and roared defiantly: "We didnae vote furrit, and we're naw huvvin' it!"

Simon Pia wrote: "As for Soapy, when he cried 'We didnae vote for it and we're no havin' it', close your eyes and it was John

The Results

Inman in a kilt... And for Wendy... who else but Snow White..."

Perhaps the irony of his outburst escaped him. After all, no-one had voted for Section 28 either.

The turnout of Brian Souter's glorified opinion poll, shunned by the Electoral Reform Society and using an outdated voters register; disenfranchising students and anyone who moved about a lot, was 32% or 34% depending on whether you included in the total numbers polled (3,970,712) the eight per cent of envelopes returned by the post office undelivered. (Given the £2m PR campaign, that ought to have disappointed the organisers. Even a previous postal ballot in Scotland on the privatisation of water services in Strathclyde attracted a 71.5% response and the nuclear waste repository postal ballot in the Highlands was as much as 69%)! Out of 1,272,202 returns, there were 11,356 spoilt ballots and 11,856 empty envelopes (each about one per cent). The 'referendum' suggested that 166,406 voted for repeal (13%) and 1,094,440 voted against repeal (86%). Overall, this suggested 70% of Scots rejected the 'Keep the Clause' campaign, either by binning the ballot or by voting for repeal. With the vote for retaining Section 28 barely half the claimed readership of the *Daily Record*, Wendy Alexander was defiant: "Two out of three Scots voters rejected, binned or simply ignored this glorified opinion poll. More and more Scots have come to see that this is not about schools. It never was about our schools. It's about the character of our society and whether Scotland is tolerant", she said.

The gay community's *Pink Paper* quoted Pete Mooray from the Electoral Reform Society who advised: "The turnout should be a mandate of 50 per cent to validate a referendum". Tim Hopkins of the Equality Network remarked: "Something like 70% to 75% of people in Scotland have either thrown their ballot paper away or have voted to repeal Section 28 and that's the most significant thing" and Rozanne Foyer of the Scottish Trades Union Congress added: "We have been utterly opposed to this ballot from the very beginning. It has been nothing more than a cynical attempt to undermine our democratic processes and its execution has been insecure, unfair and ill thought-out".

Malcolm Dickson wrote in *The Herald:* "...Only those opposed to repeal bothered to vote in any numbers. That they can claim this as a victory is ludicrous. Suppose...

fundamentalist... Brian Souter had put his financial weight behind a referendum asking the Scottish people whether they wanted to repeal the unique privileges enjoyed by Roman Catholics, in alone of all religions, having their own State-funded schools. What if this campaign had had the rabid support of the tabloid press, where alternative viewpoints are rarely, if ever, expressed? What then? I fancy his enthusiasm for populist referenda would be a lot less keen. Religious fundamentalists are a dangerous breed. Because they take their creed, whatever it might be, literally, and also often selectively, they are almost impossible to reason with. Indeed reason is implicitly condemned by the elevations of faith above all else. They are right and they have the word of God to back them up. Such conviction allows them to see all of those not of their persuasion as sinners, infidels, heathens, or whatever other pejorative description comes in most handy. This in turn, they believe, gives them the divine right to interfere in the lives of others. Tolerance and liberalism are seen, not as virtues, but as vices. This justified the cruelty of the Inquisition, the brutality of the Crusades, and today the barbarity of the Taliban. Thank goodness that we have a democratically elected secular Parliament to protect us from these men of God".

Soon after the result, the *Herald* reported the results of a System Three poll, which showed a 10 per cent lead for Labour over the SNP, its nearest rival on first ballot preferences. The results demonstrated a very hollow victory for Brian Souter. From "Media House Strategic Communications", Jack Irvine wrote to the *Herald* in disgust. "It is ludicrous to suggest a Government that has ignored over 1,000,000 voters can possibly be gaining strength in the polls. If Mr Dickson had submitted this paper to the Media House Public Affairs Unit, he would have been awarded a C - with the comment, 'good try but avoid postulating on unverifiable data'." Professor Chris Eynon, Managing Director of System Three in Edinburgh replied: "...If our approach is so flawed, why was Media House happy for System Three to use the same methodology in a poll on its behalf in Tony Blair's Sedgefield constituency? I do not recall the results to that poll being issued with a health warning over suspect interviewing method".

The *Scottish Express* declared: "Fewer than 1 in 3 say they want to keep the clause" after finding "a sizeable majority of

The Results

people decided not to take part in the survey..." The paper revealed the entire population of the isle of Mull hadn't received ballot forms until after the deadline. 'Keep the Clause' blamed the Royal Mail. The editorial stamped: "If Scotland is not sick and fed up of the interminable wrangle over the Section 28 repeal by now then it should be" and went on to give a thumbs-down to McMahon's amendment or any future concessions the Executive might make, bending to Brian Souter's threats.

The Scottish Parliament Local Government Committee, on the last day of debate on the Ethical Standards Bill at stage two, unanimously approved the repeal of section 28. Of the two 'marriage is best' amendments, Brian Monteith's was defeated by 10 votes to one, with only the Tory Committee member, Keith Harding voting in favour. Michael McMahon's amendment was defeated by seven votes to three with one abstention. The three who voted for McMahon's amendment were Keith Harding (Tory), Jamie Stone (LibDem) and himself, Michael McMahon (Labour). Donald Gorrie (LibDem), Gil Paterson (SNP), Kenny Gibson (SNP), Sylvia Jackson (Labour), Johann Lamont (Labour), Trish Godman (Labour) and Bristow Muldoon (Labour) voted against his amendment. Only Colin Campbell (SNP) abstained. Despite Liberal Democrat Jamie Stone's support for the amendment, Souter attacked the Liberal Democrats as "politically correct" and suggested in the *Scottish Sun* that "someone should get them and give them a good verbal doing round the back of the bike sheds".

The next day, the embittered *Record's* front page featured a picture of two fingers held up with the caption: "WENDY'S TWO FINGERS TO THE LOT OF YOU". And declared: "HELL MEND THEM... The government who happily rode to power on 100,000 less Scottish votes are more interested in the opinion of people who couldn't be bothered to put a form in an envelope and post if off for free..." adding threateningly: "They're asking for trouble". The *Scottish Sun* roared with indignation: "For each Cabinet member who STILL wants to repeal Clause 28 one hundred thousand Scots voters say: To hell with you". After accusing the Executive of shifting their position, the *Record* insisted "this debate is no longer so much about allowing the promotion of homosexuality in schools as a campaign to force the Government to do the same for marriage". Speaking for the so-called 'moral majority', Brian Souter

RELIGIOUS FASCISM

promised: "We are going to make a hell of a nuisance of ourselves" and promised he was about to embark on a prolonged guerrilla war. *Record* columnist, 'Brigadier' Brown praised the "increasingly impressive Brian Souter" while the editorial wrote bitterly: "How bizarre that a government who rightly realise the vote-winning potential of a wholesome family man at No 10 are determined to do nothing to bolster the institution he embodies... What do women want most - a partner with government-approved paternity leave or a man who'll marry them?" 'Brigadier' Brown reaffirmed his old-fashioned and homophobic stance when he went on to write about members of the Cabinet dressing casually: "When I started in national newspapers, we were expected to wear dark suits, white shirts and plain ties... But are we really ready for Peter Mandelson straight from clubbing in his Julian Clary gear? When they start carrying handbags, I'm changing my vote".

The *Scottish Sun* was not intending to take defeat quietly either and laid its whole front page out like an optician's chart, demanding of the Scottish Executive: -

"A
RE
YOU
BLIND
DEAFAND
BONKERSTOO?"

Posing as a bastion of the nation's morality, the *Scottish Sun* editorial begged: "Never in the field of human decency have so many been so badly served by so few... We told THEM they were off their rockers. Again and again and again and again". But, "they put us - by which we mean the Brian Souter campaign, the Scottish Sun, the vast majority of the people AND our children - through the inconvenience of a private referendum... And if the figure of 87 per cent isn't conclusive, then the moon's made of cheese. Honestly, the sheer arrogance of the Scottish Executive beggars belief. And so we had 11 men and women good and true sticking two fingers at us AGAIN, as if nothing had happened. These were the same people who approached every right-on organisation with an axe to grind for their opinion, and got it by return of post... As Corporal Jones in Dad's Army would have

The Results

been quick to say: They don't like it up 'em. Well, they've had it up 'em - one million, ninety four thousand, four hundred and forty times. We, the simple voters, may not be as smart as them. We may not be as cool as they like to think they are. But we don't want our kids taught gay lessons in schools. And we told 'em".

Brian Souter told the *Scottish Sun* he had been subjected to a barrage of attacks and threats from "extremists". He added that a "live BULLET" (their emphasis) had been sent with a ballot paper and claimed campaigners had tried to block him and his family from making their way to church.

The *Sun's* political reporter Andrew Nicoll wrote: "It's just one symptom of the touchy-feely, everything is allowed, musn't offend anybody, multi-culturalism that's so fashionable in Government now. And it's tripe".

The *Scottish Daily Mail* was incandescent with rage. "SHAMEFUL", they boomed off the front page, even taking the unusual step of devoting a whole page to their editorial over "an extremely serious situation" declaring: "Scotland's parliament has broken its covenant with the Scottish people". Referring to the Executive's consultation process, the *Mail* accused the First Minister of being "economical with the truth". (Rich indeed coming from a paper forced to issue yet *another* public apology for an inaccuracy that appeared in a news story only the day before)! Editor Ramsay Smith and his reporters, Ian Smith and Hamish McDonell, had worked hard to prevent the repeal of Section 28; now the paper turned their frustration on the Scottish Conservatives who they insisted could have "launched a crusade to defend family values and so have established themselves as the voice of Middle Scotland". They rebuked MSPs for launching: "A root-and-branch attack on all institutions of traditional morality and social cohesion, to be replaced by the soulless political correctness whose anarchic product is the growing underclass in society". In its report, Valerie Riches from the controversial Family and Youth Concern squealed: "If the politicians ignore a result like this it would seem we are living in a pseudo-fascist state". A full-page interview with Brian Souter under the heading: "A million reasons to keep fighting" had him explaining: "Family is everything" while an "electoral expert", John Curtice, professor of politics from Strathclyde University, added "Mr Souter has got the headline he wants, that a million Scots are in favour of retaining Section 28. I would not like to be in Wendy Alexander's shoes right now". In the *Scotsman*, the words of Professor Curtice took on an altogether different tone: "Brian Souter got his headline... But in truth he got little else for his money... For if a million Scots voted for Clause 28, well over two million decided to ignore the ballot... In short the referendum has produced a low turnout and an apparently biased result. It is doubtful whether the outcome has done much to strengthen the Keep the Clause's campaign".

Scottish editions of the *Daily Telegraph* declared a "poll boost for Section 28" on the front page. The editorial satisfied itself that attempts by the "...Scottish media to discredit the Keep the Clause campaign..." had "manifestly backfired". They warned: "Cardinal Winning, Mr Souter and their allies should stand firm against repeal". As the poll results had been read out, the *Telegraph's* Alan Cochrane overheard a young reporter from the *Independent* sigh: "Well, here we are in the homophobic capital of the world". Cochrane took issue, insisting the campaign had merely tapped into Scotland's "innate conservatism... We Scots are not all 'homophobes'. Just ordinary people, with ordinary concerns about our children's education".

The *Times* editorial pointed a finger at Wendy Alexander, suggesting the matter had been "ineptly handled... igniting a fire storm". The London-based Murdoch broadsheet claimed it would have been more reassuring to see the committee embrace the McMahon amendment; an amendment they wrongly suggested was "endorsed by Stonewall..." They insisted "a similar bargain struck by David Blunkett, the Education Secretary, with leading Church of England bishops is the right device for improved legislation in the same sphere at Westminster". Giddy with her success amongst unelected clerics in the House of Lords, Baroness Young later rejected this 'bargain'.

In the *Times*, reporter Andrew Pierce scathingly wrote how "dozens of gay rights groups, from the Establishment-favoured Stonewall... to groups catering for leather fetishists and lesbian collectives, produced ambitious information campaigns in anticipation of reform". Amongst a host of other "radical" literature that "most" gay groups had apparently privately conceded had "seriously damaged" the "battle" was Phace West and its "guide to 'cruising' for sex in public places with explicit references"; Bi-g-les "which offered advice to children as young

The Results

as 12" and Healthy Gay Scotland with their "guide on coming out". The latter stated: "There are plenty of things that you can do and enjoy like kissing, hugging and oral sex, masturbation, touching each other and anal sex". Neither Phace West, Bi-g-les nor Healthy Gay Scotland had produced information campaigns in anticipation of reform but continued to work under the current emergency with professionals to get appropriate information to those that needed it.

Before becoming President of the National Secular Society, as *Gay Times's* MediaWatch columnist, Terry Sanderson wrote: "As the religious Right has found... It is very easy to create the image of the sinister homo. There is no law to stop you saying whatever you want about gay people, however nasty and defamatory. Other minorities may have protection against hate mongering. We have none. All that is needed is the money to disseminate the propaganda, and a few newspapers willing to frighten the punters, and the referendum is in the bag. And each time a referendum on a gay issue is lost, equality is pushed further from our grasp and our public image irreparably damaged. Those citizens who had previously been of an indifferent live-and-let-live frame of mind suddenly find themselves taking an active anti-gay stance. They have become convinced - often by malevolent and dishonest advertising - that their children are at risk or that society is about to be damaged in some way by homosexuals. Tolerance rarely figures in these campaigns. Souter's cohort, Cardinal Winning, was pushing his own nasty agenda throughout all this, and was a willing accomplice in these weeks of consistent distortion, exaggeration and scare-mongering. The Daily Record, too, became the organ of hostility, using its power to promulgate a totally one-sided version of the debate".

Brian Souter said Scotland's politicians should not try to turn Scotland into Sweden. Robbie Dinwoodie suggested in the *Herald*: "Perhaps Mr Souter should finance a referendum on that idea, and see what the result is. A tolerant broad-minded liberal country where folk know how to party versus a wee theocracy run according to the whims of an evangelical Protestant and a Cardinal. Abba versus Kenneth McKellar. You decide... So what are the 'customs and conventions embodying the fundamental values' of our community? The fur coats and absent knickers of the 'you'll have had your tea' capital? The 'see you, Jimmy' of the city that gave the world the Glasgow kiss? The international brotherhood and philandering of Burns? Or the stern moral gaze of Knox? You would have thought that as a heavily paid-up supporter of the SNP, the transport tycoon would have welcomed comparisons with an independent nation across the North Sea, but apparently not. We are to have none of their damned Swedish practices here..."

Ian Bell wrote in the *Scotsman:* "By his account, Mr Souter is an extremely tolerant man who just happens to have a lengthening list of things he will not tolerate. As Mr Jack Irvine's PR knitting circle will attest, he is also a very generous man. Mr Souter has not only stopped tolerating things on his own behalf but he is prepared to do it for the rest of us, too".

The *Scottish Mirror* avoided a Section 28 cover story altogether. Their Scottish Political editor Lorraine Davidson, former communications director for the Labour Party in Scotland reported that: "Bus tycoon Brian Souter last night threatened to keep on boring the Scottish public with his moral crusade... The Scottish Executive employs an army of spin doctors - led by David Whitton. Whitton, the Executive's official spokesman, has the added advantage of having worked alongside Jack Irvine. If anyone should have been able to second guess his every move, it should have been Whitton. But his lacklustre team failed to deliver a single front page headline promoting the Government's view... Brian Souter blundered yesterday by saying he would call off his campaign if the Government introduced the same guidelines on the issue as England. Little did he realise London's early promise to stress the importance of marriage has failed to materialise. The Executive could have capitalised on his mistake and offered him a deal. But the advisers are so dozy they did not even realise Souter had scored an own goal. The bus tycoon has now vowed to continue his crusade. He has now admitted what many of us had suspected - his moral stand goes much further than just the issue of Clause 28. He will spend much more of his vast wealth telling us how we should live our lives".

When Catholic Labour backbencher Jim Murphy embarrassed Jack Irvine's Media House by questioning the work they did for the £3.4m budget, particularly PR work for the Scotland Against Drugs (SAD) campaign, it soon became clear that Donald Dewar's spokesman, David Whitton, had been in charge of the SAD account while he worked for Jack Irvine from 1996 to 1998. David Macauley had been a director of SAD before

The Results

he joined Jack Irvine at Media House. Three months after Macauley left SAD, Jack Irvine's Media House said it no longer wanted to represent the organisation. By 2006, the doors were closed on the publicly-funded advisory group after most of its functions were transferred to a new body, The Scottish Centre for Healthy Working Lives.

The *Scottish Express's* front page featured a strained expression on Souter's face and the caption: "HAPPY NOW, MR SOUTER?" The *Express* believed "each vote Mr Souter secured for his Keep the Clause campaign has cost him £2 of his personal fortune... He has spent £500,000 on his advertising trailer campaign, more than £1million on staging the poll and another £500,000 on newspaper adverts". Their editorial was defiant. "We make our opinions on such matters clear at the ballot box, not some millionaire's whim... That, Mr Souter, is how we do things in this country. And, if you still don't like it, the answer is clear, stand as an MSP next time round and see how many people support you - when it really counts".

There was nothing left but for Glasgow's *Evening Times* to reveal how tattooed 18-year-old Aberdeen supporter, Tony Rowe had streaked onto the Hampden pitch in Glasgow in a match against Rangers with 'Keep Section 28' splashed across his back. The *Evening Times* cheerfully reported how he had raised £600 for charity after being given a "stern warning" by police.

Aberdeen's *Evening Express* columnist Scott Begbie discovered: "The results of a website survey to sound out Scottish kids' opinions were released this week. It shows that the majority of them want Section 28 scrapped. If we have to listen to any part of society on such a crucial issue, shouldn't it be the ones who are affected most?"

In yet another poll, this time for ITV Teletext, 2,041 people called to register a vote on whether the Executive should listen to the electorate over Section 28. 90 per cent voted 'yes' and 10 per cent voted 'no'.

A phone-in on TalkSport radio in the evening had a caller expressing his concern for a friend who was gay and effeminate. He believed his friend already faced discrimination every day and wondered how in the present climate he would be able to get up in the morning.

By Thursday, 1 June 2000, the *Record's* front page was given over to "Wendy's marriage 'con trick'". Apparently, "the Scottish

RELIGIOUS FASCISM

Cabinet descended into chaos over the result of the Keep the Clause referendum" and were now "squirming to get themselves off the hook on Section 28". The *Record* also reported how Brian Souter was preparing a "family celebration day" later in the month. "The event at Strathclyde Country Park near Glasgow on June 24 is intended as a day to celebrate marriage and the family... Entertainment at the free-entry event is to feature a gospel choir. Brian Souter is to make a short address there". To ensure its success, amongst the star line-up was Baroness Janet Young!

R S Stephen wrote to the *Fraserburgh Herald:* "When Christians march in the name of Jesus Christ they are given infinite power for victory, Acts 1.8. ...Brian Souter is in the driving seat and is offering free buses for all the people to a great Family Action Day picnic with bairns' entertainments and the London Gospel choir and speakers on family values all free at Strathclyde Country Park, Hamilton, and he has now declared this to be a victory celebration rather than a S28 protest rally! Years ago when I saw Cardinal Thom Winning reprove the BBC and Tony Blair etc over the abortion of 5,000,000 unborn UK bairns I felt God had raised him to do battle with the politically correct do-gooder elitist mob. The war is far from over but Winning is winning with the people behind him. Hallelujah".

The *Scottish Daily Mail* warned: "Day by day, the liberties of ordinary people are eroded by... militant gay rights crusaders..."

Simon Pia, in his *Scotsman* Diary claimed Jack Irvine's Media House had the "wizard wheeze" of mooning at MSPs on the Mound. "First in line to volunteer were Tom Cassidy and David McAulay, until Jack Irvine told them not to be so bloody stupid. Could they not see this would be construed as promoting homosexuality?"

With all eyes on marriage, religionists rallied behind MSP Brian Adam, the Parliament's only Mormon who co-sponsored the Catholic MSP Michael McMahon's attempt to promote the institution. Adam was attempting to introduce an amendment along similar lines to McMahon's when the Bill came back for its third and final reading. The Mormons from the Church of Jesus Christ and Latter-Day Saints planned an assault on Scotland in 2001. The U.S. church appointed its first ever public relations officers, a husband and wife team to forge links with local groups and councils.

The Results

With the burgeoning promotion of marriage, single parents were swept under the wheels. A White Paper on family law promised unmarried fathers the same rights as those who were married, causing the *Scottish Daily Mail* to cast around for anyone singing from their hymn-sheet. "...Divorce goes up unless you strengthen marriage", insisted Gordon Macdonald of Christian 'family values' group CARE. Father Danny McLaughlin for the Catholics chipped in with: "...Making divorce easier is not helpful as far as supporting marriage is concerned. It is lessening the value of marriage". And Tory Phil Gallie asked: "What evidence is there to suggest that speedier divorces will benefit children?"

Ian Smith, the *Scottish Daily Mail* Political Reporter predicatably found "fury over McLeish 'marriage U-turn'" in the Scottish Executive's Family Law White Paper. It had been drawn up by Deputy First Minister Jim Wallace, who had dropped any mention of marriage, originally inserted by Henry McLeish in a previous draft, indicating that the White Paper was not the best place to discuss its merits. The *Mail* reported "the Executive was pursuing a politically correct agenda aimed at undermining the institution of marriage", adding, in an instant; "the Executive also plans to legalise gay group sex". The Executive was planning to comply with European rulings and lift the ban on gay men having group sex. (It was already legal for heterosexuals). The *Mail* said the Church of Scotland was calling it "a dilution of Scotland's moral values". Mrs Ann Allen, on behalf of the Board of Social Responsibility declared: "We would oppose group sex of any nature. It is a cheapening of the whole sexual act and to make such activity legal is giving out the signal that it is acceptable to society. I am sure the vast majority of people would not see such activity as moral". The *Mail* went on to report how "Christian and family values groups are to demand that Mr McLeish explain his moral views..." And, in the next day's edition: "The Christian Institute is contacting 2,000 churches to garner support..." The *Scottish Mail's* reporter Eddie Barnes, (a former editor of the *Scottish Catholic Observer*) found "the Scottish Executive was attacked last night for caving in to European legislation and ushering through more liberal laws governing homosexual practices". As if nobody in Scotland ever wanted equality in law, the *Scottish Daily Mail*, and its new Scottish editor Ian MacGregor, screamed: "Ministers bow to Europe to legalise gay group sex".

Familiar voices demanded Britain stand up to Europe. "...They should fight it in the courts and protect our youngsters", insisted Gordon Macdonald of Christian group CARE. The tabloid mimicked the political posturing of thirties Nazi propaganda by linking the interests of minorities to greater evils: "If it is passed by the Scottish parliament, whole swathes of Scottish legislation will be changed to comply with EU Convention rights... It could mean an early release for several long-serving murderers..." The conviction of "yet another" homosexual child abuser, David Murphy, forced the *Mail* to remind readers of a string of more recent cases of men abusing boys. The burgeoning cases of abuse in Catholic institutions and heterosexual cases of abuse were brushed aside even though only two days before a 38-year-old man from Beith had been jailed for raping and abusing two little sisters. "Nobody wants to create a witch hunt..." they implored "but... The Scottish Executive... has a need to raise its game. Recent scandals make its preoccupation with legalising the promotion of homosexuality in schools and lowering the age of homosexual consent particularly inappropriate..."

Hamish Macdonell scorned "about £11,000 of taxpayers' money" being spent on the Scottish Executive's Equality Strategy in the *Scottish Mail*. He claimed it had been "derided as 'politically correct nonsense'." Macdonell didn't explain exactly by whom, but we could guess. Gerald Warner was wheeled in for an "analysis". He wrote: "This can only be an attempt to classify homosexuality as a disability, similar to physical disadvantages, rather than as a sexual preference... With marriage under attack from plans for faster divorce and same sex weddings, is the Scottish Executive out to ruin the traditional family?" Warner frothed: "A parliament which was supposed to busy itself with improving health, education and other vital services, in close partnership with the Scottish people, has become totally obsessed with a politically correct crusade to alter the moral map of Scotland beyond recognition".

Professor J P Duguid from Inverness wrote to the *Scotsman* to offer his guidance on marriage. "Women should be persuaded not to have children until they obtain a reliable, supportive husband, and unmarried pregnant girls should offer their newborn babies for adoption. However desirable may be the self-esteem of unmarried mothers and homosexual youths, it is less

The Results

important than the good upbringing of the majority of children and future citizens".

After senior Ministers confided in the *Scottish Daily Express* their readiness to accept that non-legal guidelines should stress the importance of marriage, the tabloid lost its patience. The editorial slammed the Executive, calling it "spineless". Referring to Brian Souter the front page begged: "PLEASE GET HIM OFF OUR BACKS..." and fumed at the Executive's prevaricating, suggesting: "...They should have met fire with fire".

By Friday, 2 June 2000, Section 28 was still top of the news agenda in Scotland. The press pounced on Cardinal Winning's article, marking his 75th birthday in the *Scottish Catholic Observer*. He wrote: "I am ashamed of our politicians and the way they have behaved and the things that they have done over the last year. I think it has been an utter failure... They can talk as much as they like about what they have achieved but in the big issues they have achieved nothing. They have given me the impression that there is a very liberal agenda out there and come hell or high water they are going to see it through and they are aided and abetted by many of the people in the media". Aiding and abetting Winning, Scotland's biggest-selling tabloid, the *Record* quoted him saying: "It's up to society to show that they do not accept the libertarian agenda the Parliament are proposing... Gay sex is wrong, because such behaviour is not good for the human person. Far from liberating a person, it ensnares them in a lifestyle that can never respond to the deepest longings of the human heart". As he strengthened the growing alliance with other churches, Winning defended Brian Souter: "He is not trying to ram things down other people's throats. He is just promoting the Kingdom of God which is equally valid to the Muslims, the Hindus and the Sikhs".

Aberdeen's *Press and Journal* picked up on the comments of Canon Kenyon Wright, a veteran devolution campaigner, when he called Winning's comments a "gross exaggeration".

Pop star Elton John hit back at Winning in the *Spectator* magazine. "Cardinal Winning, and his ignorance, is totally representative of why people are turning away from the Church. I am astonished to be told by Cardinal Winning that my sexuality is not good for me. He argues that homosexuality 'ensnares them in a lifestyle that can never respond to the deepest longings of the human heart'. From what practical perspective does he form this point of view? As a cardinal and presumably a celibate and solitary individual, how can he possibly be in a position to judge...? The reality is that homosexuals have no choice - and no amount of hectoring or hypnosis can make us change". The *Scottish Sun* reported that Sir Elton "who openly admits he is gay" took a "pop at Winning", while the 'Sexfinder General', Monsignor Tom Connolly added: "We would say that Sir Elton's views are eminently predictable. The Cardinal would not wish to dignify them with a response".

The *Scotsman's* editorial blasted Winning for his "absolutist" tone that smacked "of the language of the United States' so-called Christian Right - a tone that does not belong in the more mature world of British politics". Skipping over the taxbreaks and millions of taxpayers' money spent annually on religion in the NHS and education, the editorial rather surprisingly suggested "perhaps the executive was mistaken in allowing Section 28 to become such a defining issue in its first term, ahead of the things that affect us all, such as health and education". Even the right-wing *Daily Telegraph's* commentator admitted other business had to go on while the media was transfixed by the Section 28 circus. The *Scottish Mirror's* editorial called Winning a "sour Father" and the *Scottish Express* blasted: "We elect our politicians and we can dismiss them from office if they do not please us. We cannot do the same with churchmen". Backing Winning's remarks, the *Scottish Mail,* on the other hand, insisted: "He is right. With some honourable exceptions, sections of the Scottish media have in their eagerness to embrace the so-called New Scotland creed, allowed themselves to be carried along on the bandwagon of political correctness driven by the Scottish Executive and parliament". Forgetting for one moment the purpose of the *Thought for the Day* slot, reserved exclusively for religionists, they added: "Even BBC Radio's Good Morning Scotland has become infected with this propagandist attitude". They quoted a Catholic Church spokesman who told them: "It is unacceptable for the slot to be abused in such a way that the genuinely felt concerns of the vast majority of Scotland's Christians are being rubbished". Hamish Macdonell had his copy boxed-in with his portrait, borrowing eighties Tory jargon to illustrate his view on "the Holyrood obsession with the politically-correct at the expense of the politically important". He complained "liberalism appears to

The Results

be running riot", adding, "Ministers declared Section 28 a 'badge of shame' and immediately alienated anybody who wanted to see it retained".

The *Times* Scottish Political Reporter Jason Allardyce suggested Winning's comments had put the Executive under "severe strain" and believed "the erosion of Catholic support for Labour could lead to the loss of Scottish Parliament and Westminster seats". Allardyce was referring to the west of Scotland, where the SNP posed "a strong challenge". An influential group within the Catholic Church had already distanced itself from Cardinal Winning's controversial attack on the Scottish Parliament and called into question whether he had, in fact, spoken for all of Scotland's Catholics. He was not - as the media persistently portrayed him – the 'leader of the Scottish Catholics' at all, but the Archbishop of Glasgow and the President of the Catholic Bishops' conference. Bishops were only sovereign within their own area. Peter Lynch, a Stirling University academic who co-edited a book on the Catholic experience in Scotland claimed all the available data showed the Catholic population quite liberal - tolerant of abortion, contraception and divorce.

Scottish editions of the *Daily Telegraph* also posted a story on Winning's comments on their front page, causing columnist Alan Cochrane to feel "condemned to write about Section 28 until the crack of doom... Try as we might, we hacks are forced to return to it again and again and again... Tony Blair and Alastair Campbell have already taken Wendy Alexander, the communities' minister, to task in the severest terms over her handling of the issue. And it would be remarkable if she were not feeling the strain. She is. Yesterday's all-out assault from the cardinal will only add to her cup of woe. So, if I have bad dreams about Sections 28, can you imagine what Wendy's nightmares are like?" Wendy Alexander denied the allegations which were most likely planted by a political rival.

Cardinal Winning's comments drew a sharp response from Ronald Campbell from Melrose in the *Herald's* letters: "Cardinal Winning's ideal past, to which he obviously wishes to take this country, is the Irish Republic of the 1950s, a grey and dismal place, ruled by the crozier, where the people suffocated - and left in their tens of thousands. There is an old saying that 'Scotland will never change until the last minister is strangled with the last copy of the Sunday Post'. It needs to be updated, and should now be: 'Scotland will never enter the modern world until the last cardinal is strangled with the last copy of The Daily Record on the last Stagecoach bus".

Russell Ramsay from Irvine had a useful question to ask in the *Herald:* "If the institution of Christian marriage is so important, why is Cardinal Winning not married? Of course, the celibacy of the priesthood is an aid to maintaining power over the flock, like the dog-collars, robes, gowns and other distinctive paraphernalia so beloved by the clergy. And if marriage and celibacy are both acceptable modes of behaviour why is celibacy not to be promoted in schools and why is it impossible for any other form of loving relationship to be accepted".

Journalist, Alan Taylor observed in *Scotland on Sunday:* "...One of the girls in The Prime of Miss Jean Brodie fantasised about eliminating sex from 'Edinburgh and environs', which would not have been difficult. Sex in those days cropped up in newspapers carefully camouflaged in euphemism. The correct technical phrases were to be found, such as 'intimacy took place' and 'plaintiff was in a certain condition'. Females who were up for sex were not called 'Miss' or 'Mrs', they were referred to by their surnames: 'Willis was remanded in custody...' 'Roebuck', said counsel, 'was discovered to be in a certain condition'. Sandy Stranger's campaign in Jean Brodie was a conspicuous failure however and, not surprisingly, she ended up in a convent".

A battle had now broken out amongst the Scottish Conservative Party ahead of an election for a deputy chairman, with the emergence of a right-wing faction. Bill Walker, the 72-year-old homophobic former MP for Tayside North announced he would be standing for the position of deputy chairman of the Party. A few weeks later and the *Scottish Mail's* Hamish Macdonell was able to report on his victory. He won with a majority of over 1,000 votes and was backed by only one of the 19 Tory MSPs, winning almost half of the 7,357 votes cast by party members. On Bill Walker's meeting with former Prime Minister Margaret Thatcher during 1999's Tory Party Conference, Macdonell wrote: "Mr Walker managed to detain the former Premier for a few seconds, long enough to tell her: 'You were wonderful, marvellous, wonderful', before Lady Thatcher was escorted away. Even as she disappeared into the distance, Mr Walker was gazing

The Results

after her, beaming and murmuring 'marvellous, wonderful' to himself'.

By Sunday, 4 June, Gerald Warner opened his *Scotland on Sunday* column with his most vitriolic attack on gays yet. "Greetings, fellow homophobes and bigots - all 1,094,440 of you!" He wrote that the Executive "has arrogated to itself the right to control the education of our children and to hand them over to the missionary zeal of the homosexual lobby. A rebarbative subculture which, until recently, carried out its cloacal practices in subterranean public lavatories, is now enthroned as a 'lifestyle' of equal - no, greater - validity than marriage. Moral considerations apart, that is a potential death sentence. During an Aids pandemic, any extension of homosexual influence is deadly. Spotty teenagers, unsure of themselves in the company of girls, will readily find a sympathetic mentor to offer them tea, sympathy and a reappraisal of their sexual orientation. Homosexual recruiting sergeants have the persistence of Mormons. Once insecure youths have been inveigled, the next Big Lie is the myth of 'safe sex'. For legal reasons, this term has lately been modified to 'safer sex' - the condom culture. Prophylactics were designed to act as barriers to human sperm which, in relation to the HIV virus, resembles the Loch Ness Monster in size. The virus measures 1-10,000th part of a millimetre, while the inherent flaws in latex rubber are more than 50 times larger. It is like driving a golf-ball into a football net. You will not find homosexual activists advertising this fact to confused youngsters: 'Come on in, the water's lovely!' is the message". His disgust at the apparent failure of the Executive, with its "assorted bidie-ins", (an Aberdeen expression referring to unmarried couples living together), "social includers and fag hags" to give legal status to marriage over and above all other relationships to children in schools was encapsulated in more homophobic mocking. "Marriage? Ye gods! Isn't that something that chaps do in public conveniences and then have to resign from their clubs?" On the "ghastly neologism... 'Homophobe'," he castigated "Tory and other pro-Clause spokesmen" for infuriating the public "by spending four and a half minutes explaining that they are not 'homophobes' and about 30 seconds expounding their case. That is as hypocritical as the Executive's ludicrous claims". He was adamant that "the majority of people are indeed so-called homophobes - with good reason". A "healthy and natural fear - of the corruption of children and of an aggressive minority representing 2.8% of the population gaining a disproportionate influence in government..." A letter to the editor from David C Purdie of Loanhead appeared the following week: "I have been respectably married to the same member of the opposite sex for over three decades... Gerald Warner has... scaled the heights of splenetic invective and plumbed the depths of prejudice and mendacity. His piece was nauseating, irrational and totally unacceptable in any paper which lays claim to being a quality broadsheet".

My letter to *Scotland on Sunday's* editor, John McGurk asked them to correct the statement that HIV can enter condoms like "a golf ball into a football net". All the best scientific evidence categorically states that condoms are the best protection against the virus. A letter appeared beneath mine from (Rev) Alex Muir from Inverness who wrote: "He and His Son exclusively and hurtfully insist that sexual intercourse should be confined to heterosexual monogamous marriage". Muir warned ministers at the General Assembly that if they believe in the Day of Judgement, "they must be hoping that they'll meet, not their God and Father of the Lord Jesus Christ, but the Eternal Essence of Political Correctness or some such being". Ronald J MacDonald responded to my letter the following week: "As totally safe abstinence from homosexual intercourse is apparently not an option for Garry Otton, his touching faith in inherently flawed condoms as the best protection against HIV which science can provide served merely to confirm the frightening complacency which has led, and which will continue to result, in the early deaths of millions".

The World Health Organisation (WHO) has made it clear that the male latex condom is the single, most efficient, available technology to reduce the sexual transmission of HIV and other sexually transmitted infections and a critical element in a comprehensive, effective and sustainable approach to HIV prevention and treatment.

Old Mother Burnie gave her response to a "petrified" man who thought he might already have contracted the HIV virus through unsafe sex in South Africa in her problem page in the *Record*. "...Married men should keep their zips up, shouldn't they? That's the best protection going".

The Results

In the *Scottish Mail on Sunday*, representing the Glasgow Kelvinside constituency, Westminster MP George Galloway made Scottish television news after challenging Brian Souter in his column: "Instead of lurking behind his billboards and his big money, he could stand against me at the general election. After all, my constituency is a near perfect microcosm of the new Scotland; home to playwrights and shipwrights, caulkers and burners from the Clyde yards to 'fancy dancers' from the Royal Scottish Ballet. My constituency has some of the best and some of the worst housing in Scotland, some of the richest and most expensively educated people and some of the poorest in the land. Don't 'target' me Brian; put your name on the ballot paper against me, and subject yourself to the same spending limits as other democratic election candidates. I think it's time to lance this boil of big money. Now don't be a 'sissy', Soapy, come out and fight me like a man". Jack Irvine accused George Galloway in the *Record* of acting "like a dance hall ned" and reminded him: "One little word and we could all pack our bags and go home - marriage". He told the *Sunday Herald*: "I can categorically state that Brian will not stand for parliament, ever, but if George wants to resign and fight a by-election over the issue I'm sure that someone from Keep the Clause, or one of the ethnic groups, will be happy to take him up on it". Jack Irvine added cosily: "Brian and I are holding our fire at the moment".

By 2010, a Muslim was indeed standing in George Galloway's former constituency for the SNP, the political party backed by Brian Souter.

Whatever George Galloway thought about Brian Souter, Section 28 was an issue he felt Labour should have compromised over. He told the press he would not have prioritised the repeal, saying: "It sent out the wrong message…" The MP warned: "I think the mixture of big money and bigotry has to be guarded against and fought because now it has become a sort of Frankenstein's monster. It started as a slightly eccentric Scottish businessman who had a point of view concerning regulations on sex education. Now it's become a nascent, US-style Moral Majority campaign. Power has intoxicated Souter and those around him… It is homosexuals today, it could be Catholics tomorrow, it could be immigrants, it could be refugees, it could be Muslims, it could be anything. It could be any minority, and that is the point". After Galloway became an MP and leader of the Respect political party for Bethnal Green and Bow, some members were forced to pass a motion at the party conference calling it unacceptable that their manifesto didn't contain any reference to gay equality which opponents claimed was a compromise to appease Muslim voters and Respect's main donor, Dr Mohammed Naseem of the Islamic Party of Britain.

Jack Irvine's full-page advertisement for Media House in media magazine the *Drum* quoted the *Scottish Mirror's* Lorraine Davidson, who had asked how Jack Irvine could "single-handedly" dominate the Scottish news agenda for so long. Irvine used his advertisement to brag: "We gave the client and the media what they wanted. The only person who didn't get what they wanted was you".

Scotland on Sunday reported how Souter was planning a new set of "hard-hitting" posters to go up in Scotland's central belt, where he found support. He said: "The issue we are going to draw attention to is that the New Labour Scottish Executive does not believe that marriage is central to the teaching of sex education". The *Sunday Herald* reported that the "opening salvo" had been fired "in an electoral battle between moral fundamentalism and mainstream politics in Scotland with the millionaire Brian Souter threatening to fund candidates to stand against sitting Labour MPs". Souter warned: "The parliamentary voting records of Scottish MPs are to be checked in the coming weeks to judge their record on family values".

Svetlana Rolink, a pro-marriage fanatic from Airdrie, travelled to the Scottish Executive in a horse and carriage, wearing a wedding dress and a Wendy Alexander mask, to hand them her suggestions on how the Executive could promote marriage.

Wendy Alexander responded to Brian Souter's morality campaign in the *Sunday Mail* saying: "It can only lead to closed minds and cold hearts. Money should not buy influence. If the principles of the religious right were to run riot in Scotland, we'd ban abortion, label kids illegitimate and restore hanging, all in the name of family values..." The *Sunday Mail* drew an analogy with US multi-millionaire Howard Ahmanson Junior who promoted family values. "He pumps money into Colorado-based group Focus on the Family, which shares Souter's beliefs on gay rights and abortion, is against gun control and rejects the theory of evolution".

The Results

Iain Macwhirter also attacked the Executive in the *Sunday Herald*: "They've drawn so many lines in the sand, only to abandon them. At first, ministers said last November that the guidelines on sex education were adequate and would not be reviewed. Now they are being reviewed by the McCabe committee. In February, the Scottish Executive said there would be no replacement clause for Section 28. In March they tabled one. In April, ministers were adamant that the guidelines on sex education would not be made legally binding. In May the Executive made the guidance statutory. Finally, we were assured by Donald Dewar that there would be no inclusion of marriage in any guidelines. It looks as if there will be before June is out... If we have ministers sitting weekly in 'cabinet' then the least we can expect is that they do what ministers are paid to do: govern. Instead, we have the pathetic hole-in-the-wall gang of ex-cooncillors fixing and botching. The men who run the inner cabinet of the Executive have instincts and reflexes wholly unsuited to their new role".

The Scottish Executive showed weakness and naïvety in caving in to the demands of those who supported the promotion of marriage when they should have learnt the lessons of their counterparts in Westminster. In the Houses of Parliament, the repeal of Section 28 had been utterly botched by a lack of commitment to reform; allowing the legislation to originate from the House of Lords and not the House of Commons, where the Government could have used the Parliament Act to force it past Baroness Young and her militant Christian-inspired blockade.

David Aaronovitch gave a wry view from London for the *Sunday Herald*. "What is going on up there? We English can hardly hear ourselves think for you lot quarrelling... Those on the left had been hoping Scotland could set an example in creating a modern, liberal, social democracy. To be honest, we thought you were better than us... We'd forgotten the other Scotland: the censorious, puritanical country of priests and ghillies... You've somehow allowed the national debate to become dominated by cardinals and tycoons - and the secular Burns, who would have repealed Section 28 with a gay wave of his pen, to be out-shouted by John Knox... Churches are given privileged treatment. Their fundraising has charitable status; their schools are allowed state subsidies. If they are to become involved in politics, this must change. But who in Scotland is arguing for this?"

RELIGIOUS FASCISM

On Monday, 5 June 2000, Ian Smith reported in the *Scottish Daily Mail:* "Family values campaigners are preparing to turn the next General Election into a battleground over sexual morality by putting up independent candidates. A number of family values groups, which have mushroomed since the Scottish Executive's decision to repeal Section 28, are meeting in Glasgow tonight to draw up a strategy". These were Ayub Khan's Multi-Faith Coalition, Patrick Rolink of the Airdrie Family Action Group, and Hugh Lynch of the Falkirk-based Family Action Movement. Both Rolink and Lynch headed the 'Keep the Clause' roadshows. In the *Scotsman*, Ian Maxwell of One Parent Families Scotland wrote to the editor expressing his disappointment at not being invited to their strategy meeting.

In yet another special supplement of letters concerning Section 28, Isobel Lindsay from Biggar wrote to the *Herald* to say: "If the Parliament supports a legal obligation on schools to promote marriage, among the first victims of this witch-hunt are likely to be teachers. The logic will be that if teachers have a legal obligation to promote marriage, they will be unable to do this if pupils know they are divorced or living outwith marriage with a sexual partner".

Ian O'Bayne from Glasgow wrote suggesting: "...The apparent belief of the 'Keep the Clause' campaigners that the private behaviour and lifestyle choices of young people in Scotland today can be significantly affected either by the retention of 'Section 28' or (now) by the substitution of carefully constructed sex-education guidelines is about as realistic as the medieval conviction that the earth is flat".

Mark Park from East Kilbride asked the *Herald:* "Are we to return to the days of stigmatising children born out of wedlock, incarcerating single mothers in asylums, and visiting their so-called sins on innocent children?"

The *Sunday Herald* printed an open letter sent in by Tony Gurney: "When I burn a bull on the altar as a sacrifice, I know it creates a pleasing odour for the Lord (Leviticus 1:9). The problem is my neighbours. They claim the odour is not pleasing to them. How should I deal with this? I would also like to sell my daughter into slavery, as it suggests in Exodus 21:7. In this day and age, what do you think would be a fair price for her? I know I am allowed no contact with a woman while she is in her period of menstrual uncleanliness (Lev. 15:19-24). The problem is, how

The Results

do I tell? I have tried asking, but most women take offence. Lev. 25:44 states that I may buy slaves from the nations around us. A friend of mine claims this applies to the English but not the Irish. Can you clarify? Then there is my neighbour, who insists on working on the Sabbath. Exodus 35:2 clearly states he should be put to death. Am I morally obligated to kill him myself? A friend of mine feels that even though eating shellfish is an abomination (Lev. 10:10), it is a lesser abomination than homosexuality. I don't agree. Can you settle this? And Lev. 20:20 states that I may not approach the altar of God if I have a defect in my sight. I have to admit that I wear reading glasses. Does my vision have to be 20/20, or is there some wiggle room here?"

With the battle to repeal Section 28 in mind and after seeing London's holocaust exhibition at the Imperial War Museum, human rights campaigner, Peter Tatchell was sufficiently moved to remark: "Never again? Fifty-five years after the defeat of Nazism, minorities are still being scapegoated and demonised - even in Britain". The previous day, in New Cross, London, Dutch-born gay florist Jaap Bornkamp was stabbed to death in a homophobic attack. It was a tragic shock to his aged mother and his sister Gerda Bos who begged for support in solving the murder. Two days later, on Tuesday, 6 June, David Copeland filled the papers again with his appearance in court, fourteen months after he had bombed a gay bar in London's Soho.

The *Scottish Sun* carried a story of alleged censorship in the in-house magazine of the Scottish Parliament: "A magazine aimed at Scotland's MSPs has dumped a Keep the Clause advert in case it upsets Wendy Alexander and the Scottish Executive". *Holyrood* magazine editor John Macgill supposedly "dropped the ad because he feared a Labour backlash". The *Record* declared: "Government chiefs were last night accused of bullying a tiny magazine..." after it dropped its £1,500 full-page ad on the back page. The cartoon depicted Brian Souter, Jack Irvine, a member of the ethnic community and a million voters of Souter's 'referendum' trailing behind the Saltire while MSPs Donald Dewar, Jim Wallace, Wendy Alexander, Sam Galbraith and Susan Deacon were pictured in grey, holding what looked like a tattered white flag of surrender at half-mast. It was an opportunity for the *Record* to remind readers: "Ministers are scared over the backlash from the million Scots who voted against their plans to allow gay sex lessons in classroom".

RELIGIOUS FASCISM

'Brigadier' Brown, who also wrote regularly for *Holyrood* magazine, resigned from the magazine in a huff. He told the *Record* where he had a regular column: "Acting in this manner goes against everything I have believed in for all these years". (The *Record* otherwise censored personal ads submitted by lesbian, gay, bisexual and people of transgender). *Holyrood* editor John Macgill explained that he pulled it because he didn't like the advert, which, as an editor, was entirely his prerogative. The *Scottish Mail* accused the magazine of "compromising its editorial independence" and a spokesman for 'Keep the Clause' told them: "It is a sad day when the politicians are trying to silence free speech and open debate in this way".

On Wednesday, 7 June, MSP Brian Adam's attempt to have marriage included in school guidelines on sex education failed. The *Record's* letters' page, Voice of Scotland, carried two letters denouncing Wendy Alexander. The next day, the event was overshadowed by a sea of floral print on the front page of the *Daily Mail* as "stony faced and pinched-lipped" members of the Jerusalem and jam-pot Women's Institute "...HUMILIATED A PRIME MINISTER". A small minority who encouraged slow-handclapping and heckling of their guest speaker, Tony Blair, had led the protest. The 'Brigadier' told *Record* readers he thought; "it shows something wonderful has happened to the WI", and 'Old Mother' Burnie cried: "If ever there's another world war, I think I know who I want on the front line - the ladies of the Women's Institute. They are national treasures... Quite what Tony Blair thought he was doing lecturing that lot with his empty platitudes beats me. You don't patronise dames like these with spin-doctor speak about family values. They live those values, Tony. They've done their best to instil them in their children and their grandchildren - and then had to watch as the politicians undermined it all, bit by bit or even clause by clause". Alastair Campbell, the Prime Minister's official spokesman took most of the blame and subsequently spent less time briefing the press amid growing criticism of New Labour's spin-machine.

As the repeal of Section 28 drew closer, the *Record* declared: "Time is now running out for campaigners battling the repeal of Section 28". The tabloid turned on the Liberal Democrat MSP for Mid Scotland and Fife, Keith Raffan, who woke up to the headline: "WE KNOW WHERE YOU LIVE, MATE!" Carlos Alba reported how "retired engineer George Lyndsay" had been

The Results

"stunned" and "open-mouthed" after his MSP had called on him at his home, supposedly, "to give him a dressing down over Clause 28". The *Record* headlined: "HEAVY-HANDED: SECTION 28 BACKER TOLD TO STICK TO GARDENING". Keith Raffan pointlessly tried to explain to the *Record* that he had been receiving e-mails from Mr Lyndsay that had become "increasingly immoderate, over-the-top, intemperate in language and, quite frankly, offensive. I went to see him because I thought that was the best way of dealing with it because he was e-mailing me two or three times a week". Mr Lyndsay otherwise claimed: "He had come to tell me personally that my letter was offensive and insulting. He then went on to slate Brian Souter. He thought he had got his comeuppance because his share prices were falling. He said Cardinal Winning was a bigot who speaks for a very small minority in the Catholic Church. Then he went on to say he was surprised I was as young as I am because the views I hold are normally associated with older people". The tabloid picked up the story again a few days later when they discovered, as a former Tory MP in 1987, Raffan had voted for Section 28. The *Record* jeered: "He even voted down a Labour amendment which sought to discourage 'discrimination against any homosexual person' and 'to protect the civil rights of any such person'." A spokesman for 'Keep the Clause' advised the *Record*: "politicians adopt the mantle of political correctness when it suits them". The same could have been said of the *Record* which, before Martin Clarke took over the reigns, described Section 28 as a "backward and repressive measure... very nasty prejudices creeping out of the woodwork..." and "a sledgehammer to crack a few nuts".

Agony Aunt 'Old Mother' Burnie's 'Your Life' page featured a woman who had written to her for advice on her son who had "suddenly decided he's gay". It wasn't so much the advice that deserved criticism as the accompanying picture produced by the *Record* of a young man in a frilly pinafore pouring a cup of tea with the caption: "I hope they can accept me the way I am".

As "thousands" of people attended Pentecost 2000, billed as the biggest multi-faith Christian gathering in Scotland, at Hampden Park in Glasgow, the *Record* advertised how religion was good for your sex life. Following research by Dr Tim LaHaye in Los Angeles, they declared: "Religious wives have sex more often and enjoy it more than non-religious married women..."

Labour MP Ben Bradshaw reported Christian Action Research and Education (CARE) - an organisation widely used by the Scottish press - to the Charity Commission after it withdrew a female student intern from his office because the MP was openly gay. CARE was already under investigation by the parliamentary commissioner for standards, Elizabeth Filkin, for supplying parliamentary researchers to MPs. With funds of around £3m annually, the Christian organisation was opposed, amongst other things, to sex outside marriage. They also advised children not to take part in Hallowe'en trick-or-treating since they believed it to be satanic in origin. Bradshaw was subjected to an "interrogation" by two CARE officers who asked questions about his sexuality. Other MPs working with graduates supported by CARE at this time were Labour Treasury minister Stephen Timms, David Stewart and Andy King; Tory MPs Gary Streeter, Caroline Spelman and James Gray, and, of the Lib-Dems, Alan Beith and Professor Steven Webb.

By 2012, a group of scientists in Glasgow, calling themselves C4ID, were in schools promoting Intelligent Design and creationism, a belief the world was created in six days. Financially based in Guernsey, its supporters believed that Noah's Ark was real and women were made from Adam's rib. The group's president was Professor Norman Nevin OBE, a geneticist at Queen's University in Belfast, and its vice-president was Dr David Galloway, a vice-president of the Royal College of Physicians and Surgeons and a member of the Lennox Evangelical Church in Dumbarton. Their director, a former HM inspector of schools and education officer for CARE, Dr Alastair Noble, told the *Sunday Herald:* "We are definitely not targeting schools, but that doesn't mean to say we may not produce resources that go to schools". He also denied this was in any way religious, adding: "I think people are afraid of this debate because they sense it's religion from the back door. They see it as an invasion of science with religion, but it most certainly is not that". No formal guidance existed in Scotland to stop creationism being taught as fact in schools.

By Saturday, 10 June, at the important Educational Institute of Scotland's (EIS) annual conference in Dundee, the EIS voted overwhelmingly in support of the abolition of Section 28. It went

The Results

unreported in the *Record*. Jim Whannel, a gay human rights supporter and Glasgow primary headteacher told the conference how 'Keep the Clause' was a low point in Scottish history: "What they have done is try to create an artificial danger, and then suggest measures to try to prevent this danger. The cardinal talks about perversion. There is no greater perversion in society than incitement to hatred, and that is what we must resist". Ronnie Smith, the general secretary of EIS said: "The simple truth is that, before the clause was enacted, during its existence and after its repeal, teachers always have handled - and will continue to handle - issues surrounding sex education and sexuality with a high degree of sensitivity and professional care... We are on dangerous ground here. Schools are places of learning and they must never be allowed to become the battlefield upon which politicians fight to save their political face, or others play out their dreams for what they think is their ideal society".

While the debate smouldered, the *Sunday Mail* reported a blackmail attempt after 54-year-old Agnes Imrie threatened to hand over a compromising gay video of Allan Parker, a manager of a Lloyds TSB bank in Glasgow's Byers Road, to his employers. The father of a six-year-old boy, Parker had been married to her daughter Carol for five years. His mother-in-law was said to have been incensed at having forked out thousands of pounds for what turned out to be a sham wedding. Parker called the police and they gave him a case of real bank notes on top of blank ones to hand over to her. Agnes Imrie was arrested. The *Sunday Mail* reported: "Parker has bought a luxury flat in the trendy Merchant City area of Glasgow, which is now a popular district of gays".

On Monday, 12 June, both the *Record* and *Scottish Mail* warned thousands of children would be withdrawn from schools if sex education guidelines to replace Section 28 did not give marriage enough prominence. The *Record* described this as a "new threat" by the Multi-Faith Coalition, an ethnic alliance of Muslims, Hindus, Sikhs and some other faiths that would result in children being placed in Catholic schools if there was "any hint of homosexuality being promoted in the new guidelines". A spokesman for 'Keep the Clause' told the *Record:* "If the committee do not recognise marriage in the hierarchy of relationships, the war will go on". It was an interesting new alliance, especially given when in only a few months the Italian press would be awash with news of how Cardinal Biffi had called for Muslims to be barred from Italy "to save the country's identity". He said: "Europe must return to Christianity or Islam will win". His comments came only a week after the Vatican declared that non-Catholic churches and faiths were "defective". Far from distancing itself from Cardinal Biffi's views, the Vatican called him "one of Italy's most important theologians".

By Wednesday, immune from any legal restraints and vindicated by the London-based Advertising Standards Authority, new billboard posters went up over Scotland. "POLITICALLY CORRECT MADNESS" they bellowed in the familiar red on black. With a torn photo of a couple at the altar the poster spat: "THIS GOVERNMENT THINKS IT'S ACCEPTABLE TO PROMOTE HOMOSEXUALITY, BUT NOT MARRIAGE!" In the *Scottish Mail*, Jack Irvine said: "Every time we use a hard-hitting message it seems to drive our message home. The latest campaign is another weapon in our armoury". The *Mail* reported how vans featuring the posters were circling the Scottish parliament building.

Labour MSPs were paged to attend an emergency meeting on Thursday, and by the next day, Friday, 16 June, Section 28 once again dominated the front pages of the Scottish press as the Government made yet another concession.

The *Daily Record* gloated from its front page: "KIDS WILL BE TAUGHT MARRIAGE".

Chapter Eight
Keeping Marriage and Schools for Christians

But you've gotta make your own kind of music
Sing your own special song,
Make your own kind of music even if nobody
Else sings along".
Mamas and Papas

Caving-in to the demands of Christian campaigners demanding the promotion of heterosexual marriage, the McCabe committee – excluding gays, but not religionists - put aside recommendations for non-legally binding guidelines; agreeing instead to uphold the importance of marriage and parenting in legally binding guidance issued to all Scottish schools. The reference to 'stable family relationships' would remain in the guidelines. Some saw this as a botched exercise in semantics. "Government in amazing Section 28 climbdown", the *Daily Record* crowed with a picture of Souter's now familiar face sternly looking out from the cover. The tabloid reported: "Labour backbenchers attended a secret meeting last night to rubber stamp the dramatic move which comes after pressure from the Keep the Clause campaign funded by Stagecoach tycoon Brian Souter". With it being still light after 10pm, the words "last night" looked strangely out of place in early editions distributed by children to cars stopping at traffic lights, to pub customers or people on the streets. The *Record* editorial in later editions declared: "At last they see sense... Inch by reluctant inch, the Scottish government is being forced in the direction of a sensible stance on Section 28... The committee they set up in a public relations attempt to spike Brian Souter's national referendum has favoured the parents and the one-million-plus who voted to Keep the Clause". And, following the advice of Keep the Clause almost word for word, they added: "It would still be wise to wait and be sure the formula on marriage is acceptable - and, most importantly, is written into the guidance, which is enforceable in law". The *Record* was quite satisfied "the government impaled themselves on a sword of their own making... all because they couldn't bring themselves to use the word 'marriage'." Scottish Education Minister, Sam Galbraith said: "We never, ever ruled out statutory guid-*ance*. Guide-*lines* are the contents, guid-*ance* is about the conduct, and that's important".

The 50-page report contained the key-phrase in a section headed: "Effective Sex Education". Local authorities would legally be required to observe "an awareness of the importance of stable family life and relationships including the responsibilities of parenthood and marriage". Under the heading: 'Social Inclusion and Diversity', this is what it said: -

2.53 Scotland is a diverse society. Within that society, there is a range of different family relationships. The most common relationship is that of marriage. This is supported by churches, religious groups and others in Scottish society. They see marriage as the ideal to which they aspire. However, others in Scottish society have different styles of relationships and family life which they regard as equally valid.

2.54 Teachers will be aware that each class will contain pupils from a variety of family backgrounds. Teachers should ensure that they treat all children with respect and sensitivity when covering these areas of the curriculum. Lack of awareness of diversity can lead to prejudice and discrimination which may lead to bullying. Bullying of any type affects self-esteem and can impact on educational achievement.

2.55 School sex education has a role to play at the appropriate age and stage in discussing the myths and stereotypes around gender, sexuality and sexual orientation issues, both as a means of preventing harassment and bullying and as an opportunity to engender a respect for and understanding of diversity.

2.56 School sex education needs to be sensitive to the fact that young people may find it particularly difficult to speak openly with their parents or carers about their sex, sexuality and sexual orientation matters. It is therefore important that school sex education provides accurate and factual information about sexuality and sexual orientation matters as well as developing a strong anti-bullying stance on this matter.

2.57 Children living in a range of different family groupings might also be vulnerable to bullying as a result of their home circumstances and schools should be aware of the needs of these children and give sensitive recognition to their family units. Schools, parents and pupils can refer to the Anti-Bullying Network for advice and guidance on these matters.

On 'Sexual orientation' the report said: -

5.25 As young people mature, they experience a range of feelings which affect their attitudes, behaviours and personal relationships.

5.26 As they enter adolescence, most begin to develop feelings of a sexual nature towards members of the opposite sex. Some develop similar feelings towards members of their own sex. Some young people become aware of their sexual orientation at a relatively early age while others take longer. For a number, the process is fraught with uncertainty, confusion and anxiety. It is important that teachers show understanding of these issues and are sensitive to protecting and supporting vulnerable young people as they come to terms with their feelings and work out how best to deal with them.

5.27 All young people should be helped to understand, at an appropriate age, that different people can have different sexual orientations. Teachers have an important role to play in enabling young people to consider such issues and to discuss them in an open, sensitive and non-discriminatory way in order that all young people may develop understanding of these differences. The central purpose should be to promote understanding and mutual respect for one another, regardless of orientation. This approach is considered an important way of encouraging respect for and valuing the diversity of, human life.

5.28 Opportunities for discussion may arise within class through a planned session on relationships or sexual development; through a response to a specific incident or as a result of an incidental question or comment by a pupil. Teachers may be approached by an individual pupil regarding concern about the pupil's sexual orientation; teachers should respond in a similar manner, i.e. sensitive and non-judgemental and, where appropriate, indicate sources of support either within the school or external to the school.

The central recommendations of the working group were laid out in the report: -
1. The Scottish Executive should adopt the key principles and aims for sex education identified by this Working Group, incorporate them in the guidance circular, and consult on the terms of this guidance.
2. Summary guidance on available curricular advice and materials should be developed by the Scottish Executive and be made available to schools.
3. The Scottish Executive should offer guidance to local authorities and schools on effective consultation with parents.
4. The Scottish Executive should produce a parent's leaflet explaining the nature and purpose of sex education, its place within health education, and the importance of its relationship to Personal and Social Education and Religious and Moral Education. This should be available in Braille and other languages.
5. The Scottish Executive should organise seminars for key personnel from local authorities to help prepare the local response to the statutory guidance.

The *Scottish Sun's* headlined beamed: "SECTION 28 CAVE-IN..." and reported, "Repeal of Section 28 is expected to go through on Wednesday. But the Executive has already been forced into a string of concessions over safeguards for schoolchildren. Education Minister Sam Galbraith has so far agreed to legally enforce guidance which gives parents the right to veto sex education. Now marriage will be included in the same legal framework". The *Sun* boasted: "Ms Alexander and fellow ministers claimed to have 80 per cent support for repeal until the Scottish Sun revealed they had lobbied gay clubs and the British Potato Council but not school boards".

The *Scottish Daily Mail* trumpeted: "MARRIAGE BROUGHT BACK IN SECTION 28 U-TURN". Hamish Mcdonell quoted Brian Souter who crowed: "The power of public opinion has triumphed". He insisted that the concession "will be viewed with anger and disappointment by the gay lobby". The paper soon began describing it as "a clause stressing the importance of marriage".

Although its editorial tried to back its headline: "A VICTORY FOR COMMON SENSE" in its Saturday edition, there could be no concealing the *Daily Record's* bitterness over its

Keeping Marriage and Schools for Christians

failure to keep the Clause. They suggested 'Keep the Clause' had been "fully vindicated", and claimed they were "toasting victory" while brushing over the fact Brian Souter hadn't even managed to get "the importance of marriage" written into statute let alone keep the clause! The editorial snapped: "Education Minister Sam Galbraith, Communities Minister Wendy Alexander and Health Minister Susan Deacon are lucky they have not been made to pay the price for their political ineptitude and pig-headedness. They spat in the face of public opinion and are left looking incompetent". The sound of popping corks was replaced by a grumbling editorial admonishing how the key principles and aims for sex education "leave a lot to be desired. Bluntly, they tend towards politically-correct mush... The fine line between discussing homosexuality and active approval - the promotion of homosexuality in the classroom which took Scottish parents to the barricades in the first place - is still there". The *Record* warned: "The bottom line is that Section 28 is being repealed. From now on, it is for parents to make sure their children are taught what they want them to be taught - and, after all the public fury, woe betide any school that pushes too far". The editorial added in bold letters: "PARENTS MUST STAY ON ALERT". Reporter Carlos Alba insisted: "Teachers will be told to stress the value of marriage..." although marriage was unlikely to get treated any differently from other relationships. The *Record* also reported that Wendy Alexander "said she was willing to accept defeat" when what she actually said was: "I believe we have a unanimous recommendation from the working party which we will be delighted to accept".

The *Scottish Sun* was disappointed Wendy Alexander told 120 politicians, policemen and community workers at Strathclyde University: "Yet again we have newspapers obsessed with the Section 28 issue. You may have heard that the Parliament is arrogant - even that some Ministers are arrogant. It's a press myth!" The *Scottish Sun* featured a photograph of Wendy Alexander pursing her lips and a bold headline calling her: "TWO-FACED WENDY".

The *Record* reported how in England: "...The Government have given in on two key areas in the row over sex education in schools. Out goes a reference to 'stable relationships' which Keep the Clause campaigners fear would give gay partnerships exactly the same status as marriage. In comes a new power which will allow school governors and head teachers to ban material from AIDS helplines, health centres or family planning clinics which they fear could influence youngsters during a vulnerable time in their lives. The concessions have been made in the Learning and Skills Bill".

After the Scottish Education Minister, Sam Galbraith, issued his statement of acceptance of the committee's findings; he refused to be photographed with Cardinal Winning when he coincidentally attended the same function as him in Bishopbriggs, outside Glasgow. The pro-Section-28 campaigners spoke in unison. Brian Souter told the *Record:* "After a long, hard battle, I am relieved common sense has finally prevailed". The *Scottish Mail* reported Conservative Brian Monteith insisting: "Wendy Alexander, the High Priestess of Political Correctness is now in an untenable position". The *Scottish Express* reported Cardinal Winning's spokesman Ronnie Convery's reaction to the committee's findings: "Today is a victory for common sense. We would have preferred that the Clause remained, but we consider it significant that marriage is to be enshrined in statute". In the same paper, the SNPs Nicola Sturgeon said: "I believe the debate can be settled on this basis..." Ann Allen from the Kirk's Board of Social Responsibility said: "This would give a very positive message and clear indication of the importance of marriage in our society..." The Scottish Schools' Board Association, which had a member on the committee, said: "Back in January, this is what we were asking for and the working party has certainly delivered" while Tory MSP Phil Gallie grunted: "...What the Executive should be doing is simply burying their ideas and leaving Section 28 well alone".

The *Scottish Daily Mail's* editorial also issued warnings to parents. "The parents and other concerned citizens of Scotland - Scottish Daily Mail readers prominent among them - have slowed but not halted the juggernaut of political correctness. To that extent, there are grounds for satisfaction. Public gratitude is also due to Brian Souter, Cardinal Winning and the many other people who contributed to the limited victory that this Government concession represents". After investing so much time and energy in their mendacious campaign, the *Scottish Mail* was also bitter. "Moreover, the fact remains that Section 28 - the legal safeguard against the promotion of homosexuality - will be repealed. The onus now lies with vigilant parents to protest if a local authority breaches the new guidance on sex education". The *Scottish Mail* reported: "The compromise was largely down to the persuasive powers of one man - John Oates, the Catholic Church's representative on the working party reviewing the guidelines". Under the heading "forced to end the fighting", the tabloid also reported: "Government sources in London disclosed the Prime Minister's advisers exerted pressure on the Scottish Executive to head off the damaging row over Section 28..." Tony Blair had been in Scotland the previous day but refused to answer questions on Section 28 when he paid a visit to Donald Dewar, still recovering after his heart operation.

The *Scottish Daily Express* believed Wendy Alexander had promised repeal of Section 28: "With an arrogance which was breathtaking..." The editorial boasted how it had always hoped "sex education would be balanced and that marriage and family values would be at the core of the teaching".

In the *Scottish Daily Mail*, the ubiquitous Mrs Katie Grant wailed: "What has marriage got to do with Section 28..." or the "crusade against the largely mythical bullying of homosexuals in schools?" Quick to respond from the privilege of her major media platform, she advised: "The answer is that the liberal elite by whom we are governed, of whom Ms. Alexander is an archpriestess, never tell the full story. The full story, the true agenda, has to be dragged out of them little by little". Mrs Grant gave the 'm' word the full roses-round-the-porch treatment. "...Nobody in the Scottish Executive has spoken with conviction about the joys of marriage... To reiterate as Disraeli did, that... 'there is nothing happier than a happy marriage': or to encourage teenagers obsessed with the moment to read Laurie Lee's moving recollections of the old couple who became 'as alike as cherries, having taken and merged, through their years together, each other's looks and accents...' Removing the concept of an ideal, achievable relationship was if anything harmful rather than beneficial. Those who believe in marriage, and that includes many single parents and gay people, have suddenly realised how far the drift towards the 'anything goes' school of relationships has taken us". In tones that begged a return to the moral vigilantism of more than a century ago, Katie Grant warned: "People are now suspicious. They have now realised that behind Wendy Alexander's small frame was hidden a truck load of explosives... Let us not be complacent. That truck load of 'anything goes' explosives may be too damp to go off at present but it still remains parked just outside the school gates waiting for another opportunity". The very next day, reports circulated of the militant anti-abortion group Precious Life distributing 50,000 leaflets graphically describing terminations to children outside school gates.

Fed to children from converted buses loaded with hi-tech equipment, DVDs and printed propaganda, parked outside the school gates, Christianity had long since breached that defence to proselytise in the classroom.

In 2013, shocked parents discovered an extremist religious sect had been rubbishing evolution and brainwashing their children entirely without their knowledge for eight years. The US Church of Christ had got into a non-denominational primary school in East Kilbride in 2005 when a head teacher invited them in to minister to pupils. They targeted Kirktonholme Primary School as a "mission" and had several members helping with classes, working as classroom assistants, assisting with homework and accompanying children on activities outside the school.

The Church of Christ posted videos on Youtube suggesting that they were the only true representatives of Christianity in Scotland and it was their mission to save the rest of the country. Followers were told Scotland was a spiritual wasteland where only 700 of a population of 5.1 million were practising Christians. (The reality was that there were 700 Church of Christ parishioners in 20 branches UK-wide). The sect had also managed to infiltrate a nearby special needs school at Greenburn. Preacher Alex Gear was on the chaplaincy team at Kirktonholme Primary School and arranged for the West Mains Church of Christ to minister there.

One of the members of the church, Evelyn Graciano, 22, from Mexico, echoed Pat Robertson who had said in 1999 that Scotland was a "dark place" overrun by homosexuals when she described Scotland as "a place full of darkness and emptiness that is in a big need of Jesus". She was reported in the *Record* telling pals she used classes to get into the heads of Kirktonholme pupils saying: "They all are very receptive and willing to listen and learn. Hopefully at least we can let the kids know who Jesus is. Maybe someday that seed we've planted can be grown by God." A key member of the church's Adventures in Missions (AIMS) Team Scotland was Texan, Jared Blakeman, who sought to indoctrinate

Keeping Marriage and Schools for Christians

kids and implant the Church of Christ's version of Christianity on Scots.

The scandal only surfaced in 2013 when a five-year-old showed his parents books he was given as a present from the Church of Christ in school for all the money the children had raised for their expansion. The dad explained that his son had burst into tears when he tried to take the books away. "When I asked why he was crying, he said the man who gave them to him told him they were really, really important".

School chaplain Alex Gear had written to the Church of Christ headquarters praising the school staff at Kirktonholme for having "gone the extra mile" to make his group welcome – and told how pupils had raised money to build a new church. He wrote: "Many of you will know Kirktonholme Primary have been raising funds to help with our church building fund. Yesterday, just before the worship service finished, I was presented with a check for $350 from the children. They had been collecting change and saving it up for us". Gear also praised author Kyle Butt for giving him "absolutely fantastic material on creation and exposing the myth of evolution" to take back to Scotland. The West Mains Church of Christ were part of the school chaplaincy team, spoke to the children in Assembly and handed their books out to the children.

The two books *How Do You Know God Is Real?* and *Truth Be Told: Exposing the Myth of Evolution* were written by US evangelist Kyle Butt who had graduated from a private Churches of Christ university with degrees in Bible and Communications. According to online reviews, *Truth Be Told* was "written and designed to prepare and equip students to deal with false evolutionary assumptions that often make their way into many science books used in schools", adding, "This book will excite, encourage, and inform students who want to know the truth. In the end, that truth leads the honest student to the fact that this magnificent universe did not evolve, but rather was created by an all-powerful God." In other words, it was creationist material designed to undermine scientific knowledge using spurious evidence of rock art to back claims that humans used dinosaurs as beasts of burden and boarded Noah's Ark. The book was accompanied by illustrations of dinosaurs pulling carts and being ridden by men. Children were persuaded that if evolution was true, dogs would give birth to animals that were half-dog and half-cat. Another one of Kyle Butt's books was *Homosexuality – Sin, or Cultural Bad Habit?* The books were printed by the Apologetics Press based in Montgomery, Alabama; the company was closely affiliated to the Church of Christ. Apologetics Press enjoyed some notoriety after firing its long-term director Bert Thompson following allegations of sexual misconduct with a young man. No charges were brought after a grand jury in Montgomery County heard accusations of inappropriate sexual contact by Thompson with a 17-year-old, but his wife of 33 years, Rhonda, filed for divorce. Interim executive director Dave Miller said the organization, which had a $1million annual budget, intended to proceed "undaunted by Satan". He added, "We are deeply grateful for Doctor Thompson's longstanding warfare against the sinister doctrine of evolution and with his eloquent affirmation of the biblical account of Creation". In support of Apologetics Press, elders of Palm Beach Lakes Church wrote: "We implore you to increase your financial and moral support to Apologetics Press for the next two years then make an evaluation. We are confident the Lord will bring unparalleled results through the new leadership, its renewed focus and its amazingly talented staff".

The Scottish Secular Society's Professor Paul Braterman found within the first five pages of *Truth Be Told*, "nine major errors of scientific fact or logic" adding, "their content is contrary to the whole of present-day science, and to the principles and requirements of guidance from the Scottish Department of Education, and the Curriculum for Excellence. Their arguments are a re-hash of a long-refuted 'creation science', a 20th century heresy that has its roots in Henry Morris's *Genesis Flood*, and in Seventh Day Adventism, rather than in mainstream Christianity".

It also transpired that a notable pro-creationist who worked with Answers in Genesis, Dr Nagy Iskander, sat on the education committee of South Lanarkshire Council which was responsible for Kirktonholme Primary School. Iskander had also sat on the Chaplaincy team at Caulderhill School.

In Scotland, according to law, three unelected religious affiliates had to sit on every one of Scotland's 32 education committees. One from the Catholic Church, one from the Church of Scotland, and one chosen from another religion. In the Western Isles and Shetlands it had to be four clerics or affiliates. In 19 of the committees, the Church of Scotland boasted it held the balance of power to make decisions.

Keeping Marriage and Schools for Christians

Efforts by the Scottish Secular Society to petition the Scottish Parliament in 2013 recommending children should no longer be enrolled in Religious Observation by default had been stonewalled. The organisation argued that RO should be an opt-in arrangement after parents were properly informed what worship was conducted, who was carrying it out and how often.

On the distribution of creationist material and at the time the Scottish Secular Society's petition was being put before Parliament, SSS Chair, Caroline Lynch said: "A book written to undermine education was allowed into the hands of 5-year-olds because of the combined efforts of a complacent Head and American Creationists. We hope that this debacle gives pause to the ministers on the Public Petitions Committee who are considering our petition to change Religious Observance to opt in. Should our petition be enacted into law, it would stop future abuses like this from occurring." The Scottish Secular Society's Robert Canning reported: "The boy's parents had sent him to Kirktonholme – a non-denominational school – to be educated: to gain an understanding of the real world around him, and its past, and to be taught skills useful for living in it. Yet, along with the rest of his class, he had spent some of that afternoon, not being educated, but being enticed to believe in a religion which his parents do not follow, and without their knowledge."

Kirktonholme's two head teachers Sandra McKenzie and Liz Mockus were removed from the school and redeployed. South Lanarkshire Council promised to launch a full investigation.

As repeal of Section 28 drew closer, a lesbian contributing to Stonewall's *Caused by the Clause* expressed her relief the campaign had ended: "I was aware that despite an informative opinion poll conducted by The Herald which showed Scottish Catholics to be marginally more tolerant of homosexuality than the general population, many of the lesbian and gay population still came to view Catholics as the 'enemy'. Winning's views are not shared by all Catholics in Scotland... I think many folk on many levels have been deeply hurt by the 'debate'. I still believe however that the political solution is a huge step forward and the fact that no one has 'won' or 'lost' completely may be the beginning of a healing".

A man in his 60s also wrote to Stonewall offering a more positive account of the Catholic Church during the campaign. "In my church where people had gathered after the service to have a cup of tea and a chat, a woman I didn't know slapped down a torn-off sheet from a certain tabloid demanding that 'everyone sign that' – no explanation; no nothing! I asked the group simply to think before signing and went on to explain what it would mean to minorities in Scotland if Section 28 were retained. People heard me in puzzled silence and then turned to the priest who was also having a well-deserved 'cuppa'. His comment was: 'It's a viewpoint to consider; it's up to you to decide if you want to sign it or not'. He rightly gave no pressure either way; no hostility to either perspective, not then or afterwards. Several weeks later the group for lesbian and gay Catholics, of which I am a long-standing member, was invited to the church to talk and listen to anyone there who wanted to meet us, and do you know what? Lots of people came and we received a warm welcome".

Peter Mullan, the award-winning star of *My Name Is Joe* warned in the *Herald* of "an attempt by the Roman Catholic Church to turn Scotland into a theocratic state". Mullan had been preparing a script for a film project called *The Magdalene Sisters*, which followed the plight of four young women incarcerated by their families, priests or orphanages in Ireland's Magdalene laundries to atone for their sins. The laundries were a place for unmarried mothers, victims of rape or the simple-minded to work 364 days a year without pay. Here, they were beaten, starved, humiliated, raped or had their children forcibly taken away by the so-called Sisters of Mercy, a group of celibate women who imagined themselves 'Brides of Christ'. Thousands of women lived and died there before the last Asylum closed in 1996 and, in 2011, the UN Committee Against Torture demanded Ireland investigate and compensate the victims. Mullan said: "I have had barriers put in my way in even trying to research the subject…" Despite heavy condemnation from the Vatican, the film went on to win the award for best film at the Venice Film Festival.

The Scottish theatre community, in their solidarity with campaigners for the repeal of Sections 28, held a benefit performance of *Death in Venice* at Glasgow's Citizen's Theatre with proceedings going to the arts organisation MCT Theatre Company and Glasgay!, both of which had had their funding suspended by Glasgow City Council following legal action brought about by the Christian Institute and Mr and Mrs Strain.

Keeping Marriage and Schools for Christians

The *Herald's* editorial found "lessons for all of us in the long-running, nasty, and, frankly, increasingly tiresome debate about Section 28 which, we trust, is now drawing to a close".

The *Sunday Herald* cried with relief: "So farewell then, Section 28. After months of Scotland's very own jihad waged by the combined forces of Souter/Winning/Irving/the Daily Record (Big Money, Big God, Big Mouth, Big Homophobia), the war is over... And with that, we sign off on the defunct clause".

The *Sunday Post's* editorial declared it: "A victory for family values", but took a soft line on the changing face of families. "If they re-form in a different way at least it means we have kept some kind of anchor in the great sea change going on around us".

With old habits dying hard, *Scotland on Sunday* attacked Wendy Alexander: "She has been forced to back down almost completely, damaging her own credibility on the way by denying she is backing down at all".

Scottish Nationalist Party leader, Alex Salmond, writing in his column in the *Scottish News of the World* supported Nicola Sturgeon MSP and presented the committee's stance as a vindication of SNP policy. Andrew Wilson wrote in the *Sunday Mail*: "The issue has been a tale of two women - Labour Minister Wendy Alexander who caused the whole fiasco, and the woman who calmly showed the way through the mess, the SNP's Nicola Sturgeon". In Iain Macwhirter's column in the *Sunday Herald*, he wrote: "...Money is becoming the root of all evil in political parties these days. In the age of post-ideology politics, it is increasingly the money men who call the shots. As the parties lose their mass membership base, and have to fund ever more expensive media campaigns, the way to find out what is really happening is to follow the money. Brian Souter has been a major benefactor in the SNP in the past, and the Nationalists had to tread very carefully through the Section 28 controversy to keep him onside. It is a credit to Alex Salmond that he didn't waver on the commitment to repeal the clause, even as Souter was covering Scotland with the Keep the Clause billboards. But as leader of an impoverished party he wouldn't have been human if Souter's cash hadn't weighed heavily on his mind. In the end, Salmond's attempt to play marriage guidance counsellor between Souter and the Scottish Executive seems to have worked. But it was a close call".

RELIGIOUS FASCISM

Clearly aimed at embarrassing the leadership before the repeal of Section 28, another telephone poll was commissioned by 'Keep the Clause'. It had been polled just before the Government's U-turn. In the *Scottish Daily Mail*, Hamish Macdonell described "Section 28 poll misery for Labour". Voters were asked: "The policy of the Labour Party in Scotland is to repeal Section 28. Will this make you more likely to vote Labour in the next general election, less likely or will it make no difference?" The *Mail* reported: "Seven per cent said they were more likely to vote Labour because of the party's repeal plans; 22 per cent said it made them less likely to vote Labour while 66 per cent said it made no difference". The press papered over the cracks. "...The voting intentions showed the electorate have turned against Labour in large numbers... Voters are still unhappy", the *Mail* declared. "Labour faced losing more than a fifth of their support in Scotland if they had failed to back down over Section 28..." and would be "leaped-frogged by the SNP if they had pressed ahead with their unpopular plans", wrote Carlos Alba in the *Record*. "One in five voters would have turned against Labour at the next election had they not caved-in over Section 28... And 12 per cent of Labour voters would have dumped the party..." wrote Tariq Tahir in the *Scottish Sun*. Despite a full 10 per cent difference between the *Sun* and the *Mail* estimating the numbers prepared to 'dump' Labour, the reality turned out to quite different at the election the following year, in the summer of 2001: Labour romped home with a massive majority. In the run-up to the General Election on 7 June 2001, R S Stephen wrote again to the *Fraserburgh Herald:* "In the Section 28 referendum, 1.2 million Scots voted against the Lib Lab SNP parties who are determined to promote Gay propaganda in our schools. So now is your chance to get revenge. Only the Tories are against Gay promotion". After apparently witnessing mysterious zodiacal signs representing Satan arising out of a Scottish Executive letter-heading, he added: "Vote carefully; study policies. Only the Tory party says it 'will take back our seas or come out of Europe'. God does not allow neutral non-voting so be sure and vote." Soon after a disappointing election result in Scotland, millionaire John Paul Getty donated £5m to the Conservative Party to help them on their way.

The Tories had planned to make a bid to persuade the Executive to place a higher emphasis on marriage in guidelines, but this was only destined to be included in the so-called 'guidance' and not in the bill itself. Brian Monteith's move was later defeated by 100 votes to 20. Iain Macwhirter's commentary in the *Herald* was sharp. "So, who won the war of the Clause? Section 2a is being scrapped; the guidelines haven't changed; marriage is given no greater status than it had before. If this is a victory for Keep the Clause, one wonders what it would have regarded as a defeat". He also had some harsh words reserved for that latest U-turn performed by the Executive. "Of course, the 'guidance' versus 'guidelines' controversy still rages. But it's not only in Gaelic that the two words have identical meanings. The 'guidance' given to local authorities is that the 'guidelines' should be observed. Neither the substance, nor the legal status of the guidelines have changed. This whole ridiculous exercise in semantics has been about nothing… Whisper it, but the great 'concession' last week from the Education Minister Sam Galbraith was nothing of the kind. Marriage has always been referred to in the guidelines on sex education in schools. The whole marriage issue has been a red herring - a convenient one as it happens since it got the Scottish Executive off the hook… Brian Souter said the people of Scotland 'didnae vote for it, and we're no huvvin it!' But, it seems that they are huvvin' it after all".

The *Daily Record* meekly avoided any mention of the forthcoming debate on the repeal of Section 28. 'Brigadier' Brown grumbled: "The hallmark of the first year of the Parliament has been the concentration on the Executive's personal politically-correct hobby horses and side issues".

Siezing an opportunity to lash out at the 'gay lobby', the *Record* chanced upon a personal observation made in an e-mail sent by *ScotsGay* editor, John Hein. "I'm sorry to have to interject a sour note into the celebrations for the repeal, in Scotland, of Section 28. Following a lengthy campaign, largely initiated by the Edinburgh-based Equality Network but supported by Outright Scotland, various ad hoc groups, Trades Unions, etc., the Scottish Parliament is likely to vote tomorrow (Wednesday) for the Repeal of Section 2A as it is known in Scotland. Campaigners in Scotland intend to mark the passing of the clause with a fairly low key media event - simply the unveiling of a giant banner saying 'BYE BYE SECTION 28' immediately in front of the Scottish Parliament on The Mound. However, the London-based Stonewall Lobby Group Ltd has now effectively contrived to hijack UK media coverage by arranging a London media circus - free alcohol is being offered to people who turn up and don kilts at a bar in Soho. Apart from the cultural and gender insensitivity involved - stereotyping (largely male) Scots as wearers of Highland Dress with all the overtones of the Kailyard is problematic - the truth is that Stonewall has contributed very little if anything to the Scottish campaign". The *Record* stormed: "...As Dewar waded into the limelight, gay rights campaigners stormed in. They were at each other's throats last night as celebrations descended into farce... Gay pressure groups in Scotland and London were bickering over who had done more to bring about their 'victory'."

On Wednesday, 21 June 2000, the public gallery in the Scottish Executive was fairly quiet, most of the seats were empty and no 'Keep the Clause' demonstrators were in sight. At 6.23pm, during the debate on the Ethical Standards in Public Life bill, Section 2a (aka Section 28) of the Local Government Act 1986 was sent on its way by a majority of 99 to 17, with 2 abstentions. The whole Tory group voted against repeal. Wendy Alexander said: "Repeal is not and never has been about the promotion of homosexuality in our schools. Nor is repeal about political correctness or even marriage. It is about building a tolerant Scotland". There was a spontaneous round of applause from almost everyone in the chamber. All eyes were now focused on what replaced it.

The *Scottish Sun* shrugged: "MSPs finally abolished controversial Section 28 yesterday - after less than an hour's debate... Smiling Communities Minister Wendy Alexander shook hands with colleague Frank McAveety and embraced Sam Galbraith as the 99-17 majority result was announced".

The *Herald* reported: "Section 28 is finally consigned to history... with the words 'this Bill will remove a badge of shame'". The paper quoted Brian Souter's prepared statement: "I believe the fight has been very worthwhile and it is good to see marriage placed at the centre of statutory guidance for future generations of Scots. At the end of the day, the values we have fought for are priceless".

In Stonewall's *Caused by the Clause*, an elderly man returned a touching personal testimonial reflecting on the campaign to 'Keep the Clause', declaring: "I had never seen a country so filled with hate and fear since the Second World War. I was five when

Keeping Marriage and Schools for Christians

the war began and from then until it ended, I felt the same fear as I did during the whole of the Clause 28 farce. I have a gay son and my heart was breaking for his mental agony and also for every gay person who was being subjected to this".

The *Scottish Daily Mail* printed all the names of the MSPs who voted to repeal Section 28 and those who did not. The Tory MSPs, of course, all voted to keep Section 28. They were: Bill Aitken, Alex Ferguson, Phil Gallie, Annabel Goldie, Keith Harding, Nick Johnston, Lyndsay McIntosh, Brian Monteith, David Mundell, Murray Tosh, John Young, David McLetchie, James Douglas-Hamilton, David Davidson, Alex Johnstone, Jamie MacGregor and John Scott. There were two Tories absent from the debate: Ben Wallace and Mary Scanlon. So were Jamie Stone, Ian Jenkins and Robert Brown for the Liberal Democrats. Robert Brown, who had voted on every division, including the one on the Tory amendment, and supported its repeal throughout, felt the passage of the bill itself was by now a formality and asked to leave early to attend a meeting in Glasgow with the agreement of the business manager. Ian Jenkins also had a long-standing prior engagement. (I e-mailed Jamie Stone to ask why he stayed away from the vote, but he did not respond and gave no explanation). Also absent were SNP MSP's Richard Lochead and Andrew Welsh, Labour MSPs Sarah Boyack and Donald Dewar and SSP MSP Tommy Sheridan. SNP MSPs Fergus and Winnie Ewing were present, but both abstained.

There was a subtle irony in having "Camilla in the pink" on the front page of the *Scottish Daily Mail* and "OUT fair and square" on the front page of the *Record*, which turned out to be a story on England's football defeat. But the battle was not over yet. Before the Ethical Standards in Public Life bill gained its Royal Assent; there would be a barrage of bitter recrimination and retaliation.

The next day there was no clause-related front-page story from the pro-Section-28 papers. The *Daily Record* instead just weighed in on the Scottish Executive and so-called 'gay lobby' in its editorial: "They just couldn't leave it alone. They had to gloat. They had to get out the banners. They had to claim a compromise as a triumph. Worst of all, they had to tell the people of Scotland: 'Yah, suckers! We conned you'... Sadly, the Scottish government and gay rights campaigners are hell-bent on keeping the row going. Instead of seeking to heal the divisions, they are working hard at widening them". On the supposed special status of marriage, the editorial claimed: "The government and the gay rights lobby are playing a stupidly self-destructive game by undermining that". The tabloid warned: "If they think it will now be plain sailing from here until the next election, they can forget it. The real weapon deployed against all politicians will not be a bus tycoon's poster campaign, referendum or any private initiative. It will be a sound trouncing at the polls by a disillusioned electorate. It should have been kiss-and-make-up, but the government want forget-and-shut-up. The Scottish people will not forget - and we won't be shut up".

Tom 'Brigadier' Brown also reacted angrily in the *Record*, with a pece ominously headed: "They think it's all over... we'll see... Sticks and stones and all that, name-calling doesn't bother me. But when Mr Smug in a small-circulation Scottish newspaper numbers you among the 'Forces of Darkness', you have to laugh". Against the background of a ferocious tabloid campaign and with billboard posters pasted up across Scotland, 'Brigadier' Brown complained it was impossible for him to have a rational debate about homosexuality because "the immediate reaction from the gay lobby is shrieking hysteria". Despite misunderstanding the physical nature of gay relationships, anal penetration being widespread amongst heterosexuals too, Brown felt handicapped "...because you cannot talk about what homosexuals actually do. The mechanics of homosexual 'love-making', involving every orifice except the one nature made for sex, is distasteful and unhealthy. That's why the majority of people do not want their children to be involved in it. But how do you explain that without being crudely offensive? As a father and grandfather, I want my family to be happy. I don't think the homosexual way of life will give them that. The homosexual lobby may call it prejudice, but it is a genuinely held, and not unreasonable, point of view. Their reaction was to spit venom and obscenely compare themselves to the persecuted and martyred. Another revelation has been the undue influence of a tiny self-appointed elite in politics, the media and the establishment in Scotland - and their contempt for popular feeling... But there are no winners and losers on Section 28, and any triumphalism could provoke a backlash".

The *Scottish Daily Mail* cried: "How can this be called a victory...? Any ministers or MSPs who are tempted to pop champagne corks over the successful repeal of Section 28 are seriously deluded... It is the devolved parliament which has shot itself in the foot. Holyrood has had its say; eventually it will be the turn of the electorate - a consideration which may make the champagne taste rather flat". Gerald Warner commented on the Scottish parliament's "pyrrhic victory". He snarled: "...The voices of repeal displayed time again that their 'tolerance' dripped with venom... MSPs adamantly rejected inclusion of marriage in the ironically entitled Ethical Standards in Public Life Bill. That was just after Wendy Alexander, in a final burst of Orwellian doublespeak, had declared that repeal of Section 28 was not and never had been about promotion of homosexuality in schools. Since that is all that the Section itself is about, her weasel words are transparently false. The Executive is not only insulting the opinions of the electorate, but also its intelligence".

Reporter Hamish Macdonnel mourned the death of a regular source of material for the *Scottish Daily Mail* to vent their homophobic malice. "The Scottish parliament last night defiantly ignored the overwhelming weight of public opinion by voting to scrap Section 28". His co-worker, Ian Smith, turned to attempts at repealing Section 28 south of the border in England and Wales as part of the Local Government Bill. Having completed committee stage for the second time, it was soon to be fully debated in the House of Commons. Blocked by a recalcitrant House of Lords, repeal was unlikely until after the next election.

The *Fraserburgh Herald* editorial shrieked: "Solved with honour!" It declared Wendy Alexander written off as "the worst of the lot", and the Executive had "...now done an about-face and agreed that with the statutory sex education guidelines, teachers will be obliged to promote the importance of marriage".

Robert McNeil wrote in the *Scotsman:* "And so farewell, Clause 28. Or 2a. Or whatever you were called. You brought forth bigots without number. You were a mere form of words but you wreaked more misery than a badger-baiting act at a children's party. For the Conservatives, it was the last crack of the whip, as it were. Still keen to have a last twang at fear's suspenders, they brought forth an amendment in parliament yesterday which had all the usual pious twaddle about love and marriage going together like a horse and cabbage... And so to Wendy Alexander, the wee sacrificial lamb who has borne the brunt of Brian Souter's righteous ravings... The crux of her case was that political principles could not be bought by busmen with little room upstairs".

In the *Daily Record*, Dave King produced a report headed: "DONALD LEADS THE GLOATERS" which suggested ministers were lining up to take credit for repeal. On Wendy Alexander he wrote: "After spending much of the year hiding from the furore, she tried to present herself as a heroine". First Minister Donald Dewar "made his first public appearance since his heart operation to give tame interviews to two TV stations. And he couldn't resist boasting that the Executive had delivered on its promise to scrap the law preventing the promotion of homosexuality in schools". (Dave King was later offered the post of deputy to Henry McLeish's spokesman, Peter McMahon. King turned down the offer to become the *Record's* deputy political editor).

The pro-Section-28 tabloids responded to repeal in an orgy of 'political incorrectness'. The *Sun* shed tears for the 'daughters' - using inverted commas - of gay partners, Barrie Drewitt and Tony Barlow. After the children were bought a couple of toy Mercedes and matching Tommy Hilfiger bottles, the *Sun's* editorial cried: "We feel for these two girls. We find their plight upsetting and shocking".

The 'left-leaning' and gay-friendly London mayor Ken Livingstone got a roasting for telling London police chief Sir John Stevens he wanted parents of murdered black teenager Stephen Lawrence to have a generous payout. "Stand up to him, Sir John. The man's dangerous".

Westminster's concern - led by Tessa Jowell MP - over the rise in eating disorders partly brought on by the portrayal of thin women in the media also evoked the ire of the *Sun's* editorial. The *Daily Mail* submitted to "LUNACY OF THE TV WEIGHT WATCH POLICE" on its front page. "Nanny Tessa, you're just being absurd", wrote Ann Leslie in her column; Edward Heathcoat Amory did a double-page spread on "Britain's most spineless public body", the Independent Television Commission, for not listening to the opinion of the *Daily Mail* on "Channel Filth" (Channel Five) and there was a report on where the money was going from the Princess Diana Memorial Fund. "It has adopted a policy of targeting ethnic minority groups, which it feels are often deterred from applying for grants". There was also a story on how Tony Blair had "failed" the country and another piece on how the shape of the hands revealed - amongst other things - your sexual orientation.

The *Scottish Daily Mail* and *Daily Record* both advertised Brian Souter's rally in Strathclyde Park near Hamilton. The *Scottish Mail* suggested - with the late Baroness Young as their star attraction - that it was expected to attract thousands while the *Record* estimated 5,000 and illustrated their fantasy with a three-quarter-page photograph of a huge gathering at Glastonbury! After the event, *Scotland on Sunday* rather enthusiastically estimated 5,000 had indeed attended. (A few hundred might have been more accurate). Brian Souter said: "Please can you let us know in advance of the next election if you are planning any more surprises so we can express our views at the ballot box... We will be watching this government with great care and will have absolutely no hesitation in re-mobilising our coalition if the views of the Scottish people are ignored by Ministers at the parliament at Holyrood". The *Record* promised: "As a final gesture, a beacon for family values will be lit and Souter will claim: 'Section 28 may have been the wake-up call but the numbers here show the strength of feeling that exists. We want to protect our children, to encourage them to do good, to teach them our values... For them we light this beacon'."

At the same time, Tim Hopkins of the Equality Network was addressing the March for Diversity in Edinburgh and assured everybody "this was not a war against those who supported Section 28. They had been misled... The real losers are the campaigners for Keep the Clause". Wendy Alexander sent a message of support to the crowd: "Clause 28 was a badge of shame that did nothing to protect children. But it stigmatised many. It has no place in our society. That is why the Scottish parliament decided to repeal this piece of institutionalised discrimination". On stage, Bill Spiers, the STUC leader, attacked David McLetchie, leader of the Scottish Conservatives, over a diabtribe against Wendy Alexander which he called "the cheapest and most personal attack on a Minister I have ever witnessed." McLetchie had referred to Wendy Alexander at the Scottish Tory Party Conference as "the high, or should I say low, priestess of political correctness. What a hypocrite she is. Two weeks ago she went to her brother's wedding but when it comes to the Scottish Parliament and what is taught in our schools she apparently believes that marriage has the moral equivalence of a one-night stand".

A few years later, David McLetchie was distancing himself from sleaze allegations by resigning from his £30,000-a-year post at the law firm Tods Murray after it emerged he had lodged a parliamentary motion backing the new Edinburgh Royal Infirmary without declaring his firm represented the consortium that built the hospital. In a similar case, he had failed to reveal his law firm represented the Royal Highland and Agricultural Society which opposed the proposed expansion of Edinburgh Airport. McLetchie had signed a parliamentary motion rejecting parts of the plan. McLetchie's day finally came when it was revealed he had charged taxpayers £10,448 in taxi bills since he had become an MSP. He was accused of using taxis to transport him to and from his offices at Tods Murray. (He was not alone. Labour MSP Gordon Jackson who the *Record* had bragged was not towing their line over the repeal of Section 28 had, as a director of Kilmarnock Football Club, charged the taxpayer for a trip from his home to Ibrox to watch his team play against Rangers). David McLetchie died in 2013 after a battle with cancer.

The Scottish Conservative Party imploded when another senior Tory, Brian Monteith, was forced to resign the party whip after admitting sending emails to *Scotland on Sunday* urging the paper to call for McLetchie's resignation despite appearing on television praising the former leader's time in office. There followed a string of allegations against other Tory members before McLetchie was replaced by Annabel Goldie, who was elected as the new Scottish leader of the Conservatives.

In a fit of wishful thinking, the *Scottish Daily Mail* cried: "As the gloss rubs off New Labour's promises, Conservatism is re-emerging as a credible and - for increasing numbers of voters - an attractive alternative".

Hamish Macdonell penned a story in the *Scottish Mail*, (also carried by the *Record*) explaining how the Executive coalition had been attacked over "£4,000 of public cash... spent on an overnight 'strategy' session at the four-star MacDonald Houstoun House Hotel in West Lothian". The *Record* suggested. "DONALD AND WENDY GO ON £4,000 AWAY DAYS". They included a full run-down of the menu: "Ministers would have tucked into delicacies such as gravadlax, smoked duck, Aberdeen Angus fillets and chocolate terrines..."

Keeping Marriage and Schools for Christians

The *Daily Record* ran another front-page story on Section 28, this time claiming 'Keep the Clause' would be challenging the Scottish Executive in the courts. 'Keep the Clause' alleged Prime Minister Tony Blair had unfairly influenced the debate during his brief visit to Scotland by accusing their campaign of "astonishing propaganda" and dismissing their fears as "complete and total nonsense". Not missing an opportunity for another editorial on the subject, the *Record* added: "Dewar, Alexander and their cohorts could be forced to face the courts and Court of Session judges - a prospect which will have them shaking in their boots. But as we have said before, they have only themselves to blame". In desperation, 'Keep the Clause' also threatened to take issue with the way Section 28 was being repealed, suggesting that it was a reserved matter and as such, should have been dealt with by Westminster. Interestingly, Brian Souter later issued another press release distancing himself from the original press release from Media House, while both the Catholic Church and the Christian Institute indicated they did not favour a legal challenge.

In another headline, the *Record* shrieked: "NEW SCHOOLS TO QUESTION PUPILS ON SEX LIVES". 64 community schools in Scotland were planning to question pupils on all aspects of their lives including eating habits and if they wore condoms. Ann Hill from the Scottish School Boards' Association told the tabloid: "Do we really want children to be quizzed about their sexual behaviour at school?" Conservative Tino Ferri of the teaching union National Association of Schoolmasters and Union of Women Teachers (NAS/UWT) said: "This is really going too far. The sex lives of pupils are outwith the remit of the school" and Brian Monteith thought Donald Dewar had "lost his marbles".

At London's 50,000-strong gay Mardi Gras that summer, 10-foot puppets of Cardinal Winning, Brian Souter and Baroness Young took to the stage. Souter's puppet declared: "Look at all these nasty homosexuals", and Baroness Young's turned on a kissing couple saying: "We can't have that!" Angela Mason of Stonewall turned on them both: "We've all heard what you've had to say, now listen to what we have to say. We will get an equal age of consent, we will win the fight against prejudice, we will be seen for the real families we are and Section 28 will be repealed".

RELIGIOUS FASCISM

In the *Sunday Herald*, Iain Macwhirter wrote: "Journalists, this one included, would be happy never to write about the damn clause ever again. The Scottish public long ago made its excuses and left, and even the keepers of the clause have developed indignation fatigue".

Scotland on Sunday, with sources working closely with 'Keep the Clause' confirmed the cost of Souter's campaign: "The total cost of his campaign, which involved a private referendum, was £2m". Souter described the money as "well spent".

Sir Michael Rifkind delivered a Party Political broadcast on TV for the Scottish Conservative and Unionist Party. With the saltire flying to rousing music, he charged the Labour administration with being "obsessed with Section 28".

The *Scottish Daily Mail* printed a string of letters supporting the Conservatives. Gwen Walker of Peterhead reminded everyone "only one party voted against the repeal of Section 28... The Conservative Party's MSPs all voted for the parents and children of Scotland". J Lynn of Inverness warned: "MSPs may well be smirking about abolishing Section 28. Maybe they will be smirking on the other side of their faces at the next election". And A Parker of St Andrews advised: "Let the 1.1 million Scots go to the polling station, get their voting forms and write across them: 'Pay Back Time - remember section 28/2a'".

Catholic radio host Michael Kelly invited Scots Tory, the late Phil Gallie onto his one-hour programme on Clyde 2. Gallie had appeared in the *Scottish Sun* saying that: "Labour talks about being family friendly and keeping children safe, then they give way to a minority whose self-interest goes beyond the bounds of decency where children are concerned". Abandoning any pretence of impartiality as programme host, Kelly tried to explain to the Equality Network's Tim Hopkins how "left-handedness..." unlike being gay, "doesn't lead to any social consequences..." On being gay, Kelly added: "I'm not saying discriminate, I'm saying don't promote it as an equal value to society as a relationship..." He expressed the opinion that the point "most" people were trying to make was: "You shouldn't be giving children the choice. You may be landed with being homosexual and shouldn't be discriminated against if you are – but you shouldn't suggest to kids that they've got a choice to pick one or the other". Quite where he got the idea that sexual

Keeping Marriage and Schools for Christians

orientation was chosen like jellybeans at a pic n' mix counter he didn't say.

Cardinal Winning's views were welcomed in Glasgow's *Evening Times*. "THERE IS MUCH TO COMMEND HIS BROAD VIEW OF SOCIETY AND DEFENCE OF TRADITIONAL VALUES" they cooed. For someone who didn't have sex, Winning certainly had a deep interest in the subject. "I know the pressures of a sex-ridden society…" he advised the *Scottish Mail*. In his interview in the Glasgow *Evening Times* he confessed there were "very well-organised and resourced forces at work in our society which are Hell-bent - and I use those words advisedly - on destroying the Christian family". In a thinly-veiled warning to gay activists, he advised "you will not conquer" and suggested "the system should be promoting and buttressing marriage". Winning stayed tight-lipped about Father Fitzsimmons who was removed from his Lothian parish after two teenagers claimed he molested them, or Father Murphy who quit his Lochgilphead parish to marry his housekeeper, or Canon Joseph Terry who was jailed for indecency against four girls while he was a priest in the diocese of Argyll and the Isles, or the Bishop of Argyll and the Isles, Roddy Wright who left the church to marry a divorcee after revealing he already had a teenage son by another woman. At his 50th anniversary sermon, Glasgow Lord Provost Pat Lally hosted a reception for Winning in the City Chambers attended by Donald Dewar and Alex Salmond. Cardinal Winning told the *Evening Times:* "My dream for Scotland is that the new millennium will see us rid our country of discrimination, whether based on creed or colour". (But, of course, not on sexual orientation).

Getting the repeal of Section 28 in England and Wales, encapsulated in a Local Government Bill, past the House of Lords would have meant overturning the Conservative majority and appointing more liberal supporters. Or, as the *Mail* put it: "Manipulating the House of Lords with its toady supporters". Baroness Janet Young led the fight in the House of Lords. Lady Young told the *Mail:* "If Clause 28 is repealed, local authorities will be free once again to start funding appalling material. The floodgates will be open and taxpayers will be paying for it all". Under a picture of her labelled "Triumph: Young" which was almost unrecognisable, probably taken when she was in her thirties, the Baroness told the *Record* – which conveniently juxtaposed the story with a report on the "pervert list" (the Sex Offenders' Register) - that Scotland should continue the fight by making Section 28 a key election issue. The *Mail's* editorial warned: "Even if the Government succeeds, it is likely to be a pyrrhic victory. Pro-clause peers could, in revenge, wage guerrilla warfare against the rest of the local Government Bill..." and if the Government lost, "...it would mean that schoolchildren in England and Wales would continue to enjoy protection from homosexual propaganda denied to children in Scotland". The *Mail* insisted that Scottish children had now been "stripped of protection by their own parliament". In a profile in *Scotland on Sunday*, Lady Young hinted her crusade had only just begun. "I think there is far more to this whole debate than the particular issue of Section 28. I think our whole society is really at a watershed... I look at my family, my three daughters, they are all grown up, they've been married for some time - even my grandchildren have grown up. But they are all Christian families and they live by Christian beliefs. I do find this an enormous strength and comfort - I think we all do. We are a very united family... Yes I know a lot of gay people. Well not a lot, but I know gay people. Of course they are very charming, very gifted, very clever and I often think really very unhappy people". Maybe she spoke from personal experience? We will never know. She passed away in September 2002.

It was a stormy and emotional debate in the House of Lords on the evening of 24 July 2000, lasting more than two hours. Former MP Michael Brown witnessed the debate for the *Pink Paper*: "Some came on sticks, some on walking frames and some in motorised wheelchairs. One wore an eye patch. Several had deaf aids and one even had an ear trumpet... We must endure these pathetic war-dances. Until, that is, Tony Blair summons up the courage to ignore the *Daily Mail* and the focus groups and force the repeal of Section 28 down their Lordships' throats and up their collective backside". The House of Lords decided to keep the Clause by 270 votes to 228. 64 of those voting to retain the law were hereditary peers. Former Conservative Prime Minister Lady Thatcher was amongst them. She said: "It was due to Janet's belief and determination that we won this vote and people are absolutely behind her. She has been terrific from the start to the finish and we owe a great deal to her".

Keeping Marriage and Schools for Christians

Forgetting Northern Ireland - which never had Section 28 - the *Daily Record* cried: "...It leaves Scotland as the only part of the UK to abolish the law, which prevents local authorities promoting homosexuality in schools". Brian Souter told the tabloid: "It vindicates the Daily Record campaign". The *Sun* saw it as "a huge victory for The Sun's campaign to keep the clause in the Local Government Bill", declaring, righteous with indignation, that: "The voice of decency and reason has spoken" opposite a picture of topless Leilani, 20, from Bournemouth, while the *Daily Mail* bragged: "Last night's landmark vote in Westminster marks a victory for the Daily Mail, which has campaigned to retain Clause 28 as a safeguard against gay propaganda being fed to impressionable minds". Lady Young was "delighted" and praised the *Mail's* efforts: "The Daily Mail has played a great role in all of this and it has made a big difference in winning the argument". Others joined in the praise, including the controversial Iqbal Sacranie of the Moslem Council of Britain and Chief Rabbi Dr Jonathan Sacks. (Socranie later refused to condemn a 'fatwa', or death threat issued by Sheikh Omar Bakri Mohammed who headed the fanatical *Al-Muhajiroun* against the gay Muslim group *Al-Fatiha).*

In the *Scottish Mail,* Gerald Warner wished Scotland had an unelected House of Lords because "schoolchildren south of the Border will continue to enjoy protection from homosexual propaganda and associated dangers, which is now denied to children in Scotland". Brushing aside news of Concorde ploughing into a Parisian hotel, the *Scottish Mail's* editorial was taken up with Section 28 "splitting the moral and legislative cohesion of the Union, thus preparing the way for full-blooded separatism... If the Prime Minister wants to be accepted by voters as pro-family, he must drop his overstated pro-homosexual programme, once and for all". The *Mail* declared a "dangerous drift into separatism" between Scotland and the rest of the UK because "laws on protection of children from homosexual propaganda" had been repealed.

The *Daily Record* called it: "CLAUSE CRISIS" as Blair "THROWS IN THE TOWEL ON SECTION 28" and "abandoned" efforts to repeal Section 28 in England and Wales. The *Sun* gleefully declared a "crushing blow" for Blair who had "admitted defeat".

RELIGIOUS FASCISM

Peter Tatchell had another opportunity to confront religious leaders as they left the National Holocaust Memorial Day Commemoration at Westminster Central Hall in London on Saturday, 27 January, 2001. Slipping through the security cordon, Tatchell challenged the Chief Rabbi, Jonathan Sacks, Catholic leader, Cardinal Murphy O'Connor and the Archbishop of Canterbury, George Carey, over their support for Section 28 and opposition to an equal age of consent. Tatchell first confronted the Chief Rabbi, telling him: "I hope you will remember the words of tolerance and compassion spoken here tonight next time there is a vote on gay human rights. Your support for Section 28 causes great pain to the gay community". Dr Sacks fronted an expression of contrition before replying: "Peter, I hear the pain of the gay community". Tatchell replied: "If you hear our pain, please do not vote again to support discrimination against homosexuals. Don't deny us human rights". The Chief Rabbi replied: "Thank you Peter, I am listening". Special Branch officers surrounded Tatchell and radioed for reinforcements. But he walked towards the exit and they let him go. As soon as the police had turned their backs, Tatchell again slipped through the security cordon and approached the Archbishop of Canterbury and Cardinal Murphy O'Connor. He told them: "Your support for discrimination against homosexuals colludes with the prejudice that makes possible awful crimes like the Holocaust. It is wrong for you to endorse the humanitarian values of this commemoration, and then continue to oppose the repeal of Section 28 and the equalisation of the age of consent". The Cardinal and Archbishop were non-committal: "Yes, I understand what you are saying", said a momentarily distracted Dr Carey. Cardinal O'Connor's only response was to murmur: "Very well. We will see".

After this second security alert, Special Branch officers saw Tatchell to the main exit. But stooping down and mingling with the crowd, he re-infiltrated the main lobby once again and confronted a beaming Conservative leader, William Hague and his startled wife Ffion. Tatchell asked Hague: "Please remember tonight's message of tolerance and compassion next time there is a vote on Section 28". Hague replied: "Thank you, Peter. Don't worry, I will", before beating a hasty retreat. In 2010, as Foreign Secretary, Hague accepted the resignation of his advisor, Christopher Myers, following Internet allegations they'd shared a hotel room during the election campaign. His robust denial was accompanied by highly personal comments that he and his wife had suffered "multiple miscarriages" trying to start a family.

Tatchell narrowly missed challenging Prime Minister Tony Blair as he left the hall. In his keynote address to the Holocaust Memorial Day commemoration, Blair notably omitted the Nazi persecution of homosexuals. Speaking about the lessons of the Holocaust for future generations, Blair mentioned the need to fight racism and anti-Semitism, and the importance of defending the human rights of every person "regardless of race, religion or the colour of their skin", but avoided any mention of challenging prejudice based on sexual orientation or disability.

"There is absolutely no excuse for the way Tony Blair ignored the suffering of gay people and the need to combat homophobia", said Tatchell who, despite 30 years of writing and campaigning on Holocaust issues, was initially excluded from the ceremony on the grounds he was a security risk. He added: "These religious leaders are homophobes and hypocrites. They endorse the human rights theme of Holocaust Memorial Day, yet they campaign against gay human rights at every opportunity".

Terry Sanderson, Mediawatch correspondent for *Gay Times* was appalled by the homophobic outpourings from the *Daily Mail's* English editions. "The Daily Mail – which could curdle the milk of human kindness at a hundred paces – must have spent a small fortune on its ongoing campaign against the repeal of Section 28. Not a day goes by that the paper doesn't manage to come up with some new homophobic angle. On February 5th it was: "The gay rights campaigner with an OBE and her links to a group of anarchist bombers that you won't find on her CV". This related to Stonewall's Angela Mason. It said nothing about her past that hasn't already been said, and was deeply dishonest in its presentation. On February 14th the Mail gave us: "Why wrongs don't make gay 'rights'." February 19th: "Gay sex laws must stay now". February 21st: "Catholic chief backs gay propaganda ban". February 23rd: "Labour peers still defiant in battle of Section 28". February 29th: "Church grassroots fury at gay law 'deal'." March 5th: "This sad betrayal of the family". March 6th: "Let gays 'cruise for sex' say Norris and Dobson". March 7th: "Moslem threat to boycott schools if Section 28 goes". March 9th: "Keep Clause 28. Premier is told by majority of his constituents"… and on and on and on: a relentless catalogue of distortion, invention and slander".

South of the border, stories of Scotland's victory were coloured by the repeal's tortuous passage, inspiring aggressive challenges to the Labour Government's attempts to repeal the law in England and Wales. Homophobia was rife both inside and outside Parliament. In the early hours of the morning of 9 July, gay petrol attendant, Scott Newman was found dead in a courtyard in Bishop's Stortford, England, murdered by a single blow to the head. He was found with his trousers round his ankles and a 44-pound concrete block lying across his legs. Found near his body were the two hearing aids Scott Newman wore to combat a severe hearing disability. A 34-year-old father of two, 'bi-curious' Scotsman, Patrick O'Hagan was later arrested and convicted of manslaughter. He confessed to the court: "I was curious to see what it was like, just for the experience really". He was jailed for seven years. On the same day, a 25-year-old gay man in London was in hospital fighting for his life after an artery was severed in his neck by broken glass in a horrific attack carried out by a gang of youths.

In another incident, Ian Wilmott and his friend were severely beaten with clubs in broad daylight in a Manchester park. Wilmott just happened to be the chairperson of the National Advisory Group on Gay and Lesbian Policing. He wrote in the *Pink Paper* on eight years of research: "...When anti-gay prejudice and misinformation is aired by the media, hate-motivated attacks increase. There is a correlation between so called 'soft homophobia' peddled by politicians, the press and broadcast media, and the 'hard hatred' typical of physical attack and assault. Baroness Young has used her privileged position in the House of Lords to foster an atmosphere of lies about lesbians and gay men, and to infer that we pose a threat to young people by wanting to 'promote' our lifestyles. She has polarised the debate about educating young people in our schools so that any accurate and realistic information about lesbian and gay sexuality is now entirely off the agenda..."

Pink Pampers, a gay hairdresser in Brighton was vandalised for a third weekend in a row. The shop was daubed with the words 'batty men' and a brick was thrown through the window. It was suggested to the owners they changed the colour of the shop exterior.

Keeping Marriage and Schools for Christians

In Cardiff, David Fenner, a gay man had to have 18 staples in his head and seven stitches in his wrist after his homophobic brother battered him with an ashtray in a second attack in the home David shared with his partner and mother. The conditions of the bail meant Christopher Fenner was still able to turn up at the home to visit his mother.

In Edinburgh there was a brutal rape of a 32-year-old man by two men.

In Holland Park in London, nine men were battered in attacks linked to gangs of teenagers on school holidays.

Also in London, when an attacker spotted blind Denny Ryder, star of docu-soap *Paddington Green*, walking with his stick along the street near where he lived, he shouted: 'You're the gay bastard off Paddington Green' before punching him twice in the face. Denny lost all his front teeth, had £30 stolen and needed seven stitches. He had already lost his sight in a previous mugging.

In Exeter, a mob of around fifty teenagers chased five gay men leaving a gay pub hurling homophobic abuse. The five took refuge in a house while the mob besieged the house, attempted to break down the door and smashed the back window of a car parked in a driveway.

In Plymouth, 26-year-old Richard Young, who had returned to the Royal Navy after being sacked for being gay left a gay bar with his boyfriend. Two passengers of a car got out and attacked them, leaving Richard with a fractured skull, broken jaw and two smashed eye sockets. Surgeons hoped to reconstruct Richard Young's face using titanium plates. Suspects Wayne Glanville, 29 and Jason Leslie, 31 were cleared of all charges after police errors caused the case to collapse. Jason Leslie was found 'not guilty' after Judge Sean Overend ruled the video evidence of an indentification parade with Leslie wearing a white sleeveless vest could not be shown to the jury and was inadmissible after Young had described his attacker as wearing a white sleeveless vest and having well-defined arm muscles. Wayne Glanville was cleared after two exhibits, a vest and shirt sent to the police forensic laboratory and requested by the defence, went missing. The judge ruled that the missing items might have been used by the defence to show whether there had been a mistake in the identification.

19-year-old Steven Fields was sentenced to seven years for killing a 26-year-old rugby player, Troy Comins. He was found bleeding to death in an alleyway off Whitstable High Street on the evening of November 22, 2000 and died later of a single stab wound to the chest. He claimed Comins had made sexual advances to him. DNA tests showed DNA matching Comins was found on Field's genitals. The jury acquitted Fields of murder and instead found him guilty of the lesser charge of manslaughter.

At a Pride March in Leicester, three members of the National Front were arrested. Two men were found guilty of public order offences and the third for carrying an offensive weapon.

In London, a 21-year-old Somalian refugee, Anwar Ahmed was hacked to death by Muslims simply for being gay.

Echoing an increase in attacks in Scotland, the *Pink Paper's* editorial admitted: "Rarely a week goes by without the Pink Paper newsdesk hearing about someone being victim of a homophobic attack".

The attacks were not aimed at gay men alone. A transsexual from Saltcoats in Ayrshire told the *Scottish News of the World*: "I wish people would leave me alone. I'm given a miserable time... I went out wearing a pink top. Some binmen saw me in front of the grocers and jeered and juggled coconuts in front of their chests... Suddenly a pellet hit me near the elbow and I saw somebody run away... It was extremely frightening". Former Scots Guard, Ian MacDougall said it was safer being a soldier in Ulster than a transsexual in Saltcoats. The tabloid appeared more interested in how hormone replacement "gave him a 40in bust..."

Incitement to hatred blistered across the Scottish media. In Gerald Warner's Saturday Essay in the *Scottish Mail* he heralded the House of Lords as "that last democratic check". As an entirely unelected body, of course, it is anything but democratic. He then turned on the "debilitating influence of Europe" and its new laws and regulations that were "imposed upon the British people; laws about which we were never consulted; which were included in no election manifesto and for which we never voted... Are we, really and truly, living any longer in a democratic society?" Because of Section 28, he warned the ballot box would be boycotted on a large scale and hinted at trouble on the streets: "...Opposition may take an extra-parliamentary form; that the parliament might be brought to heel by huge, organised manifestations of public discontent. Brian Souter's Keep the

Keeping Marriage and Schools for Christians

Clause campaign was a possible portent of things to come". From Associated Newspapers to Scotsman Publications, Gerald Warner belted out his views. In *Scotland on Sunday* he asked: "Is there an adequate supply of tar and feathers in the country?" Attacking education minister Sam Galbraith over an exams crisis, he blasted: "This is a parliament of scoundrels… It is a pity that the parliament did not feel able to devote a fraction of the attention it gave to promoting sodomite propaganda in schools, to the more basic responsibility of ensuring that the examination system was viable". In desperation Warner begged: "The only other option is to organise resistance to the devolved dictatorship… Public opinion would have to mobilise in an extra-parliamentary context. The Keep the Clause campaign might prove to be the precursor of more heavyweight crusades… Tanks on the lawn and goose-stepping formations of a People's Army outside the window are not indispensable accessories to the extinction of democracy…"

In London, Stonewall came in for some heavy criticism from former *Boyz* editor, *Express* writer Simon Edge in the *Pink Paper*: "When Stonewall announced its support for the pro-marriage guidelines in the Learning and Skills Bill, many of us warned that this might leave us worse off than before. We could end up with a new law requiring teachers to stress the importance of marriage with the old Section 28 still on the statute book. Stonewall chose to ignore such warnings, but that is precisely what has now happened. Stonewall, with its slavish faith in New Labour and its refusal to listen to constructive criticism, must also take the blame. After three years of the gay-friendliest government ever, it has failed to win one single legislative reform. Instead, it has galvanised a cast-iron coalition against us and alienated an otherwise indifferent population. There could have been a proper campaign around Section 28, drawing the full lessons of the Soho bomb and Copeland trial. There could have been a real push into hostile newsrooms, which paid such dividends when the age of consent was first debated. There could have been outreach to the other political parties, not just New Labour. Most importantly, it could have drafted a one-clause bill on the Irish model, getting rid of anti-gay discrimination at a stroke, and avoiding the disastrous piecemeal approach which has played into the hands of Young. It is time to say out loud what many have been saying in private for months. Angela Mason is

RELIGIOUS FASCISM

inept and arrogant and her leadership of Stonewall since New Labour came to power has been disastrous. For the good of the community she should resign".

Angela Mason responded, saying: "With regard to the new Sex and Education Relationship guidelines, they clearly emphasize stable relationships. Baroness Young complained that they only mentioned marriage three times... For the first time ever gay sexuality is discussed".

Local government minister Hillary Armstrong called for unity within the gay community and praised Angela Mason. Turning on Baroness Young she said: "One of the most peculiar things about their campaign for Section 28 is that we have answered all their arguments and anxieties about schools, and they went right through just not hearing it... The worst aspect of this whole thing is how some members of the House of Lords have been attacking lesbians and gay men as if it's open season. The rhetoric has been appalling... The church and the press have fed off each other".

In Scotland, the Bill repealing Section 28 in Scotland received its Royal Assent on Monday, 24 July, and became the Ethical Standards in Public Life etc. (Scotland) Act 2000 - the 8th Act of the new Scottish Parliament. However, the section of the Act repealing Section 28 would not be activated until the new sex education guidance and other materials had been issued to education authorities and schools. This was not expected to happen until 2001, so it was not quite over yet. Gerald Warner shrieked in *Scotland on Sunday*: "This clause is no more... It is dead... This is a deceased democracy!" It was all too much: "Christ has been supplanted by Mammon and every other horned beast... This country has sunk to unprecedented depths of barbarism and degeneracy". He joined Tory leader William Hague, capitalising on the murder of 10-year-old Peckham boy, Damilola Taylor. "When the West Indians first came to this country, they were among the stoutest pillars of the community. While the indigenous population began its long slide into decadence in the Sixties, corrupted by cynicism and permissiveness, the black population remained idealistic, patriotic and law-abiding". But as one young person told Carlos Alba in the *Sunday Times Scotland:* "People get stabbed in Wishaw every weekend, but it's got nothing to do with race. It's religious - Celtic v Rangers. (Catholic v Protestant) If you want to see violence come down here after the next Old Firm game". It certainly wasn't decadence or permissiveness that murdered 'Little Man' Damilola Taylor, who believed God would protect him. The gangs that mauraded the weak and vulnerable inside and outside the gates of Oliver Goldsmith's School chased him and called him gay.

On Tuesday, 25 July 2000, the *Scottish Sun* was bubbling over with an exclusive: "STAGECOACH BOSS IN GAY VICE STING". 51-year-old William Hinckley, a married man with three children, was charged with having attempted to call an escort agency to privately arrange sex with a black male escort. In the 'sting' operation performed by police in Houston, Texas, Hinkley was arrested. Police denied 'entrapment', suggesting the idea would have to have been planted in the defendant's mind first. In this case, they insisted the idea was already there when Hinkley rang the agency. His defence lawyers, DeGuerin and Dickson, who represented Waco cult leader David Koresh, argued media coverage had ruined Hinckley's life. William Hinkley was a Stagecoach senior executive. His wife, who lived at their home in Cumbria, knew nothing about the incident until the day before the story appeared. Hinckley had made a call from the Omni Hotel to the escort agency on June 28 at 9.50pm and told the undercover cop he wanted 'all of it'. Hinkley was forced to resign from Stagecoach. The charge stated that he offered and agreed to engage in 'deviant sex', which was defined, as either oral or anal sex. Hinkley was charged with 'moral turpitude', a crime that carried a sentence of up to 180 days in jail or a $2,000 fine. Hinkley admitted the offence and was fined $1,500. His boss, Brian Souter was said to be furious.

Brian Souter had problems of his own. Stagecoach profits were down so much that the company was no longer in the FTSE 100 index. Plans to buy a 35% stake in Italy's largest bus company, Sogin had already been pulled, hopes of a network of airports were dashed and Prestwick Airport was up for sale. Stagecoach's 60% stake in Hong Kong's Road King had been written off; the City was doubtful if the investment in Coach USA was a good buy and the sudden, unexplained resignations of group chief executive Mike Kinski and the executive chairman of Coach USA, Larry King, didn't help. Shareholders were jittery over Souter's involvement in the 'Keep the Clause' campaign and thought he had taken his hands off the wheel.

RELIGIOUS FASCISM

In June 2000, Stagecoach announced it was writing off £85m of its £140m investment in Chinese toll roads operator Road King Infrastructure, signalling the latest of a series of exits from acquisitions which included Swebus, its Swedish bus operation, which was sold at a loss. It was even suggested that Stagecoach might exit altogether from Road King. Porterbrook, Souter's rail leasing business had already been sold. On Thursday, 15 June, after the City had seen Brian Souter's full-year's results for running Stagecoach, the *Scotsman's* Business View chided: "If Stagecoach's share price were a bus, the police would have pulled the driver over for suspected drink-driving this week. Ten per cent up over Monday and Tuesday, 10 per cent down yesterday..." The *Herald's* business Comment suggested: "Stagecoach needs a complete overhaul - not a puncture repair kit - and it will be a long while before it is firing on anything like all cylinders again... Stagecoach is a sorry tale". Shares had plunged 11% after Stagecoach presented falling profits in its UK business and announced Coach USA would take another year to sort out. After Forbes Global, one of the world's most respected business publications published a feature that cast doubt over Souter's business acumen in May 2002; they were threatened with legal action over what were claimed by Stagecoach to be "spectacular" innaccuracies.

In January 2001, Stagecoach finally sold Glasgow Prestwick International airport to a New Zealand investment firm for £33.4m. Souter's company had paid £41m for it in 1998. News of the sale still failed to impress the City and another plunge in Stagecoach's profits soon followed when Brian Souter's rail subsidiaries lost £2m, revenues fell by a third, and Coach USA was hit by driver shortages. Stagecoach had still done well out of Prestwick: in 2013 the Scottish Government would buy the airport from Infratil for just £1. Brian Souter's sister Ann picked up Infrati's other airport at Manston in Kent for the same price.

By the summer of 2001, even the *Record* was forced to announce "Souter's skid into the red". Reporter Jon Clements put down Souter's £500m reversal in fortunes to "a barrage of blunders and bad publicity". Souter had transformed a profit of £182.3m into a £316.5m loss! The value of the stake he and his sister Ann Gloag held had fallen by more than £1billion from £1.25billion two years previously to just £187m. Souter blamed the rail chaos after the Hatfield train crash and the cost of buying Coach USA.

By July 2002, Brian Souter and Ann Gloag together lost £70m as shares in Stagecoach collapsed. At their peak, the pair's combined wealth was estimated at £1.03bn when the company's shares peaked at £14.29 each. Souter's 160 million shares were now worth £22.4m and Gloag's 105 million shares £14.7m. Keith Cochrane quit as chief executive with a £552,000 pay-off after Coach USA continued to underperform, and Brian Souter took over the day-to-day running of the operation in a bid to turn around its fortunes. Souter's chairman, Bob Spiers confronted Souter with the problems at Coach USA that chairmans Larry King, Barry Hinkley, Randy West and Keith Cochrane had all been unable to sort out, Brian Souter prepared for a new role as chairman. As Bob Spiers spoke at their board meeting, Souter was reported doodling the faces of two clocks on a pad in front of him. Time was running out. City investors were losing patience. Shares tumbled, despite the announcement that taxpayers were likely to have to fork out £465m to Virgin Rail in order to repair faulty tracks on the UK's west coast line. The Strategic Rail Authority (SRA) ordered the payment after the effectively bankrupt Railtrack failed to upgrade the West Coast main line on time. Chairman and chief executive of the SRA was the son of Roger Bowker, one of Souter's trusted executives, Richard Bowker was a former co-chairman of Virgin Rail when it became part-owned by Stagecoach. As head of the SRA, he wasn't allowed to have anything to do with Stagecoach or Virgin for the first six months in his new post. An evangelical Christian himself, he travelled to Perth to speak at the Church of the Nazarene. Bowker was good for Souter. He stabilised Stagecoach's share price by relieving Virgin of the duty to pay around £1.5billion in franchise premiums and gave it £106m extra subsidy for some of its crumbling network. He planned to curtail other companies' services to give Virgin more room for growth. He put aside his own official policy of reducing costs by competitive tendering to give Stagecoach exclusive negotiations for a new Isle of Wight franchise and even awarded a £29m subsidy to Stagecoach's already well-subsidised South West Trains. By 2012, Stagecoach and Network Rail were in an alliance, jointly operating trains and tracks used by the South West Trains in deals which were rolled out elsewhere across the network, including ScotRail.

Suddenly, in October 2002, an unidentified investor sold nearly five per cent of the company at a knock-down price of 9.75 a share. Stagecoach's battered share price plunged 44%. Fingers were pointed at US investment house, Franklin Templeton a non-family shareholder with almost 10.2% of the issued share capital. Others shareholders included Marathon Asset Management (4.35%), Standard Life Assurance (3.99%), Merrill Lynch Investment (3.12%) and Legal & General Assurance (3.07%). Brian Souter and Ann Gloag, once worth about £1bn, now had a combined shareholding of just £38.9m. Souter offloaded around 50% of ailing Coach USA's assets. After purchasing the Hong Kong Citybus operation for £181m in 1999, Souter sold it for £176m to help cut debts. Citybus had gone the way of Stagecoach's operations in Sweden, Portugal, Australia and Africa, and Prestwick Airport in Ayrshire. Now all that was left overseas was a small bus company in New Zealand. Adding to Souter's troubles, undercover traffic commissioners had monitored 742 Stagecoach buses for seven weeks in Exeter in 2002. They reported 82 not seen in service and 123 either more than one minute early or five minutes late. In Scotland, he and his sister, Ann Gloag still held 90% of Scotairways. (In 2006, Brian Souter and Ann Gloag more than doubled their money when they sold their shares in the airline back to the founders, Merlyn and Roy Suckling).

In 2002, Stagecoach's budget coach operation's joint venture between megabus.com and Scottish Citylink was referred by the Office of Fair Trading to the Competition Commission. The OFT said the joint venture had led to a loss of competition where their services overlapped. Meanwhile, megabus.com offered fares as low as $1 between Chicago and eight Midwest cities in the US as Souter made a determined effort to recover his lost fortunes. The Stagecoach company report and accounts were nonetheless upbeat. Profits at South West Trains had surged 38% to £137m and Stagecoach's overall net profits rose by £9.4m to £140.6m. With more than one in eight South West Trains services running late during the rush-hour peaks, commuter groups didn't share the same enthusiasm for the news. Brian Souter was the biggest beneficiary. He received a total of £6.7m, including £5.8m in dividends from his shareholdings in the company, and was paid a base salary of £499,000 topped up by £408,000 of cash and share bonus awards. As a non-executive director, Ann Gloag received a £4.6m dividend cheque and a £38,000 fee for attending board meetings. RMT rail union general secretary Bob Crow assured the press: "If Stagecoach bosses can afford to pay themselves £15m in salaries and bonuses, then our members will be looking forward to the substantial pay rises they are due in the next pay round". Stagecoach went on to sell their London bus operations to Australia's Macquarie Bank for £263.6m.

In 2010, shares soared 3.4 per cent after Stagecoach won a £100m victory following a bitter battle for government subsidies. Although Stagecoach lost its claim over the use of car park revenues in subsidy calculations, they successfully argued that its South West franchise should be granted revenue support from April 2010 in a case heard by the rail industry arbitrator. The Department for Transport lost their claim that the franchise contract specified any payments did not kick in until February 2011. Brian Souter had been confident enough to warn long before the successful outcome: "We will end up with a very large cheque". While the government offer revenue support to rail franchises to cover shortfalls in targeted income, the franchise stood to pay more to the government if they outperformed. Experts predicted Stagecoach to benefit to the tune of £100m.

After the 2004 payout, in December 2006, Stagecoach shareholders prepared themselves for another big bonus. Cash rich, the company made a massive pay-out. As 15% owner of Stagecoach, Brian Souter was reported paying himself a handsome £60m Christmas bonus while his sister Ann with 11% got £44m.

The timing couldn't have been worse for Stagecoach pension holders. Stagecoach had shut its final salary pension scheme to new staff members. There was a funding shortfall of £103m by the end of October 2006. There had already been a one-off contribution of £57m from Stagecoach and they had reached an agreement with scheme trustees to add another £50m to that. Although the company agreed to maintain final salary benefits for existing members, it still meant Stagecoach and their staff were making higher contributions. It was hoped the deficit would have been eliminated within five years. Grahame Smith, the STUC's general secretary thought it "shocking" and train union ASLEF's chief, Kevin Lindsay, who looked after members working for Stagecoach's South West Trains, wasn't best pleased either, calling it a "disgrace". He told the *Herald*: "In this day and age when pensions are top of the political agenda it is immoral for two multi-millionaires to take more money when the pension fund is in deficit". The company had made huge gains after selling its London bus operations to Australia's Macquarie Bank.

Brian Souter and Ann Gloag were beaten by the magic of Harry Potter's creator, JK Rowling into ninth place in the *Sunday Times Scotland's* Rich List in 2006 with a joint personal fortune estimated at £395m.

Brian Souter sustained further losses, along with Sir Bill Gammell and Angus Grossart's nephew, Hamish Grossart, chairman of IndigoVision, when Digital Bridges - a company promising to revolutionise the way we play games on our mobile phones and trading under the brand, I-Play - was sold to Oberon Media for less than the investors paid for it.

Nonetheless, in 2009, the family's private investment group, Souter Investments, teamed up with Argent Energy's management to buy the bio-diesel company with a £25m annual turnover, converting tallow and cooking oil into fuel for transport in Motherwell. With a portfolio of 120 investments worth around £400million including luxury boat builder Sunseeker, Souter went on to chalk up even bigger successes. By 2011, with 14 million users, Megabus.com had made tremendous inroads into the US market, covering a further 11 cities in the US.

From his father's redundancy pay-off and the purchase of two second-hand buses, Brian Souter went on to build Stagecoach into an empire employing 30,000 with an annual turnover of £2 billion.

Estimated at the time to have a personal fortune of around £200m, Brian Souter's sister, Ann Gloag was living in the £1.3m, 19,500 acre; 23-bedroomed, Beaufort Castle estate in Beauly, which she had bought off Lord Lovat in 1995. She too would attract her fair share of media attention. In 2003 Ann Gloag took to court two tenants on her estate, a former policeman and his wife, Ian and Patricia Hamilton, who had been renting for 12 years at £60-a-week, a three-bedroom Coach House property. She wanted to stop them mowing a lawn and planting shrubs on a small plot adjacent to their cottage. Gloag never talked to tenants on her estate. Two years after she had tried to repossess the property she now insisted that the plot of land, measuring 20 yards by six, along with nearby barn and carport; was hers. She sought an interdict limiting the Hamiltons to their house and its immediate garden. The couple claimed the protected tenancy, including rights to the disputed areas, had been agreed with Lord Lovat. Gloag faced some harsh criticism from the Hamiltons' solicitor advocate who twice accused her of lying in court over whether there had been padlocks on the outbuildings prior to buying the property and over the location of 'large red stones' placed by the Hamiltons near to the Coach House. Gloag told the court that she had scuffed the car on one of the stones she had hit. "There were about half a dozen and they were spread out. There was a bit of a jolt. I was concerned with the fact that there were small children in the car". Mr Hamilton shook his head when Gloag pointed to where the stones had been in a photograph and the Hamilton's solicitor advocate pointed out the stones had been on the other side of the track. Gloag disagreed. She said it had been the passenger side of the Range Rover that had been hit, "unless", she added indignantly, "I had taken up the continental style of driving". The solicitor advocate wondered if maybe it wasn't the stones that were a danger to the small children but the manner of her driving. Mrs Gloag denied it. The court learned that she had instructed her caretaker to remove the stones with a bulldozer the day before the Hamiltons received a letter from her solicitors in Perth complaining about them. Gloag said it wasn't a "huge concern" to her the Hamiltons' plants had been damaged "given that I didn't think the plants should be there anyway". The Hamiltons suggested in court that there might have been more progress if Mrs Gloag had talked to him and his wife. Mrs Gloag insisted she had no communication with any of her tenants and her advocate, Eric Robertson, said, "Are you seriously suggesting that a landowner should come in and talk about these matters over a cup of tea?" Mr Hamilton replied: "Yes I do, I do indeed". Reporting the case in *Scotland on Sunday*, Jason Allardye tagged on to the end of his report: "While both parties continue to give competing versions of events about what has gone on in the Highlands, what is not in question is that the Mercy Ships that Gloag supports have allowed life-changing operations to take place. The entrepreneur has helped not only with her money but also with her time, working on board and drawing on her experience as a nurse. Gloag said: 'Even as a little girl it seemed right to donate part of my pocket money to starving children in Africa. Then, when I became a nurse, even though we were very poorly paid, it was the most natural thing in the world to continue with my giving'." Gloag sought and won her interdict in addition to her legal costs, estimated at around £20,000, which cost the Hamiltons their life savings. At Inverness Sheriff Court, Sheriff Donald Booker Milburn accused them of lying during the three-day hearing and said: "I could not help thinking of Humpty-Dumpty's words in Through the Looking Glass: 'When I use a word it means just what I choose it to mean – neither more nor less'. Mr Hamilton is saying that his use of the word 'surrounding' means 'to the east of.' I do not accept this.

The ruling came at a time when Gloag had had her latest application for up to £10,000 of grant money to improve houses on her estate turned down by Highland Council.

10 days after the court ruling, the Hamiltons wrote to Sheriff Principal Stephen Young in Aberdeen. Mrs Hamilton expressed her concern that the hearing had been unfair. That Sheriff Booker Milburn had from the outset made his feelings about the case known in court and that it was hard to accept that they had been completely wrong in everything they had said. She wrote: "The sheriff listened politely to the persuer's case and witnesses, questioning in a very minor way their statements... Our own evidence was questioned, interrupted and ridiculed; our solicitor was continually interrupted and was not allowed to finish his statements or even his pleadings in law. I was given the impression throughout that our case was a bore, of no consequence and that the plight of an ordinary family who had been stupid enough to use pension funds and life savings to fund this case was of absolutely no concern".

The couple were advised to seek further legal advice.

By 2004, Ann Gloag had her lawyers write to one of the last tenants on her Highland estate. Mr Slater's tenancy was not a protected tenancy under the Rent (Scotland) Act, 1984: his tenancy was a contractual assured tenancy under the Housing (Scotland) Act, 1988, which from 2004 was to become a statutory assured tenancy under that act. This type of tenancy derives purely from statute and not common law and differed in various material ways from a protected tenancy. (All the other tenants were in tied cottages or on month-to-month leases). How much Mr Slater understood this is not clear. John Slater, 67, was an

Keeping Marriage and Schools for Christians

eccentric character who had raised money for charity walking from Land's End to John o'Groats barefoot and in pyjamas and had previously lived in caves off Wester Ross. He had supported the Hamiltons through their court case and had lived over 10 years on the estate. Gloag's Edinburgh solicitors explained that the purpose of serving the notice was to terminate Mr Slater's contractural assured tenancy so that his only entitlement to reside at Stables Cottage would be for as long as he was a statutory assured tenant. They added that this would not be an eviction since court approval would be needed for that, but changes to the lease would allow Gloag to increase his rent and allow her estate to impose new terms to his contract. Clearly worried, he explained: "I just want to live here quietly". Gloag's lawyers wrote to the *Herald*, which had covered the story, to explain: "The fact is that Mr Slater will continue to enjoy security of tenure under the 1988 act provided of course, as with any tenant, that he observes the requirements of his tenancy. Mr Slater can readily obtain reassurance on this point from his laywer, so we are unclear as to why he is expressing concerns as to the security of his tenancy".

Keeping Beaufort Castle estate in Beauly, Ann Gloag decided to sell her Perthshire mansion, Balcraig House in Scone which went on the market with FPD Savills at offers over £1.8m and was expected to fetch £2m. The property, situated in 11 acres, had three floors, a separate bothy cottage, a staff flat, nine bedrooms, a swimming pool, tennis courts and a gym.

Only a year after purchasing a Category A mansion, awarded the highest level of government protection, Kinfauns Castle by the River Tay in 2005 for £4m, Ann Gloag submitted a planning application for a £20m golf and leisure project in the grounds, to include a 6,551-yard championship course which landed her in the news again. Gloag had erected a mile-long, seven-foot high; barbed-wire security fence around almost half of the 30-acre estate without planning permission. Grassland and woods, once accessible to walkers through gates were now firmly padlocked. The Ramblers Association of Scotland called the fence 'outrageous' and the Architectural Heritage Society of Scotland objected in the 'strongest possible terms' to Perth and Kinross Council.

Under a new editor, *Scotland on Sunday* didn't appear to be nearly so accommodating about Ann Gloag and her brother's issues. The broadsheet blasted: "They are seen by some as hard-nosed bureaucrats who will readily order a wall ripped down if it's inches out of place. But a different side to Scotland's planning officials emerged when they came face-to-face with the country's second-richest woman". Gloag was under investigation by Historic Scotland after it emerged that Dave Stubbs, Perth and Kinross council's access officer had opposed the erection of the 12-acre wire-mesh enclosure but changed his mind after receiving a letter from her lawyer, Peter Watson, which explained: "Mrs Gloag has privacy issues which she wants respected". Stubbs wrote to Paul Kettles, the council's area planning enforcement officer: "Remember this one. No word about the erection of a 6ft fence". Kettles alerted his boss, Ian Sleith, the council's head of development control who wrote: "Owner will not be happy with numerous people inspecting interior of her home, indeed I have had a personal request it is me! I am ready to recognise the importance of privacy to this particular individual. So can I suggest enforcement officer, planning officer and Historic Scotland all inspect at same time if at all possible and by arrangement?" With only five days to raise objections, unsurprisingly, there were none when council officials – under delegated powers - recommended planning permission should be passed. (It would normally take 21 days). Historic Scotland was furious they had not been entitled to raise objections to the fence round the Category A mansion. Gloag won her battle after Perth and Kinross Council refused to review its decision, which meant Historic Scotland was left without any authority to have it pulled down.

Gloag went further and challenged the Executive's right-to-roam legislation in an attempt to stop members of the public wandering on to her land at all. (Following pressure from the Ramblers' Association, Rangers Football Club owner David Murray had also been challenged by Perth and Kinross Council for erecting a gated barrier around his retreat in Bridge of Earn without permission, a claim he strenuously denied). The Ramblers' Association publicly begged for funds to challenge Ann Gloag in court, fearing she would set a precedent that could be exploited by other landowners. After Sheriff Michael Fletcher trudged round her property in his Wellington boots he returned to court to listen to an independent security adviser, paid by Gloag, who told the court that the fence was the minimum security measure he would have advised. A former superintendent of Grampian Police said she owned valuable artefacts and jewellery at the castle and also suggested that the fence was the minimum security measure he would have advised. Representing Ann Gloag, Jack Irvine told the court that his client had been the victim of "gross intrusion" that had been "really quite disgusting", adding that, "it's really quite extraordinary the amount of attention she gets, the volume of inquiries by the media and the interest in her private life. There just seems to be this insatiable interest by the media in everything she does". He said he had notified the Press Complaints Commission several times of stories he disapproved of, including one in the *Sun*. Ms Wilson, for the council, asked Mr Irvine: "Is it not somewhat disingenuous, given your experience and background in the newspaper industry, to suggest that a high-profile businesswoman like Ann Gloag would not merit the attention and interest of journalists?" Mr Irvine replied: "I am a reformed character. I'm not a journalist anymore".

Challenged in court by the Ramblers' Association Scotland - who were keen to ensure the efficacy of the right-to-roam legislation - and Perth and Kinross Council, Ann Gloag went on to become the first private individual to successfully argue that right-to-roam legislation should not apply to her land. Sheriff Michael Fletcher returned a judgement that the nature of the building and its prominence meant that a larger section of land around her home was required to ensure her family's privacy and enjoyment. (Section 6 of the Act allowed for land to be made exempt for reasons of privacy or enjoyment by the owner). Whilst the Act allowed for privacy, location and "other characteristics" to be taken into consideration, Sheriff Michael Fletcher was critical of the vagueness of the Act. Critics suggested the case would most likely be challenged in the Court of Session before finishing up in the House of Lords. The Ramblers' Association Scotland and Perth and Kinross Council were ordered by Sheriff Michael Fletcher to pay Gloag's costs. (She was represented by Levy and McRae). The bill for her legal costs came to £161,000 which she promised to donate to charity. Dennis Canavan, a former MSP who had been instrumental in getting the Land Reform (Scotland) Act 2003 onto the statute books called the judgement "a gross distortion" adding it was "flouting the will of the Scottish Parliament". In court, Gloag was condemned by John Campbell QC, representing the Rambers' Association, for treating court proceedings with a lack of respect, accusing her of being "accustomed to having her own way" after she declared it "inconvenient" she attended the court case she herself had brought.

Finally, Ann Gloag made a settlement – secretly under a confidentiality clause negotiated by her lawyers - with land access campaigners over the costs of taking her to court. The Ramblers' Association, a charity, appealed to its members to help pay the substantial court bill.

Life at Beaufort Castle wasn't always as secret as Ann Gloag might have liked. Her daughter Pamela was married there to her husband Eddie Gray in 2003 in a ceremony performed by David Souter only months after he had been fined £125 and ordered to compensate his ex-wife, also called Pamela, for aggressive behaviour. In 2009, during a Christmas at the castle, he was thrown out after an argument broke out. The matter ended up in court where Sherriff Michael Fletcher was made aware that it had not been the first time his wife had been subjected to aggressive bullying by her husband.

A new six-bedroom villa with a separate three-bedroom bungalow for a carer set the scene for a new round of objections from neighbours and Forestry Commission Scotland who warned that if the planning application went ahead it would ruin an area of ancient woodland. Perth and Kinross Council disagreed. Part of the condition for winning their approval was that she paid a £12,790 'education contribution' fee to fund improvements at nearby Kinnoull Primary School.

After successful applications for a six-bedroomed mansion and a three-bedroomed house on her estate, Gloag wasn't so lucky with plans for three terraced houses by Kinfauns Castle or a row of new homes by a former steading near the castle on a green belt site of great landscape value. Permission had originally been granted in 2008 but since building work hadn't started it became the subject of a further application. Architectural Heritage Society of Scotland wrote to planners to say: "This proposal breaches just about every planning policy for the location".

Ann Gloag made one of Britain's biggest donations to a Christian charity, giving £4 million to convert old car ferries into 'Mercy Ships' or floating hospitals, relief centres and Christian missionary bases. She also established an orphanage and school in

Keeping Marriage and Schools for Christians

Kenya and a women's refuge centre. Lord Ian McColl, a former adviser in the House of Lords to former Conservative Prime Minister John Major, headed the charity in the UK. Gloag sat on the international board of the Texas-based Mercy Ships. She also donated money through her Balcraig charity. Whilst the charity performed outreach work in communities by building clinics and centres for sexual health education, surgeons apparently did not perform operations on HIV patients. A spokesperson explained to the *Scotsman:* "The medics believe it is too easy to be sidelined by the AIDS problem. The virus has killed 20 million Africans in 19 years. Every year, the same numbers die from dirty water, bad sanitation, malaria and tuberculosis".

Patrons of the Mercy Ships included John Major and his wife Norma. As Prime Minister, Major supported Section 28 and launched the infamous 'Back to Basics' morality campaign, sacking ministers caught having extra-marital affairs. (It was later disclosed he had enjoyed a long-standing sexual affair with fellow minister, Edwina Currie).

In 2005, Gloag met the wives of the world's most powerful men at the G8 summit held at Gleneagles, lunching with Laura Bush, Ludmila Putin and Cherie Blair. She was chosen as one of four 'opinion formers' to discuss world poverty at the event along with Dr Josephine Munthali, a Malawian who lived in Edinburgh and worked for the Scottish Catholic International Aid Fund.

After being awarded an OBE in 2004, in October 2009, Ann Gloag received the United Nation's first ever Susan B Anthony Humanitarian Award in honour of her international charity work. Anthony was one of the US's best known human rights campaigners and the only woman to be featured on a US coin. Mary Singletary, president of the National Council of Women of the United States, said the honour had been established to recognise those who were dedicated to making a difference in people's lives, communities or the state of the world. Gloag said she was "humbled" and said "helping to improve the lives of others truly enriches my life".

By June 2011, Brian Souter was knighted in the Queen's Birthday Honours List for services to transport and the voluntary sector, initiating almost 3,000 protests within a few days on a Facebook page begging it be withdrawn. Under Bruce Waddell's editorship, the *Daily Record* appeared to wash its hands of the campaign they had taken to their heart. Sir Brian was described as a man "also known for his failed campaign to keep Section 28, the law which banned teachers and pupils from discussing homosexuality in schools". Sir Brian was reported to be delighted with his award, praising the Stagecoach team and his wife Betty's efforts with the Souter Charitable Trust. He told the BBC: "They really don't seek any publicity but they do some really, really good work". Whilst the leader of the Scottish Parliament, Alex Salmond, insisted the nomination was made by a group of civil servants and not the SNP, the UK Cabinet Office insisted the nomination came directly from the Scottish government. A spokesman for the First Minister claimed this was a reference to the Scottish government's independent Honours Committee. Another excuse given was that Buckingham Palace rules banned publishing more details as it related to the exercise by Her Majesty of Her prerogative of honour.

The findings of former Lord Advocate, Lord Fraser, later cleared Alex Salmond of having any part in knighting Brian Souter. It was met with claims of 'whitewash' by some Labour activists who said the report failed to address all the issues, while Souter accused them of "mischief-making". The problem centred round Labour's demand to know why Alex Salmond wrote a letter denying his government had any involvement when the permanent secretary sat on the judging panel. They also wanted to know why the Scottish Government was refusing a Freedom of Information request to publish all the relevant papers. Shortly after the nomination was made, Brian Souter said he would donate £500,000 to the SNP.

However, the Scottish Information Commissioner found that the SNP had indeed failed to comply with the law in its refusal to release documents revealing communications between Sir Brian Souter and the SNP on the grounds it would 'prejudice' relations with the UK government.

Suddenly, at 9am on Thursday, 31 August 2000, Martin Clarke, the editor of the *Daily Record* "resigned". With plummeting sales figures and low staff morale on the tabloid, most media observers suspected he had been fired. His own record of tantrums, foul mouth, petulance and aggressive manner would not be missed. One senior journalist said: "You can hardly move in this place without being tripped up by the smiles". Prime Minister Tony Blair was said to have been very happy with the news, unlike Gerald Warner. His column in *Scotland on Sunday*

Keeping Marriage and Schools for Christians

announced we had all woken up "in Totalitaria" and launched another blistering attack on the repeal of Section 28, comparing the Scottish Executive with Ceausescu's Romania and demanding the heads of ministers Sam Galbraith, Susan Deacon and Wendy Alexander. Martin Clarke went home to his Scottish Catholic wife Veronica, who was said to have influenced his rabid campaign to prevent the repeal of Section 28, before taking up the post of editor-in-chief of Associated Newspapers – owners of the *Daily Mail* - in Ireland. The *Sunday Herald's* Mediawatch column noted that he would be editing *Ireland on Sunday* and wrote: "We recommend that staff at the youthful paper acquire hard hats, flak jackets, earplugs and rawhides". He would be promoted to editor of the MailOnline which by 2011 was the second most visited English-language newspaper website worldwide.

Clarke's departure had centred on the *Herald* grabbing an exclusive on Rangers' signing of Ronald de Boer, which had him up against the management after he was said to have gone "ballistic" at deputy sports editor Alan Rowan, who, along with his sports editor Jim Traynor, threatened to resign. Clarke's salary was reported to be around £250,000 per annum and he was thought to have taken twice that amount as a pay-off. Peter Cox, the editor of the *Sunday Mail*, who was more faithful to the Labour administration, immediately replaced Martin Clarke as editor of the *Daily Record*. I was immediately re-assured that "the juggernaut that is the Record is about to change course" and Cox went on to halve the circulation loss Clarke had created. It would be, however, over a year later before gay people would be seen advertising in the paper's personal columns under columns discreetly headed: 'Men Seeking Men' and 'Women Seeking Women'. It was a short reign. By 2003, he was sacked and replaced by the editor of the *Scottish Sun*, Bruce Waddell. Jack Irvine described the appointment: "Shit hot".

By the end of 2000, Martin Clarke had a new column in the *Scottish Daily Mail*. It wasn't long before he was using his columns to attack Wendy Alexander, bragging Section 28 had killed off any chance of Donald Dewar's favourite becoming First Minister. "In many ways this is Wendy's hard cheese"; he scoffed. On the demise of Section 28, he huffed: "As the long awaited replacement for Section 28, the Scottish Executive unveils new 'non-judgmental' sex education guidelines which put every relationship on an equal moral footing and suggest only that

455

some groups, such as churches, still think marriage is important. Which is rather like telling kids some people still think smashing up a bus shelter is a bit off".

Martin Clarke proved his abilities to write were as questionable as his abilities to edit when he introduced a soap based on Holyrood in the *Scottish Mail* called "Deidenders" after the popular BBC soap *Eastenders*. Set in a pub on Edinburgh's Mound it featured, of course, "bossy barmaid, Wacky Wendy" who delivered such lines as: "Who are you calling hen, you sexist old man?" and "Sloppy Susan, the local sexual health outreach worker…" who asked: "Can I interest you in some free condoms and a guide to gay Edinburgh?" and, when the offer was declined, retorted: "Homophobe. Take a couple home for the weans then…"

In the absence of Section 28, the public themselves were urged to act as moral vigilantes. When a picture of a young woman holding up an unrolled condom appeared in a handbook for the Guides Association, the Church, with the help of the *Sunday Mail*, now under the editorship of Alan Rennie, demonstrated their vigilantism. The Guides were "under fire". Mrs Ann Allen of the Kirk's Board of Social Responsibility was wheeled in to tell the *Sunday Mail* that Girl Guides needed "a moral map, not how to use a condom". The Catholic Church issued a warning to parents over the manual and sought a meeting with the Guides Association. Father Danny McLaughlin bemoaned "the diminishing role of religion in the Guides" and, after scanning the handbook, Guide leader Penny Thomson wailed: "The word 'marriage' is nowhere to be found. Nor can I find the word 'wife'. It seems young women in the Guides will become 'partners'." Martin Clarke used his column in the *Scotsman* to question the absence of marriage in the manual while *Sunday Mail* reporter Lynn McPherson found a Guide with a nose-ring on the front cover of the handbook and groups encouraged to invite family planning clinics to meetings "to talk about relationships, discuss prostitution and ask MPs why single-sex marriages are illegal". Her report was accompanied by a saluting Guide in uniform, harking back to days of hockey-sticks and goose-stepping to brass bands, with the caption: "Innocent: The traditional image of Guides".

John McGurk, editor of *Scotland on Sunday*, resigned from a brief stint editing the *Scotsman* in 2006, not long after Johnston

Keeping Marriage and Schools for Christians

Press bought the group. His former employee, Aidan Barclay, offered him the post of managing editor of Telegraph Group papers, the *Daily Telegraph* and the *Sunday Telegraph*, the right-wing papers which were now owned by the Barclays brothers, before he took a big pay-off and became a consultant with a PR firm.

Tom 'Brigadier' Brown left the *Daily Record* and appeared briefly in *Scotland on Sunday* before hitting the hay after his brand of religious proselytising began to lose its shine.

Ramsay Smith, editor of the *Scottish Daily Mail*, moved to Jack Irvine's Media House as a political consultant and soon took up a new post as the Glasgow editor of the *Scotsman* before becoming executive director of Media House. In 2002, David Montgomery, former chief of the Mirror Group, fronted a bid to buy the *Herald* with Jack Irvine as his Scottish adviser. Montgomery had a reputation as a costcutter, but shareholder pressure over Mirror Group's poor performance after its merger with Trinity newspaper group led to his departure with a £1.13m payoff.

Jack Irvine was later joined by Allan Hogarth, who had previously worked with Irvine on the board of the Scottish North American Business Council before standing as a Tory party candidate and becoming head of media relations at business lobbying group CBI Scotland. He joined Media House as director of government affairs with the intention of helping the firm secure more government business.

In 2004, one of 'Keep the Clause's 'celebrity supporters', hairdresser Taylor Ferguson was cleared of recklessly and culpably firing a shotgun close to a children's horse-riding lesson that was held in neighbouring stables. A horse had bolted and thrown the 13-year-old rider who had to be rushed to hospital with severe bruising. Ferguson told the court he had been shooting rabbits from his bathroom window at his house in Mugdock, near Glasgow, saying: "When there is an excess of rabbits you need to deal with them". The riding instructor, Lynne Shovelin told the court that Ferguson had previously threatened to "go and shoot his gun if she did not lower her voice and that she had 'been warned'." Ferguson admitted he had asked her to keep her voice down. He was found 'not guilty' of reckless conduct by Sheriff Robert Younger. Outside the court, Ferguson expressed his relief it was all over, adding: "It ends an extremely difficult period for my family. I would like to thank my clients

RELIGIOUS FASCISM

and all who supported me, especially my wife Anne". The owner of the stables, David Ralston told the press: "He knows what he did and he will have to live with that".

One of Brian Souter's 'referendum' sponsors, Donald Macdonald, chairman of Macdonald Hotels was awarded an OBE in 2005 but faced legal action in the same year when Elizabeth Irons, a former director of corporate affairs and director of marketing and communications for the hotel chain claimed she had faced sexual discrimination. She alleged that she was unfairly dismissed and subjected to disability discrimination, bullying and harassment. She took her claim to an employment tribunal, arguing that she had been paid up to £50,000 a year less than male colleagues in an equivalent role, before the company struck an eleventh hour deal.

Macdonald again found himself in the news after trying to wrest back his group's lucrative management contract for the timeshare resort of Loch Rannoch Highland Club. Macdonald offered to pay the owners up to £2,000 for holiday weeks which he claimed were being traded for £150 on ebay. It was an offer many owners would find difficult to refuse. The only condition was that they hand over their legal title of ownership and all voting rights at Loch Rannoch to Macdonald Resorts, putting the group in control by using the proxy votes. Macdonald had lost his flagship resort when its owners took majority control of the five-person committee and with the backing of the owners, sacked Macdonald and handed the running of the resort to owner-run company TMSL which promptly introduced new services and cut the management fees by 16%. By the end of the first year the owner-led company had made a small surplus and its lodges went on to win three-star and four-star grading by VisitScotland inspectors. Amongst other penalties, Macdonald responded by barring everyone who used the Loch Rannoch resort from using the swimming pool and the bar of its adjacent hotel. His attempt to gain control of the committee through "a genuine offer made by me on behalf of Macdonald Resorts in the spirit of trying to restore Loch Rannoch to the fine holiday destination it once was" failed. In a letter sent to owners who had accepted, the chairman wrote: "Whilst I have been very heartened by the response to our offer, which showed that it appealed to over a third of owners, the acceptance condition stated in our terms and conditions has not been met. Accordingly, the offer has now lapsed. I wish to express my gratitude to you for supporting the initiative. To that end I would like to offer you, free of charge, and subject to availability and conditions, full dinner, bed and breakfast, for two persons at The Macdonald Four Seasons Hotel at Aviemore". The letter concuded: "If you wish to give us further support I enclose a proxy form... if you are agreeable to completing and signing it". When the owners attempted to place the letter on their website, Macdonald's lawyers at Tods Murray (Tory leader, David McLetchie's firm), warned the letter was copyright and couldn't be reproduced. Unfortunately, for Macdonald Resorts, the letter did not contain any copyright warning and TMSL were entitled to go ahead and release the contents of the letter. Macdonald Resorts suggested their concerns were primarily over any subsequent editing of the letter and continued to withhold management fees for the 163 holiday weeks in its ownership and pursue a legal claim against the three lay committee owner members for more than £800,000. Macdonald Hotels told the *Herald* that the committee's view had "no credence when over one-third of the ownership either wished to sell their weeks or see a change in the management regime".

Another of the sponsors of Brian Souter's opinion poll, Pat Grant OBE went on to encounter problems when her refridgeration company, Norfrost, went into administration. Although sales amounted to £13m in 2004, the company had been making a loss for three years. Caithness and Sutherland Enterprise had handed Norfrost a loan of £1.2m secured against the firm's assets.

In 2005, former sponsors, Vera and Gerald Weisfeld of the What Everyone Wants chain sold their ostentatious, mock ancient Roman, eight-bedroomed mansion, complete with a porch and free-standing Ionic columns, not dissimilar to the Temple of Portunos, for £2.6m through Savills. The Verace-inspired interior with sweeping double-staircase, marble floors, underground swimming pool with Greek columns and a ballroom with fibre-optic lighting to give the impression of a star-filled sky was on the 35-acre estate in Stratford-upon-Avon. It was a holiday home. It had originally taken three years to sell the property, built in 1999 by an Iranian businessman whose wife hated it, forcing him to sell it to the Weisfelds for a £500,000 loss. The Weisfelds also owned homes in Australia and Bridge of Weir in Scotland.

RELIGIOUS FASCISM

Another sponsor, Tom Hunter, Scotland's richest man, went on to be portrayed in the media as something of a philanthropist and dismissed reports that he had discussed a £60m business acquisition, drunk, in a Monaco nightclub toilet. Sir Tom also denied being drunk at Nicky's Beach Bar in St Tropez during a similar discussion with Jon Wood in 2003. He was asked to explain himself to the High Court in London where he and fellow Scottish businessman, Chris Gorman (himself caught in something of a ménage a trois in a Florida nightclub toilet in 2011) fought a £100m lawsuit. They were being sued by two former co-owners of high street chain, Gadget Shop. The dispute related to Tom's purchase of Birthdays, the greetings card chain which he purchased through his West Coast Capital Investment vehicle. His partners in Gadget Shop, Peter Wilkinson and Jon Wood, believed they had been cut out of the deal. Although it had been sold at a loss, they wanted back their shares at the time of its purchase. The legal wrangle cost 750 jobs. During the trial, Tom was accused of "suspect business ethics and business morals" and a "complete lack of probity and commercial morality". In court, Jon Wood was accused of being a liar and of wasting court time in an attempt to embarrass Sir Tom in public.

In 2006 Sir Tim Hunter topped the *Sunday Times Scotland* Rich List with a personal fortune estimated at £780m. He pledged to give away £1billion with the words: "With great wealth comes great responsibility" and "I am not going to hide it under a bushel". He didn't have to. By the time the recession hit in 2009 he was forced to seriously modify his ambitions.

Another of Souter's sponsors, the Catholic entrepreneur Sir Tom Farmer, was awarded the Andrew Carnegie Medal of Philanthropy in 2005 for providing support to communities all over the world in promoting self-sufficiency and personal development through his Farmer Foundation. He also went on to support Brian Souter again in 2011 in opposing the SNP government's efforts to consult on introducing same-sex marriage. After SNP donor Sir Brian warned against creating a "Babylonian" society where sex is seen as "primarily a recreational activity", Sir Tom, also a wealthy SNP sponsor, felt moved to warn the *Sunday Herald*, that the SNP had "alienated" itself from "large parts of the population".

Keeping Marriage and Schools for Christians

By May 2000, editor Tim Luckhurst had left the *Scotsman* in the hands of Rebecca Hardy, who later went on to edit the *Sun*. Hardy wasn't shy about homophobic headlines as editor of the *Sun*, demonstrated on the front page when Elton John married David Furnish: "Elton takes David up the aisle". She wasn't exactly choosy about who wrote for the *Scotsman*, either. Ex-*Daily Record* editor Martin Clarke had his own column, in addition to one he already had in the *Scottish Daily Mail*. Linda Watson-Brown, a rabid anti-porn campaigner who believed all men were potential rapists, appeared almost daily. Perhaps Hardy thought Watson-Brown was in touch with the Scottish psyche. Watson-Brown would write: "Surely all journeys with children on board should provide entertainment appropriate for the youngest passenger? No matter if a plane has only one three-year-old who sleeps for ten hours, it is no excuse for any film above a U certificate". Linda Watson-Brown hated laddish magazines like *GQ* and *Loaded* that showed: "Gynaecological illustrations of dehumanised women". She begged readers to anonymously send their letters of disgust to her so she could pass them on to newsagents W H Smith as a punishment for re-introducing erotica after only a five-year break. Anyone who disagreed was dismissed as a "stultifying... intellectually-challenged... pro-pornographer..." Walking into Arnold Clark's car showroom to test-drive a Citroën, Linda Watson-Brown found: "...If I chose to take a test drive in one of their vehicles, I would be rewarded with a gift voucher for the nation's most visited pornographic outlet... A young man informed me that I didn't have to spend the £10 voucher on pornography. He also, helpfully, told me that some people like pornography and that he did not think his boss would be interested in my concerns".

Linda Watson-Brown attacked Yves Saint Laurent's Opium advertisement featuring model Sophi Dahl lying on her back "in the buff wearing only her shoes and jewellery". One parent, seeing it displayed near a secondary school told the *Glaswegian:* "I want it removed pronto". Linda Watson-Brown agreed: "...Leaning back, legs open at a ridiculous angle". Dahl was a woman "pretending to enjoy her own body... Her spread-eagled, created pose says more about the sad dupes we are believed to be by the advertising industry... Opiate of the people - pornography is the new religion". The complaints received by the Advertising Standards Authority over this advertisement, however, fell far short of those received over Books Online's advertisement of a naked couple sitting reading a book. Their message? Sex is good, but reading's better!

Linda Watson-Brown, who admitted she had no problem with censorship, would have no doubt cheered the hundreds of protesters from various churches who sent 283 written objections and stormed a council meeting to stop Margaret McCracken from opening a sex shop in Ayr before the spring of 2001. Despite assurances that goods requiring a licence would be kept at the back, no entry would be given to anyone under 21 and the windows - as required by law - would be completely blacked out, the Licensing Board refused to give Ms McCracken a licence. One tearful woman claimed her son had become addicted to pornography, changing and distorting his personality until he had become "sinful". A minister advised that sex was God's gift to loving couples and allowed them to express their love in a caring way within marriage. An elderly lady describing herself as a born-again Christian lectured the Board for five minutes on the state of their "immortal souls" before promising them: "I'll pray for you. I'll pray that you'll be saved from this evil".

After the British Board of Film Classification's president, Andreas Whittam Smith, suggested there ought to be more sex shops, Watson-Brown labelled them places that sold "pornography" for "grown-ups who just happen to get aroused by images of exploitation and degradation". There were only two licensed sex shops - or "pervert's paradises" as Watson-Brown called them - in Scotland, both in Edinburgh. "...Do we ignore the problem, or wait until the likes of Andreas Whittam Smith puts a sex shop on every High Street in Scotland?" Watson-Brown warned the sight of 'pornographic' pictures on the Internet took only a few seconds to view "but a lifetime to wipe out".

Campaigning against 'pornography' in the *Scotsman*, day after day, she highlighted new campaigns: "Can I really justify writing about this again? Too damn right I can..." she sniffed in one article. And, in the unlikely event you found it hard to make your censorious voice heard in Scotland, or if you had any information "about the tentacles the sex industry has into other areas, let me know. I am still receiving letters about last year's WH Smith campaign – maybe it's time for another", she added. And for anyone e-mailing her, she promised: "I will compile an information sheet for readers who want to know just what their magazine company is producing besides recipes..."

With a crusading zeal, Watson-Brown insisted, "many Scotsman readers are extremely nice, and I have evidence to prove it... They are also jolly good at taking up some of the many crusades which get suggested in this page... In the past week, I have had letters telling me that a major car manufacturer has defended the use of naked women on its calendars as 'a bit of fun to brighten up the day... And WH Smith has still not replied to more than one angry complainant asking how our favourite porn-peddler is allowed to get away with sponsoring so many education events and children's competitions. This, I'm sorry to say, is par for the course. Don't give up, and keep me informed. Good luck!" Rattling collecting cans during Comic Relief soon had the priggish porn-seeker lengthening her skirt. Watson-Brown was "alarmed" by "very young women in our city centres wandering along in schoolgirl and nurses' uniforms, adorned with suspenders and stockings, shaking collecting tins and asking complete strangers for money... It is a disgrace" she gasped.

Throughout the campaign, there were those who had surmised on the death of the First Minister, Donald Dewar. Iain Macwhirter had written in the *Sunday Herald*: "The really scary resignation scenario – the Nightmare on Holyrood which Labour MSPs are desperately trying not to talk about – is the possibility that Donald Dewar might himself throw in the towel. Could it happen? In his sixties, fatally wounded politically, and with an administration in meltdown, this is a man with little to look forward to except years of exhausting work rewarded by personal vilification. Might he just walk? Prime Ministers aren't meant to do that... But no-one said anything about First Ministers..."

On 10 October 2000, First Minister Donald Dewar collapsed on the steps of Bute House, his official Edinburgh residence. He continued to conduct meetings into the afternoon before his condition began to rapidly deteriorate. Despite his initial protests, his advisor, David Whitton recommended calling a doctor. Donald Dewar died the next day in hospital. He was 63.

It might have come as something of a relief to Gerald Warner, who had written earlier on in the year, mockingly, of Dewar being put down: "As he slumped there, his head resting on his paws, the whites of his eyes rolling fearfully, bereft of any quality of life he may once have enjoyed, nobody with a scintilla of pity could have resisted the claims of Sad Donald to a merciful release". Tom 'Brigadier' Brown had written: "Supposing – heaven forfend! – Donald Dewar fell under a Stagecoach bus..." As far back as January, 2000, Brown had been laying the ground for Henry McLeish's promotion. "At the moment, there is just one real contender – Henry McLeish, who has quietly but efficiently positioned himself as the only frontline Minister in the Scottish Cabinet with a safe pair of hands". But just how 'safe' were those hands? Henry McLeish benefited from the support he gained from the *Daily Record* and was soon chosen to be the new First Minister. His favourite *Record* columnist, Tom Brown was rewarded. He was first asked if he wanted the job of Henry McLeish's special advisor, but Brown's reputation alarmed the Liberal Democrats on the coalition. Instead, he was offered the job of becoming Henry McLeish's speechwriter. McLeish was forced to offer assurances that Brown would be restrained. Within days, Brown had written in his column in the *New Statesman* of proposed policy shifts and cabinet posts before McLeish had even announced them to his cabinet! Wendy Alexander, Donald Dewar's protégé and once tipped to be his deputy, became the Enterprise and Lifelong learning minister. Martin Clarke, still obsessed with marriage, remarked dryly in his column: "Wendy Alexander was promoted to Minister for Enterprise and Lifelong learning. She didn't get married. There was a wee stushie about something called Section 28, which the government replaced with guidelines on sex education. They don't mention marriage". Sam Galbriath, who also supported repeal of Section 28, was demoted to environment before he tendered his resignation due to ill health. Tom McCabe - whose partner was the *Scottish Mirror's* political editor, Lorraine Davidson – became Minister for Parliament. He was widely regarded as a tough operator and Henry McLeish's 'fixer'. One advisor to McLeish told the press; Tom McCabe's job would be to 'dump the crap'. McCabe, earning £77,000 per annum, later courted further controversy when - despite having a new £310,000 house with four bedrooms, three dining rooms, two en-suite bathrooms and a chauffeur-driven car in affluent Bothwell, Lanarkshire – he was awarded a £9,500 annual grant from the Scottish Executive towards buying or renting a flat in Edinburgh. The grant helped pay for a £150,000 three-bedroom penthouse in Powderhall, which McCabe would have been entitled to sell at any time, pocketing the profit. An MSP can claim a housing allowance if they live more than 90 minutes from parliament. McCabe did not originally qualify, but managed to persuade chiefs to make him an exception. He claimed this would save on his hotel bills when he was forced to stay overnight in Edinburgh; however, it transpired that his hotel bills in one year totalled just £2,784, plus £423 for travel, much less than the £9,500 grant he would have been entitled to claim to buy a property. Tom McCabe received a basic MSP's wage of £42,493 plus a Cabinet Minister's allowance of £35,538. As Labour's business manager, McCabe also sparked a protest when he attempted to become the sole judge of whether someone had stepped out of line and what their punishment should be in the Executive. Normally MSPs had to explain themselves to a party group.

In 2005 Tom McCabe provoked further outrage when plans were formalised to allow John Duncan, a right-wing Republican congressman and Presbyterian elder from Tennessee to escort a Scottish Executive delegation on a six-day Tartan Week tour of the US funded by the taxpayer. Duncan had compared green groups to Nazis when they opposed his support for drilling in the Arctic National Wildlife Refuge; backed calls to pull the USA out of the United Nations; complained there was too much homosexuality in America and was a favourite amongst Christian groups like the Christian Coalition, founded by Pat Robertson and gun groups. He was also expected to meet Jack McConnell. Tartan Week had already provoked controversy by its association with homophobic Mississippi senator Trent Lott who declared homosexuality an addiction that could be cured.

By 2011, Tom McCabe had lost his Holyrood seat in Hamilton, Larkhall and Stonehouse to the SNP, but the following year he landed himself a politically neutral policy role with the staunchly Labour Glasgow City Council earning just short of £50,000 a year. He had played a key role in Labour's successful local election campaign in Glasgow.

Defending his new position as First Minister Henry McLeish's speechwriter; Tom 'Brigadier' Brown focused on criticism that he was taking up a post that might be compromised by his writing for the *Record*. In his Holyrood column in the *New Statesman* he bragged of the "compliments" that were showered upon him: "The Sunday Herald described me as having 'macho, populist, politically incorrect tabloid credentials...'" He sniped: "I find that it is mainly those journalists who slant their reports to suit their proprietors' right-wing politics who most piously purport to be purveyors of the untainted truth, pretending there is no connection between what they write and what their bosses want". There had been little in the way of criticism from Brown of his former editor, Martin Clarke until now. Following some derisory comments by Martin Clarke in the *Scotsman* on journalists who work too closely with politicians, Brown sneered: "I had to remind myself that this was the same Clarke (ex-Daily Mail) who, although his politics are somewhere to the right of Norman Tebbit, managed to edit the leftish Daily Record for two years, during which time he continued to employ me and happily relied on my Labour contacts". Brown soon left the *Daily Record*, but the old Christian soldier's entrenched views still popped up in newspapers like the *Scottish Mail, Scotland on Sunday* or any paper that would have him.

One of the first things McLeish did when he was in office was to summon health minister Susan Deacon, who oversaw Healthy Respect, a £3m sexual health pilot project. He told her it was not the kind of thing he wanted his administration to be part of. Deacon had given an interview to the *Scotsman* magazine and McLeish didn't like it. In future, all questions on the subject of sex went through Peter MacMahon, McLeish's special adviser, while Tom McCabe controlled all Executive communication. McLeish set about appeasing the Catholic Church, first with a visit to the Vatican in December 2000 and then a 'bonding' session at Bute House with Susan Deacon, Cardinal Winning and the moderator of the Church of Scotland where it was reported they talked over shortbread and wine about everything but sex.

By the autumn of 2001, after just one year in office, Henry McLeish's head was on the block after he was embroiled in the notorious 'Officegate' scandal. Strict rules had been established to prevent publicly funded premises like constituency offices being used for political activism. McLeish denied he gave Fife Central Labour Party use of his offices at Hanover Court in Glenrothes, Fife, and of his secretary - salaried by the taxpayer - in the run-up to two local authority elections. Nonetheless, details of his offices were printed on election campaign leaflets. He made strenuous denials on Scottish television and admitted that if charges made against him were true, it would be a very serious matter.

Keeping Marriage and Schools for Christians

One of Henry McLeish's constituents, Andrew Duncan, frustrated by the lack of response from his MP, marched to his constituency office in Fife, where he was based. He wanted to air his grievances over a land deal that had turned sour, involving Fife Council and a lawyers' firm with strong links with Labour, Digby Brown. He was surprised to find Digby Brown sharing McLeish's office. The law firm had become the centre of allegations of cronyism after Lord Hardie, when lord advocate, appointed some of Digby Brown's personnel as sheriffs. Their satellite office had no phone, fax or e-mail. McLeish was entitled to an allowance of up to £51,572 to pay for his parliamentary office in Fife. Although he insisted he made no personal gain from the £4,000 a year he received from Digby Brown, he failed to declare the income and allowed payments from Digby Brown to be made directly into his own bank account. Labour spin-doctor Peter McMahon rushed to the aid of Henry McLeish after it was revealed he had been secretly sub-letting his constituency offices whist claiming the full rental costs on his Westminster expenses. "I don't see any conflict of interest in Henry sub-letting the office" McMahon said, adding later: "The money is not just for rental but for everything in the office, including the staff". On BBC's *Question Time* McLeish admitted he had no idea how much money he received in rent for his offices. All the same, after having let his upstairs offices for ten years - including to Fife Regional Council, the local authority which McLeish led from 1982 to 1987, Labour-supporting lawyers and a government-funded charity which employed his election agent - it was estimated McLeish had pocketed around £36,000, an amount he eventually said he would pay back. He was initially asked to pay back £9,000 to the Commons Fees Office. Henry McLeish never recovered from the scandal and after details of a sixth sub-let to the Third Age Group, a lunch club for the elderly, at his offices emerged, he forestalled a vote of no confidence by resigning as First Minister on Thursday, 8 November 2001.

The Third Age Group was a charity funded by Fife Council. McLeish's wife, Julie, had been one of a number of senior officials who had authorised £40,000 to be paid to the Third Age Group a year after the charity had wound up. Council officials shredded all documents relating to these payments, and, although the Audit Commission identified failings, they still claimed the money had been properly apportioned. McLeish was once again under scrutiny in the summer of 2002 when it was reported that he had used taxpayers' money – which he had insisted he would never accept – to pay off almost £39,000 of the money wrongly claimed for his constituency office back to the House of Commons Fees Office. McLeish and other Scottish MPs in Westminster had been offered a 'golden handshake' of £30,000 to give up their seats there to prevent 'dual mandating'. McLeish was later reported to have benefitted after selling his four-bedroomed villa in St Andrews in Fife for £400,000 – less than six years after he purchased it for £175,000. He expected to pick up a package worth £24,000 when he stood down as an MSP in 2003, plus a £34,000 pension as a former First Minister. He purchased for £285,000 a home in Cellardyke, a fishing village in Fife which was sold for £465,000, and went on to purchase a luxurious £500,000 home in St Andrews. Henry McLeish's memoirs, *Scotland First: Truth and Consequences* was published in 2004 but sold few copies. It was reported that only four people turned up to his book signing at a Glasgow store.

Another one of the 'Big Macs', Jack McConnell, was education chief in McLeish's cabinet. A former employee of lobbying firm Beattie Media, Jack McConnell was himself no stranger to controversy, since, as finance minister, he endured the 'Lobbygate' scandal after being accused of offering clients access to ministers. An investigation cleared him of any wrongdoing. Jack McConnell replaced Henry McLeish to become Scotland's third First Minister. McConnell faced a low point in his career in November 2000 when, with his wife Bridget, he faced a press conference to explain an affair he had had with a Labour Party worker. He was once again in the firing line and facing a police investigation in 2002 when it was revealed that payments by the Iron and Steel Trades Council union of £375-a-quarter were paid into a controversial development account which McConnell used to cover a variety of expenses, including the cost of his leadership campaign against McLeish. These donations to the Motherwell and Wishaw Labour Party, in the heart of Lanarkshire, by the union, were not declared to the electoral commission and they should have been. Former treasurer Liz Wilson was later charged with embezzling £11,000 from the funds. McConnell and local Labour MP Frank Roy were both cleared following an internal investigation. McConnell's political base, Lanarkshire, was riddled with sectarianism, cronyism and Labour in-fighting. By his own

Keeping Marriage and Schools for Christians

admission, Scotland faced opposition within Lanarkshire to the sort of reforms that were designed to tackle racism, sectarianism and by default, homophobia. Once the £11,000 black hole in McConnell's constituency accounts of unaccounted donations from union and private donations and affiliation fees emerged, so too did news of a fund-raising dinner for McConnell's election campaign which appeared undeclared in the accounts. One generous diner was a known drug baron.

McConnell faced criticism again in 2006 from Green campaigners and senior councillors in Aberdeenshire after US tycoon Donald Trump was engaged in numerous phone calls and at least two meetings in the US with McConnell when he wanted to build a £300m golf course, luxury hotel and housing on the Menie estate, a stretch of environmentally sensitive coastline north of Aberdeen. At a cost of £4,800 out of the public purse, Trump was taken on a helicopter ride over the centuries-old beach, home to nesting wildfowl, wild geese and songbirds, while memos revealed the Scottish Executive were prepared to meet the £40,000 - £50,000 cost of a feasibility study of a golf course here. Neil Hobday, Trump's UK project manager, used his middle name to purchase property on the site to avoid paying an inflated price. McConnell was accused of putting too much effort into impressing rich businessmen rather than looking after Scotland's long-term interests.

After McConnell lost the 2007 Scottish election for Labour by just one seat to the SNP, it became clear that Wendy Alexander might replace him as leader of the Labour Party in Scotland. He stood down on 15 August 2007 to spend a few years working for an organisation set up by former US President Bill Clinton and Tom Hunter, the Clinton Hunter Development Initiative in Malawi and Rwanda. Within four hours, Wendy Alexander announced she would stand to lead the Labour Party in Scotland. Her campaign would be led by Tom McCabe.

With the help of Brian Souter, who contributed at least £500,000 to the SNP's campaign, Alex Salmond became the new First Minister. He snubbed a debate on gay equality attended by all Scottish political parties, including the Tories, and backed the demands of Catholic adoption agencies - putting their dogma before the well-being of children in their care - to turn away gay couples.

RELIGIOUS FASCISM

After the 2007 election win, the SNP hosted a lavish reception at Bute House with its generous allies in attendance – including Brian Souter and Sir Tom Farmer - at a cost to the taxpayer of £1,446.50. Salmond had already engaged in behind-the-scenes talks with Catholic leaders, and SNP minister Fergus Ewing went on to hold private talks with Souter's charity, the Souter Charitable Trust (STC), whose aim was "the advancement of religion", to discuss a return to the discredited, pro-abstinence drug policy similar to one promoted by 'Keep the Clause's' David Macauley, only this time Souter's charity was proposing the administration of neuro-electric therapy – sending an electric current to the brain - to addicts. The controversial treatment had been developed in the sixties by Scottish neurosurgeon Dr Meg Patterson. The SNP also quickly dropped their resolution to do away with bus de-regulation and were further criticised for not putting out to tender plans to offer a hovercraft service across the Firth of Forth linking Edinburgh and Fife. Stagecoach looked likely to benefit. The company sought £3.3m of funding until the service became profitable. In 2008, Labour demanded an Audit Scotland probe after learning that the SNP-led Fife council – led by Peter Grant, who had stood for election as an MP in Glenrothes supporting Catholic demands for the Human Fertilisation and Embryology Bill - earmarked £1m of public money for the transport project. This was likely to go ahead if Stagecoach presented a full business plan and Edinburgh City Council, also SNP-led, committed a further £1m to the project. However, plans were eventually shelved after a plan to build a port at Portobello was rejected by councillors in Edinburgh. Souter was reported to have been "scunnered" after Stagecoach had spent £500,000 on the project and council-run regional transport body SEStran contributed £92,000 of public funds. The service would have greatly benefitted the east of Scotland's local communities and businesses.

At the annual Cardinal Winning Education Lecture at the University of Glasgow in 2008, Alex Salmond said that Scottish schools could learn from the strong moral values he claimed were being taught in Catholic primary and secondary schools. He promised to make it his mission to put ethics and moral values at the heart of Scottish education, giving his "unswerving support" for more 'faith' schools. Attacking opponents of sectarian schools, he praised Catholic schools as "second to none".

Keeping Marriage and Schools for Christians

Salmond warned: "For too long the attitude of some has been, at best, grudging acceptance of Catholic education and, at worst, outright hostility. It is time for that attitude to be finished in Scottish society". Instead of addressing a resistance to promote greater diversity within Catholic education, Salmond instead proclaimed: "We must celebrate – not tolerate – diversity and distinctiveness within our education system". Further praising Catholic education, he said: "When we consider the ideals – the values – that we should foster in Scotland's young people, we can think of the words inscribed on the mace of the Scottish Parliament. Words that help describe the values for our whole democracy: Justice, wisdom, integrity and compassion, values that are – and have always been – at the heart of Catholic education in Scotland".

Soon, in an article in the *Scottish Catholic Observer*, Alex Salmond was promising the Catholic Church he would do all he could to secure them exemptions from equality legislation that permitted same-sex couples to adopt. Later, in a deal struck between the Church and health and education officials, a vaccine against cervical cancer caused by the human papilloma virus (HPV), passed on during sex - was to be administered to schoolgirls without any accompanying safer sex advice mentioning condoms offered protection against other sexually transmitted diseases. Not only that, the mention of condoms was removed from leaflets going out to *all* Scottish schools, even non-denominational ones. Under a new editor, even *Scotland on Sunday* was rattled: "Alex Salmond's administration should take particular care in matters such as these, given that the SNP's biggest donor is a man well known for his conservative views on sexual education in schools. The health of Scotland's young people is too important to be the subject of any horsetrading".

After his meeting with Muslim leaders at Bute House and in a nod to demands for separate schools for them too, he promised: "My advocacy for faith-based education extends beyond Catholic schools". (The Green Party stood virtually alone in its resistance to such religious privileges). Divisions amongst Muslims, the treatment of women, forced marriages and female circumcision were all conveniently brushed under the carpet in the stampede to portray religious solidarity. By 2008, Salmond had decided to award £215,000 in public funds to the Scottish Islamic Foundation (SIF), a company the SNP helped set up which was led by SNP activist Osama Saeed, the SNP's parliamentary candidate for the Glasgow Central constituency, who was campaigning to secure the support of its large Muslim population. The organisation also included other SNP activists and members of Saeed's family. Osama Saeed had been heavily criticised for his support for the restoration of an Islamic Caliphate, which would absorb existing states around the world into a Shari'a "superstate"; for urging Dundee's Muslim community not to cooperate with Tayside Police's Special Branch community contact unit; and for his support for separate Muslim schools. Most of the funding was earmarked for an IslamFest in Glasgow. SIF later received a further £190,000 from the Race, Religion and Refugee Integration Fund (RRRI) which supported organisations assisting ethnic minority communities, despite being the only one of 33 organisations that was neither a company nor charity at the time they applied for funding.

In July 2008 alone, the SNP-controlled government had awarded £100,000 to Connecting and Empowering Communities, run by Glasgow's Scottish Council of Jewish Communities; £130,000 to the Festival of Spirituality and Peace, organised by the Church of St John the Evangelist in Edinburgh; £190,000 to Glasgow's Youth Community Support Agency for its Faith Exploration Services; and £130,000 to Edinburgh Interfaith Association's Interfaith Development Project to sort our their squabbles.

A law in Scotland, passed by Westminster, ensured religionists had a powerful voice in schools. Section 124 of the Local Government etc. (Scotland) Act 1994 insisted that where an education authority - and there were 32 of them in Scotland - appointed a committee, the persons appointed by them had to include three clerics: one from the Roman Catholic Church; one from the Church of Scotland and one other (or two others in the Orkney Islands, Shetland Islands and Western Isles).

Soon after being elected First Minister in November 2001, Jack McConnell chose a new health minister: Malcolm Chisholm. It took Chisholm almost a year to set up an expert group just to prepare a draft strategy for the long promised 'guidelines'. Chaired by Professor Phil Hanlon, the team included Father Joseph Chambers, whose job it was to ensure the aims of the Catholic Church were met. The watered-down draft for the Sexual Health Strategy, promising better access to contraception and abortion services, was finally published in 2003. At first, Father Joe Chambers threatened he would write a report of his own before begrudgingly signing off the document.

As if to demonstrate the extent of cognitive dissonance amongst Catholics, former *Scottish Catholic Observer* editor, Eddie Barnes, reassured readers: "I could show you the letters I've got from gay priests thanking us for our coverage of Section 28". As Scottish political editor for *Scotland on Sunday* he flagged up "sex clinics in rural schools plan". The Sexual Health Strategy had promised to ensure all pupils had access to advice and support, condoms and the so-called 'morning-after pill'. The *Scottish Daily Mail* warned the strategy was "sure to trigger a renewed battle between ministers and moral campaigners over sex education". Peter Kearney told the *Herald*: "From the date Cardinal O'Brien's article was published, (in the *Sunday Times Scotland*, labelling the strategy "state sponsored child abuse") we had more public debate in the 10 days following than in the 10 months previous. To say he raised awareness of it would be an understatement". Oddly, when the strategy was out, the Catholic-Church-supporting *Scottish Mail* hardly had a word to say about it. Where were the 'storms', the 'fury' and the 'outrage'? Instead, the story that dominated the papers that morning was the conviction of Luke Mitchell for the murder of Jodi Jones. Mitchell, a disturbed Goth had attended St David's, a Catholic school that had already experienced the suicide of a 13-year-old girl who had hung herself in her bedroom in Dalkeith. Her friends claimed she'd been a victim of bullying. School inspectors saw nothing wrong with the school and left praising its 'good standard of education within a very caring and supportive atmosphere'.

Professor Phil Hanlon admitted the final draft for Scotland's Sexual Health Strategy was not radical enough but seemed resigned to pressure from moral conservatives. It was finally put out to consultation in November 2003, the closing date being February 2004, later extended to March, and after Archbishop Mario Conti's attack on the Executive's strategy, postponed until April. When Cardinal Keith O'Brien warned of the "graphic imagery" that was to bombard pre-school and primary education in *Sunday Times Scotland*, Labour ministers went through the final draft once more to see if there was anything else they could drop to appease the Catholic Church. Once the coalition partners, the Liberal Democrats, had seen the changes awarding Catholic schools opt-outs from the strategy and accompanying notes with the Cardinal's concerns next to his name, another re-draft was ordered with the help of half-a-dozen Labour ministers. The LibDems refused to sign. Their health spokesman, Mike Rumbles, referred to a private meeting between health minister Andy Kerr and Cardinal Keith O'Brien: "What I have a problem with is private meetings that lead to policy changes. I'd like to have known about that meeting in advance".

Mario Conti returned to the *Sunday Herald* writing about why we should all treat sex holistically in schools "and not exclusively as a medical issue". This might have been a good thing if it meant being more open and honest about all aspects of sexuality, but no. He offered the same boiled sweet in a different wrapper: No sex please: we're Catholics. Conti was happy that the strategy had taken on board his insistence that it contained "clear educational guidelines..." The problem was, the "appropriate information" provided by Catholic schools with its "emphasis on the moral and ethical framework within which we view this great gift" excluded lesbians, gays, bisexuals and the transgendered or any self-defining heterosexual who occasionally engaged in gay sex. Conti was happy the strategy had taken so long to "get the right answer". He bragged it was a blow to "political correctness" and added in his address: "I would define the victory, if victory there must be, as being one for good sense. For that the Executive deserves our thanks". That 'thanks' was owed to the 'abstinence-plus'-supporting Scottish health minister, Andy Kerr, who told the *Scottish Daily Mail:* "We respect the right of faith groups and others to hold onto and promote their religious, moral and spiritual values".

Cardinal Keith O'Brien had had a private meeting with Kerr, undated and unminuted, three days before Christmas, not long after O'Brien had warned in the Scottish parliament that gays were 'captives' of 'sexual aberrations' whilst he himself was indulging in them. The Sexual Health Strategy was now transformed into what Conti described as an "impressive document... Gone are the ambiguous language of political correctness and provocative neologisms; the talk of 'celebrating sexual diversity' and tackling 'heterosexism'... Gone is the 'safe-sex' mantra; replaced with the altogether wiser rhetoric of 'abstinence plus'." Gone too was the wind out of the *Scottish Mail's* sails. So, while Hanlon's Expert Group recommended a

Keeping Marriage and Schools for Christians

special sex tsar to co-ordinate the implementation of the strategy, Kerr made do with a National Sexual Health Advisory Committee, led by him, and following on from a recent announcement that £300m would be spent on sexual health south of the border, Kerr pledged just £15m. Sam Galbraith told the *Sunday Herald:* "We have backed down again to the Catholic Church, and this cannot continue. Until the Labour Party gets over its fear of the Church, we will never make progress in these areas. Political parties that don't confront organisations eventually fail". The church had the 'guidelines' they wanted. Family planning workers could be barred from entering their schools at the insistence of head teachers, effectively giving Catholics a veto. Iain Macwhirter shook his head in his column in the *Sunday Herald:* "Abstinence plus what? Abstinence plus rampant promiscuity? Abstinence plus judicious sexual exploration? Abstinence plus a bit on the side now and again? The Executive sexual health policy is an oxymoron: just say no – except when you say yes". This had been five years in the making, cumulating in a cash injection of £15m of public money, only some of which would go to centres helping pregnant teenagers. Even that was still too much for the Catholic hierarchy, who always had the *Mail* to bang its drum for them when they wanted something. Cash for abortions had their spokesman, Peter Kearney telling readers: "This is a staggering investment in approaches which have demonstrably failed. To plough good money after bad on such a scale is very worrying". He added: "The Scottish Executive must translate its rhetoric on abstinence into reality by giving equally serious financial support to groups offering abstinence-based advice". The discredited application of abstinence programmes in the US was unlikely to knock Scotland from the top of the league for unwanted pregnancies and sexually transmitted infections. In the five years Scotland had waited for 'guidelines', Herpes and Chlamydia had gone up by 50% amongst teens, over 38,000 young women had became pregnant and 16,000 had abortions. By 2008, as Scotland dithered over pertinent sex education and an estimated 5,300 people were counted as living in Scotland with HIV, a survey by the National AIDS Trust revealed Scots the UK's most ignorant nation on issues surrounding the transmission of the HIV virus. Almost a third (31%) of people in Scotland failed to recognise that sex between a man and a woman without a condom exposed them to a risk of becoming infected by the HIV virus, compared to 21% across the rest of the UK. As much as 35% of Scots didn't know the same was true of sex between men compared to 26% across the UK. In fact, Scots only scored equally with the rest of the UK when 31% correctly identified sharing needles as a way of contracting the HIV virus.

Determined to get their way over Abstinence Plus, the *Scottish Daily Mail* picked at the scab. Their 'political editor' Ian Smith declared "anger over cash for youth group offering children secret abortions". In an ideal world, girls as young as 13 who became pregnant could count on the support of their parents. But this didn't always happen. They were often completely alone, fearful of their parents and desperate for help. In such cases, Caledonia Youth was there for them. £701,000 to assist Caledonia Youth was not a lot in real terms, but enough for the *Mail* to moan: "Critics said the figures undermined Mr Kerr's claim that the strategy was focused on encouraging school children to avoid underage sex... The funding row has derailed the Executive's attempts to appease critics, particularly the Catholic Church..." With an already large majority of Catholics ignoring what their bishops told them, it begged the question, just exactly who were these 'critics?' It turned out to be the ubiquitous Catholic propagandist Peter Kearney and campaigner Eileen McCloy, a mother of ten from Glasgow.

Soon a new abstinence programme was introduced into Catholic schools in Scotland, paving the way for a two-tier sex education system. The Executive funded a new £170,000 initiative entitled *Called to Love*, developed by Healthy Respect and the Scottish Catholic Education Service (SCES), which set itself against "artificial contraception", and promoted marriage and the sanctity of human life.

Some in the Church of Scotland coveted the Catholic Church's successes, demanding they all sat up and took note. Rev Ian Watson, Professor Andy McGowan and Rev Bill Wallace were the ringleaders of their new group, Forward Together. Bill Wallace was on record as once telling the *Scotsman* all "genital sexual acts should be within the marriage bond and nowhere else".

Despite millions ploughed into abstinence-only sex education in the USA during the presidency of George W Bush, it was proven to be a catastrophic failure with greater numbers going on to have unprotected sex. That didn't stop uniformed

Keeping Marriage and Schools for Christians

school-kids, driven by coaches from all over the Catholic diocese of Paisley, filling an assembly hall at St Andrew's Academy to watch mouthy, abstinence-only zealot Pam Stenzel poison their minds with fear and anxiety over sex in 2013. Pam Stenzel was a student of controversial Jerry Falwell's Liberty University and counselled young women at crisis pregnancy centres run by pro-life organizations. With money drying up after President Obama was elected, Stenzel's company Enlighten Communications continued to cash-in on promoting abstinence with her company earning $268,799 in 2011.

I found my way into St Andrew's Academy to watch her frighten schoolchildren into abstinence under the watchful eye of their Religious & Moral Education teachers, Father Tom Boyle and Michael McGrath from the Scottish Catholic Education Service. After explaining to the children that HIV could kill you, Stenzel warned them: "Condoms are not safe". I tried to discuss what I had just heard to Michael McGrath who was sitting behind me with two others. I was surprised only by how quickly they closed ranks. "You're misrepresenting us... She did not say that... She said condoms protect against HIV". Tracy Clark-Flory writes on Salon.com: "Here's a direct quote from Stenzel on that topic: "Condoms aren't safe. Never have been, never will be."

Stenzel barely took a breath as she rattled off sexually transmitted infections over the heads of the children. "HPV-genital warts-syphilis-gonorrhoea-herpes-chlamydia-vulvodynia-Hep B-Hepatitis-HIV-and HPV", before finally roaring, "30 per cent of STI's are incurable!"

Before predictably wheeling in heterosexual marriage ("God created") and anti-choice propaganda, the all-American mom squeezed in a joke and won a few laughs from her audience before turning on them to warn that if they had sex outside a virginal marriage, "you will pay"! She repeated: "No one has ever had more than one partner and not paid." The audience were reeled in, but her delivery was patronising and smug. She recounted how she once asked a puzzled boy where his vulva was. Silent pause. Then she yelled: "YOU DON'T HAVE ONE!" Everyone laughed with her. I was now understanding a comment I overheard her make to one of the teachers before she went on stage: "The kids are great! The people I have trouble with are adults." She apologised to the kids if sounded like she disliked the male gender. On stage behind her a banner displayed a clue to her behaviour, it read: "We are not some casual product of evolution. Each of us is the result of a thought of God." It contrasted with the sordid reality she owed to her own existence: Stenzel's mother was 15-years-old when she became pregnant after being raped. Pam was given up for adoption. "My life isn't worth any less than any of yours just because of the way I was conceived, and I did not deserve the death penalty because of the crime of my father", she says.

Stenzel was invited by Fertility Care Scotland, a charity that had a clinic at the Southern General Hospital where two Catholic nurses would later win a fight not to be involved in abortions. Fertility Care promoted the 'Billings Ovulation Method of Natural Fertility Regulation' which used "knowledge about your own fertility to achieve or avoid a pregnancy" offering a "method of natural family planning" described as "a reliable alternative to contraception." Better known as *coitus interruptus* or the withdrawal method, many Scots gave it the name of a train station just before Edinburgh's main station, Edinburgh Waverley and referred to it as 'getting off at Haymarket.'

I was assured by teacher Sam McFaddon that parents had all given their express permission for their children to be at Pam Stenzel's talk. One young boy I spoke to from St Ninian's School begged to differ. With a roll of his eyes he told me in a quiet voice that he'd been sent by his teacher. He sat quietly in his chair with the other children in his class and some parents who had accompanied them and listened to Stenzel describe girls on the beach in their bikinis: "If the sun doesn't touch it – no son must touch it!"

Death and disease cropped up more than condoms in Stenzel's tirade. So did so-called 'Purity rings' that the 'princesses, daughters of the king of kings' could wear until they had found a male virgin. As for the girls, she warned them: "You contract Chlamydia one time in your life, cure it or not, there is about a 25 per cent chance that you will be sterile for the rest of your life."

The 'sex lady', as she called herself, promised the children she would answer every email that was sent to her and would help them with any problem they had.

After her session, children were rewarded with soft drinks and snacks while photographs of pupils from different schools were taken posing with her on stage. One girl was so disturbed by the event, she needed counselling.

Keeping Marriage and Schools for Christians

Stenzel has received sharp criticism from Sexuality Information and Education Council of the United States (SIECUS), who challenged some of the myths she peddled, like telling children sex would put them at risk of getting warts "for the rest of your life" and confusing their young minds by adding "you can't know if you have viral infections." SIECUS advised: "The majority of HPV infections cause neither genital warts nor cervical cancer but, instead, resolve themselves spontaneously without medical intervention. Even HPV infections that cause warts can resolve without treatment." On infertility, Stenzel said: "Girls, please hear this, this is primarily going to affect the girls: infertility, the ability to have children, has risen over 500 per cent in 10 years." SIECUS attacked this too in their report: "Although the media has focused a great deal of attention on infertility in recent years, much of this is tied to the fact that women are delaying pregnancy well into their 30s and 40s, in fact, research suggests that infertility rates have remained unchanged."

Pam Stenzel was not interested in telling the truth. Addressing an audience at a fundamentalist conference called "Reclaiming America for Christ" in 2003 she rejected the idea that abstinence education should be judged by its effectiveness. "People of God," she implored, "can I beg you, to commit yourself to truth, not what works! I don't care if it works, because at the end of the day I'm not answering to you, I'm answering to God!"

On the DVD Stenzel peddled, 'Sex Still Has a Price Tag', SIECUS warned it is based "on fear and shame; designed to control young people's sexual behavior by instilling in them feelings of dread, guilt, and embarrassment." The report argued that "in both her tone and her words, Stenzel appears to have an intense dislike or at least distrust of the young people she is speaking to, and seems to see her goal as that of a drill sergeant or prison guard who is there to keep them in line and dole out punishment. Stenzel relies on inaccurate statistics and passes off gross exaggerations and complete falsehoods as fact." SIECUS concludes that her curriculum represents "the worst kind of abstinence-only-until-marriage programming."

Although a massive improvement from its former self, the *Daily Record* still had issues with sex after the sudden disappearance of editor Martin Clarke. By way of example, on one day following repeal of Section 28, the tabloid was saturated with sex scandals involving men. There were allegations against Jonathan King, responsible for such plastic 45s as 'Everyone's Gone to the Moon' and 'I Don't Want to be Gay'; a court case involving another alleged 'paedophile ring' in a small Ayrshire village; and, in a front-page exclusive that once again pointed at the Catholic Church's difficulties over sex, there was the: "SCANDAL OF GAY PORN PRIEST". The latter was apparently a "depraved and sickening story that will shock Scotland". Father Jim Nicol had downloaded pictures of gay erotica and posted one of him having sex. The *Record* attacked the Church for reacting with "blind complacency" and failing "to take obvious measures to protect their flock", although quite what measures and what exactly anyone needed to be protected from, was unclear. In a moment of shameless hypocrisy the tabloid condemned the priest for pursuing unconventional methods of meeting guys, perhaps forgetting how long it had itself been discriminating against lesbians, gays, bisexuals and people of transgender by not allowing them to seek partners in its personal ads. "WHY IS PERVERT STILL A PRIEST?" the tabloid begged before trumpeting: "THANK GOD HE'S GONE!" after Nicol resigned. Cardinal Winning, who had vowed he would set up a 'shop-a-priest' hotline, had apparently failed to contact police when he learned of Nicol's activities. A religious clinic in the States and a special unit in Glasgow both had their hands outstretched to 'help' 46-year-old Father Jim Nicol but the Church's appointed 'counsellor', Alan Draper, was one of the first to contact the police, believing Nicol was "sexually out of control" and "got police in on the case, fearing some of the men in the pictures might be under age". A picture of Jim Nicol having sex and wearing a kilt had the *Record* fretting: "...Other material found on the machine was too sordid to be described here". The *Record* was soon back in finger-wagging mode: "...Father Nicol's behaviour is beyond contempt... Sordid and sickening... Shamelessly... Habitually carrying out lewd and indecent sex acts with young men". But as hard as the tabloid tried to imply otherwise, the sex was both consensual and performed with young men of a legal age.

By October 2000, there was a split in the 'Keep the Clause' camp. Former *Record* reporter Carlos Alba reported in the *Sunday Times Scotland*: "Hardline Keep the Clause campaigners have rounded on their former patron, Stagecoach tycoon Brian

Souter". Hugh Lynch's Family Action Movement (FAM), described as "a militant offshoot" of 'Keep the Clause' was fielding its own candidate in the Falkirk West by-election. Up until now, 'Keep the Clause' activists had no problem with Lynch's contributions. Brian Souter instead gave his backing to the SNP, who supported repeal of Section 28, and got Jack Irvine to explain how he was "realistic enough" to know FAM was only likely to field "a few hundred votes". Hugh Lynch wrote in the *Herald*: "FAM is the only party which actively promotes family values and condemns the politically correct, gay, irresponsible, useless, Deaconite policies which have damaged the lives of our young people..." and with scant regard to widespread religious activism, added: "Gay rights activists have infiltrated all of the political parties, and Blair's Cabinet has, at least, four gays on board, which means that the direction, control, and policy-making of the party are strongly influenced by gay rights priorities rather than family interests".

Right up to repeal of Section 28 and beyond, Wendy Alexander continued to be mercilessly maligned. "SHAPE UP OR SHIP OUT... McLeish warning to hapless Wendy", snapped the *Scottish News of the World*. "I confess that the wee lady scares me", cried Bill Greig in the *Scottish Sunday Express*. "Wendy baiting may yet become a national sport", giggled Iain Martin in *Scotland on Sunday*. Referring to Britain's Foot and Mouth epidemic, Martin Clarke in the *Scottish Daily Mail* sniped: "Henry McLeish told prospective American tourists not to worry about the 'little problem' they may have heard we've been having here in Scotland. Seems a remarkably casual way to dismiss Wendy Alexander to me". Nonetheless, she was rated top Scottish parliamentarian by Channel Four and walked away with a handsome glass trophy. (Unfortunately, she only got as far as Heathrow Airport before dropping it!) To the conservative elements across all parties in Scotland, 'wee Wendy' was perceived as dangerous: she was Donald Dewar's favourite; she was talented; she was too close to the position of First Minister: and worst of all, she was a woman. A catalogue of smears followed almost everything she did. When she turned down Henry McLeish's offer of the water portfolio, which wasn't helped when McLeish's adviser, Peter McMahon made the announcement public before she had even been informed, Alexander had already been doing more work than McLeish with less staff and had, quite rightly, blown the whistle. She also had the job of running Labour's election campaign in Scotland. Then there was her appointment of Rod Lynch as chief executive of Visitscotland. After it was discovered he held another executive position, he was sacked after just four days. Wendy Alexander contined to be unfairly pilloried. Andrew Nicoll, the *Scottish Sun's* political reporter wrote: "...They say Wendy Alexander has a brain the size of a planet. What they forgot to mention is that a lot of planets are just swirling balls of poisonous gas... (The First Minister, Henry McLeish) will dump her as soon as the General Election is over". It appeared she had the temerity to be working in a parliament with very strong women doing a lot of hard work while weak men briefed the press against them. Soon, what should have been "a matter of principle" became a "tantrum" from a "bossy" woman with a "petulant manner". According to Wilson's Week in the *Sunday Mail*, "Wendy threw a tantrum at the prospect of having to justify Labour's soaring water taxes. She stamped and puffed and hollered so loud Henry backed down". Shortly after, 39-year-old civil servant Andrew Baird, who had previously worked with Sir Malcolm Rifkind, was moved to another department over an apparent inability to work with her. According to the *Scottish Mail*, she would "frequently nag him to work to her rules".

The head of the civil service in Scotland was the permanent secretary at the Scottish Executive, Muir Russell, (now Sir Muir Russell). The civil service endured an uneasy relationship with the Scottish Executive, and Muir Russell's relationship with Donald Dewar was described as cool. Russell and his department were criticised for being deeply conservative and stalling law reform. After his job as head of the housing department with additional responsibility for constitution under John Major's Conservative Government, he was seconded as part-time director of Stagecoach between 1992 and 1995. When he took early retirement to take up the post of principal of Glasgow University in 2002, the *Scottish Daily Mail* penned an editorial expressing a deep regret at his passing. It was unlikely Sir Muir would have shared that regret, at least, not financially anyway. At only 53 he had obtained a severance package which included an immediate pension of more than £50,000 plus a lump some of more than three times that amount. His new post carried a salary and pension contribution package of around £180,000. Wendy

Keeping Marriage and Schools for Christians

Alexander and Donald Dewar's special advisor both had conflicts with Muir Russell. After Russell suggested organisational and managerial changes within the civil service he tried to by-pass Alexander by going straight to the First Minister. Donald Dewar was not impressed.

In 2005 Wendy Alexander reflected on her experiences as an MSP in the *Sunday Herald:* "Law-making powers had just been returned to Scotland after 300 years, and the question before the new parliament was whether to attempt to repeal discriminatory laws in step with reform in the rest of the UK. If our 'principled' choice had been for insitutionalised discrimination to remain enshrined in Scottish law while it was being tackled in the rest of the UK, what would that have said about our nation, its leaders and our vision for Scotland...? Repeal was never our top priority; it was simply one section in one of the 11 bills that we tackled in our first year – a year in which, despite the din, we were never diverted from lifting children out of poverty, building new schools and hospitals, planning new homes and creating jobs. It was others who chose to elevate this issue to the top of their agendas... Today, our public life still needs nurturing, and the power of public relations – when rooted in scaremongering – has been exposed as ephemeral. Parental concerns have been successfully allayed and Scotland is becoming a more tolerant land". After her resignation from First Minister Jack McConnell's cabinet, citing a need to 'move on', Wendy Alexander was appointed a visiting professor at Strathclyde Business School, based at Strathclyde University in Glasgow. Apart from a few newspaper articles and her parliamentary and constituency duties as an MSP, she withdrew almost completely from public life. Alexander later admitted: "I think being a woman in politics is harder. Nobody talks about Sam Galbraith's earrings, dinner dates or fertility". She later married Professor Brian Ashcroft, an adviser to the Scottish Executive and policy director of the Bank of Scotland's economic think tank, the Fraser of Allander Institute, which was also based at Strathclyde University.

In 2007, long after the 'Keep the Clause' debacle was over, Wendy Alexander became leader of Scottish Labour. Her press officer (or spin doctor) was journalist Brian Lironi. He penned a particularly nasty piece on a gay cop in the *Sunday Mail* in 2004. As open-minded as a ball and clawed foot under the cover of a walnut dressing table, Lironi's report exposed the young cop doing nothing more than acting as a host and giving out towels and sandwiches in a gay sauna in Edinburgh. "PC Delwyn Williams, 32, resigned from the force on Friday after his astonishing double life was exposed", the report sniffed with satisfaction. Williams faced a criminal inquiry. Reporters Jane Hamilton and Brian Lironi, described "an undercover reporter", too ashamed to expose himself in more ways than one, popping along to the No 18 sauna in Edinburgh to be shown around by Delwyn Williams, by all accounts, courteous and helpful to the shy, prudish man from the *Sunday Mail*. "Williams showed our reporter three small rooms, which he said were available for anyone who wanted to have sex. There is also a dark room and a 'sling' room with leather straps suspended from the wall about half way up... Eight middle-aged men were sitting naked. (The stairway was) decorated with posters of nearly-naked men". But what did they expect? Posters of Esther Williams and Deanne Durbin? Men in smoking jackets flicking through *Horse and Hounds*? Delwyn even added: "There are two other gay saunas in Edinburgh. You might want to try them too". The *Sunday Mail* grabbed a fresh towel after coming back for more, gasping: "Another investigator who visited the sauna was propositioned for sex three times in an hour. ...Two men, both in their 50s, were sitting in the Jacuzzi chatting... Williams joked that our reporter would have to 'dis-robe' before he could be shown the rest of the sauna. Several other men were lying around wearing only towels... Later, a second reporter sitting in the sauna was asked three times by different people within an hour if he wanted sex. He refused all offers and left". Returning for yet a third time, the *Sunday Mail* appeared somewhat surprised after finding the premises "still open for business". A "police source" told them: "There have been stories in the past which have embarrassed the force but this is on another level". The licence holder, Kathleen Dykes, reasoned with the hysterical *Mail* employees over the constable's moonlighting: "It was a great job for a gay man. Any straight man would be more than happy to work on a desk if they were going to meet a potential 50 women in a towel every day".

Brian Lironi was also behind the *Sunday Mail's* headline: "MAKE PORN A HATE CRIME". The story was a piece of self-flagellation over some "sex abuse summit" militant feminists had called to work towards getting men's magazines pulled off newsagents' shelves. Lironi described the notorious, shelf-clearing

Keeping Marriage and Schools for Christians

Scottish Women Against Pornography (SWAP), led by Catherine Harper of the Scottish Women's Coalition, as "Scotland's leading experts". Ms Harper told the *Sunday Mail:* "The message of all pornography is that women secretly wish to be raped and abused and enjoy the treatment they receive. We view pornography as sexual hatred in the same way racist material is regarded as incitement to racial hatred... It is about providing a more equal society and a safer place for women and children". Just how one-sided the debate was going to be was captured in the report's quote from Elaine Smith MSP: "We need to hear from academics who work in this field about whether they think pornography is harmful and how serious a problem it might be. We don't expect any of them to say it is a good thing so the next question will be what we can do about it".

Wendy's spin doctor, Brian Lironi lasted barely a week in his post. He went on to work for Glasgow mayor, Steven Purcell. Glasgow might not yet have had its girly magazines pulled off newsagents' shelves, but it did have a reputation for prosecuting men seeking to pay for sex, forbidding exhibitions of erotica in its conference centre, prohibiting the sale of erotic DVDs in the few sex shops that could get a licence, banning Scotland's only gay magazine in its gay centre for carrying 'unsuitable content' and enforcing a ban on the Monty Python film *Life of Brian* for thirty years.

Wendy Alexander and her brother, Douglas Alexander, the Secretary of State for International Development, were accepted for membership of the secretive British-American Project (BAP) which had its first three conferences funded by the late, far-right oil magnate, J Howard Pew. BAP was launched by former Republican President, Ronald Reagan and religious media mogul, Rupert Murdoch, and now boasted an influential fellowship of over 1,000 members from both sides of the Atlantic. It was set up in 1985 as the British-American Project for the Successor Generation, an organisation for rising stars in - amongst others - the world of business, politics and media. Although more recently doing its best to play down its Christian-Right image of grooming right-leaning British and US youth as leaders, for an organisation inviting so many journalists into its membership, it was still little known to the public. The centrepiece of the organisation in 2007 was a four-day conference on Faith and Justice centred in Newcastle.

RELIGIOUS FASCISM

J Howard Pew and his family nurtured a bewildering array of US right-wing publications, campaigns and organisations besides BAP. Amongst them were the Christian Freedom Foundation, the Christian Economic Foundation, the Gordon-Conwell Theological Seminary and The Presbyterian Layman, a proselytising organisation engaging with "ethical and moral issues in cultural, economic and political affairs as Christ's active disciples". With billions of dollars of assets, the family have worked with Sun Oil, Weyerhaeuser, Standard Oil, Placid Oil, the CIA, SIL International, (another Christian organisation) and Wycliffe, an aggressive, proselytising Christian mission dedicated to churning out the Bible in every conceivable language for the "Bibleless people" of the World it believed "as a result of sin, are alienated from God and each other, and therefore in need of reconciliation". According to Gerard Colby and Charlotte Dennett in their book *Thy Will be Done, The Conquest of the Amazon*, together, these companies were guilty of plundering rich resources like oil in the Amazon to the near-genocidal detriment of its indigenous peoples.

Wendy Alexander's leadership of Scottish Labour was dogged by scandal from the moment of her election when it was revealed Jersey tycoon entrepreneur Paul Green had twice donated £950 to the party's Holyrood election campaign. Green was not a UK resident: therefore his donation was in breach of electoral law. In the course of their investigations, the *Sunday Herald*, from a document they attributed to Alexander's husband, Professor Brian Ashcroft, revealed another donor as Moir Lockhead, the chief executive of transport giant First Group contributing £995, five pounds less than the £1,000 ceiling permissible. The *Sunday Herald* claimed the payment was made through Labour MP John Lyons, yet, curiously, a spokesman for Lockhead denied making any such contribution.

Barely a year later, by June 2008, Wendy Alexander announced she was standing down as leader of Scottish Labour after facing a one-day ban from parliament for breaking donation rules by failing to declare them to her leadership campaign on her register of interests. As MSP for Paisley North, she always insisted she had been wrongly advised by standards committee clerks and branded the Scottish Parliament Standards Committee's decision, chaired by a Nationalist MSP, as "partisan". She said: "My pursuers have sought the prize of

Keeping Marriage and Schools for Christians

political victory with little thought to the standing of the parliament. Some may feel they have achieved a political victory but wiser heads will surely question 'at what price?'"

Gerald Warner was in a buoyant mood in *Scotland on Sunday:* "So farewell then, Wendy Alexander. The uncanny silence, the laryngitis-imposed whisper, at First Minister's Questions last Thursday were a presage of her demise. The batteries in the drumming bunny had finally run out. It seems as if we had been deaved by that hectoring voice for all our lifetimes; in reality it was only since 1999 when the Chamber of Horrors opened on The Mound, later to migrate to Holyrood. La Alexander's career has been a chronicle of the triumph of ego over capability; in that respect it is a parable of our politics since devolution".

When it was announced Northern & Shell publisher Richard Desmond had bought Express Newspapers; he was attacked as a "Porn king... Porn merchant... Porn magnate... Peddler of Porn..." even a "Porn magnet"! *(sic)* The Scottish media went into shock. Apart from owning gay magazine *Attitude*, Northern & Shell was described as a company "that peddles female nudity..." Richard Desmond had bought the paper that once delivered to its readers stories of the Perfumo scandal. The *Scottish Daily Express* was Scotland's top-selling newspaper in the 60s and was edited over the period of the Section 28 storm by Kerry Gill. The *Scottish Daily Star* was also included in the bundle.

Thinking, somehow, that one more socially and politically conservative owner contributed to greater diversity, the *Daily Mail's* dogs nipped at the heels of their competitor, the *Daily Express*, in their editorial. "The Mail Group recently sought to buy the Express titles, believing that we had the resources and professionalism to restore them to their former glory thus contributing to the diversity of the British newspaper market". *The Mail* explained: "...Newspapers are different. They are part of the fabric of our society, with an immense influence for good or ill. The values they promote do matter". Bel Mooney wrote in the *Mail* to celebrate WH Smith's decision not to stock sexy magazines again and berated the speed with which Richard Desmond had secured the *Express:* "...As simple as a potential molester selecting one of Mr Desmond's magazines from the top shelf that seems to be spreading through our newsagents like a disease". Grasping the bannisters of her version of hetero-normative behaviour, she scoffed: "The difficulty in writing about them here is the lack of decent words to describe the content... One photo-set displays an extremely fat, rather plain, sad-looking black woman, over 50, with a white toyboy. Pale, weedy, embarrassed, he looks about 19 and his nakedness is, if anything, more humiliating than hers. The ugly, vaguely racist pictures degrade both participants and it is hard to imagine who would find them sexy". Leafing through one of Richard Desmond's sexy magazines, she found an 80-year-old woman: "Someone's grandmother, I thought - someone who should be treated with respect... One or two of the readers' wives look as if they might be enjoying themselves, but maybe that's because it hasn't occurred to them to ask why the men they live with want to spread them across glossy pages for other men to masturbate over. Was this part of the deal when they made their vows, or at least decided to move in? Normal women are shy when they have to see the gynaecologist. Yet these women look normal..." Advertising standards watchdog, the Advertising Standards Authority, slammed the publishers of the *Daily Mail*, Associated Newspapers after they sent out leaflets saying: "Do you really want an X-rated paper in your home?"

The failure of the Church to uphold Section 28 was indicative of its failure to survive as a politically-motivated organisation in a changing world. The Church of Scotland's Board of National Mission found, in 2002 that the Kirk had lost the "right to be heard". Indeed it had. During the 30s, one in four people was a member whilst by 2000, with only 607,000 members, it was losing up to 19,000 members a year. By 2050, it was estimated the Kirk would cease to exist. (The Catholic Church in Scotland fared no better, with numbers of those attending mass plummeting). Due to the stock market crash in 2002, the Church of Scotland threatened to axe jobs and sell assets after losing £70m off its £330m assets. The Church of Scotland's Board of Social Responsibilty announced it would close a string of nursing homes to save money. When the Board announced they would close Leslie House near Glenrothes in Fife and move 92-year-old May Vettraino, who suffered from dementia, and 16 other residents, May's 63-year-old son Ross told reporters: "I would never have expected the Board of Social Responsibility to behave in such an uncaring and un-Christian way. It just beggars belief". Perhaps May Vettraino might have preferred the Church of Scotland's luxury hotel with swimming pool and private beach, reached by an elegant wooden bridge imported from Italy, on the Sea of Galilee. The interior was cooled by the pastel shades of glazed stucco walls and filled with Charles-Rennie-Mackintosh-style chairs on polished marble floors.

By 2006, the Scottish Executive realised they could no longer ignore their responsibility to ensure young gays and bisexuals were able to access sexual education that was appropriate to them. In the face of such issues regularly coming up in the classroom, teachers were to be given the green light to discuss how a gay person could access safer sex information; the emotional side of gay relationships; the law of consent and where gay people might obtain further support, all within the framework of the Sexual Health and Relationships Education (SHARE) programme for secondary schools. The programme's key messages encouraged respect for others and urged youngsters to delay sex until they were ready. By now, only *Scotland on Sunday* and the *Scottish Daily Mail* were on hand to take up the cudgels for the militants. With a track record of slanted reporting on issues of sexuality in the *Scottish Mail*, Kate Foster, now *Scotland on Sunday's* chief reporter, penned a report under the heading: "Schools told to give pupils gay sex advice". Foster garnered quotes from the Catholic Church who told her the move was "appalling, outrageous and utterly unnecessary". Jack Irvine accused the Executive of reneging on their promise "not to promote gay sex in schools". Dr Alastair Noble, education officer for evangelising 'Christian' charity CARE for Scotland, demanded to see the proposals "in advance of circulation to evaluate them" and ensure they "emphasise the importance of stable family life and the importance of marriage". The *Scottish Daily Mail's* Stuart Nicolson insisted: "Schoolchildren are to be given explicit gay sex lessons under a new education scheme" before turning to Eileen McCloy, a Catholic mother of ten who had pulled her ten-year-old son out of sex education classes because they were too explicit. Heading a campaign group calling itself Not With My Child, Mrs McCloy was indignant: "We were told there would be safeguards to make sure there was not proselytising of homosexuality in schools. Promises that parents would be consulted and would have the right to withdraw their children from classes they did not think were appropriate are not worth the paper they are written on".

RELIGIOUS FASCISM

Chapter Nine
Curtains for Section 28!

He would swing out
At the chequered ball
But they pick him last
Because he always kicks
At invisible goals a foot
To the left of the real one.
Edwin Morgan, former Scottish Makar *(Poet Laureate)*

Prior to Parliamentary appraisal of the Ethical Standards in Public Life etc (Scotland) Act 2000, Ministers undertook - before commencing repeal of Section 2a (Section 28) of the Local Government Act 1986 - to publish new materials on sex education. These publications featured: *A Guide for Parents and Carers; Guidance for Schools and Local Authorities on Effective Consultation with Parents and Carers; A Summary of National Advice on Sex Education; and A Circular to Directors of Education: Standards in Scotland's Schools etc Act 2000 – Conduct of Sex Education in Scottish Schools*. Mike McCabe, who chaired the original Working Group on Sex Education, set up to review the curriculum guidelines, oversaw the revision and produced a second and final draft, which was published on 16 June 2000. The Reference Group, included representatives from the Scottish School Boards' Association, Scottish Parent Teacher Council, Health Education Board for Scotland, Learning Teaching Scotland and the Scottish Executive Education Department.

With the evangelical Alan Smith installed as its new chairman, The Scottish School Boards' Association pounced on the Executive's consultation document: *A Guide for Parents and Carers*. Smith warned the *Scotsman:* "The promotion of homosexuality is still a fear amongst parents..." A statement from the SSBA declared: "It was considered that there was not enough reference to marriage within the leaflet". Alan Smith was later appointed to the Religious and Moral Education Committee at the Scottish Executive. Ann Hill became chief executive of the SSBA and joined a ministerial review group looking at replacing the SSBA and SPTC and creating a single national body to represent parent's views on their children's education. After the report was released, Hill told the press: "This is an excellent report which draws on the strength of involving parents in the education of their children".

Marriage was soon back on the agenda after the *Scottish Daily Mail* was thrown into a panic on its front page: "CHURCHES' ANGER AS MINISTERS 'IGNORE' MARRIAGE". The Executive's refusal to give marriage special status was met with the rattling of tambourines and several days of fulminating copy delivered by Hamish Macdonell. For the Catholic Church it was "unacceptable". For the Church of Scotland it was "inadequate". And once again, the Scottish Executive was "at odds with public opinion…" The *Mail* warned them to be wary. "Public tolerance is wearing thin…" They accused the Executive of having "ratted on its commitment to religious groups", alleging that they were "not going to pay any heed to such significant voices as the Catholic Church and the Church of Scotland…" Ann Allen from the Board of Social Responsibilty waved "a survey" showing 92 per cent of young people seeing marriage as their ultimate goal. Tory leader Brian Monteith demanded Jack McConnell - widely regarded as having supported the mention of marriage in guidelines - to explain himself. Juxtaposed with a piece on why Mustique's flamboyant Colin Tennant never married Princess Margaret, the editorial asked: "What is wrong with our devolved government that it cannot bring itself to give marriage anything approaching parity with 'alternative' lifestyles…? Why is marriage effectively outlawed? Do majorities no longer have any rights?" Mrs Katie Grant leapt on the subject in *Scotland on Sunday:* "It says something remarkable about marriage, given the invective poured on it by unhappy individuals, that it still stubbornly refuses to go down the plughole. …The real truth is that although many people cock theirs up, marriage is a very good idea".

Katie Grant would change. Writing for *Scottish Review* in a more enlightened frame of mind in 2013 she admitted "we have

Curtains for Section 28!

come to understand homosexuality not as a threat but as a natural condition. My children accept it without surprise. Their children will accept it without remark... I cannot support a church which believes that gay marriage will undermine the future of humanity, as Pope Benedict has claimed. If he means the human race, this is clearly nonsense. The human race is rather more robust than he supposes... Gay marriage is no different from heterosexual marriage".

The Scottish Executive finally published the new guidelines for sex education for education authorities, schools and parents on 23 March 2001, as the independent Working Group on sex education advised they should have done back in the summer of 2000. They were non-statutory, therefore without the force of law. Two major concessions had been made. Firstly, children were to be taught the importance which the churches placed on marriage and a stable family life (as if, by now, anyone could have been in any doubt)! Secondly, Catholic schools could issue supplementary guidelines to their teachers, giving their position on homosexuality. With Pope Benedict calling it 'intrinsically disordered', representing an 'inclination towards an intrinsic moral evil', and Cardinal Winning calling it a 'perversion', those supplementary guidelines were expected to be tougher than Section 28. Also released was a statutory guidance circular for education authorities on sex education. Now that these documents were published, section 34 of the Ethical Standards in Public Life etc (Scotland) Act 2000, could be enacted and Section 2a of the Local Government Act 1986 (Section 28), would be repealed. One section of the guidance, which did have the force of law, suggested that sex education formed a key element of personal, social and health education in schools and was an important part of children's preparations for adult life. It stated that the purpose of sex education was to provide knowledge and understanding of the nature of sexuality and the processes of human reproduction within the context of relationships based on love and respect. The guidance stated that sex education should develop understanding and attitudes which would help pupils to form relationships in a responsible and healthy manner. The guidance stated the importance of sex education programmes being well matched to pupils' needs and levels of maturity and that teaching materials should be selected with great care and sensitivity to the age and understanding of the pupils. The guidance also stated that programmes of sex education should present facts in an objective, balanced and sensitive manner within a framework of sound values and an awareness of the law on sexual behaviour and that pupils should be encouraged to appreciate the value of stable family life, parental responsibility and family relationships in bringing up children and offering them security, stability and happiness; that pupils should also be encouraged to appreciate the value of commitment in relationships and partnerships including the value placed on marriage by religious groups and others in Scottish society. At the same time, they stated that teachers must respect and avoid causing hurt or offence to those who come from backgrounds that do not reflect this value and that all pupils should be encouraged to understand the importance of self-restraint, dignity, respect for themselves and the views of others. The guidance stated that sex education should be encouraged to recognise the physical, emotional and moral implications and risks of certain types of behaviour and to accept that both sexes must behave responsibly. The circular also included the key principles and aims of sex education set out by the independent Working Group, including the need to develop an appreciation for respect for diversity and the need to avoid prejudice and discrimination.

It rained on Thursday, 29 March 2001; the day Section 28 was officially repealed in Scotland. The whole country was in the grip of a foot and mouth epidemic with the media ablaze with stories and images of burning funeral pyres of dead farm animals. Lost in the pages of the *Scottish Sun* was a report: "Work pals beaten for being 'gay'." The thugs, Mark Robertson and Vincent Demarco, both 20-year-olds, had beaten two workmates, Kenneth McLellan and Ian Crew while they walked home together after a night out in Edinburgh. One received a broken ankle; the other was kicked in the head. Robertson and Demarco simply thought the two lads were gay. It was reported Demarco had told the police: "It was a square go and I won, poofs get away with everything". A Sheriff awarded them both community service.

On that day, while the space station Mir was hurtling towards Earth for a crash landing, the *Scottish Daily Mail* otherwise turned its attention on the front page to: "MARRIAGE U-TURN IN NEW SEX GUIDE FOR

Curtains for Section 28!

SCHOOLS... The Scottish Executive says it will place far stronger emphasis on the benefits of marriage than expected in the advice to teachers... Ministers had previously decided the new guidance would not place strong emphasis on the importance of marriage. However, after talks with Cardinal Thomas Winning, leader of Scotland's Roman Catholics, Education Minister Jack McConnell ordered a rethink". Father Joe Chamber, of the Catholic Education Commission told them: "...There is definitely room for improvement here". The Christian Institute claimed they had examples of material that could slip through the guidance. The *Scottish Mail* dutifully carried an example on the front-page the very next day: "PUPILS' SEX GUIDE SHOCK". This was described as a "new twist". But it wasn't. *The Primary School Sex and Relationship Pack* approved by the Executive and already widely used, taught kids the definition of words they were already familiar with in the playground. These words included, for example "lesbian", which was defined as "A woman who has a sexual relationship with another woman". Hardly rocket science. The *Mail's* editorial went delirious. "Children as young as nine are being taught how to use condoms; told to write stories about lesbian families; contraception 'kits' are to be demonstrated to them by teachers; and detailed descriptions of homosexual sex (formerly banned under Section 28) feature in the education 'pack'." The tabloid once again trawled through the new guidance in search of marriage. "Although it mentions marriage three times, it does not give it any preference..." With the battle cry for extra vigilance, the *Mail* issued a clear warning: "Parents are now in the front line as regards monitoring what their children are taught in school as sex education".

The Scottish media was already an efficient moral vigilante. In its more conservative guise, on the day Section 28 was consigned to the dustbin of history in Scotland, the *Scotsman* pounced on a "pervert's primer" that "reads like the lurid index of a pornographic magazine". The editorial declared; "a line has been crossed" which was "all too obvious to every parent". Healthwise's out-of-print publication *Taking Sex Seriously* was not intended to be handed out to children, but to sex education teachers. That didn't stop the *Scotsman's* lurid headline: "Do you want your child to be exposed to this?" They listed activities such as anal intercourse, using sexual toys, S&M, partner swapping, kissing, and fellatio. The broadsheet labelled Healthwise "controversial", and reporter Kate Foster and Andrew Denholm lined-up anyone prepared to condemn it. Valerie Riches of Family and Youth Concern said: "This is exactly why we are trying to keep the clause and why it shouldn't have been repealed in Scotland. Some of the acts listed are clearly of a homosexual nature". Michael Willis of Parent Truth Campaign, "who fought against the repeal of the clause", gasped: "...Modesty, commonsense and decency are being eroded away". Danny McLoughlin promised this wouldn't be used in Catholic schools before adding with some regret that "there are parts of the country where there is no provision for Catholic education". Phil Gallie for the Tories said: "Sex education should be about the human body and reproduction". An unnamed SNP spokesman called the material "inappropriate" and the Christian Institute's Colin Hart declared he would let parents know about "the condom demonstrations, the gay sex lessons and the general lack of any sense of decency" before picking out the best bits of *Taking Sex Seriously* and sending them to 2,000 churches and running off a report to all the Scottish MPs and MSPs.

In a section labelled "commonsense", the *Scotsman's* education editor, Seonag Mackinnon blamed Britain's high rate of teenage pregnancy on liberal sex education programmes. The editorial fumbled in the dark for a light switch. "Sex education was introduced in schools to guide the young in childbirth and in the basics of sexual behaviour in the context of stable and loving relationships. The latest proposals, spanning discussion of sadism, sexual toys, multiple partnering and tying up, can lay no claim to such a justification". The editorial squealed: "It treats all activities as equal and equivalent... It raises those activities that degrade human beings and treat them as no more than sexual objects for the infliction of pain and abuse to the level of normalcy". This debate highlighted how the educational challenge of sex education or the needs of pupils was increasingly being used as a catalyst for the anxieties of an adult society unable to cope with the realities of a world were adolescents had access to a much greater choice of sex and sexual expression through the Internet.

On 8 June 2001, Cardinal Winning had a heart attack. He made a speedy recovery and was sent home but within 48 hours,

Curtains for Section 28!

on the morning of 17 June, 2001, he was found dead by his housekeeper of over thirty years Mrs McInnes.

Following the death of Baroness Young in 2002, on 10 July 2003, the House of Lords in England defeated an amendment put forward by Baroness Blatch replacing Section 28 in England and Wales with parental vetting of sex education in schools by 180 to 130. The former Conservative Prime Minister Margaret Thatcher was in attendance, her first appearance in the chamber since her husband Denis's death. Ben Summerskill of Stonewall said: "Stonewall has worked long and hard to have this deeply offensive law overturned. Today's vote was a triumph for twenty-first century tolerance over nineteenth century prejudice". The Office of the Deputy Prime Minister issued a statement following the Lords' decision. "The Government very much welcome the House of Lords vote to support repeal of Section 28. We have always said this is an unnecessary piece of legislation which is deeply offensive to many people and which stigmatises certain lifestyles. This is another step towards a more tolerant and fair society".

On 18 November 2003 section 122 of the Local Government Act 2003 finally repealed Section 28 in England and Wales.

The Conservative Party under David Cameron's leadership would be filled with remorse for voting against legislation to repeal Section 28. Francis Maude – whose gay brother Charles had died from an AIDS related illness in 1993 - was interviewed in *Gay Times* and admitted its introduction did the Party a great deal of harm, confessing that MPs who voted for its introduction were simply following orders, adding: "The truth is most MPs don't necessarily think a huge amount about a lot of the bills they're voting on. If you're a Minister, which a lot of us were at the time, you've got your huge portfolio of stuff and you're absolutely on top of all that; and the other stuff, you're not, sort of, spending a huge amount of time thinking about... most people are simply voting on something they're whipped on to vote". Amongst those who had voted for the retention of Section 28 were David Cameron, Kenneth Clarke, Mark Francois, Chris Grayling, William Hague, Patrick McLoughlin, Andrew Mitchell, George Osborne, Sir George Young and, of course, Francis Maude.

RELIGIOUS FASCISM

Outside Scotland, as soon as Conservative Prime Minister David Cameron's coalition cabinet took over the reins in 2010, Christian Education Secretary Michael Gove's flagship policy of rolling out more religious schools took off. He would breathe new life into the ghost of Section 28. New rules were introduced for headteachers to ensure children were 'protected from inappropriate teaching materials and learnt the nature of marriage and its importance for family life and for bringing up children'. It seemed almost with intention that the mention of marriage appeared under Section 28 of this new agreement. This 'model funding agreement' was to be a template used by all the new acadamies and 'free' schools set up by 'faith' groups, parents and charities which started off in their hundreds and were soon mushrooming into their thousands. Such an explicit endorsement of marriage in the curriculum brought a response from the National Secular Society which itself faced ever-growing obstacles and chastisement for defending the UK against religious privilege. President, Terry Sanderson said: "For children brought up by unmarried parents or single parents, being told that marriage is the only valid family arrangement will be totally contradictory to everything they know about the world. It opens the door for religious schools to teach a really narrow version of what constitutes an acceptable relationship. It is telling our children that their own family structure is somehow inferior. A lot of church schools would love to do that and this gives them license to do it". The Government was making a departure from the previous guidelines which stated that children should learn the nature and importance of marriage and of stable relationships for family life and bringing up children. The reference to 'stable relationships', which alluded to gay couples and those living outside marriage, was dropped. If headteachers broke the rules, or ended up being legally challenged by religious parents, funding for the school or academy could be lost.

In 2012, Michael Gove warned that the Equality Act, which prohibited discrimination on the grounds of sexual orientation, did not extend to the school curriculum. The door was open for homophobic teaching materials to be allowed into schools. At a Roman Catholic school in Lancashire, a US evangelist distributed leaflets, including a booklet called 'Pure Manhood: How to become the man God wants you to be" after his talk to children. The booklet discussed a boy dealing with "homosexual

Curtains for Section 28!

attractions" which it suggested might "stem from an unhealthy relationship with his father, an inability to relate to other guys, or even sexual abuse". The booklet claimed "scientifically speaking, safe sex is a joke" suggesting "the homosexual act is disordered, much like contraceptive sex between heterosexuals. Both acts are directed against God's natural purpose for sex – babies and bonding". Gove insisted: "The education provisions of the Equality Act 2010 which prohibit discrimination against individuals based on their protected characteristics (including sexual orientation) do not extend to the content of the curriculum. Any materials used in sex and relationships education lessons, therefore, will not be subject to the discrimination provisions of the act". A review of guidelines on what was appropriate for schools to teach had been abandoned when the last electon had been called. A new coalition of faith groups and politicians, the Religious Education Council of England and Wales was quickly formed to promote the value of religious education in schools.

In Scotland after the repeal of Section 28, the *Scottish Daily Mail* never tired of running homophobic campaigns. On 10 August 2006, the day British police foiled a terrorist plot threatening to blow passenger planes from the sky, the paper filled its front page with a story by their 'home affairs editor', Graham Grant about supposed "outrage over new 'equality' plans: SCHOOLS TOLD TO TEACH GAY SEX". It was to be one of many stories compiled by this journalist in support of the Catholic Church's rethink of their strategy which now appealed for sympathisers to support a campaign to 'protect religious freedoms' and fight a 'politically correct orthodoxy'. Cardinal Keith O'Brien, embroiled in a gay sex scandal of his own in 2013, would describe same-sex marriage as a 'grotesque subversion' that would 'shame the UK in the eyes of the world'. He pledged to go one step further in an article in the same paper four days later when he suggested faith schools would ignore the Equality Act 2006 prohibiting discrimination on the grounds of sexual orientation. The newspaper warned: "The Cardinal's declaration effectively draws up battle lines that threaten a re-run of the controversy over the repeal of Section 28". O'Brien claimed that treating gays equally would "pit the powerful against the vulnerable" adding that "the Church must speak out, not just for its own freedoms but the freedoms of all". It was clearly a case of everyone being equal; but some being more equal than others. His hypocritical words came at a time when police figures revealed homophobic crime in Scotland, which included serious and indecent assaults, threats and extortion, vandalism and breach of the peace had risen by a staggering 150% since 2003, just two years after Section 28 had been repealed in Scotland.

By 2013, whilst same-sex marriage was undergoing a second consultation, Brian Souter appeared on BBC's *Question Time* discussing what would be taught in schools on gay marriage. An organisation calling itself Scotland for Marriage argued that the legislation was as controversial as abortion and parents had a right to remove their children from classes where it was discussed. Christian organisation, CARE for Scotland submitted their objections to the consultation exercise on how equal marriage would be implemented and told the *Scotsman:* "Concerns have been expressed that should so-called same-sex marriage be introduced it is likely that children will taught in school that marriage can be between two people of the same sex... To raise a generation of children with such a subjective view of marriage is a huge social experiment which is likely to result in severely detrimental consequences... Arguably, it may even increase the occurrence of homosexual relationships." The spectre of Section 28 once again loomed on the Scottish horizon.

Although the unpleasant statute was laid to rest in Scotland, England and Wales, it took a further three years for the Isle of Man to vote to drop its version of Section 28: Section 38. On 1 March 2006, the island's parliament, the House of Keys, voted 12 to 9 in favour of repeal. The Isle of Man's Education Minister, David Anderson had tried to argue that it was wrong to equate gay relationships with straight couples, and Section 38 offered 'good guidelines' on the teaching of sexuality.

Outside the old seven-storey red-glass office block that had once housed the *Daily Record* at Anderston Quay in Glasgow, that wet Thursday in March when Section 28 was finally repealed in Scotland, JCBs smashed through twisted supports and reinforced concrete, floor by floor. They ploughed effortlessly through the swing-doors that once ejected editor, Martin Clarke. They drilled through the floor where he once sat and pummelled through the glass windows he looked out. Where once editors and journalists sat taking notes, hanging onto every word of moral arbiters and religionists, vertical blinds hung helplessly like broken teeth,

Curtains for Section 28!

hanging out of vacant windows: gaping mouths of broken concrete and twisted steel. Clouds of concrete dust were lifted in the wind and scurried down the Broomielaw under Kingston Bridge and across the river Clyde. A new building would soon go up in its place; a fresh, new design that reflected a bright, new, young Scotland.

The public didn't vote for Section 28, and they weren't having it.

None of the Scottish newspapers, churches or individuals who enrolled in the vitriolic campaign to prevent the repeal of Section 28 has ever apologised to the gay community in Scotland.

Epilogue
The Emergence of a New Religious Militancy

After the repeal of Section 28 came equal marriage. In their fight to prevent LGBT people jumping this final major hurdle towards full emancipation, religious reactionaries gave it all they got and lost. But there were gains.

As each day was marked by the passing of another old lady who made jam for church fêtes, or an elderly minister concerned for the sick in Africa, something cancerous had spread from the pulpits, across the chancels to the front rows: A new, smaller, hard-core, socially conservative progeny of the zealous, immigrants, individuals with mental health problems, the vulnerable, the mentally unstable, children indoctrinated in religious homes and schools and those saved by pastors from drugs, alcoholism or emotional breakdowns. The musty smell of prayer books had gone and in their place were eye-catching leaflets for evangelical Alpha courses, church 'planting' and international missions. Across the world, churches were filling their buckets with cash to oil the wheels of organisations ready to save the world from sexual degradation, permissiveness, and by default: homosexuality.

In 2013 a mob of 5,000 Christians led by priests of the Russian Orthodox Church in Tbilisi, Georgia targeted a group marking the International Day Against Homophobia (IDAHO) chanting, "trample them to death!" Police managed to evacuate most of those on the march onto municipal buses assembled in the centre of Tbilisi while protesters threw stones, beat on the windows of the buses screaming: "Drag them out and stomp on them to death." The old women carried bouquets of stinging nettles while men waved Georgian flags and crosses. It was the year Turkey collected *nul points* in the Eurovision Song Contest, storming out of the contest at the last minute after taking umbrage at Finland's entry which featured two girls kissing. The year when subway officials in Ankara asked metro passengers to "act in accordance with moral rules" after a heterosexual couple had been caught kissing on security cameras. A few hundred amorous protesters storming the station for a kiss-in were faced with riot police and pro-Islamists.

In Greece, having already gained 18 seats in the Greek parliament, fascist party Golden Dawn had their offices blessed by priests of the Greek Orthodox Church. Terence McNally's play *Corpus Christi*, depicting Jesus and his disciples as gay and living in Texas evoked the ire of both Orthodox bishops and Golden Dawn members who, before seeing the play, staged an angry protest outside the theatre. The director and production cast of *Corpus Christi* were prosecuted and faced charges of 'blasphemy'. The director's parents were disturbed by calls telling them that their son's body would be delivered to them in pieces. One of the bishops advised Golden Dawn if it changed its style to become more "mature", they could become a "sweet hope" for desperate Greeks.

In Romania, seven young people were assaulted after attending an academic debate about the history of homosexuality and a year later, 50 fascists in Bucharest went on to halt the screening of American film *The Kids Are Alright*, assaulting and filming filmgoers chanting 'death to homosexuals' before singing the Romanian national anthem and waving religious icons.

In Russia, two-thirds still found homosexuality 'morally unacceptable and worth condemning' and, according to the Pew Research Center, only 16 per cent said homosexuality should be accepted. In a country with little or no sex education in schools, backed by Patriarch Kirill of the Russian Orthodox Church, the government introduced a new federal law – much like Section 28 – against the 'propaganda of non-traditional sexual relations among minors', just one of several anti-gay measures that were introduced in a new climate of fear. Conflating paedophilia with homosexuality, Russian President Vladimir Putin repeated what many religious campaigners said about Section 28, that the new law was only about protecting children. The law also banned representing "tradition" and "non-traditional" relationships as

The Emergence of a New Religious Militancy

equally acceptable and made it an offence to say anything positive about being gay in public, even to tell a child there was nothing wrong with them being gay or being raised by parents who were gay.

Russian lawmakers allowed themselves to be taken-in by the discredited Regnerus study funded by a US Republican think-tank, the Heritage Foundation, which claimed gay parents pushed their children to suicide. An audit by an editorial board member of *Social Science Research*, the journal which published Christian Mark Regnerus's $785,000 funded study, concluded that the study should have been disqualified during the peer-review process. He called it "bullshit" and accused Regnerus of pushing a political agenda. In Poland, France and Africa, the Regnerus study was repeatedly used to attack gays. Converting from Quakerism to Catholicism, US Republican Brian Brown of the National Organisation for Marriage who had argued that legalized same-sex marriage could lead to paedophilia testified before the Russian Duma in favour of anti-gay legislation citing the Regnerus study. Days after his presentation the Russian legislative body again cited the Regnerus study and introduced a bill to ban Russian children from being adopted by same-sex couples. They were soon debating new laws to take children away from gay parents altogether.

After finding a book in Ulyanovsk children's library by Vera Timenchik called *Families. Ours and Theirs* about different family-related traditions and cultures across the world, prosecutors were called in to investigate its suitability. A spokesperson for the library was quick to reassure everyone the book had been removed.

Only weeks after a brutal murder of a 23-year-old gay man at a demonstration in Moscow to celebrate 20 years since homosexuality was decriminalised and to protest at the introduction of the new homophobic law, 30 were arrested after unfurling their rainbow flags. Several were attacked by Orthodox Christian thugs who sang hymns and crossed themselves to ward off evil. A law banning gay pride marches in Moscow for a whole century was passed before the European Court of Human Rights declared the ban illegal.

RELIGIOUS FASCISM

Two dozen masked men stormed a popular gay bar in Moscow and beat the patrons – mostly women – with fists and bottles. Some were seriously injured. On the streets, Pavel Samburov was arrested and fined 570 roubles and given 30 hours of detention for kissing his boyfriend in public. Konstantin Kostin, a member of the Holy Rus movement declared: "Gay people need medical treatment. It's simply disgusting to look at them. Russia used to be a great superpower. Now look what's become of us. Marriage is a sacred union between man and woman, and this lot want to defile the sanctitude of our country".

In a more sinister development, using the Internet, numerous victims were lured by organised gangs across Russia with a promise of a date before they were made to strip naked, tortured, humiliated and forced to come out to family and friends whilst being filmed. Footage of the assaults was posted online. In one case a man was left blinded in one eye after a gang attacked him and in another found by Human Rights Watch a man had his clothes burnt after he was abducted and handcuffed. The gang then put a gun to his head and made him rape himself with a bottle. Most of the gang members were confident enough to be filmed, knowing they were able to act with impunity. Liz MacKean, an investigative journalist who travelled to Russia to make the documentary *Hunted* for Channel 4 said, "We filmed these groups with their knowledge, and what I found shocking afterwards was that only a few asked to have their faces disguised. They all believe they are doing the right thing". Russian diplomats responded by saying that a similar film could have just as easily been made about people victimised because they had ginger hair.

In Uganda in 2010, after popular newspaper *Rolling Stone* ran a story on "100 PICTURES OF UGANDA'S TOP HOMOS" with their names and addresses and calls for the hanging of homosexuals, the efforts of Christian extremists began to bear fruit. Amongst the list of names was Kasha Nabagesera whose workshop at a hotel in Entebbe for LGBT activists was raided by the country's Ethics Minister, a defrocked Catholic priest called Simon Lokodo. Ms Nabagesera was arrested. Lododo was reported saying: "I have closed this conference because it's illegal. We do not accept homosexuality in Uganda. So go back home". Another listed homosexual was David Kato, a gay human rights activist, who within three months of the article being printed was found bludgeoned to death. An Anglican priest used his funeral to condemn homosexuality.

Uganda's *Rolling Stone* stirred hatred with stories under headlines not dissimilar to claims that laced the campaign to 'Keep the Clause', like: "WE SHALL RECRUIT 1,000,000 KIDS BY 2012," and "PARENTS NOW FACE HEARTBREAKS AS HOMOS RAID SCHOOLS". Evangelical Christian lawmakers had to be held back from putting into place new laws that would put all homosexuals to death. When President Museveni signed an Anti-Homosexuality Bill into law, the act sentenced anyone suspected of same-sex relations to life in prison. The law punished anyone associated with 'promoting' LGBT activities, be they health workers conducting HIV tests or offering advice. The punishment extended to anyone who failed to report violations of the Act to the authorities within 24 hours of the event.

The Anti-Homosexuality bill was introduced not long after a big seminar in Kampala called "Exposing the Truth behind Homosexuality and the Homosexual Agenda". It featured two rabidly homophobic speakers, Scott Lively, head of Abiding Truth Ministries in Massachusetts and author of the *Pink Swastika*, which claimed homosexuals invented Nazism and were instrumental in the Holocaust, and Dan Schmierer of the ex-gay group Exodus International. At the seminar, Lively told the audience that a powerful global gay movement had now set its sights on Africa and that the "gay agenda" was unleashing epidemics of divorce, child abuse, and HIV/AIDS wherever it gained a foothold. He warned that by permitting homosexuality, "you can't stop someone from molesting children or stop them from having sex with animals".

The Rwandan genocide was also blamed on homosexuals. Influential evangelist Rick Warren, head of California's Saddleback megachurch had already travelled to Rwanda, Kenya and Uganda declaring along the way that "homosexuality is not a natural way of life and thus not a human right". Scott Lively met with Ugandan government ministers and David Bahati who would go on to draft the Anti-Homosexuality Bill there. Bahati was connected to the secretive Christian fundamentalist organisation behind National Prayer Breakfasts, the Fellowship, which pours millions into student leadership programmes that places government and media with disciples of Jesus. According to Jeff Sharlet, a contributing editor for *Harper's*, Joe Pitts, a Republican congressman has diverted millions in US aid to Uganda from sex education programmes to abstinence programmes and evangelical revivals that included condom burnings. Africans were being duped as their traditions of not only homosexuality but the extended family or *ubuntu* was being smothered by western culture wars and a nuclear family that had more in common with *The Waltons* from rural Virginia than a family living in the African bush.

In Nigeria, the president went on to ban same-sex marriages, gay groups and any public sign of affection between people of the same sex with penalties of up to 14 years imprisonment.

As Scott Lively joined other Christians in Russia, Latvia, Macedonia, Romania, Croatia and other countries, the Center for Constitutional Rights, under laws permitting foreigners to sue American citizens who violate international law, helped the Sexual Minorities Uganda (SMUG) file a suit in a US court against Scott Lively for denying Ugandan's their human rights.

With the modernisation of Christian missions and crusades, Pat Robertson's Christian Broadcasting Network and the evangelical Trinity Broadcasting Network were both seen across sub-Saharan Africa with the addition of many other Christian-right radio networks. Rev. Dr. Kapya Kaoma, author of the investigative report *Globalizing the Culture Wars: U.S. Conservatives, African Churches, & Homophobia* wrote: "Evangelical churches and groups provide scholarships for African clerics to receive conservative theological training at U.S. institutions. They sponsor orphanages, Bible schools, universities, and social-welfare projects".

In France, the shouts and screams of thousands of mostly religious protesters coached in from the countryside shook the tables of Parisian cafés from Montparnass to Montpellier during

The Emergence of a New Religious Militancy

President Hollande's attempt to introduce marriage equality. Starting out as grass-roots organisations organised by the Catholic Church, protesters marched with right-wing politicians including a candidate for the far-right *Front National* to protest. Skinheads attacked a gay bar in Lille and masked armed men smashed another bar in Bordeaux. Raphaël Leclerc, a gay cabaret dancer was beaten unconscious in Nice, Muslims were filmed kicking and punching women protesters in Paris and Wilfred de Bruijn, a young librarian who was caught holding his boyfriend's hand sustained injuries so severe they went viral on the Internet. Despite protestations from campaigners that their campaign wasn't religiously motivated; *Le Monde* examined the 37 associations behind *Manif Pour Tous*, an anti-gay-marriage organisation led by comedienne Frigide Barjot, (literally, Frigid Bonkers), a self-styled "press officer for Jesus". 22 were described as 'empty vessels'; the rest were all religious. She warned: "Hollande wants blood, and he will get it".

Two members of France's socialist party Sylviane Bulteau and Hugues Fourage received letters threatening to kidnap their loved ones. Claude Bartolone, the head of France's National Assembly, was sent an envelope filled with gun powder and a letter signed by a radical right-wing group, saying: "Allowing marriage for all would be the same as destroying all marriage. Our methods are more radical and direct than demonstrations. You wanted war, you've got it ... If you were to carry on regardless; your political family will have to suffer physically."

Christine Boutin, president of the Christian-Democrat party and former minister under Nicolas Sarkozy hinted that violence would be justified if François Hollande did not ditch same sex marriage. Despite one Green MP having her tyres slashed in front of her house, President Hollande stuck to his election promise and brought in the legislation. Days after he signed the bill into law he 'got blood' when a member of extreme far-right group, *Printemps Français*, (French Spring), 78-year-old Dominique Venner, walked into the cathedral of Notre Dame and shot himself through the mouth. He left a note warning: "New spectacular and symbolic actions are needed to wake up the sleep walkers... We are entering a time when acts must follow words."

RELIGIOUS FASCISM

Soon, it was Frigide Barjot's turn to seek police protection after receiving a handkerchief soaked in what looked like blood. She suspected, not gay militants, but *Printemps Français*, which had gained notoriety in her demos and threatened to target "the government and all its appendices, the collaborating political parties and lobbies where the ideological programmes are developed and the organs which spread it." Barjot insisted she was not anti-gay and thought the group had turned on her after she called Venner "deranged" and "un-Catholic". John Lichfield in the *Independent* reported her saying: "I entered this fight because I knew that, otherwise, the protests would be dominated by people like them: the far right and the Catholic extremists." In many respects she was right. It was an issue the far-right and religious extremists were successfully hijacking while at the same time inciting new, shrill, liberal and atheistic voices into counter attacks. Somewhere between the conflicts of these polar opposites was the increasingly marginalised voice of a moderate secularism, chastised or ignored.

Before May was out, the first same-sex couple in France, Vincent Aubin and Bruno Boileau were married. The ceremony was performed by Socialist mayor, Hélène Mandroux despite numerous threats, including a telephone call from a man telling her to "get bodyguards." Nevertheless, within weeks, 18-year-old gay student, Clément Méric was pronounced brain-dead after an attack by a group of far-right skinheads from the group JNR *Jeune Nationaliste Revolutionnaire*.

As Hollande's socialist party fell behind in popularity, the *Front National* surged forward. Catholic and some Muslim groups opposed to same-sex marriage were back on the streets again in a Day of Anger in 2014 which attracted 17,000 from far-right and fascist movements. Journalists were chased away with chants of "Nazi state, collaborationist media". Amongst other chants picked up by the media were "Juif, la France n'est pas pour toi" (Jew, France is not for you), "Hollande or the CRIF (Jewish representative group), who is leading who?" and "Europe gay criminal Zionist". Ivan Rioufol, journalist for *Le Figaro*, wrote: "The Day of Anger has revealed the hideous face of fascist France". Hollande backed down from introducing any further equality legislation.

The Emergence of a New Religious Militancy

By 2014, Russian news agency TASS reported a French delegation of religionists, including *Manif Pour Tous*, the Catholic Bishop of Bayonne and Oloron Marc Aillet, representatives of Strasbourg-based European centre For Law and Justice and the anti-abortion and euthanasia Jerome Lejeune Foundation meeting religious leaders and delivering speeches in both houses of the Russian Parliament. The envoy of the Moscow Patriarchate at the Council of Europe Hegumen Filipp said: "All this is organized so that Frenchmen will be able to find partners in Russia for co-operation in the protection of traditional values".

In the UK, by 2010, the BNP's Nick Griffin, an Anglican who believed "nations are ordained by God", was already enjoying the exposure of an hour-long programme on Christian TV channel, Revelation. When he appeared on Sky News - facing accusations of obtaining lists of email addresses of Christians to win their support in elections - he sported a cross in his lapel. But he was yesterday's man. Nigel Farage and the UKip was soon the more respectable face for the Christian-right.

Christian proselytiser Richard Lucas, whose letters appeared so frequently in the *Scotsman* he set up his own website to show them off, declared "a party has now emerged (UKip) reflecting such previously unrepresented views." He proclaimed: "It's democracy in action – widely held views can only be excluded from the political system for so long." UKip earned more than a nod from Gerald Warner in his *Scotland on Sunday* column when, under the statement, "Ukip is the natural agent of this political euthanasia", he delivered a long article of political adoration.

In the absence of any genuine engagement with secular organisations like the Scottish Secular Society from either government or religious groups, a new bullish Christian supremacy was being manufactured in Scottish churches. It concealed a growing frustration against Islam and polarised views both for and against religion. In such a climate, extremism was thriving. With millions in grants ploughed into 'interfaith' projects, no efforts were being made to engage faith with the majority without religion who challenged by a concerted effort by government to defend and maintain religious privileges.

RELIGIOUS FASCISM

Scotland was proving ripe for unregulated proselytising. The New Life Christian Fellowship in Broxburn advised parents of children of pre-school age on its website: "Little Children's Church is NOT simply a crèche where little ones are looked after." It's a place where children "learn about God, Jesus and the Holy Spirit." The church boasted a Child Protection Policy approved by the Churches Child Protection Advisory Service. The church deplored "unbelief" which they claimed was a hindrance to supernatural healing and gave examples such as Lorna, a woman eight years into a diagnosis of multiple sclerosis, who claimed she had thrown her medication into the bin a day after 'healing' before walking around in high heels.

Kairos Church in Peterhead conducted Alpha courses, held an inevitable crèche and a 'hands-on-Bible' curriculum for children from five to 11 whilst adults attended services speaking in "other tongues".

The Destiny Church in Glasgow boasted 'cells' or 'growth' groups and also welcomed under-fives to "listen to stories." Destiny paid over £2m for a former Clydesdale Bank building in Townhead before opening a charity superstore in the former Dobbies Garden Centre outside Paisley.

The Scripture Union already had access to children in schools. They claimed on their website: "We have a team of 30 highly creative regional and associate staff who work in primary and secondary schools across Scotland." They proclaimed: "Jesus Christ as Lord and God... as Victor over Satan and all his forces."

Then there were 'Challenger' buses run by People with a Mission Ministries, parking outside primary schools. At least two of the buses contained computer stations, evangelistic DVD's, and presentations. The upstairs area contained a coffee lounge area with a 46" flat screen TV with surround-sound and mini-cinema in the front half of the buses. Their website boasted: "In subsequent Friday visits the average number of youth attending the bus was around 12 with two or three making a commitment to Christianity." The Ministries sold and endorsed *Answers*, a monthly periodical from the infamous Answers in Genesis; a well-known anti-science and young Earth creationism ministry which held regular conferences in Scotland.

The Emergence of a New Religious Militancy

Not every cleric, like the three that are made to take their place on every education committee in Scotland by law, received such unconditional acceptance. In May 2013, in Raploch, Stirling, Pastor Soloman Makhathoela was in court for calling his neighbour Catherine Kerr "white scum" after learning the mum-of-two wasn't wed. He was reported in the *Scottish Sun* telling her that in his country her kids "would be shot and hung" before turning on her fiancé, Alan Brown, to tell him "it was a fucking disgrace they had kids out of wedlock."

In the same week, Michael Voris, a Church Militant TV presenter, was invited to talk to 150 hard-core Catholics at Carfin Grotto outside Motherwell. I spoke to a young man in his early twenties who had been brought along by the leader of his church peer group. He had been shown Voris on the internet. Passionately defensive of Catholicism, he said it had rescued him from depression, suicide and pornography. He told me Voris "inspired him".

In typical Bible-belt fashion, Voris is in the Ted Haggard tradition; an unmarried Catholic apologist from Texas in a suit and tie, toupee and tan. He dismisses global warming as "pseudoscience and hyper-sensationalism" and brands many of the Catholic clerical hierarchy, "namby-pamby". He fears the Catholic Church is "falling apart" and wants "muscular Catholicism that isn't afraid to encourage battle and sacrifice." He told his audience: "We have such an intense relationship for Him we would die for Him." And that pretty much confirmed his somewhat desperate response to the collapse of the Catholic Church. "The job of the Church is not to make soup kitchens," he scoffed, "but to make saints." Voris reminded the faithful: "The Catholic Church isn't about feelings."

Perhaps he's right and the time for sentimentality over religion is over.

www.ingramcontent.com/pod-product-compliance
Lightning Source LLC
Chambersburg PA
CBHW071957150426
43194CB00008B/910